THE RULE OF LAW AT THE NATIONAL AND INTERNATIONAL LEVELS

This book aims to enhance understanding of the interactions between the international and national rule of law. It demonstrates that the international rule of law is not merely about ensuring national compliance with international law. International law and institutions (eg, international human rights treaty-monitoring bodies and human rights courts) respond to national contestations and show deference to the national rule of law. While this might come at the expense of the certainty of international law, it suggests that the international rule of law can allow for flexibility, national diversity and pluralism.

The essays in this volume are set against the background of increasing conflict between international and national legal norms. Moreover the book shows that international law and institutions do not always command blind national obedience to international law, but incorporate a process of adjustment and deference to national law and policies that are protected by the rule of law at the national level.

Volume 56 in the series Studies in International Law

Studies in International Law

Recent titles in this series

Integration at the Border: The Dutch Act on Integration Abroad and International Immigration Law
Karin de Vries

An Equitable Framework for Humanitarian Intervention
Ciarán Burke

Democratic Statehood in International Law: The Emergence of New States in Post-Cold War Practice
Jure Vidmar

International Law and the Construction of the Liberal Peace
Russell Buchan

The OIC, the UN, and Counter-Terrorism Law-Making: Conflicting or Cooperative Legal Orders?
Katja Samuel

Statelessness: The Enigma of the International Community
William E Conklin

The Reception of Asylum Seekers under International Law: Between Sovereignty and Equality
Lieneke Slingenberg

International Law and Child Soldiers
Gus Waschefort

The Contractual Nature of the Optional Clause
Gunnar Törber

Non-State Actors in International Law
Edited by Math Noortmann, August Reinisch and Cedric Ryngaert

For the complete list of titles in this series, see 'Studies in International Law' link at www.hartpub.co.uk/books/series.asp

The Rule of Law at the National and International Levels

Contestations and Deference

Edited by
Machiko Kanetake
and
André Nollkaemper

•HART•
OXFORD • LONDON • NEW YORK • NEW DELHI • SYDNEY

HART PUBLISHING
Bloomsbury Publishing Plc
Kemp House, Chawley Park, Cumnor Hill, Oxford, OX2 9PH, UK

HART PUBLISHING, the Hart/Stag logo, BLOOMSBURY and the Diana logo are trademarks of Bloomsbury Publishing Plc
First published in Great Britain 2016

First published in hardback, 2016
Paperback edition, 2018

A catalogue record for this book is available from the British Library.

Library of Congress Cataloging-in-Publication Data

Names: Kanetake, Machiko, editor. | Nollkaemper, André, editor.

Title: The rule of law at the national and international levels : contestations and deference / edited by Machiko Kanetake and Andr?e Nollkaemper.

Description: Oxford ; Portland, Oregon : Hart Publishing Ltd, 2016. | Series: Studies in international law ; volume 56 | "The contributions contained in the present volume were presented originally in an international seminar in March 2013 hosted by the HiiL and the Amsterdam Center for International Law (ACIL)." | Includes bibliographical references and index.

Identifiers: LCCN 2015045796 (print) | LCCN 2015046374 (ebook) | ISBN 9781849466677 (hardback : alk. paper) | ISBN 9781782256168 (Epub)

Subjects: LCSH: Rule of law—Congresses. | International law and human rights—Congresses. | International and municipal law—Congresses.

Classification: LCC K3171.A6 R848 2016 (print) | LCC K3171.A6 (ebook) | DDC 340/.11—dc23

LC record available at http://lccn.loc.gov/2015045796

ISBN: PB: 978-1-50992-458-5
HB: 978-1-84946-667-7

Typeset by Compuscript Ltd, Shannon

To find out more about our authors and books visit www.hartpublishing.co.uk. Here you will find extracts, author information, details of forthcoming events and the option to sign up for our newsletters.

Preface and Acknowledgements

The present volume is the result of a multi-year research project sponsored by the Hague Institute for the Internationalisation of Law (HiiL), which aims to explore the processes and consequences of the 'internationalisation of the rule of law'. The outcome of the project's first phase was published as Michael Zürn, André Nollkaemper, and Randall Peerenboom (eds), *Rule of Law Dynamics: In an Era of International and Transnational Governance* (Cambridge University Press, 2012). Building on this first volume, the present volume contains the outcome of the second phase of the project. Its aim is to identify and assess some of the patterns and consequences emerging from in the interactions between the national and international rule of law.

The contributions contained in the present volume were presented originally in an international seminar in March 2013 hosted by the HiiL and the Amsterdam Center for International Law (ACIL). The papers presented at the international seminar were selected through a rigorous process out of over 100 submissions which the ACIL had received. The analysis and argument presented in the present volume also benefited from the discussions within a research group (called 'Interfaces') organised within the ACIL.

The editors would like to thank the HiiL for supporting the research project which generated the present volume. In particular, the editors are grateful for Morly Frishman of the HiiL for his enthusiastic support in organising the aforementioned seminar and other related events and in enriching and disseminating the outcomes of the project. The editors would also like to thank Rosanne van Alebeek, Theresa Reinold, Ingo Venzke, Michael Zürn, many other colleagues of the ACIL, and the participants to the international seminar for their advice and help in the process of developing the present volume.

Contents

Part II: International Deference to the National Legal Order

Conclusion

List of Contributors

Yvonne Donders is Professor of International Human Rights and Cultural Diversity at the University of Amsterdam. She is Head of the Department of International and European Law. She received her PhD from Maastricht University. Before her current position, she was Executive Director of the Amsterdam Center for International Law (ACIL) and Programme Specialist on Economic, Social and Cultural Rights in the Division of Human Rights at UNESCO's Secretariat in Paris. She is currently member of the editorial board of the Netherlands Quarterly of Human Rights, member of the National Commission for UNESCO, member of the Human Rights Committee of the Advisory Council on International Affairs and member of the European Expert Network on Culture (EENC).

Shai Dothan is an Associate Professor of International and Public Law at the University of Copenhagen Faculty of Law affiliated with iCourts. Previously, he was a Senior Researcher at the Global Trust Project, Tel Aviv University Faculty of Law and an Adjunct Professor at the Hebrew University of Jerusalem Faculty of Law. He received his PhD, LLM, and LLB from Tel Aviv University Faculty of Law and has previously been a Post Doc at the University of Chicago and the Hebrew University. He is the author of *Reputation and Judicial Tactics: A Theory of National and International Courts* (Cambridge University Press, 2014).

Jennifer Easterday is a founder and Executive Director of JustPeace Labs. She previously was a PhD researcher for the '*Jus Post Bellum*' project at the Grotius Centre for International Legal Studies, University of Leiden. She received her JD from the University of California, Berkeley School of Law and is a member of the California State Bar. She has worked and consulted for various international NGOs, including Open Society Justice Initiative, International Criminal Law Services, and the UC Berkeley War Crimes Studies Center. She is a co-editor of *Jus Post Bellum: Mapping the Normative Foundations* (Oxford University Press, 2014).

Veronika Fikfak is a Fellow and Lecturer at the University of Cambridge and an ESRC Future Research Leader. She holds a Magister Juris (MJur) and a DPhil in Public International and Constitutional Law from the University of Oxford. Dr Fikfak previously worked at the International Court of Justice, the United Nations, the Law Commission of England and Wales, and the European Court of Human Rights. She is an Associate Member of the Lauterpacht Centre for International Law and of Cambridge's Centre for Public Law. Her monograph on the role of domestic courts in relation to international law is forthcoming with Cambridge University Press (International and Comparative Law Series, 2016).

Shotaro Hamamoto is a Professor at the Faculty of Law of Kyoto University. His prior academic appointments include teaching positions in Japan (Professor, Kobe University, 2006–9) and abroad (Professeur invité, Université Paris I, 2009 and Sciences Po Paris, 2012). He has also served as an advocate for the Japanese Government in the Whaling in the Antarctic Case (*Australia v Japan*, ICJ) and Hoshinmaru and Tomimaru Cases (*Japan v Russia*, ITLOS, 2007). He has served as the Japanese Representative to the UNCITRAL WGII (Arbitration/Conciliation) (2010–2015) and to the OECD Investment Committee (2011); as an Expert on the Advisory Group on Legal Issues, Monitoring Group of the Anti-Doping Convention of the Council of Europe (2010–2012); and as an Arbitrator on the Japan Sports Arbitration Agency (2008–).

Machiko Kanetake is an Assistant Professor of Public International Law at Utrecht University. Machiko received her PhD from Kyoto University, her LLM at the London School of Economics and Political Science (LSE), and her MA in Law from the University of Sheffield. She was also appointed a Hauser Visiting Doctoral Researcher (2010–11) of the Global Fellows Program at New York University (NYU) School of Law, a Visiting Researcher (2012) of the University of Sydney, a Visiting Fellow (2014–2015) at the Human Rights Program, Harvard Law School, and a Visiting Fellow (2015) at the Transnational Law Institute, the Dickson Poon School of Law, King's College London.

Hege Elisabeth Kjos is an Assistant Professor at the University of Amsterdam. She is Deputy General Editor of Arbitration International (Oxford University Press) and serves on the Board of Reporters for the Institute for Transnational Arbitration (country reporter for Norway) and on the Advisory Board of the Brill Research Perspectives: International Investment Arbitration. She assists in research for arbitrators and experts in investor-state arbitrations. She was previously employed at the Legal Department of the World Bank in Washington DC. Dr Kjos holds a Juris Doctor degree, a Cand Mag degree, and a Bachelor of Arts degree following studies in the United States, the Netherlands, France and Norway. She received her PhD from the University of Amsterdam, and is the author of the book *Applicable Law in Investor-State Arbitration: The Interplay between National and International Law* (Oxford University Press, 2013).

Andrew Legg is a barrister, practising from Essex Court Chambers in London, with a broad practice in commercial law, public law and international law. He received his DPhil from the University of Oxford, where he taught law for four years and lectured on the European Human Rights

Law course. He is the author of *The Margin of Appreciation in International Human Rights Law* (Oxford University Press, 2012).

Ji Li is an Associate Professor of Law at Rutgers Law School. He received his PhD in Political Science from Northwestern University, and his JD from Yale Law School, where he was an Olin Fellow in Law, Economics and Public Policy and an editor of the Yale Human Rights and Development Law Journal. Before joining the faculty at Rutgers, he worked as an associate at the New York office of an international law firm, practising corporate and tax law.

André Nollkaemper is Professor of Public International Law and Director of the Amsterdam Center for Interrnational Law at the Faculty of Law of the University of Amsterdam. He is also (external) adviser to the Minister of Foreign Affairs of the Netherlands, Member of the Permanent Court of Arbitration, President of the European Society of International Law and member of the Royal Netherlands Academy of Arts and Sciences of the Netherlands. Previously, he was a member of the Advisory Commission on Public International Law of the Netherlands and counsel at Böhler, attorneys in Amsterdam. His practical experience includes cases before the European Court on Human Rights, the Special Court for Sierra Leone, the International Criminal Tribunal for the Former Yugoslavia, the Extraordinary Chambers in the courts of Cambodia, courts of the Netherlands and consultancy for a variety of international and national organisations.

Birgit Peters is Assistant Professor of Public Law, International Law and European Law at the Faculty of Law of the University of Rostock. She holds a PhD from Humboldt-University Berlin, and an LLM from the University of London. Previously, she was a Postdoctoral Fellow and Lecturer at the Institute for Environmental and Planning Law at the University of Münster, at the Centre for European Environmental Law of the University of Bremen, and at the 'Should States Ratify Human Rights Conventions?' Project at the Norwegian Centre for Human Rights, University of Oslo. She recently edited *Constituting Europe: The European Court of Human Rights in a Global, European and National Context* (edited with Andreas Follesdal and Geir Ulfstein (Cambridge University Press, 2013).

Prabhash Ranjan is an Assistant Professor at the Faculty of Law, South Asian University, New Delhi. He received his PhD in Law from King's College London, where he studied with the benefit of a King's College London School of Law Doctoral Scholarship. He studied at the School of Oriental and African Studies (SOAS) and the University College London (UCL) for an LLM, and passed with distinction as a British Chevening scholar. Prabhash also holds a BA (Hons) in Economics and an LLB from the University of Delhi.

Stephan Schill is Professor of International and Economic Law and Governance at the Faculty of Law of the University of Amsterdam. He is Principal Investigator in a European Research Council-funded project on 'Transnational Public-Private Arbitration as Global Regulatory Governance'. He is admitted to the bar in Germany and New York, has acted as counsel before the European Court of Human Rights, and is a Member of the ICSID List of Conciliators. He is the Editor-in-Chief of the *Journal of World Investment and Trade* and the author of various books and numerous articles on international investment law and arbitration.

Mateja Steinbrück Platiše is a Senior Research Fellow at the Max Planck Institute for Comparative Public Law and International Law and previously a Marie Curie Fellow of the Institute. She is also Lecturer at the Law Faculty of the University of Heidelberg, where she is teaching on human rights. Previously, she was appointed as Lecturer at the Law Faculty of the University of Hamburg and at the Law Faculty of the Catholic University of Lille. Before joining the Max Planck Institute, she worked for several years as a Legal Officer at the European Court of Human Rights. Her other practical experience includes clerkship at the Legal Liaison Office of the United Nations Office in Geneva. After her Master Studies in international law at the University of Ljubljana, she obtained her PhD degree from the same university. She also holds an MJur degree from the University of Oxford, where she specialised in European and Comparative Law.

Rene Urueña is Associate Professor and Director of the International Law Program at the Universidad de Los Andes (Bogota, Colombia). He earned his doctorate in law at the University of Helsinki (*eximia cum laude*), and holds a postgraduate degree in economics from the Universidad de Los Andes. He has been a research fellow at the Institute of Law and Justice at New York University, a Docent of the Institute of Global Law and Policy at Harvard Law School, and a visiting Associate Professor of International Law at the University of Utah. He has twice served as expert witness before the Inter-American Court of Human Rights and is the author of *No Citizens Here: Global Subjects and Participation in International Law* (Martinus Nijhoff, 2012).

Vincent Vleugel is a PhD Researcher at the Faculty of Law of the University of Amsterdam. He holds an LLM degree in Public International Law from the University of Amsterdam, and an MSc degree in International Business from Tilburg University. He previously worked as a policy officer at the Human Rights Department of the Dutch Ministry of Foreign Affairs, with a focus on business and human rights.

Ekaterina Yahyaoui Krivenko is a Lecturer and LLM Programme Director at the Irish Centre for Human Rights (ICHR), School of Law, at the National University of Ireland, Galway. She is also an associate researcher at the Hans and Tamara Oppenheimer Chair in International Law at McGill University, Montreal, Canada. Previously, she taught at the Faculty of Law, University of Montreal. Ekaterina Yahyaoui holds a BA from Geneva University (Switzerland), an LLM from the Albert-Ludwigs University (Freiburg i Br, Germany), a DES in international relations and a PhD in international law from the Graduate Institute of International Studies (Geneva). She leads the project 'International Protection of Human Rights as a Constitutional Issue: Promises, Problems and Prospects' funded by the EU FP7 Marie Curie Career Integration Grant.

Introduction and Framework

Introduction

ANDRÉ NOLLKAEMPER

I. BACKGROUND: RULE OF LAW DYNAMICS

THE PRESENT VOLUME builds on the earlier volume *Rule of Law Dynamics in an Era of International and Transnational Governance* ('Rule of Law Dynamics').[1] That volume argued that the interaction between international and domestic law can be conceptualised as a two-way relationship. On the one hand, international law influences the contents and practice of the rule of law at the domestic level. On the other hand, the domestic rule of law standards and practices influence the development of the rule of law at the international level.

More in particular, these dynamics involve three distinct but interrelated processes: promotion, diffusion, and conversion.[2] The *promotion perspective* looks at strategies and programs of states and organisations to promote the rule of law elsewhere. One important dimension of such rule of law promotion is the process whereby international law, and more concretely, international institutions, seek to promote the rule of law at the national level.[3]

The *conversion perspective* emphasises the decisive role of reception of international legal concepts at the national level, including the transfer of a concept, the translation into the local context, but also in some cases the rejection of the norms. It asks questions about the ways in which concepts are transformed in the process of translation and about the sources of this transformation or their rejection. Of particular relevance are normative conflicts between international law and domestic law or, more generally, between international law and the national rule of law. After all, rule of law promotion does not occur in a vacuum. Rule of law reforms often conflict with, and tend to displace, existing laws.

[1] Michael Zürn, André Nollkaemper, and Randall Peerenboom (eds), *Rule of Law Dynamics: In an Era of International and Transnational Governance* (Cambridge, Cambridge University Press, 2012).

[2] For more details about these processes, Michael Zürn, André Nollkaemper, and Randall Peerenboom, 'Introduction: Rule of Law Dynamics in an Era of International and Transnational Governance' in Zürn, Nollkaemper, and Peerenboom (ibid) 1.

[3] See Helmut Philipp Aust and Georg Nolte, 'International Law and the Rule of Law at the National Level' in Zürn, Nollkaemper, and Peerenboom (ibid) 48.

The *diffusion perspective* focuses on the dissemination of the rule of law concept and asks about the causes and mechanisms that lead to this development. A key manifestation of diffusion is the boomerang effect. The reception and contestation of international norms at domestic level may create a feedback loop to the international level; in particular, to the institutions involved in rule of law promotion. In most cases, this process is not controlled by one actor or one set of actors but results from the interplay of a multiplicity of actors and forces, and in that sense, are themselves interactive and iterative processes with intended and unintended effects. These upward effects of reception and conversion in themselves can be seen as rule of law promotion—one that increasingly targets international organisations—and in that respect there is no hard distinction between diffusion and promotion.

This boomerang effect allows us to conceptualise the relationship between the international rule of law and national law in a more complex way, beyond the conception in which the international rule of law would just require compliance with the prescriptions of international law. It is precisely the expectation of full compliance that may meet with resistance and contestation at the national level. Arguably, such resistance and contestation subsequently effects how we understand the rule of law at the international level.

This process does not mean that, under influence of national conceptions of the rule of law and of feedback loops, the international rule of law becomes a copy of, or even remotely looks like, the national rule of law. The rule of law at the international level is a completely different phenomenon which is to be adjusted to the specific nature of the international legal order.[4] However, it does mean that international law itself, and indeed our understanding of the international rule of law, should take into account the interactive process with the national legal order. This may take a diversity of forms however, including both an increasing influence of rule of law principles in international law, and recognition of deference and diversity at the national level.

Rule of Law Dynamics concluded that to better understand the dynamics of rule of law development, more attention must be paid to the interaction between rule of law promotion, rule of law diffusion, and rule of law conversion. Further research could make us better understand the causal mechanisms that lead states, international organisations, and other transnational actors to adopt and comply with rule of law principles, and how that process may be supported.

[4] See, eg, Jeremy Waldron, 'Are Sovereigns Entitled to the Benefit of the International Rule of Law?' (2011) 22 *European Journal of International Law* 315.

II. THEME OF THE PRESENT VOLUME

It is here where the present volume further develops the themes of *Rule of Law Dynamics*. While international legal scholarship has produced extensive studies as to how the *national* legal order understands, contests, and accommodates international law,[5] much less recognised is the *international* perspective; namely, how the international legal order understands, contests, and accommodates the national reception of international law. The 'international' perspective allows us to situate the national legal order not merely as the venue for implementation but also as the agent for the critical revision of international law and of the universality of policies behind it. We address the critical question as to how the promotion of the rule of law, based on the standards of international law, copes with a wide variety of forms of resistance from the targets of the promotion of the rule of law, and whether international organisations have altered their strategies, programs, and practices to reflect resistance and contestation.

The present volume is induced by the fact that the increasing subject matter overlap between international and national law has led to an increasing interaction between decisions of international and national institutions. International law and institutions prescribe standards concerning, for instance, human rights, crimes, trade, and investment, which are likewise regulated by national law. The national implementation of those standards is reviewed by international institutions, such as human rights courts, criminal tribunals, investment arbitration tribunals, and non-judicial treaty-monitoring bodies. In turn, that very process of review, and the outcomes thereof, may be reviewed and contested at the national level.

This volume focuses in particular on those decisions of national actors that seek to protect, in the process of performance of international obligations, the national rule of law, and on how that may influence the content and development of the international rule of law. Practices discussed in this volume include decisions of domestic courts that contest decisions of international institutions; decisions of domestic courts to curtail immunities of international organisations; and domestic review of investment awards. The central claim of the volume is that interactions between international and national spheres demonstrate that the national legal order is not merely a venue for implementation of international obligations, but also is an agent for the development and revision of the international rule of law.

[5] See, eg, David Sloss (ed), *The Role of Domestic Courts in Treaty Enforcement: A Comparative Study* (Cambridge; New York, Cambridge University Press, 2009); Dinah Shelton (ed), *International Law and Domestic Legal Systems: Incorporation, Transformation, and Persuasion* (Oxford, Oxford University Press, 2011); August Reinisch (ed), *The Privileges and Immunities of International Organizations in Domestic Courts* (New York, NY, Oxford University Press, 2013).

There are wide differences in the degree to which domestic practices indeed challenge international laws or international decisions. In some states, domestic judicial and non-judicial actors grant precedence to international norms or seek to harmonise such prescriptions through the process of interpretation. However, in other states, actors respond to those differences in a more confrontational manner, and directly or indirectly contest international law, including the decisions of international institutions. *Ahmed* and *Kadi* in relation to the UN's listing decisions,[6] *Medellin* on the avoidance of the ICJ decision,[7] and *Horncastle* against the jurisprudence of the European Court of Human Rights (ECtHR)[8] are some prominent examples.

This collection captures these domestic contestations, and the international responses to them, not in terms of fundamental conflicts between international and national law, but rather as an essential component of the 'international rule of law'. The conventional understanding about the international rule of law tends to emphasise the need for national *compliance*, and would consider such national practices as problematic from the perspective of the international rule of law. For instance, UN Secretary-General Annan in his March 2012 report, which was prepared for the high-level meeting of the General Assembly held on 24 September 2012, almost equated national 'compliance' with the achievement of the international rule of law.[9]

Yet the relationships between the international and national rule of law are much more nuanced and interactive. The present book exposes that international law and institutions do not always command blind national obedience to international law, but incorporate the process of adjustment and deference to national law and policies that are protected by the rule of law at the national level. While this flexibility might come at the expense of the certainty of international law, the practice suggests that the international rule of law in relation to the national legal order seems to allow flexibility, national diversity, and pluralism.

[6] *HM Treasury v Mohammed Jabar Ahmed and Others; HM Treasury v Mohammed al-Ghabra; R (Hari El Sayed Sabaei Youssef) v HM Treasury* [2010] UKSC 2 (UK Supreme Court, Judgment of 27 Jan 2010); Cases C-402/05 P and C-415/05 P *Kadi and Al Barakaat International Foundation v Council of the European Union and Commission of the European Communities* [2008] ECR I-06351 (Court of Justice, Judgment of 3 Sept 2008); Joined cases C-584/10 P, C-593/10 P and C-595/10 P *Kadi v European Commission* [2013] ECR (Court of Justice, Judgment of 18 July 2013).

[7] *Medellín v Texas* (2008) 128 S Ct 1346 (US Supreme Court, Judgment of 25 March 2008).

[8] *R v Horncastle and Others* [2009] UKSC 14 (UK Supreme Court, 9 Dec 2009).

[9] Report of the Secretary-General, 'Delivering Justice: Programme of Action to Strengthen the Rule of Law at the National and International Levels', UN Doc A/66/749 (16 March 2012).

III. ROADMAP

We address the questions in 16 substantive chapters and a conclusion. Chapter one, by Machiko Kanetake, will further develop the theoretical framework on the interfaces between the national and the international rule of law. Thereafter, the volume comprises two parts. Part I consists of chapters that address *national contestations*. Part II discusses practices of international institutions that show *deference* to the national rule of law.

In chapter two, Veronika Fikfak discusses different techniques employed by domestic courts to contest the decisions of international organisations and international courts. She argues that domestic contestations facilitate a dialogue between domestic and international institutions, and strengthen, as opposed to undermine, the international rule of law and the foundations for an effective international legal order.

In chapter three, Mateja Steinbrück Platiše examines domestic judicial contestations and their impact on the international rule of law within the specific context of jurisdictional immunities of international organisations. The chapter analyses how domestic courts have resisted and restricted the grant of immunities on international organisations, and how the jurisprudence of international courts and political initiatives taken by international organisations have incrementally responded to domestic judicial contestations. For instance, domestic contestations have incrementally contributed to the development of alternative dispute settlement mechanisms; in particular, within international organisations.

In chapter four, Shotaro Hamamoto discusses the domestic review of investment arbitration awards. The chapter argues that domestic courts' contestation can be normatively justified by investment awards, and explores how domestic contestations can affect the legitimacy of international investment law.

In chapter five, Prabhash Ranjan analyses the role of non-judicial national contestations in the context of international investment law regimes. He argues that while such national contestation may appear to undermine international rule of law reflected in bilateral investment treaties, it in fact has triggered a debate on how to re-craft such treaties in a manner that balances investment protection with the host states' right to regulate in public interest. It has also activated the global community to develop innovative solutions to strengthen the adjudicative process, which will result in a more robust international investment law reflecting the principles of international rule of law.

In chapter six, Rene Urueña examines the roles of domestic non-judicial institutions in the development of the international rule of law. The chapter argues that such institutions can be seen as agents for the revision of the international rule of law; for instance, by acting as norm entrepreneurs, pushing for the development of new international norms.

In chapter seven, Ji Li discusses wider social norms that underlie domestic contestations against international law and institutions within the specific context of trade dispute resolution. He argues that the state is no more than a metaphoric actor in international affairs and that we should recognise that for resolving inter-state trade disputes, the real actors are government officials embedded in their respective social and cultural backgrounds. This chapter argues that domestic social norms that govern the choice of dispute resolution mechanisms play a significant role in determining how states resolve trade disputes, formally or informally.

In chapter eight, the first chapter of part II, Birgit Peters discusses various conversations between the ECtHR and national courts on the implementation and interpretation of the European Convention on Human Rights (ECHR). The chapter highlights the effects of the dialogue between international and national judges on the jurisprudential development of the ECHR and demonstrates that domestic courts' contestation and international courts' responses have been incrementally formalised and methodised within the context of the ECHR.

In chapter nine, Shai Dothan analyses constraints which seem to circumscribe the interpretive discretion of the ECtHR. These suggest that the Court should show deference to the policies of the state whose behaviour is scrutinised; that it should limit its demands from that state to the obligations it took upon itself when it ratified the EcHR; and it should follow the consensual view within Europe, the so-called 'emerging consensus'. Dothan argues that if the ECtHR would apply these interpretive constraints, it would serve the values of the international rule of law and it would show proper deference to the national rule of law.

In chapter ten, Andrew Legg focuses on the margin of appreciation which fosters a dialogue between domestic and international institutions. The doctrine of the margin of appreciation is a key to the interface between international and national legal orders in the sphere of human rights law. This chapter considers the impact that the margin of appreciation has for different conceptions of the international rule of law.

In chapter eleven, Machiko Kanetake analyses the notion of subsidiarity as a key component that sustains a dialogue between domestic and international institutions and thereby develops the international rule of law. It argues that the concept of subsidiarity allows us to assess the practice of international institutions that pay deference to the national rule of law and the political legitimacy behind it. This chapter further assesses whether the idea of subsidiarity contributes to the legitimacy of international institutions and their jurisprudence.

In chapter twelve, Ekaterina Yahyaoui Krivenko addresses the question of how international human rights law, and more broadly the international rule of law, preserves national diversity while ensuring the universal standards of human rights and their legal certainty. The chapter analyses this tension between the universality and diversity in the specific context of reservations to human rights treaties.

In chapter thirteen, Yvonne Donders and Vincent Vleugel explore the interaction between states and the Committee on the Elimination of Discrimination against Women (CEDAW) and their relevance for the development of the international rule of law. The chapter analyses to what extent and how the constructive dialogue between the CEDAW and states enables states to reiterate, revisit, or be challenged on the value of particular cultural norms and practices in relation to international human rights, while at the same time progressively developing consensus and certainty about the meaning of these rights. The chapter also discusses whether this process could strengthen the clarity and predictability of international human rights law as a constitutive element of the international rule of law.

In chapter fourteen, Hege Elisabeth Kjos analyses how arbitration tribunals show deference to domestic court decisions in evaluating those decisions against investment treaty standards in cases brought by foreign investors against host states. The chapter also considers to what extent such deference to national court decisions may contribute to the development of the rule of law.

In chapter fifteen, Jennifer Easterday analyses international institutional deference in the context of post-conflict peace agreements. Easterday argues that the imposition of international rule of law on domestic systems vis-à-vis peace agreements can be counter-productive. The chapter argues that in the face of the criticisms of neo-colonialism, international institutions cannot simply 'impose' their rule of law standards in post-conflict situations. Institutions need to defer to national standards and actors.

In chapter sixteen, Stephan Schill demonstrates that the interdependence and mutual deference between international and national law in the areas of international energy law qualifies our understanding of the rule of law. Conceptualising the various interfaces as a division of labour between national and international actors and instruments leads the author to revise the compliance-based understanding about the international rule of law and see it not as embodying the idea of the rule of international law, but as part of an overarching concept of the global rule of law that is formed through interactive processes of mutual control in which national and international law, national and international actors, and different understandings of the rule of law in national and international law relate to one another. The chapter illustrates the idea of division of labour with the interaction of domestic and international law governing international energy relations.

Chapter seventeen contains the conclusions of the volume.

1

The Interfaces Between the National and International Rule of Law: A Framework Paper

MACHIKO KANETAKE

I. INTRODUCTION

THE INTERFACES BETWEEN national and international law create opportunities for mutual self-reflection. The interfaces are the points where the actors, norms, and procedures belonging to respective legal orders connect and interact with one another. The possibilities for interactions and mutual self-reflection have been expanded by the subject matter[1] overlap between national and international law. International law prescribes standards concerning, for instance, human rights, crimes, trade, investment, public health, and environmental conservation, which are equally governed by national law.[2] International law also enforces those standards through adjudicative venues such as human rights courts, criminal courts and tribunals, and investment arbitration tribunals.

National and international law regulating the exercise of authority are no exception to this subject matter overlap. Such an area of law generally represents the idea of the 'rule of law' which, in this chapter, is defined as

[1] In this chapter, a 'subject matter' is not the same as the 'substance' of law. The subject matter denotes factual or legal scenarios which sustain the need for legal regulation, and with respect to which law extends its regulatory reach. For instance, environmental degradation or the need for environmental conservation is a broad subject matter of environmental law. The subject matter of the 'rule of law' is the exercise of authority by institutions in a society.

[2] See, eg, William Twining, *Globalisation and Legal Theory* (Cambridge, Cambridge University Press, 2000); Joseph HH Weiler, 'The Geology of International Law: Governance, Democracy and Legitimacy' (2004) 64 *Zeitschrift für ausländisches öffentliches Recht und Völkerrecht* 547, 559–61. The subject matter extension of international law into domestic regulatory agendas would likely continue, and the future of international law may indeed lie in its ability to guide and direct domestic actors to act in prescribed ways: see Anne-Marie Slaughter and William Burke-White, 'The Future of International Law Is Domestic (or, the European Way of Law)' (2006) 47 *Harvard International Law Journal* 327.

the regulation of the exercise of authority.[3] *Both* national public law and international human rights law regulate how the government ought to exercise its authority against individuals and entities within its jurisdiction. While the national and 'international'[4] rule of law are both indispensable components of global governance,[5] the overlap has given rise to greater chances of conflict between the two branches of the rule of law. For instance, the rights of detained foreign nationals are regulated by domestic public law (constitutional, administrative, and criminal law) and international human rights treaties and the Vienna Convention on Consular Relations.[6] The parallel regulation created the series of avoidances and conflicts; the US courts interpreted relevant domestic laws and the Vienna Convention (eg, *Breard*).[7] The interpretation was contested by the International Court of Justice (ICJ) in *LaGrand* and *Avena* and by the Inter-American Court of Human Rights (IACtHR),[8] which further invited domestic avoidance in *Medellin*.[9]

Broadly, the interfaces between the national and international rule of law can be analysed from *three* different angles: (1) how the *national* rule of law understands, accepts, and resists the international rule of law; (2) how the *international* rule of law understands, accepts, and resists the national rule of law; and (3) how the interactions can be understood and evaluated from *external* (outside) angles. International scholarship has produced

[3] For the definition of the rule of law in this chapter, see further section II below. This chapter employs the rule of law as an umbrella notion, which is open to the inclusion of both formal and substantive requirements. This chapter's approach is inductive: namely, to induce the meaning of the rule of law through legal practices. At the same time, at an analytical level, this chapter presupposes possible formal and substantive elements of the rule of law developed at the domestic level. By relying on the list of possible rule of law elements as an analytical tool, the present chapter attempts to identify and understand the rule of law materialised in the actual legal practices.

[4] In this chapter, the 'international' rule of law concerns *international law* regulating the exercise of authority by states, international organisations, and other subjects of international law. It does *not* matter which *relations* the rule of law purports to regulate. Namely, the 'international' rule of law may purport to regulate not only state-to-state relations, but also government-individual relations, or the relations between international organisations and individuals.

[5] As Schill critically argues, national and international law should not be captured only from a confrontational angle; they often serve to achieve common goods: see ch 16 (Schill) of this volume.

[6] Vienna Convention on Consular Relations, 24 April 1963, 596 UNTS 261 (entered into force 19 March 1967) Art 36.

[7] eg, *Breard v Greene* (1998) 523 U.S. 371 (US Supreme Court, 14 April 1998).

[8] *LaGrand (Germany v United States)* [2001] ICJ Reports 466; *Avena and Other Mexican Nationals (Mexico v United States of America)* [2004] ICJ Reports 12; *The Right to Information on Consular Assistance in the Framework of the Guarantees of the Due Process of Law* (1999) Inter-Am Ct HR (Ser A) no 16 (1999) (Advisory Opinion OC-16/99 of 1 Oct 1999).

[9] *Sanchez-Llamas v Oregon* (2006) 548 U.S. 331 (US Supreme Court, Judgment of 28 June 2006); *Medellín v Texas* (2008) 128 S Ct 1346 (US Supreme Court, Judgment of 25 March 2008). See also *Request for Interpretation of the Judgment of 31 March 2004 in the Case concerning Avena (Mexico v United States of America)* [2009] ICJ Reports 3 (Judgment of 19 Jan 2009).

extensive studies on the *national* reception of international law, including the international rule of law.[10] Much less recognised is the *international* reception; namely, how the international rule of law understands, accepts, or resists the national rule of law.[11] Now that UN General Assembly resolutions have given recognition to the rule of law at *both* the national and international levels,[12] it is worth examining the question of how the international rule of law finds connection with domestic rule of law practices.

This chapter and volume aim to capture the interfaces from the international perspective. It considers how the national rule of law has any feedback effect on the international rule of law. This angle of this chapter and volume is a response to the critical need for situating the national legal order, not merely as the venue for implementation, but as the agent for the critical revision of the international rule of law[13] and of the universality of policies behind it.[14] This chapter, together with other chapters in

[10] eg, David Sloss, 'Domestic Application of Treaties' in D B Hollis (ed), *The Oxford Guide to Treaties* (Oxford, Oxford University Press, 2012) 367; David Sloss, 'Treaty Enforcement in Domestic Courts: A Comparative Analysis' in D Sloss (ed), *The Role of Domestic Courts in Treaty Enforcement: A Comparative Study* (Cambridge; New York, Cambridge University Press, 2009) 1; Dinah Shelton (ed), *International Law and Domestic Legal Systems: Incorporation, Transformation, and Persuasion* (Oxford, Oxford University Press, 2011). Domestic cases on the application of international law are most comprehensively collected by the Oxford Reports on International Law in Domestic Courts (ILDC) available at: http://opil.ouplaw.com/home/oril.

[11] Among the limited existing studies is Shany's work on the jurisdictional relations between national and international courts. Shany demonstrates that both international and domestic courts avoid or resolve jurisdictional conflicts by stressing the foundational dualism between international and national judicial decisions, resorting to the jurisdictional hierarchy, or by the application of 'comity' which represents the integrative, pragmatic, and flexible approach to the jurisdictional competition: see Yuval Shany, *Regulating Jurisdictional Relations Between National and International Courts* (Oxford, Oxford University Press, 2007).

[12] *2005 World Summit Outcome* UN Doc A/RES/60/1 (24 Oct 2005) para 134. Since 2006, the General Assembly has adopted resolutions entitled 'The Rule of Law at the National and International Levels': see, eg, UN Doc A/RES/61/39 (18 Dec 2006).

[13] Benvenisti and Downs argue that national courts' active application of international law has also signalled to international courts that the national courts are no longer passive recipients of the decisions of the international tribunals but rather equal partners: Eyal Benvenisti and George W Downs, 'National Courts, Domestic Democracy, and the Evolution of International Law' (2009) 20 *European Journal of International Law* 59, 68.

[14] See Mattias Kumm, 'International Law in National Courts: The International Rule of Law and the Limits of the Internationalist Model' (2003) 44 *Virginia Journal of International Law* 19 (suggesting that to situate domestic courts simply as enforcement fora for the international rule of law may be problematic, as it tends to leave the politics behind the international rule of law unchecked); Jean D'Aspremont, 'The Systemic Integration of International Law by Domestic Courts: Domestic Judges as Architects of the Consistency of the International Legal Order' in O K Fauchald and A Nollkaemper (eds), *The Practice of International and National Courts and the (De-)Fragmentation of International Law* (Oxford, Hart Publishing, 2012) 141 (noting that, while the systemic integration of international law in theory places domestic courts in a position to integrate international law, such a one-sided constitutionalist view may not be appropriate). In a similar vein, see Armin von Bogdandy and Ingo Venzke, 'In Whose Name? An Investigation of International Courts' Public Authority and

this volume, analyse the critical feedback from national judicial and non-judicial actors on international legal practices and the international rule of law, and highlight how international law and institutions pay deference to political legitimacy attached to the national rule of law.

The chapter begins with an overview of the concept of the international rule of law, by classifying the *relations* regulated by it as well as the established *elements* of the international rule of law (section II below). The subject matter overlap between the national and international law concerning the regulation of the exercise of authority has invited confrontational and avoidant practices on the part of domestic courts (section III). The confrontational national reception, however, provides normative, conceptual, and political feedback on the international legal order (section IV). As several chapters in this volume further elaborate upon,[15] the international rule of law has then been re-establishing its interfaces with the national rule of law by preserving national competences and, at the same time, making the elements of the international rule of law less formalistic (section V). Despite the national and international claim of hierarchy, the actual manner in which the international rule of law interacts with national law is much more nuanced and heterarchical. The heterarchical interactions have the benefit of preserving the flexibility and national diversity; at the same time, they give rise to questions about the certainty, and whether international law could provide the credible regulatory framework for the international reception of the national rule of law (conclusion).[16]

Its Democratic Justification' (2012) 23 *European Journal of International Law* 7 (suggesting that domestic constitutional organs will retain a critical role in relieving the legitimacy questions levelled against international courts' authority).

[15] See, eg, chs 2 (Fikfak) and 3 (Platiše) of this volume. Fikfak suggests that domestic contestations facilitate a dialogue between domestic and international institutions and have led to incremental procedural changes within international institutions. Platiše argues that domestic contestations have incrementally contributed to the development of alternative dispute settlement mechanisms within international organisations.

[16] This chapter focuses on the interactions between the national and international legal orders. These two legal orders by no means exhaust multiple normative layers in international society. The study of multiple layers of transnational norms, notably done by the NYU-based 'global administrative law' initiative, has the benefit of identifying normative phenomena which could not be captured by the traditional legal lens. At the same time, to capture multiple normative layers as one set of study injects the greater plurality into the concept of law, unless one uses a more loose term of 'norms'. Kingsbury puts forward an extended positivist concept of law, which is empirically identified by social facts, and normatively screened by the publicness requirements: see Benedict Kingsbury, 'The Concept of "Law" in Global Administrative Law' (2009) 20 *European Journal of International Law* 23. At the moment, global administrative 'law' is not (yet) standing on the established rule of recognition (about law), in the same way as is 'international law': see ibid 29–30.

II. THE INTERNATIONAL RULE OF LAW

A. Relations Regulated by the International Rule of Law

As 'a principle of governance'[17] nurtured historically in the domestic legal order,[18] the rule of law primarily regulates the relations between the national government and individuals under its jurisdiction. While the scope of the governmental entities and the applicability of the rule of law to private entities which exercise de facto governmental authority may still be disputed, a historically embedded general idea is that the core addressee of the rule of law is the national government.

With respect to the 'international' rule of law, however, it is by no means clear whose relations it purports to regulate in the first place. This elementary ambiguity stems from the absence of centralised governmental authority in international society, which has traditionally made the rule of law a less pressing issue therein. This no longer holds true; the growth and reinvigoration of international organisations and international courts ('international institutions')[19] have brought the rule of law into the familiar language at the international level.[20]

[17] Report of the Secretary-General, 'The Rule of Law and Transitional Justice in Conflict and Post-conflict Societies' UN Doc S/2004/616 (23 Aug 2004) para 6.

[18] The modern elements of the rule of law were first formulated by AV Dicey. Three meanings of the rule of law developed by Dicey are: (1) the rule by regular law, and not by arbitrary power; (2) equality before the law; and (3) the protection of individual rights by judicial decisions: Albert Venn Dicey, *Introduction to the Study of the Law of the Constitution* (Indianapolis, Liberty Fund, 1982) 110–22. For the earlier roots of the rule of law, see Brian Z Tamanaha, *On the Rule of Law: History, Politics, Theory* (Cambridge, Cambridge University Press, 2004) 7–31 (chs 1–2) (Greek, Roman, and Medieval roots); Simon Chesterman, 'An International Rule of Law?' (2008) 56 *American Journal of Comparative Law* 331, 334–36 (referring to Sir Edward Coke, Samuel Rutherford, and Thomas Hobbes).

[19] In this chapter, 'international institutions' include international organisations (including their political and judicial organs) and international courts established by treaties (such as the ECtHR). Apparently, there are a number of differences among these 'international institutions'. (1) eg, international organisations possess *international personality*, while international courts generally do not. (2) Also, there are *political* institutions (political organs of international organisations, such as the UN Security Council), and *judicial* institutions (judicial organs of international organisations, such as the ICJ, and other international courts). While these differences must be taken into account for the analysis of the interfaces, the focus of this chapter is to provide the framework, on the basis of which I further pursue individual analyses.

[20] This has produced studies such as the NYU-based 'global administrative law' initiative, and the Max Planck Institute's studies on 'international public authority', which aim at establishing the rule of law and accountability for the exercise of authority by international institutions. See Benedict Kingsbury, Nico Krisch, and Richard B Stewart, 'The Emergence of Global Administrative Law' (2005) 68 *Law and Contemporary Problems* 15; Armin von Bogdandy and others (eds), *The Exercise of Public Authority by International Institutions: Advancing International Institutional Law* (Heidelberg, Springer, 2009); Armin von Bogdandy and Ingo Venzke (eds), *International Judicial Lawmaking: On Public Authority and Democratic Legitimation in Global Governance* (Berlin; New York, Springer, 2012).

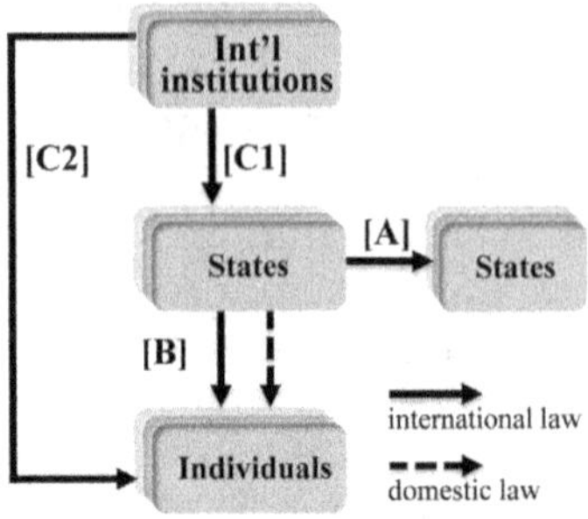

Figure 1: The international rule of law: Relational categorisation

Broadly, the international rule of law concerns three levels of relations: [A] horizontal state-to-state relations, [B] authority exercised by the government against individuals and non-state entities, and [C] authority exercised by international institutions, which [C1] *review* or [C2] effectively *replace*[21] governmental decisions against individuals and non-state entities. By reviewing and effectively replacing the governmental authority, international institutions exercise their authority indirectly (in the case of [C1]) and directly ([C2]) against individuals. (See Figure 1 regarding the three levels of the international rule of law.)

This chapter primarily focuses on the *third* level (indicated as [C] in Figure 1): namely, the international regulation of authority exercised by international institutions. Nevertheless, it would be necessarily intertwined with the *second* level (indicated as [B] in Figure 1), because international institutions review the government's exercise of authority based upon the standards of review which may differ from those accepted under domestic law. The distinction between three different levels of the international rule of law bears significance when one considers the interfaces between the national and international rule of law. It is important because the degree of subject matter connection between the national and international rule of law varies depending on the level of the international rule of law to which one refers.

The international rule of law is most commonly understood as the regulation of horizontal relations between states (ie, the relations indicated as [A] in Figure 1). At this level, the subject matter connection between the national and international rule of law would be the least extensive among

[21] In a formal sense, international institutions cannot 'replace' governmental decisions; international decisions are rendered under international law, while domestic decisions are made under domestic law. Yet international institutions effectively replace governmental decisions when the institutions make decisions against individuals, and such decisions are internationally binding on member states which have authority over those subjects.

the three. The rule of law developed in order to constrain governments and protect individuals within a national legal system is different from the regulation of state-to-state relations. While both regulate the exercise of authority by governments, they differ in terms of subjects against whom authority is exercised, the substance of decisions governed by the rule of law, and their wider legal and political contexts. The subject matter *dis*connection renders Jeremy Waldron's observation particularly pertinent here. As pointed out by Waldron, in this first scenario, the rule of law at the international level ought not to be constructed as protecting sovereign states and their freedom in the same manner as does the domestic rule of law for individuals and their autonomy.[22] The two branches of the rule of law address very different regulatory relations.

By contrast, the subject matter overlap between the national and international rule of law would be extensive if the latter is used for the regulation of governmental authority exercised against individuals and non-state entities (ie, the relations indicated as [B] in Figure 1). International human rights law is a prominent example. An extensive body of treaties and customary international law purport to regulate how the government ensures the protection of rights of individuals. Another example may be international investment law, in that it regulates host states' authority exercised against foreign investors.[23] The key principles of international investment law find parallel presence in domestic public law (administrative and constitutional law), which enables both theoretical comparison and practical conversion between the two areas of law.[24]

The regulation of the exercise of *international* authority (ie, the relations indicated as [C] in Figure 1) can be situated in the middle of these two scenarios. Human rights courts, such as the European Court of Human Rights (ECtHR) and the IACtHR, *review* the human rights compatibility of governmental decisions vis-à-vis individuals. In restricted cases, international criminal courts and tribunals, including the International Criminal

[22] Jeremy Waldron, 'Are Sovereigns Entitled to the Benefit of the International Rule of Law?' (2011) 22 *European Journal of International Law* 315. See also Janne E Nijman, 'Non-State Actors and the International Rule of Law: Revisiting the "Realist Theory" of International Legal Personality' in M Noortmann and C Ryngaert (eds), *Non-State Actor Dynamics in International Law from Law-Takers to Law-Makers* (Farnham, Ashgate, 2010) 91, 97–100 (observing that the beneficiaries of the rule of law are human individuals, and that such rule of law (perhaps inherently) has a substantive element of justice).

[23] On the interactions in the area of international investment law, see further chs 4 (Hamamoto), 5 (Ranjan), and 14 (Kjos) of this volume.

[24] See the 'comparative public law' approach suggested by Schill: Stephan W Schill, 'International Investment Law and Comparative Public Law–An Introduction' in SW Schill (ed), *International Investment Law and Comparative Public Law* (Oxford, Oxford University Press, 2010) 3; Stephan W Schill, 'Fair and Equitable Treatment, the Rule of Law, and Comparative Public Law' in SW Schill (ed), *International Investment Law and Comparative Public Law* (Oxford, Oxford University Press, 2010) 151.

Court (ICC), the International Criminal Tribunal for the former Yugoslavia (ICTY), and the International Criminal Tribunal for Rwanda (ICTR), effectively *replace*[25] governmental decisions by rendering orders against the accused individuals and witnesses without being intermediated by states. Political organs can also replace governmental authority in limited circumstances. For instance, the UN Security Council's sanctions committees designate specific individuals as the targets of global asset freeze measures.[26] Although the asset freeze must be implemented by member states, as far as the prescription of individual targets is concerned, the UN Security Council's sanctions committees prescribe specific individuals and entities as targets of asset freeze. The quantitative and qualitative extension of review and replacement by international institutions is part of the broader political movement initiated by the UN, the World Bank, and other international organisations to promote the rule of law.[27]

At this third level, there is a subject matter *dis*connection between the national and international rule of law in terms of the kind of *institutions* which exercise authority, in that the former regulates the government, and the latter addresses international institutions. Yet the subject matter disconnection is mitigated, insofar as the exercise of authority by international institutions bears resemblance to the exercise of authority by national government, with respect to *subjects* against which authority is indirectly and directly exercised (ie, individuals), and the *substance* of decisions rendered by the institutions.

B. Elements of the International Rule of Law

i. Rule of Law Elements

Having overviewed the relations governed by the international rule of law, the next inquiry is its elements. Whether national or international,

[25] The meaning of 'replacement', see (n 21). The effective replacement takes place only in extraordinary circumstances, in the sense that jurisdiction of the ICC is complementary to national criminal jurisdictions and conditioned on the unwillingness or inability of member states; and that the establishment of the ICTY and ICTR was possible as the UN Security Council determined the existence of a 'threat to the peace' under c VII of the UN Charter.

[26] Between 1994 and February 2014, the UN Security Council instigated 20 sanctions targeting specific individuals and entities. For the summary and analysis of each sanctions regime, see Jeremy Matam Farrall, *United Nations Sanctions and the Rule of Law* (Cambridge, Cambridge University Press, 2007). For the analysis of UN-targeted sanctions from the perspective of the 'interfaces' between national and international rule of law, see further Machiko Kanetake, 'The Interfaces between the National and International Rule of Law: The Case of UN Targeted Sanctions' (2012) 9 *International Organizations Law Review* 267.

[27] eg, the UN provides a post-conflict state with the assistance to draft a rule of law-based constitution and legal mechanisms that support it: see Laura Grenfell, 'The UN and "Rule-Of-Law Constitutions"' (2012) Working Paper no 1.6, Centre for International Governance

the rule of law is one of the lexicons about which few raise an objection as a matter of abstract ideal,[28] but on which many disagree on more specific content. While I do not discount the controversy over the definition, this chapter moves its attention to the consideration of more specific elements. In this chapter, the rule of law is employed as an umbrella notion, which can in theory cover both formal and substantive requirements.[29] A drawback of contemplating the rule of law as embracing both formal and substantive requirements may be to dilute the distinct function of the rule of law per se.[30] Yet the focus of this chapter and volume is *not* to settle the theoretical definition of the rule of law. Rather, this chapter and volume intend to derive the notion of the rule of law from the actual *practices* of national and international law and of interactions between the two legal orders. In identifying the rule of law materialised in practice, I analytically rely upon the major rule of law elements adopted at the national level, and see if they can be found in international legal practices. The reliance upon the national rule of law does not mean that the national rule of law is actually transferable to the international level, or that there indeed exists the overarching rule of law for national and international institutions. What the national concept provides is analytical support for ascertaining the development of the international rule of law.

'Formal' requirements under the umbrella of the rule of law typically include: law-based decision-making (namely, the 'rule by law' requirement),[31] the independence of the judiciary,[32] and democratic and participatory decision-making,[33] as well as certain non-substantive qualities of the law, such as non-retrospectivity, openness, and certainty of law.[34]

and Justice, Canberra. Such rule of law assistance is not to review or replace governmental authority, but it is part of the broader rule of law movement.

[28] At least within the UN fora, the rule of law as an ideal is hard to object to. It is so especially since the UN General Assembly recognised it in 2005 as one of the universal and indivisible core values and principles of the UN: *2005 World Summit Outcome* (n 12) para 119.

[29] The distinction between 'formal' and 'substantive' requirements was articulated by Paul Craig: Paul Craig, 'Formal and Substantive Conceptions of the Rule of Law: An Analytical Framework' (1997) *Public Law* 467. The distinction was further progressively graded by Brian Z Tamanaha, in accordance with the 'thinner' and 'thicker' axes: Tamanaha, *On the Rule of Law* (n 18) 91, and chs 7–9.

[30] See Joseph Raz, 'The Rule of Law and its Virtue' (1977) 93 *Law Quarterly Review* 195, 195–96, 210–11; Craig, 'Formal and Substantive Conceptions of the Rule of Law' (n 29) 468–71, 487 (observing that Raz and Dworkin seem to agree on this point).

[31] Dicey, *Introduction to the Study of the Law of the Constitution* (n 18) 110–13 (first requirement). See Chesterman, 'An International Rule of Law?' (n 18) 342 (a 'government of laws' as the first core definition of the rule of law).

[32] See Chesterman' (n 18) 342 (the second and third core definition); Raz, 'The Rule of Law and its Virtue' (n 30) 200–01 (fourth and seventh principles). In addition to these requirements, one may also add some other formal elements, such as the equality before the law, and the access to courts.

[33] See Tamanaha (n 18) 91, 99–101.

[34] Raz (n 30) 198–99 (first principle); Tamanaha (n 18) 93–99.

'Substantive' elements, on the other hand, require the content of the law and law-based decisions to conform to justice and the protection of individual rights.[35] Each element can of course be defined in a number of different ways.[36] One requirement can also be both formal and substantive. For instance, democracy—although controversy persists as to whether democracy is a possible component of the rule of law—could be defined procedurally as popular election, or more substantively, as the respect for human rights.[37]

ii. The Formalistic and Thin International Rule of Law

The application of these elements to the regulation of international authority (indicated as [C] in Figure 1, section II(A)) exposes the thin character of the international rule of law.

There is already broad recognition that the rule of law applies at the international level,[38] and international organisations are not exempt from it. In the 'Declaration of the High-level Meeting of the General Assembly on the Rule of Law and the National and International Levels' adopted in September 2012,[39] the General Assembly recognised that 'the rule of law applies to all States equally, *and to international organizations, including the United Nations and its principal organs*'.[40]

Among the rule of law elements listed in section B(i) above, it is well established that the 'rule by law' element applies to international organisations. The decisions of international organisations are governed by a constituent instrument. Even such a highly political organ as the UN

[35] See Tamanaha (n 18) ch 8 (substantive theories). On the relationships between formal and substantive elements, see Randall P Peerenboom, 'Varieties of Rule of Law: An Introduction and Provisional Conclusion' in Randall P Peerenboom (ed), *Asian Discourses of Rule of Law: Theories and Implementation of Rule of Law in Twelve Asian Countries, France, and the U.S.* (London; New York, Routledge, 2004) 1, 5–6 (observing that a state's adoption of a formal conception of the rule of law reflects a particular conception about substantive elements).

[36] eg, the 'rule by law' requirement could be met by every modern state if it only required (whatever) laws to be adopted. See Tamanaha (n 18) 92–93; Raz (n 30) 197. By contrast, if it is contrasted with the rule by 'arbitrary power' as Dicey did, it may serve to restrict the use of public powers for private ends. See Dicey (n 18) 110, 120. See also Raz (n 30) 203.

[37] See Brett Bowden and Hilary Charlesworth, 'Defining Democracy in International Institutions' in B Bowden, H Charlesworth, and J M Farrall (eds), *The Role of International Law in Rebuilding Societies After Conflict: Great Expectations* (Cambridge; New York, Cambridge University Press, 2009) 90, 90–100 (analysing various international statements regarding the definition of democracy).

[38] *2005 World Summit Outcome* (n 12) para 134. Since 2006, the General Assembly has adopted resolutions entitled 'The Rule of Law at the National and International Levels': see, eg, UN Doc A/RES/61/39 (18 Dec 2006).

[39] UN GA Res adopted on 24 Sept 2012, 'Declaration of the High-level Meeting of the General Assembly on the Rule of Law at the National and International Levels' UN Doc A/RES/67/1 (30 Nov 2012).

[40] ibid para 2 (emphasis added).

Security Council is bound by law,[41] as reiterated by the Appeals Chamber of the ICTY in *Tadić*.[42] The same 'rule by law' element should also apply to international courts, whose mandates are much more restricted than (the political organs of) international organisations. The independence of the judiciary is implicit in the function of judicial bodies,[43] and the independence of judges is often explicitly provided in relevant treaties.

Yet beyond this, it is difficult to identify an established rule of law element. First, this 'rule by law' requirement itself is understood in a formalistic manner, in that it does not exclude the arbitral exercise of power by political organs.[44] The selection of judges through international politics can also call into question the qualifications, independence, and impartiality of international judges.[45]

Second, other major formal and substantive requirements of the rule of law have yet to be established. The decision-making processes of international organisations are certainly not democratic, in the sense that they do not ensure elections and equitable representation.[46] Also, there remains uncertainty as to whether international organisations are bound by international human rights law. One may observe that the human rights obligation attaches *a priori* to the legal personality of international organisations enjoyed under international law.[47] However, international personality has, in principle, no predetermined content in international law.[48] The presumption that international organisations are born with no predestined entitlement and obligations is, of course, increasingly subject to qualification by the development of common rules on international

[41] As the International Court of Justice (ICJ) affirmed at the outset of the UN, the 'political character of an organ cannot release it from the observance of the treaty provisions established by the Charter when they constitute limitations of its powers': *Admission of a State to the United Nations (Charter, Art 4)* [1948] ICJ Reports 64 (Advisory Opinion of 28 May 1948).

[42] The Tribunal observed 'neither the text nor the spirit of the Charter conceives of the Security Council as *legibus solutus* (unbound by law)': *Prosecutor v Duško Tadić*, 2 Oct 1995, International Criminal Tribunal for the former Yugoslavia, Appeals Chamber, Decision on Jurisdiction, no IT-94-1-AR72, para 28 (in relation to the Council's power under Art 39 of the UN Charter).

[43] eg, the UN Security Council, a political organ, cannot review the individual decisions of judicial organs such as the ICTY which was established by the Council itself.

[44] See Chesterman (n 18) 351.

[45] See von Bogdandy and Venzke, 'In Whose Name?' (n 14) 32–36.

[46] See Robert O Keohane, 'The Concept of Accountability in World Politics and the Use of Force' (2003) 24 *Michigan Journal of International Law* 1121, 1136.

[47] August Reinisch, 'Developing Human Rights and Humanitarian Law Accountability of the Security Council for the Imposition of Economic Sanctions' (2001) 95 *American Journal of International Law* 851, 858–59; Nigel D White, *The Law of International Organisations* (2nd edn, Manchester, Manchester University Press, 2005) 217. Similarly, Henry G Schermers and Niels Blokker, *International Institutional Law Unity Within Diversity* (4th rev edn, Boston, Martinus Nijhoff Publishers, 2003) 1002; Felice Morgenstern, *Legal Problems of International Organizations* (Cambridge, Grotius Publications, 1986) 32.

[48] Schermers and Blokker, *International Institutional Law Unity Within Diversity* (n 47) 990, 992–93; White, *The Law of International Organisations* (n 47) 40–41.

organisations.[49] Yet the variance among international organisations has so far hampered the development of substantive rules, such as human rights law, into the corps of common institutional rules. Unless the constitutive instruments of international organisations specifically mandate them to ensure respect for international human rights law, it would be difficult to argue, in a general sense, the institutional human rights obligations.

III. NATIONAL RECEPTION OF THE INTERNATIONAL RULE OF LAW

Despite the formalistic and thin character of the international rule of law, international organisations and courts often direct and specify how the government ought to exercise its authority vis-à-vis individuals under its jurisdiction. This subject matter extension leads us to consider how national legal practices—which are built upon the national rule of law—understand, accept, and reject international institutions, international law constituting them, and, overall, the international rule of law on which international institutions and international law are based.

A. The Gap and Asymmetry in the Rule of Law

The formalistic and thin international rule of law governing the authority of international institutions has created a *gap* with the more substantive and thicker national rule of law. The gap between two branches of the rule of law has then solicited confrontational and avoidant national responses to the decisions of international institutions. The gap is problematic especially for domestic courts, which are circumscribed both by the national rule of law and international obligations owed by their states.[50]

Despite this gap, international institutions review and replace governmental authority based upon the more substantive and thicker element of the rule of law. The widely cited definition of the rule of law given by the UN Secretary-General in 2004 in part illustrates the *asymmetry* in the international rule of law for the regulation of *governmental* authority

49 Some examples include an ultra vires doctrine, the legal personality of international organisations, an implied power doctrine, interpretation of constituent instruments, and a series of rules on immunities and privileges: see Dapo Akande, 'International Organizations' in M D Evans (ed), *International Law* (3rd edn, Oxford, Oxford University Press, 2010) 252, 255–76.

50 In this sense, domestic courts are therefore placed in a 'double bind': see André Nollkaemper, *National Courts and the International Rule of Law* (Oxford; New York, Oxford University Press, 2011) 13–15.

on the one hand (indicated as [B] in Figure 1, section II(A) above), and that of *international* authority on the other (shown as [C] in Figure 1). The UN definition encompasses such elements as accountability to laws, independent adjudication, consistency with human rights standards, fairness, the separation of powers, participation, legal certainty, and legal transparency.[51] This expansive list is described as 'almost certainly go[ing] beyond what states would actually implement'.[52]

B. The Claim of Ultimate Authority

While it is true that national courts demonstrate their amenability to international law and proactively invoke international law as leverage to challenge governmental decisions,[53] the amenability of domestic courts has thus been compensated by a growing number of confrontational and avoidant practices.[54]

Domestic courts normally claim their ultimate authority to determine the relationships with international law at the domestic level based on the

[51] Report of the Secretary-General, 'The Rule of Law and Transitional Justice in Conflict and Post-conflict Societies' (n 17) para 6.

[52] Simon Chesterman, '"I'll Take Manhattan": The International Rule of Law and the United Nations Security Council' (2009) 1 *Hague Journal on the Rule of Law* 67, 68.

[53] See Eyal Benvenisti, 'Reclaiming Democracy: The Strategic Uses of Foreign and International Law by National Courts' (2008) 102 *American Journal of International Law* 241. Domestic courts employ international law as an interpretive aid, even if they are *not* obligated to do so to: see Robert Howse and Ruti Teitel, 'Beyond Compliance: Rethinking Why International Law Really Matters' (2010) 1 *Global Policy* 127, 132 (observing that the influence of international law in domestic law (and before domestic courts) cannot be reduced to the 'compliance' of international law). The interpretive rules commonly employed by domestic courts, such as consistent interpretation, and systemic integration, facilitate the presence of international law before national courts: see further Nollkaemper, *National Courts and the International Rule of Law* (n 50) ch 7 (Consistent Interpretation); D'Aspremont, 'The Systemic Integration of International Law by Domestic Courts: Domestic Judges as Architects of the Consistency of the International Legal Order' (n 14).

[54] Domestic courts directly and indirectly review the decisions of international organisations and the judgments of international courts. See, eg, August Reinisch, *International Organizations Before National Courts* (Cambridge; New York, Cambridge University Press, 2000); Erika De Wet and André Nollkaemper, 'Review of Security Council Decisions by National Courts' (2002) 45 *German Yearbook of International Law* 166; August Reinisch (ed), *Challenging Acts of International Organizations Before National Courts* (Oxford, Oxford University Press, 2010) chs 1–5. Judicial avoidance and contestations were accompanied by wider political oppositions against the promotion and the diffusion of the rule of law by international law and institutions: see, eg, Michael Zürn, Andre Nollkaemper, and Randy Peerenboom (eds), *Rule of Law Dynamics: In an Era of International and Transnational Governance* (Cambridge, Cambridge University Press, 2012); Anne Peters, 'The Globalization of State Constitutions' in J E Nijman and A Nollkaemper (eds), *New Perspectives on the Divide Between National and International Law* (Oxford; New York, Oxford University Press, 2007) 251.

authorising rule of domestic law.[55] The *Görgülü* case[56] before the German Constitutional Court is an illustrative example; the Court affirmed that it had the ultimate authority to determine the compatibility of the judgments of the ECtHR with its constitutional provisions. In the UK, the Supreme Court in *Horncastle* also observed that 'it is open to [the] court to decline to follow the Strasbourg decision' when a decision of the Strasbourg Court fails to sufficiently accommodate particular aspects of the UK's domestic process,[57] adding further to the international feedback of such national resistance as being a 'valuable dialogue' between the UK Court and the Strasbourg Court. In Spain and France, judges likewise secure their interpretive discretion to determine whether and how ECtHR judgments have effect in the domestic settings.[58]

C. Techniques and Bases for National Avoidance and Contestations

Specific techniques and grounds under which domestic courts avoid and contest the decisions of international institutions vary depending on whether those decisions are rendered by political or judicial institutions, whether states have monist or dualist traditions, the kind of treaties involved, and the wider political and judicial climate surrounding the judges. While the grounds cannot be exhaustively elaborated upon, here I refer to four legal techniques and grounds on the basis of which courts limit the domestic effect of the decisions of international organisations and courts.

First, domestic courts may deny the *domestic applicability* of particular decisions in the first place. In a 'monist' state, in which international agreements automatically acquire domestic validity, domestic courts encounter the question of whether or not particular international treaties are directly applicable (or so-called self-executing-treaties).[59] A well-known case in

[55] Domestic lawyers often employ the vertical narratives, regarding national constitutions as the ultimate source of authority of law, and expecting domestic courts to reject international decisions that are inconsistent with fundamental domestic principles: see Shany, *Regulating Jurisdictional Relations Between National and International Courts* (n 11) 6.

[56] 2 BvR 1481/04 (Judgment of 14 Oct 2004) (Decision of the Federal Constitutional Court), English translation available at: http://bverfg.de/entscheidungen/rs20041014_2bvr148104en.html. For analysis, see Matthias Hartwig, 'Much Ado About Human Rights: The Federal Constitutional Court Confronts the European Court of Human Rights' (2005) 6 *German Law Journal* 869.

[57] *R v Horncastle and Others* [2009] UKSC 14 (Judgment of UK Supreme Court, 9 Dec 2009) [11] (Lord Phillips).

[58] See Nico Krisch, 'The Open Architecture of European Human Rights Law' (2008) 71 *Modern Law Review* 183.

[59] The conditions under which international treaties have direct applicability vary according to states and their domestic courts. It is nevertheless possible to derive some common conditions for direct effect: the *subjective* element that parties have not excluded the direct

this regard is *Medellin*, in which the US Supreme Court observed that ICJ decisions were not automatically enforceable as domestic law.[60] In monist states, domestic courts are generally endowed with the power to tentatively block the application of particular treaties in the domestic settings, while, in dualist states, such power is, in principle, entrusted to the hands of legislative and executive bodies.

Second, judges can also *interpret* international law as more favourable to domestic law and political interests. This was illustrated, for instance, by the US Supreme Court in *Sanchez-Llamas*.[61] In this case, the US Supreme Court interpreted Article 36(2) of the Vienna Convention on Consular Relations as requiring the conformity of the *treaty provision* with domestic laws and regulations.[62] This interpretation is contrasted with the ICJ's reading of the same article in *LaGrand*, in which the ICJ regarded the provision as requiring the conformity of *national law* with the treaty.[63] The ICJ emphasised giving 'full effect' to the conventional rights, while the US court stressed the condition 'in accordance with the laws and regulations of the receiving State'. Both arguments may be defended by reference to the terms of Article 36(2) of the Vienna Convention.

The third is the principle of *separation of power* at the domestic level. Domestic courts may avoid or contest the specific decisions of international institutions by leaving the political branches to decide whether

applicability of the treaty as a whole, and the *objective* elements that treaty provisions are precise and complete enough to be applied by domestic courts. See Nollkaemper (n 50) 134–38; Yuji Iwasawa, *International Law, Human Rights, and Japanese Law: The Impact of International Law on Japanese Law* (Oxford, Clarendon Press, 1998) 44–49. See also *A and B v Government of the Canton of Zurich, Appeal Judgement, Case no 2P273/1999* ILDC 350 (CH 2000) (Switzerland, Federal Supreme Court, 22 Sept 2000) (denying the direct applicability of ICESCR provisions).

[60] *Medellín v Texas* (n 9) 1356–65. In a similar vein, the US courts in *Corus Staal* have rejected the direct applicability of the reports of the Dispute Settlement Body (DSB) of the World Trade Organization (WTO): *Corus Staal BV v Department of Commerce*, Appeal judgment (2005) 395 F 3d 1343 (Fed Cir 2005); ILDC 1649 (US 2005) (US, Court of Appeals for the Federal Circuit, 21 Jan 2005) 1348 (quoting *Timken Co v United States*, 354 F3d 1334, 1344 (Fed Cir 2004)). Likewise, *United States v Lombardo and ors, Ruling on Motion to Dismiss* (2007) Case no 2:07-CR-286 TS (D Utah); ILDC 1055 (US 2007) (US, District Court of Utah, Central Division, 13 Dec 2007). In these cases, the US courts have regarded WTO reports as non-binding (on the US) and non-self-executing (before US courts). This approach is contrasted with the interpretive use of WTO DSB reports by a NAFTA Chapter 19 bi-national panel: *In the Matter of Certain Softwood Lumber Products from Canada, Final Affirmative Antidumping Determination* (2005) File no USA-CDA-2002-1904-02 (Art 1904 Binational Panel Review under NAFTA, 9 June 2005) 39–43. For details, see Shany (n 11) 56–60, 83–84.

[61] *Sanchez-Llamas v Oregon* (n 9).

[62] See ibid 347–48. Art 36(2) of the Vienna Convention on Consular Relations reads in full: 'The rights referred to in paragraph 1 of this article shall be exercised in conformity with the laws and regulations of the receiving State, subject to the proviso, however, that the said laws and regulations must enable full effect to be given to the purposes for which the rights accorded under this article are intended': Vienna Convention on Consular Relations (n 6) Art 36(2).

[63] *LaGrand (Germany v United States)* (n 8) 497–98, para 91.

or how the rules can be given effect to in the domestic legal order.[64] In *Ahmed*,[65] the UK Supreme Court found that the executive orders (the Terrorism Order and the Al-Qaida and Taliban Order), which implemented the UN Security Council's sanctions regimes on terrorist financing, were ultra vires and unlawful. The Court so decided on the ground that the Parliament did not empower the executive to override fundamental rights.[66] In this case, the Court therefore upheld the parliamentary supremacy, as Lord Phillips observed, in determining whether and how international measures should be imposed at the domestic level when fundamental rights were affected.[67]

Finally, the *protection of fundamental rights* has been an important legal basis of contestations. Courts often invoke the safeguarding of human rights as a basis for which they directly or indirectly review the decisions of international organisations. The aforementioned *Ahmed* case before the UK Supreme Court is one example. The Court upheld fundamental rights as well as parliamentary supremacy, and, by so doing, effectively reviewed the human rights compatibility of the listing decisions of the UN Security Council's targeted sanctions regimes. Human rights used as the standards of (indirect) review by domestic courts are often no longer parochial national conceptions, but often substantively formulated by international human rights law regulating governmental authority.[68]

IV. CHARACTERISING THE POINTS OF CONNECTION BETWEEN THE NATIONAL AND INTERNATIONAL RULE OF LAW

A brief overview of national avoidance and contestations then brings us to the question as to how domestic legal practices, including confrontational ones, have any feedback effect on the international rule of law.

[64] See Eyal Benvenisti, 'Judicial Misgivings Regarding the Application of International Law: An Analysis of Attitudes of National Courts' (1993) 4 *European Journal of International Law* 159 (the use of political question and act of state doctrine).

[65] *HM Treasury v Mohammed Jabar Ahmed and Others; HM Treasury v Mohammed al-Ghabra; R (Hari El Sayed Sabaei Youssef) v HM Treasury* (2010) [2010] UKSC 2 (UK Supreme Court, Judgment of 27 Jan 2010).

[66] See, eg, ibid [45], [61] (Lord Hope).

[67] ibid [157] (Lord Phillips). The aforementioned *Medellin* is also combined with the separation of power argument with respect to the effect of the President's Memorandum on the domestic enforceability of the ICJ judgment. The US Supreme Court held that it is up to the Congress to decide whether a non-self-executing treaty (in this case, the ICJ judgment) could be enforceable at the domestic level: see *Medellín v Texas* (n 9) 1368.

[68] See André Nollkaemper, 'The European Courts and the Security Council: Between Dédoublement Fonctionnel and Balancing of Values: Three Replies to Pasquale De Sena and Maria Chiara Vitucci' (2009) 20 *European Journal of International Law* 862, 868–70.

A. Legal

A classic answer to the question of how national legal practices connect with international law would be that under international law, national rule of law practices are, after all, part of *state practices*,[69] which contribute to the creation of new customary international law[70] or new treaty interpretations.[71] National legal practices may also form part of the general principles of law.[72] National case law may also qualify as *opinio juris*.[73] Before international courts, judicial decisions, possibly including those of national courts,[74] would be invoked as subsidiary means for the determination of rules of international law.[75]

From these traditional points of view, the practices of national courts against the decisions of international institutions inevitably connect with international law as part of state practice. For instance, the ECtHR makes considerable use of domestic (case) law in the interpretation and development of the Convention.[76] Nevertheless, these classic modes of interaction

[69] See Anthea Roberts, 'Comparative International Law? The Role of National Courts in Creating and Enforcing International Law' (2011) 60 *International & Comparative Law Quarterly* 57, 61–64 (pointing out a dual role of domestic courts to create law as state practice, and to enforce established international law).

[70] Hersch Lauterpacht, 'Decisions of Municipal Courts as a Source of International Law' (1929) 10 *British Year Book of International Law* 65; Robert Jennings and Arthur Watts (eds), *Oppenheim's International Law* (9th edn, Harlow, Essex, Longman, 1992) 41; ILA, Statement of Principles Applicable to the Formation of General Customary International Law, principle 9, reproduced in ILA, Report of the Sixty-Ninth Conference (2000); Benedetto Conforti, *International Law and the Role of Domestic Legal Systems* (Dordrecht, Martinus Nijhoff Publishers, 1993) 79 ('domestic court decisions constitute one of the most important categories of custom-shaping State behaviour'). See further Nollkaemper (n 50) 267–71.

[71] Treaty interpretation can be developed through subsequent practice which establishes the agreement of the parties regarding its interpretation: Vienna Convention on the Law of Treaties, 23 May 1969 (entered into force 27 Jan 1980) 1155 UNTS 311, Art 31(3)(b).

[72] See Statute of the International Court of Justice, 26 June 1945, 39 AJIL Supp 215 (1945) (entered into force on 24 Oct 1945) (1945) Art 38(1)(c). It has indeed been argued that judicial review or the access to information might form part of the general principles of law. For the analysis of judicial review, see Erika de Wet, 'Judicial Review as an Emerging General Principle of Law and its Implications for the International Court of Justice' (2000) 47 *Netherlands International Law Review* 181. On the access to information and the principle of transparency, see Devika Hovell, 'The Deliberate Deficit: Transparency, Access to Information and UN Sanctions' in J Farrall and K Rubenstein (eds), *Sanctions, Accountability and Governance in a Globalised World* (Cambridge, Cambridge University Press, 2009) 92.

[73] Hersch Lauterpacht observes that the decisions of municipal courts within a particular state, 'when endowed with sufficient uniformity and authority, may be regarded as expressing the *opinio juris* of that State': Hersch Lauterpacht, *The Development of International Law by the International Court* (Cambridge, Cambridge University Press, Originally Published in 1958, 1982) 20.

[74] See ibid.

[75] See ICJ Statute (n 72) Art 38(1)(d). Regarding the ICJ's reference to domestic court decisions, see André Nollkaemper, 'The Role of Domestic Courts in the Case Law of the International Court of Justice' (2006) 5 *Chinese Journal of International Law* 301.

[76] Paul Mahoney, 'The Comparative Method in Judgments of the European Court of Human Rights: Reference back to National Law' in G Canivet, MT Andenæs and

apply only to a very limited extent with respect to the development of the international rule of law concerning the regulation of international authority; the standards of review applied by domestic courts are often for those applicable to the national government and not to international institutions per se.

B. Normative, Conceptual, and Political

Domestic avoidance and contestations may rather contribute to the development of the international rule of law in normative, conceptual, and political terms. For instance, if domestic courts refer to each other's decisions,[77] the inter-judicial communication may even create *norms* which are yet to become part of formal international law but which affect the way international organisations and international judicial institutions render their decisions.

Another possibility is a *conceptual* connection. National law and the decisions of national courts may be translated into international law by analogy.[78] The analogical reasoning is widely used in judicial practices as well as in the process of treaty-making.[79] Traditionally, the analogical travelling of national law to international law was limited to 'private law'.[80] Nevertheless, as the exercise of authority by international institutions

D Fairgrieve (eds), *Comparative Law before the Courts* (London, British Institute of International and Comparative Law, 2004) 135.

[77] Judicial dialogue can be broadly defined as the reference in the reasoning of a court to the decisions rendered by other national (or regional or international) courts ('foreign' decisions) which the court is not obligated to follow. For transnational judicial dialogue in general and its role in the development of international law, see further, eg, Anne-Marie Slaughter, 'A Global Community of Courts' (2003) 44 *Harvard International Law Journal* 191; Christopher A Whytock, 'Transnational Judicial Governance' (2012) 2 *St John's Journal of International and Comparative Law* 55; Benvenisti and Downs, 'National Courts, Domestic Democracy, and the Evolution of International Law' (n 13) (observing that the loose form of inter-judicial coordination has contributed to the mitigation of fragmentation of norms within the international legal systems). There is, however, the methodological weakness of the discretionary cross-citation of foreign judgments by domestic courts: see Roberts, 'Comparative International Law?' (n 69). See also ch 9 (Dothan) of this volume. Dothan observes that judicial dialogue among states, as well as the emerging consensus doctrine adopted by the ECtHR, are based upon the weak assessment of national practices.

[78] For the different types of analogical reasoning, and the practices of international courts, see Robert Kolb, *Interprétation et création du droit international: Esquisses d'une herméneutique juridique moderne pour le droit international public* (Brussels, Bruylant, 2006) 710–56.

[79] See, eg, the 'legal borrowing' in the making of climate change treaties: Jonathan B Wiener, 'Something Borrowed for Something Blue: Legal Transplants and the Evolution of Global Environmental Law' (2000) 27 *Ecology Law Quarterly* 1295.

[80] Hersch Lauterpacht, *Private Law Sources and Analogies of International Law: With Special Reference to International Arbitration* (Union, NJ, The Lawbook Exchange, Ltd, 1927).

shares similarities with that of governmental authority, there is the growing possibility of applying a 'public law' analogy.[81]

The most likely mode of feedback on the development of the international rule of law is *political*. If domestic courts legally prejudice national implementation of international decisions, their effectiveness would be simply undermined if states encountered legal impediments to their implementation.[82] Yet the political impact that each national court decision may produce is by no means uniform. It varies, first, by the geopolitical location in which the courts reside. In addition to the effect of decisions themselves, judges' specific reasoning and narratives also determine the extent to which domestic court decisions foster political momentum and any changes in judicial interpretation at the international level.

The different modes of connection and feedback involve *different actors* and their *differing roles*. In a classic 'state practice' mode of connection, the participants are limited to those actors whose conduct is attributable to a state. Domestic courts' decisions are merely part of a collection of the possibly contradictory acts of state. At the *normative* point of connection, on the other hand, the role of judicial branches may carry greater weight than that of non-judicial branches of the government. At the *normative* point, non-governmental entities, by contesting international decisions, can also participate in the development of transnational norms. The *theoretical* point of connection generally requires international adjudicative bodies in executing the theoretical interaction. Finally, at the *political* point of connection, the international political significance of national courts varies depending upon their geographical location. Suppose that the well-known *Kadi* decisions, which indirectly reviewed the listing decisions of the UN Security Council's targeted sanctions, were rendered by the court of a small state, that the state is not a well-known advocate of the rule of law, and that the decisions were not readily available in English. In this case, national (regional)[83] contestations might have brought far more

[81] See Aleksandar Momirov and Andria Naude Fourie, 'Vertical Comparative Law Methods: Tools for Conceptualising the International Rule of Law' (2009) 2 *Erasmus Law Review* 291. While Momirov and Fourie do not specifically distinguish between 'private law analogy' and 'public law analogy', their 'vertical comparative law methods' largely concern public law comparison.

[82] eg, *Kadi* and other national and EU court decisions against the listing decisions of the UN Security Council's sanctions committees create legal impediments to national implementation and undermine the operational effectiveness of sanctions regimes: see Kanetake, 'The Interfaces between the National and International Rule of Law: The Case of UN Targeted Sanctions' (n 26) s 3.3.4. Political interactions also occur between national and international courts; national courts' support to particular international judgments contributes to the enhancement of the legitimacy and effectiveness of international courts in question: see Shai Dothan, 'How International Courts Enhance Their Legitimacy' (2013) 14 *Theoretical Inquiries in Law* 455, s II.

[83] Within the binary national-international classification, this chapter situates the decisions of EU courts on the 'national' side. Apparently, the national-international classification

moderate progress in the regulation of the UN Security Council's listing decisions.

V. INTERNATIONAL RECEPTION OF THE NATIONAL RULE OF LAW

National contestations and avoidant practices may have therefore brought incremental changes to the international reception of the national rule of law. The international reception of national law would of course vary depending on cases. Here, I simply refer to two interrelated responses by which international institutions interact with the national rule of law.

A. The Distribution of Competences

i. Principle of Subsidiarity

The first manner is to keep a distance from the national rule of law by creating the *distribution of competence.*[84] More specifically, international institutions have been adopting the idea of 'subsidiarity' as a technique or basis to avoid conflicts between national practices and international law, and to preserve the autonomy of member states (and their cultural identity) from international law and the decisions of international institutions.[85]

The idea and language of subsidiarity is relatively unfamiliar to international law, as contrasted with EU law, which formally introduced subsidiarity.[86] This unfamiliarity may be largely because international law

does not sit easily with EU law which is considered as autonomous and has many distinct characteristics. Yet the purpose of this chapter is to examine how the rule of law regulating international authority has developed through the interactions with other legal orders, and, for that purpose, this chapter situates the decisions of the EU courts on the national side.

[84] Here, I prefer to use 'competence' rather than 'jurisdiction'. While these two English terms can be used interchangeably, 'jurisdiction' is more often invoked as a matter of general fields, while 'competence' is more likely used for *particular* cases which in principle meet the general jurisdictional requirement: see Gerald Fitzmaurice, 'The Law and Procedure of the International Court of Justice, 1951-4: Questions of Jurisdiction, Competence and Procedure' (1958) 34 *British Year Book of International Law* 1, 8–9.

[85] On subsidiarity, see further ch 11 of this volume.

[86] Introduced in 1993 by the Maastricht Treaty; Presently, Consolidated Version of the Treaty on the Functioning of the European Union (TFEU) Art 5. See generally, eg, George A Bermann, 'Taking Subsidiarity Seriously: Federalism in the European Community and the United States' (1994) 94 *Columbia Law Review* 331; Graínne de Búrca, 'Proportionality and Subsidiarity as General Principles of Law' in U Bernitz and J Nergelius (eds), *General Principles of European Community Law* (The Hague, Kluwer Law International, 2000) 95, 101–12; Theodor Schilling, 'A New Dimension of Subsidiarity: Subsidiarity as a Rule and a Principle' (1994) 14 *Yearbook of European Law* 203.

developed primarily for the regulation of relations between supposedly symmetrical sovereign states, and without a higher, superior authority. Due to this decentralised structure, there was no strong need for legally restraining and counterbalancing the authority exercised by 'higher' governance units. However, the regulatory extension of international law into domestic regulatory agendas has created the asymmetrical interactions for which international law claims its supremacy (as represented by Article 27 of the Vienna Convention on the Law of Treaties). This has increasingly injected the idea of subsidiarity into international law as a potential principle to guide the allocation of competences between national and international institutions.

Subsidiarity commonly refers to a 'principle which guides the allocation and exercise of public authority in systems of multi-level governance'.[87] Subsidiarity gives preference to the decision-making at a particular (and usually lower) level of governance. By so doing, the principle of subsidiarity is, in a way, to counterbalance the claim and exercise of superior authority by the higher level of governance units, and protects the autonomy of decision-making at the lower level and its political and cultural identity.[88] It is originated in Catholic thought, which upholds the autonomy of lesser communities for human flourishing. The flourishing of persons requires the (subsidiary) space of social and cultural communities, which must be safeguarded against, for instance, political bodies.[89] While the principle of subsidiarity is now applied in different political contexts, it can still be traced back to the Catholic Church's original notion, in that one of its main values remains to be the preservation of the autonomy of individuals and their communities.

While 'subsidiarity' per se is still an unfamiliar term, international law and the practices of international institutions accommodate a number of examples which can be regarded as the realisation of the notion of subsidiarity. For instance, the complementarity principle of the ICC can be seen as a specific application of the subsidiarity principle protecting the autonomy of states, and indirectly, that of individuals.[90] Also, the way the ICTY implemented the 'Completion Strategy' seems to have effectively introduced the principle of complementarity (and thus the idea of subsidiarity) into the practice of the ICTY.[91]

[87] Isabel Feichtner, 'Subsidiarity' in R Wolfrum (ed), *Max Planck Encyclopedia of Public International Law* (New York, Oxford University Press, 2008) online edn at: http://mpepil.com, para 1.

[88] See ibid paras 3, 5.

[89] See Jonathan Chaplin, 'Subsidiarity: the Concept and the Connections' (1997) 4 *Ethical Perspectives* 117–20.

[90] See Feichtner, 'Subsidiarity' (n 87) para 28.

[91] Fausto Pocar, 'Completion or Continuation Strategy? Appraising Problems and Possible Developments in Building the Legacy of the ICTY' (2008) 6 *Journal of International Criminal Justice* 655.

ii. Margin of Appreciation

The margin of appreciation[92] developed by the ECtHR as a judicial doctrine is one of the manifestations of the idea of subsidiarity.[93] The similar deferential review is also seen in the jurisprudence of the IACtHR—albeit not as explicitly as it is in the case of the ECtHR. The ECHR mechanisms premise that there is the institutional division of power between national and international institutions, and that the international mechanisms are subsidiary to the activities of contracting parties themselves.[94]

The justifications[95] for the doctrine are both pragmatic and value oriented. National authorities and courts are, in general, better equipped to collect and analyse evidence or other data, and this generates the inclination of international courts to support the findings of national authorities.[96] Yet the margin of appreciation also signals the judicial institutions' deference to value-pluralism, cultural diversity, and democratic decision-making.[97] In the *Handyside* case, the ECtHR pointed out that 'it is not

[92] For the detailed analysis of the margin of appreciation, see ch 10 (Legg) of this volume.

[93] The ECtHR observed that: the Court 'cannot assume the rôle of the competent national authorities, for it would thereby lose sight of the subsidiary nature of the international machinery of collective enforcement established by the Convention': *Case 'Relating to Certain Aspects of the Laws on the Use of Languages in Education in Belgium' v Belgium (Merits)* App nos 1474/62 et al Ser A no 6 (ECtHR, Judgment of 23 July 1968) [I.B.10]. Referred to in: *Handyside v United Kingdom* App no 5493/72, (1976) 1 EHRR 737, (1979) 1 EHRR 737 (ECtHR, 7 Dec 1976) [48]. *Handyside v UK*, a seminal case for the margin of appreciation doctrine, already contained the key factors that sustain the judicial invocation of the margin of appreciation: see ibid. See James A Sweeney, 'Margins of Appreciation: Cultural Relativity and the European Court of Human Rights in the Post-Cold War Era' (2005) 54 *International & Comparative Law Quarterly* 459, 471–75; Paolo G Carozza, 'Subsidiarity as a Structural Principle of International Human Rights Law' (2003) 97 *American Journal of International Law* 38. See also Yutaka Arai-Takahashi, 'Disharmony in the Process of Harmonisation?—The Analytical Account of the Strasbourg Court's Variable Geometry of Decision-making Policy Based on the Margin of Appreciation Doctrine' in M Andenas and C Andersen (eds), *Theory and Practice of Harmonisation* (Cheltenham, Edward Elgar Publishing Ltd, 2012) 95, 104–05; Janneke Gerards, 'Pluralism, Deference and the Margin of Appreciation Doctrine' (2011) 17 *European Law Journal* 80, 104; Andrew Legg, *The Margin of Appreciation in International Human Rights Law Deference and Proportionality* (Oxford, Oxford University Press, 2012) 61–62.

[94] Sweeney, 'Margins of Appreciation' (n 93) 471–75.

[95] The justifications are wider than a strictly legal basis, and may belong to the sphere of judicial politics. Based upon an extensive analysis of cases, Legg argues that the margin of appreciation is the judicial practice that pays difference to one or more of the 'second-order' (external) reasons: democratic legitimacy, the common practice of states, and expertise: Legg, *The Margin of Appreciation in International Human Rights Law Deference and Proportionality* (n 93) 17, and chs 4–6.

[96] See Arai-Takahashi, 'Disharmony in the Process of Harmonisation?' (n 93) 105, 111–12; Legg (n 93) 27–29. In the seminal case of *Handyside*, the Court observed that '[by] reason of their direct and continuous contact with the vital forces of their countries, State authorities are in principle in a better position than the international judge to give an opinion … on the "necessity" of a "restriction" or "penalty"' under Art 10(2) of the ECHR: *Handyside v United Kingdom* (n 93) [48]. See Legg (n 93) 27–29.

[97] Arai-Takahashi (n 93) 105–06, 111. Democratic legitimacy is used in favour of the national margin of appreciation where the legislative body has decided a balance between

possible to find in the domestic law of the various Contracting States a uniform European conception of morals'.[98] The absence of uniformity then justifies judicial deference to democratic legitimacy.[99] The deference to democratic legitimacy is one way to alleviate the democratic deficit in the operation of international judicial bodies themselves.[100]

The margin has the effect of preserving diversity among member states, except for the protection of minorities, for which international human rights law rather obligates states to engage in cultural preservation.[101] The acceptance of the national margin does not, however, signify the total exclusion of the review by international judicial institutions.[102] The margin could be better understood as achieving the universality of human rights law at an abstract level, while preserving the differences among states at the more concrete level.[103]

The delicate manner in which international courts keep distance from national law can also be found outside human rights adjudicative venues. In the *LaGrand* case, the ICJ was, in principle, prepared to say that a domestic law was the cause of the violation of an alleged obligation to provide assurances of non-repetition.[104] Nevertheless, the ICJ concluded that the violation of Article 36(2) of the Vienna Convention on Consular Relations was 'caused by the circumstances in which the procedural default rule was applied, and not by the rule as such',[105] and thus carefully

two competing private rights, or has stricken the balance between public and private rights: Legg (n 93) 83–90.

[98] *Handyside v United Kingdom* (n 93) [48].

[99] This may be already illustrated by the fact that the ECtHR makes particular reference to the legislator among domestic organs to whom the margin is accorded. See ch 11 (Kanetake) of this volume.

[100] Yuval Shany, 'Toward a General Margin of Appreciation Doctrine in International Law?' (2005) 16 *European Journal of International Law* 907, 919–21.

[101] See Legg (n 93) 93–96; Eyal Benvenisti, 'Margin of Appreciation, Consensus, and Universal Standards' (1999) 31 *New York University Journal of International Law and Politics* 843, 849. See also ch 13 (Donders and Vleugel) of this volume.

[102] While the domestic margin of appreciation limits the European review and thereby allows manifold national practices, the ECtHR signals that it 'goes hand in hand with a European supervision': *Handyside v United Kingdom* (n 93) [49]. Delmas-Marty observes that the European human rights law manifests both 'controlled national sovereignty' (the extension of the ECHR's regulatory coverage) and the 'relative European primacy' (a self-limitation of European supervision): see Mireille Delmas-Marty, *Towards a Truly Common Law: Europe As a Laboratory for Legal Pluralism* (Cambridge, Cambridge University Press, 2002) 73, 113.

[103] Legg (n 93) 40–50 (drawing on Raz' conception of 'thin' morality).

[104] *LaGrand (Germany v United States)* (n 8) [125] (regarding Germany's fourth submission to provide assurances).

[105] ibid [125]. The Court also made sure to note that the choice of means to allow the review and reconsideration of the conviction and sentence 'must be left to the United States' ([125]). It is also noted that the terms of Art 36(2) themselves accommodate the margin which could be used to defend both international and domestic courts. In *LaGrand* (see [91]), the ICJ regards this provision as requiring the conformity of national law to international standards. The US Supreme Court, on the other hand, eg, in *Sanchez Llamas* (n 9), understands Art 36(2)

avoided the general assessment of domestic law. The case of *LaGrand*[106] seems to illustrate that the Court is well aware that the international court is generally not well positioned to consider the matters of domestic law.[107]

In a similar vein, in *Avena*,[108] while the ICJ found the breach by the US of Article 36 of the Vienna Convention,[109] the Court left it to the US to determine how the state implements the review and reconsideration.[110] An interesting part of this judgment is nevertheless the delicate balancing exercises that the ICJ did at the interface with the domestic criminal law. The Court not only emphasised the need for 'effective' review and reconsideration of sentence and conviction, but also effectively denied the use of clemency procedure as an appropriate means of review and reconsideration.[111] The ICJ's judgment in *Avena* therefore demonstrates how international courts try to keep a delicate balance between mandating and not mandating how domestic procedures ought to be.

The cautious stance of the ICJ in *Avena* is somewhat contrasted with the much more interventionist remedial orders issued by the IACtHR (as a result of its finding of treaty violations). The IACtHR, originally modelled after the ECtHR, has developed remedial practices to order and monitor domestic judicial processes in a way much less deferential to states than those developed under the ECtHR.[112] More specifically, the IACtHR has been engaging in a 'quasi-criminal review' by ordering, specifying, monitoring, and guiding national criminal prosecutions.[113] In 1996, the Court began to obligate the punishment of those responsible as part of its remedial orders,[114] and, in its subsequent decisions, it further added that the prosecutions must be effective, and specified how the state in question ought to conduct investigation and prosecution.[115] The IACtHR

as requiring the conformity of the application of the Convention with domestic law. Both arguments may be defended by reference to Art 36(2).

[106] *LaGrand (Germany v United States)* (n 8).

[107] See Nollkaemper, 'The Role of Domestic Courts in the Case Law of the International Court of Justice' (n 75) 318 and fn 94.

[108] *Avena* (n 8).

[109] Vienna Convention on Consular Relations (n 6) Art 36.

[110] In this case, Mexico asked for the annulment of the conviction and sentences of Mexican nationals. In rejecting Mexico's request, the ICJ observed that the relationships between the treaty violations and the domestic convictions/penalties are for the US courts to determine in the process of review and reconsideration: see *Avena* (n 8) paras 122, 131.

[111] ibid para 143.

[112] Alexandra Huneeus, 'International Criminal Law by Other Means: The Quasi-Criminal Jurisdiction of the Human Rights Courts' (2013) 107 *American Journal of International Law* 1.

[113] ibid.

[114] *El Amparo Case, Reparations (art 63(1) American Convention on Human Rights)* (1996) Inter-Am Ct HR (Ser C) no 28 (1996) (Judgment of 14 Sept 1996) [64] ('4. Decides that the State of Venezuela shall be obliged to continue investigations into the events referred to in the instant case, and to punish those responsible').

[115] See, eg, *Myrna Mack Chang Case* (2003) Inter-Am Ct HR (Ser C) no 101 (2003) (Judgment of 25 Nov 2003). See further Huneeus, 'International Criminal Law by Other Means' (n 112) 5–12.

also ordered states to reform their criminal codes and military justice systems.[116]

The differences in the jurisprudential development of two regional human rights courts may in part reflect the maturity of the domestic rule of law reviewed by the international human rights courts. The IACtHR was confronted with mass state-sponsored violations of fundamental rights and the discouraging compliance record, while the ECtHR oversees a group of relatively well-functioning democracies committed to the rule of law.[117] The systematic human rights violations in the Latin American states encouraged the international human rights court to step in domestic procedures in a much more specific and unconditional way.

B. Substantive Accommodation

While the preservation of national competences is one way international courts respond to conflicting national practices, international institutions also engage in *substantive accommodation* by interpreting and developing the international rule of law in line with the national rule of law.

Political institutions have been incrementally developing their own decision-making procedures by adopting the elements of participation and transparency. For instance, the UN Security Council and its sanctions committees, which have invited well-known domestic contestations, have been developing their listing procedures in accordance with the principle of fairness and transparency, and established the petition procedures accessible to the designated individuals and entities.[118] These political changes can be seen as efforts on the part of international institutions to render the international rule of law for the regulation of international authority less formalistic.

Judicial institutions also make substantive accommodation, by alleviating the gaps between the national rule of law and international standards on the regulation of governmental authority. The margin of appreciation is often combined with the substantive changes in the doctrines and principles of international human rights law. For instance, the ECtHR has been

[116] See, eg, *Radilla Pacheco v Mexico* (2009) Inter-Am Ct HR (Ser C) no 209 (Judgment of 23 Nov 2009). See further Huneeus, 'International Criminal Law by Other Means' (n 112) 20–22.

[117] Huneeus (n 112) 5–6.

[118] On the development of the fairness and transparency principles and their concrete realisation, see, eg, Machiko Kanetake, 'Enhancing Community Accountability of the Security Council through Pluralistic Structure: The Case of the 1267 Committee' (2008) 12 *Max Planck Yearbook of United Nations Law* 113; Clemens A Feinäugle, 'The UN Security Council Al-Qaida and Taliban Sanctions Committee: Emerging Principles of International Institutional Law for the Protection of Individuals?' in A Bogdandy and others (eds), *The Exercise of Public Authority by International Institutions*, vol 210 (Berlin; Heidelberg, Springer, 2010) 101.

interpreting the 'legality' requirement and the associated 'rule of law' concept differently from the UK, Germany, France, and other member states.[119] The domestic laws of territorial states and other member states have been invoked for the interpretation of the legality principle and the elements of crimes as interpreted by the ICTY, ICTR, and ICC.[120]

Overall, these examples illustrate the delicate interplay between the national rule of law and the decisions of international institutions which review or replace governmental authority. They attempt to preserve the space for national democratic decision-making, while maintaining the universality of international law. International institutions also made some incremental efforts to improve their own decision-making procedures in order to alleviate contestations from the guardians of the national rule of law.

VI. CONCLUSION: TOWARDS THEORETICAL AND NORMATIVE APPRAISAL

It was in 1950 that the International Law Commission (ILC) observed that 'many of the provisions of international law serve[d] little purpose in national law'.[121] This remark no longer represents the extent to which the subject matter of international law presently overlaps with the regulatory agendas of domestic law.[122] As noted in section II of this chapter, international institutions, which are circumscribed only by the formalistic and thin international rule of law, review and replace governmental authority, based upon the assumption that governmental authority would have to be constrained by the thick requirement of the rule of law. The gap between the national and international rule of law, and the asymmetry within the international rule of law, have invited domestic contestations against the decisions of international institutions, as briefly overviewed in section III of this chapter. Domestic contestations, connected through

[119] Geranne Lautenbach, *The Concept of the Rule of Law and the European Court of Human Rights* (Oxford, Oxford University Press, 2013).

[120] See further Harmen van der Wilt, 'National Law: A Small but Neat Utensil in the Toolbox of International Criminal Tribunals' (2010) 10 *International Criminal Law Review* 209; Harmen van der Wilt, 'Domestic Courts' Contribution to the Development of International Criminal Law; Some Reflections' in T Ingadottir and others (eds), *Impact of International Courts on Domestic Proceedings in Mass Atrocity Cases* (2012) Amsterdam Law School Research Paper no 2012; Yuval Shany, 'Seeking Domestic Help: The Role of Domestic Criminal Law in Legitimizing the Work of International Criminal Tribunals' (2013) 11 *Journal of International Criminal Justice* 5.

[121] ILC, Report of the International Law Commission (1950) II *Yearbook of the International Law Commission* 364 at 370, para 53 (regarding Art 24 of the Statute of the ILC).

[122] See, eg, Twining, *Globalisation and Legal Theory* (n 2); Weiler, 'The Geology of International Law: Governance, Democracy and Legitimacy' (n 2) 559–61.

normative, theoretical, and political points (as analysed in section IV), have given rise to the opportunity for international law and the international rule of law to revise their relations with the national rule of law (as observed in section V).

The sketch of the national and international reception finally brings us to the *third* angle about the interfaces; namely, how can we theoretically understand and normatively evaluate the interfaces between the national and international rule of law, from slightly distant standpoints? This is the opportunity to critically recapture the practices as well as to revise our own perspectives with which to understand and evaluate those practices.

A. Theoretical Understanding About the Interfaces

The theoretical understanding about the interfaces has developed from the classic monism-dualism debates (Triepel and Kelsen) regarding the abstract relations between two legal orders.[123] As a matter of formal relations domestic and international legal orders, the proposition of dualism[124] to separate them still has a powerful explanatory force. Even when a treaty specifies how it should be implemented under domestic law, the formal legal effect of international law within the domestic legal order is contingent on an authorising rule of domestic law (and vice versa).[125] While the formal separation of two legal orders remains a useful starting point, the more substantive interactions between two legal orders have rendered the formal dualistic perspective on national and international legal orders increasingly mismatched with the reality of inter-order interfaces.

[123] The traditional monism-dualism argument was not necessarily about understanding how two legal orders interact in the actual legal practices, but about advocating political agendas from which to doctrinally or hypothetically organise the inter-order relationships. Kelsen observed that the question of primacy between national and international law is guided by ethical or political preferences: Hans Kelsen, *Principles of International Law* (Clark, New Jersey, The Lawbook Exchange Ltd, 1952) 447. See also Richard A Falk, *The Role of Domestic Courts in the International Legal Order* (Syracuse, Syracuse University Press, 1964) 170 (regarding the debate as a doctrinal logic advocated primarily by European scholars to fuse sovereignty with international obligations); George Rodrigo Bandeira Galindo, 'Revisiting Monism's Ethical Dimension' in J Crawford and S Nouwen (eds), *Select Proceedings of the European Society of International Law. vol 3 (2010)* (Oxford, Hart Publishing, 2011) 141.

[124] The monism-dualism classification is used in two different contexts: (1) to see the relationships between national and international law from a distance, and provide a general theory about the relationship, and (2) to describe a particular state's policy with regard to the effect of international law under its domestic law: Sloss, 'Treaty Enforcement in Domestic Courts: A Comparative Analysis' (n 10) 6. Here, the term 'dualism' is used in the *former* sense (ie, general theory, as opposed to particular states' policy).

[125] See Janne Nijman and André Nollkaemper, '12. Beyond the Divide' in JE Nijman and A Nollkaemper (eds), *New Perspectives on the Divide Between National and International Law* (Oxford, Oxford University Press, 2007) 341, 341–42.

The monism-dualism theory has thus been substituted by the more recent debates on constitutionalism and pluralism.[126] While these terms could be defined in multiple ways,[127] one basic dichotomy concerns the question of *hierarchy* as to which *institutions* have the final say, and which *norms* have the superior status.

As I have noted above, domestic courts claim and reserve the ultimate authority to determine the effect of international law in their own legal orders by reference to constitutional principles. International courts likewise reserve their final say about the effect of domestic law in their legal orders.[128] Such determination is ultimately based upon international law, which claims its supremacy over domestic law, as represented by Article 27 of the Vienna Convention on the Law of Treaties.[129] Also, before international courts, national law is officially regarded as mere 'facts' and does not occupy any space in the legal construction.[130] In this respect, there is

126 For the analysis of constitutionalism in global spheres, see, eg, Anne Peters, 'The Merits of Global Constitutionalism' (2009) 16 *Indiana Journal of Global Legal Studies* 397; Antje Wiener and others, 'Global Constitutionalism: Human Rights, Democracy and the Rule of Law' (2012) 1 *Global Constitutionalism* 1. For pluralism, see, eg, Armin von Bogdandy, 'Pluralism, Direct Effect, and the Ultimate Aay: On the Relationship between International and Domestic Constitutional Law' (2008) 6 *International Journal of Constitutional Law* 397; Krisch, 'The Open Architecture of European Human Rights Law' (n 58); Nico Krisch, *Beyond Constitutionalism: The Pluralist Structure of Postnational Law* (Oxford, Oxford University Press, 2010). There is also a considerable literature regarding the pluralistic (ie, non-hierarchical) relationships between EU law and national law: see, eg, Mattias Kumm, 'Who is the Final Arbiter of Constitutionality in Europe?: Three Conceptions of the Relationship Between the German Federal Constitutional Court and the European Court of Justice' (1999) 36 *Common Market Law Review* 351; Neil Walker, 'The Idea of Constitutional Pluralism' (2002) 65 *The Modern Law Review* 317.

127 Pluralism can be used as a matter of *multiplicity* or as the absence of clear-cut *hierarchy*. This chapter uses the term in a latter (hierarchical) sense. As Krisch observes, pluralism rejects the practical feasibility and normative desirability of the overarching legal framework, and emphasises the 'heterarchical interaction of the various layers of law': Krisch, *Beyond Constitutionalism* (n 126) 23.

128 One illustration is *Hirst (No 2)* before the ECtHR: *Hirst v United Kingdom (No 2)* App no 74025/01, ECHR 2005-IX (ECtHR, Grand Chamber, Judgment of 6 Oct 2005). In *Hirst v UK (No 2)*, the ECtHR observed that, while states must be allowed a wide margin of appreciation (ibid [60], [82]), it is ultimately for the Strasbourg Court to determine in the last resort whether the Convention's requirements have been complied with (ibid [62]). On this basis, the ECtHR concluded that the general restriction on the rights to vote exceeded any acceptable margin of appreciation (ibid [82]). In *Hirst (No 2)*, the ECtHR decided upon the question whether the Representation of the People Act in the UK, under which a convicted person is legally incapable of voting in any parliamentary or local election, was compatible with Art 3 of Protocol No 1 to the ECHR. The ECtHR held that a blanket ban on the prisoners' voting rights violated the right to free elections.

129 Vienna Convention on the Law of Treaties (n 71) Art 27.

130 *German Interests in Polish Upper Silesia (Germany v Poland)* 1926 PCIJ (Ser A) no 7 (PICJ, 25 May 1925) [52] ('municipal laws are merely facts which express the will and constitute the activities of States, in the same manner as do legal decisions or administrative measures. The Court is certainly not called upon to interpret the Polish law as such'). For the 'factual' status of national law, see further Carlo Santulli, *Le statut international de l'ordre juridique étatique: étude du traitement du droit interne par le droit international* (Paris, Editions A Pedone, 2001) 258–77.

clearly hierarchy in terms of the ultimate authority to determine the interfaces, and the ultimate legal basis for the determination.

Yet what national and international institutions actually do in order to resolve normative conflicts is much more subtle, and cannot be reduced to the presence of hierarchy. Domestic courts try to avoid conflicts by interpreting international law in such a way that it does not contradict domestic law, and by leaving the issue to the executive's decisions, based upon the separation of power. The reception of international institutions cannot be reduced to the hierarchy either. They avoid conflicts by preserving national competences, and also by incrementally absorbing some of the rule of law requirements into the regulation of international authority. The picture we can draw with respect to the interfaces thus appears to be much more heterarchical than claimed by national and international institutions.

B. Normative Appraisal of the Interfaces

The theoretical understanding finally leads us to evaluate interfaces from the broader question of legitimacy. Have the heterarchical interactions rendered the decisions of international institutions and the international rule of law more certain, participatory, and democratic?

On the one hand, the heterarchical interactions have an advantage of preserving flexibility. They also help alleviate the democratic deficit of international law and institutions. Behind national contestations and avoidance always lies the democratic (il)legitimacy of international law and institutions in the eyes of the national guardians of the rule of law. To secure the space for national competences for the matters regulated by international law would be one way to defer to political legitimacy attached to national law.

On the other hand, if the interfaces should be understood as heterarchical, this may also suggest that law, including international law, fails to provide rules as to how international law and institutions respond to conflicting national practices and how conflict between them can be resolved.[131] The margin of appreciation doctrine could be one illustrative example. The difficulty in predicting when and how precisely the doctrine ought to be applied may support the characterisation of the doctrine as

[131] See André Nollkaemper, 'Inside or Out: Two Types of International Legal Pluralism' in J Klabbers and T Piiparinen (eds), *Normative Pluralism and International Law: Exploring Global Governance* (Cambridge; New York, Cambridge University Press, 2013) 94, (critically observing that the paradigm of (external) pluralism seems difficult to reconcile with the interests of stability of the international legal system).

a (judicial) policy standard, rather than a legal rule.[132] While the heterarchical interactions preserve national diversity and alleviate democratic deficit, there remains the greater uncertainty in the manner in which international institutions and international law interact with potentially contradictory national law.

One possible way to alleviate the uncertainty and reclaim the regulatory role of international law could be to identify the rules, which are akin to 'conflict-of-laws', that regulate the international reception of conflicting national legal practices. Traditionally, the law of conflict-of-laws (also referred to as private international law) is applied against 'horizontal' state laws and concerns transnational 'private' legal disputes.[133] Yet attempts have been made to extend the conflict-of-laws 'approach' to the regulation of legal conflicts between 'non-horizontal' orders (eg, between EU law and member states' national law),[134] including disputes in 'public' law (eg, human rights). It has been put forward as a perspective to account for the treatment of international law in domestic courts; namely, the *national* reception of international law,[135] and, to a limited extent, as a possible approach to the *international* reception of domestic law.[136] The conflict-of-laws approach accepts the pluralistic inter-order interactions and yet still aims at ensuring the certainty and justice for affected individuals and entities.[137] The conflict-of-laws approach, albeit still an issue for future studies, may have the potential of achieving greater consistency in the interactions between multiple layers of law without disturbing the foundational non-hierarchical setting that sustains and enriches the interactions between the national and international rule of law.

Overall, we have witnessed the delicate interplay between the actors, norms, and procedures at the interfaces between the national and international rule of law. National avoidance and contestations signal deficiencies in the decisions of international institutions and the formalistic and

132 Arai-Takahashi (n 93) 96–98.

133 See Florian Rödl, 'Democratic Juridification Without Statisation: Law of Conflict of Laws Instead of a World State' (2011) 2 *Transnational Legal Theory* 193, 200–01.

134 The approach has been put forward to regulate three types of legal conflict: horizontal, vertical, and diagonal. (1) Horizontal conflicts occur between different state laws; (2) vertical conflicts are those between a state law and EU law; and (3) diagonal conflicts arise between a state law and EU law, which do not directly conflict one another, but nevertheless make potentially conflicting demands. See Christian Joerges, Poul F Kjaer, and Tommi Ralli, 'A New Type of Conflicts Law as Constitutional Form in the Postnational Constellation' (2011) 2 *Transnational Legal Theory* 153, 155; Renate Mayntz, 'The Architecture of Multi-Level Governance of Economic Sectors' *MPIfG Discussion Paper 13/2007* 23–24.

135 Karen Knop, Ralf Michaels, and Annelise Riles, 'International Law in Domestic Courts: A Conflict of Laws Approach' (2009) Cornell Law Faculty Working Papers. Paper 69.

136 See Krisch, *Beyond Constitutionalism* (n 126).

137 See Alex Mills, *The Confluence of Public and Private International Law* (Cambridge, Cambridge University Press, 2009).

thin international rule of law regulating such institutions. The confrontational national reception, and the international responses to it, further point to the need for a nuanced understanding about the hierarchical relationships between the national and international legal orders. As noted at the beginning of this chapter, the interfaces are the venues for learning and self-reflection. They continue to revise the way in which national and international institutions exercise authority, develop the national and international rule of law, and further revise the theoretical and normative accounts on the interfaces between the national and international rule of law.

Part I

National Contestations in the Critical Revision of the International Rule of Law

2

Judicial Strategies and their Impact on the Development of the International Rule of Law

VERONIKA FIKFAK

I. INTRODUCTION

HOW DOMESTIC COURTS give effect to international law is becoming increasingly pertinent to the international legal order as the rules of international law are becoming 'inward' looking.[1] Scholars describe domestic courts as 'the natural first port of call for adjudicating … international claims by private parties'[2] and 'the only judicial institution likely to adjudge the legality of important controversies about the application of international law'.[3] Even more, domestic courts are the key enforcement mechanism when it comes to the implementation of decisions of international institutions in their domestic legal orders. The International Court of Justice (ICJ) in *LaGrand* identified US internal organs, including domestic courts, as organs that should enforce the holding of the international court.[4] Many other international institutional decisions—such as the international criminal tribunals' requests to surrender individuals as witnesses or suspects to their jurisdiction—also depend on domestic courts to ensure their effectiveness.[5]

[1] Antonios Tzanakopoulos, 'Domestic Courts in International Law: The International Judicial Function of National Courts' (2011) 34 *Loyola of Los Angeles International and Comparative Law Review* 133, 138.

[2] André Nollkaemper, *National Courts and the International Rule of Law* (Oxford; New York, Oxford University Press, 2011) 11–12.

[3] Richard Falk, *The Role of Domestic Courts in the International Legal Order* (Syracuse, Syracuse University Press, 1964) 172.

[4] *LaGrand (Germany v United States of America)* [1999] ICJ Reports 9 (Provisional Measures, Order of 3 March 1999) 16, [28].

[5] See Antonio Cassese, 'On the Current Trends towards Criminal Prosecution and Punishment of Breaches of International Humanitarian Law' (1998) 9 *European Journal of International Law* 2, 13.

The greater dependence of international law on domestic courts has, however, created a *dilemma* for national judges in their relations with the rule of law. On the one hand, domestic courts are increasingly expected to act as a guardian of the *international* rule of law by ensuring domestic *compliance* with international law.[6] Domestic courts are often considered 'as agents of the international legal order, in the service of the international rule of law',[7] and as a '*key component* in the protection of the international rule of law'.[8] Scholars are calling on domestic judges to extend their commitment to the rule of law from domestic to international law.[9] When dealing with international law claims, domestic courts, because of their commitment to the rule of law, are expected to 'perform the international function of upholding rights and duties grounded in international law'.[10]

On the other hand, domestic courts are entrusted to safeguard constitutional principles and, more broadly, the *national* rule of law. This may result in disapproving of the national executive's decisions which implement international law if such decisions do not conform to the national rule of law standards. An independent judiciary is often considered as an important element of the rule of law, and domestic courts uphold the rule of law by reviewing authority exercised by governmental bodies. To uphold the national rule of law and act as a check on executive power may put the enforcement of international decisions into question. National judges, therefore, often face the dilemma between enforcing international law and exercising an independent judicial function over the executive.

This chapter analyses how judges have responded to this dilemma. Through the analysis of judicial strategies, this chapter ultimately reconsiders our understanding about the international rule of law. It argues that the international rule of law should not only be captured as ensuring

[6] See Eyal Benvenisti, 'Judicial Misgivings Regarding the Application of International Law: An Analysis of Attitudes of National Courts' (1993) 4 *European Journal of International Law* 159, 160.

[7] Nollkaemper, *National Courts and the International Rule of Law* (n 2) 8.

[8] ibid 304 (emphasis added). Other authors put forth the rule of law argument: eg, see Anne-Marie Slaughter, 'International Law in a World of Liberal States' (1995) 6 *European Journal of International Law* 503, 511; HF van Panhuys, 'Relations and Interactions Between International and National Scenes of Law' (1964) 112 *Recueil des Cours* 1, 46.

[9] Anne-Marie Slaughter, 'A Typology of Transjudicial Communication' (1994) 29 *University of Richmond Law Review* 99, 137.

[10] Richard B Lillich, 'The Proper Role of Domestic Courts in the International Legal Order' (1970) 11 *Virginia Journal of International Law* 9, 12. National judges are anticipated to give force to international norms, and to ensure that domestic organs abide by their international commitments: see Nollkaemper (n 2) 11–12; Antônio Augusto Cançado Trindade, *The Access of Individuals to International Justice* (Oxford; New York, Oxford University Press, 2011) 51, 54; Antônio Augusto Cançado Trindade, 'Exhaustion of Local Remedies under the UN Covenant on Civil and Political Rights and Its Optional Protocol' (1979) 28 *The International and Comparative Law Quarterly* 734, 335.

national *compliance* with international law; the international rule of law also preserves the space for *dialogue* between national organs and international institutions. In this chapter, I analyse domestic court cases on the decisions of the UN Security Council's Sanctions Committee against Al Qaeda to designate individuals and entities as the targets of asset freeze measures.[11] In the absence of basic due process protections before the UN Security Council, the listed individuals turned to domestic courts to challenge the legality of states' measures to implement these international measures on the basis of *inter alia* the individuals' fundamental rights. National courts encountered the dilemma between ensuring national compliance with the international decisions and upholding individuals' fundamental rights and the national rule of law standards. To uphold the individuals' claims might have 'call[ed] the whole system of targeted United Nations sanctions into question'.[12] It was difficult to circumvent this dilemma since the obligations imposed by the UN Security Council and the Al Qaeda Sanctions Committee were so specific in their instructions that virtually no discretion was left to the domestic implementing organ in giving force to the international decision.

In section II below, I describe the position of domestic courts in relation to the international and national rule of law. As illustrated in section III, domestic courts in some cases conduct 'strong' review of implementing measures against the 'fundamental' tenets of the domestic legal order. Paradoxically, by not directly referring to international norms, domestic courts can indirectly review and challenge the decisions of international institutions according to such tenets. At the same time, as discussed in section IV, domestic courts also engage in 'weak' review according to deferential standards of review. These 'strong' and 'weak' review techniques employed by domestic courts have elicited dialogues and responses from international institutions; such an interaction then calls for the revision in the compliance-based understanding about the role of domestic courts in developing the international rule of law.

[11] The basic frameworks are established under the UN Security Council's Resolutions 1267, 1333, and 1390: see UN Doc S/RES/1267 (15 Oct 1999) para 4; UN Doc S/RES/1333 (19 Dec 2000) paras 8, 10, 11; UN Doc S/RES/1390 (28 Jan 2002) para 2. In June 2011, the sanctions regime was split into two: for Al Qaeda, UN Doc S/RES/1989 (17 June 2011); for Taliban, UN Doc S/RES/1988 (17 June 2011). On the UN's targeted sanctions, see generally, eg, Jeremy Matam Farrall, *United Nations Sanctions and the Rule of Law* (Cambridge, Cambridge University Press, 2007).

[12] 1267 Sanctions Committee, 'Threats to international peace and security caused by terrorist acts' S/PV.5446, 26; the Austrian representative speaking before the SC on behalf of the EU.

II. DOMESTIC COURTS' DILEMMA WITH REGARD TO THE RULE OF LAW

A. Upholding the International Rule of Law

On the international level, the international rule of law is described as requiring first and foremost 'compliance with international law'.[13] The 2012 UN Secretary-General's report on the rule of law, prepared for the UN General Assembly's high-level meeting, noted that states consider compliance as the primary concern for the upholding of the international rule of law. In a similar manner, international scholars and judges insist that the international rule of law 'requires compliance by the State with its obligations in international law, the law which … governs the conduct of nations'.[14]

Those authors who regard compliance with international law as an element of the international rule of law sometimes situate *domestic courts* as agents of the international rule of law. Nollkaemper points out that '[i]n virtually all fields of international law, compliance with international law is not possible without a meaningful connection to the domestic arena'.[15] The decisions of domestic courts can lead their state to violate international law; in this respect, scholars imply that domestic courts may be indirectly bound to obey international law imposed on their state. But the rule of law argument scholars make goes beyond the need to prevent a violation of international law. Rather, it is about 'empowering national courts and providing the conditions for the effectiveness of international law'.[16] Beyond compliance, international law relies on national courts 'to make it effective'.[17]

The role of domestic courts is considered important precisely because they potentially remedy the lack of centralised enforcement mechanisms in the international legal order.[18] The international legal order has no

[13] Report of the Secretary-General, 'Delivering Justice: Programme of Action to Strengthen the Rule of Law at the National and International Levels' UN Doc A/66/749 (16 March 2012) paras 11–13. '2005 World Summit Outcome' UN Doc A/RES/60/1 (24 Oct 2005) para 134. Since 2006, the General Assembly has regularly adopted resolutions entitled 'The Rule of Law at the National and International Levels': see, eg, UN Doc A/RES/61/39 (18 Dec 2006).

[14] Lord Bingham, 'The Rule of Law' (2007) 66 *Cambridge Law Journal* 67, 81–82.

[15] Nollkaemper (n 2) 301.

[16] ibid 12.

[17] ibid 301.

[18] Unlike municipal law, the international legal order is not a unitary government system with an enforcement mechanism: see Mary Ellen O'Connell, 'Enforcement and the Success of International Environmental Law' (1995) 3 *Indiana Journal of Global Legal Studies* 47, 47. See also Percy Ellwood Corbett, *Law and Society in the Relations of States* (New York, Harcourt, Brace, 1951) 68; Robert Jennings and Arthur Watts (eds), *Oppenheim's International Law* (9th edn, Harlow, Essex, Longman, 1992) 11 ('there is no central government above the governments of the several states, which could in every case secure the enforcement of

centralised judicial system, such as the case of the Court of Justice in the European Union (CJEU) in the European Union (EU). Instead, over the last half-century, the international legal order has been populated with an increasing number of international courts and tribunals which have jurisdiction over a specific type of international law dispute and whose competencies often overlap.[19] Without the highest court to resolve conflicts and the conflicting interpretations of international law, the content of international rules remains disputed and fragmented.[20]

The lack of regular enforcement mechanisms[21] had traditionally led to the ultimate question about the 'legal' quality of international law.[22] Since the 'legal functions within [the international] community have never been organised', to this day the 'international community does not have at its disposal the legal means to enforce international rules effectively and impartially'.[23] International law is still described as a 'law without a sword',[24] a 'weak' and 'primitive' type of law.[25] The lack of physical enforcement of binding international law or international decisions led some to question not only the effectiveness of international law but also its

the rules of international law'). Conforti observed the statement '*ni loi, ni juge, ni gendarme* remains … largely accurate'): Benedetto Conforti, *International Law and the Role of Domestic Legal Systems* (Dordrecht, Martinus Nijhoff Publishers, 1993) 4. The proliferation of international judicial bodies has not led to corresponding procedures for the coercive enforcement of international rules: see ibid 5.

[19] Yuval Shany, *The Competing Jurisdictions of International Courts and Tribunals* (Oxford, Oxford University Press, 2003).

[20] Even more, the proliferation of international judicial bodies has not led to corresponding procedures for the coercive enforcement of international rules: see Conforti, *International Law and the Role of Domestic Legal System* (n 18) 5. If anything, some argue, 'there has been a regression in this respect': ibid.

[21] Corbett, *Law and Society in the Relations of States* (n 18) 68.

[22] Math Noortman *Enforcing International Law: From Self-Help to Self-Contained Regimes* (London, Ashgate Publishing, 2005) 2ff; Lori Fisler Damrosch, 'Enforcing International Law Through Non-Forcible Measures' (1997) 269 *Recueil des Cours* 9, 19, referring to sceptics and critics but without quoting who.

[23] Conforti (n 18) 10.

[24] GF Will 'The Perils of Legality' (*Newsweek*, Sept 1990) 66 in response to Daniel Patrick Moynihan *On the Law of Nations* (Harvard, Harvard University Press, 1990).

[25] Lillich, 'The Proper Role of Domestic Courts in the International Legal Order' (n 10) 12, citing Lambertus Erades and Wesley Gould *The Relation Between International Law and Municipal Law in the Netherlands and in the United States* (New York, Oceana Publications, 1961) 223; Friedrich Kratochwil 'The Role of Domestic Courts as Agencies of the International Legal Order' in RA Falk, F Kratochwil and S Mendlowitz (eds), *International Law, A Contemporary Perspective* (Boulder, CO, Westview, 1985) 236, though he rejects the primitive nature. See also Friedrich Kratochwil, 'Thrasymmachos Revisited: On the Relevance of Norms and the Study of Law for International Relations' (1964) 37 *Journal of International Affairs* 343; Lassa Oppenheim, *International Law: A Treatise, vol 1, 'Peace'* (3rd edn, London, Longmans, 1920) 11–12 ('A law is the stronger, the more guarantees are given that it can and will be enforced. … [International law] must be a weaker law than Municipal Law, as there is not, and cannot be, an international Government above the national ones which could enforce the rules of International Law in the same way as a national Government enforces the rules of its Municipal Law'.).

legal credential. Damrosch describes critics' view of the international legal order as a 'system so woefully deficient in means for compelling compliance [that it] can hardly qualify as "law"'.[26] D'Amato and O'Connell also raise the direct question: 'Is international law really "law"?'[27]

This is where domestic courts come in as potential venues that in part mitigate the problem of enforcement in international law. National courts 'may indeed compensate for the lack of international courts as a systemic force in the protection of the international rule of law'.[28] Given the 'structural weaknesses in the international legal system'[29] and 'the lack of international courts',[30] domestic courts can be seen as the key organ to 'perform the international function of upholding rights and duties grounded in international law'.[31] National courts can indeed decide international claims which are in whole or in part based on a rule of international law.[32] Courts can, for example, apply and interpret international rules and give them domestic effect directly or indirectly through consistent interpretation. By so doing, national courts necessarily seek to determine the content of international rules. Overall, domestic courts 'play a role in the interpretation, determination, and development of international law'[33] while simultaneously remedying the deficiency or lack of enforcement in the international legal order.

B. Upholding the National Rule of Law

While domestic courts are expected to extend their 'commitment to the rule of law' from domestic to international law,[34] judges are also supposed

[26] Damrosch, 'Enforcing International Law Through Non-Forcible Measures' (n 22), though the phrase is not footnoted and there is no reference to any specific commentators.

[27] Anthony D'Amato, 'Is International Law Really "Law"?' (1984–85) 79 *Northwestern University Law Review* 1293, 1296; Anthony D'Amato, *Jurisprudence: A Descriptive and Normative Analysis of Law* (Dordrecht, Martinus Nijhoff Publishers, 1984) 119–22, traces the command theory of law from Hobbes through Bentham and Austin though he later rejects that law needs enforcement to be law. Linking the label 'law' with enforcement comes from an understanding of prescriptions in terms of constraints. According to Kelsen, for example, 'law' is distinguished from other norms by 'sanctions'; a 'threatened evil'. From this perspective, reminiscent of a criminal law understanding of legal norms, 'law' is a constraining force and functions as a sanctioning system of norms. Actors follow rules largely out of fear of threatened sanctions. Through the threat of negative consequences 'law' influences the actors' decision-making processes and thus makes them behave in a certain manner. Hans Kelsen, *Principles of International Law* (New York, Rinehart, 1959) 4.

[28] Nollkaemper (n 2) 8.

[29] Richard Falk, *The Role of Domestic Courts in the International Legal Order* (Syracuse, Syracuse University Press, 1964) xi.

[30] Nollkaemper (n 2) 8.

[31] Lillich (n 10) 12.

[32] Nollkaemper (n 2) 9.

[33] ibid 10.

[34] Slaughter, 'Typology' (n 9) 137.

to independently scrutinise the political branches' decisions according to constitutional principles and other domestic laws. The independence of the judiciary is one of the formal elements of the rule of law at the domestic level.[35] In fact, 'it is hard to conceive of a rule of law domestically without independent courts'.[36] In order to hold the executive to account, domestic judges have to act as a 'neutral arbiter',[37] detached 'from political entanglements and by abstention from injecting itself into the clash of political forces in political settlements'.[38] As Trinidade argues, of 'utmost importance is the autonomy and independence of judicial organs from executive influence, with a direct bearing on the effectiveness of the local remedies to be exhausted'.[39]

The independence of judicial organs at the domestic level may *both* encourage and discourage the domestic implementation of international law and the decisions of international institutions. On the one hand, judges may proactively employ international law in settling disputes or interpreting relevant domestic law even if legislative and executive organs are unwilling to give effect to the particular rules of international law. As the guardians of the rule of law, domestic courts may be encouraged to apply international rules even against public powers and to review 'the legality of national acts in the light of international obligations and to ensure rule-conformity'.[40] The international commitment of the state is treated as a constraint on the government's power.[41] This position of domestic courts was welcomed already two decades ago by the International Law Institute in Paris in its resolution on the treatment of international law before domestic courts. The Institute called 'upon national courts to become independent actors in the international arena, and to apply international norms impartially, without deferring to their governments'.[42]

[35] See Simon Chesterman, 'An International Rule of Law?' (2008) 56 *American Journal of Comparative Law* 331, 342 (the second and third core definition); Joseph Raz, 'The Rule of Law and its Virtue' (1977) 93 *Law Quarterly Review* 195, 200–01 (fourth and seventh principles).

[36] Nollkaemper (n 2) 5.

[37] Friedrich V Kratochwil, 'The Role of Domestic Courts as Agencies of the International Legal Order' in Falk, Kratochwil, and Mendlovitz (eds), *International Law* (n 25) 236, 242.

[38] *Baker v Carr* 369 US 186 (1962) (US Supreme Court, 26 March 1962) 267 (Frankfurter dissenting).

[39] AA Cançado Trindade, 'Exhaustion of Local Remedies in International Law and the Role of National Courts' (1978) 17 *Archiv des Völkerrechts* 333, 336.

[40] Nollkaemper (n 2) 10. Scholars observe that courts have to remember their 'commitment to the rule of law' and to use 'law as both a shield (from political interference) and a mask (to hide their political agenda)': Alex Mills and Tim Stephens, 'Challenging the Role of Judges in Slaughter's Liberal Theory of International Law' (2005) 18 *Leiden Journal of International Law* 1, 12.

[41] *Minister for Immigration and Ethnic Affairs v Teoh* (1995) 183 CLR 273 (HCA) [28] (Mason CJ and Deane J), insisting that international law is a 'legitimate guide'.

[42] Anne-Marie Slaughter, 'Judicial Globalization' (2000) 40 *Virginia Journal of International Law* 1103, 1104; Benedetto Conforti and Rapporteur, 'The Activities of National Judges and

On the other hand, the independence of judicial organs may discourage national judges from giving effect to international law. International law and international institutional decisions are implemented at the national level normally by the acts of the domestic executive (or legislature). If domestic courts subject the implementing domestic measures to the full judicial scrutiny as required by the rule of law argument, domestic courts may find it necessary to reject the executive's (or legislature's) efforts to give effect to international law or a decision of international institutions. The latter will be illustrated with the example of the implementation of the decisions of the UN Security Council in section III.

This creates the aforementioned dilemma for domestic courts. For the purpose of the international rule of law, national courts play a crucial role in ensuring their states' compliance with international law and facilitating its effectiveness. At the same time, the rule of law at the domestic level requires the judicial review of the national implementing measures, which sometimes necessitates national judges to go against the executive's (or legislature's) efforts that give effect to international law and institutional decisions.

III. 'STRONG' REVIEW BY DOMESTIC COURTS

A. Applying the Stringent Standards of Review

In remedying the dilemma sketched in the previous section, domestic courts employ different strategies in deciding upon cases involving the executive's decisions to implement international institutional decisions. This chapter adopts Mark Tushnet's distinction between 'strong' and 'weak' review, and distinguishes domestic court decisions according to: the degree of deference in the courts' review; the existence of common terms of reference, and the responses received from other organs.[43]

Domestic courts conduct so-called 'strong' reviews of implementing measures according to the 'fundamental' tenets of the domestic legal order. Illustrative here are a series of national and EU court decisions concerning the decisions of the UN Security Council's Al Qaeda Sanctions Committee's decisions to designate individuals. Domestic and EU courts reviewed the implementing measures for the Committee's decisions on the basis of the measures' compatibility with the protection of fundamental

the International Relations of Their State' (1993) 65-I *Yearbook of the Institute of International Law* 327, 327–448; Institut de Droit International, 'Resolution: The Activities of National Judges and the International Relations of their State, 65-II YB IIL 318–23 (1994)' (1994) 65-II *Yearbook of the Institute of International Law* 318, 318–23.

[43] See Mark Tushnet, 'Dialogic Judicial Review' (2009) 61 *Arkansas Law Review* 205.

human rights—which can be seen as one of the 'fundamental' tenets of the domestic legal order. A widely-known decision is *Kadi* before the EU courts; the CJEU in *Kadi I* (2008) set aside the General Court's judgment, and engaged in the 'full review' of the implementing measures.[44] In *Kadi II* (2013), the CJEU augmented the extent of 'full review'.[45] The CJEU's decisions also determined the direction of similar domestic and EU court decisions concerning the implementation of the Al Qaeda sanctions regime.

National courts succeeded in conducting 'strong' reviews, not directly against international decisions, but against the decisions of the EU institutions to give effect to the international decisions. By not directly aiming at the international decisions, domestic courts were able to subject the decisions of international institutions to scrutiny according to the protection of fundamental rights, and indirectly challenged the international institutional decisions. For instance, in *Al-Qadi*, the Turkish Council of State was asked to review the legality of the sanctions imposed on Al-Qadi's assets pursuant to the Al Qaeda sanctions regime.[46] Rather than reviewing the relevant resolutions of the UN Security Council or the decisions of its Sanctions Committee, the Turkish Court evaluated the legality of the implementing measure taken by the Turkish Council of Ministers. A similar approach was adopted in the cases of *A, K, M, Q, G* and separately in *Hay*.[47] In these two cases, the UK courts reviewed the Al-Qaida and Taliban (United Nations Measures) Order 2006 implementing the Al Qaeda sanctions regime and Security Council Resolution 1373 (2001). Likewise, in *Abdelrazik*, the applicant complained about the Canadian government's decision not to allow him to return to Canada or give him financial support after his having been added to the Sanctions Committee's list. Justice Zinn in *Abdelrazik* did not review the travel ban or asset freeze under the Al Qaeda sanctions regime, but rather the government's decision not to permit his travel. And in *Nada*, Swiss courts reviewed the authorities' refusal to remove the plaintiff from the list of individuals and entities who were subjected to sanctions under the Al Qaeda sanctions regime.

Obviously, the review of domestic administrative and legislative measures makes perfect sense given that the institutional decisions of the UN

[44] Cases C-402/05 P and C-415/05 P *Kadi and Al Barakaat International Foundation v Council of the European Union and Commission of the European Communities* (2008) [2008] ECR I-06351 (ECJ, Judgment of 3 Sept 2008, 'Kadi I').

[45] Joined cases C-584/10 P, C-593/10 P and C-595/10 P *Kadi v European Commission* (2013) (ECJ, Judgment of 18 July 2013, 'Kadi II') [114]–[30].

[46] *Kadi*, Judgment E 2002/984, K. 2006/4795 (cited in ILDC 311 (TR 2007) [F6]–[7]; Fifth report of the Monitoring Team, UN Doc S/2006/750, Annex III, para 11; Sixth report of the Monitoring Team, UN Doc S/2007/132, Annex I, para 8) (Turkey, Council of State, 10th Division, 4 July 2006).

[47] *A, K, M, Q & G v HM Treasury* (2008) [2008] EWHC 869 (Admin) (UK, High Court of Justice, 24 April 2008); *Hay v HM Treasury* [2009] EWHC 1677 (Admin) (UK High Court of Justice, 10 July 2009).

Security Council's subsidiary organs have no validity or applicability at the domestic level unless such decisions are given effect by national implementing measures.[48] International decisions usually do not specify the way according to which the obligations are given effect by states. The implementing measure almost always acts as an 'essential prerequisite'[49] to make operative at home the decisions of the UN Security Council and potentially other international organisations.

Whilst the argument of incorporation—and of what domestic courts are bound by—is a formal reason why domestic courts review implementing measures rather than international decisions,[50] the national courts' reliance on the domestic implementing acts provides an important and pragmatic benefit; such reliance works as a tool that enables the courts to distance themselves from reviewing the decisions of international institutions whilst, at the same time, adopting the very intrusive standards of review for decisions of domestic implementing organs. In fact, by neglecting to address the link between the international and domestic measure (and remaining ignorant of the potential 'strict' nature of the international decision), courts are often able to disregard the international origin of the measure and review an exclusively domestic measure. As a consequence, in the above examples, national courts managed to exercise review, and, in some cases, declared the implementing measures void and even ordered the executive to undertake specific measures without elaborating on what position such a judicial pronouncement might put the executive in on the international level. For example, in *Sayadi and Vinck* concerning the UN Security Council's sanctions regime mentioned above, the Belgian Court of First Instance ordered the Belgium government to request Sayadi and Vinck's delisting, even though it was obvious that the state would not readily be successful in achieving the delisting of these individuals since the information gathered against them had been supplied not only by Belgium but also by other countries.[51] The limited involvement of Belgium in the initial listing processes of Sayadi and Vinck did not stop the Brussels Court of First Instance from requesting the government's

[48] Vera Gowlland-Debbas, 'Implementing Sanctions Resolutions in Domestic Law' in Vera Gowlland-Debbas (ed), *National Implementation of United Nations Sanctions—a Comparative Study* (Leiden, Martinus Nijhoff Publishers, 2004) 34.

[49] Andrea Bianchi, 'Assessing the Effectiveness of the UN Security Council's Anti-Terrorism Measures: The Quest for Legitimacy and Cohesion' (2006) 17 *European Journal of International Law* 881, 895.

[50] Especially when decisions impose particular measures against individuals, eg, such as the freezing of assets. Gowlland-Debbas, 'Implementing Sanctions Resolutions in Domestic Law' (n 48) 34.

[51] It is also noted that, at the time, only the state that requested the listing could ask for delisting. If the designation comes from several countries, the delisting needs to be agreed on. The requirement to consult with the designating state is still in force today. Fact Sheet on Delisting, available at: www.un.org/sc/committees/1267/fact_sheet_delisting.shtml, para 6.

delisting efforts.[52] Similarly, in *Abdelrazik*, the Canadian Federal Court, having found that the executive's decision not to allow Abdelrazik's return to the country was illegal, ordered the government to provide an emergency passport and the airfare necessary for Abdelrazik to return to Canada.[53] As demonstrated by these domestic cases, national courts, by distancing themselves from international institutional decisions, can employ the intrusive standards of review and order the proactive governmental action to remedy the violation.

B. Eliciting International Responses

Although national courts tend to insist on the autonomous nature of the domestic legal order in which they render decisions,[54] the reality is that the courts' actions in one jurisdiction may have an important effect on other jurisdictions, and more broadly, on the international legal order. For instance, courts in other jurisdictions could follow the actions of courts in Canada, Belgium, Turkey, and Switzerland and tailor their own review of implementing measures after these courts. Such cross-jurisdictional impact can both enhance and undermine the effectiveness of international institutional decisions. In the example of national cases (mentioned in the previous section) concerning the Al Qaeda sanctions regime, the cross-jurisdictional impact could considerably undermine the effectiveness of the sanctions regime as a whole. In relation to potentially confrontational decisions of the EU courts, the Monitoring Team established for the Al Qaeda sanctions regime noted, as early as 2005, that 'one or more potentially negative court decisions … could hamper enforcement efforts'[55] not only in the 27 member states of the EU, but also outside the EU. '[T]he precedent of a decision that invalidated the sanctions, especially one affecting so many States, might lead to similar problems in other States'.[56] As the Monitoring Team acknowledged, if states were unable to enforce the international decisions without violating their own

[52] In the end, it was precisely the information provided by other countries that prevented the Committee from according Belgium's request to delist the couple in question. They were finally delisted on 20 July 2009 (UN Press Release SC/9711 of 21 July 2009).

[53] *Abousfian Abdelrazik v The Minister of Foreign Affairs and the Attorney General of Canada* (2009) 2009 FC 580; [2010] 1 FCR 267 (Canada, Federal Court, 4 June 2009) [160].

[54] Especially interesting was the assertion of an 'autonomous legal order' by the Court of Justice of the European Union. *Kadi I* (n 44) [300].

[55] 'Second Report of the Analytical Support and Sanctions Monitoring Team Appointed Pursuant to Resolution 1526 (2004) Concerning Al-Qaida and the Taliban and Associated Individuals and Entities' UN Doc S/2005/83 (15 Feb 2005) para 58.

[56] 'Report of the Analytical Support and Sanctions Monitoring Team Pursuant to Resolution 1735 (2006) Concerning Al-Qaida and the Taliban and Associated Individuals and Entities' UN Doc S/2008/324 (14 May 2008) para 40.

(or EU laws), this would 'fundamentally [affect]' or 'erode the authority of the Council'.[57] By putting domestic law before international law, domestic judges therefore threaten to undermine the effectiveness of international law and international institutional decisions.

IV. 'WEAK' REVIEW BY DOMESTIC COURTS

A. Applying the Deferential Standards of Review

Domestic courts engage in 'strong' review of legislation and executive action when they review such an action on the basis of—as Tushnet argues—the constitutional provisions and other higher domestic laws. Such a review could lead national judges to find a violation, strike down the relevant legislation or executive decisions, and even to order the executive to undertake a specific action in order for the government to comply with the relevant law.

In contrast to this 'strong' approach, Tushnet proposes that domestic courts engage in 'weak' review by adopting deferential standards of review. Tushnet characterises weak review as an assessment of another organ's actions in a manner that elicits a response from this organ and thus establishes a dialogue between the two organs as to the meaning of the norm in question.[58] The elements of weak review are, as noted above, the deferential manner in which review is undertaken by the court, the common terms of reference (ie, international rules) with which the court engages the attention of the other organ, and finally, the response received from the other organ.[59] These elements can be found in domestic courts' assessments of international decisions.

Domestic courts can apply a generous standard of review towards the decisions of international institutions or presume that the relevant international institutions have complied with the law. Courts can also argue that they are not reviewing but simply interpreting the international decisions.

[57] 'Tenth Report of the Analytical Support and Sanctions Implementation Monitoring Team Submitted Pursuant to Resolution 1822 (2008) Concerning Al-Qaida and the Taliban and Associated Individuals and Entities' UN Doc S/2009/502 (2 Oct 2009) para 45. See also 'Third Report of the Analytical Support and Sanctions Monitoring Team Appointed Pursuant to Resolution 1526 (2004) Concerning Al-Qaida and the Taliban and Associated Individuals and Entities' UN Doc S/2005/572 (9 Sept 2005) para 54; 'Eleventh Report of the Analytical Support and Sanctions Implementation Monitoring Team Established Pursuant to Security Council Resolution 1526 (2004) and Extended by Resolution 1904 (2009) Concerning Al-Qaida and the Taliban and Associated Individuals and entities' UN Doc S/2011/245 (13 April 2011) para 30.

[58] Tushnet, 'Dialogic Judicial Review' (n 43); Mark Tushnet, 'Weak-Form Judicial Review and Core Civil Liberties' (2006) 41 *Harvard Civil Rights-Civil Liberties Law Review* 1, 6, 14.

[59] Tushnet (n 43).

For example, in *Nada*, while the Swiss Federal Supreme Court admitted that domestic courts' powers were limited when reviewing international decisions, the Court still held that the domestic court had the power to review the compatibility of the UN Security Council measures with 'les règles impératives du droit international'.[60] Nada's assets had been frozen according to Swiss measures following the adoption of Security Council Resolutions 1267 (1999) and 1333 (2000) and the listing of the individual on the consolidated list in 2001. The Swiss Federal Supreme Court affirmed the decision of the Federal Tribunal, which stated that although the court may enjoy the limited power to review the compatibility of Security Council acts with *jus cogens*,[61] the right of property and the procedural guarantees of a fair trial did not belong to the core of peremptory rights;[62] on this basis, the court had to refrain from exercising review over the decision to put Nada on the list of targeted persons.[63] The Swiss Court's decision is still relevant and significant for the purpose of this chapter, however, in that the national court employed, albeit in a limited sense, international law and its *jus cogens* as the standards with which the domestic court assessed the UN's international decisions.

Yet the use of international law as a standard of review often lowers the intensity of review conducted by national courts. Domestic judges assume a role of protecting only the peremptory rules of international law, leaving the international institution to secure the legality of its actions with regard to non-peremptory rules of international law. The standard of scrutiny adopted by domestic courts vis-à-vis international decisions in this context is a deferential one. To employ *jus cogens* norms as the standards of review also involves the difficulty of identifying the norms and establishing their content; in the absence of a clear and agreed conception of *jus cogens* rules,[64] it is highly unlikely that domestic courts would identify a rule as a peremptory norm or indeed find a violation of such a norm.

Another manner in which domestic courts' review is deferential to international institutions is that the courts often presume that an international

[60] Constitution of the Swiss Confederation of 1999, Arts 193.4 and 194.2.

[61] *Youssef Nada v State Secretariat for Economic Affairs and Federal Department of Economic Affairs, Administrative appeal judgment* (2007) Case No 1A.45/2007, DTF 133 II 450; ILDC 461 (CH 2007) (Switzerland, Federal Supreme Court, First Public Law Chamber, 14 Nov 2007) [7].

[62] ibid [7.3].

[63] *cf* Case T-306/01 *Ahmed Ali Yusuf and Al Barakaat International Foundation v Council of the European Union and Commission of the European Communities* (2005) (CFI, Judgment of 21 Sept 2005). Having found that the interference with the applicant's right to property and fair trial had not been disproportionate, it found that no breach of *jus cogens* had taken place and dismissed Kadi's claim.

[64] Antonios Tzanakopoulos, 'Domestic Court Reactions to UN Security Council Sanctions' in A Reinisch (ed), *Challenging Acts of International Organizations Before National Courts* (Oxford; New York, Oxford University Press, 2011) 54, 62. Tzanakopoulos observes: 'Given the notorious difficulty (and disagreement) as to the qualification of certain rules of *jus cogens* … and the significant indeterminacy of norms at such a high level of abstraction': ibid.

institutional decision complies with relevant legal norms. In *Rukundo v Switzerland* before the Swiss Federal Supreme Court, a Rwandan citizen appealed against the Swiss government's decision to transfer him to the International Criminal Tribunal for Rwanda (ICTR). He argued that the ICTR could not guarantee the right to a fair trial as enshrined in the European Convention on Human Rights (ECHR) and the International Covenant on Civil and Political Rights (ICCPR) because the international tribunal was subject to severe dysfunctions relating to the management and the functioning of the tribunal; on this basis, he claimed that Switzerland could not allow his transfer.[65] Whilst the relevant Security Council resolution clearly laid down the duty of states to cooperate with the ad hoc international criminal tribunal, the resolution did not specify whether the tribunal would be bound by the fair trial guarantees applicable in the case of criminal proceedings.[66] The Swiss Federal Supreme Court held that whilst extradition or transfer would only be allowed to states or institutions that guaranteed the respect for minimal procedural rights, there was a presumption that such rights were ensured at the ICTR. In this context, the Swiss Court further noted that important improvements had been made in the functioning of the ad hoc international criminal tribunal and that the applicant had not presented sufficient evidence to rebut the presumption that the international proceedings before the ICTR guarantee human rights protection.[67]

Applying such a presumption of legality to international judicial decisions not only shifts the burden of proving a violation of a legal norm onto the applicant, but also affirms a certain understanding about international institutions; that is, the understanding that international bodies do not have the intention to carry out actions that violate international human rights standards, peremptory norms of international law, non-derogable rights, or those that are not strictly proportionate.[68] This reading of international decisions means that domestic courts have to be persuaded by clear and explicit language that the international institution intended to violate the aforementioned legal standards before they are willing to exercise review or contemplate finding that a violation of these legal standards has taken place.

[65] *Emmanuel Rukundo v l'Office Federal de la Justice*, Swiss Federal Supreme Court (3 Sept 2001) No 1A.129/2001, [3b].

[66] 'Report of the Secretary-General Pursuant to Paragraph 2 of Security Council Resolution 808 (1993)' UN Doc S/25704 (3 May 1993) para 106.

[67] See *Emmanuel Rukundo v l'Office Federal de la Justice* (n 65). A similar presumption was applied also by a Dutch court in *Slobodan Milošević v The State of the Netherlands* (2002) 41 ILM 86 (Netherlands, The Hague District Court, 31 Aug 2001).

[68] *Nabil Sayadi and Patricia Vinck v Belgium* (2008) UN Doc CCPR/C/94/D/1472/2006 (views of the Human Rights Committee under Art 5, para 4, of the Optional Protocol to the ICCPR) (29 Dec 2008). The 4 criteria for interpreting the UN Charter and SC decisions were set out by Sir Nigel Rodley: ibid 36 (Sir Nigel Rodley, concurring).

The third manner in which domestic courts exercise deferential review lies in the courts' interpretation of international institutional decisions. In *Othman*,[69] for example, UK courts reviewed the decision of the UK Secretary of State for Work and Pensions which had implemented UN Security Council Resolution 1333 (2000) as well as related regulations of the then European Community (EC), and pursuant to which social benefits to the applicant, who was listed as a terrorist suspect under the so-called Taliban list, were suspended. The domestic judge recognised that although the assets of the individual could be frozen, the Security Council resolution had to be read as including an implicit humanitarian limitation which would allow minimum payments to be made to the applicant in order to provide for his basic needs or 'bare necessities of life'.[70] Collins J observed as follows:

> I would read this regulation subject only to the proviso that the member State is entitled, and indeed perhaps bound, to ensure that the effect of applying the regulation is not so as to mean that the individual in question, in this case the Claimant, has because of having no means of support, reached a situation where his health and perhaps his very life are at risk.[71]

The judge continued to hold that these minimum payments were to be made without recourse to the Taliban Sanctions Committee which would not be in a position to make a speedy determination:

> It seems to me that it would be quite absurd to think that that sort of matter would have to be determined by the United Nations through the Taliban Sanctions Committee. Quite apart from anything else, I very much doubt if a decision would be able to be obtained particularly speedily in that way. That is not intended as criticism; it is merely a recognition of the realities of the situation.[72]

Collins J interpreted the strict Security Council resolution (and EC regulation) in a way in which individuals' health and very life would have to be protected. Prior to this *Othman* case, the UN Security Council did not fully address this issue, and given that the listed individuals were not allowed to appeal to the Council's Sanctions Committee to raise this question by themselves, the Security Council arguably did not intend such individuals to have the opportunity to have their 'bare necessities' considered. Through interpretation of the Security Council's silence, however, Collins J concluded that there was no doubt that the state had a duty and a prerogative to ensure a humanitarian safety net for Othman.

[69] *R (on the application of Othman) v Secretary of State for Work and Pensions* [2001] EWHC Admin 1022; [2001] All ER (D) 413 (Nov) (Judgment of UK High Court, 28 Nov 2001).

[70] ibid [60].

[71] ibid [57].

[72] ibid [61].

It is in the deferential yet engaging approach of Collins J's reasoning that 'the power of interpretation' as a crucial element of 'achieving the desired outcome'[73] becomes apparent. In *Othman*, Collins J is very clear in affirming that he supports the enforcement of the Security Council's resolutions and sanctions regimes. In relation to 'bare necessities' he states: 'I use the expression "bare necessities of life" advisedly, because I fully recognise that the Claimant is not entitled to anything more than that'.[74] With this, the judge clearly expresses deference to the international institution and never second-guesses the Security Council's competence to decide what is in the security interest of the international community. The judge does not claim responsibility to replace the Sanctions Committee's (or the executive's) reading of the international norm with his own.

At the same time, Collins J explains why the involvement of the domestic court is necessary. He notes that the UN Security Council would not ensure a speedy resolution of their situation, a factor that is crucial if bare necessities are to be ensured. Specifically he notes that this observation is not intended as 'criticism' of the Sanctions Committee but 'recognition of [the] realities of the situation'. That Collins J wishes to avoid a conflict with the international institution is even more apparent when we consider the fact that the judge could have noted that individuals could not appeal to the Sanctions Committee[75] without the help of the state, and that thus domestic courts were the only forum where such claims could be made and brought to the attention of the public at large. But the judge avoids painting such a picture of the court, presenting his role merely as drawing the international institution's attention to the issue that may have escaped its attention. In this context, therefore, the domestic court is portrayed as effectively helping the international institution strengthen the legitimacy and efficacy of its anti-terror measures by finding its actions consistent with 'the law of humanity'.[76]

B. Eliciting International Responses

What relevance do these examples of deferential review have for domestic courts' role in relation to the international rule of law? The key that enables domestic courts to act both as a check on the executive and, at the same time, to uphold international law as 'law' lies in the other two

73 Bianchi, 'Assessing the Effectiveness of the UN Security Council's Anti-Terrorism Measures' (n 49) 916.

74 *Othman* (n 69) [60].

75 This was the case until the adoption of Council Resolution 1730 in late 2006, which allowed individuals to petition for delisting: UN Doc S/RES/1730 (19 Dec 2006).

76 *Othman* (n 69) [56]. See also Thomas M Franck, *The Power of Legitimacy among Nations* (New York, Oxford University Press, 1990).

elements of weak review—the use of a common terms of reference with which the court engages the attention of the other organ, and the dialogue with that institution.[77] Domestic courts' deferential review, when it is combined with these two characteristics of weak review, contributes to the development of the international rule of law within the international legal order and, it does so without challenging the authority of international institutions.

First, domestic courts speak to international institutions by making use of the same terms of reference—international law, thus enforcing international law as 'law'. When they undertake weak review, it is consistency with international norms that they seek. In *Nada*, *Kadi*, *Yusuf*, international decisions are evaluated against international peremptory norms; in *Rukundo*, the courts reviewing fair trial guarantees refer to Article 6 of the ECHR and to the equivalent norm in the ICCPR; and finally, in *Othman*, Collins J inquiries into the consistency of Othman's situation with Articles 3 and 8 of the ECHR.[78] In the end, he finds it unnecessary to rule on these norms since the English common 'law of humanity' as expressed by Lord Ellenborough allows him to 'save [Othman] from starving'.[79] His approach may appear domestic; however, as case law shows in the implementation of the Refugee Convention and the application of the relevant domestic legislation, 'the law of humanity' has been regularly used instead of the international equivalent to ensure the 'humanitarian safety net' to refugees and asylum seekers.[80] The reference to common law cannot be attributed to anything else but previous case law.

Second, the review undertaken by courts resembles efforts to interpret consistently two legal norms within the same legal order. In this context, the domestic court assumes that the international institution ensures protection of 'fundamental procedural human rights', that it complies with norms that are lower than *jus cogens* or that it does not intend to violate 'the law of humanity'.[81] In comparison to strong review, the addressee of this exercise of consistent interpretation is therefore the international institution. The assumptions, presumptions, or reading-in of intent speak directly to the international institution. Even when a domestic court

[77] Tushnet (n 43).

[78] *Othman* (n 69) [63]–[64], [11].

[79] *R v Inhabitants of Eastborne* (1803) 4 East 103, 107 (Lord Ellenborough CJ).

[80] *Othman* (n 69) [52] (citing *R v Hammersmith & Fulham London Borough Council, ex parte M* (1997) 30 HLR 10).

[81] ibid [56]; 'Fourth Report of the Analytical Support and Sanctions Monitoring Team Appointed Pursuant to Security Council Resolutions 1526 (2004) and 1617 (2005) Concerning Al-Qaida and the Taliban and Associated Individuals and Entities' UN Doc S/2006/154 (10 March 2006) 46, paras 8–9; 'Fifth Report of the Analytical Support and Sanctions Monitoring Team Appointed Pursuant to Security Council Resolutions 1526 (2004) and 1617 (2005)

appears to disagree with the international institution, this disagreement is expressed through consistent interpretation, by imputing to the institution a very specific (and potentially non-existent) intent.[82]

Such a review, as scholars predict, engages the international institution—as well as the executive organ which implements its decision—in a dialogue.[83] When in late 2001 Collins J rendered his interpretation of the SC Resolution 1267 in *Othman*, the Monitoring Group of the Sanctions Committee brought this concern to the attention of the Committee and the SC.[84] By the end of 2002, a new resolution had been adopted by the SC (SC Resolution 1452), which provided for a humanitarian exception to the SC Resolution 1267, allowing individuals on the consolidated list to be provided with basic expenses.[85] Although *Othman* is not explicitly mentioned in the report of the Monitoring Group—note that at the time, the states were not yet required to report on their implementation efforts and therefore on the litigation before their courts[86]—the 'humanitarian exception' was signalled to the Group by states, 'which are seeking to determine how to respond to challenges made through judicial procedures to allow access to frozen funds ostensibly needed to obtain civilian necessities'.[87] It is on the basis of these concerns that the Group advised the Committee to 'establish procedures regarding the possible granting of humanitarian exceptions'.[88]

The type of review employed by the domestic courts appears to have played a major role in this respect. Namely, if initially, the Monitoring Team saw '[t]he many legal challenges to the measures … and the threat of more' as 'a serious impediment to the success of the sanctions regime',[89] in 2009 it asserted that the Committee could benefit 'from consideration

Concerning Al-Qaida and the Taliban and Associated Individuals and Entities' UN Doc S/2006/750 (20 Sept 2006) 48, para 5.

[82] *Abdelrazik* (n 53).

[83] Tushnet (n 43); Tushnet, 'Weak-Form Judicial Review and Core Civil Liberties' (n 58) 6, 14.

[84] 'Second Report of the Monitoring Group Established Pursuant to Security Council Resolution 1363 (2001) and Extended by Resolution 1390 (2002)' UN Doc S/2002/1050 (20 Sept 2002) para 42.

[85] SC Resolution 1452 (2002), which allows for extraordinary expenses provided that such determination has been notified by the relevant state(s) to the Sanctions Committee and has been approved by the Committee.

[86] The reporting by states commences in SC Resolution 1455 (2003) and a litigation annex is added to the Monitoring Group reports from 2005.

[87] 'Second Report of the Monitoring Group Established Pursuant to Security Council Resolution 1363 (2001) and Extended by Resolution 1390 (2002)' (n 84) para 42.

[88] ibid para 136.

[89] 'Second Report of the Analytical Support and Sanctions Monitoring Team Appointed Pursuant to Resolution 1526 (2004) Concerning Al-Qaida and the Taliban and Associated Individuals and Entities' (n 55) para 50.

of listings by the courts'.[90] The Group argues that 'national and regional courts provide a forum for listed persons', where additional information can be brought to the fore and where their grievances can be expressed.[91] Given their access to information and to the individuals affected, domestic courts 'may allow a better evaluation of the strengths or weaknesses of the cases against [these individuals], especially when the challenge is brought in the courts of the designating States, which will likely have the most information against them'.[92] But no review has 'persuasive value in itself for the Committee'.[93] Instead,

> the Committee may value the opinion of a national court that has *carefully evaluated reasons* for listing as stated by the Committee and has accorded *appropriate deference* to its fact-finding and decision-making prerogatives. In cases where such court decisions exist, the Team recommends that the Committee give them due weight when reviewing the corresponding listing.[94]

Domestic courts' review of international decisions, therefore, has to pay *appropriate deference* to the international institution.[95] Before a domestic court will receive a response from the Security Council, the Sanctions Committee has to be sure that it remains 'the body ultimately in charge of designations'[96] and the body that 'makes the final decision' in relation to delisting.[97] The Committee cannot 'cede [its] role to others'[98] and the SC cannot accept any review that appears to 'erode its absolute authority to take action on matters affecting international peace and security, as enshrined in the Charter'.[99] Only a domestic court that expresses 'significant deference' to the international institution can '[expect] to

[90] 'Ninth Report of the Analytical Support and Sanctions Monitoring Team, Submitted Pursuant to Resolution 1822 (2008) Concerning Al-Qaida and the Taliban and Associated Individuals and Entities' UN Doc S/2009/245 (13 May 2009) para 23.

[91] ibid para 28.

[92] ibid.

[93] ibid para 29.

[94] ibid.

[95] Yuval Shany, 'Toward a General Margin of Appreciation Doctrine in International Law?' (2005) 16 *European Journal of International Law* 907, 921–22.

[96] 'Report of the Analytical Support and Sanctions Monitoring Team Pursuant to Resolution 1735 (2006) Concerning Al-Qaida and the Taliban and Associated Individuals and Entities' UN Doc S/2008/324 (14 May 2008) para 46.

[97] 'Second Report of the Analytical Support and Sanctions Monitoring Team Appointed Pursuant to Resolution 1526 (2004) Concerning Al-Qaida and the Taliban and Associated Individuals and Entities' (n 55) para 56.

[98] 'Tenth Report of the Analytical Support and Sanctions Implementation Monitoring Team Submitted Pursuant to Resolution 1822 (2008) Concerning Al-Qaida and the Taliban and Associated Individuals and Entities' (n 57) para 42.

[99] 'Eighth Report of the Monitoring Team pursuant to resolution 1526 (2004) and extended by resolutions 1617 (2005) and 1735 (2006)', S/2008/324, 'Report of the Analytical Support and Sanctions Monitoring Team Pursuant to Resolution 1735 (2006) Concerning Al-Qaida and the Taliban and Associated Individuals and Entities' (n 96) para 41.

influence' it 'to any significant degree'.[100] At most, therefore, domestic courts can draw the international institution's attention to an incompatibility, an error or an oversight, and frame its judgment as a suggested reading of the international decision.[101]

In addition, the requirement of *'carefully evaluated reasons'* relates to how the domestic court explains its decision. In this context, the international institution will not consider persuasive a decision of a national court that evaluates a listing pursuant to a criminal law standard 'set out under national law'.[102] Indeed, domestic courts can achieve compliance with international law without ever mentioning or thinking about international law.[103] But when it comes to review of international decisions, national and regional standards are often 'too high for the Committee to meet'. What is needed instead is an institution that 'bring[s] targeted sanctions regimes into line with principles of international law'.[104] Is this not a direct call to domestic courts to evaluate or rather interpret international decisions against international law?[105]

The willingness to engage with the domestic courts and to respond to their interpretation of the law means that the Security Council has accepted the role of the domestic courts in the making of international law. If international decisions are to be examined against international law,[106] then those who review and interpret them will help make new international law. The international law that comes out of this process is an 'international law of collaboration',[107] an international law in which rules

[100] 'Ninth Report of the Analytical Support and Sanctions Monitoring Team, Submitted Pursuant to Resolution 1822 (2008) Concerning Al-Qaida and the Taliban and Associated Individuals and Entities' (n 90) para 29.

[101] Mark Tushnet, 'Alternative Forms of Judicial Review' (2003) *Michigan Law Review* 2781, 2797; James B Thayer, 'Origin and Scope of the American Doctrine of Constitutional Law' (1893) 7 *Harvard Law Review* 129.

[102] 'Ninth Report of the Analytical Support and Sanctions Monitoring Team, Submitted Pursuant to Resolution 1822 (2008) Concerning Al-Qaida and the Taliban and Associated Individuals and Entities' (n 90) para 29.

[103] Damrosch observes: 'Assuming that the standards under United States constitutional law are at least as high as what international law requires, a judicial decision under constitutional rule would bring about full compliance with the international rule. No question of "enforcing international law" needs to arise': Damrosch (n 22) 156.

[104] 'Tenth Report of the Analytical Support and Sanctions Implementation Monitoring Team Submitted Pursuant to Resolution 1822 (2008) Concerning Al-Qaida and the Taliban and Associated Individuals and Entities' (n 57) para 41.

[105] Tushnet argues that a dialogue needs to be established therefore about what the law means. Tushnet, 'Weak-Form Judicial Review and Core Civil Liberties' (n 58) 3, 17.

[106] If courts can review international decisions for compatibility with international law, this means that the supremacy of the international decisions is no longer guaranteed. If the international decision is not consistent with higher international law, there is no guarantee that it will be enforced. The supremacy conferred by domestic courts is enjoyed by international law; not decisions of the international institution.

[107] Dan T Coenen, 'A Constitution of Collaboration: Protecting Fundamental Values with Second-Look Rules of Interbranch Dialogue' (2000) 42 *William and Mary Law Review* 1575.

are formed no longer only by strictly defined subjects of international law (international institutions and states), but also by national organs such as domestic courts. Inevitably, such a role also protects the international rule of law. Domestic courts apply international law and in doing so, act as a check, not only on their executive. More importantly, by engaging with the international institution in a discussion about the content of international law, they also help draw the international institution's attention to protections accorded by international law to individuals and thus contribute to a higher protection of the international rule of law.

V. CONCLUSION

If international scholars arguing in favour of domestic courts' acting as 'agents' of the international legal order in the protection of the international rule of law expect courts to uphold the legal nature of international law and keep a check on the executive, then the judiciary's recourse to domestic law clearly fails to live up to their expectations. Domestic courts seized to adjudicate challenges to implementing measures enforcing international decisions usually have recourse to the traditional strong review. In this context, they often strike down executive implementing measures or order for this political branch to undertake specific action to comply with domestic rights protection. Although this review acts as a check on the executive, in situations where states are under a 'strict' international obligation, it often fails to ensure sufficient protection for the individual, as the obligation arises from the international level. This impasse is further complicated by domestic courts' unwillingness to refer to international law but to instead use domestic law as a standard against which implemented measures are evaluated. As a consequence, their review is couched in a separate, autonomous legal order and can be isolating to the state, often leading it to have to choose between performing its international obligations or violating domestic law.

For domestic courts to act as supporting the international rule of law, their review has to uphold international law. In this chapter, I argued that instead of such a strong review, domestic courts should adopt a weaker approach, an approach in which domestic courts give up their power to have a final word. Instead, their review should pay deference to the authority of the international institution and employ international law as a standard against which to evaluate the legality of international or implementing measures. Only such a review can both act as a check on the executive which brought the measure into domestic law and engage with the international institution.

This last element is particularly important. Given the 'strict' nature of the international obligation imposed by the international decision, weak review enables domestic courts to talk directly to the original decision-maker. By paying 'appropriate deference' to the international institution and explaining their reasons for re-interpretation or reading-in, domestic courts can provide 'carefully evaluated' arguments to the international institution about how its decision ought to be amended to comply with international rights protections. By employing international law as common terms of reference, domestic courts can avoid national particularities and speak to the international institution in a language it understands. This, in turn, establishes a dialogue between domestic courts and the international institution, a dialogue in which both domestic courts and the international institution are willing to participate in and resolve their rights disagreements, a dialogue that can lead to greater rights protection and to an international law of collaboration.

3

The Development of the Immunities of International Organisations in Response to Domestic Contestations

MATEJA STEINBRÜCK PLATIŠE*

I. INTRODUCTION

FOR A LONG time, international organisations were entrusted only with limited activities and employed relatively few members of staff. International rules and standards that they adopted were primarily addressed to states and regulated highly specialised and narrow fields of social activity.[1] In cases where organisations committed wrongful acts, such acts therefore usually remained limited to the narrow fields of their activity and directly affected only a limited number of individuals and other private parties. As a result, claims against international organisations were rarely brought before domestic courts. When such disputes did arise, the courts dealt with them on a case-by-case basis, and the question of jurisdictional immunities of organisations before domestic courts was not a major concern.[2]

With the increase of international organisations in their number, size, and power, immunities began to be regulated on the international level. When the United Nations was established, the provisions of the UN Charter granted the organisation legal personality as well as privileges

* This chapter is based on the author's research on the Responsibility of International Organisations for Human Rights Violations, which has received funding from the People Programme (Marie Curie Actions) of the European Union's Seventh Framework Programme (FP7/2007–20013) under REA grant agreement no PIEF-GA-2011-299446.

[1] Jan Klabbers, *An Introduction to International Institutional Law* (2nd edn, Cambridge; New York, Cambridge University Press, 2009) 14–20; Joseph HH Weiler, 'The Geology of International Law: Governance, Democracy and Legitimacy' (2004) 64 *Zeitschrift für ausländisches öffentliches Recht und Völkerrecht* 547, 549–52.

[2] Michael Singer, 'Jurisdictional Immunity of International Organizations: Human Rights and Functional Necessity Concerns' (1995) 36 *Virginia Journal of International Law* 53, 59.

and immunities that are necessary for the fulfilment of its purposes.[3] Constituent instruments of a variety of other international organisations and their implementing treaties contain similar provisions.[4] Such formulations of the scope of immunities gave ground to the doctrine of functional necessity, according to which organisations enjoy such immunities as are necessary for the exercise of their functions in fulfilment of their purposes.[5]

Practice has shown, however, that international organisations commonly rely on their immunities before domestic courts without at the same time subjecting themselves to alternative dispute settlement mechanisms that could review claims against organisations. The hesitance of international organisations to settle disputes with individuals and other private parties thereby results in a systematic deprivation of remedies for the claimants, who are often left without a forum that could entertain their claims, either on the domestic or international level.[6] Moreover, such hesitance of organisations poses a problem for domestic courts, which are faced with two conflicting obligations under international law: on the one hand, they are bound to grant immunities to international organisations;[7] on the other hand, they are bound to grant access to court and the right to a remedy to individuals and other private parties.[8] Furthermore, access to justice as a human right is often constitutionally protected and forms a vital part of the domestic rule of law,[9] according to which an exercise of public authority over individuals and other private parties should be subjected to judicial review.[10]

In the present chapter, I will examine the response of domestic courts to the conflicting international obligations and evaluate the impact that

[3] Charter of the United Nations, 26 June 1945, 1 UNTS XVI (entered into force 24 Oct 1945) Art 105(1). In the second paragraph, a similar provision is added with respect to representatives of member states and the UN officials; see also the Convention on the Privileges and Immunities of the United Nations, 13 Feb 1946, 1 UNTS 15 (entered into force 17 Sept 1946), which further elaborated the immunities of the organisation.

[4] See, eg, Convention on the Privileges and Immunities of the Specialized Agencies, 33 UNTS 261 (entered into force 2 Dec 1948); Charter of the Organization of American States, 119 UNTS 3 Art 133; Statute of the Council of Europe, 87 UNTS 103, ETS 1 Art 40.

[5] See more detail in s II(D) of the present chapter.

[6] For one of more recent examples, see the statement of the UN Secretary General Ban Ki-moon of 21 Feb 2013 claiming immunities for the UN with respect to the Haiti cholera outbreak allegedly caused by UN troops, available at: www.un.org/sg/statements/?nid=6615.

[7] See also s II(A) of the present chapter.

[8] See s III(A) of the present chapter.

[9] For the right to access to court and the right to a remedy as constitutional rights, see examples discussed in ss III(A) and (B) of the present chapter.

[10] For the lack of judicial review over acts of international organisations as part of a general problem of legitimacy of international organisations, see Armin von Bogdandy, Philipp Dann and Matthias Goldmann, 'Developing the Publicness of Public International Law: Towards a Legal Framework for Global Governance Activities' in A von Bogdandy and others (eds), *The Exercise of Public Authority by International Institutions: Advancing International Institutional Law* (Heidelberg; London; New York, Springer, 2009) 1379–80.

the domestic practice has had on the development of the immunities of international organisations. On the basis of such an examination I will try to ascertain the role that domestic courts can play in interpretation, application and enforcement of international law. For that purpose, I will first analyse in section II some theoretical and practical reasons for the increasing difficulties of domestic courts to grant immunities to international organisations. In section III, I will explore how domestic courts respond to these difficulties in the context of human rights law and constitutional law; in particular, by challenging the absolute scope of the organisations' immunities. The effect of the domestic courts' practice on international law will be studied in section IV, where I will focus on those international actors that have addressed the legality and legitimacy of domestic courts' challenges to the absolute scope of the immunities. On the basis of the analysis of the domestic courts' practice in section III and its reception in international law in section IV, I will attempt to sketch in section V a normative framework under which domestic courts are able to influence the development of international law and the law of immunities of international organisations in particular. Thereby, I will try to show that in addition to the role of domestic courts in ensuring the rule of law domestically, their potential to contribute to the international rule of law should also be acknowledged. This dual role of domestic courts can prevent public authority over individuals, exercised either on the domestic or international level, from escaping a judicial review. By way of conclusion, I will assess the relevance of such development for the future interaction of domestic courts with international institutions and for the legal orders to which these courts and institutions belong.

II. THE CREEPING IMMUNITIES OF INTERNATIONAL ORGANISATIONS

In order to explain the domestic courts' practice in granting immunities to international organisations, I will first examine the theoretical and practical difficulties that domestic courts face when an international organisation, as one of the parties to the proceedings, invokes its right to immunities. Conceptually, these difficulties can be divided into four different but interrelated problem areas, which I discuss in turn under the following sections: the traditional lack of distinction between different acts of international organisations (section A); the lack of dispute settlement procedures alternative to the domestic proceedings (section B); the growing powers of international organisations (section C); and the traditional interpretation of immunities as covering all the acts that an organisation may adopt in accordance with its functions (section D). I will try to show that, cumulatively, these trends and traditional concepts require domestic courts to grant immunities in a growing number of policy areas and therefore lead to creeping immunities of international organisations.

A. Lack of Distinction Between Acts *de iure imperii* and *de iure gestionis*

While a large number of legal instruments[11] grant immunities to international organisations to the extent necessary for the fulfilment of the organisation's purposes, they do not define which acts of international organisations are covered by such immunities. The interpretation of the scope of their immunities has therefore not been without controversy, and has led to different, sometimes even contradicting conclusions. International organisations, on the one hand, usually assert that nothing less than absolute immunity will satisfy the requirement of functional necessity.[12] Domestic courts, on the other hand, have been much less unequivocal in interpreting the scope of immunities.[13] Their interpretation may differ from one judge to another,[14] from one country to another,[15] and has also changed over time.[16] In general, however, domestic courts used to be very generous in granting absolute immunities to international organisations,

[11] The law relating to privileges and immunities of international organisations is sometimes compared to a 'labyrinth' of treaties and other legal instruments, including domestic legislation, see Klabbers, *An Introduction to International Institutional Law* (n 1) 155. For an early discussion of that problem, see David B Michaels, *International Privileges and Immunities: A Case for a Universal Statute* (The Hague, Martinus Nijhoff, 1971).

[12] See, eg, submission by the Organization of American States as well as amici curiae briefs filed by the UN, the International Bank for Reconstruction and Development, the Inter-American Development Bank and the International Telecommunications Satellite Organization in the case *Broadbent v Organization of American States* (US Court of Appeals) 628 F 2d 27 (DC Cir 1980); *OSS Nokalva, Inc v European Space Agency*, Appeal Judgment, 617F 3d 756 (3rd Cir 2010) ILDC 1580 (US 2010); *Killeen v International Centre of Insect Physiology and Ecology* (First Instance, High Court of Nairobi) Civil Case 1737 of 2002, ILDC 77 (KE 2005); *General Secretariat of the African, Caribbean and Pacific Group of States v BD* (Belgian Court of Cassation, Final appeal Judgment) Cass nr C 07 0407 F, ILDC 1576 (BE 2009).

[13] For a general study, see August Reinisch, *International Organizations Before National Courts* (Cambridge; New York, Cambridge University Press, 2000) 206.

[14] cp, eg, the judgments of different Dutch courts in the Case no 295247/HA ZA 07-2973 *Mothers of Srebrenica et al v The State of the Netherlands and the United Nations* (2008) (Netherlands, District Court in The Hague, Judgment of 10 July 2008); Case no 200022151/01 *Mothers of Srebrenica et al v The State of the Netherlands and the United Nations* (2010) (Court of Appeal in The Hague, Judgment of 30 March 2010); *Mothers of Srebrenica v Netherlands and United Nations, Final appeal judgment* (2012) LJN: BW1999; ILDC 1760 (NL 2012) (Netherlands Supreme Court, 13 April 2012). See also s IV of the present chapter.

[15] cp, eg, *African Development Bank v Mr X* (French Court of Cassation, Appeal Chamber) no 04-41012, ILDC 778 (FR 2005) with *Weinstock v Asian Development Bank and Others* (US District Court) civil action no 1:05-CV-00174, 13 July 2005 (US 2005).

[16] For the US jurisdiction, cp the old precedent in *Atkinson v Inter-American Development Bank*, Appeal Judgment, 156 F 3d 1335 (DC Cir 1998) with a new precedent as established in *Nokalva* (n 12).

often arguing that only the broadest scope of immunities could ensure their independent functioning.

Granted, when organisations began to appear, they had quite limited functions, were intended for very special purposes, and had a fragile position vis-à-vis states.[17] The protection of their independent functioning therefore required a broad scope of immunities, most often an absolute one. Moreover, the immunities of international organisations used to be assimilated with the immunities of states, which also at that time enjoyed absolute immunities.[18] In that respect, the International Organizations Immunities Act, enacted by the United States in 1945, catches well the spirit of the time, in that it provides that '[i]nternational organisations … shall enjoy the same immunity from suit and every form of judicial process as is enjoyed by foreign governments'.[19]

However, state immunities began increasingly to be limited to their acts *de iure imperii*, leaving the state acts *de iure gestionis* outside their scope. Domestic courts interpreted such limitation as necessary for 'the rule of law'[20] and 'fairness to plaintiffs'.[21] In particular, the limitation was based on the argument that absolute immunities led to a denial of legal remedies for individuals for the vindication of their rights against the state in the matter of both contract and tort.[22]

On the other hand, no such distinction has been established with respect to international organisations. Despite the fact that a number of scholars addressed the possibility of distinguishing between commercial and public acts of international organisations,[23] domestic courts have often remained hesitant in applying that doctrine. Indeed, the distinction has

[17] C Wilfred Jenks, *International Immunities* (London; New York, Stevens, Oceana Publications, 1961) 40–41.

[18] Singer, 'Jurisdictional Immunity of International Organizations' (n 2) 58–65.

[19] 22 US Code § 288a(b)(1994); the UK Diplomatic Privileges (Extension) Act 1944 similarly provides for immunity to be accorded to international organisations to the same extent as to states; *Yearbook of the International Law Commission* (1977) vol II, pt 1, 152; likewise, the Swiss Federal Council declared in 1919: 'Il est naturel que la Société des Nations jouisse des mêmes privilèges et immunités que tout Etat avec lequel nous entretenons des relations diplomatiques'; cited in Pierre Freymond, 'Remarques sur l'immunité de juridiction des organisations internationales en matière immobilière' (1955–56) 53 *Freiedens-Warte* 365, 366.

[20] Hersch Lauterpacht, 'The Problem of Jurisdictional Immunities of Foreign States' (1951) 28 *British Year Book of International Law* 220, 220.

[21] James Crawford, 'International Law and Foreign Sovereigns: Distinguishing Immune Transactions' (1984) 54 *British Yearbook of International Law* 75, 77.

[22] ibid.

[23] Nicolas Valticos, 'Les contrats conclus par les organisations internationales avec des personnes privées, Rapport provisoire et projet de résolution—Rapport définitive et projet de résolution' (1977) *Annuaire de l'institut de Droit International* 1, 3; Henry G Schermers, 'International Organizations, Legal Remedies against Acts of Organs' in Rudolf Bernhardt (ed), *Encyclopedia of Public International Law*, vol II (2nd edn, North-Holland, 1995) 1318, 1318. For a contrary view, see Rosalyn Higgins, *Problems and Processes: International Law and How We Use It* (1994) 93.

been occasionally revisited by some domestic courts; for example, in the case of *the League of Arab States v TM*, in which the Court of Appeals in Belgium held that the employment dispute of the claimant with the international organisation concerned *actium iure gestionis*, to which immunity does not attach under customary international law.[24] Nevertheless, such distinction does not seem to be generally accepted, and domestic courts still commonly grant immunities also for those acts that could be classified as having *de iure gestionis* character.[25]

B. Lack of Dispute Settlement Procedures

Another important difference between the regimes of state immunity and the immunity of international organisations is that organisations are generally not subject to compulsory jurisdiction of any international tribunal that could compensate for the lack of jurisdiction by domestic courts over claims against international organisations. While victims of human rights violations can, as a rule, bring their claims against the offending state before domestic courts of that state, such 'domestic' remedies are rarely available within international organisations. Their internal dispute settlement mechanisms are, for the most part, still in their nascent stage, if they are available all.[26] Indeed, certain international instruments, such as the Convention on the Privileges and Immunities of the United Nations,[27] expressly require that the organisation makes provisions for appropriate modes of settlement of disputes arising out of contracts or other disputes of a private law character to which the organisation is a party.[28] The Convention thereby clearly establishes a duty to provide for

[24] *League of Arab States v TM* (Belgian Court of Cassation) ILDC 42 (BE 2001); the distinction can also be traced in the case law of some other countries; in particular, in the newer case law of the US following the adoption in the *Nokalva Case* (n 12); for a Russian example, see *State Tax Service v (Anonymous) An International Organization, Decision on 'nadzor review'* ILDC 26 (RU 2001) (Russia, Supreme Commercial Court, 18 Jan 2001); for a Mexican example, see *Instituto Latinoamericano de la çommunicatión educative*, Amparo en Revisión 348/2001, Reg no 17498, Novena Época, Semanario Judicial de la Federation y su Gaceta, Tomo XVII, Marzo de 2013.

[25] From many examples, see, eg, *Maruba SCA Empresa de Navegación Marítima v Itaipú* (Argentinian Supreme Court, 5 Feb 1998) SCM 1109 XXIX; *Company Baumeister Ing Richard L v O*, (Austrian Supreme Court) ILDC 362 (AT 2004); see also *Prewitt Enterprises Incorporated and Similarly situated purchasers of petroleum products in the United States v Organization of Petroleum Exporting Countries* (US Court of Appeals) 353 F 3d 916 (11th Cir 2003); see generally Cedric Ryngaert, 'The Immunity of International Organizations before Domestic Courts: Recent Trends' (2010) 7 *International Organizations Law Review* 121, 126.

[26] These are usually limited to administrative tribunals competent to settle employment disputes between an international organisation and its members of staff; see discussion in s IV of this chapter.

[27] UN Immunities Convention (n 3).

[28] ibid Art VIII (29).

remedies available to the victims. Yet, the UN, just as many other international organisations, has still not yet fully implemented its obligation to provide for dispute settlement procedures which should mitigate for its immunity before domestic courts.[29]

C. Growing Powers

While international organisations have, on the one hand, claimed absolute immunities before domestic courts, and have consistently remained hesitant to subject themselves to alternative dispute settlement procedures, they have, on the other hand, grown in their number and size, and expanded their scope of activities and policy fields. Today, organisations regulate a broad range of matters that previously belonged to the state's exclusive domain. In particular, since the end of the Cold War era, they increasingly influence domestic political and legal processes and increasingly limit the realm in which national self-government can take place.[30] With the extended powers entrusted to them, the situations have increased in which also individuals can be affected by the exercise of their authority. In particular, legal acts of international organisations are no longer addressed primarily to states, but increasingly also to other actors, including individuals. The most well-known examples in which individuals have been negatively affected include the targeted sanctions adopted by the UN Security Council,[31] the lack of adequate legal protection of individuals concerning the decisions and actions of various UN bodies and agencies, such as the UN High Representative for Bosnia and Herzegovina,[32] and the actions of the Kosovo Force (KFOR), the NATO-led peacekeeping force in Kosovo.[33] At the same time, international organisations rely on the axiom of international law that domestic law, even constitutional law, cannot serve as a justification for non-compliance with international legal obligations, which includes the acts of international organisations.[34] International organisations thus broaden their powers and competences,

[29] See also s IV of this chapter.

[30] Mattias Kumm, 'The Legitimacy of International Law: A Constitutionalist Framework of Analysis' (2004) 15 *European Journal of International Law* 907, 910–17.

[31] Clemens A Feinäugle, 'The UN Security Council Al-Quaida and Taliban Sanctions Committee: Emerging Principles of International Institutional Law for the Protection of Individuals' (2008) 9 *German Law Journal* 1513, 1539. On domestic contestations against the UN Security Council's sanctions regimes, see ch 2 (Fikfak) of this volume.

[32] Richard Caplan, 'Who Guards the Guardians? International Accountability in Bosnia' (2005) 12 *International Peacekeeping* 463.

[33] John Cerone, 'Minding the Gap: Outlining KFOR Accountability in Post-Conflict Kosovo' (2001) 12 *European Journal of International Law* 469.

[34] Vienna Convention on the Law of Treaties, 23 May 1969, 1155 UNTS 311 (entered into force 27 Jan 1980) (1969) Art 27.

increasingly exercise international public authority,[35] and insist on the absolute immunities from jurisdiction and enforcement before domestic courts. By doing so, international organisations, I assert, correspondingly broaden their immunity claims.

D. The Role of the Functional Necessity Argument

Such creeping of immunity claims by international organisations may be seen as a result of the concept of their functional personality, which grants them international legal personality to the extent required to perform their functions. Legally, international organisations are therefore unable to act beyond their functional personality. Any act not covered by such a limited functional personality is considered ultra vires.[36] While enjoying functional personality, international organisations enjoy also functional immunity, which covers all the acts in the performance of their functions.[37] And since organisations can only act within the scope of their functional personality—so the argument goes—there is no room left for the acts for which immunity could be denied. Such view necessarily leads to the requirement of absolute immunities of international organisations.[38] Interpreted in this way, the criterion of functional necessity can therefore hardly play a role in circumscribing the immunity of international organisations. Instead, it allows immunity to be granted to international organisations in all circumstances, given that the organisations will always be deemed to act within the scope of their duties.[39]

III. CONTESTATIONS BY DOMESTIC COURTS

While the cases in which domestic courts denied immunities to international organisations on the ground that the reviewed acts were not *de iure*

[35] von Bogdandy, Dann and Goldmann, 'Developing the Publicness of Public International Law' (n 10) 1376–1400.

[36] *Certain Expenses of the United Nations (Article 17, Paragraph 2, of the Charter)* [1962] ICJ Reports 151 (Advisory Opinion of 20 July 1962) 168.

[37] See generally Peter HF Bekker, *The Legal Position of Intergovernmental Organizations: A Functional Necessity Analysis of Their Legal Status and Immunities* (Dordrecht; Boston, M Nijhoff, 1994).

[38] August Reinisch and Ulf Andreas Weber, 'In the Shadow of Waite and Kennedy: The Jurisdictional Immunity of International Organizations, The Individual's Right of Access to the Courts and Administrative Tribunals as Alternative Means of Dispute Settlement' (2004) 1 *International Organizations Law Review* 59, 63 (quoting Seidl-Hohenveldern in an unpublished report to the ILA Committee on State Immunity, referred to in Final Report on State Immunity, ILA Buenos Aires Conference 1994, 475).

[39] Emmanuel Gaillard and Isabelle Pingel-Lenuzza, 'International Organisations and Immunity from Jurisdiction: to Restrict or to Bypass' (2002) 51 *International and Comparative Law Quarterly* 1, 10.

imperii seem to be rather sporadic, a rather new line of domestic courts' practice appears to be a more persistent objection to the traditional rule on absolute immunities of international organisations. The new trend concerns the practice of some domestic courts to condition the grant of immunities to an international organisation on the fulfilment of certain human rights standards by that organisation. Hence, in cases where a lawsuit is brought against an organisation for an alleged breach of human rights, domestic courts increasingly condition their abstention from review on the availability of some alternative review mechanism to which the victim can have recourse. Before turning to the analysis of particular court decisions, it is necessary to refer to a broader context of such a development. For that purpose, I will try to show that the recent contestations by domestic courts correlate with the development of the human rights law that is applicable to the immunity cases (section A) as well as with the development of a related courts' practice, particularly developed in Europe, which contests strict compliance with acts of international organisations in case they do not meet certain basic human rights standards (section B). The influence of these two developments on the contestations of domestic courts to absolute immunities of international organisations will be analysed in section C.

A. Revisiting the Compatibility of Immunities with Human Rights

The recent challenge of domestic courts to absolute immunities of international organisations may be seen as a domestic response to the extension of public powers of international organisations discussed in the previous sections and the resulting legitimacy concerns with respect to the authority exercised by organisations over individuals and other private parties. At the same time, this trend corresponds also to the developments in human rights law; in particular, with respect to the right of access to court and the right to a remedy. A deprivation of access to court in order to determine the individual's civil rights and obligations will raise important human rights issues on the international level and pose serious constitutional problems in many legal systems.[40] The right of access to court and the right to a remedy are granted, *inter alia*, under Articles 8 and 10 of the 1948 Universal Declaration of Human Rights,[41] under Articles 2(3) and 14(1) of the 1966

[40] Mauro Cappelletti, *The Judicial Process in Comparative Perspective* (Oxford, Clarendon Press, 1989); Karl Heinz Schwab and Peter Gottwald, 'Verfassung und Zivilprozess' in WJ Habscheid (ed), *Effektiver Rechtsschutz und verfassungsmaässige Ordnung* (Bielefeld, Gieseking-Verlag, 1983) 1; Reinisch, *International Organizations Before National Courts* (n 13) 290–313.

[41] GA Res 217A (III) UN Doc A/810 (1948), 71; the interpretation of the right to fair trial as covering the right of access to court follows, *inter alia*, from the draft text of the article, which originally provided that '[e]veryone shall have access to independent and impartial tribunals

International Covenant on Civil and Political Rights,[42] under Article 6 and 13 of the European Convention on Human Rights,[43] and under Article 8 and 25 of the American Convention on Human Rights;[44] the right to be heard is also granted under Article 7 of the African Charter on Human and Peoples' Rights.[45] These rights are considered today as having the status of a customary rule of international law.[46]

Yet, despite the development of these human rights, jurisdictional immunities are commonly considered as remaining unaffected by the adoption of the human rights instruments. Thus, as for the *state* immunity, the International Court of Justice (ICJ) decided in *Jurisdictional Immunities of the State*[47] that under customary international law, as it presently stands, a state was not deprived of immunity by reason of the fact that it allegedly committed serious violations of international human rights law or the international law of armed conflict. In the judgment, the ICJ relied on the findings of the European Court of Human Rights (ECtHR) in *Al-Adsani*[48] and *Kalogeropoulou*,[49] that there is no acceptance yet in international law of the proposition that states were no longer entitled to immunity in respect of civil claims for damages brought against them in another state for gross violations of human rights.[50]

However, it is questionable to what extent these findings, with respect to state immunity, can be applied to immunities of international

in the determination of any criminal charge against him, and of its rights and obligations'; Report of the UN Human Rights Commission, ECOSOC Official Records, third year, Sixth Session, E/600, Annex A.

[42] UN Treaty Series, vol 999, 171; see also the statement of the UN Human Rights Committee, which views access to court as an inherent part of the right to a fair trial; 'CCPR General Comment no 13: Equality Before the Courts and the Right to a Fair and Public Hearing by an Independent Court Established by Law' HRI/GEN/1/Rev.9 (vol I) (13 April 1984) para 3.

[43] Convention for the Protection of Human Rights and Fundamental Freedoms, 4 Nov 1950, ETS 5, 213 UNTS 221 (1950); see also *Golder v the United Kingdom* App no 4451/70, Ser A18 (ECtHR, 21 Feb 1975) [36]; *Osman v the United Kingdom* App no 23452/94, ECHR 1998-VIII (ECtHR, Grand Chamber, 28 Oct 1998) [136].

[44] American Convention on Human Rights, 22 Nov 1969, 1144 UNTS 123, OAS Treaty Series no 36 (1969).

[45] African Charter on Human and Peoples' Rights, 1520 UNTS 217.

[46] In the case of *Rubio v the Universal Postal Union*, the ILO Administrative Tribunal also noted that refusal to entertain the [applicant's] case would be denial of due process and contrary to general legal principles; ILOAT, 10 July 1997, Judgment no 1644, [12].

[47] *Jurisdictional Immunities of the State (Germany v Italy : Greece intervening)* [2012] ICJ Reports 99 (3 Feb 2012).

[48] *Al-Adsani v the United Kingdom* App no 35763/97, ECHR 2001-XI (ECtHR, Grand Chamber, 21 Nov 2001).

[49] *Kalogeropoulou and Others v Greece and Germany* App no 59021/00, ECHR 2002-X (ECtHR, 12 Dec 2002).

[50] *Immunities* Case (n 47) 139; see also the Report on Jurisdictional Immunities of States and their Property, prepared by the working group of the International Law Commission; in particular, Annex to the Report of the ILC on the work of its Fifty-first Session, A/54/10, paras 6, 7.

organisations. The growing authority of international organisations vis-à-vis individuals and private parties, their virtually absolute immunities before domestic courts, and their reluctance to subject themselves to other dispute settlement mechanisms have therefore led judges and scholars alike to respond to the broad immunity claims. They developed the idea of restricting the immunity of international organisations with the requirement of an alternative protection for the claimant.

B. The Requirement of an Alternative Protection in the *Solange* Jurisprudence

In essence, the idea of an alternative protection requirement is to ensure that domestic courts would abstain from human rights review of the acts of an international organisation only if the organisation itself provides for some other review mechanism which may be considered to be an adequate alternative protection to the one granted to the claimant by domestic courts. The requirement of ensuring such alternative human rights protection to the claimant vis-à-vis an organisation has been interpreted as binding primarily the forum state, thereby commonly avoiding the question of whether and to what extent the organisation itself is bound to respect human rights in general and the right of access to court and the right to a remedy in particular.

The requirement was first developed in the context of a human rights review of domestic acts that had implemented acts of international organisations. Judicial review of acts of international organisations was thereby sought incidentally in legal proceedings to which organisations were not parties. If we understand it as a response to the growing powers of international organisations, it is not surprising that the first important challenge of domestic courts was directed against a supranational organisation, the European Community (EC), which had pioneered in the extending of its powers and competences, including those affecting human rights. The requirement for an alternative protection was most clearly expressed by the German Constitutional Court in its co-called *Solange I* decision of 1974,[51] in which the Court accepted the subjecting of EC acts to a human rights review 'as long as' Community law does not ensure an alternative, comparably adequate fundamental rights protection as granted under the German Constitution.[52] In its follow-up decision of 1986, the

[51] *Internationale Handelsgesellschaft v Einfuhr- und Vorratstelle für Getreide und Futtermittel* [1974] CMLR 540 (Germany, Federal Constitutional Court, 29 May 1974).

[52] See also Andreas Haratsch, 'Die Solange-Rechtsprechung des Europäischen Gerichtshofs für Menschenrechte' (2006) 66 *ZaöRV* 927–47 and Reinisch and Weber, 'In the Shadow of Waite and Kennedy' (n 38) 74.

so-called *Solange II*,[53] the German Constitutional Court reviewed anew the standards of human rights protection granted by the EC and established, conversely, that the organisation had developed an equal level of human rights protection, as granted under the German Constitution, including the remedies available before the European Court of Justice (ECJ). As it stated, the procedural rules of the ECJ satisfied the due process requirements of a state subject to the rule of law, including the right to be heard. On that basis, the German Constitutional Court justified the abstention from human rights review of the German judiciary over the acts of Community organs 'as long as' such equal protection would be ensured by the organisation.

The *Solange* jurisprudence was more or less explicitly followed by other domestic courts and found its counterpart particularly in the Italian Constitutional Court, which held, ever since its *Frontini* judgment of 1973, that the EC acts cannot derogate from certain fundamental principles or inalienable rights of persons.[54] Such fundamental principles and inalienable rights are 'counter-limits' to the limitations of sovereignty that follow from the state membership in the international organisation. Thus, when the state institutions exercise sovereign powers, they must respect the fundamental values and principles of the constitution; one cannot accept a complete renunciation of those values and principles when powers are attributed to the European institutions.[55] At a later stage, an alternative protection requirement was developed by domestic courts also in the cases brought directly against international organisations, in which the organisations appeared as parties to the dispute before domestic courts and invoked their right to immunities.

C. The Requirement of an Alternative Protection in Immunity Cases

Following the *Solange* decisions, the German Constitutional Court was soon prepared to apply the test of an alternative protection of human rights also in cases brought directly against international organisations, which invoked their immunities from jurisdiction before the German

[53] *In reapplication of Wünsche Handelsgesellschaft, Federal Constitutional Court* [1987] 3 CMLR 225 (Germany, Federal Constitutional Court).

[54] *Frontini v Ministero Delle Finanze*, case 183/73 (Italian Constitutional Court, judgment of 27 Dec 1973) trans in [1974] 2 CMLR 386, 387.

[55] For the discussion, see Armin von Bogdandy, 'The European Union as a Human Rights Organization? Human Rights and the Core of the European Union' (2000) 37 *Common Market Law Review* 1307; Paul Craig and Gráinne de Búrca, *The Evolution of EU Law* (1st edn, Oxford, Oxford University Press, 1999) 201–05; Henry G Schermers and Denis F Waelbroeck, *Judicial Protection in the European Union* (The Hague, Kluwer Law International, 2001).

courts. For example, in the case against the European Organisation for the Safety of Air Navigation (EUROCONTROL),[56] the German Constitutional Court granted the organisation's plea for immunity from suit only after it established that the ILO Administrative Tribunal was competent to hear the case over the employment dispute between the organisation and the claimant, and that the tribunal provided an adequate alternative remedy to the claimant. As it stated, the grant of organisation's immunity before the German courts did not violate minimum requirements of the rule of law principle contained in the German Constitution.[57] Similarly, the Swiss Supreme Court described the obligation to provide for alternative remedy as a 'counterpart' to the jurisdictional immunity enjoyed by international organisations.[58] The Italian courts developed a restrictive approach towards the granting of immunity to international organisations in cases such as *FAO v INPDAI*.[59] The American courts, too, have acknowledged that the grant of immunity to international organisations may conflict with constitutional law demands of providing a claimant with a forum for the settlement of disputes. Thus, in the *Weiner* case,[60] the Criminal Court of the City of New York sought to strike a fair balance between the UN's right to immunity and the constitutional right of American citizens of access to court.[61] The Argentinian courts have balanced organisations' right to immunities with the individual's right of access to justice in cases such as *Duhalde v World Health Organisation (WHO) and Panamerican Health Organisation*,[62] as have Colombian courts in cases such as *Velásquez v the UN High Commissioner for Human Rights*.[63]

It is true that, in the end, most domestic courts ultimately uphold the immunities of international organisations, after they review, with more or less scrutiny, the effectiveness of alternative remedies that organisations offer to the claimants. However, there are some examples where a domestic

[56] *Hetzel v EUROCONTROL* (Federal Constitutional Court, Second Chamber, 10 Nov 1981) 2 BvR 1058/79, BVerG, 63; see generally Bardo Fassbender, 'The Jurisprudence of the Federal Constitutional Court regarding the constitutionality of supranational acts of international organisations' in A Reinisch (ed), *The Privileges and Immunities of International Organisations in Domestic Courts* (Oxford, Oxford University Press, 2013) 123–31.

[57] *EUROCONTROL* case (n 56) [22].

[58] *Groupement d'Entreprises Fougerolle et consorts v CERN* (1ère Cour civile du tribunal fédéral Suisse, 21 déc 1992) ATF 118 Ib 562.

[59] *FAO v INPDAI* (Supreme Court of Cassation, 18 Oct 1982) [1982] UNJYB 234, 235; see also *FAO v Colagrossi* (Corte di Cassatione, 18 May 1992) no 5942 [1992] RivDI 407.

[60] *People v Mark S Weiner*, 378 NYS 2d 966 (Criminal Court of the City of New York, NY County, 19 Jan 1976) [1976] UNJYB 249.

[61] See, similarly, in *Urban v the United Nations*, 768 F 2d 1497, 1500 (DC Cir 1985).

[62] *Duhalde, Mario Alfredo v Organisatión Panamericana de la Salud-Officina Sanitaria Panamericana*, (Argentinian Supreme Court, 31 Aug 1999) D 73 XXXIV, Accidente-ley 9688, CSJN.

[63] *Diana María Gamarra Vélasquez v la Officina del Alto Comisionado de la Natciones Unidas para los Derechos Humanos en Colombia-Sub-officina Bucaramanga* (Columbian Constitutional Court) T-667/11, expediente T-3136840, 8 Sept 2011.

court did not grant immunities and did allow court proceedings against the organisation. For instance, in *UNESCO v Boulois*,[64] a French appellate court rejected a plea of immunity after it established that the granting of immunity would inevitably prevent the individual from bringing his case to court. According to the French court, such a situation would be contrary to public policy because it constitutes a denial of justice and a violation of the European Convention on Human Rights.[65]

Moreover, after the requirement of alternative protection has been endorsed also by international institutions and by the ECtHR in particular, such examples became more common, especially by states parties to the European Convention. In a number of cases, the Convention has been directly invoked, such as in *Siegler v Western European Union*, in which the Belgian Court of Appeals applied the *Waite & Kennedy* test and ultimately denied entitlement to immunity to the international organisation.[66] The gradual acceptance in international law of the idea of restricted immunities of international organisations thus provided domestic courts with a legal basis to challenge the immunities, additional to the legal basis they may find under their domestic law or under general international human rights law. Such additional legal basis further encouraged domestic courts to review the compliance of international organisations with human rights and the rule of law standards.

IV. RECEPTION IN INTERNATIONAL LAW

The challenges of domestic courts to the acts of international organisations that may violate human rights and to their immunities from domestic legal proceedings have not been rejected at the international level as breaches of international law. Instead, they have been acknowledged by international courts (section A) and other international institutions (section B) as legal and legitimate contestations to international acts adopted by international organisations that escape certain minimum human rights standards. Moreover, it seems that the content and scope of such minimum human rights standards applicable to international organisations

[64] *UNESCO v Boulois* Tribunal de grande instance de Paris (ord Rèf), 20 Oct 1997, Rev Arb (1997) 575; Cour d'appel Paris (14e Ch A) 19 June 1998, XXIV a Yearbook Commercial Arbitration (1999) 294; Rev Arb (1999) 343.

[65] For a development of the relevant jurisprudence in France, see August Reinisch, 'Privileges and Immunities' in J Klabbers and Å Wallendahl (eds), *Research Handbook on the Law of International Organizations* (Cheltenham; Northampton, MA, Edward Elgar, 2011) 144, 144–45.

[66] *Siegler v WEU* (Brussels Labour Court of Appeal, Judgment of 17 Sept 2004) Journal des Tribunaux 2004, 617, ILDC 53 (BE 2003).

has been developed in a continuous interaction between domestic and international institutions (section C).

A. Reception by International Courts

On the international level, the domestic human rights concerns first resonated in the treaty provisions that provide for an obligation of international organisations to waive immunity where their immunity might otherwise lead to denial of justice.[67] Moreover, some arbitration panels have started to protect the right of a private party to access to justice by interpreting an organisation's immunity from suit as entailing its duty to arbitrate.[68]

Unsurprisingly, the international human rights bodies then took the lead in developing the argument that international organisations should provide for an alternative forum of human rights protection to the one available by domestic courts. Such an argument was first adopted by the European Commission of Human Rights. In *M & Co v the Federal Republic of Germany*;[69] the Commission started with the observation that the European Convention on Human Rights does not prohibit a state party to the Convention from transferring powers to international organisations. Nonetheless, if a state accepts obligations under the Convention and subsequently concludes another international agreement which disables it from performing its obligations under the first treaty, the state would be responsible for any resulting breach under the first treaty. In the opposite case, as the Commission stated, 'the guarantees of the Convention could wantonly be limited or excluded and thus deprived of their peremptory character'.[70] In the end, the Commission declared the complaints against the contested EC act inadmissible; yet it did so only after it found that a sufficiently developed system of human rights protection was available to the claimant by the EC, including the remedies before the ECJ.

The requirement of an alternative protection within an international organisation was later embraced by the ECtHR, which in 1999 issued three

[67] See, eg, Art IV(1)(a), Annex 1 to the Convention for the Establishment of the European Space Agency, Paris, 30 May 1975, 14 ILM (1975), 855; see also Art V, s 20, where the obligation to waive the immunity is provided with respect to the UN officials, in case the immunity would 'impede the course of justice'.

[68] For an early example, see *A (organisation internationale) v B (société)*, ICC Arbitration Award, 14 May 1972, Case no 2091, Revue de l'Arbitrage (1975) 252, in which the panel held: 'L'immunité de juridiction accordée a un organisme international qui n'a pas de juridictions propres oblige celui-ci a recourir a un arbitrage pour le litiges soulèves par son activité'.

[69] *M & Co v the Federal Republic of Germany* App no 13258/87, (1990) 64 DR 138 (European Commission of Human Rights, 9 Feb 1990).

[70] ibid. Similarly, see *Heinz v Contracting Parties who are also Parties to the European Patent Convention* App no 12090/92, (1994) 76–A DR 125 (European Commission of Human Rights, 10 Jan 1994).

landmark decisions. In the *Matthews case*,[71] the ECtHR reaffirmed that the states remained responsible for ensuring the respect for the Convention rights even after the transfer of competences to international organisations. Since the ECtHR established that the applicant was left with no remedies to challenge the legality of the EC act, that is, neither before domestic courts nor before the ECJ, it found the breach of the Convention.

This approach matured into the concept of restrictive immunities of international organisations in the cases *Waite and Kennedy*[72] and *Beer and Regan*.[73] In these cases, the ECtHR recognised that the grant of immunities to an international organisation can lead to an infringement of an individual's right of access to court, unless it is mitigated by the availability of an adequate alternative means of redress. While recalling that the right of access to court is not an absolute right but might be subject to limitations,[74] the ECtHR held that such limitations should, however, not restrict the right of access to court to such an extent that the very essence of the right would be impaired. Moreover, the ECtHR ruled that the limitations must pursue a legitimate aim and be proportionate with respect to the means employed and the aim sought. When applying that compatibility test to the grant of immunities to the respective organisation, the ECtHR held that the immunities were an essential means of ensuring the proper functioning of international organisations, free from unilateral interference by individual governments, and therefore accepted that a corresponding restriction of the individual's right of access to court by the grant of immunities pursued a legitimate aim.

However, as to the requirement of proportionality, the Court stressed that 'a material factor in determining whether granting immunity is permissible is whether the applicants had available to them reasonable alternative means to protect effectively their rights under the Convention'.[75] In the case at hand, the ECtHR found that the requirement of alternative dispute settlement mechanisms was fulfilled, since the European Space Agency had established an internal appeals board. Although some observers criticised the ECtHR for not taking a step further and reviewing—with more scrutiny—the effectiveness of the alternative remedies,[76] these three

[71] *Matthews v the United Kingdom* App no 24833/94, (1999) ECHR 1999-I (ECtHR, Grand Chamber, 18 Feb 1999).

[72] *Waite and Kennedy v Germany* App no 26083/94, (1999) ECHR 1999-I (ECtHR, Grand Chamber, Judgment of 18 Feb 1999).

[73] *Beer and Regan v Germany* App no 28934/95, unpublished (ECtHR, Grand Chamber, 18 Feb 1999).

[74] See esp *Golder v the United Kingdom* App no 4451/70, Ser A18 (ECtHR, 21 Feb 1975).

[75] *Waite and Kennedy v Germany* (n 72) [68].

[76] Jean-François Flauss, 'Droit des immunités et protection internationale des droits de l'homme' (2000) 10(3) *Revue suisse de droit international et de droit européen* 299, 323; August Reinisch, 'Waite and Kennedy v. Germany, Application No. 26083/94; Beer and Regan v. Germany, Application No. 28934/95' (1999) 93 *American Journal of International Law* 933.

judgments—namely, *Matthews*, *Waite and Kennedy*, and *Beer and Regan*—nevertheless represent a milestone in building an analytical framework to test the legality and legitimacy of immunity grants to international organisations.

The idea that an individual should receive an 'equivalent protection' within an international organisation as it is granted to him by the state party to the Convention was further elaborated in the *Bosphorus* case.[77] Without any express reference to the *Solange* jurisprudence of the German Constitutional Court and its followers, the ECtHR applied the principle of equivalent protection as developed by domestic courts. It held that when a state complies with its international obligations and its membership obligations within an international organisation, such an act may be justified only 'as long as' the relevant organisation is considered to protect fundamental rights, as regards both the substantive guarantees offered as well as the mechanisms controlling their observance, in a manner which can be considered at least equivalent to that provided for by the Convention. If such equivalent protection is provided by the organisation, the presumption will be that the state has not departed from the requirements of the Convention when it does no more than implement legal obligations flowing from its membership in the organisation.[78] The case law was developed further in the cases such as *Gasparini*[79] and *Michaud*,[80] and has been recently shaped also with respect to the UN. That case law will be examined in more detail under section IV(C).

In 1999, also, the ICJ addressed the relevance of internal legal remedies of international organisations in the light of their immunities. In its advisory opinion on the *Immunity from Legal Process*,[81] it viewed the obligation to provide for alternative internal redress mechanisms as being a corollary to the UN's right to immunity. It held that the organisation may itself be responsible for the acts of its agents acting in their official capacity. According to the Court, the question of immunity from legal process is thereby distinct from the duty of compensation for any damages incurred as a result of the official acts of their agents, and the claims arising therefrom should be settled in accordance with appropriate modes of settlement due to be established by the UN.[82] This seems to be an important development from the ICJ's earlier *Effects of Awards* case,[83] in which the Court considered

[77] *Bosphorus Hava Yollary Turizm ve Ticaret Anonim Sirketi v Ireland* App no 45036/98, ECHR 2005-VI (ECtHR, Grand Chamber, 30 June 2005).

[78] ibid [155].

[79] *Gasparini v Italy and Belgium* App no 10750/03 (ECHR, Decision of 12 May 2009).

[80] *Michaud v France* App no 12323/11, ECHR 2012 (ECtHR, 6 Dec 2012).

[81] *Difference Relating to Immunity from Legal Process of a Special Rapporteur of the Commission on Human Rights* [1999] ICJ Reports 62 (Advisory Opinion of 29 April 1999).

[82] ibid para 66.

[83] *Effect of Awards of Compensation Made by the United Nations Administrative Tribunal* [1954] ICJ Reports 47.

the UN's obligation to provide for alternative legal remedies only in the specific context of employment disputes, by asserting that it would

> hardly be consistent with the expressed aim of the Charter to promote freedom and justice for individuals [...] that the United Nations should afford no judicial or arbitral remedy to its own staff for the settlement of any disputes which may arise between it and them.[84]

Thus, the lack of remedies against the UN may not only amount to a violation of human rights of the individual, but has been found in the employment-related case before the ICJ to conflict also with the provisions of the UN Charter.

B. Reception by Other International Institutions

The idea that a state should balance its obligations towards an international organisation with its obligation towards the individual has received a wide support among scholars,[85] and eventually found its expression in the Draft Articles on Responsibility of International Organizations (DARIO), which were adopted by the International Law Commission (ILC) in 2011.[86] The ILC afforded the principle a general application and, expressly relying on the *Waite & Kennedy* and *Bosphorus* jurisprudence of the ECtHR, stated in Article 61 that a state member of an international organisation incurs international responsibility if, by taking advantage of the fact that the organisation has competence in relation to the subject matter of one of the state's international obligations, it circumvents that obligation by causing the organisation to commit an act that, if committed by the state, would have constituted a breach of the obligation.[87] Moreover, in Article 45(2) of the DARIO, the ILC adopted the requirement that the internal legal remedies established within organisations need not only be available, but also effective, if the victims of human rights abuses were expected to use them.[88]

[84] ibid para 57.

[85] International Law Association, Accountability of International Organizations (1996–2004) Final Conference Report, Berlin 2004, 41 and 46, available at: www.ila-hq.org/en/committees/index.cfm/cid/9; see also Ian Brownlie, 'The Responsibility of States for the Acts of International Organizations' in M Ragazzi (ed), *International Responsibility Today: Essays in Memory of Oscar Schachter* (Leiden; Boston, Martinus Nijhoff, 2005) 361; Olivier De Schutter, 'Human Rights and the Rise of International Organizations: The Logic of Sliding Scales in the Law of International Responsibility' in J Wouters and E Brems (eds), *Accountability For Human Rights Violations By International Organisations* (Antwerp, Intersentia, 2010) 51.

[86] 'Draft Articles on the Responsibility of International Organizations' ILC Report, Sixty-third Session UN Doc A/66/10 (3 May 2011).

[87] See the commentary to the Article, where the relevant passage from *Waite & Kennedy* is quoted verbatim; ibid 94.

[88] ibid 71–74. In order for the remedy to be considered as effective, however, it does not need to be judicial; see, eg, Erika de Wet, 'Holding International Institutions Accountable:

In the same vein, the Venice Commission of the Council of Europe addressed in its opinion concerning the Office of the High Representative for Bosnia and Herzegovina the issue where no effective remedies are available for human rights violations by an international organisation that administers the territory.[89] The Commission established that the acts of the High Representative should comply with international standards and found it unacceptable, as a matter of principle, that the High Representative's decisions directly affecting the rights of individuals were not subject to a fair hearing or at least the minimum of due process and scrutiny by an independent court. The situation may therefore not last forever, but 'the day must come when such decisions are made subject to full judicial control and made the responsibility of the proper national institutions'.[90] The lack of remedies available against international organisations has been criticised also by the Parliamentary Assembly of the Council of Europe, which recommended a number of measures to be implemented by states and international organisations, including the adoption of binding mechanisms for monitoring organisations' compliance with human rights standards.[91]

The requirement to provide for an alternative human rights protection has thus increasingly been acknowledged also by international organisations themselves. The obligation to provide access to alternative dispute settlement procedures has most clearly been acknowledged with respect to the members of staff of international organisations.[92] Today, such right of employees is interpreted by administrative tribunals of international organisations as a general legal principle binding upon their international organisation.[93] Apart from international civil servants, other private parties may now in certain cases bring a claim against some organisations by availing themselves of their internal dispute settlement mechanisms. For instance, the challenges by domestic court to unsatisfactory human

The Complementary Role of Non-Judicial Oversight Mechanisms and Judicial Review' (2008) 9 *German Law Journal* 1987. However, DARIO also left significant gaps with respect to the human rights protection: see Armin Von Bogdandy and Mateja Steinbrück Platiše, 'ARIO and Human Rights Protection: Leaving the Individual in the Cold' (2012) 9 *International Organizations Law Review* 67.

[89] European Commission for Democracy through Law, Opinion on the Constitutional Situation in Bosnia and Herzegovina and the Powers of the High Representative, Sixty-second Session, CDL-AD (2005) 004, Venice, 11–12 March 2005.

[90] ibid para 97.

[91] See Resolution 1979 (2014) and Recommendation 2037 (2014); Accountability of international organisations for human rights violations, together with the Report of the Committee on Legal Affairs and Human Rights, Doc 13370, 17 Dec 2013.

[92] See esp *Chadsey v Universal Postal Union*, ILO Administrative Tribunal, 15 Oct 1968, Judgment no 122 and *Rubio v the Universal Postal Union* (n 46).

[93] Early examples include *Waghorn* v *ILO*, [1957] ILOAT Judgment no 28; *Mendaro v IBRD*, 1985 World Bank Administrative Tribunal Reports Judgment no 26, 9; *Franks v EPO*, [1994] ILOAT Judgment no 1333.

rights protection within the EC contributed importantly to the development of the legal remedies that are available today to private parties within the EU.[94] Since 1993, private parties can also bring certain claims against the World Bank, which established the Inspection Panel in order to assess whether an action or omission of the Bank that directly affects the rights or interests of the claimants follow the Bank's operational policies and procedures.[95] The World Bank's example was followed by the Inter-American Development Bank, the Asian Development Bank, the European Bank for Reconstruction and Development, and the African Development Bank, which have all established their internal inspection panels.[96] After the Inspection Panel of the World Bank was criticised for failing to meet a number of the standards of an effective internal remedy,[97] the World Bank complemented in 2001 its internal mechanisms with a sanctions procedure, which can be deployed in case of corruption and fraud by individuals and companies involved in the activities of the Bank. While the sanctions procedure is of a limited scope with regard to the admissibility of claims *ratione personae* and *ratione materie*, some authors refer to the mechanism as a good example of internal remedies of international organisations because it features a number of elements of a judicial dispute settlement mechanism.[98]

These procedural developments to accommodate the claims of private parties do not necessarily mean that international organisations also expressly acknowledge their being bound by human rights or the international rule of law in general. Nonetheless, examples may increasingly be found in the official documents of international organisations, such as in the UN Declaration of the High-Level Meeting of the General Assembly on the Rule of Law at the National and International Levels, which states that

> the rule of law applies to all states equally, *and to international organizations, including the United Nations and its principal organs*, and that respect for and

[94] See also the process of the accession of the EU to the European Convention on Human Rights, as finalised in 2013, available at: www.coe.int/t/dghl/standardsetting/hrpolicy/Accession/Meeting_reports/47_1(2013)008rev2_EN.pdf.

[95] For a general overview of the panel's work, see The International Bank for Reconstruction and Development/The World Bank, *Accountability at the World Bank, The Inspection Panel, 10 Years On* (2003); see also the Inspection Panel homepage, available at: http://web.worldbank.org/WBSITE/EXTERNAL/EXTINSPECTIONPANEL/0,menuPK:64132057~pagePK:64130364~piPK:64132056~theSitePK:380794,00.html.

[96] For an overview, see Sigrun I Skogly, *The Human Rights Obligations of the World Bank and the International Monetary Fund* (London, Cavendish Publishing Ltd, 2001) 180–85.

[97] ibid 180–81; Ariel Buira (ed), *Challenges to the World Bank and IMF: Developing Country Perspectives* (London, Antham Press, 2003; Karel Wellens, *Remedies against International Organizations* (Cambridge, Cambridge University Press, 2004) 185ff.

[98] Laurence Boisson de Chazournes and Edouard Fromageau, 'Balancing the Scales: The World Bank Sanctions Process and Access to Remedies' (2012) 23 *European Journal of International Law* 963.

> promotion of the rule of law and justice should guide all of their activities and accord predictability and legitimacy to their actions. We also recognize that *all persons*, institutions and entities, public and private, including the state itself, are accountable to just, fair and equitable laws and are *entitled without any discrimination to equal protection of law* [emphasis added].[99]

It may therefore be observed that the contestations of domestic courts, supported by various international institutions, contribute to the raising of human rights standards being respected by international organisations. Whether, and how promptly, these examples will develop into a general trend will also depend, again, on the practice of domestic courts and their dialogue with international courts and other international institutions. The interdependence between the development of domestic courts' practice and the practice of international institutions merits a closer empirical analysis, which I will carry out in the following section, as well as some theoretical considerations on the conceptual relationship between these institutions, which I will try to sketch in section V.

C. From Reception to Interaction

It seems that international courts and other international institutions have been prepared to address also the concern raised by certain domestic courts as to whether a restrictive regime of immunities of international organisations should apply also to the UN. Indeed, it is not settled yet whether a uniform regime should be applied with respect to all organisations alike, regardless of the differences in their membership, institutional structure, legal position, functions, powers, and mandates. In particular, the UN has been considered as occupying a special place in the international legal community due to its distinguished mandate and powers. For instance, with respect to the acts and omissions of the United Nations Interim Administration Mission in Kosovo (UNMIK) and the NATO's KFOR operating in Kosovo pursuant to a UN Security Council resolution, the ECtHR recalled in the *Behrami* and *Saramati* cases[100] that the powers entrusted to the UN under Chapter VII of the UN Charter were fundamental to the mission of the UN to secure international peace and security. Their implementation by the member states should therefore not be subject to the scrutiny of the ECtHR, as this could compromise the effective conduct of the UN operations.[101]

[99] UN Doc A/67/L 1, para 2; see also the relevant Resolution of the Council of Europe's Parliamentary Assembly and the Report of the Committee on Legal Affairs and Human Rights (n 91).

[100] *Behrami and Behrami v France; Saramati v France, Germany and Norway* App nos 71412/01, and 78166/01 (2007) (ECtHR, Admissibility Decision of 2 May 2007).

[101] ibid [149].

This has led the Dutch Supreme Court to conclude in the *Mothers of Srebrenica* case[102] that the acts and omissions of the UN Protection Force (UNPROFOR), the UN peacekeeping force deployed in the former Yugoslavia and acting under Chapter VII, could not be subjected to the *Waite and Kennedy* test.[103] Instead, it held that the immunity should be granted to the UN even if alternative legal remedies might not be available to the individuals whose rights the UNPROFOR allegedly breached. In this sense, the Dutch Court declared the UN's immunity as being absolute.[104]

In the subsequent proceedings before the ECtHR, the Strasbourg Court later endorsed the decision of the Dutch Supreme Court.[105] While acknowledging that the victims of the Srebrenica genocide were left with no remedy before the domestic courts and before the UN, it nevertheless refused to apply the *Waite and Kennedy* test to the case at hand. It rather reaffirmed its position taken in the cases of *Behrami* and *Saramati* and considered that to bring the UN operations taken under Chapter VII of the UN Chapter within the scope of domestic jurisdiction would be to allow individual states, through their courts, to interfere with the fulfilment of the key mission of the UN in the field of international peace and security.

While the ECtHR refused to apply the requirement of an alternative protection with respect to the UN in the immunity case, it did, however, apply that requirement in the cases that challenged domestic implementation of the UN acts. The two relevant cases both concerned domestic measures implementing the UN Security Council decisions on targeted sanctions adopted under Chapter VII of the UN Charter, and have been importantly influenced by the practice of domestic courts following the *Solange* jurisprudence of the German Constitutional Court. In express terms, the ECtHR has been influenced also by the decision of the Court of Justice of the EU (CJEU) in the *Kadi* case, in which the CJEU established that the implementation of the targeted sanctions of the UN Security Council would violate human rights granted under the EU legal order; in particular, the right to a fair trial and the right to a remedy.[106] Thus, in the *Nada* case[107] the ECtHR found that the UN law did not prevent judicial review of domestic implementation of the acts adopted by the UN

[102] *Mothers of Srebrenica v Netherlands and United Nations, Final appeal judgment* (n 14).

[103] With regard to the *Waite and Kennedy* case, see s IV(A) of this chapter.

[104] *Mothers of Srebrenica v Netherlands and United Nations, Final appeal judgment* (n 14) [4.3.6].

[105] *Stichting Mothers of Srebrenica and Others v The Netherlands* App no 65542/12 (ECtHR, Decision of 11 June 2013).

[106] Cases C-402/05 P and C-415/05 P *Kadi and Al Barakaat International Foundation v Council of the European Union and Commission of the European Communities* [2008] ECR I-06351 (ECJ, Judgment of 3 Sept 2008). See also Juliane Kokott and Christoph Sobotta, 'The Kadi Case—Constitutional Core Values and International Law—Finding the Balance?' (2012) 23 *European Journal of International Law* 1015.

[107] *Nada v Switzerland* App no 10593/08 (ECtHR Grand Chamber, Judgment of 12 Sept 2012).

Security Council under Chapter VII of the UN Charter. It therefore held that Switzerland violated the right of access to court granted by the Convention, in that it failed to ensure the claimant effective remedies against the implementation of the UN sanctions. Subsequently, the ECtHR established in the *Al-Dulimi et Montana Management* case[108] that the UN failed to ensure equal protection of human rights. Therefore, the 'Bosphorus presumption', wherein an implementation of an act of an international organisation by a member state is considered to be in conformity with the Convention, did not apply with respect to the UN.[109]

It may therefore be concluded that the ECtHR counts on domestic courts to review acts adopted by international organisations in light of their compliance with human rights standards and to allow the domestic implementation of only those acts that do not result in a violation of the individual's right to a remedy. Thus, even if the ECtHR may not have itself the power to review internal remedies available within the UN, it nevertheless obliges domestic courts to exercise such a review. Indeed, it sounds like an invitation for domestic courts to complement the judicial review of the international court and to compensate for the lack of the ECtHR's jurisdiction over international organisations.

Similar incentives for such compensatory domestic judicial review come also from other international institutions. For example, with regard to the targeted sanctions of the UN Security Council, the UN General Assembly 'urge[d] States, while ensuring full compliance with their international obligations, to include adequate human rights guarantees *in their national procedures* for the listing of individuals' [emphasis added].[110] National procedures thereby include court proceedings.[111] The UN Special Rapporteur joined that call to domestic courts by stating that:

> [a]s long as there is no independent review, (…) judicial or quasi-judicial decisions by the Security Council should be interpreted as being of preliminary rather than final character, it is essential that listed individuals and entities have access to the domestic judicial review of any measure implementing the sanctions.[112]

108 *Al-Dulimi and Montana Management Inc v Switzerland* App no 5809/08 (ECtHR, 26 Nov 2013). Note, however, that the case is currently pending before the Grand Chamber of the Court.

109 See also Anne Peters, 'Article 25' in B Simma and others (eds), *The Charter of the United Nations: A Commentary*, vol I (3rd edn, Oxford, Oxford University Press, 2012) 761–854, 842, where the author argues that indirect judicial control of decisions of the UN Security Council by domestic courts in such a case does not amount to a violation of Art 25 of the UN Charter.

110 UN GA Res 63/185, Protection of human rights and fundamental freedoms while countering terrorism (3 March 2009) UN Doc A/RES/63/185 para 20.

111 Peters, 'Article 25' (n 109) 841.

112 The Report of the Special Rapporteur on the promotion and protection of human rights and fundamental freedoms while countering terrorism, UN GA A/65/258 (6 Aug 2010) 18.

This trend may be seen as reflecting an increasing interdependence and interaction of domestic courts and international institutions in the protection of human rights and promotion of the international rule of law vis-à-vis the acts of international organisations. The common normative assertion of these institutions is thereby that acts of organisations can be challenged either at the occasion of their implementation at the domestic level—that is, in legal proceedings against the state that adopts the implementing acts—or in legal proceedings brought directly against the organisation, if the organisation is not granted immunities due to its failure to provide for alternative means of redress.

V. SKETCHING A NORMATIVE FRAMEWORK FOR INTERACTION BETWEEN DOMESTIC COURTS AND INTERNATIONAL INSTITUTIONS

In section V, I will try to set a normative framework in which the interaction and mutual influence of domestic courts and international institutions is legally possible and legitimately desirable. Some of the core elements of that framework will be discussed under the following three sections, starting with the interdependence of legal sources on which the domestic and international authorities rely (section A). In section B, I will try to show that the contestations of domestic courts to absolute immunities of international organisations and their reception by international authorities have a common normative basis. That common basis is the quest for the international rule of law, according to which any exercise of public powers, including those exercised by organisations, should be based upon authority conferred by law and must be controlled by law; in particular, by certain fundamental human rights.[113] In section C, I will explore the separation of powers that emerges between the domestic and international institutions, and the principle of subsidiarity that guides the allocation and exercise of powers among these institutions.

A. Interdependence of Legal Sources

A brief overview of decisions taken by domestic and international courts and other international institutions might suggest that the demand

[113] von Bogdandy, Dann and Goldmann (n 10); Gianluigi Palombella and Neil Walker, *Relocating the Rule of Law* (Oxford, Hart Publishing, 2009); Mattias Kumm, 'International Law in National Courts: The International Rule of Law and the Limits of the Internationalist Model' (2003) 44 *Virginia Journal of International Law* 19, 22; André Nollkaemper, *National Courts and the International Rule of Law* (Oxford; New York, Oxford University Press, 2011) 8–10.

to limit immunities granted to international organisations came from domestic courts. However, as already suggested in the previous section, such an endeavour seems to be the common undertaking of these institutions. For example, after the ECtHR delivered its judgment in the *Waite and Kennedy* case, domestic courts were given a new impetus and a legal basis for assessing whether, to what extent, and under what conditions they may deny the immunities to international organisations. Moreover, while many domestic courts' decisions that dealt with the right of access to justice for employees of international organisations predate the *Waite and Kennedy* jurisprudence of the ECtHR, such national decisions, on the other hand, follow the ICJ Opinion in the *Effects of Awards* case, in which the ICJ articulated the UN's obligation to provide for legal remedies to its own staff.

The scope of immunities and the obligations arising therefrom for states and international organisations has therefore been shaped in a more or less explicit dialogue between domestic and international courts. They have served each other as a legal source, on the basis of which, on the one hand, international courts' decisions have been implemented by national courts, and, on the other hand, national court decisions have produced legal effects in international law and could be taken into account by international courts. Thus, at the domestic level, the practice of domestic courts was guided and in some respects determined by international human rights law as interpreted by international courts; in particular, by the ECtHR's interpretations of unjustified limitations of the right of access to court and the right to a remedy. Domestic courts have thereby complied with decisions of international courts in accordance with the respective constitutive instruments of international courts.[114] Moreover, decisions of the European and other international courts not only produce legal effects for the particular states that are parties to the dispute (effects *inter partes*), but may affect also normative expectations of all other states that could potentially be parties to a similar dispute.[115]

At the international level, decisions of domestic courts have been relevant for international courts to the extent that they can be viewed as part of state practice and therefore considered as evidence of international

[114] See, eg, Art 46 of the European Convention on Human Rights and Art 59 of the Statute of the ICJ; see also Vienna Convention on the Law of Treaties (n 34) Art 27.

[115] Armin von Bogdandy and Ingo Venzke, *In wessen Namen? Internationale Gerichte in Zeiten globalen Regierens* (Berlin, Suhrkamp, 2014). See also the dissenting opinion of Judge Sir Robert Jennings in *Continental Shelf (Libyan Arab Jamahirija v Malta)*, Application to Intervene [1984] ICJ Reports (Judgment) 3, and the declaration of Judge Simma in the case *Accordance with International Law of the Unilateral Declaration of Independence in Respect of Kosovo* [2010] ICJ Reports 403.

customary law that international courts have to apply in their decisions.[116] Moreover, domestic courts also determine general principles of law, which, international courts, in turn, must apply in their decision making. Furthermore, according to Article 38 of the Statute of the ICJ, judicial decisions of domestic courts are considered as subsidiary means for the determination of rules of law. Thus, even when domestic courts are seen as merely complying with an international obligation, they necessarily also interpret that international obligation and thereby make a systemic contribution to the development of international law. Decisions of domestic courts are therefore not only facts of which international courts may take notice, but fulfil a legal function in that they can determine, with finality, legal rights and obligations under international law.[117] An increasing number of scholars therefore consider domestic courts as agents of the international legal order.[118] The challenge to the immunities of organisations by domestic courts, which is examined in this chapter, is thus a prime example of the role that domestic courts have played in applying, interpreting, and developing international law.

B. The Rule of Law as a Common Normative Basis

The challenge to immunities should be seen as a part of broader contestations of legitimacy of international organisations and international law in general.[119] In this context, the respect for human rights may be considered as one of the criteria for legitimacy of every international act. Thus, it has been questioned whether an international rule should be disregarded in case it constitutes a sufficiently serious violation of countervailing normative principles, such as procedural principles of adequate participation and accountability, the international rule of law, and fundamental human

[116] Anthea Roberts, 'Comparative International Law? The Role of National Courts in Creating and Enforcing International Law' (2011) 60 *International and Comparative Law Quarterly* 57–92.

[117] Nollkaemper, *National Courts* (n 113) 8–10.

[118] Christoph Schreuer, *Die Behandlung internationaler Organakte durch staatliche Gerichte* (Berlin, Duncker und Humblot, 1977); Antonio Cassese, 'Remarks on Scelle's Theory of Role Splitting (dedoublement fonctionnel) in International Law' (1990) 1 *European Journal of International Law* 210, 210; Yuval Shany, 'Dédoublement fonctionnel and the Mixed Loyalties of National and International Judges' in F Fontanelli, G Martinico and P Carrozza (eds), *Shaping Rule of Law Through Dialogue: International and Supranational Experiences* (Groningen, Europa, 2010) 27.

[119] Jürgen Habermas, 'Konstitutionalisierung des Völkerrechts und die Legitimationsprobleme einer verfassten Weltgesellschaft' in W Brugger and others (eds), *Rechtsphilosophie im 21 Jahrhundert* (2008); Armin von Bogdandy and others (n 10); Anne Peters, 'Compensatory Constitutionalism: The Function and Potential of Fundamental International Norms and Structures' (2006) 19 *Leiden Journal of International Law* 579–610; Simon Chesterman,

rights protection.[120] That discussion has not been limited to scholarly work, but presents precisely the core of the dialogue between domestic and international institutions as empirically evidenced and presented in sections III and IV of the present chapter. The international rule of law as it can be construed on the basis of that dialogue thereby requires, *inter alia*, that the exercise of powers by an international organisation conforms to certain fundamental human rights standards.[121] Moreover, in case an international organisation contravenes its legal obligations, either under international or domestic law,[122] it should be held responsible for its acts on the basis of the law. In particular, that last requirement, however, reveals one of the structural deficiencies of international law; namely, the lack of compulsory and independent judiciary that could review complaints about human rights violations committed by international organisations.

C. The Separation of Powers and the Principle of Subsidiarity

The role of the international judiciary that could review the compliance of international organisations with human rights has increasingly been taken over by domestic courts. While domestic courts have always been the first forum for adjudicating rights and obligations of private parties, they are becoming also the first forum for international claims by these parties and emerge as subjects of the international normative framework.[123] They interpret, determine, and apply human rights and the international rule of law standards to international organisations and thereby exercise a complementary function to the one entrusted to international courts with respect to states. International and domestic courts therefore complement one another in the protection of human rights. Indeed, it may seem almost a paradox that while international courts monitor observance of human rights by domestic courts and other domestic authorities, domestic courts monitor observance of human rights by international authorities. Deficits

'UNaccountable? The United Nations, Emergency Powers and the Rule of Law' (2009) 42 *Vanderbilt Journal of Transnational Law* 1509–41.

[120] cp Kumm, 'The Legitimacy of International Law' (n 30) 917; Ernest A Young, 'The Trouble with Global Constitutionalism' (2003) 38 *Texas International Law Journal* 527; Jed Rubenfeld, 'The Two World Orders' (2003) 27 *The Wilson Quarterly* 22. See also the reasoning of domestic and international courts in the above discussed cases such as *Solange I*, *Kadi*, and *Nada*.

[121] Helen Keller and Andreas Fischer, 'The UN Anti-terror Sanctions Regime under Pressure' (2009) 9 *Human Rights Law Review* 257; Erika De Wet and André Nollkaemper (eds), *Review of the Security Council by Member States* (Antwerp, Intersentia, 2003).

[122] On responsibility of international organisations under national law, see August Reinisch, 'Accountability of International Organizations According to National Law' (2005) 36 *Netherlands Yearbook of International Law* 119.

[123] Nollkaemper (n 113) 12.

in the protection of human rights and the rule of law standards, and more broadly, deficiencies in the checks and balances between different authorities within one legal system are thereby compensated for by another legal system. What is most noteworthy in that development is that the separation of powers is not only being established between the authorities belonging to the same legal order, but between the authorities belonging to different legal orders. Such a development therefore presents a new stage in the growing interdependency between different legal systems.

However, despite the complementary function played by domestic courts in protecting human rights against violations by international organisations, domestic courts can hardly be considered as the most appropriate fora for adjudication. One reason is that international organisations can thereby be subjected to interferences and unilateral control by a forum state, particularly by their host state, which can affect their independence and proper functioning.[124] Another danger is that the choice for domestic courts as a venue for settling such disputes may lead to a fragmented and differentiated jurisprudence, even with regard to the same organisation that could be sued with respect to the same subject matter in different states. That can compromise the necessary legal certainty in the protection of international organisations as well as their victims.[125] In case of employment disputes between organisations and their employees, domestic courts might also lack sufficient expertise in applying international administrative law.[126] Furthermore, even when the immunities can be set aside in a particular legal proceeding—for example, due to a waiver by the relevant international organisation—the question still remains what enforcement measures may be considered as appropriate for the implementation of a court decision against the organisation.[127] Perhaps the most important is, however, the concern that if each and every state were allowed to scrutinise the acts of international organisations and

[124] This has been the primary reason for concluding the treaties on privileges and immunities; see Edwin H Fedder, 'The Functional Basis of International Privileges and Immunities: A New Concept in International Law and Organization' (1960) 9 *The American University Law Review* 60, 60–69. In that sense, also the waiver of immunities is regulated; for a standard provision, see Art IV, s 14 of the Convention on the Privileges and Immunities of the United Nations, which states that '[p]rivileges and immunities are accorded to the representatives of members not for the personal benefit of the individuals themselves, but in order to safeguard the independent exercise of their functions in connection with the United Nations'.

[125] That would add to the fragmentation in the field of human rights law with respect to enforcement of human rights obligations of states; see, in a positive tone, Laurence R Helfer, 'Forum Shopping for Human Rights' (1999) 148 *University of Pennsylvania Law Review* 285.

[126] August Reinisch, 'The Immunity of International Organizations and the Jurisdiction of their Administrative Tribunals' (2008) 7 *Chinese Journal of International Law* 285.

[127] The treaties on privileges and immunities of international organisations thereby distinguish the waiver of immunity from submission to the jurisdiction of a domestic court for the purposes of execution. Art II, s 2 provides, similar to other treaties on immunities, that '[i]t is, however, understood that no waiver of immunity shall extend to any measure of execution'.

domestic acts that implement those international acts, the binding quality of international acts could be called into question.[128] The protection of human rights against violations by international organisations at the domestic level can therefore be unsatisfactory and the establishment of effective human rights protection mechanisms at the international level is considered necessary.

The role of domestic courts in the settlement of disputes with international organisations should be seen only as a means of last resort. I propose that the exercise of adjudicative powers by domestic courts be guided by the principle of subsidiarity. The principle of subsidiarity has so far been best known as the central principle of European constitutionalism, which requires that in areas that do not fall within the EU exclusive competence, the EU shall act if and in so far as the objectives pursued by the EU's action could not be sufficiently achieved by individual states.[129] The principle of subsidiarity is also one of the fundamental principles underpinning the system of human rights protection under the European Convention on Human Rights.[130] In that context, it means that the principal task of ensuring respect for human rights as granted under the Convention lies with states and that the ECtHR can and should intervene only if domestic authorities fail in that task.[131] Moreover, while at present, subsidiarity is not widely recognised as one of the general principles of international law, it has been increasingly invoked as a political and legal principle that should govern the allocation and exercise of powers by other international organisations and in case of multilevel governance in general.[132] With the purpose to mediate between the tendency of a higher level of governance to impose a centralised unity and the tendency of a lower level of governance to protect local differences, the principle establishes the preference of the lower level of governance. Thereby, it aims to protect individual autonomy, cultural identity, democratic governance, national sovereignty, and efficiency.[133] The higher governance level may, however, take action if

[128] With respect to review of the acts adopted by the UN Security Council, see Peters (n 109) 840.

[129] Art 5(3) of the Treaty on European Union and Protocol (no 2) on the Application of the principles of subsidiarity and proportionality.

[130] On the principle of subsidiarity, see also chs 8 (Peters) and 11 (Kanetake) of this volume.

[131] High Level Conference on the Future of the European Court of Human Rights, Interlaken Declaration of 19 Feb 2010.

[132] Kumm (n 30); Andreas Føllesdal, 'Subsidiarity' (1998) 6 *Journal of Political Philosophy* 231; Paolo G Carozza, 'Subsidiarity as a Structural Principle of International Human Rights Law' (2003) 97 *American Journal of International Law* 38.

[133] See, however, Kees van Kersbergen and Bertjan Verbeek, 'The Politics of Subsidiarity in the European Union' (1994) 32 *Journal of Common Market Studies* 215, where the authors argue that the apparent consensus on the concept of subsidiarity has been gained only by its obfuscation.

those particular interests cannot satisfactorily be fulfilled at a lower governance level.[134]

As the domestic and international practice discussed in this chapter suggests, a range of powers and competences have been transferred to international organisations, including the competence to establish human rights mechanisms that should ensure compliance of organisations with human rights standards. Yet, domestic courts have not been discharged of every right and responsibility to exercise their judicial review in that legal field. While the primary responsibility to ensure respect for human rights and the right to a remedy, in particular, now lies with international organisations, domestic courts may, and should, continue to exercise at least a limited judicial review of acts of international organisations and their implementation at the domestic level in order to ensure that individuals are not left without any means of redress. The principle of subsidiarity may legitimise domestic courts in seizing jurisdiction and denying immunity to international organisations if, and 'as long as', international dispute settlement mechanisms, including internal remedies available within organisations, are missing or do not meet the standard of effective alternative remedies for the protection of human rights.

VI. CONCLUSION

While 'judicial dialogue', 'cross-fertilisation', and other notions describing the influence that domestic and international courts have on each other have already become almost a term of art, the impact of domestic courts on other international institutions is not well researched. Indeed, the interaction between domestic and international judicial authorities is more intense, especially if compared with a side role that has been given so far to domestic courts by some other international institutions. Yet, this seems to be changing. Not only are domestic courts gaining a more prominent standing vis-à-vis international judiciary, they are also strengthening their legal—and political—standing vis-à-vis international organisations in general. Due to the lack of judicial review of acts of international organisations at the international level, domestic courts are increasingly complementing international judiciary by reviewing the legality and legitimacy of such acts as well as their implementation at the domestic level. The present chapter has shown that such a kind of domestic review can no longer be seen merely as a unilateral act of a state, but rather as a task of

[134] Isabelle Feichtner, 'Subsidiarity' in Rudiger Wolfrum (ed), *The Max Planck Encyclopedia of Public International Law* (Oxford, Oxford University Press, 2008) online edn, available at: www.mpepil.com; George A Bermann, 'Taking Subsidiarity Seriously: Federalism in the European Community and the United States' (1994) 94 *Columbia Law Review* 331–456.

domestic courts that is acknowledged by international courts and other international institutions. However, since domestic review of acts of international organisations bears a number of weaknesses, such a challenge to immunities of international organisations by domestic courts should only be interpreted as a temporary and residual device that may only be admissible in case, and as long as, victims of human rights violations committed by an international organisation are left with no alternative means of redress.

4

Domestic Review of Treaty-Based International Investment Awards: Effects of the Metalclad *Judgment of the British Columbia Supreme Court*

SHOTARO HAMAMOTO*

I. INTRODUCTION

THE RAPID PROLIFERATION of international investment treaties and the ensuing 'explosion' of investor-state arbitration spurred a backlash from a certain number of states.[1] Negative reactions to investment treaties and investor-state arbitration take various forms. With respect to individual arbitral decisions, a losing respondent state may simply refuse to implement the award without advancing any legal arguments[2] or by pointing out conflicting international obligations incumbent upon it to justify its non-compliance.[3] More fundamentally, states may attempt to modify the rules by way of authentic interpretation,[4] amendment, or

* The present study is dedicated to the memory of the late Professor Akira Kotera: see (n 22) below.

[1] Michael Waibel and others (eds), *The Backlash against Investment Arbitration* (Alphen aan den Rijn, Kluwer Law International, 2010). With regard to the backlash against investor-state arbitration, see also ch 5 (Ranjan) of this volume.

[2] It seems that Kazakhstan did not justify its refusal to comply with the award rendered on 7 Oct 2003 by an ICSID tribunal in *AIG v Kazakhstan*, ICSID ARB/01/6. See *AIG Capital Partners Inc v Kazakhstan* [2005] APP.L.R. 10/20, in which the High Court of Justice in the United Kingdom refused to execute the award due to sovereign immunity.

[3] The European Commission issued an order obliging Romania to suspend the implementation of the award rendered on 11 Dec 2013 in *Micula v Romania* (ICSID ARB/05/20), considering that the payment of compensation as required by the ICSID tribunal would constitute an unlawful state aid under the EU law. European Commission, 'State aid SA.38517(2014/C) (ex 2014/NN)—Romania Implementation of Arbitral award Micula v. Romania of 11 December 2013', 1 Oct 2014, C(2014) 6848 final.

[4] See 'Interpretation of the Free Trade Commission of Certain Chapter 11 Provisions', available at: www.state.gov/documents/organization/38791.pdf, based on NAFTA Art 1131(2).

renegotiation of investment treaties.[5] They may even decide to leave the system by terminating investment treaties.[6]

Another possibility is to take procedural steps to have the arbitral decision annulled or set aside. With respect to the International Centre for the Settlement of Investment Disputes (ICSID) arbitration, states as well as investors frequently request annulment of awards (ICSID Convention, Article 52) with which they are not satisfied. There exist a number of studies on the roles, effects, and limits of the ICSID annulment system.[7] However, there are relatively few studies on the roles and effects of domestic courts in non-ICSID procedures.[8] In non-ICSID cases,[9] a court in the jurisdiction of the seat of arbitration may set aside the award and a court in the jurisdiction where a winning party to arbitration applies for the enforcement of the award may refuse to enforce it.[10] In these situations, the question arises how domestic court decisions setting aside or refusing to enforce the arbitral award influence the following arbitral tribunals dealing with the same or similar issues.

One of the reasons explaining why there has been a relatively small number of studies addressing this question seems to be about the lack of information and precedent. Andrew Newcombe's *Investment Treaty Arbitration* lists some 'set aside/review proceedings' undertaken before domestic courts,[11] but the number is considerably small in comparison to

[5] See the speech delivered by the South African Minister of Trade and Industry in an UNCTAD meeting on 25 Sept 2012, available at: www.dti.gov.za/delegationspeechdetail.jsp?id=2506; Arif Havas Oegroseno (Indonesian Ambassador to Belgium), 'Revamping bilateral treaties' (*Jakarta Post*, 7 July 2014) available at: www.thejakartapost.com/news/2014/07/07/revamping-bilateral-treaties.html.

[6] See James Harrison, 'The Life and Death of BITs' (2012) 13 *Journal of World Investment & Trade* 928; Tania Voon and others, 'Parting Ways: the Impact of Mutual Termination of investment Treaties on Investor Rights' (2014) 29 *ICSID Review* 451.

[7] Shotaro Hamamoto, 'New Challenges for the ICSID Annulment System: Another Private-Public Problem in the International Investment Dispute settlement' in R Wolfrum and I Gätzschmann (eds), *International Dispute Settlement: Room for Innovations?* (Heidelberg, Springer, 2013) 393; R Doak Bishop and Silvia M Marchili (eds), *Annulment under the ICSID Convention* (Oxford, Oxford University Press, 2012); Emmanuel Gaillard and Yas Banifatemi (eds), *Annulment of ICSID Awards* (Huntington, Juris Publishing, 2004).

[8] Albert Jan van den Berg, 'Should the Setting Aside of the Arbitral Award be Abolished?' (2014) 29 *ICSID Review* 271–72; Walid Ben Hamida, 'Investment Treaties and Domestic Courts' in J Werner and AH Ali (eds), *A Liber Amicorum: Thomas Wälde* (London, Cameron May, 2009) 69; Matthias Scherer and others, 'Domestic Review of Investment Treaty Arbitrations: The Swiss Experience' (2009) 27 *ASA Bulletin* 256–79; Noah Rubins, 'Judicial Review of Investment Arbitration Awards' in F Ortino (ed), *Appeals and Challenges to Investment Treaty Awards* (London, BIICL, 2006) 75–81; Noah Rubins, 'Judicial Review of Investment Arbitration Awards' in T Weiler (ed), *NAFTA Investment Law and Arbitration* (Ardsley, Transnational Publishers, 2004) 359–90.

[9] Including ICSID Additional Facility arbitrations. See ICSID Arbitration (Additional Facility) Rules.

[10] Vladimír Balaš, 'Review of Awards' in P Muchlinski and others (eds), *The Oxford Handbook of International Investment Law* (Oxford, Oxford University Press, 2008) 1125, 1136.

[11] Investment Treaty Arbitration, at: www.italaw.com/browse/set-aside-review-proceedings.

that of publicly available non-ICSID arbitrations. Furthermore, except for the British Columbia Supreme Court's decision,[12] which will be explained in the following section of this chapter and which partially set aside the arbitral award of the *Metalclad v Mexico* case,[13] no domestic court has set aside an award rendered in treaty-based investment arbitration, according to publicly available information as of March 2015.[14]

The present chapter does not pretend to fill this lacuna or cover all aspects of domestic review of treaty-based international investment arbitral awards. Instead, this chapter provides a follow-up study of the 2001 British Columbia Supreme Court's decision that, as noted above, partially set aside the *Metalclad* award. This national procedure to set aside the award is to be characterised as threefold national contestations to an international procedure. The arbitration was instituted under the North American Free Trade Agreement (NAFTA). One of the three member states, Mexico, filed the request to set aside the award rendered against it. A court of another member state, Canada, with which the request was filed, partially set aside the award. In addition, Canada submitted opinions to support Mexico's request and the United States welcomed the Court's judgment.[15] In other words, all three states parties supported the partial setting aside of the award. The objective of this threefold national contestation was certainly not limited to questioning the validity of the *Metalclad* award. The states parties filed or supported the request for setting aside the award because they considered that the *Metalclad* award, if it was left as it stood, would negatively affect future cases in which they would be the respondent. How effective, then, was the three NAFTA states parties' contestation against the *Metalclad* award? This is the question to be dealt with in the present study.

Following a brief account of the *Metalclad* award and the British Columbia Supreme Court's judgment (section II below), this chapter will analyse the domestic judgment's effects on subsequent NAFTA Chapter 11 arbitrations (section III). Its effects on subsequent non-NAFTA cases will

[12] *Mexico v Metalclad*, 2001 BCSC 664, 2 May 2001.

[13] *Metalclad v Mexico*, ICSID ARB(AF)/97/1, Award 30 Aug 2000.

[14] See Ben Hamida, 'Investment Treaties and Domestic Courts' (n 8) 83. The arbitral award in *BG v Argentina* was vacated by a US Court of Appeals (*Argentina v BG*, 665 F.3d 1636 (DC Cir 2012)) but the decision of the Court of Appeals was later reversed by the US Supreme Court (*BG v Argentina*, 134 S Ct 1198, 5 March 2014).

[15] Canada submitted a brief to the British Columbia Supreme Court, in which it argued that 'the Tribunal has elevated one purpose of the NAFTA above others by creating a new transparency obligation'. *Mexico v Metalclad, Outline of Argument of Intervenor Attorney General of Canada*, 16 Feb 2001, para 33. The United States favourably quoted the relevant part of the *Metalclad* judgment in its rejoinder on jurisdiction that it submitted to the *Methanex* tribunal in the month following the British Columbia Supreme Court's judgment. *Methanex v USA, Rejoinder Memorial of Respondent United States of America on Jurisdiction, Admissibility and the Proposed Amendment*, 27 June 2001, at 32.

complement our study (section IV). Our brief survey will indicate an almost complete lack of effects of the British Columbia Court's judgment. Such absence of effects of domestic contestation in this field derives from a systemic limit inherent to the investor-state arbitration: the domestic courts act as courts of review but not as courts of appeal (section V).

II. THE *METALCLAD* CASE

Both the arbitral award and the British Columbia Supreme Court's judgment have been widely discussed[16] and a very brief account is sufficient here. Metalclad, an enterprise of the United States, purchased a Mexican enterprise through its affiliate companies, with a view to the acquisition, development, and operation of the Mexican enterprise's hazardous waste transfer station and landfill in Mexico. Prior to the purchase, the Mexican federal government and the government of the federated state in which the landfill would be built issued construction and operation permits. When Metalclad inquired, prior to its purchase of the Mexican enterprise, as to the necessity for municipal permits, federal officials assured it that it had all that was needed to undertake the landfill project. However, the municipality ordered the cessation of all building activities due to the absence of a municipal construction permit. Metalclad filed an application for the permit with the municipality, which, however, rejected the application, despite the positive audit of the site carried out by the Mexican federal organ in charge of the protection of the environment. Although the federal authorities granted Metalclad an additional permit authorising the expansion of the landfill capacity, the operation of the landfill was precluded by the opposition of the municipality and of the federated state.[17]

The tribunal found that these contradictory acts of the federal and local governments of Mexico constituted a violation of NAFTA Article 1105 ('Minimum Standard of Treatment')[18] for the following reason:

> [t]he absence of a clear rule as to the requirement or not of a municipal construction permit, as well as the absence of any established practice or procedure

[16] Chris Tollefson, 'Metalclad v. United Mexican States Revisited' (2002) 11 *Minnesota Journal of Global Trade* 183; Alain Prujiner 'L'expropriation, l'ALENA et l'affaire Metalclad' (2003) 5 *International Law FORUM du droit international* 205; Henri C Alvarez, 'Setting Aside Additional Facility Awards: the Metalclad Case' in Gaillard and Banifatemi (eds), *Annulment of ICSID Awards* (n 7) 267; Todd Weiler, 'Good Faith and Regulatory Transparency: the Story of Metalclad v. Mexico' in T Weiler (ed), *International Investment Law and Arbitration* (London, Cameron May, 2005) 701.

[17] *Metalclad v Mexico* (n 13) paras 2, 29, 31, 35, 40, 43, 44, 50, 57, 59.

[18] NAFTA, Art 1105, in relevant part, provides: 'Article 1105: Minimum Standard of Treatment

1. Each Party shall accord to investments of investors of another Party treatment in accordance with international law, including fair and equitable treatment and full protection and security'.

> as to the manner of handling applications for a municipal construction permit, amounts to a failure on the part of Mexico to ensure the transparency required by NAFTA.[19]

Article 1105, providing a fair and equitable treatment (FET) clause, does not expressly refer to transparency. However, the tribunal considered it to be an element of the FET obligation because '[p]rominent in the statement of principles and rules that introduces the Agreement [NAFTA] is the reference to 'transparency' (NAFTA Article 102(1))'.[20]

Mexico filed a request for setting aside the award with the Supreme Court of British Columbia, where the seat of arbitration was situated. The Court accepted the request and set aside the part of the award regarding Article 1105. According to the Court:

> the Tribunal did not simply interpret the wording of Article 1105. Rather, it misstated the applicable law to include transparency obligations and it then made its decision on the basis of the concept of transparency … [T]he Tribunal was referring to Article 102(1), which sets out the objectives of the NAFTA in clauses (a) through (f). Transparency is mentioned in Article 102(1) but it is listed as one of the principles and rules contained in the NAFTA … Article 102(2) provides that the NAFTA is to be interpreted and applied in light of the objectives set out in Article 102(1), but it does not require that all of the provisions of the NAFTA are to be interpreted in light of the principles and rules mentioned in Article 102(1).[21]

To put it simply, the Court considered that the requirement of transparency did not constitute an element of the FET obligation under NAFTA

[19] *Metalclad v Mexico* (n 13) para 88.

[20] ibid para 76.

NAFTA, Art102 provides: 'Article 102: Objectives

1. The objectives of this Agreement, as elaborated more specifically through its principles and rules, including national treatment, most-favored-nation treatment and transparency, are to:
   a. eliminate barriers to trade in, and facilitate the cross-border movement of, goods and services between the territories of the Parties;
   b. promote conditions of fair competition in the free trade area;
   c. increase substantially investment opportunities in the territories of the Parties;
   d. provide adequate and effective protection and enforcement of intellectual property rights in each Party's territory;
   e. create effective procedures for the implementation and application of this Agreement, for its joint administration and for the resolution of disputes; and
   f. establish a framework for further trilateral, regional and multilateral cooperation to expand and enhance the benefits of this Agreement.
2. The Parties shall interpret and apply the provisions of this Agreement in the light of its objectives set out in paragraph 1 and in accordance with applicable rules of international law'.

[21] *Mexico v Metalclad* (n 12) paras 70–71.

Article 1105. This judgment aroused fierce criticism from investment law experts, who condemned what they regarded as a gross deviation from the rules on treaty interpretation under international law.[22] Interestingly, however, contrary to the generally critical attitude of commentators, all the states parties to NAFTA were in favour of setting aside the *Metalclad* award.[23] One might then suppose that the subsequent tribunals would have followed the interpretation adopted by the British Columbia Supreme Court and supported by all NAFTA states parties. The story is, however, a bit more complicated than that.

III. EFFECTS OF THE BRITISH COLUMBIA COURT'S JUDGMENT ON SUBSEQUENT NAFTA CHAPTER 11 ARBITRATION

A. Tribunals Following the BC Court's Judgment

The judgment of the British Columbia Supreme Court was followed by at least one of the subsequent NAFTA Chapter 11 tribunals. In *Feldman v Mexico*, the investor of US nationality owned and controlled a Mexican company which engaged in the export of Mexican cigarettes. When the company started its operation in 1990, the export of cigarettes was free from excise tax and the company received rebates, as the relevant Mexican legislation provided that when cigarettes were purchased in Mexico at a price that included the tax and subsequently exported, the tax amounts initially paid could be rebated. Following various changes in the legislation and administrative acts that affected the operation of the company, the legislation was amended in 1997 to bar rebates to cigarette resellers such as the company in question, and the Mexican tax authorities required the company to repay the rebates that it had received.[24] The US investor

[22] Rudolf Dolzer and Christoph Schreuer, *Principles of International Investment Law* (2nd edn, Oxford, Oxford University Press, 2012) 150, fn 143. See also Alvarez, Setting Aside Additional Facility Awards' (n 16) 267, 281; Weiler, 'Good Faith and Regulatory Transparency' (n 16) 717–18; Campbell McLachlan and others (eds), *International Investment Arbitration* (Oxford, Oxford University Press, 2007) 241, fn 198; Akira Kotera, 'Regulatory Transparency' in Muchlinski and others (eds), *The Oxford Handbook of International Investment Law* (n 10) 617, 630; Roland Kläger, *'Fair and Equitable Treatment' in International Investment Law* (Cambridge, Cambridge University Press, 2011) 104. Many authors simply note the existence of the judgment of the British Columbia Supreme Court without giving it any particular consideration. See Ioana Tudor, *The Fair and Equitable Treatment Standard in the International Law of Foreign Investment* (Oxford, Oxford University Press, 2008) 176, fn 119; Andrew Newcombe and Lluís Paradell, *Law and Practice of Investment Treaties* (Alphen aan den Rijn, Kluwer Law International, 2009) 293, fn 306; Jeswald W Salacuse, *The Law of Investment Treaties* (Oxford, Oxford University Press, 2010) 238, fn 133.

[23] See (n 15).

[24] *Feldman v Mexico*, ICSID ARB(AF)/99/1, Award 16 Dec 2002, paras 6–23.

brought arbitration, alleging that the measures taken by Mexican authorities constituted indirect expropriation (NAFTA Article 1110).

In accordance with NAFTA Article 2103, which generally excludes tax measures from coverage under NAFTA, Article 1105 is not applicable to the measures in question. However, the tribunal was led to examine whether the measures met the requirements of due process and Article 1105 as provided in Article 1110(1)(c).[25] The claimant argued that the actions taken by the Mexican Ministry of Finance and Public Credit were so arbitrary as to constitute expropriatory actions, as the Ministry had concluded an oral agreement with it to permit the rebates.[26] The tribunal, though expressing its sympathy with the claimant's argument, rejected it for the following reasons:

> While the transparency in some of the actions of [the Mexican Ministry of Finance and Public Credit] may be questioned, it is doubtful that lack of transparency alone rises to the level of violation of NAFTA and international law, particularly given the complexities not only of Mexican but most other tax laws. The British Columbia Supreme Court held in its review of the *Metalclad* decision that Section A of Chapter 11, which establishes the obligations of host governments to foreign investors, nowhere mentions an obligation of transparency to such investors, and that a denial of transparency alone thus does not constitute a violation of Chapter 11 ... While this Tribunal is not required to reach the same result as the British Columbia Supreme Court, it finds this aspect of their decision instructive.[27]

The tribunal also indicated that the investor should have sought a formal administrative ruling on the applicability of tax rebates since oral or informal opinions were not binding on the tax authorities under the Mexican law.[28]

B. Tribunals Taking Distance from the British Columbia Court's Judgment

It is notable that *Feldman v Mexico* is the only case in which the tribunal clearly adopted the approach taken by the British Columbia Supreme

[25] NAFTA, Art 1110(1): 'No Party may directly or indirectly nationalize or expropriate an investment of an investor of another Party in its territory or take a measure tantamount to nationalization or expropriation of such an investment ("expropriation"), except:

(a) for a public purpose;
(b) on a non-discriminatory basis;
(c) in accordance with due process of law and article 1105(1); and
(d) on payment of compensation in accordance with paragraphs 2 through 6'.

[26] *Feldman v Mexico* (n 24) para 125.
[27] ibid para 133.
[28] ibid para 134.

Court. In *Waste Management v Mexico*, the tribunal attempted to give a general and abstract interpretation of NAFTA Article 1105. According to the tribunal:

> the minimum standard of treatment of fair and equitable treatment is infringed by conduct attributable to the State and harmful to the claimant if the conduct is arbitrary, grossly unfair, unjust or idiosyncratic, is discriminatory and exposes the claimant to sectional or racial prejudice, or involves a lack of due process leading to an outcome which offends judicial propriety—as might be the case with a manifest failure of natural justice in judicial proceedings or a complete lack of transparency and candour in an administrative process.[29]

Although the tribunal referred to the British Columbia Supreme Court's judgment in the context of its analysis of NAFTA Article 1110,[30] it curiously ignored the judgment when it interpreted Article 1105 in the aforementioned paragraph. It thus implicitly took distance from the *Metalclad* judgment to conclude that the conduct of the host state involving 'a complete lack of transparency and candour in an administrative process' might result in a violation of the FET obligation provided in Article 1105. However, the tribunal did not examine whether the Mexican authorities' conduct involved 'a complete lack of transparency and candour' and rejected the claimant's argument on other bases.[31] *Apotex Holdings v USA* took a similar position, quoting the *Waste Management* award.[32] In *Clayton v Canada*, the tribunal, while explicitly referring to the Canadian government's position excluding the requirement of transparency from the scope of NAFTA Article 1105,[33] referred to the above-quoted '*Waste Management* epitome' of the FET obligation as 'particularly influential' and 'particularly apt'.[34] The tribunal found a violation of Article 1105 because the investor 'was denied a fair opportunity to know the case it had to meet' due to 'the unprecedented approach' taken by the host state government.[35] This is not far from a direct application of the transparency standard without naming it.

Cargill v Mexico seems at first glance to follow the British Columbia Supreme Court's judgment, since the tribunal held that the '[c]laimant ha[d] not established that a general duty of transparency is included in the customary international law minimum standard of treatment owed to foreign investors per Article 1105's requirement to afford fair

[29] *Waste Management v Mexico*, ICSID ARB(AF)/00/3, Award 30 April 2004, para 98.

[30] ibid paras 154, 159.

[31] ibid paras 100–40.

[32] *Apotex Holdings v USA*, ICSID ARB(AF)/12/1, Award 25 Aug 2014, paras 9.44, 9.49–9.51.

[33] *Clayton v Canada*, PCA 2009-04, Award on Jurisdiction and Liability 17 March 2015, paras 401, 407.

[34] ibid paras 442–43, 588.

[35] ibid para 590.

and equitable treatment'.[36] However, it also said that the violation of Article 1105 '[might] relate to a lack of due process, discrimination, a lack of transparency, a denial of justice, or an unfair outcome'.[37] This apparent contradiction is cleared up with a closer reading of the award. The claimant invoked the *Tecmed* award and its notoriously demanding interpretation of the FET obligation so as to allege that the 'general duty of transparency' constituted part of the FET obligation. In response, the tribunal stated that the lack of transparency 'must be "gross,", "manifest," [or] "complete"' to constitute a violation of NAFTA Article 1105 and emphasised that 'this standard is significantly narrower than that present in the *Tecmed* award'. In other words, the tribunal considered that a 'gross', 'manifest', or 'complete' lack of transparency may bring about a violation of Article 1105, while a relatively minor lack of transparency does not, contrary to what the claimant affirmed referring to the *Tecmed* award. It is also to be noted that the tribunal did not refer to the British Columbia Supreme Court's judgment except where it quotes the respondent's allegations.[38]

In *Merrill & Ring v Canada*, the tribunal decided not to discuss the content of the FET obligation in detail[39] but showed some hesitation, as *obiter dicta*, in following the *Metalclad* judgment as follows:

> [W]hile a requirement for transparency may not at present be proven to be part of the customary law standard, as the judicial review of *Metalclad* rightly concluded, it is nonetheless approaching that stage. Indeed, it would be difficult today to justify the appropriateness of a secretive regulatory system.[40]

The tribunal did not have to say anything on the *Metalclad* case since it avoided entering detailed discussions on the FET obligation. It nevertheless felt it necessary to voice serious reservations regarding the judgment of the British Columbia Court.

C. Disputing Parties' Arguments

In cases where the tribunal did not express its position concerning the question whether the lack of transparency in governmental conduct may constitute a violation of the FET obligation under NAFTA Article 1105, disputing parties often discussed it.

[36] *Cargill v Mexico*, ICSID ARB(AF)/05/2, Award 18 Sept 2009, para 294.

[37] ibid para 285.

[38] ibid para 264.

[39] The tribunal found it useless to examine whether Art 1105 had been violated because the claimant did not prove damages to the satisfaction of the tribunal. *Merrill & Ring v Canada*, Award 31 March 2010, paras 243–46, 266.

[40] ibid para 231.

In *Methanex v USA*, the claimant, relying on the *Metalclad* and *Waste Management* awards, argued that a complete lack of transparency and candour in the Californian administrative process that had banned the product that the claimant had been producing constituted a violation of the FET obligation under NAFTA Article 1105.[41] The respondent, although it alleged that the tribunal could not deal with the claim because the issue was belatedly raised,[42] accepted the above mentioned synthesis provided by the *Waste Management* award.[43] The US thus considered that a 'complete lack of transparency and candour in an administrative process' might constitute a violation of the FET obligation under NAFTA Article 1105. The tribunal did not deal with this issue,[44] but it must have been, in any case, difficult for it to find any lack of transparency in the conduct of the Californian authorities, given the facts of the case.[45]

In *Glamis Gold v USA*, the claimant argued that measures which lack transparency violated the customary international law obligation to provide fair and equitable treatment.[46] The respondent, while invoking the British Columbia Supreme Court's judgment to argue that there is no stand-alone rule of transparency under NAFTA Article 1105, admitted that there may be transparency aspects within the customary international law minimum standard of treatment.[47] The tribunal rejected the claimant's argument, but it is to be noted that the claimant submitted a rather peculiar argument on transparency. As the tribunal pointed out, the claimant admitted the procedural transparency of the measures in question. What the claimant characterised as a lack of transparency was the change in applicable domestic legal rules that had affected the stability of the legal framework within which the claimant-investor operated.[48] This allegation was rejected for the lack of specific assurances on the part of the respondent to maintain the stability of the legal framework.[49] The tribunal thus did not deal with the question whether 'a complete lack of transparency and candour in an administrative process' violates the FET obligation.

[41] *Methanex v USA*, Transcript, Day 8, 16 June 2004, at 1945.

[42] ibid Transcript, Day 9, 17 June 2004, at 2145, 2149.

[43] ibid Transcript, Day 9, 17 June 2004, at 2153.

[44] ibid pt IV, ch C, paras 12, 26.

[45] The ban in question was introduced following a series of scientific research and public hearings. See ibid pt IV, ch D, paras 14–15. See also Alberto Alvarez-Jiménez, 'The Methanex Final Award' (2006) 23 *Journal of International Arbitration* 427, 429.

[46] *Glamis Gold v USA*, Award 8 June 2009, para 572. This argument obviously takes into account the NAFTA Free trade Commission's Note of Interpretation (2001), which states that '[t]he concept[] of "fair and equitable treatment" […] do not require treatment in addition to or beyond that which is required by the customary international law minimum standard of treatment of aliens': available at: www.state.gov/documents/organization/38790.pdf.

[47] *Glamis Gold v USA* (n 46) para 578.

[48] ibid para 575, note 1169; para 798.

[49] ibid paras 801–02.

In *Chemtura v Canada*, the claimant invoked the *Waste Management* award to argue that the lack of transparency and candour in the Canadian authorities' dealing with the investor violated NAFTA Article 1105.[50] It also emphasised that the British Columbia Supreme Court's judgment was isolated.[51] The respondent referred to the judgment as 'persuasive guidance' to argue that the customary international minimum standard does not include a requirement of 'total transparency'.[52] Although Canada stated that transparency is not part of customary minimum standard treatment,[53] it admitted that transparency would play some role in the context of NAFTA Article 1105, referring to the *Waste Management* award without criticising it.[54] The tribunal, while taking note of these allegations submitted by the disputing parties,[55] did not examine whether transparency constituted part of the fair and equitable treatment under NAFTA Article 1105. However, one can safely say that the tribunal would, in any case, not have accepted the claimant's argument, since it stated that the claimant did not establish that the Canadian authorities had acted in breach of due process standards.[56]

In *Grand River v USA*, the claimant invoked the *Metalclad* and *Waste Management* awards to allege that the host state failed to ensure a transparent and stable framework for the investor's activities.[57] The US quoted the British Columbia Supreme Court judgment to reject the notion of transparency as an element of the fair and equitable treatment under NAFTA Article 1105.[58] The tribunal did not directly deal with the question, but implicitly recognised the relevance of transparency to Article 1105. The dispute arose out of the host state's measures that affected the activities of the claimants as indigenous people, ie, the production and sales of tobacco.[59] The tribunal held that, even though there might exist a rule of customary international law requiring the host state to consult indigenous

[50] *Chemtura v Canada*, Memorial of the Claimant/Investor, 2 June 2008, paras 347, 364; Reply of the Claimant/Investor, 15 May 2009, paras 399–401.

[51] Reply (n 50) para 397.

[52] *Chemtura v Canada*, Counter-Memorial of the Government of Canada, 20 Oct 2008, paras 835–39.

[53] *Chemtura v Canada*, Rejoinder Memorial of the Government of Canada, 10 July 2009, para 189.

[54] *Chemtura v Canada*, Rejoinder (n 53) para 191: 'Rather than establishing "transparency" as an independent element of customary MST [minimum standard treatment], the comment [of the Waste Management tribunal] appears illustrative of other behaviour which might breach customary MST'.

[55] *Chemtura v Canada*, Award, 2 August 2010, paras 112, 115.

[56] ibid para 162.

[57] *Grand River v USA*, Claimants' Memorial, 10 July 2008, para 202; Award 12 January 2011, para 179, 189.

[58] *Grand River v USA*, Counter-Memorial of Respondent, 22 Dec 2008, at 100–01.

[59] *Grand River v USA*, Award, 12 Jan 2011, para 212: 'Retail tobacco businesses are in many Indian reservations across the country, constituting important sources of income and catalyzing other economic activity among indigenous communities'.

peoples on such issues, the investor as an individual was not in a position to require such consultation.[60] The tribunal thus considered that a certain degree of transparency could be required under Article 1105.

In *Gallo v Canada*, the same pattern was repeated: the investor relied on *Waste Management*[61] and the host state on the British Columbia Supreme Court judgment.[62] The tribunal, however, did not deal with the issue, as it found that it did not have jurisdiction over the claims.[63]

The arguments submitted by the disputing parties as well as the decisions handed down by the tribunals indicate that a certain degree of transparency is required under NAFTA Article 1105. This trend is confirmed by other tribunals instituted on the basis of other investment treaties.

IV. EFFECTS OF THE BRITISH COLUMBIA COURT'S JUDGMENT UPON SUBSEQUENT NON-NAFTA CASES

The requirement of transparency is almost always considered to be part of the FET obligation out of the NAFTA context.[64] Out of the context of NAFTA, there are six tribunals that referred to the *Metalclad* award to conclude that the requirement of transparency constitutes part of the FET obligation. In other words, these tribunals did not hesitate to rely on a vacated arbitral award. None of them, however, paid the slightest attention to the British Columbia Court's judgment, which had set aside the award on which they relied.

The earliest example is *OEPC v Ecuador*. The investor was entitled to reimbursement of the value added tax paid on domestic transactions necessitated to carry out its investment activities but was later disqualified from such reimbursements.[65] The tribunal noted that '[t]he tax law was changed without providing any clarity about its meaning and extent and the practice and regulations were also inconsistent with such changes' and found that the host state violated the FET clause contained in the Ecuador-US BIT, relying on the *Metalclad* tribunal's finding that the failure to ensure a transparent and predictable framework for the investor's business planning constituted a violation of the FET obligation under Article 1105 NAFTA.[66] The award does not touch upon the British Columbia Court's judgment. Similarly, the tribunals in *LG&E v Argentina*, *Biwater and Tanzania*,

[60] ibid paras 210, 213.

[61] *Gallo v Canada*, Investor's Memorial, 1 March 2010, para 393.

[62] *Gallo v Canada*, Counter-Memorial of the Government of Canada, 29 June 2010, para 286.

[63] *Gallo v Canada*, Award, 15 Sept 2011, para 359.

[64] Patrick Dumberry, *The Fair and Equitable Treatment Standard* (Alphen aan den Rijn, Kluwer Law International, 2013) 180. See cases referred to in (nn 67–68) below.

[65] *OEPC v Ecuador*, LCIA Case No UN3467, Final Award, 1 July 2004, paras 29–35.

[66] ibid paras 184–86.

Bayindir v Pakistan, *Micula v Romania*, and *Gold Reserve v Venezuela* relied on the *Metalclad* award to find that a breach of the FET obligation may arise from the host states' behaviour, lacking transparency, while making no reference to the British Columbia Court's judgment.[67]

In fact, whether or not referring to the *Metalclad* award, the requirement of certain degree of transparency is almost always considered to be part of the FET obligation.[68] One may consider that this is irrelevant to the effects of the British Columbia Court's judgment, which is NAFTA-specific, and that the requirement of transparency is not part of the FET obligation under NAFTA Article 1105, which is tied with customary international law obligation because of the interpretation adopted by the Free Trade Commission of the NAFTA a few months after the said judgment.[69]

However, as the *Saluka* tribunal stated, 'the difference between the Treaty standard [of the FET laid down in the Czech-Netherlands BIT] and the customary minimum standard, when applied to the specific facts of a case, may well be more apparent than real'.[70] As a matter of textual

[67] *LG&E v Argentina*, ICSID ARB/02/1, Decision on Liability 3 Oct 2006, para 125, fn 31; *Biwater v Tanzania*, ICSID ARB/05/22 Award 24 July 2008, para 602; *Bayindir v Pakistan*, ICSID ARB/03/29, Award 27 August 2009, para 178; *Micula v Romania* (n 3) paras 519, 531, 533; *Gold Reserve v Venezuela*, ICSID ARB(AF)/09/1, Award 22 Sept 2014, para 128, fn 35; paras 574, 609.

[68] *Bogdanov v Moldova*, SCC, 22 Sept 2005, para 4.2.4.4; *Saluka v Czech Republic*, Partial Award 17 March 2006, paras 288, 302–09; *Siemens v Argentina*, ICSID ARB/02/8, Award 6 Feb 2007, paras 297–98; *Rumeli v Kazakhstan*, ICSID ARB/05/16, Award, 29 July 2008, para 609; *LESI-Astaldi c Algérie*, CIRDI Aff No ARB/0-5/3, sentence, le 12 novembre 2008, para 151; *Nortzucker v Poland*, Second Partial Award 28 Jan 2009, para 12; *Lemire v Ukraine*, ICSID ARB/06/18, Decision on Jurisdiction and Liability 14 Jan 2010, paras 262, 284; *Roussalis v Romania*, ICSID ARB/06/1, Award 7 Dec 2011, para 314; *Bosh v Ukraine*, ICSID ARB/08/11, Award, 25 Oct 2012, para 212.

[69] (n 4) above.

[70] *Saluka v Czech Republic* (n 68) para 291. A number of tribunals find no difference between the treaty standard of fair and equitable treatment and the customary international law standard of minimum treatment. *OEPC v Ecuador* (n 65) para 190; *CMS v Argentina*, ICSID ARB/01/8, Award 12 May 2005, paras 278, 284; *Duke Energy v Ecuador*, ICSID ARB/04/19, Award 18 Aug 2008, para 337; *Siemens v Argentina* (n 68) para 299; *Rumeli v Kazakhstan* (n 68) para 611; *El Paso v Argentina*, ICSID ARB/03/15, Award 31 Oct 2011, para 336. Although several tribunals found that the FET obligation stipulated in the applicable investment treaty was (or could be) 'autonomous' and different from the customary international law standard of minimum treatment, the difference is 'more apparent than real'. There are five groups of such tribunals; the first group considers the difference to be rather conceptual and of no practical relevance (*Biwater v Tanzania* (n 67) paras 592–93; *Total v Argentina*, ICSID ARB/04/1, Decision on Liability 27 Dec 2010, para 125; *SAUR c Argentine*, Affaire CIRDI No ARB/04/4, décision sur la compétence et sur la responsabilité, le 6 juin 2012, paras 491, 494; *Deutsche Bank v Sri Lanka*, ICSID ARB/09/2, Award 31 Oct 2012, paras 418–19); the second group points out that the (possible) difference is not relevant at least in the given case (*Impregilo v Argentina*, ICSID ARB/07/17, Award 21 June 2011, paras 285–89); the third group mentions the difference but is silent about the requirement of transparency (*Enron v Argentina*, ICSID ARB/01/3, Award 22 May 2007, para 258; *CAA & Vivendi v Argentina*, ICSID ARB/97/3, Award 20 Aug 2007, para 7.4.5; *Sempra v Argentina*, ICSID ARB/02/16, Award 28 Sept 2007, para 302; *EDFI v Argentina*, ICSID ARB/03/23, Award 11 June 2012, para 1003); the fourth group seems to deal with the requirement of transparency as that of customary international

interpretation, it is difficult to see no element of transparency in the 'fair and equitable' treatment. Furthermore, as the *Tecmed* tribunal stated, the content of the FET obligation should be determined in light of 'the good faith principle established by international law'.[71] It is difficult to deny that the good faith principle requires no degree of transparency in the behaviour of the host state.[72] We can and should argue about how transparently the host state is obliged to behave under the FET obligation stipulated in the applicable investment treaty[73]—and the *Tecmed* award cannot be free from criticism in this respect[74]—but it is simply excessive to say that the requirement of transparency is totally out of the scope of the FET obligation, as indicated by a number of arbitral awards examined in this section. It follows that arbitral tribunals have not paid heed to the British Columbia Court's judgment, which ousted the requirement of transparency from the scope of the FET obligation.

V. CONCLUSION

Sornarajah regrets that 'events since the [*Metalclad*] judgment have shown that the adherents of the expansionary view were in no way deterred'.[75] He is surely right in that the line of arbitral jurisprudence, as examined in the present study, does not follow the British Columbia Supreme Court's judgment and considers that the requirement of transparency constitutes part of the FET obligation.[76] However, is it appropriate to criticise the arbitral decisions examined in the present study for adopting an 'expansionary' view?

law (*Paushok v Mongolia*, Award on Jurisdiction and Admissibility 28 April 2011, para 304 ('Legislative assemblies of all countries'); and the fifth group considers the requirement of transparency as part of the 'autonomous' FET obligation without making it clear whether such exists also under customary international law (*OKO v Estonia*, ICSID ARB/04/6, Award 19 Nov 2007, paras 241–42; *Lemire v Ukraine* (n 68) paras 253, 262, 267, 284). In any case, none of these tribunals has considered that the requirement of transparency was only part of the autonomous treaty standard and not of customary international law.

[71] *Tecmed v Mexico*, ICSID ARB(AF)/00/2, Award 29 May 2003, para 154.

[72] The extremely comprehensive and demanding interpretation of the FET clause adopted by the *Tecmed* tribunal.

[73] See Stephan W Schill, 'Fair and Equitable Treatment, the Rule of Law, and Comparative Public Law' in SW Schill (ed), *International Investment Law and Comparative Public Law* (Oxford, Oxford University Press, 2010) 168–69.

[74] Zachary Douglas, 'Nothing if Not Critical for Investment Treaty Arbitration' (2006) 22 *Arbitration International* 27.

[75] Muthucumaraswamy Sornarajah, *The International Law on Foreign Investment* (3rd edn, Cambridge, Cambridge University Press, 2010) 350.

[76] Even Patrick Dumberry, who affirms that the NAFTA arbitral jurisprudence does not consider transparency as a 'stand-alone obligation under Article 1105', admits that the tribunals take into account the concept of transparency when examining whether there is a violation of Art 1105. Dumberry, *The Fair and Equitable Treatment Standard* (n 64) 179.

Why does the *Metalclad* judgment exert little influence over the subsequent tribunals, while the vacated part of the *Metalclad* award continues to be quoted and relied on? Although it is impossible to specify the reasons with complete certainty, it is to be remembered that the British Columbia Supreme Court's argument had a major flaw in its application of the rules on treaty interpretation.[77] In addition and more fundamentally, since the Court set aside the award for 'making reference to Article 102',[78] it did not consider the question whether the FET clause itself encompasses the requirement of transparency,[79] and if so, how transparently the host state ought to act under the FET obligation. No matter how restrictively the term 'fair and equitable treatment' is to be interpreted, it is difficult to conclude that neither fairness nor equity contains any element of transparency whatsoever, and the NAFTA states parties, which unanimously support the *Metalclad* judgment, are nevertheless led to accept that a complete lack of transparency and candour might constitute a violation of the FET obligation. Thus, the central question is how transparently the host state ought to act under the FET obligation. The *Metalclad* judgment failed to deal with this central question.

It is, however, doubtful whether the British Columbia Court could have done otherwise, if it was unsatisfied with the original award. It was bound to act as a court of review and not as a court of appeal. The review procedure—whether the ICSID annulment system or the review by domestic courts—has an inherent systemic limit: the review instance is entitled to set aside arbitral awards for procedural reasons but is not tasked with checking and rectifying errors in the application of the law.[80] This is not surprising at all because the treaty-based investment arbitration has been introduced so as to 'delocalise' the procedure or, in other words, to prevent any intervention of domestic state organs, including courts and tribunals. Therefore, if any of the states parties to an investment treaty wish to prevent certain evolution of arbitral jurisprudence, they have to change the rules of the game themselves, by amending or denouncing the applicable investment treaty.[81]

[77] (n 22) above.

[78] *Mexico v Metalclad* (n 12) para 72.

[79] See Christopher F Dugan and others (eds), *Investor-State Arbitration* (Oxford, Oxford University Press, 2008) 522.

[80] As for the ICSID annulment system, see (n 7). Non-ICSID arbitral awards may be set aside in accordance with the law of the seat of arbitration, which usually does not give the domestic courts the power to carry out substantive review (*révision au fond*). See UNCITRAL Model Law on International Commercial Arbitration, 2006, Art 34. Domestic courts may refuse to enforce non-ICSID arbitral awards only on strictly limited legal bases. See Convention on the Recognition and Enforcement of Foreign Arbitral Awards, Art 5.

[81] (n 1) above.

5

National Contestation of International Investment Law and the International Rule of Law

PRABHASH RANJAN

I. INTRODUCTION

THE PURPOSE OF this chapter is to analyse the impact of national contestation of international investment law on 'international' rule of law elements embodied in international investment law. This chapter focuses on Bilateral Investment Treaties (BITs), which are at the heart of international investment law, amount to more than 3000 treaties so far, and are regarded as its most important source.[1] BITs are treaties signed bilaterally by two countries to protect investments made by investors of both countries.[2] The first BIT was signed in 1959 between Germany and Pakistan.[3] Since 1959 to the end of 2013, a total of 3236 BITs have been concluded.[4] This mass of BITs has generated a significant volume of cases which arise out of disputes between foreign investors and host states and

[1] Rudolf Dolzer and Christoph Schreuer, *Principles of International Investment Law* (Oxford, Oxford University Press, 2012) 13; Jeswald W Salacuse, 'The Treatification of International Investment Law' (2007) 13 *Law and Business Review of the Americas* 155, 157.

[2] Jeswald W Salacuse, 'BIT by BIT: The Growth of Bilateral Investment Treaties and Their Impact on Foreign Investment in Developing Countries' (1990) 24 *The International Lawyer* 655. For a general discussion on BITs, see Muthucumaraswamy Sornarajah, *The International Law on Foreign Investment* (Cambridge, Cambridge University Press, 2004) 204–314; Dolzer and Schreuer (n 1); Andrew Newcombe and Lluís Paradell, *Law and Practice of Investment Treaties* (The Hague, Kluwer, 2009) 1–73; Jeswald W Salacuse, *The Law of Investment Treaties* (Oxford, Oxford University Press, 2010); Kenneth J Vandevelde, *Bilateral Investment Treaties: History, Policy and Interpretation* (Oxford; New York Oxford University Press, 2010). In this chapter, investment chapters in Free Trade Agreements (FTAs) are also included within the ambit of BITs.

[3] Vandevelde, *Bilateral Investment Treaties* (n 2) 1.

[4] This includes 2902 stand-alone investment treaties and 334 investment chapters in FTAs: UNCTAD, *World Investment Report–Investing in the SDGs: An Action Plan* (New York; Geneva, United Nations, 2014) 114.

cover a wide array of regulatory measures of the host state.[5] BITs impose restraints on the arbitrary exercise of power of host states with respect to foreign investors by recognising principles of non-discrimination and fair and equitable treatment.[6] They also allow for protection of these rights through an independent dispute resolution system (investment treaty arbitration).[7] Imposition of such restraints on the arbitrary exercise of power by the state and an independent dispute resolution system are integral components of the rule of law, both at the national and international levels. This has situated BITs as important elements in understanding the meaning of the international rule of law in the context of foreign investment.

The chapter starts by discussing the potential elements of the international rule of law and analyses whether international investment law has adopted some of the core elements of international rule of law (section II below). This forms a useful background to explore the impact of national contestation on the elements of international rule of law. In last few years, many states have contested (parts of) international investment law in the belief that restrictions imposed by BITs on the exercise of the states' public power are too severe and cripple their ability to regulate in the public interest. Contestations emanate not just from developing countries in Latin America, Africa, and Asia but also from developed countries such as the United States, Canada, Norway, and Australia. Various countries have given up their membership of the International Centre for the Settlement of Investment Disputes (ICSID), alleging that the investor-state dispute resolution system is biased against host states to the advantage of foreign investors.[8] There are also extreme cases in which countries took steps to renounce BITs (some Latin American countries and South Africa).[9] A few countries have decided to exclude the investor-state dispute resolution mechanism from their BITs in order to safeguard state sovereignty. At the same time, some countries have adopted an engaging form of national contestation by conducting a national review of BITs (section III).

These varied modes of national contestations have triggered a debate on how to re-craft BITs in a manner that balances investment protection with the host states' right to regulate in the public interest. The debate has

[5] From a negligible number in early-1990s, the total number of treaty-based cases rose to 568 by the end of 2013—UNCTAD, 'Recent Developments in Investor State Dispute Settlement', IIA Issue Note no 1 (2014) available at: http://unctad.org/en/PublicationsLibrary/webdiaepcb2014d3_en.pdf.

[6] See s II of this chapter.

[7] ibid.

[8] eg, Venezuela views ICSID as favouring interests of Transnational Corporations: see Sergey Ripinsky, 'Venezuela's Withdrawal from ICSID: What it Does and Does not Achieve' (Investment Treaty News, 13 April 2012) available at: www.iisd.org/itn/2012/04/13/venezuelas-withdrawal-from-icsid-what-it-does-and-does-not-achieve/.

[9] See s III of the chapter.

then encouraged the global community to develop innovative solutions to strengthen the adjudicative process (section IV). While national contestations appear to undermine the international rule of law, this chapter observes that they do not do so (section V); rather, as will be discussed below, national contestations provide an opportunity for a critical revision of the elements of international rule of law.

II. INTERNATIONAL INVESTMENT LAW AND THE INTERNATIONAL RULE OF LAW

Before discussing national contestation of international investment law, we need to conduct an overview the elements of the international rule of law in the context of international investment law. This is important because national contestation targets these very elements of international rule of law. This section first discusses and identifies the potential elements of the international rule of law (A), and then determines to what extent these elements are reflected in international investment law (B).

A. Elements of the Rule of Law

In 2005, the United Nations General Assembly (UNGA) adopted the 2005 World Summit outcome, which recognised the need for universal observance to and implementation of the rule of law at both the national and international levels.[10] The references to the 'rule of law' are by no means novel in the UN's documents.[11] The use of the term 'rule of law' can be traced back to the 1970s.[12] A noteworthy development in the UN from 2005 is, however, that states have so expressly embraced the objective of the 'international' rule of law.[13] This has led to scholarly debates that endeavour to delineate the meaning of the international rule of law.[14] Most scholars understand the rule of law at the international level in the formal sense

[10] '2005 World Summit Outcome' UN Doc A/RES/60/1 (24 Oct 2005) para 134. See also UN Doc A/RES/63/128 (15 Jan 2009).

[11] International Law Association (2012), Sofia Report, Islamic Law and International Law.

[12] 'Declaration on Principles of International Law Concerning Friendly Relations and Co-operation among States in accordance with the Charter of the United Nations', GA res 2625, Annex, 25 UN GAOR, Supp (No 28) UN Doc A/5217 at 121 (1970).

[13] André Nollkaemper, *National Courts and the International Rule of Law* (Oxford; New York, Oxford University Press, 2011) 1. See also the Report of the Secretary-General, 'The Rule of Law at the National and International Levels' UN Doc A/63/64 (12 March 2008).

[14] James Crawford, 'International Law and the Rule of Law' (2003) 24 *Adelaide Law Review* 3; Simon Chesterman, 'An International Rule of Law?' (2008) 56 *American Journal of Comparative Law* 331; Nollkaemper, *National Courts and the International Rule of Law* (n 13); Stéphane Beaulac, 'The Rule of Law in International Law Today' in G Palombella and N Walker (eds), *Relocating the Rule of Law* (Oxford; Portland, OR, Hart Publishing, 2009) 197.

and not in the substantive sense.[15] For instance, Kumm argues that the international rule of law needs to be distinguished from the international rule of *good* law and that at the international level it should be understood narrowly.[16] Accordingly, attempts have been made to examine whether the formal core values of the rule of law are to be found in the international legal system.[17] It has been argued that across cultures and political systems it is the formal notion of the rule of law that is applicable and accepted, which is consistent with 'how' the rule of law is articulated at international fora.[18]

The following elements are generally considered to be central to the formal version of the rule of law. First, exercise of public power must be controlled by law and should be based upon authority conferred by law;[19] second, the requirement of formal legality, such as rules, must be set out and applied in a manner that meets a certain threshold of predictability and clarity;[20] third, public powers cannot set or change the law at will—they have to act within the powers conferred by law;[21] and fourth, there must be a process of independent adjudication in order to ensure accountability of exercise of public power.[22] Some scholars also argue that rule of law requiring exercise of powers, such as changing the law, should conform to fundamental civil and political rights.[23] This, arguably, goes beyond the formal version of the rule of law and points towards the substantive notion of the rule of law.[24]

[15] Beaulac, 'The Rule of Law in International Law Today' (n 14) 201; Chesterman, 'An International Rule of Law?' (n 14) 333; Mattias Kumm, 'International Law in National Courts: The International Rule of Law and the Limits of the Internationalist Model' (2003) 44 *Virginia Journal of International Law* 19. On 'formal' and 'substantive' rule of law, see Paul Craig, 'Formal and Substantive Conceptions of the Rule of Law: An Analytical Framework' (1997) *Public Law* 467. See also Brian Z Tamanaha, *On the Rule of Law: History, Politics, Theory* (Cambridge, Cambridge University Press, 2004) 91. See also 'Framework Paper', ch 1 (Kanetake) of this volume (pointing out the formalistic character of the international rule of law).

[16] Kumm, 'International Law in National Courts' (n 15) 22.

[17] Beaulac (n 14).

[18] Chesterman (n 14) 342.

[19] Nollkaemper, *National Courts and the International Rule of Law* (n 13) 3; Chesterman (n 14) 342; Kumm (n 15) 22; Beaulac (n 14) 204–05.

[20] Beaulac (n 14) 205–06.

[21] Nollkaemper (n 13) 4. See also Gianluigi Palombella, 'The Rule of Law Beyond the State: Failures, Promises, and Theory' (2009) 7 *International Journal of Constitutional Law* 442, 442–67.

[22] Chesterman (n 14) 342; Beaulac (n 14) 204–05; Nollkaemper (n 13) 5. See also Crawford, 'International Law and the Rule of Law' (n 14) 10.

[23] Nollkaemper (n 13) 4. See also Ernst-Ulrich Petersmann, 'International Rule of Law and Constitutional Justice in International Investment Law and Arbitration' (2009) 16 *Indiana Journal of Global Legal Studies* 513, 516–18.

[24] On this point, it is also argued that a formal conception of international rule of law 'tends to privilege the value of order over that of justice' and 'requires that the rules adopted through designated sources be observed, but tells us nothing about the character of those rules': Bhupinder Singh Chimni, 'Legitimating the International Rule of Law' in J Crawford and M Koskenniemi (eds), *The Cambridge Companion to International Law* (Cambridge, Cambridge University Press, 2012) 290.

Scholars disagree over whether these formal components of the rule of law are reflected in the *international* legal system. Beaulac, on the one hand, argues that 'the extensive body of international legal rules in many substantive areas' limits the exercise of discretionary and arbitrary power by states in their international relations.[25] On the other hand, scholars such as Chesterman observe that the fragmentation of the legal order undermines rule of law concepts such as clarity.[26] Crawford, while recognising that there are practical problems in ensuring absence of arbitrary power at the international level,[27] recognises that 'we are growing into the rule of law at international level' and that this is happening 'in some fields more than others'.[28]

Disagreements also persist with regard to specific elements of the rule of law, such as the equal application of law and a process of independent adjudication at the international level. Beaulac, on the basis that 'normativity on the international plane applies equally to all states',[29] argues that states are not only equal in terms of the application of legal norms, but also the participation in the creation of international norms.[30] On the other hand, Chesterman, while discussing this feature of the rule of law in the international context, raises the important question of 'who the true subject of law is'.[31] Chesterman suggests that the development of the international rule of law would require more general application of international law to states and other entities.[32]

With regard to an independent judicial mechanism for the enforcement of international norms, some argue that this element is satisfactorily reflected at the international level. On the other hand, others observe that the advancement of the rule of law at the international level requires greater acceptance of the compulsory jurisdiction of the International Court of Justice (ICJ) and other independent tribunals, and 'confirmation that international law applies to international organisations in general and to the UN Security Council in particular'.[33]

Taking into account these contrasting observations, this chapter analyses the presence and meaning of the aforementioned four elements of the rule of law in the international investment law regime. Given the complex

[25] Beaulac (n 14) 207.
[26] Chesterman (n 14) 359.
[27] Crawford, 'International Law and the Rule of Law' (n 14) 10.
[28] ibid.
[29] Beaulac (n 14) 211.
[30] ibid.
[31] Chesterman (n 14) 360.
[32] ibid.
[33] ibid 359.

understanding of the substantive notions of international rule of law, the chapter is restricted to the formal notions of international rule of law.[34]

B. Elements of the Rule of Law in International Investment Law

While the concept of the rule of law in the context of international investment law has attracted some academic discussion,[35] the existing studies have yet to fully address the fundamental question as to whether and how international investment law materialises the key elements of the international rule of law. For example, some authors argue that international investment law will strengthen the international rule of law without specifically explaining whether international investment law is a component of international rule of law.[36] Some authors consider international investment law to be a component of international rule of law, but with respect merely to a few BIT provisions.[37] Another study limits the discussion of the international rule of law in the context of international investment law to just one issue only—whether international investment law contains legal rules that meet a certain threshold of predictability and certainty.[38] In an attempt to remedy some of the shortfalls of existing studies, we will

[34] While this chapter restricts itself to discussing the formal and not substantive notion of international rule of law, this is not to say that the substantive notion is not important. But there is no consensus on what is a substantive notion of international rule of law.

[35] See L Yves Fortier, 'Investment Protection and the Rule of Law: Change or Decline?' in R McCorquodale (ed), *The Rule of Law in International and Comparative Context* (London, British Institute of International and Comparative Law, 2010) 119; Charles N Brower and Lee A Steven, 'Who Then Should Judge: Developing the International Rule of Law under NAFTA Chapter 11' (2001) 2 *Chicago Journal of International Law* 193; Charles N Brower and Stephan W Schill, 'Is Arbitration a Threat or a Boom to the Legitimacy of International Investment Law' (2009) 9 *Chicago Journal of International Law* 471; Stephan W Schill, 'Fair and Equitable Treatment under Investment Treaties as an Embodiment of the Rule of Law' (2006) Institute for International Law and Justice Working Paper 2006/6 (Global Administrative Law Series); Thomas W Wälde, 'The Present State of Research Carried Out by the English-Speaking Section of the Centre for Studies and Research' in P Kahn and T Wälde (eds), *Les aspects nouveaux du droit des investissements internationaux/New Aspects of International Investment Law* (Leiden; Boston, Martinus Nijhoff Publishers, 2007) 63; Gus Van Harten, 'Investment Treaty Arbitration, Procedural Fairness, and the Rule of Law' in S Schill (ed), *International Investment Law and Comparative Public Law* (Oxford, Oxford University Press, 2010) 627. An exception to this is: Thomas Schultz and Cédric Dupont, 'Investment Arbitration: Promoting the Rule of Law or Over-Empowering Investors? A Quantitative Empirical Study' (2014) *European Journal of International Law* forthcoming. Their study specifically, categorically, and separately deals with role of the international investment law regime in promoting national rule of law and international rule of law.

[36] Brower and Steven, 'Who Then Should Judge' (n 35).

[37] Schill (ed), *International Investment Law and Comparative Public Law* (n 35). Schill talks about the FET provision in BITs as an embodiment of international rule of law.

[38] Schultz and Dupont, 'Investment Arbitration: Promoting the Rule of Law or Over-Empowering Investors? A Quantitative Empirical Study' (n 35).

discuss each of the four rule of law elements listed above[39] in the context of international investment law.

i. Subjecting the Exercise of Public Power to Law

The first formal element of the rule of law is arguably to subject the exercise of public power to law. If one situates this notion in the context of international investment law, BITs are indeed part of international legal mechanisms that impose conditions on the host state's exercise of public power in order to prevent undue interference with the rights of the foreign investor. In other words, they control the exercise of regulatory power of the host state. BITs do so in various forms; they prohibit both direct and indirect expropriation of foreign investment unless such expropriation is in the public interest, due process has been followed, and fair and equitable compensation has been given to the foreign investor. BITs also restrict host states from discriminating against a foreign investor in favour of a domestic investor or in favour of another foreign investor in order to ensure equality of competitive conditions. BITs obligate countries to permit transfer of funds related to investment; mandating host states to accord fair and equitable treatment to foreign investment.

According to Schill, the fair and equitable treatment provision in BITs 'can be understood as embodying the rule of law as a standard that the legal systems of host states have to embrace in their treatment of foreign investors'.[40] He advocates using the comparative public law methodology to identify common features of the rule of law recognised in major legal domestic systems and in other international legal systems in order to concretise a fair and equitable treatment standard in BITs.[41] The fair and equitable treatment standard in BITs reflects institutional and procedural dimensions of the rule of law such as the possibility of recourse to courts for adjudication of the foreign investors' rights, legal security, and protection of legitimate expectations.[42] At the same time, Klager points out that developing the content of the fair and equitable treatment in BITs by adopting a comparative rule of law approach is difficult because of the controversial understanding of the rule of law within domestic legal systems, which, in turn, makes it difficult to deduce common elements that could constitute international rule of law.[43]

[39] See section II(A) above.
[40] Schill (n 35) 159.
[41] ibid 174–76.
[42] ibid 182.
[43] Roland Klager, *Fair and Equitable Treatment in International Investment Law* (Cambridge, Cambridge University Press, 2012) 125–27.

Resolving this issue is beyond the scope of this chapter. Nonetheless, it can be said that the fair and equitable treatment provision in BITs, along with other provisions, imposes restrictions on the host state's exercise of public power with respect to foreign investment. Some even argue that international investment law, by restricting state action, safeguards the interests of the international community and thus serves a constitutional function.[44] While opinion may be divided on such a constitutional function, the fact that BITs impose restrictions on the exercise of public power of states shows that international investment law embodies an important formal component of the rule of law. Such restrictions on the exercise of public power have been described, in the context of the investment chapter of the North American Free Trade Agreement (NAFTA), as establishing 'a rule-based investment regime in which foreign direct investment can thrive'.[45]

ii. Predictability and Clarity

This brings us to consider a more intricate question as to whether and how international investment law realises the second formal element of the rule of law: the predictability and clarify of law itself. Let us try to consider the predictability and clarity of, first, the manner in which international investment law is 'set out' and, second, the way in which it is 'applied'.

International investment law is a complicated assembly of more than 3000 BITs and thus is deeply fragmented in nature and also incoherent and inconsistent,[46] which, arguably, undermines clarity in law.[47] At the same time, the observation about it varies depending on the level of abstraction about the identification of legal rules. Most BITs contain common elements, such as fair and equitable treatment (FET), most favoured-nation (MFN) and national treatment, and protection from illegal expropriation. These common elements do provide formal clarity for foreign investors as well as host and home states in that these rules are accessible and understandable to their addressees.[48] This does not mean that the more concrete

[44] Stephan Schill, *The Multilateralization of International Investment Law* (Cambridge, Cambridge University Press, 2009) 373.

[45] Brower and Steven (n 35) 193.

[46] Christoph Schreuer, 'Coherence and Consistency in International Investment Law' in R Echandi and others (eds), *Prospects in International Investment Law and Policy* (Cambridge; New York, Cambridge University Press, 2013) 391.

[47] See Chesterman (n 14) 356. Chesterman argues that fragmentation of the legal order undermines clarity—an important aspect of the rule of law.

[48] Schultz and Dupont (n 35).

meanings of rules given in most BITs are clear-cut; it is often the case that little guidance is given about their content.[49]

Opinions differ as to the extent of predictability and clarity in the application of international investment law—or in other words, over whether it is applied in a coherent and consistent fashion so as to create 'dependable guideposts' for the actions of foreign investors, host, and home states.[50] Some authors are of the view that BIT rules have become more precise and hence by implication, more predictable because of the 'ever more elaborate interpretations of relevant law rendered by international arbitrators sitting in investor-state disputes'.[51] However, arbitral tribunals have not been consistent in giving meaning to the commonly found terms in most BITs. There are examples where similar set of facts[52] or even the same provision of a BIT[53] has been interpreted differently by tribunals. This inconsistency in interpretation undermines the predictability of international investment law investment treaty arbitration[54] because it has failed to evolve dependable guideposts. It is also argued that because of the lack of an appellate review in international investment law, there has been a failure to minimise the risk of inconsistent arbitral awards.[55] The 'application' of international investment law thus casts doubt on the extent to which BITs materialise the element of 'predictability and clarity' in their legal practice.

iii. Public Powers Cannot Set or Change the Law at Will

The third formal element of the rule of law is a mechanism with which to protect public powers from setting or changing the law at will. In the

[49] The best example of such a broad and vague provision in BITs is the FET provision—see Vandevelde (n 2) 203; Sornarajah, *The International Law on Foreign Investment* (n 2) 349.

[50] Schultz and Dupont (n 35).

[51] Jose Alvarez, *Public International Law Regime Governing International Investment* (Brill; Nijhoff, The Hague, 2011) 25.

[52] The most commonly stated example of this is the 'Lauders case' where two arbitration tribunals gave different decisions on essentially the same set of facts for disputes brought under two different IIAs. The cases are: *CME Czech Republic BV v Czech Republic*, 13 Sept 2001, 14(3) World Trade and Arbitration Material 109 and *Lauder (Ronald) v Czech Republic*, 3 Sept 2001, 4 World Trade and Arbitration Materials 35.

[53] The Argentine cases on Art XI of the US-Argentina BIT are a good example of such inconsistency. Charles H Brower II, 'Obstacles and Pathways to Consideration of the Public Interest in Investment Treaty Disputes' (2009) 1 *Yearbook on International Investment Law and Policy* 347, 343–48. Also see Jürgen Kurtz, 'Adjudging the Exceptional at International Law: Security, Public Order and Financial Crisis' (2010) 59 *International and Comparative Law* Quarterly 325.

[54] See generally Stephan W Schill, 'Deference in Investment Treaty Arbitration: Re-conceptualizing the Standard of Review' (2012) 3 *Journal of International Dispute Settlement* 577.

[55] S Susan D Franck, 'The Legitimacy Crisis in Investment Treaty Arbitration: Privatizing Public International Law Through Inconsistent Decisions' (2005) 73 *Fordham Law Review* 1521.

context of BITs, this means having a mechanism to prevent states from amending or terminating BITs without recourse to legal rules. A few BITs indeed provide the process to be followed for amending the treaty.[56] One such example is Article 13(4) of the Chinese Model BIT of 2003, which provides that '[t]his Agreement may be amended by written agreement between the Contracting Parties. Any amendment shall enter into force under the same procedures required for entry into force of the present Agreement'.[57] In case the BIT is silent on this issue, rules regarding the amendment given in the Vienna Convention on Law of Treaties (VCLT) apply.[58] In principle, BITs and relevant international law therefore provide the mechanisms that require states to amend BITs though an agreement, and not at the will of just one country.

Also, many BITs provide procedures to be followed regarding the termination of BITs. For example, according to Article 16(1) of the Indian Model BIT, countries can terminate the BIT by giving a one-year notice.[59] Interestingly, despite the termination, the BIT shall continue to be effective for a further period of 15 years from the date of its termination in respect of investments made or acquired before the date of termination of the treaty.[60] The UK Model BIT of 2005 goes a step further and states that, despite termination, the BIT provisions shall be effective with regard to foreign investments made while the treaty is in force for a period of as long as 20 years after the date of termination and without prejudice to the application thereafter to the rules of general international law.[61]

These provisions ensure that, even if a country terminates its obligation under the treaty, it cannot escape liability for its sovereign regulatory actions for foreign investments made when the treaty was in force for the next 10 or 15 or 20 years. Similarly, for these years and for foreign investment made when the treaty was in force, the BIT provisions will continue to control the exercise of public power of the host state. Once the extended period of protection is over, public power of the host state in terms of

[56] Salacuse, *The Law of Investment Treaties* (n 2) 136.

[57] See Agreement Between the Government of the People's Republic of China and the Government of [...] on the Promotion and Protection of Investments in Dolzer and Schreuer, *Principles of International Investment Law* (n 1) 358.

[58] See Vienna Convention on the Law of Treaties, 23 May 1969, 1155 UNTS 311 (entered into force 27 Jan 1980) (1969) pt IV (Arts 39–41). Art 39 of the VCLT allows amendment of treaties by agreement between the parties and further states that the rules laid down in pt II of VCLT (Conclusion and Entry into Force of Treaties) apply to such a treaty except in so far as the treaty may otherwise provide.

[59] Indian Model Text of Bilateral Investment Promotion Agreement (BIPA): http://finmin.nic.in/the_ministry/dept_eco_affairs/icsection/Indian%20Model%20Text%20BIPA.asp.

[60] See Art 16(2) of the India Model BIT. In some instances this period is of 10 years. See Art 13(3) of the Chinese Model BIT of 2003.

[61] See Art 14 of the UK Model BIT of 2005. Also see Art 13(3) of the German Model BIT of 2008.

regulating foreign investment will not be subject to international treaty law, which, arguably, would weaken the international rule of law though the protection of foreign investment under customary international law would continue to exist. However, it is important to note that even if a host country terminates one of its BITs, foreign investors can still take advantage of the BIT protection by restructuring their investments so that it falls under another BIT of the host state.[62]

iv. Independent Adjudication of Disputes

Finally, the fourth element of the formal rule of law is a process of independent adjudication with which to ensure accountability of exercise of public power. Whether international investment law effectively embodies this element of the rule of law is a contentious issue.

The vast majority of BITs contain investment arbitration clauses and thereby provide for adjudication of investment disputes before an international tribunal. This covers both state-state arbitration and investor-state arbitration. Under the state-state arbitration, one party to the treaty can bring a claim against the other country. The investor-state dispute settlement provisions allow an individual foreign investor to directly bring a claim against the host state challenging its exercise of public power.[63] Most BITs allow foreign investors to bring claims against the host state even without exhausting local remedies.[64] In the large majority of BITs, these investor-state dispute settlement clauses offer unequivocal consent to arbitration to investors who are nationals of the other contracting state.[65] Whether the consent is unequivocal or not depends on the actual wording of the BIT. For example, phrases such as the contracting party 'hereby consents' or where the dispute 'shall be submitted' to arbitration imply an offer of unequivocal consent to arbitration.[66] This consent to arbitration, often, covers 'any dispute concerning an investment', which is quite

[62] Schill, *The Multilateralization of International Investment Law* (n 44) 373.

[63] See the discussion in Dolzer and Schreuer (n 1) 235–310; Salacuse, *The Law of Investment Treaties* (n 2) 353–92.

[64] Dolzer and Schreuer, ibid, 265. Also see *Helnan v Egypt*, Decision on Annulment 14 June 2010, paras 43–57; *Generation Ukraine, Inc v Ukraine*, Award 16 Sept 2003, para 13.4.

[65] Christoph Schreuer, 'Consent to Arbitrate' in P Muchlinski and others (eds), *The Oxford Handbook of International Investment Law* (Oxford, Oxford University Press, 2008) 832, 835–36. Also see Vandevelde (n 2) 433–39.

[66] See Art 8(1) of the Agreement Between the Government of United Kingdom of Great Britain and Northern Ireland and the Government of the Democratic Socialist Republic of Sri Lanka, 13 Feb 1980. Also see Dolzer and Schreuer (n 1) 258; Jan Paulsson, Arbitration Without Privity (1995) 10 *ICSID Review—Foreign Investment Law Journal* 235; *RosInvest v Russia*, Award on Jurisdiction 1 October 2007, paras 56–75; *Millicom v Senegal*, Decision on Jurisdiction 16 July 2010, paras 56 and 61–66.

broad, covering not just treaty breaches but also contractual breaches.[67] A foreign investor may accept this offer, for example, by instituting ICSID arbitral proceedings against the host state.[68]

The unequivocal consent to arbitrate by the host states in the large majority of BITs is a very important aspect from the perspective of the international rule of law. It ensures that states could be held accountable for the exercise of their public power by a third party ie, an international tribunal, which will have the power to review the action of the host state—whether executive, judicial, or legislative.[69] Indeed, it has been argued that arbitrators in investor-state dispute settlements foster the international rule of law by the independent and impartial application of the governing law.[70]

On the other hand, some question the independence and impartiality of the investment treaty arbitration mechanism primarily because of the unique way in which investment treaty arbitration engages with issues of public law.[71] As it has been discussed above, investment treaty arbitration addresses disputes between private foreign investors and the host state over a state's sovereign conduct or exercise of public power (public law questions) using a private law adjudicative model to settle international commercial arbitration disputes.[72] In other words, investment treaty arbitration also involves privately appointed party arbitrators where the procedure depends upon the rules of arbitration that the foreign investor elects, similarly to in international commercial arbitration.[73] Further, only foreign investors can bring claims against the host states and not the other way round, which gives rise to the apprehension that arbitrators will interpret the law in favour of claimants because their future arbitral appointments depend on foreign investors using the system.[74] Also, it is argued, that investment treaty arbitration lacks typical institutional safeguards for impartiality and independence, such as security of tenure for

[67] Vandevelde (n 2) 433. Also see Art 9(1) of the Indian Model BIT; Art 9(1) of the Chinese Model BIT; Art VIII(1) of the Cambodia-Vietnam BIT.

[68] See *Generation Ukraine v Ukraine*, Award 16 Sept 2003, paras 12.2 and 12.3.

[69] Andreas Kulick, *Global Public Interest in International Investment Law* (Cambridge; New York, Cambridge University Press, 2012) 93. See also Schil (n 44) 374.

[70] Brower and Schill, 'Is Arbitration a Threat or a Boom to the Legitimacy of International Investment Law' (n 35) 497. See also Petersmann, 'International Rule of Law and Constitutional Justice in International Investment Law and Arbitration' (n 23) 518.

[71] Van Harten, 'Investment Treaty Arbitration, Procedural Fairness, and the Rule of Law' (n 35).

[72] Private foreign investors and host states are not in a reciprocal relationship but in a regulatory relationship.

[73] See Franck, 'The Legitimacy Crisis in Investment Treaty Arbitration (n 55) 1543–44. See also Gus Van Harten, *Investment Treaty Arbitration and Public Law* (Oxford; New York, Oxford University Press, 2007).

[74] Van Harten, *Investment Treaty Arbitration and Public Law* (n 73).

those who decide disputes and the prohibition of outside remuneration.[75] These factors, it is argued, create an apprehension of bias in favour of claimants (foreign investors) and cast doubts about whether the investment treaty arbitration is an impartial adjudicative system that embodies the critical element of international rule of law.[76]

It is also argued that because the genesis of investment treaty arbitration is international commercial arbitration, which embodies confidentiality,[77] it lacks transparency[78]—a very important aspect of the rule of law. Thus, despite public interest and exercise of public power being involved in investment treaty arbitration claims, host states often do not divulge details about these claims to their citizens;[79] oral hearings are not accessible to the public; and final decisions are made public only with the consent of the parties.[80] Also, investment treaty arbitration lacks a system of appellate review, as discussed earlier, and thus has no provision to correct inconsistent decisions, which, in turn, poses a question as to the 'legitimacy' of the entire dispute resolution system.[81]

In sum, it can be said that the dispute resolution provision in international investment law is not perfect and needs improvement. Nevertheless, what needs to be appreciated is that international investment law has a dispute settlement provision that can hold states accountable for the exercise of public power—something, which is missing from many other spheres of public international law. This is a system that has been frequently used by foreign investors to enforce the accountability of host

[75] ibid. Also see Alan Scott Rau, 'Integrity in Private Judging' (1997) 38 *South Texas Law Review* 485, 521–22; Barnali Choudhury, 'Recapturing Public Power: Is Investment Arbitration's Engagement of the Public Interest Contributing to the Democratic Deficit?' (2008) 41 *Vanderbilt Journal of Transnational Law* 775, 818–21.

[76] Van Harten (n 35). See also Vicki Been and Joel Beauvais, 'The Global Fifth Amendment?' (2003) 78 *New York University Law Review* 30.

[77] For more on confidentiality in international commercial arbitration, see Ileana M Smeureanu, *Confidentiality in International Commercial Arbitration* (The Hague, Kluwer Law International, 2011).

[78] Choudhary, 'Recapturing Public Power' (n 75) 786. On the issue of confidentiality in investment treaty arbitration also, see Fortier, 'Investment Protection and the Rule of Law' (n 35); Guillermo Aguilar Alvarez and William W Park, 'The New Face of Investment Arbitration: NAFTA Chapter 11' (2003) 28 *Yale Journal of International Law* 365, 370; Organisation for Economic Cooperation and Development (OECD), 'Transparency and Third Party Participation in Investor-State Dispute Settlement Procedures' (2005) OECD Working Papers on International Investment, no 2005/01 available at: http://dx.doi.org/10.1787/524613550768; Craig Forcese, 'Does the Sky Fall? NAFTA Chapter 11 Dispute Settlement and Democratic Accountability' (2006)14 *Michigan State Journal of International Law* 315, 317; Franck (n 55) 1544–45.

[79] A good example of this is from India—more than a dozen foreign corporations have brought BIT claims against India, yet the Indian government has not made any information available regarding the nature of these claims and the public interest at stake.

[80] Forcese, 'Does the Sky Fall?' (n 78) 55; Franck (n 55) 1545.

[81] Franck, ibid.

states. Moreover, the significance of the investor-state dispute settlement system in fixing accountability of host states under international investment law, from an international rule of law perspective, needs to be appreciated by comparing it with the existing alternatives such as using local courts or using diplomatic protection to adjudicate disputes between foreign investors and host states. Access to local courts to fix states' responsibility might not be an attractive proposition for a variety of reasons such as domestic courts not being independent, lack of impartiality,[82] application of domestic law over international law in certain situations, and so forth.[83] Similarly, diplomatic protection where the home country espouses the case of the foreign investor before the host state is also not an attractive proposition because the home country might decide not to espouse the case of the foreign investor for political reasons and even if it espouses the case, it retains control over how the claim will be made and what settlement will be accepted.[84] Thus, from an international rule of law perspective, both access to local courts and use of diplomatic protection are weak mechanisms to hold states accountable for the exercise of their public power.

On the basis of the above discussion, there could be different views on the question of whether and how international investment law embodies the formal elements of the rule of law. It can be said that it has adopted some elements better than others. After having shown that international investment law contains certain elements of international rule, though to different degrees, we now proceed to examine the national contestation of international investment law and its impact on the international rule of law.

III. NATIONAL CONTESTATION

We now turn our focus to national contestation of international investment law by states and the impact that this could have on the elements of formal international rule of law embodied in international investment law. The discussion here will first provide the context and background to this national contestation (A) and then explain how states have contested international investment law (B).

[82] On lack of impartiality, see *Loewen Group Inc v United States*, ICSID ARB (AF)/98/3, 19 July 2002.

[83] Dolzer and Schreuer (n 1) 235; Salacuse, *The Law of Investment Treaties* (n 2) 357–58.

[84] Salacuse, ibid, 358. On diplomatic protection also, see Mavrommatis Palestine Concessions Case, PCIJ, Ser A, No 2, 12; *Barcelona Traction, Light and Power Co, Ltd (Belgium v Spain)* [1970] ICJ Reports (Judgment, 5 Feb 1970) 3, 44.

A. Context and Background to National Contestation

Before understanding the actual national contestation of international investment law, it is imperative to provide a context and background to such contestations. We divide this discussion on context and background into two parts. The first part focuses on the impact of international investment law on the domestic rule of law as a background to national contestation. The second part discusses the nature of investment treaty arbitration awards as the background to national contestation.

i. Impact of International Investment Law on the Domestic Rule of Law

There has been a debate on whether international investment law has positively or negatively impacted the domestic rule of law. On the one hand, it is contended that BITs, through investment treaty arbitration, strengthen the rule of law in the host state.[85] The argument is that BITs, through investment treaty arbitration, protect foreign investment by replacing dysfunctional courts (courts that have limited respect for rule of law) in countries that have a weak legal system.[86] Such substitution, it is observed, results in improvement of the regulatory quality of investment protection in the host state, thus bringing the host state to firmer adherence with the rule of law.[87] On the other hand, such positive appraisal has been challenged by a more critical account that the BIT legal regime 'constitutes a legal enclave of sorts' (by benefiting international claims available only to foreign investors and not to domestic investors) and has 'systematically subverted the evolution of robust rule of law institutions in the developing world'.[88] According to the critical view, the rule of law due to the BIT legal

[85] See the arguments in Gus Van Harten, 'Five Justifications for Investment Treaties: A Critical Appraisal' (2010) 2(1) *Trade, Law and Development* 1. See also Mary Hallward-Driemier, 'Do Bilateral Investment Treaties Attract Foreign Direct Investment? Only a Bit … and They Could Bite' (June 2003) available at: http://elibrary.worldbank.org/doi/pdf/10.1596/1813-9450-3121.

[86] Susan D Franck, 'Foreign Direct Investment, Investment Treaty Arbitration and Rule of Law' (2007) 19 *Pacific McGeorge Global Business and Development Law Journal* 337.

[87] Jan Paulsson, 'Enclaves of Justice', Conference Paper, Rule of Law Conference at University of Richmond School of Law (12 April 2007); Franck, 'Foreign Direct Investment, Investment Treaty Arbitration and Rule of Law' (n 86) (2006) 370; Julie A Maupin, 'Public and Private in International Investment Law: An Integrated Systems Approach' (2014) 54(2) *Virginia Journal of International Law* 367. On this, see also Tom Ginsburg, 'International Substitutes for Domestic Institutions: Bilateral Investment Treaties and Governance' (2005) 25(1) *International Review of Law and Economics* 107. In this regard, also see a recent empirical study throwing light on this functional aspect of investment treaty arbitration: Schultz and Dupont (n 35).

[88] Ronald J Daniels, 'Defecting on Development: Bilateral Investment Treaties and the Subversion of the Rule of Law in the Developing World' (Draft 23 March 2004), previously available at: www3.unisi.it/lawandeconomics/stile2004/daniels.pdf (link no longer working).

regime is subverted because 'the foreign investors rationally refrain from championing good and generalised rule of law reforms in the developing state, preferring instead to protect their interests by relying on the BIT rule of law enclave'.[89] In other words, the argument is that since investment treaty arbitration replaces domestic courts when it comes to protecting the interests of foreign investors, it disincentivises the reform of institutions at the domestic level and weakens the capacity of domestic institutions. Some also see this replacement as an onslaught on the domestic judicial mechanism of the host state where the foreign investor bypasses domestic legal system and uses investment treaty arbitration.[90]

ii. Nature and Kind of BIT Disputes Between Foreign Investors and Host States

In the last decade or so, BIT disputes between foreign investors and host states have covered a very wide array of regulatory measures. They concern, for instance, environmental policy,[91] sovereign decisions regarding privatisation,[92] regulatory issues related to supply of drinking water,[93] urban policy,[94] monetary policy,[95] laws and policies related to taxation,[96] policies related to re-organisation of public telephone services,[97] industrial policy related to sectors like media,[98] financial services,[99] banking,[100]

[89] ibid. See also Mark Halle and Luke Eric Peterson, *Investment Provisions in Free Trade Agreements and Investment Treaties: Opportunities and Threats for Developing Countries,* (Colombo, UNDP Regional Centre, 2005) 23–24.

[90] eg, in the case of India, in an investment treaty arbitration award called *White Industries v India,* the foreign investor whose claim regarding enforcement of an international commercial arbitration award was yet to be decided by the Indian courts, and the foreign investor successfully challenged the delay in enforcement as a violation of India's obligations under the India-Australia BIT.

[91] *Metalclad Corporation v United Mexican States* 5 ICSID 236; *Methanex Corporation v United States of America* (2005) 44 ILM 1345.

[92] *Eureka BV v Republic of Poland,* ICSID ARB/01/11, 19 Aug 2005.

[93] *Biwater Gauff Ltd v United Republic of Tanzania,* ICSID ARB/05/22, 24 July 2008.

[94] *MTD Equity v Republic of Chile* (2005) 44 ILM 91.

[95] *CMS Gas Transmission Co v Argentina,* ICISD ARB/01/8; *CMS Gas Transmission Company v Argentina,* ICSID ARB/01/8 (Annulment Proceedings); *Enron Corporation v Argentina,* ICSID ARB/01/3; *Enron Creditors Recovery Corp v Argentina,* ICSID ARB/01/3 (Annulment Proceeding); *Sempra Energy International v Argentina,* ICSID ARB/02/16; *Sempra Energy International v Argentina,* ICSID ARB/02/16 (Annulment Proceedings); *LG&E Energy Corporation v Argentina,* ICISD ARB/02/1; *Continental Casualty Company v Argentina,* ICSID ARB/03/9.

[96] *Occidental Exploration and Production Co v Republic of Ecuador,* LCIA UN 3467; *EnCana Corporation v Ecuador,* London Court of International Arbitration, 3 Feb 2006; *Feldman v Mexico,* ICSID ARB(AF)/99/1.

[97] *Telenor Mobile Communications v Republic of Hungary,* ICSID ARB/04/15.

[98] *CME v Czech Republic,* UNCITRAL Arbitration Proceedings, 3 Sept 2011; *R S Lauder v The Czech Republic,* 9 ICSID Reps 66, 3 Sept 2001.

[99] *Fireman's Fund Insurance Company v Mexico,* ICSID ARB(AF)/02/01, 17 July 2006.

[100] *Saluka Investments v The Czech Republic* (Partial Award), UNCITRAL, 17 March 2006.

energy,[101] public postal services,[102] electricity services,[103] motorway construction,[104] and tourism.[105] In addition to these regulatory areas, there have been instances where a host country's important public interest measures, such as public health[106] and sovereign debt restructuring,[107] have been challenged by foreign investors as potential breaches of BITs. The most sensitive have been the investment treaty arbitration (ITA) cases against Argentina,[108] where foreign investors challenged Argentina's regulatory measures to safeguard its economy from a complete collapse as a violation of Argentina's obligations under different BITs. There have also been cases where ITA tribunals have adjudicated over the actions of the judiciary.[109]

The fact that foreign investors challenge the sovereign actions of host states under BITs should not come as a surprise because that is what BITs are meant to do—to hold states accountable for the exercise of their public power while dealing with foreign investment. However, adjudication of such a large and wide gamut of sovereign regulatory measures by ITA tribunals as potential breaches of BITs has the potential to affect a large part of the population of the host state (for example, if a health measure is found to have breached the BIT, the state could remove the health measure affecting the local population) and may involve the award of substantive damages to foreign investors,[110] resulting in diversion of taxpayers' money to foreign investors, and generate a backlash or contestation against international investment law.[111] This backlash has been further fuelled by the

[101] *Duke Energy Electroquil Partners v Republic of Ecuador*, ICSID ARB/04/19, 18 Aug 2008.

[102] *United Parcel Service of America v Canada*, Arbitration Under Chapter 11 of NAFTA, 24 May 2007.

[103] *Nykomb Synergetics v Republic of Latvia*, Stockholm Chamber of Commerce, 16 Dec 2003.

[104] *Bayindir Insaat Ticaret VeSanayi AS v Islamic Republic of Pakistan*, ICSID ARB/03/29.

[105] *Waguih Elie George v Egypt*, ICSID ARB/05/15, 1 June 2009.

[106] *Philip Morris Asia Ltd v The Commonwealth of Australia*, UNCITRAL, PCA 2012-12.

[107] *Abaclat and Others v Argentina*, ICSID Case No ARB/07/5, Decision on Jurisdiction and Admissibility, 4 August 2011.

[108] *CMS v Argentina; CMS Gas Transmission Company v Argentina*, (Annulment Proceedings); *Enron Corporation v Argentina; Sempra Energy International v Argentina; LG&E Energy Corporation v Argentina; Continental Casualty Company v Argentina* (n 95).

[109] *Saipem SpA v Bangladesh*, ICSID ARB/05/7, 30 June 2009.

[110] eg, in *CME Czech Republic BV v Czech Republic* (n 98), Czech Republic paid US $ 355 million to CME in damages for violating the IIA on account of adopting a regulatory measure. As per one study on NAFTA—to date, Canada has paid damages to the tune of $ CAD 157 million to NAFTA claimants; Mexico has paid damages of more than $187 million; interestingly, the US has not paid any damages, as it has never lost a NAFTA case. Also all three NAFTA countries have incurred significant costs in defending their claims—Canadian Centre for Policy Alternatives (2010), NAFTA Chapter 11 Investor-State Disputes available at: www.policyalternatives.ca/sites/default/files/uploads/publications/National%20 Office/2010/11/NAFTA%20Dispute%20Table.pdf.

[111] LT Wells 'Backlash to Investment Arbitration: Three Causes' in M Waibel and others (eds), *The Backlash Against Investment Arbitration* (The Hague, Kluwer Law, 2010) 341. Also

fact that in instances involving a similar set of facts,[112] the same provision of a BIT[113] has been interpreted differently depending on tribunals. This inconsistency has led to a contestation, as is reflected in the writings of academics[114] and the actions of civil society organisations.

B. Different Forms of National Contestation

The contestation discussed above however went further than academic debates, and has been reflected in the action of states.[115] It is not a coincidence that many states that have contested against international investment law have been those against whom foreign investors have brought BIT claims.[116] As will be explained in this section, the national contestation of international investment law by states has taken different forms.

i. Pulling Out of the System

Some states have adopted the most dramatic and extreme form of contestation by terminating their BITs and thus, pulling out of international investment law.[117] One such country is Ecuador, which has witnessed the

see Stephan Schill, 'Enhancing International Investment Law's Legitimacy: Conceptual and Methodological Foundations of a New Public Law Approach' (2011) 52 *Virginia Journal of International Law* 57, 69 (observing that 'the extent to which investment treaties limit a state's regulatory powers and subject the exercise of such powers to liability claims by foreign investors may become the litmus test for the future viability of the system'). See also Franck (n 55); Van Harten (n 73) 63; 757; Asha Kaushal, 'Revisiting History: How the Past Matters for the Present Backlash Against the Foreign Investment Regime' (2009) 50(2) *Harvard International Law Journal* 491; Robert Howse, 'Sovereignty, Lost and Found' in W Shan and others (eds), *Redefining Sovereignty in International Economic Law* (Oxford, Hart Publishing, 2008) 72–73; Choudhary (n 75); Suzzane A Spears, 'The Quest for Policy Space in New Generation of International Investment Agreements' (2010) 13 *Journal of International Economic Law* 1037.

112 The most commonly stated example of this is the 'Lauders case' where two arbitration tribunals gave different decisions on essentially the same set of facts for disputes brought under two different BITs. The cases are: *CME Czech Republic BV v Czech Republic* and *Lauder (Ronald) v Czech Republic* (n 52).

113 See Brower II, 'Obstacles and Pathways' (n 53) for diverging jurisprudence on Art XI of the US-Argentina BIT.

114 In this regard, see the public statement issued by many leading academics on ITA: Public Statement on the International Investment Regime (31 Aug 2010) available at: www.osgoode.yorku.ca/public-statement-international-investment-regime-31-august-2010/.

115 Omar E Garcia-Bolivar, 'Sovereignty vs Investment Protection: Back to Calvo?' (2009) 24(2) *ICSID Review: Foreign Investment Law Journal* 464, 470–74.

116 These countries include Bolivia, Ecuador, Venezuela, South Africa, India, and so forth.

117 Even if a country terminates its BITs, which is the most important source of international investment law, customary international investment law will continue to apply for the protection of foreign investment.

third-highest claims by foreign investors after Argentina and Venezuela.[118] In 2008, Ecuador denounced nine of its BITs.[119] In July 2009, the Russian Federation terminated the provisional application of the Energy Charter Treaty.[120] South Africa has started terminating its BITs. In September 2012, it terminated its BIT with Belgium and Luxembourg and then terminated the BITs with Spain and Germany in 2013.[121] This decision to terminate BITs was made after reviewing its entire BIT programme in light of an investment treaty arbitration challenge from foreign investors for South Africa's Black Empowerment Programme.[122] This challenge prompted South Africa to review its BIT programme and to conclude that it would prefer to have a single domestic legislation aimed at simultaneously protecting foreign investment and South Africa's right to regulate instead of BITs.[123] Venezuela had sent a notice terminating its BIT with Netherlands because it felt that the particular BIT came in the way of implementing policy changes in its energy sector.[124] Recently, Indonesia expressed the intention to terminate all of its 67 BITs.[125]

Termination of BITs means that exercise of public power will not be subject to treaty law anymore. Though it will continue to be subjected to customary international law, this is quite inadequate in protecting foreign investment. In other words, termination of BITs is a frontal attack on a very important component of formal international rule of law embodied in the international investment law regime.

ii. Denunciating or Modifying Investor-State Dispute Settlement Mechanisms

Another form of national contestation is directed at changing or altering the investor-state dispute settlement mechanism. There have been

[118] Allen & Overy, 'Ecuador Establishes Commission to Audit its Bilateral Investment Treaties' (13 Nov 2013) available at: www.allenovery.com/publications/en-gb/Pages/Ecuador-establishes-Commission-to-audit-its-Bilateral-Investment-Treaties.aspx.

[119] World Investment Report, *Global Value Chains: Investment and Trade for Development* (Geneva; New York, United Nations, 2013) 108. Ecuador has also established a commission to audit its BITs: see Allen & Overy, 'Ecuador Establishes Commission to Audit its Bilateral Investment Treaties' (n 118).

[120] Amelia Hadfield and Adnan Amkhan-Banyo, 'From Russia with Cold Feet: EU-Russia Energy Relations, and the Energy Charter Treaty' (2013) 1(1) *International Journal of Energy Security and Environmental Research* 1.

[121] Sean Woolfrey, 'Another BIT Bites the Dust' (30 Oct 2013) available at: www.tralac.org/discussions/article/5342-another-bit-bites-the-dust.html.

[122] *Piero Foresti, Laura de Carli & Others v The Republic of South Africa,* ICSID ARB(AF)/07/01.

[123] Woolfrey, 'Another BIT Bites the Dust' (n 121).

[124] Luke E Peterson, 'Venezuela Surprises Netherlands With Termination Notice of BIT' (16 May 2008) available at: www.iareporter.com/articles/20091001_93.

[125] Termination Bilateral Investment Treaty available at: http://indonesia.nlembassy.org/organization/departments/economic-affairs/termination-bilateral-investment-treaty.html.

instances of countries denunciating the Convention on the ICSID.[126] Bolivia and Ecuador gave up their membership of ICSID,[127] and in 2012, Venezuela sent a notice to the World Bank denouncing the ICSID Convention.[128] These examples are of countries that denunciated not only individual BITs but also the most important convention that provides for investor-state dispute settlement.

On the other hand, there are also instances where countries have not terminated BITs, but have decided not to have the investor-state dispute resolution mechanism but only a state-state dispute settlement mechanism. An example is Australia,[129] which decided not to have investor-state dispute settlement mechanisms in a clear response to the notice given by Philip Morris (Asia) Limited challenging Australia's tobacco regulations.[130]

In terms of the international rule of law discussion, this means that while Australia is willing to subject the exercise of its public power to international treaty law, it wishes to change the method by which it will be held accountable for this. It could be argued, however, that this cannot be said to be an attack on the international rule of law component on enforcement embodied in international investment law because Australia is only opposing the method of fixing accountability for exercise of public power and not fixing accountability as such.

In India, in the aftermath of the investment treaty arbitral award issued against India—*White Industries v India*[131]—it was suggested by one arm of the Indian government (Ministry of Commerce) that India should

[126] Convention on the Settlement of Investment Disputes Between States and Nations of other States.

[127] For detailed discussion on the legal effect of these denunciations, see Antonios Tzanakopoulos, 'Denunciation of the ICSID Convention under the General International Law of Treaties' in R Hofmann and CJ Tams (eds), *International Investment Law and General International Law: From Clinical Isolation to Systemic Integration?* (Baden-Baden, Nomos Publishers, 2011) 75. Both Bolivia and Ecuador have faced many ITA disputes so far: see the list of cases on the Investment Treaty Arbitration, available at: http://italaw.com/.

[128] ICSID News Release, 'Venezuela Submits a Notice Under Article 71 of the ICSID Convention' (26 Jan 2012) available at: http://icsid.worldbank.org/ICSID/FrontServlet?requestType=CasesRH&actionVal=OpenPage&PageType=AnnouncementsFrame&FromPage=Announcements&pageName=Announcement100. Venezuela has also faced many ITA disputes: see the list of cases on the Investment Treaty Arbitration, available at: http://italaw.com/.

[129] US-Australia FTA does not contain investor-state dispute resolution. See Gillard Government Trade Policy Statement, 'Trading Our Way to More Jobs and Prosperity' (April 2011).

[130] 'Philip Morris Sues Australian Government over Tobacco Laws' (*The Guardian*, 21 Nov 2011) available at: www.guardian.co.uk/world/2011/nov/21/philip-morris-australia-tobacco-laws. Although, the new Australian government, then led by Tony Abbott, has decided that it will decide on investor-state dispute settlement provisions on a case-by-case basis, thus signalling a change in the previous policy. See Luke Nottage, 'Investor-State Dispute Settlement Back for Australia's Free Trade Agreements' (*Japanese Law in Asia-Pacific Socio-Economic Context*, 17 Dec 2013) available at: http://blogs.usyd.edu.au/japaneselaw/2013/12/isds_back.html.

[131] *White Industries Australia Limited v Republic of India*, UNCITRAL, Final Award 30 Nov 2011.

not include investor-state arbitration provisions in future BITs in order to ensure that India's sovereign measures are not challenged under the investor-state dispute settlement mechanisms.[132] However, this is not India's official position.[133]

Opposition to investor-state dispute settlement is certainly an attack on the kind of enforcement mechanism that is preferred in international investment law.[134] The history of BITs shows that the inclusion of the investor-state dispute settlement provision in these treaties was to remedy one of the great deficiencies of customary international law's lack of an '*effective and binding mechanism to resolve investment disputes*'[135] and thus the inability to hold states accountable for the exercise of their public power.

iii. Recalibrating BITs

This form of national contestation is aimed at tweaking and adapting existing BITs or rebalancing existing BITs to ensure that foreign investment is protected from arbitrary state action without undermining the ability of host states to regulate in the public interest.[136] There are quite a few examples of this from the newer treaties that states have negotiated. For example, the Japan-Papua New Guinea BIT of 26 April 2011 contains provisions that permit prudential measures relating to financial services, and temporary safeguard measures to deal with balance-of-payments and external financial difficulties, even in contravention of national treatment.[137] Another example is from the final draft of the Central America-Dominican Republic Free Trade Agreement (CAFTA-DR) where the MFN provision is limited to establishment, acquisition, expansion, management, operation

[132] Asit Ranjan Mishra, 'India May Exclude Clause on Lawsuits from Trade Pacts' (*Livemint*, 29 Jan 2012) available at: www.livemint.com/Home-Page/dTXmHa0mYUyRrFko4H-biLP/India-may-exclude-clause-on-lawsuits-from-trade-pacts.html.

[133] ibid. See also Mihaela Papa, 'Emerging Powers in International Dispute Settlement: From Legal Capacity Building to a Level Playing Field' (2013) 4(1) *Journal of International Dispute Settlement* 83, 103.

[134] For criticism of Australia's approach, see Jürgen Kurtz, 'Australia's Rejection of Investor-State Dispute Settlement: Causation, Omission and Implication' (2012) 27(1) *ICSID Review: Foreign Investment Law Journal* 65; Luke Nottage, 'Throwing the Baby out with the Bathwater: Australia's New Policy on Treaty-Based Investor-State Arbitration and its Impact on Asia' (2013) 37(2) *Asian Studies Review* 253.

[135] Salacuse, *The Law of Investment Treaties* (n 2) 137.

[136] Muthucumaraswamy Sornarajah, 'Mutations of Neo Liberalism in International Investment Law' (2011) 3(1) *Trade, Law and Development* 203, 229. Also see Federico Ortino, 'Refining the Content and Role of Investment "Rules" and "Standards": A new Approach to International Treaty Making' (2013) 28 *ICSID Review: Foreign Investment Law Journal* 152, 157. For more on the recalibration phase of international investment law, see Jürgen Kurtz, 'The Shifting Landscape of International Investment Law and its Commentary' (2012) 106 *American Journal of International Law* 686.

[137] See the Japan-Papua New Guinea BIT, Arts 17 and 21.

and the like and does not include matters related to dispute settlement—a clear indicator of rejecting the ruling given in *Mafezzini v Kingdom of Spain* and thus prohibiting an expansive interpretation of MFN.[138]

India, for example, has decided to review all its existing BITs in order to rebalance investment protection with the right of the host state to regulate in the interest of non-investment objectives.[139] In 2001, NAFTA Free Trade Commission (FTC)—a body composed of the representatives of all the three NAFTA states—issued a note of interpretation aimed at limiting and rejecting the expansive interpretation given by arbitral tribunals on the meaning of fair and equitable treatment (FET),[140] thus showing the contestation in the form of clarifying the rule that restricted the state's public power. Canada, in response to the concerns expressed by the civil society on the effect of investment treaties on Canada's regulatory power, adopted a new model BIT in 2004.[141] Even Norway developed a new model BIT in 2008, in response to concerns related to BITs and host states' regulatory power.[142] However, Norway is yet to adopt this model since concerns arose that it does not balance investment protection with regulation.[143] The Czech Republic has renegotiated more than 20 BITs following its accession to the EU in May 2004, which was aimed at ensuring consistency between those treaties and EU law.[144] Some recent Chinese BITs, in response to concerns over the possibility of investment tribunals broadly interpreting concepts such as 'indirect expropriation', provide that regulatory measures for the protection of public welfare shall not constitute an indirect expropriation.[145]

In 2004, the US adopted a new model BIT in an effort to address the apprehensions that the 1994 model BIT did not balance investment protection with regulatory power.[146] The change in the approach of the US

[138] For more on this, see Efraim Chalamish, 'The Future of Bilateral Investment Treaties: A De Facto Multilateral Agreement?' (2009) 34(2) *Brooklyn Journal of International Law* 303, 331.

[139] For more on this, see Prabhash Ranjan, 'India and Bilateral Investment Treaties—A Changing Landscape (2014) 29 (2) *ICSID Review—Foreign Investment Law Journal* 219.

[140] Salacuse, *The Law of Investment Treaties* (n 2) 225.

[141] Andrew Newcombe, 'Canada's new model Foreign Investment Protection Agreement' (Aug 2004) available at: http://italaw.com/documents/CanadianFIPA.pdf.

[142] 'Norway Proposes Significant Reforms to its Investment Treaty Practices' (*Investment Treaty News*, 27 March 2008) available at: www.iisd.org/pdf/2008/itn_mar27_2008.pdf.

[143] 'Norway Shelves its Draft Model Bilateral Investment Treaty' (*Investment Treaty News*, 8 June 2009) available at: www.iisd.org/itn/2009/06/08/norway-shelves-its-proposed-model-bilateral-investment-treaty/.

[144] UNCTAD, *World Investment Report—Global Value Chains: Investment and Trade for Development* (New York; Geneva, UN, 2013) 108.

[145] See Free Trade Agreement between the Government of New Zealand and the Government of the People's Republic of China, 28 May 2004, Annex 13. For a full discussion on new trends in investment treaty making, see Stephan W Schill and Marc Jacob, 'Trends in International Investment Agreements, 2010–11: The Increasing Complexity of International Investment Law' (2013) 3 *Oxford Yearbook of International Investment Law and Policy* 141.

[146] See Kenneth J Vandevelde, *US International Investment Agreements* (New York; Oxford, Oxford University Press, 2009) 64–82 for a detailed description of the third wave of the US

towards BITs came about when foreign investors started suing the US government for BIT violation.[147] Even after the adoption of the 2004 model BIT, the Obama administration announced that it would 'review the implementation of our FTAs and BITs to ensure that they advance the public interest'.[148] Elucidating further on this, the Chairman of the Sub-committee on Trade of the Committee on Ways and Means, while holding a hearing on investment obligations in US BITs, said:

> concerns have been expressed regarding these investment provisions. These concerns include: whether our FTAs and BITs give foreign investors in the United States greater rights than U.S. investors have under U.S. law; whether the FTAs and BITs give governments the 'regulatory and policy space' needed to protect the environment and the public welfare;[149]

In other words, concerns were expressed as to whether BITs unduly restricted the exercise of public power of the US. The US finally adopted a new model BIT in 2012.[150]

This kind of contestation would change the nature of the first element of formal international rule of law discussed in this chapter. By recalibrating their BITs, countries are still willing to subject the exercise of their public power to law. However, the manner of this subjection is undergoing some change. The newer generation of BITs that attempt to rebalance investment protection with the host country's right to regulate are more deferential to the exercise of public power of the host state and provide more explicit carve-outs for domestic public spaces in host states.

IV. INTERNATIONAL IMPACT OF NATIONAL CONTESTATIONS

The contestation by states has activated the global community to find innovative solutions to the challenges posed to the international investment

BIT programme focusing on the conditions that made the US change its approach towards BITs. Also see Spears, 'The Quest for Policy Space in New Generation of International Investment Agreements' (n 111) 1038.

[147] Vandevelde, US International Investment Agreements (n 146) 64–65. Jose Alvarez has argued that the change in the US approach to BITs was due to the realisation within the US that it could be at the receiving end of foreign investment flows. See Jose Alvarez, 'The Once and Future Foreign Investment Regime' in M Arsanjani and others (eds), *Looking to the Future* (Leiden; Boston, Martinus Nijhoff, 2011) 607, 625–26.

[148] Hearing Before the Committee on Ways and Means, US House of Representatives, One Hundred Eleventh Congress, First Session, 14 May 2009, Serial 111-20 (US Government Printing Office 2010) at 2, available at: www.gpo.gov/fdsys/pkg/CHRG-111hhrg53473/pdf/CHRG-111hhrg53473.pdf.

[149] Hearing Before the Committee on Ways and Means (2010), ibid. See also 2012 US Model Bilateral Investment Treaty, *Treaty Between The Government of the United States of America and the Government of [Country] Concerning the Encouragement and Reciprocal Protection of Investment*, available at: www.state.gov/documents/organization/188371.pdf.

[150] 2012 US Model Bilateral Investment Treaty, ibid.

law regime. Before focusing on the reaction of ITA tribunals to this national contestation, this section discusses how international investment law has responded to the national contestation.

A. Impact on Scholarship

Academic writings in the field of international investment law clearly show the impact of this national contestation. There is a greater focus on mapping and outlining several ways in which one can understand international investment law, including a public or private international law paradigm or a public law paradigm.[151] Also more and more writings are appearing on how to rebalance foreign investment protection with a host country's regulatory power.

While some writings merely diagnose this problem,[152] some also propose a cure to the problem. So far, the scholarship has produced three kinds of cures to the problems that states have brought to light through their contestation, ie, the problem of BITs and investor-state dispute settlement unduly encroaching upon the regulatory power of the host state. The first kind of cure relates to modifying or revising the BIT provisions—something that states have already started doing (recalibration of BITs discussed above).[153] This reaction recognises that while the exercise of public power of states that affects foreign investment should be restricted through BITs, this restriction should not unduly encroach upon the exercise of public power for public welfare.[154] Some argue for the reform and reinvigoration of BITs in order to strike a balance between investment protection and the host state's right to regulate.[155] National contestation of international investment law has also triggered proposals to reform and improve investor-state dispute settlement.[156] These proposals range from debating revision of BITs for improving the dispute settlement mechanism

[151] See Van Harten (n 73); Anthea Roberts, 'Actors and Analogies Shaping the Investment Treaty System' (2013) 107 *American Journal of International Law* 45–94; Maupin, 'Public and Private in International Investment Law' (n 87).

[152] See various papers published in Waibel and others (eds), *Backlash Against Investment Arbitration* (n 111).

[153] See Kurtz 'The Shifting Landscape of International Investment Law (n 136).

[154] See Ortino 'Refining the Content and Role of Investment (n 136).

[155] Peter Muchlinski, 'Towards a Coherent International Investment System: Key Issues in the Reform of International Investment Law' in Echandi and others (eds), *Prospects in International Investment Law and Policy* (n 46) 411; Kate Miles, *The Origins of International Investment Law* (Cambridge; New York, Cambridge University Press, 2013) 351, 351–72.

[156] On this question, see Jean E Kalicki and Anna Joubin-Bret, 'Introduction TDM Special Issue on "Reform of Investor-State Dispute Settlement: In Search of a Roadmap"' (2014) 11 *Transnational Dispute Management* (TDM); and other contributions in the special issue.

to increasing the transparency of the investor-state tribunals to establishing a system of appellate review in international investment law.[157]

The second kind of cure offered by some is to interpret BITs in a manner that is supportive of the host country's right to regulate. This puts the onus on arbitrators and not on countries to balance investment protection with the host country's regulatory power. In this regard, some authors argue for conceptualising international investment law as part of a public law system and using tools such as proportionality in balancing investment protection with the host state's regulatory power.[158] Some also argue that investor-state dispute settlement tribunals should use deferential judicial review like margin of appreciation in reviewing the conduct of the state with respect to BITs.[159] Others debate on different standards of review that investor-state dispute settlement can use and argue that standards developed within the WTO could be used as possible models in investor-state dispute settlement.[160] Arguments have also been made to conceptualise the investment treaty system (international investment law) through the lens of judicial review in order to develop a methodology that properly balances investment protection with the sovereign right to regulate.[161]

The third kind of cure relates to improving the institutional design of arbitral dispute settlement. It has been argued that arbitrators in international investment law are appointed on a case-by-case basis and many a times may act as counsel in similar sort of disputes thus raising issues related to conflict of interest.[162] Hence, it has been proposed that a world

[157] See ibid.

[158] Benedict Kingsbury and Stephan W Schill, 'Public Law Concepts to Balance Investors' Rights with State Regulatory Actions in the Public Interest—the Concept of Proportionality' in SW Schill (eds), *International Investment Law and Comparative Public Law* (Oxford, Oxford University Press, 2010) 75; Caroline Henckels, 'Indirect Expropriation and the Right to Regulate: Revisiting Proportionality Analysis and the Standard of Review in Investor-State Arbitration (2012) 15(1) *Journal of International Economic Law* 223; Andreas Kulick, *Global Public Interest in International Investment Law* (Cambridge; New York, Cambridge University Press, 2012) 168–224; Ursula Kriebaum, 'Regulatory Takings: Balancing the Interests of the Investor and the State' (2007) 8 *Journal of World Investment and Trade* 717. See also Santiago Montt, *State Liability in Investment Treaty Arbitration* (Oxford, Hart Publishing, 2009).

[159] Caroline Henckels, 'Balancing Investment Protection and the Public Interest: The Role of the Standard of Review and the Importance of Deference in Investor-State Arbitration' (2013) 4 *Journal of International Dispute Settlement* 197; William W Burke-White and Anreas Von Staden, 'Private Litigation in Public Law Sphere: The Standard of Review in Investor-State Arbitrations' (2010) 35 *Yale Journal of International Law* 283; Julian Arato, 'Margin of Appreciation in International Investment Law' (2014) 54 *Virginia Journal of International Law.*

[160] Valentia Vadi and Lukasz Gruszczynski, 'Standards of Review in International Investment Law and Arbitration: Multilevel Governance and Commonweal' (2013) 16 *Journal of International Economic Law* 613.

[161] Federico Ortino, 'The Investment Treaty Arbitration as Judicial Review' (2013) 24(3) *American Review of International Arbitration* 437.

[162] Vaughan Lowe, 'Regulation or Expropriation' (2002) 55 *Current Legal Problems* 447, 464–65. Also see Philippe Sands, 'Conflict and Conflicts in Investment Treaty Arbitration: Ethical Standards for Counsel' in C Brown and K Mills (eds), *Evolution in Investment Treaty Law and Arbitration* (Cambridge, Cambridge University Press, 2011) 19.

investment court be created to act as an impartial and independent adjudicator to settle investor-state disputes.[163] Arguably, the absence of an appellate system in investor-state dispute settlement, which could correct the divergent interpretations of different arbitral tribunals and hence enhance certainty and predictability in the system, is also responsible for the problems affecting international investment law.[164] Thus, it has been proposed that an appellate mechanism be built for investment treaty arbitration.[165]

B. Reaction of ITA Tribunals and Arbitral Institutions

It might not be easy to determine that investment treaty arbitration tribunals have reacted to national contestation, because an arbitral tribunal will rarely say that a particular award is a reaction to the contestation of states to international investment law. However, one can still discern some signals from investment treaty arbitration tribunals. Many tribunals have recognised the right of the host state to adopt 'non-discriminatory', 'good faith' regulation in public interest without attracting any international liability.[166]

Similarly, many ITA tribunals have rejected overtly expansive investment-friendly alternatives and preferred a more balanced interpretation, showing deference to the host states especially when it comes to judging its domestic issues. This has been seen, for example, in the context of the interpretation of the fair and equitable treatment (FET) provision in BITs. The tribunal in *Parkerings v Lithuania*[167] stated that

> It is each State's undeniable right and privilege to exercise its sovereign legislative power. A State has the right to enact, modify or cancel a law at its own discretion. Save for the existence of an agreement, in the form of a stabilisation clause or otherwise, there is nothing objectionable about the amendment brought to the regulatory framework existing at the time an investor made its investment.[168]

[163] Van Harten (n 73).

[164] Franck (n 55) 1521.

[165] ibid. Further proposals to improve the institutional design and its functioning are establishing a 'roster' for the composition of the 'tribunal': Joachim Karl, 'International Investment Arbitration: A Threat to State Sovereignty' in Shan and others (eds), *Redefining Sovereignty in International Economic Law* (n 111) 225; allowing for amicus curiae submissions; allowing non-parties to have access to arbitral proceedings. See generally Barnali Choudhury, 'Recapturing Public Power' (2008) 41 *Vanderbilt Journal of Transnational Law* 775, 818–21.

[166] *Methanex Corporation v Mexico*, NAFTA Award 3 August 2005; *Tecmed v Mexico*, ICSID ARB/AF (00)/2.

[167] *Parkerings-Compaginet v Lithuania*, ICSID ARB/05/08, Award 11 Sept 2007.

[168] ibid para 334. Also see *BG Group v Argentina*, UNCITRAL, 24 December 2007, para 298; *Lemire v Ukraine*, ICSID Case No ARB, /06/18, 28 March 2011, para 285.

Similarly, the tribunal in *Impregilo v Argentina* said that 'The legitimate expectations of foreign investors cannot be that the State will never modify the legal framework, especially in times of crisis, but certainly investors must be protected from unreasonable modifications of that legal framework'.[169]

Similarly, other tribunals have been deferential to states. For example, in *Frontier Petroleum Service Ltd v Czech Republic*, the arbitral tribunal acknowledged that 'States enjoy a certain margin of appreciation in determining what their own conception of international public policy is'.[170] In *Continental Casualty v Argentina*, the arbitral tribunal held that states should have a 'significant margin of appreciation' to address issues of 'public order and essential security interest'.[171]

Some tribunals have also increased transparency and inclusivity to some extent; for example, the tribunal in *Suez v Argentina*[172] authorised petitioners to apply for leave to make amicus curiae submissions. Similarly, in the context of NAFTA, there have been few examples of transparency—for example, portions of the oral hearings were simultaneously broadcast and opened to the public in both *Methanex v USA*[173] and *UPS v Canada*.[174] Recently, the United Nations Commission on International Trade Law (UNCITRAL), in order to boost transparency in investment treaty arbitration and its accessibility to the public, has adopted new rules on transparency in treaty-based investor-state arbitration.[175]

V. CONCLUSION

This chapter has shown that international investment law, in its present form, possesses some elements of the formal conception of international rule of law notwithstanding the debate on the extent of these rules being reflected. Some may argue that the national contestation of international investment law is undermining the formal element of international rule of

[169] *Impregilo v Argentina*, ICSID ARB/07/17, 21 June 2011, para 291.

[170] *Frontier Petroleum Service Ltd v Czech Republic*, Final Award 12 Nov 2010, para 527, available at: www.italaw.com/documents/FrontierPetroleumv.CzechRepublicAward.pdf.

[171] *Continental Casualty Company v Argentine Republic*, ICSID ARB/03/09, 5 Sept 2008, at para 181 available at: http://italaw.com/documents/ContinentalCasualtyAward.pdf.

[172] *Suez, Sociedad General de Aguas de Barcelona, SA and Vivendi Universal, SA v Argentine Republic*, ICSID ARB/03/19.

[173] *Methanex Corp v United States*, Amicus, US Department of state available at: www.state.gov/s/l/c5821.htm.

[174] See *United Parcel Serv of Am, Inc v Canada (US v Ca.)* Decision Regarding Amicus Intervention available at: www.state.gov/documents/organization/6033.pdf.

[175] UNCITRAL Rules on Transparency in Treaty Based Investor-State Arbitration (effective from 1 April 2014) available at: www.uncitral.org/uncitral/en/uncitral_texts/arbitration/2014Transparency.html.

law as found in international investment law. However, this would be too sweeping. A more nuanced conclusion would be that on-going national contestation of international investment law provides opportunities for a critical revision of the formal elements of international rule of law. While some countries have followed an extreme approach, which could be compared to pulling out of the system altogether, many other countries are contesting this regime through more nuanced approaches such as changing the degree of restriction on the exercise of their public power that affects foreign investment so as to have more deference in deciding questions of public welfare. Similarly, the new treaty practice is becoming increasingly more complex and detailed with countries being more specific about the content of the rules, which, over a period of time, will lend more predictability and clarity to the application of international investment law. Finally, this national contestation has forced all actors (the academic community and arbitral tribunals) to fundamentally rethink many critical issues and to find solutions to provide greater deference to host states in exercising their public power without compromising on protection of foreign investment, which is anything but weakening international rule of law.

6

Domestic Non-Judicial Institutions in the Development of the International Rule of Law

RENÉ URUEÑA

I. INTRODUCTION

THE LAST COUPLE of decades have seen the emergence of global regulation without the medium of treaties, treaty-based institutions, international customary law, or more fundamentally, the traditional expression of state consent. Regulatory networks (such as the Basel Committee on Banking Supervision),[1] public-private entities (such as the International Organization for Standardization (ISO)),[2] and purely private entities (such as the Fédération Internationale de Football Association (FIFA)[3] or privatised public utilities at the transnational level),[4] among many others, have become crucial players in determining the distribution of global regulatory power today. Domestic agencies, such as the US Environmental Protection Agency, also emerged as influential actors in regulating issues which are of global concern.

These networks, entities, and agencies reveal a transformed global regulatory landscape that features, for instance, private actors exercising public powers, informal norms that carry the weight equivalent to that of formally binding instruments, and decentralised networks of regulation. However, the traditional doctrine of international legal sources seems

[1] See Anne-Marie Slaughter and David Zaring, 'Networking Goes International: An Update' (2006) 2 *Annual Review of Law and Social Science* 211.

[2] See Jan Klabbers, 'Reflections on Soft International Law in a Privatized World' (2005) 16 *Finnish Yearbook of International Law* 313 (exploring soft law regulation by the ISO).

[3] See Lorenzo Casini, *Il diritto globale dello sport* (Milan, Giuffrè, 2010).

[4] See Bronwen Morgan, *Water on Tap: Rights and Regulation in the Transnational Governance of Urban Water Services* (Cambridge, Cambridge University Press, 2011).

to be an unreliable map to navigate this new reality.[5] Hence, there has been renewed interest from some international legal scholars to rethink it. Just as a cartographer who has recently discovered GPS technology tries to include new islands or straits in ever-more accurate maps, recent academic projects try to factor in new forms of law-making in their ever-expanding legal charts, pondering their risks and opportunities, and suggesting ways to make them more democratic or accountable.[6]

Part of this new cartography has also turned to *domestic* law. Global regulatory governance often relies on domestic laws and institutions to enhance its effectiveness. National laws and institutions could be complements of traditional international legal institutions, and sometimes substitutes for international norms and institutions. This makes domestic law a crucial variable in understanding the new landscape referred to above. As power shifts towards a decentralised network of global governance, the role of domestic law in the international legal system becomes of crucial importance. This is due, in part, to a matter of effectiveness and legitimacy: on the one hand, these modes of governance rely more than ever on enforcement by domestic institutions. On the other hand, they often lack a direct claim to legitimacy (even under the diffuse form of state consent); consequently, these new technologies of governance often rely, as we will discuss in this chapter, on the legitimacy of domestic institutions.

Most of existing scholarship on the role of the domestic legal order is focused on domestic *courts*. The existing studies concern either (1) the domestic *judicial* reception of international law or (2) the international reception of domestic *judicial* decisions.[7] The first angle has triggered scholarship focused on the domestic rule of law: how, when, and why is international law applied by domestic courts? This line of scholarship has dominated the discussion in the US ('will international law undermine our democratic rule of law?'),[8] in Latin America ('will international law

[5] The traditional sources of international law are treaties, custom, and general principles: Statute of the International Court of Justice, 26 June 1945, 39 AJIL Supp 215 (1945) (entered into force on 24 Oct 1945) (1945) Art 38(1).

[6] See, eg, Joost Pauwelyn, Ramses A Wessel and Jan Wouters, 'An Introduction to Informal International Lawmaking' in J Pauwelyn, R Wessel and J Wouters (eds), *Informal International Lawmaking* (Oxford, Oxford University Press, 2012) 13. See also Armin von Bogdandy and Ingo Venzke, 'Beyond Dispute: International Judicial Institutions as Lawmakers' in A von Bogdandy and I Venzke (eds), *International Judicial Lawmaking: On Public Authority and Democratic Legitimation in Global Governance* (Berlin; New York, Springer, 2012) 3.

[7] On these different angles from which we analyse the interactions between the domestic and international rule of law, see ch 1 (Kanetake) of this volume.

[8] For an argument holding that international law suffers from a democratic deficit that makes it unfit for domestic integration, see John O McGinnis and Illya Somin, 'Should International Law Be Part of Our Law' (2006) 59 *Stanford Law Review* 1175. Against this view, proposing that, for any nation consciously to ignore global standards not only would ensure constant frictions with the rest of the world, but also would diminish that nation's ability to invoke those international rules that served its own national purposes, see Harold Hongju

bolster our democratic rule of law?'),[9] and has hit Europe with a bang ever since the *Kadi* cases.[10] The second, more recent, angle is concerned with the international rule of law: how do domestic courts contribute or undermine the rules of international law? Are domestic courts the missing link of enforcement in international law? What normative criterion could national courts use when deciding cases such as *Kadi* or *Medellín*,[11] if they are not to simply give supremacy to domestic law, but rather to contribute to the international rule of law?[12]

This chapter is a contribution to this second line of research. It examines the interfaces between the international and national legal orders from the perspective of the international rule of law; more specifically, it explores how such interaction may develop international law, and pose challenges to the compliance-based approach to the international rule of law. As contrasted with existing studies, this chapter rejects the excessive focus on courts, and argues that non-judicial institutions are as important as courts for developing, as well as understanding, the international rule of law.

In one sense, non-judicial institutions are a site for compliance with international law. It is often non-judicial institutions that are first responsible for implementing the orders of the international legal system by, for instance, carrying out the obligations of the treaties or paying the compensations ordered by international courts. Non-judicial institutions perform these functions as organs of their respective states. For instance, if the Ecuadorian Congress passes a domestic law that implements a human rights treaty, it is acting as an organ of a state (Ecuador) in order to comply with its international legal obligations.

Koh, 'International Law as Part of Our Law' (2004) 98 *The American Journal of International Law* 43, 43–57.

[9] See Eyal Benvenisti, 'Reclaiming Democracy: The Strategic Uses of Foreign and International Law by National Courts' (2008) 102 *American Journal of International Law* 241. See also Beatriz Sanchez, 'Cuando Los Derechos Son La Jaula: Transplante Rígido Del Soft Law Para La Gestión Del Desplazamiento Forzado' (2009) 35 *Estudios Políticos* 11, 11–32.

[10] Case T-315/01 *Yassin Abdullah Kadi v Council of the European Union and Commission of the European Communities* (2005) 2005 ECR II, (CFI, Judgment of 21 Sept 2005, 'Kadi I (CFI)'); Cases C-402/05 P and C-415/05 P *Kadi and Al Barakaat International Foundation v Council of the European Union and Commission of the European Communities* (2008) [2008] ECR I-06351 (ECJ, Judgment of 3 Sept 2008, '*Kadi I* (ECJ)'); Case T-85/09 *Kadi v European Commission and Council of the European Union* (2010) [2010] ECR II-05177 (EGC, Judgment of 30 Sept 2010, 'Kadi II (EGC)'); Joined cases C-584/10 P, C-593/10 P and C-595/10 P *European Commission and Ors* v. *Kadi v* (2013) (ECJ, Judgment of 18 July 2013, '*Kadi II Appeal* (ECJ)', not yet reported). See the special issue of the International Organizations Law Review, in Ramses A Wessel, 'Introduction to the Forum—The Kadi Case: Toward a More Substantive Hierarchy in International Law' (2008) 5 *International Organizations Law Review* 323. See also Rene Uruena, 'International Law as Administration: The UN's 1267 Sanctions Committee and the Making of the War on Terror' (2008) 4 *International Organizations Law Review* 321.

[11] *Medellín v Texas* (2008) 128 S Ct 1346 (US Supreme Court, Judgment of 25 March 2008).

[12] See André Nollkaemper, *National Courts and the International Rule of Law* (Oxford, Oxford University Press, 2011).

This chapter proposes a different take on the matter. It situates non-judicial institutions as sites for making and contesting international law. The chapter reads non-judicial institutions as global actors in their own right—much in the same way as we have come to understand the role of domestic courts. Nonetheless, the contribution of non-judicial institutions needs to be understood in reference to a different framework from that applicable to courts: while theories of supremacy, direct effect, and legal pluralism have proven useful to understand the role played by courts, this mindset is of limited use in the case of non-judicial institutions. The goal of this chapter is to engage with the specific patterns in which non-judicial institutions effect the creation and development of law as a limit to, and an instrument of, global power. The chapter argues that, just as our understanding of the international rule of law was incomplete without domestic courts, it is now important that we consider domestic non-judicial institutions as part of the equation.

The chapter starts off by overviewing why and how non-judicial institutions matter for the international rule of law (section II). It then explores three forms in which non-judicial domestic institutions influence global regulatory governance. First, the chapter considers how non-judicial institutions invoke international law to promote accountability (section III). Second, this chapter discusses the role of non-judicial institutions as models for global regulatory governance, and as an increasingly intense form of influence (section IV). Section V explores the role of non-judicial institutions as international law-makers, focusing on the *implementation* of the directive adopted by the Basel Committee on Banking Supervision, which is not a domestic institution in itself, but rather a transnational actor composed of domestic non-judicial institutions, such as central banks and other national authorities concerning financial regulation. By way of conclusion, the chapter discusses the impact of researching non-judicial institutions on our understanding about the international rule of law.

II. NON-JUDICIAL INSTITUTIONS IN REGULATORY INTERNATIONAL LAW

The UN General Assembly's recognition in 2005 of the rule of law at *both* the national and international levels[13] has generated debate on the international rule of law. Yet the discussion itself is by no means novel; William Bishop, for instance, published an article on the 'international

[13] '2005 World Summit Outcome' UN Doc A/RES/60/1 (24 Oct 2005) para 134. Since 2006, the UN General Assembly has been adopting resolutions entitled 'The Rule of Law at the National and International Levels': see, eg, UN Doc A/RES/61/39 (18 Dec 2006).

rule of law' already in 1960.[14] Traditionally, the notion has been understood as being separate from its domestic counterpart. While the idea of interlinking the international and domestic rule of law has been around for some years (for example, in the work of Richard Falk),[15] the truth is that until very recently such an idea remained markedly marginal. Its current revival seems to be connected to the overall 'regulatory' turn of international law, which is characterised by the creation, through international norms, of public authoritative obligations on non-state actors, or the establishment of authoritative measures to enforce such duties.[16] The well-known instances of global regulatory governance include forestry,[17] public utilities,[18] and, as we will explore in depth in this chapter, financial regulation.[19]

How is this 'regulatory' international law related to the linkages between domestic and international rule of law? The answer lies in some of the most salient international legal scholarship produced recently, including global administrative law,[20] global constitutionalism,[21] and the project on international public authority,[22] among others. For all their differences, these projects share a concern with the fact that, in the context of the regulatory turn, power is affecting peoples' lives in a transnational fashion, without being subject to significant legal controls. Of course, such exercises of power are oblivious of the strict separation between domestic and international law; as a consequence, the rule of *domestic* law will not be enough to control the exercise of this transnational power, and the

[14] See William W Bishop, 'The International Rule of Law' (1960) 59 *Michigan Law Review* 553. For a recent restatement of the division thesis, see Brian Z Tamanaha, *On the Rule of Law: History, Politics, Theory* (Cambridge, Cambridge University Press, 2004) 127–36.

[15] Richard A Falk, *The Role of Domestic Courts in the International Legal Order* (Syracuse, Syracuse University Press, 1964) 65 ('Domestic courts are agents of a developing international legal order, as well as servants of various national interests; this double role helps to overcome the institutional deficiencies on a supranational').

[16] See Jacob Katz Cogan, 'The Regulatory Turn in International Law' (2011) 52 *Harvard International Law Journal* 322. See also Joseph HH Weiler, 'The Geology of International Law—Governance, Democracy and Legitimacy' (2004) 64 *Zeitschrift Für Ausländisches Öffentliches Recht Und Völkerrecht* 547.

[17] Errol Meidinger, 'The Administrative Law of Global Private-Public Regulation: The Case of Forestry' (2006) 17 *European Journal of International Law* 47.

[18] Bronwen Morgan, 'Turning off the Tap: Urban Water Service Delivery and the Social Construction of Global Administrative Law' (2006) 17 *European Journal of International Law* 215.

[19] Michael S Barr and Geoffrey P Miller, 'Global Administrative Law: The View from Basel' (2006) 17 *European Journal of International Law* 15.

[20] For an introduction, see Benedict Kingsbury, Richard B Stewart, and Niko Krisch, 'The Emergence of Global Administrative Law' (2005) 68 *Law and Contemporary Problems* 15.

[21] For an introduction, see Jan Klabbers, 'Setting the Scene', *The Constitutionalization of International Law* (Oxford, Oxford University Press, 2009) 1.

[22] For an introduction, see Armin von Bogdandy, 'General Principles of International Public Authority: Sketching a Research Field' in A von Bogdandy and others (eds), *The Exercise of Public Authority by International Institutions* (Heidelberg, Springer, 2010) 727.

rule of *international* law (understood as inter-state law), will be unable to do so as well. The domestic rule of law would often be blind and helpless before global exercises of power, while the mere international (in the sense of inter-state) rule of law would be equally at a loss facing international norms that pierce the sovereign veil and affect individuals directly. In this context, if we are to think of the rule of law in any significant sense, it therefore makes sense to think of it as a normative standard that covers both the domestic *and* the international spheres—a *global* rule of law, understood as the normative standards that regulate the exercise of global power though both domestic and international norms.

Courts are of crucial importance in the construction of this new *global* rule of law. They have proven to be a key site of deployment of rules in order to hold accountable those in power (both domestic and international).[23] However, in the context of a 'regulatory' international law, the actual deployment of international norms occurs mostly through non-judicial institutions. There are at least two reasons for this. The first one is *technical expertise*. As international law has grown to be fragmented in specialised regimes, it is increasingly the case that technical experts in the different areas of specialisation are called to design, contest, and implement international norms. At the domestic level, this kind of expertise is often found in non-judicial institutions: experts at Ministries of the Environment discuss climate change norms,[24] central bankers discuss financial standards,[25] and both are then called to design regulation to implement whatever norms are ultimately adopted, and to enforce them. While courts also hold a specific kind of expertise to apply—namely, formal dispute resolution on the basis of binding law—such particular expertise is not the sole site of international law-making and contestation in global governance. In complement, non-legal and technical expertise fosters regulatory networks and other models of non-binding decision-making at the global level, which are relevant for understanding the role of law in global governance[26]—an angle that mostly bypasses courts.

The second and more important reason why the actual deployment of international norms occurs through non-judicial institutions is *multi-level governance*. In the context of the regulatory turn of international law, the effectiveness of international norms is often dependent on a complex

[23] For the role of domestic courts in holding international decisions to account, see chs 2 (Fikfak), 3 (Platiše) and 4 (Hamamoto) of this volume.

[24] See the case-study of law-making by experts in the context of climate change in Stephen J Toope and Jutta Brunnée, *Legitimacy and Legality in International Law: An Interactional Account* (Cambridge, Cambridge University Press, 2010) 126–219.

[25] Narissa Lyngen, 'Basel III: Dynamics of State Implementation' (2012) 53 *Harvard International Law Journal* 519.

[26] See generally David Kennedy, 'Challenging Expert Rule: The Politics of Global Governance' (2005) 27 *Sydney Law Review* 5.

interaction among global, regional, national, and sub-national levels of governance.[27] In this context, courts are not effective 'multilevel' players, as their approach tends to be exclusive; a court claims for itself absolute power within the confines of its jurisdiction,[28] and its decision is not supposed to be 'multilevel'. While a national court may end up having to interact and conflict with other national, regional, and supranational courts,[29] these conflicts are precisely the ones which are to be solved[30] and are often framed as problems of fragmentation that require answers of comity or judicial dialogue.[31] In contrast, multilevel governance is not an issue of fragmentation, but one of expressly encouraged cooperation among different levels of governance, which is undertaken through techniques such as distribution of competences, delegations of power, and so forth. Courts are often ill-suited for this sort of horse-trading, as the logic of their jurisdiction (absent some version of *forum non conveniens*)[32] is exclusive. Overall, in a world where the implementation of international norms seems to favour multilevel governance, non-judicial institutions are better placed to do the deed than are courts.

III. NON-JUDICIAL INSTITUTIONS AS PROMOTERS OF ACCOUNTABILITY

Domestic non-judicial institutions strategically invoke international law in holding both domestic public bodies and international institutions

[27] In fact, the original concern with 'multilevel' governance in Europe was connected with the ability of sub-national (non-judicial) units, such as regions, establishing direct contact with the (non-judicial) supranational level of governance, such as the Commission. See Simona Piattoni, 'Multi-level Governance: A Historical and Conceptual Analysis' (2009) 31 *Journal of European Integration* 163, 166–70.

[28] This angle has been explored before in Martti Koskenniemi, 'Hegemonic Regimes' in M Young (ed), *Regime Interaction in International Law: Facing Fragmentation* (Cambridge, Cambridge University Press, 2012) 305.

[29] In Europe, see Aida Torres Perez, *Conflicts of Rights in the European Union: A Theory of Supranational Adjudication* (Oxford, Oxford University Press, 2009). In Latin America, see René Urueña, 'Global Governance Through Comparative International Law?: Inter-American Constitutionalism and the Changing Role of Domestic Courts in the Construction of the International Law' (2013) New York University, Jean Monnet Working Paper Series no 21.

[30] See Karen Knop, Ralf Michaels, and Annelies Riles, 'International Law in Domestic Courts: A Conflict of Laws Approach' (2009) 103 Cornell Legal Studies Research Paper No 09016. Similarly, see Karen Knop, 'Here and There: International Law in Domestic Courts' (1999) 32 *New York University Journal of International Law and Politics* 501.

[31] This is the overall answer proposed in Joost Pauwelyn, *Conflict of Norms in Public International Law: How WTO Law Relates to Other Rules of International Law* (Cambridge, Cambridge University Press, 2003). Similarly, see William Thomas Worster, 'Competition and Comity in the Fragmentation of International Law' (2008) 34 *Brooklyn Journal of International Law* 119.

[32] Such is the answer now being proposed to solve courts' shortcomings in a fragmented world. See Joost Pauwelyn and Luiz Eduardo Salles, 'Forum Shopping before International Tribunals: (real) Concerns, (im) Possible Solutions' (2009) 42 *Cornell International Law Journal* 77.

accountable, which in turn would be instrumental in strengthening the international rule of law as a whole. Such accountability may be horizontal, in the sense that they keep *domestic* powers accountable under international law (A), or vertical, in the sense that they keep *international* powers accountable under international law (B).

A. Horizontal Accountability

i. Human Rights Institutions

International human rights law is one of the bodies of international law which non-judicial institutions have frequently invoked in order to promote accountability at the national level. Just as domestic courts have played a crucial role in promoting accountability under international human rights standards,[33] so too are non-judicial institutions able to hold public powers accountable. However, their techniques and challenges of legitimacy, as we will see below, differ from those of courts.

The key players here are national human rights institutions (NHRI), which can be defined generally as 'state bodies with a constitutional and/or legislative mandate to protect and promote human rights'.[34] They are part of the 'State apparatus and are funded by the State'.[35] NHRI are a common feature in most democracies, ever since the UN's Economic and Social Council (ECOSOC) invited member states to 'consider the desirability of establishing information groups or local human rights committees within their respective countries to collaborate with them in furthering the work of the Commission of Human Rights'.[36] In 1991, the first international workshop on National Institutions for the Promotion and Protection of Human Rights took place in Paris, from which a set of principles (so-called the Paris Principles)[37] emerged. Such principles provide the criteria according to which the International Coordinating Committee of National Institutions for the Promotion and Protection of Human Rights accredits NHRIs. As of February 2013, there are 69 accredited NHRIs,[38]

[33] See Beth A Simmons, *Mobilizing for Human Rights: International Law in Domestic Politics* (Cambridge, Cambridge University Press, 2009) 129–35.

[34] United Nations, *National Human Rights Institutions: History, Principles, Roles and Responsibilities* (New York, United Nations, 2010) 10.

[35] ibid.

[36] ECOSOC Res 2/9, 21 June 1946.

[37] United Nations, *National Human Rights Institutions* (n 34) 31.

[38] See Office of the United Nations High Commissioner for Human Rights (OHCHR), 'OHCHR and NHRIs', available at: www.ohchr.org/en/countries/nhri/pages/nhrimain.aspx.

and more than a hundred are not yet accredited before the International Coordinating Committee. NHRIs' specific shape and powers are heterogeneous, as they include human rights commissions, human rights ombudsmen, hybrid institutions, consultative and advisory bodies, and research institutes, among many others.[39] The key point, though, is that they are all national institutions, other than courts, that protect and promote human rights at the national level.[40]

NHRIs are instrumental in promoting their states' general compliance with international law. They can lobby for the ratification of relevant treaties, review domestic legislation, and adopt reports on whether it complies with international human rights standards.[41] More importantly for our purposes, NHRIs also promote the strategic use of international law to promote accountability, as they increasingly rely on international human rights instruments to undertake their domestic legal mandate. As Richard Carver has shown, the mandate of new generation NHRIs is more likely to include a reference to international human rights law,[42] which encourages NHRIs to invoke international legal instruments to hold governments accountable.

This possibility is even more evident in regions such as Latin America, where two phenomena converge: (1) strong, constitutionally created NHRIs; and (2) constitutional texts that are often generous in integrating international human rights norms, but are less clear about which norms, specifically, become part of domestic law. Indeed, emerging from the hardships of dictatorship and civil wars, most states in the region adopted new constitutions in a couple of decades: Argentina (1994), Bolivia (1994 and 2009), Brazil (1988), Colombia (1991), the Dominican Republic (1994, 2002, and 2010), Ecuador (1996, 1998, and 2008), Nicaragua (1987), Paraguay (1992), Peru (1993), and Venezuela (1999). Most of these constitutions create a strong NHRI, tailored after the Portuguese *Provedor de Justica* and the Spanish *Defensor del Pueblo*, which have been often called 'hybrid human rights ombudsman',[43] as they have the power to protect and promote human rights, and also to monitor government administration. Similarly, such constitutions recognise international human rights law as an important aspect of their respective domestic systems.

[39] United Nations (n 34) 15.

[40] Linda C Reif, *The Ombudsman, Good Governance, and the International Human Rights System* (Leiden, Martinus Nijhoff Publishers, 2004).

[41] See Linda C Reif, 'Building Democratic Institutions: The Role of National Human Rights Institutions in Good Governance and Human Rights Protection' (2000) 13 *Harvard Human Rights Journal* 1, 14.

[42] Richard Carver, 'A New Answer to an Old Question: National Human Rights Institutions and the Domestication of International Law' (2010) 10 *Human Rights Law Review* 1.

[43] Reif, 'Building Democratic Institutions: The Role of National Human Rights Institutions in Good Governance and Human Rights Protection' (n 41) 13.

While some constitutions, such as Argentina's,[44] expressly identify the international legal norms that will become part of domestic law, most constitutions in the area are not clear about the issue. This indeterminacy greatly empowers NHRIs, who are then able to invoke international human rights standards, even if their belonging to the domestic legal system is unclear, and hold public powers accountable under international law. Such possibility, in turn, becomes more relevant in the context of a new generation of NHRIs that have emerged in the region, which hold the competence to monitor and handle specific complaints against public powers. Hence, we find NHRIs that investigate individual cases against public powers and monitor their conduct—and they do so on the basis of an open-ended integration of international law in the domestic system, which they shape as their needs require.

ii. Accountability and Policy Review by Other Non-Judicial Institutions

Outside NHRI, a wide range of non-judicial institutions strategically invoke international law in order to review governmental policies outside judicial settings.[45] Besides holding domestic powers accountable for their acts (such as NHRIs), these other domestic non-judicial institutions also routinely engage in the review of law and policy adopted by domestic powers, still on the basis of international law. This process is not analytically different from the role played by NHRIs; however, the institutional structure that it implies seems to be particular enough to justify separate attention, at least in two senses: first, policy review by non-judicial institutions occurs *ex ante*, whereas NHRI typically act after the human rights violation has been committed. Second, policy review is often undertaken

[44] See Art 75(22) of the 1994 Constitution. See, eg, Supreme Court of Argentina, *Verbitsky, Horacio s/habeas corpus*, V 856. XXXVIII, 9 Feb 2004, paras 5, 13, 39, and 57; Llerena, Horacio Luis s/abuso de armas y lesiones arts. 104 y 89 del Código Penal -causa No 3221-, L. 486. XXXVI, 17 May 2005, paras 7, 22, and 28; Dieser, María Graciela y Fraticelli, Carlos Andrés s/ homicidio calificado por el vínculo y por alevosía-causa No 120/02-, D 81 XLI. 6 Aug 2006, opinión del Procurador, at 5.

[45] In the US, such review found support in the 1990s in the context of the debates on judicial supremacy in the interpretation of the US Constitution. In this debate, some questioned judicial supremacy: Mark Tushnet, *Taking the Constitution Away from the Courts* (Princeton, NJ, Princeton University Press, 2000) 6–32; Keith E Whittington, 'Extrajudicial Constitutional Interpretation: Three Objections and Responses' (2002) 80 *North Carolina Law Review* 773. Others defended judicial supremacy: Larry Alexander and Frederick Schauer, 'On Extrajudicial Constitutional Interpretation' (1996) 110 *Harvard Law Review* 1359; Larry Alexander and Frederick Schauer, 'Defending Judicial Supremacy: A Reply' (2000) 17 *Constitutional Commentary* 455. For those who upheld the idea that supremacy of the Constitution does not necessarily mean the supremacy of the Supreme Court's constitutional interpretation, it is a positive phenomenon that non-judicial institutions routinely engage in constitutional interpretation and that such a practice leads constitutional standards to permeate each and every decision of public power: see Mark Tushnet, 'The Hardest Question in Constitutional Law' (1996) 81 *Minnesota Law Review* 1, 25–28.

by either the executive or the legislative, which triggers a separate set of political dynamics, if compared with NHRIs. It is possible to distinguish two different forms of review: executive and legislative.

a. Review by Executive Organs

Executive review occurs when an independent (or at least, relatively independent) executive agency is empowered to review domestic law or policy on the basis of international law. Such a review mostly lacks the effect of actually striking down the legislation, as that would empower the head of the executive branch to have the ultimate say over the legislature.[46] However, it may have substantive impact in the eventual adoption of law or policy, thus facilitating accountability of domestic officials under international law.

One example of executive review is the US Office of Legal Counsel (OLC).[47] The OLC is part of the US Justice Department, but the Attorney General has formally delegated to it the legal advice-giving part of his statutory responsibility.[48] The OLC has no enforcement or litigation responsibilities, but is only responsible for giving the president legal advice. One crucial aspect of the OLC is that it is generally perceived as independent and authoritative; its opinions carry an important weight and impose a presumption of legality that is hard to rebut. Working for the Office is one the most prestigious legal positions in the US government.[49] The OLC's green light provides legal cover to laws and policy, while its denial casts an important shadow of doubt on the legality of the issue at stake.[50]

The OLC routinely provides constitutional comments on bills,[51] executive orders, and regulations calling for Attorney General review.[52] In all of these roles, the OLC employs *international law*, as applicable under US law, as its relevant standard to undertake the review if the case so requires. A well-known example of the OLC's reference to international law is its infamous 'torture memos'.[53] The memos provided the legal basis for

[46] That is the case, eg, in the US. See Cornelia Pillard, 'The Unfulfilled Promise of the Constitution in Executive Hands' (2005) 103 *Michigan Law Review* 676.

[47] The idea of the OLC as an example of non-judicial review is adopted from Mark Tushnet, 'Non-Judicial Review' (2003) 40 *Harvard Journal on Legislation* 453, 468–79.

[48] See 28 USC §§ 511, 512 (2004), and 28 CFR § 0.25(b) (2005).

[49] See Jack L Goldsmith, *The Terror Presidency: Law and Judgment inside the Bush Administration* (New York, WW Norton & Company, 2007) 141–49.

[50] Pillard, 'The Unfulfilled Promise of the Constitution in Executive Hands' (n 46) 712–14.

[51] This function is often referred to as 'bill clearance'. See Tushnet, 'Non-Judicial Review' (n 47) 469–72.

[52] Pillard (n 46) 714.

[53] The memos are a set of three briefs drafted in August 2002; one prepared by John Yoo (then the Council of the OLC) and two by Jay S Bybee (then the head of the OLC) for Alberto Gonzalez, who was then Attorney General. Available at: http://dspace.wrlc.org/doc/bitstream/2041/70966/00355_020801_003display.pdf; www.gwu.edu/~nsarchiv/NSAEBB/NSAEBB127/020801.pdf.

so-called 'enhanced interrogation techniques' and laid out the OLC's interpretation of the 1984 Convention against Torture (CAT) and of the International Criminal Court's (ICC) jurisdiction regarding harsh techniques of interrogation that could be construed as torture. This review implied, in effect, a review under international law of one of central elements of the 'War on Terror'. The OLC argued that the CAT defined torture in the 'exact same terms' as US law did: if a technique did not qualify as torture under US law, then by definition it did not fall under CAT. Another question concerned whether an interrogation that was deemed lawful under US law, but was carried on in the territory of a state party to the ICC, could lead to international criminal prosecution. The OLC responded in the negative: since the US is not party to the Rome Statute, it 'cannot be bound by the provisions of the ICC, nor can the US nationals be subject to ICC prosecutions'.

From the perspective of international law, the OLC's interpretation of international law may be considered flawed.[54] Yet the OLC's review of the 'enhanced interrogation' policy still provided the legal basis for a crucial development that affected the international rule of law; due to the OLC's stature as independent and authoritative, their non-judicial review was taken seriously and gave legal basis to several key aspects of the 'War on Terror'.[55] Similarly, in early 2002, the OLC had delivered three opinions to the Attorney General outlining the applicability of the 1949 Geneva Conventions to the conflict against Al-Qaeda, particularly about 'enemy combatants' and the prisoner of war status of enemy fighters captured by the US and its allies.[56] According to the OLC, the Geneva Convention did not apply to detainees from the war in Afghanistan, an opinion that had much impact on the protection of individual rights in the fight against terrorism.

The examples of the OLC's 'torture memos' and Geneva Conventions opinions show the crucial role of non-judicial institutions in reviewing domestic powers on the basis of international law. It is difficult to understand crucial examples of the lack of international legal accountability, such as extraordinary renditions or the prison in Guantanamo, without understanding the role played by the OLC and its executive review. If we

[54] See Philippe Sands, 'Terrorists and Torturers' in M Cohn (ed), *The United States and Torture: Interrogation, Incarceration, and Abuse* (New York, New York University Press, 2011) 261, 268–72.

[55] See, eg, the narrative in Jack L Goldsmith, *The Terror Presidency: Law and Judgment inside the Bush Administration* (New York, WW Norton & Company, 2007) 141–76. See also the narrative in Donald Rumsfeld, *Known and Unknown: A Memoir* (New York, Sentinel, 2011) ch 40 ('Law in the Time of War').

[56] Available at: www.gwu.edu/~nsarchiv/NSAEBB/NSAEBB127/02.01.09.pdf; www.gwu.edu/~nsarchiv/NSAEBB/NSAEBB127/02.01.22.pdf; www.gwu.edu/~nsarchiv/NSAEBB/NSAEBB127/020207.pdf.

overlook domestic non-judicial institutions, our map of the international rule of law is bound to be incomplete.

b. Review by Legislative Bodies

The legislature also conducts review on the basis of international law. A few domestic legal systems establish special parliamentary commissions that review legislation or policy on the basis of the Constitution. Such a mechanism often allows review on the basis of international law. There are a few examples, including China,[57] Ethiopia,[58] and Finland. One of the most interesting examples in this regard is the Finnish Constitutional Law Committee (CLC) in terms of its independence and political standing.

The CLC is part of the Eduskunta (Parliament) and has at least 17 members of parliament.[59] Its task is to give an opinion on the constitutionality of legislation prior to its adoption and, most important for our purposes, on whether such legislation is in line with international human rights standards. Despite its political mandate, and due in part to the fact that Finland lacks a constitutional court, the CLC is the most authoritative body interpreting the Constitution; the CLC is indeed the source of legal accountability in ensuring the constitutionality of legislation, including under EU law and other international obligations. While the opinions of the CLC are not binding, just as the aforementioned OLC in the US, the Finnish Committee is perceived to be independent and authoritative in its mandate, and its opinions are treated in practice as obligatory by the Eduskunta and other authorities.[60]

Unlike the Latin American constitutions mentioned above, Finland does not have a system of direct integration of international human rights standards.[61] However, under Article 74 of the Constitution, the CLC must review legislation on the basis of the Constitution as well as on its relation to international human rights treaties. Exercising such power, for instance, the CLC reviewed a legislative proposal to penalise belonging to a criminal organisation on the basis of the European Convention of Human Rights and the 1966 Convention on the Elimination of All Forms of Racial

[57] See Guobin Zhu, 'Constitutional Review in China: An Unaccomplished Project or a Mirage' (2009) 43 *Suffolk University Law Review* 625.

[58] See Chi Mgbako and others, 'Silencing the Ethiopian Courts: Non-Judicial Constitutional Review and Its Impact on Human Rights' (2008) 32 *Fordham International Law Journal* 259.

[59] See Finnish Constitution, Art 35(2).

[60] See Tuomas Ojanen, 'EU Law and the Response of the Constitutional Law Committee of the Finnish Parliament' in P Wahlgren (ed), *Constitutional Law* (Stockholm, Stockholm Institute for Scandinavian Law, 2007) 203, 205–07.

[61] See Martin Scheinin, 'Finland' in M Scheinin (ed), *International Human Rights Norms in the Nordic and Baltic Countries* (The Hague, Martinus Nijhoff Publishers, 1996) 257.

Discrimination.[62] Moreover, the CLC has adopted the practice of routinely invoking the EU Charter of Fundamental Rights when reviewing legislation that implements EU measures.[63] As such, the CLC is a non-judicial organ that holds Finnish powers accountable on the basis of international law by reviewing domestic legislation.

B. Vertical Accountability

The aforementioned role of non-judicial institutions is in the 'horizontal' accountability processes; in each case, non-judicial institutions hold accountable powers *within* their own state. Arguably, the same logic could apply to a 'vertical' process of accountability, whereby non-judicial institutions hold accountable international institutions on the basis of international law. From the perspective of veritable global rule of law, in which the distinction between domestic and international law is truly erased, the possibility of such vertical accountability seems coherent. There is no reason why domestic non-judicial institutions would be, as a matter of principle, in a different position from that of domestic courts when it comes to holding global institutions accountable under international law. If we make the argument for domestic courts to exercise such power, we must accept that non-judicial institutions should be able (in principle, and technicalities notwithstanding) to do the same.

However, this idea sounds unorthodox at the very least. For instance, the very mandate of the aforementioned NHRIs seems to limit its scope to the domestic setting, and thus seems to be restricted to holding domestic institutions accountable under domestic and international law. And yet, in the context of the regulatory turn of international law, it is increasingly clear that international norms may affect directly the human rights of individuals. Consider the example of targeted sanctions adopted by the UN Security Council, which have affected individuals. Could the relevant NHRI hold accountable the European Commission or the Security Council, for that matter? Could a non-judicial institution purport to review the Security Council's resolution? On the one hand, the obvious answer is on the negative: limited territorial jurisdiction would be a barrier. And yet, it should be recalled that the European Court of First Instance availed itself of the jurisdiction to review the legality of Security Council resolutions on the basis of *jus cogens*.[64] Could an NHRI make a similar argument, thus

[62] See Perustuslakivaliokunta *PeVL 10/2000 vp;* as referred in Veli-Pekka Hautamaki, 'Authoritative Interpretation of the Constitution: A Comparison of Argumentation in Finland and Norway' (2002) 63 *Electronic Journal of Comparative Law* 1, 11–12.

[63] Ojanen, 'EU Law and the Response of the Constitutional Law Committee of the Finnish Parliament' (n 60) 212.

[64] *Kadi I* (CFI, 2005) (n 10) [209]–[31].

engaging in vertical accountability of international institutions that violate *jus cogens?* Surely, that could be the case. That line of reasoning, though, has the same advantages, and faces the same challenges, if it is made by a court or by a non-judicial institution; advantages and challenges that have been widely debated *à propos* the *Kadi* case. Considering that there is nothing distinct about non-judicial institutions in this context, this chapter moves to an issue where domestic non-judicial institutions do have a distinct appeal: serving as models of international institutions.

IV. DOMESTIC NON-JUDICIAL INSTITUTIONS AS MODELS FOR GLOBAL REGULATORY GOVERNANCE

One of the central themes of the regulatory turn in international law is how the international legal order has pierced sovereignty and affected the domestic legal and political landscape. Domestic non-judicial institutions are no exception to this theme, and much thought has gone into describing the influence of international regulatory regimes on domestic systems. For example, one of the central focuses of global administrative law studies is to develop insights on possible global standards of transparency, reason-giving, and participation for domestic non-judicial institutions.[65]

This approach is distinctively top-down. Domestic institutions are not always on the receiving end of the equation. They also serve as *models* for formal international institutions and other international regulatory regimes. While domestic courts are being rediscovered as possible sites for critical revision of international law, national non-judicial institutions are still perceived as the actors disciplined by international law; namely, international scholarship tends to regard the domestic regulatory agencies as the sites for adopting trade restrictive measures or implementing an international environmental treaty. When not perceived as subjects to be disciplined, non-judicial institutions are framed as domestic particularities accommodated by the international legal order—a nod to a certain flexibility in the different ways of complying with international law.[66] Domestic courts are, in that sense, often understood as the manifestation of the universal, while non-judicial institutions are regarded as the expressions of the particular, which need to be disciplined or accommodated by international law.

[65] See, eg, Sabino Cassese, 'Global Standards for National Administrative Procedure' (2004) 68 *Law and Contemporary Problems* 109; Richard B Stewart and Michelle Ratton Sanchez Badin, 'The World Trade Organization: Multiple Dimensions of Global Administrative Law' (2011) 9 *International Journal of Constitutional Law* 556, 569–74.

[66] It is interesting to note that just some 40 years ago, that was the role given to domestic courts in international law. See, eg, Falk, *The Role of Domestic Courts in the International Legal Order* (n 15) 65–70.

This view on the role of domestic institutions, particularly of non-judicial institutions, is based upon a sharp distinction between the domestic and the international legal orders. The view also assumes that international law develops in parallel to domestic law and that the two legal spheres intersect as fully formed and static regimes. The reality is quite different, however; international law is shaped by domestic law, which is influenced in turn by its international equivalent, on a continuous basis. This is also true with regard to domestic non-judicial institutions. While they are certainly influenced by international regulatory regimes, they also often provide a model for the development of those very global institutions that influence domestic institutions themselves. In that sense, non-judicial institutions are models for the institutions we entrust with the international rule of law.

An example of this dynamic is the development of the UN after the Second World War. As Elizabeth Borgwardt,[67] Aparicio Caicedo Castillo,[68] Mark Mazower,[69] and Anne-Marie Slaughter[70] have shown, the institutions that grew to be the cornerstone of the international order in the post-war world order were in fact modelled after New Deal sensibilities, projecting the idea of Roosevelt's regulatory state and its institutional layout to the international setting. Non-judicial institutions played a crucial role in this context. The New Deal created a regulatory framework in the US that was characterised by the overwhelming importance of non-judicial institutions in regulating society.[71] The emergence of domestic regulatory agencies such as the Federal Communications Commission, expert administrative offices, and the whole institutional framework developed for the New Deal then served as a model for the UN. This framework was brought to the international arena, and influenced the basic layout of the UN and the Bretton Woods institutions. Domestic non-judicial institutions, in this sense, served as inspiration and model for what would later become the institutional basis of the international order.

[67] See Elizabeth Borgwardt, *A New Deal for the World: America's Vision for Human Rights* (Cambridge, Belknap Press of Harvard University Press, 2005) 70–87.

[68] See Aparicio Caicedo Castillo, *El new deal del comercio global: Génesis ideológica del ordenamiento económico de la posguerra* (Madrid, Unión Editorial, SA/Instituto Juan de Mariana, 2012) 163–80.

[69] Mark Mazower, *Governing the World: The History of an Idea* (New York, Penguin Press, 2012) 191–213.

[70] See Anne-Marie Burley (now Slaughter), 'Regulating the World: Multilateralism, International Law, and the Projection of the New Deal Regulatory State' in J G Ruggie (ed), *Multilateralism Matters: the Theory and Praxis of an Institutional Form* (New York, Columbia University Press, 1993) 125.

[71] Indeed, some of the very same people who had taken part in the New Deal transformation were leading the design of the post-war international order: see ibid 133–34; Elizabeth Borgwardt, 'Re-Examining Nuremberg as a New Deal Institution: Politics, Culture and the Limits of Law in Generating Human Rights Norms' (2005) 23 *Berkeley Journal of International Law* 401, 449–53; Mazower, *Governing the World* (n 69) 198–202.

Domestic institutions influence international regulatory regimes on a regular basis. It is in such processes that the dynamics of expertise and multilevel governance take place—through such constant interactions, global power is exercised, and it is exercised through law. This process overlaps with a vertical pattern of international law borrowing from domestic legal systems, which has been increasingly studied.[72] Scholarship on global administrative law has also posed the question of whether, and to what extent, it is possible to transplant domestic models of administrative law to global regimes.[73] However, regardless of its normative justification, the fact is that understanding domestic non-judicial institutions becomes crucial to understanding the international rule of law, not only as a matter of whether and how legal norms limit and regulate global power, but also as a question of how these very norms are instrumental to the exercise of that power.

The fact that domestic non-institutions serve as a model entails certain risks, in that it may facilitate the 'internationalisation' of domestic regulatory arrangements that could be ill-suited to global governance. It could give priority to one particular way of understanding global issues over others. For example, if we adopt the American model of non-judicial institutions as the inspiration for new global regulatory regimes, this would benefit the US whose domestic regulatory state becomes the gold standard against which global governance is measured. In that sense, non-judicial institutions as models for international regulatory institutions may be just another expression of an imperial global state in the making.[74] But the distributive implications go beyond that: adopting a particular model of domestic non-judicial institution to serve as the example for global governance may have as a result that expertise-based global NGOs are empowered, to the detriment of grass-root organisations. Or perhaps individuals gain more power with wider standing. Perhaps they lose that power as opposed to corporations. Whatever the answer, the point is that this form of inspiration is not neutral. The ways in which different models of domestic non-judicial institutions influence international law have a crucial impact on the role of law in global governance.

The international impact of particular domestic models remains to be an actual issue for states with emerging economies. As we have seen, non-judicial institutions that have historically served after World War Two

[72] In the context of climate change regulation, see Jonathan B Wiener, 'Something Borrowed for Something Blue: Legal Transplants and the Evolution of Global Environmental Law' (2000) 27 *Ecology Law Quarterly* 1295.

[73] See, eg, Richard B Stewart, 'U.S. Administrative Law: A Model for Global Administrative Law' (2004) 68 *Law and Contemporary Problems* 63.

[74] BS Chimni, 'Co-Option and Resistance: Two Faces of Global Administrative Law' (2004) 37 *New York University Journal of International Law and Politics* 799.

as a model for international law are often those from the US, and to a lesser degree, Europe. The bias in favour of institutions from the global North became even more evident in the context of the Washington Consensus, when the global expansion of the regulatory state and its institutional layout (composed mainly of non-judicial institutions) made states in the global South mere recipients of different waves of non-judicial institutions.[75]

At the same time, the historical influence of particular domestic models seems to be changing. As the neo-liberal consensus is perceived as having failed, new developmentalist policies are adopted in emerging economies (eg, India and Brazil), through the re-regulation of industries once de-regulated, and new *dirigiste* industrial policies.[76] One of the main sites where such new policies are tried, developed, and resisted is, precisely, domestic non-judicial institutions (for example, in independent regulatory agencies of public utilities, and boards of central banks, among others). Such institutions in the global South have developed certain distinct characteristics, and are more than mere transplants of their equivalent in the North: there is, in that sense, a veritable and distinct 'Regulatory State of the South'.[77] As the geopolitics of global governance shift, will non-judicial institutions from emerging economies turn out to be the new inspiration? Who could win and who could lose with the adoption of these new models? How could that affect the international rule of law?

V. DOMESTIC NON-JUDICIAL INSTITUTIONS AS INTERNATIONAL LAW-MAKERS

Domestic non-judicial institutions not only strategically invoke international law at the domestic level (as discussed in section III above) and provide a model for international institutions (section IV above); they also, simultaneously, play a key role in developing new international legal norms. Just as we saw with the case of compliance, if we focus narrowly on the traditional form of international law-making, we will not be able to fully grasp their impact on international law. We need to think outside the traditional approach to international-making.[78] Non-judicial institutions

[75] See David Levi-Faur, 'The Global Diffusion of Regulatory Capitalism' (2005) 598 *The ANNALS of the American Academy of Political and Social Science* 12.

[76] See, eg, David M Trubek, Diogo Coutinho, and Mario Schapiro, 'Towards a New Law and Development: New State Activism in Brazil and the Challenge for Legal Institutions' (2012) *University of Wisconsin Legal Studies Research Paper* 1.

[77] See Navroz K Dubash and Bronwen Morgan, 'Understanding the Rise of the Regulatory State of the South' (2012) 6 *Regulation & Governance* 261.

[78] In this sense, focus on non-judicial institutions can be seen as related to other efforts that try to theorise instances of non-traditional international law, and their challenges. See, eg, Pauwelyn, Wessel, and Wouters, 'An Introduction to Informal International Lawmaking'

have both indirect (A) and direct (B) impact in international law-making, depending on whether they require the state to which they belong to give formal consent to the norms they purport to create—or at least to not object to the creation of the new norm.

A. Indirect Impact

Let us begin by their indirect impact. First of all, the acts of domestic non-judicial institutions constitute state practice that develops international customary law.[79] Non-judicial institutions can also act as norm entrepreneurs, pushing for the development of new international norms, just as NGOs do in their own area of work.[80] In that sense, these institutions are involved in law-making and have an impact in the international rule of law. Such was the case of, for instance, with those NHRIs which worked on disability issues and, during the discussions of the Convention on the Rights of Persons with Disabilities, successfully lobbied for the inclusion of a specific domestic mechanism for monitoring compliance following closely the Paris Principles.[81] Another clear example is tax policy: domestic tax institutions aggressively use international fora, like the OECD, to develop global tax policy and achieve national tax policy goals.[82] Both examples show domestic non-judicial institutions engaging in clear processes of international law-making, much like global NGOs which, while lacking traditional law-making powers under international law, do engage in law-making activity, and have a practical impact on the international legal order.[83]

(n 6). Mapping some overlapping cases, see Christine Chinkin and Alan E Boyle, *The Making of International Law* (Oxford, Oxford University Press, 2007) 41–97.

[79] See Ian Brownlie, *Principles of Public International Law* (7th edn, Oxford, Oxford University Press, 2008) at 39.

[80] See Kathryn Sikkink and Margaret Keck, *Activists beyond Borders* (Ithaca, NY, Cornell University Press, 1998) 1–38; Kathryn Sikkink and Thomas Risse, 'The Socialization of International Human Rights Norms into Domestic Practices' in T Risse, K Sikkink and S Ropp (eds), *The Power of Human Rights: International Norms and Domestic Politics* (Cambridge, Cambridge University Press, 1999) 1; Kathryn Sikkink, 'Human Rights Advocacy Networks and the Social Construction of Legal Rules' in Y Dezalay and B Garth (eds), *Global Prescriptions: The Production, Exportation and Importation of a New Legal Orthodoxy* (Ann Arbor, University of Michigan Press, 2002) 37.

[81] Carver, 'A New Answer to an Old Question: National Human Rights Institutions and the Domestication of International Law' (n 42). See Convention on the Rights of Persons with Disabilities, 13 December 2006, 2515 UNTS 3, Art 33(2). In turn, Arts 2 and 16 of the Optional Protocol mandate a national preventive mechanism to be established as an independent organ for the prevention of torture and ill-treatment at a national level: see Optional Protocol to the Convention on the Rights of Persons with Disabilities, Arts 2, 16.

[82] Se Allison Christians, 'Networks, Norms and National Tax Policy' (2010) 9 *Washington University Global Studies Law Review* 1.

[83] For the role of NGOs in international law-making, and the ways in which they contribute to international law-making, see Chinkin and Boyle, *The Making of International Law*

A second indirect impact of non-judicial institutions in international law-making is intimately connected to their technical expertise. Contemporary structures of global governance both work through, and are deeply shaped by, practices of knowledge production. This is particularly evident where governance involves the application of an 'expert consensus' to an already-framed problem—international interventions in the sphere of economic development are a clear example; another is climate change management. But other, less obviously technocratic modes of governance, such as global trade governance, are equally structured by the tacit knowledge, habits of thought, and routinised assumptions made by policy-makers, negotiators and others actors.[84] Such patterns of knowledge production are crucial for understanding the rule of law—be it domestically, internationally or, as has been suggested here, *globally*. Expertise helps define the meaning of 'self-interest' for policy-makers, civil society, and economic actors, which is to say, it determines the power strategies that need to be controlled by law if we are to talk in any significant sense of rule by law.

The argument here is not that knowledge production directly fosters or hinders the rule of law. Instead, the point is that knowledge production defines what is *at stake* when we talk about the rule of law—and non-judicial institutions are crucial in this process. As sites of technical (ie, non-legal) expertise, non-judicial institutions tend to frame the overall discussion, which is then translated into legal terms, crystallised in treaties, or subject to adjudication. Thus, the rule of investment law, or of the law of the World Trade Organization, depends on a set of basic understandings about markets and economic rationality, which are not given, and are not legal concepts:[85] rather, they are developed by experts who, it is argued here, are often found in non-judicial institutions. Thus, if it is true that rule by international law depends in part on acceptance of that law by a given community of practice, as some constructivist readings suggest,[86] then the underlying understandings of such community become relevant: the argument being made here is that domestic non-judicial institutions are some of the most important sites where these understandings are constructed and contested.

(n 78) 52–97. My argument here is that NHRIs seem to act in much the same way, using similar techniques to achieve influence.

[84] See Andrew Lang, *World Trade Law after Neoliberalism: Re-Imagining the Global Economic Order* (Oxford; New York, Oxford University Press, 2011) 159–89.

[85] See Andrew Lang, 'The Legal Construction of Economic Rationalities?' (2013) 40 *Journal of Law and Society* 155.

[86] See Toope and Brunnée, *Legitimacy and Legality in International Law: An Interactional Account* (n 24) 59–87.

B. Direct Impact

The impact of non-judicial institutions can also be direct, in the sense that they may engage in international law-making without the formal consent of their states at the international level. This process of rule-making can be captured by the idea of regulatory networks, which was introduced by Robert Keohane and Joseph Nye in the mid-1970s[87] when they proposed that the interaction between bureaucracies below the level of head of state (such as non-judicial institutions) could explain much of the reality that was being observed in international relations at the time. They called these dynamics 'transgovernmentalism', and focused on domestic factors to explain the reasons behind transgovernmental activity. While this approach lost its explanatory power as the globalisation of political power increased, their idea of regulatory cooperation remained powerful. As the sovereign state began to lose its central place in global politics, the idea of regulatory networks seems to describe much of the new forms of law-making we observe today.

Domestic non-judicial institutions play a crucial role in that context; as Slaughter remarked in the late-1990s, '[t]he densest area of transgovernmental activity is among national regulators' and 'all the agents of the modern regulatory state ... regularly collaborate with their foreign counterparts'.[88] Regulatory networks comprise a wide range of activities. Often networks are spaces for sharing information between domestic non-judicial institutions, and coordination of their activities,[89] as is the case of the International Competition Network, which brings together competition authorities from around the world.[90] And networks are not confined to non-judicial institutions: there are networks of *judicial* institutions, which interact in a variety of ways.[91] However, it is in the process of international law-making that one more clearly sees the promise and pitfalls of

[87] Robert O Keohane and Joseph S Nye, 'Transgovernmental Relations and International Organizations' (1974) 27 *World Politics* 39. The same phenomenon is described by the commentators with a different name. Eyal Benvenisti, eg, describes similar issues as 'informal government-to-government coordination', and compares them to 'formal but non-legally binding institutions'. See Eyal Benvenisti, '"Coalitions of the Willing" and the Evolution of Informal International Law' in C Calliess, G Nolte and PT Stoll (eds), *Coalitions Of The Willing: Avantgarde or Threat?* (Cologne, C Heymanns Verlag, 2007) 1, 4.

[88] Anne-Marie Slaughter, 'The Real New World Order' (1997) 76 *Foreign Affairs* 183, 189–90. Further development of the idea is to be found in Anne-Marie Slaughter, *A New World Order* (Princeton, Princeton University Press, 2004) 36–68.

[89] See Pierre-Hugues Verdier, 'Transnational Regulatory Networks and Their Limits' (2009) 34 *Yale Journal of International Law* 113, 153.

[90] See www.internationalcompetitionnetwork.org.

[91] See Slaughter, *A New World Order* (n 88) 65–103. On judicial networks in Latin America, see Alejandra Azuero Quijano, 'Redes de Diálogo Judicial Trasnacional: Una Aproximación Empírica Al Caso de La Corte Constitucional' (2009) 22 *Revista de Derecho Público* 3.

the contribution of domestic non-judicial institutions to the international rule of law.

The Basel Committee on Banking Supervision (Basle Committee) is an example of such an instance of international law-making, where domestic non-judicial institutions (central banks and other financial authorities) adopt, through the Committee, rules that are not given formal consent by their respective state and which carry enough weight to be seen as, in effect, mandatory—regardless of their lacking in terms of legal status. Established in 1974, the Committee is a forum for cooperation on banking supervisory matters that emerged as a reaction to the failure of the Herstatt Bank in Germany and the Franklin National Bank in New York. It was originally composed by central banks governors from the G10, but has now a wider membership still composed of civil servants from national financial regulators[92] and at least one-subnational institution: the Federal Reserve Bank of the State of New York. The Committee is not an international organisation, and its secretarial and staff arrangements are provided for by the Bank of International Settlements (BIS), a formal international organisation, also based in Basel, that has served as a bank for central banks since 1930. The main objective of the Committee is to provide a forum where members can exchange information on national supervisory arrangements, improve the effectiveness of techniques for supervising international banking business, and set minimum supervisory standards in areas where they are considered desirable.[93]

Two issues have been at the centre of its activities: closing gaps on supervision, and capital adequacy. In the first area, the Committee adopts the Core Principles in Banking Supervision,[94] which allow each country's 'self-assessment' of compliance and are used by the IMF and the World Bank to assess countries' banking supervision systems and practices.[95] In the second and important area of capital adequacy (that is, capital requirements imposed on banks to absorb run-ins or abnormal losses),[96] the Committee requires bank to maintain a certain capital ratio in order to limit systemic risk in banking activities. More specifically, the Committee has

[92] The members include those from Argentina, Australia, Belgium, Brazil, Canada, China, France, Germany, Hong Kong SAR, India, Indonesia, Italy, Japan, Korea, Luxembourg, Mexico, the Netherlands, Russia, Saudi Arabia, Singapore, South Africa, Spain, Sweden, Switzerland, Turkey, the United Kingdom, and the United States.

[93] Duncan R Wood, *Governing Global Banking: The Basel Committee and the Politics of Financial Globalisation* (Aldershot, Hampshire, England, Ashgate, 2005) 22.

[94] Committee on Banking Supervision, *Core Principles Methodology* (2006). Available at: www.bis.org/publ/bcbs130.pdf.

[95] See WB and IMF (approved by Cesare Calari and Stefan Ingves), *Implementation of the Basel Core Principles for Effective Banking Supervision, Experiences, Influences, and Perspectives* (2000). Available at: www.imf.org/external/np/mae/bcore/2002/092302.htm.

[96] Wood, *Governing Global Banking* (n 93) 72.

published three Basel Capital Accords in 1988, 2004, and 2010–11, respectively. The Accords define a system for measuring capital ratios and the expected ratio for banks with international presence. While the Accords are formally non-binding, they are treated in fact as norms with crucial economic effects worldwide and provide the standards which become binding through a domestic legal act of domestic non-judicial institutions.

Despite their soft law nature, the Accords have been implemented widely.[97] Basel I was implemented by 120 countries, including the US and the EU.[98] Most importantly, perhaps, average bank capital ratios did increase around the world ahead of the Accord's final adoption in 1992.[99] Basel II, in turn, was also widely implemented; in 2006, the Financial Stability Institute did a survey among non-Committee countries and asked them about their intentions to adopt the Accord. Of 98 countries that responded, 82 had the intention of implementing[100] and, as of June 2014, 27 Committee countries had fully implemented it, including the EU and the US.[101] Basel III, however, has some problems in its implementation, due in part to the current economic climate, the perception that Basel I and II failed to prevent the financial crisis, and the fact that it is perceived as reducing the competitiveness of some powerful financial institutions.[102] As of June 2014, all Committee countries had started implementation of Basel III, and 20 had fully implemented the risk-based capital standard.[103]

Despite Basel III's bumpy ride, the general landscape of the Accords reveals a network of domestic non-judicial institutions adopting international norms that are generally complied with. This role has come under criticism due to a perceived lack of legitimacy and accountability of these sorts of networks of non-judicial institutions. Indeed, just as non-judicial institutions are able to promote domestic accountability under international law, they also seem particularly unaccountable in their role as international law-makers. Transnational regulatory networks, such as the Basel Committee, are not a transnational institution in themselves. In fact, Section 3 of the Committee's Charter expressly states that 'the BCBS does not possess any formal supranational authority. Its decisions do not have legal force. Rather, the BCBS relies on its members' commitments … to

[97] See Daniel E Ho, 'Compliance and International Soft Law: Why Do Countries Implement the Basle Accord?' (2002) 5 *Journal of International Economic Law* 647.

[98] Lawrence LC Lee, 'The Basle Accords as Soft Law: Strengthening International Banking Supervision' (1998) 39 *Virginia Journal of International Law* 1, 16.

[99] Verdier, 'Transnational Regulatory Networks and Their Limits' (n 89) 137.

[100] Financial Stability Institute, 'Implementation of the New Capital Adequacy Framework in Non-Basel Committee Member Countries' (2006) Occasional Paper No 6, 3.

[101] Basel Committee on Banking Supervision, *Progress Report on Basel III Implementation* (Basel, Bank for International Settlements, 2014) 2.

[102] Lyngen, 'Basel III: Dynamics of State Implementation' (n 25) 519–20.

[103] See Basel Committee on Banking Supervision, *Progress Report on Basel III Implementation* (n 101) 2.

achieve its mandate'.[104] In this sense, when one speaks of the Committee as a transnational regulatory network, one is also speaking of the domestic non-judicial institutions that compose it—the latter institutions acting as global actors, and not mere domestic regulators. Hence, the challenge of accountability described above. Granted, non-judicial institutions are individually accountable to domestic constituencies, as their members do belong to domestic governments.[105] And yet, serious questioning remains as to the role of non-judicial institutions as international law-makers, in at least three senses.

First, the idea that regulatory networks composed of non-judicial institutions, such as the Basel Committee, are more accountable than broader policy networks clashes with the argument that they act in the interest of a 'hypothetical global polity'.[106] After all, if such networks are accountable to their domestic constituencies, their loyalty is with them, and not with a global public interest, such as the international rule of law. As a corollary of such argument, the interaction between non-judicial institutions in the regulatory network would simply mimic the *realpolitik* of state diplomacy, because each would be pressing for their own (polity's) agenda.[107]

Second, parliamentary transnational networks are particularly weak.[108] Non-judicial institutions belonging to regulatory networks are not democratically elected and their accountability, if any at all, is due to their domestic constituencies. However, their authority does not derive from their domestic constituencies. Rather, their authority (and ultimate legitimacy) derives often from their expertise. Regulatory networks are the environment where expertise is exercised *par excellence*, and they are a prime example of Kennedy's 'background politics'.[109] Such background politics of expertise within regulatory networks are not subject to any significant scrutiny, and are in a difficult relation with a culture of transparency and accountability.

Finally, intimately connected to the last point, due to the claim to expertise of non-judicial institutions, regulatory networks are often presented as efficient mechanisms for solving global problems. However, it is less clear whether networks are *actually* solving any problems. We lack a criterion for deciding when a regulatory network is useful: of course, there will

[104] Source: www.bis.org/bcbs/charter.htm.

[105] See Slaughter, *A New World Order* (n 88) 6.

[106] See Verdier (n 89) 121.

[107] eg, Ho models 'domestic political fragmentation' (ie, the number of domestic players with veto power—for example, federalism, bicameralism, domestic regional structures, and so on) involved with implementation of the Basel Accords, and inversely correlates it with likelihood of implementation. See Ho, 'Compliance and International Soft Law: Why Do Countries Implement the Basle Accord?' (n 97) 660–70.

[108] See Slaughter, *A New World Order* (n 88) 104–30.

[109] Kennedy, 'Challenging Expert Rule' (n 26) 3–5.

be always a non-binding declaration to show, but how do we know if the problem is actually solved? The Basel Committee is, by all accounts, quite effective.[110] However, we lack a plausible counterfactual to test when regulatory networks are exercising their powers. This means that, while we will always have a non-binding resolution to view as the *product* of a regulatory network, we cannot know whether such a document is a successful or an unsuccessful outcome. Thus, even the solution-based angle of non-judicial institutions can be called into question.

VI. CONCLUSION: THE INTERNATIONAL RULE OF LAW BEYOND COMPLIANCE

This chapter has explored some of the ways in which non-judicial institutions are relevant for the international rule of law. Just as our understanding of the international rule of law is incomplete without domestic courts, it is also crucial that we consider domestic non-judicial institutions as part of the equation. A reliable map of the international rule of law requires that we widen our gaze, and consider these institutions as variables that have an impact on global issues.

Understanding the role of non-judicial institutions in global regulatory governance allows us to critically reconsider the traditional compliance-based understanding about the international rule of law. Perhaps due to our perennial anxiety derived from the dual attack of, on the one hand, Austinean positivists arguing that international law is not really 'law', and, on the other, realists denouncing its irrelevance, international lawyers have traditionally accepted that compliance, understood as the correspondence of state behaviour with international rules,[111] is one of the key issues of our discipline. The role of law in global politics is then framed as a dichotomy, asking whether states really do behave as they do because of international law or whether they follow their own self-interest that just happens to coincide with what the law says. Rationalists (which covers realists and institutionalists) would defend a version of the latter approach.[112] Most international lawyers, in turn (and certainly those that consider the international rule of law an ideal to be achieved) would consider that law does have the normative power to shape state

[110] See Kenneth Anderson, 'Book Review: Squaring the Circle? Reconciling Sovereignty and Global Governance Through Global Government Networks: A New World Order by Anne-Marie Slaughter' (2005) 118 *Harvard Law Review* 1255, 1278.

[111] See Benedict Kingsbury, 'The Concept of Compliance as a Function of Competing Conceptions of International Law' (1997) 19 *Michigan Journal of International Law* 345, 346.

[112] For a summary, see Jack Goldsmith and Daryl Levinson, 'Law for States: International Law, Constitutional Law, Public Law' (2008) 122 *Harvard Law Review* 1791, 1824–30.

preferences, thus explaining compliance. In this context, studying the role of non-judicial institutions becomes a task of finding out whether or not they facilitate compliance with the state to which they belong.

However, while compliance is doubtlessly a relevant issue, this way of framing the role of law in the exercise of global power is both too wide and too narrow to explain why domestic non-judicial institutions matter for the international rule of law. On the one hand, it is too wide because, as Kingsbury has argued, the focus on compliance is irremediably tied to the wider theory of international law held by the observer. That wider theory will entail a specific notion of compliance, which will in turn determine whether or not non-judicial institutions play a role in it. This framework tells us more about the underlying theory of international law held by the observer than about the role played by non-judicial institutions in the international rule of law.

Compliance is also too narrow a lens through which to understand why non-judicial institutions matter. It sees the state as a black box, and focuses on whether this closed entity complies with norms. Domestic non-judicial institutions do not register from this point of view because they are, after all, mere state organs whose behaviour is assessed to see whether the state as a whole complies with international law. Against this view, we need to disaggregate the state, and see domestic non-judicial institutions as independent actors that interact within the state, and with other actors outside it.

From this disaggregated perspective, the function of non-judicial institutions is not one of compliance, but of promoting accountability. This chapter also triggers one different question. If it is true that we must engage with domestic non-judicial institutions, could such an engagement transform our understanding of the international rule of law? On the one hand, the international rule of law is our constant in the analysis, and this chapter is an effort to figure out how non-judicial institutions affect it. However, as we dig deeper into the different roles played by domestic non-judicial institutions, it seems clearer that our definition of the international rule of law needs to evolve as we consider new phenomena. It seems much more plastic than expected. In this sense, the international rule of law can be understood, as Jeremy Waldron has suggested, as an essentially contested concept.[113]

Now: let us be clear that proposing that the rule of law is an essentially contested concept does not mean that all definitions are irrelevant, and neither does it imply some sort of conceptual relativism where all definitions are acceptable and none are final. The idea of essentially contested

[113] See Jeremy Waldron, 'Is the Rule of Law an Essentially Contested Concept (in Florida)?' (2002) 21 *Law and Philosophy* 137.

concepts refers to two levels of dispute.[114] First, is its *location*: the debate on the meaning of the rule of law is not restricted to the borderlines of 'hard cases' (for example, whether the protection of property should be part of the rule of law), but occurs at its core: those advancing the arguments disagree on the *essence* of the concept as well as on paradigmatic cases that may exemplify such essence.

That the debate refers to the core of the concept makes the rule of law a *complex* notion. However, complexity is not enough for essential contestedness. There is a further *normative* dimension to it: the rule of law is a desirable outcome, and all participants of the discussion on its meaning agree on that. In Waldron's words, 'everyone says that the achievement is valued as a whole, even though they disagree about the parts'.[115] The rule of law is, at the same time, the issue being discussed and the benchmark against which the conclusions are evaluated.

This combination of complexity and normativity saves us from cynicism. If the rule of law were merely a *complex* concept, then the debate would be pointless: each definition would be as valid as the next one, and only power or influence would decide which definition succeeds. However, the normative dimension of the concept, 'the sense that *somewhere* in the midst of this contestation there is an important ideal that social and political systems should aspire to',[116] engages all the participants in proposing a definition that is bound to be controversial and contested, but that is judged against the benchmark of the ideal of rule of law. Over time, through this process, some of the outlines of the achievement come into focus (for example, the international rule of law requires general laws). However, a final definition will never be reached—as further elements of the rule of law become clear, other definitions appear that will in turn be contested, and so on and so forth.

In that sense, the international rule of law is not a checklist, but a space for contestation. Far from condemning us to cynicism and immobility, the idea of the rule of law as an essentially contested concept implies that there is an active community engaged in discussing it. We have already accepted domestic courts as part of that active community. I think it is time that we consider domestic non-judicial institutions as relevant voices in that same process.

[114] ibid 148–53.
[115] ibid 150.
[116] ibid 151.

7

Interactions Between Domestic Social Norms and International Law over Trade Dispute Resolution

JI LI

I. INTRODUCTION

AT THE TIME of its establishment, the WTO Dispute Settlement Mechanism (DSM) was hailed as revolutionary progress towards the ideal goal of the international rule of law. Effective operation of the WTO DSM has since been cited as 'evidence for the hope that international law can emerge from its "twilight existence"'.[1] With compulsory jurisdiction over WTO member states and the authority to issue binding decisions, the DSM has several of the major features of a domestic court and is 'the teeth of the WTO that ensure its provisions be respected'.[2] When a dispute arises, the complaining member state, politically powerful or not, may force the responding state to negotiate by requesting a consultation. If no agreement is reached at the consultation stage, the complaining state may then request a panel, which, composed of independent experts, will review the facts and relevant WTO rules and produce a report in a timely manner. Both parties, if unsatisfied with the result, may appeal the panel report to the Appellate Body (AB), which reviews only the legal aspects of the panel ruling. An AB decision is final, and the parties are obligated to comply or otherwise risk trade retaliations authorised in accordance with the WTO rules.[3]

[1] James Bacchus, 'Groping Toward Grotius: The WTO and the International Rule of Law' (2012) 44 *Harvard International Law Journal* 533, 539.

[2] Dencho Georgiev and Kim van der Borght, *Reform and Development of the WTO Dispute Settlement System* (London, Cameron May, 2006) 16.

[3] Without appeal, a panel report becomes a binding ruling unless it is unanimously rejected by the Dispute Settlement Body.

By the end of 2013, 474 formal requests for consultation had been filed. Though the United States and the European Union are by far the most active participants in the system,[4] a growing number of developing countries have also used the mechanism to resolve trade disputes. Some developing countries are even more active than many of the developed world.[5] As of the drafting of this chapter, a majority of the disputes have been fully resolved through settlement during consultation or through litigation. A mere 10 disputes reached the stage of compliance proceedings, and non-compliance was found in only five of them.[6]

The apparent efficacy of legalism embodied in the WTO DSM, however, overshadows its incompatibility with the domestic norms of some member states that strongly emphasise non-legal dispute resolution. While adapting to the new international regime as a result of being sued by litigious states, countries with 'non-litigious' social norms continue to avoid legal resolution of their trade disputes. Such avoidance constitutes a de facto contestation of the international legal regime.[7] This chapter argues that, in response to such de facto contestation, the WTO DSM should reform its institutions in two ways. On the one hand, litigious states should be discouraged from engaging in the use of legal trickeries; on the other, non-litigious states should be provided with institutional assistance to change their negative perception of legal dispute resolution and overcome their lack of social support for using the WTO DSM. The two reforms will strengthen the efficacy of the WTO DSM and its legitimacy, which contributes to the rule of law in international trade dispute resolution.

This chapter contributes to the edited volume by exploring the interfaces of domestic social norms governing dispute resolution and the development of the international rule of law regime. Unlike most of the other chapters, which focus on how certain areas of domestic *jurisprudence* co-evolved with relevant international law, this chapter provides a theoretical model for understanding how the diversity of domestic *social norms* affects international trade dispute resolution mechanisms.

II. EXTANT LITERATURE ON THE WTO DSM

As one of the most frequently used international institutions with a quasi-judicial nature, the WTO DSM has received intensive scholarly attention.

[4] They have filed 51 cases against each other.

[5] Raúl A Torres, 'Use of the WTO Trade Dispute Settlement Mechanism by the Latin American Countries: Dispelling Myths and Breaking down Barriers' (2012) *World Trade Organization Annual Report* 1, 86.

[6] Official website of the WTO, available at: http://wto.org/english/tratop_e/dispu_e/dispu_current_status_e.htm.

[7] For a detailed summary about national contestations of international rule of law, see ch 1 (Kanetake) of this volume.

Numerous studies have explored states' use (and disuse) of the system to resolve trade disputes by studying, in particular, when and how disputes arise, escalate, and are eventually resolved. Most scholars have, so far, focused on objective and structural factors for the variance among states in terms of the use of the DSM. For instance, Guzman and Simmons argue that many developing countries lack the human, financial, and institutional capacity to fully take advantage of the WTO DSM as their wealthier counterparts do.[8] Along the same line, Busch finds legal capacity to be of critical importance to a state's dispute resolution preference.[9] In addition, the regime type is an important factor, as a government's inclination for formal dispute resolution appears to correspond with the level of its accountability to industries.[10] Such inclination can also be motivated by the use the ruling of the international tribunal to quiet domestic resistance on certain trade issues.[11] There is also evidence that being a defendant in a lawsuit significantly increases the chance that the defendant later brings a case against the plaintiff to appease domestic critics and to serve as a bargaining chip when negotiating compliance with the lost suit.[12] Moreover, Davis and Bermeo argue that developing countries participate less frequently in the disputing forum because of high start-up costs, and that past experience with the litigation system, either as a complainant or a defendant, increases the likelihood that the developing country will initiate a formal trade dispute.[13]

Given the strong ties between the state and industries in trade matters, some argue that industry features play a determinant role in a state's choice of dispute resolution mechanism. Based on a detailed study of Japan, Davis and Shirato demonstrate that industries will invest more in WTO adjudication if they are of low-velocity and the firms with a long-term time horizon expect to benefit from a victory. In addition, the study shows that political relations matter in the decision to litigate.[14]

[8] Beth A Simmons and Andrew T Guzman, 'Power Plays and Capacity Constraints: The Selection of Defendants in World Trade Organization Disputes' (2005) 34 *The Journal of Legal Studies* 557, 591–92.

[9] Marc L Busch, Eric Reinhardt and Gregory Shaffer, 'Does Legal Capacity Matter? A Survey of WTO Members' (2009) 8 *World Trade Review* 559, 576.

[10] Ji Li, 'From See You in Court—To See You in Geneva: An Empirical Study of the Role of Social Norms in International Trade Dispute Resolution' (2007) 32 *Yale Journal of International Law* 485, 504.

[11] Todd L Allee and Paul K Huth, 'Legitimizing Dispute Settlement: International Legal Rulings as Domestic Political Cover' (2006) 100 *American Political Science Review* 219, 223–25.

[12] Eric Reinhardt, 'Aggressive Multilateralism: The Determinants of GATT/WTO Dispute Initiation, 1948–1998' (2000) available at: www.isr.umich.edu/cps/pewpa/archive/archive_99/19990004.pdf.

[13] Christina L Davis and Sarah Blodgett Bermeo, 'Who Files? Developing Country Participation in GATT/WTO Adjudication' (2009) 71 *Journal of Politics* 1033, 1047.

[14] Christina L Davis and Yuki Shirato, 'Firms, Governments, and WTO Adjudication: Japan's Selection of WTO Disputes' (2007) 59 *World Politics* 274.

Because of the specific subject matter jurisdiction of the WTO DSM, some argue that certain attributes of the trade barriers and the disputes are important determinants of a state's selection of dispute resolution mechanism.[15] Guzman and Simmons find evidence that transaction costs are a main hurdle for settlement of a trade dispute.[16] If the subject matter of a dispute is such that compromise between the disputing states is difficult to obtain (eg, as in the case of safety regulations), the dispute is more likely to escalate.[17] In addition, the number of parties involved in a dispute affects the transaction costs of its resolution, and subsequently, the likelihood of dispute escalation. Thus, third-party participation reduces the chance of early settlement, but increases the plaintiff's chance of winning a legal victory.[18] In addition, Bown presents evidence that the volume of trade and the economic dependence thereof are important factors to consider.[19]

Also, as retaliation under the WTO DSM takes the form of authorised trade sanctions, the size of a winning state's economy matters indirectly through the credibility of retaliation.[20] Bown finds credible retaliation by the plaintiffs to be the most important factor that ensures compliance by the defendants.[21] He argues that potential complainants may avoid the WTO DSM because of, in addition to market size and capacity restraints, their capability to carry out retaliating policies ('vigilante justice').[22]

As summarised above, in the study of trade dispute resolution under the WTO DSM, scholars from a wide variety of perspectives analyse how certain objective political, economic, procedural, or structural factors determine a state's choice of dispute resolution mechanism. What has been under-explored is how domestic social norms impact the international dispute resolution regime. The process of perceiving a violation, blaming a rule-breaker, negotiating a settlement, filing a dispute, and/or litigating the dispute is inherently an inter-subjective process engaged by government officials, corporate leaders, and other relevant domestic and

[15] Andrew Guzman and Beth A Simmons, 'To Settle or Empanel? An Empirical Analysis of Litigation and Settlement at the World Trade Organization' (2002) 31 *Journal of Legal Studies* S205, S226–27; Davis and Shirato, ibid 297.

[16] Guzman and Simmons, 'To Settle or Empanel?', ibid, S222–23.

[17] ibid.

[18] Marc L Busch and Eric Reinhardt, 'Three's a Crowd: Third Parties and WTO Dispute Settlement' (2006) 58 *World Politics* 446.

[19] Chad P Bown, 'Participation in WTO Dispute Settlement: Complainants, Interested Parties, and Free Riders' (2005) 19 *World Bank Economic Review* 287; Pilar Zejan and Frank Bartels, 'Be Nice and Get Your Money—An Empirical Analysis of World Trade Organization on Trade Disputes and Aid' (2006) 40 *Journal of World Trade* 1021.

[20] Steve Charnovitz, 'Rethinking WTO Trade Sanctions' (2001) 95 *American Journal of International Law* 792.

[21] Chad P Bown, 'On the Economic Success of GATT/WTO Dispute Settlement' (2004) 86 *Review of Economics and Statistics* 811.

[22] Chad P Bown, 'Trade Remedies and World Trade Organization Dispute Settlement: Why Are So Few Challenged?' (2005) 34 *Journal of Legal Studies* 515.

international human actors. These individuals carry predispositions and values formed in their various domestic settings, which are different and may or may not change during the process. The differences inevitably affect how they interpret and react to the choice of dispute resolution mechanism, and subsequently, their decisions to settle or to litigate, which will affect the institutional legitimacy and efficacy of the WTO DSM. Research about the differences in domestic norms will provide directions for future institutional reforms that will enable more member states to benefit from the legalistic trade dispute resolution regime. It is puzzling that domestic social norms have largely evaded the academic radar for trade dispute resolution, despite the explosive growth of norm-based studies of international law and international relations in the past two decades.

Though the subject is generally under-explored, some literature does point to the importance of social norms for the study of the WTO DSM. Peng notes that the legalistic approach of the WTO is not consistent with the culture of East Asian countries. Under the Confucian influence, East Asian countries share an attitudinal preference for social harmony. When disputes occur, great efforts will be made to settle them.[23] Peng uses the low rates of complaints filed by East Asian countries as evidence of this regional cultural trait.[24] He suggests that the East Asian members should change their norms, adopt the legalistic approach, and sue more often.[25] McConnell takes a more structural perspective by arguing that 'the Chinese approach to dispute resolution, which favors mediation and settlement to an outside decision-maker (eg, courts), also reflects a relationship-based approach (perhaps realistically, since the court systems are unpredictable)'.[26] Other scholars, while recognising the cultural conflict, emphasise the effects of learning and observe that the East Asian countries have become more 'legally aggressive' and participated actively in the WTO DSM system.[27] The observation is consistent with the empirical evidence showing that past experience of litigating a dispute significantly increases the complainant's propensity to do it again.[28] Moreover,

[23] Shin-yi Peng, 'The WTO Legalistic Approach and East Asia: From the Legal Culture Perspective' (2000) 1 *Asian-Pacific Law and Policy Journal* 78, 89.

[24] ibid.

[25] ibid.

[26] Moira McConnell, 'From Relationships to Rules: A Comment on China's Accession to the WTO in Response to Pitman Potter's Article' (1999) 32 *Canadian Business Law Journal* 468.

[27] Henry Gao, 'Aggressive Legalism: the East Asian Experience and Lessons for China' in Henry Gao and Donald Lewis (eds), *China's Participation in the WTO* (London, Cameron May Ltd, 2005) 322; Gregory C Shaffer and Ricardo Meléndez-Ortiz, *Dispute Settlement at the WTO: the Developing Country Experience* (Cambridge, Cambridge University Press, 2010) 11; Dukgeun Ahn, 'Korea in the GATT/WTO Dispute Settlement System: Legal Battle for Economic Development' (2003) 6 *Journal of International Economic Law* 597.

[28] Davis and Bermeo, 'Who Files?' (n 13).

taking a sociological approach, Cho argues that 'under the communitarian framework, the WTO is also a reflection of the intersection of various emerging patterns of normative discourse within the WTO that are influenced by historical developments and different discursive conditions'.[29]

In short, existing studies generally focused on the three following points: (1) a specific domestic culture (particularly China) is inconsistent with the legalistic nature of the WTO DSM, (2) a specific regional culture (particularly East Asia) is incompatible with the legalism of the WTO DSM, and (3) the WTO DSM regime constitutes a framework of legal discourses in the sense that the regime evolves generally through normative intercourses among member states. What remains missing is the dynamic interaction between domestic social norms governing dispute resolution and the legalistic nature of the WTO DSM. That is: how does the WTO DSM's emphasis on legal resolution of trade disputes impact member states whose domestic social norms strongly discourage formal dispute resolution, and more importantly, how do these countries respond to the normative conflict and how does such a response in turn influence the WTO DSM? Without the understanding of the interaction, one cannot fully explain why the member states resolve their trade disputes differently. For instance, those taking the view that certain legal cultures conflict with the legalism of the WTO DSM have difficulty explaining the increasing activeness of those countries in litigating trade disputes (eg, Korea and China). Yet those who see the regime as a learning process and predict a linear development can hardly explain the fact that most of the cases filed by the adapting states are targeted at the United States and the European Union.

Recent studies by Conti have begun to fill some of these gaps. From a socio-legal perspective, Conti shows how interactions of trade officials in the international community influence dispute resolution of the member states. He argues that 'the likelihood of a dispute escalating to the panel level is determined by the configuration of the parties'.[30] In addition to the structural factors, such as trade volume and economic size, Conti shows the importance of learning and reputation to a member state's legal capacity.[31] However, Conti attributes the differences in dispute resolution behaviour mainly to a state's status as either a one-shotter or a repeated player. A repeated player is able to accumulate experience and know-how about the WTO DSM, strengthen its legal capacity, and build a litigious reputation. Thus, a repeated player routinely litigates trade disputes.

[29] Sungjoon Cho, 'Beyond Rationality: A Sociological Construction of the World Trade Organization' (2012) 52 *Virginia Journal of International Law* 321, 344.

[30] Joseph A Conti, 'Learning to Dispute: Repeat Participation, Expertise, and Reputation at the World Trade Organization' (2010) 35 *Law & Social Inquiry* 625.

[31] ibid.

In contrast, one-shotters use litigation 'in an ad hoc manner to repair or terminate a long-term relationship'.[32] Because they litigate sporadically, one-shotters are not incentivised to build a litigious reputation.[33] Conti correctly argues that in respect of how trade disputes are resolved, 'it is not the attributes of the participant that matter so much as how those attributes interact in a specific dispute'.[34]

Though Conti has made progress in exploring the inter-subjective process of trade dispute resolution, his theory is inadequate because it overlooks the effect of varying domestic social norms. Conti explains why one-shotters and repeated players behave differently and argues convincingly that the way they interact determines how trade disputes are resolved. But how do countries obtain their status as a one-shotter instead of a repeated player in the first place? Conti attributes the status difference to the number of underlying trade disputes—ie, states with sporadic disputes become one-shotters.[35] By doing so, he neglects the role of domestic norms governing dispute resolution in shaping a state's status choice. Moreover, focusing mainly on the linear process of learning and legal capacity building, Conti's theory cannot explain why certain repeated players have refrained from suing one another.

III. A NEW, NORM-BASED APPROACH

I introduce a new approach to understanding the inter-subjective process of dispute resolution under the WTO DSM. Relevant groups from different member states carry diverse sets of value and cognitive systems that were formed in their domestic settings. The systems play a critical role in member states' choice and interpretation of dispute resolution actions. In plain English, 'a person's rational choice depends on the accumulation of past decisions that have formed his dispositions and in part on the costs and benefits of his present alternatives'.[36] Past investment 'in acquiring knowledge and skills and forming social ties and group identifications affect the individual's assessment of the relative merits of current choices', and 'someone who has developed the dispositions necessary to succeed in one normative environment tends to be reluctant to major changes of the norm and will oppose any such initiatives'.[37] To be more specific,

[32] ibid.
[33] ibid.
[34] ibid.
[35] ibid.
[36] Dennis Chong, *Rational Lives Norms and Values in Politics and Society* (Chicago, Ill, University of Chicago Press, 2000) 47.
[37] ibid.

how individuals exposed to diverging information and incentives adapt depends on (1) the investment in their prior existing norms, and (2) the balance between the diverging incentives. An individual lightly invested in a prior set of norms and exposed to frequent high positive incentives for new alternative norms will adapt quickly, whereas an individual invested heavily in existing norms will adapt slowly or resist such adaptation.[38]

The WTO DSM provides the possibility of litigation as the last resort for resolving trade disputes. When a dispute arises, the disputing states face a range of options to resolve it, from negotiating a settlement, mediation, settlement during the mandatory consultation, to requesting a panel review, the report of which may be further appealed to the AB on issues of law.[39] Though negotiation does not necessarily end at the moment when a request for a panel study is filed, the decision reflects the collective preference of relevant decision-makers of both states, such as trade officials and industrial representatives, to escalate a dispute. It is obvious that, in addition to the material costs and benefits each mechanism incurs, the officials' perception regarding the proper way to resolve disputes should play an important role.

Litigation propensity has been a familiar subject for academic research. Scholars have long categorised different legal cultures and traditions into 'litigious' and 'non-litigious' ones. In a prototypical litigious country, individuals are more inclined to litigate disputes. Going to court is considered a common method for clarifying legal and contractual ambiguities and misunderstandings. Settlement out of court is regarded as more desirable than litigation for cost-saving reasons, not for any general normative preference for social harmony. By contrast, individuals in a prototypical non-litigious country exhibit strong preference for non-judicial dispute resolution because it is considered appropriate. The filing of a lawsuit is generally perceived as a strong signal of hostility and is done only to send such a message, to terminate cooperative relationships, or in extreme situations where substantial interests are at stake yet no alternatives are available. Making excessive concessions for the purpose of settling disputes is considered a virtue, and harmony is valued more than clarifying or protecting individual rights according to the law.[40]

[38] Chong's book contains a more rigorous presentation of the mechanism: ibid, 53–62.

[39] Not considering the option of bearing the loss without protesting.

[40] There are diverging views over the cause of low litigiousness. Many argue without much explanation that anti-litigation is rooted in historical cultural teachings. See, eg, Takeyoshi Kawashima, 'Dispute Resolution in Contemporary Japan' in A Von Mehren (ed), *Law in Japan: the Legal Order in a Changing Society* (Cambridge, Mass, Harvard University Press, 1963) 41. Some take a step further and point to active state role in managing and channelling social conflicts. See, eg, Frank K Upham, *Law and Social Change in Postwar Japan* (Cambridge, Mass, Harvard University Press, 1987); John Owen Haley, 'The Myth of the Reluctant Litigant' (1978) 4 *Journal of Japanese Studies* 373. Others argue that availability of thick social contexts enable disputes to be resolved through social channels, not courts.

The preceding paragraph merely describes the extreme cases of litigiousness and non-litigiousness, which are better viewed as two ends of a continuum. Most societies posit somewhere in between, at different distances towards either end. One often-discussed example of a litigious country is the United States, and a well-known relatively non-litigious country is Japan.[41] Today, even the most non-litigious communities have judicial institutions available for formal dispute resolution, and their social norms over the selection of dispute resolution mechanisms usually allow certain types of disputes to go to litigation; for instance, disputes with strangers.[42]

Individuals in litigious societies detach litigation from negative symbolic meanings. In a prototypical litigious society, going to court is viewed a routine matter for resolving disputes. The protection of legal rights and interests takes precedence over preservation of harmony. If a settlement is reached, it is likely due to low costs and expediency, not out of a sense of appropriateness or for fear of social sanctions. Trade officials from such litigious societies find home in the legalistic settings of the WTO DSM. Though settlement is still encouraged, the procedure for litigation resembles that of a domestic court. Having invested heavily in a normative system that treats litigation mechanically, officials and other stakeholders of litigious states encounter few anti-litigation incentives in the WTO DSM that may cause adjustment of their predispositions. Building a reputation of litigiousness may actually work to a member state's advantage.[43] Applying their litigious norms to trade dispute resolution, the officials and other stakeholders make decisions based on simple cost-benefit analysis, choosing the mechanism that will achieve the desirable outcome in the most timely and cost-efficient manner, while ignoring or discounting other parties' normative predispositions. To US trade officials, suing

Ellickson proposes that repeated interactions in close-knit communities resemble a repeated prisoner's dilemma game, leading to cooperation without the coercive power of legal institutions. See Robert C Ellickson, *Order Without Law How Neighbors Settle Disputes* (Cambridge, Mass; London, Harvard University Press, 1994). A recent empirical study by Ramseyer, however, suggests otherwise. J Mark Ramseyer, 'Litigation and Social Capital: Divorces and Traffic Accidents in Japan' (2014) 11 *Journal of Empirical Legal Studies* 39. Posner sees social norms as signals intended to separate groups with different attributes. According to this line of argument, avoidance of litigation may be a costly signal to differentiate the cooperative type from the non-cooperative type. See Eric A Posner, *Law and Social Norms* (Cambridge, Mass, Harvard University Press, 2000). An in-depth analysis of the literatures over the cause of non-litigious norms is beyond the scope of this study. Suffice it to say that non-litigious societies share the general normative preference for alternative dispute resolution.

[41] There is a literature disputing the normative aversion to litigation in Japan, eg, Frank K Upham, *Law and Social Change in Postwar Japan* (Cambridge, Mass, Harvard University Press, 1987); John Owen Haley, 'The Myth of the Reluctant Litigant' (1978) 4 *Journal of Japanese Studies* 378; J Mark Ramseyer, 'Reluctant Litigant Revisited: Rationality and Disputes in Japan' (1988) 14 *Journal of Japanese Studies* 111.

[42] Ellickson (n 40).

[43] Conti, 'Learning to Dispute' (n 30) 633.

the European Union is no different from suing China, though the filing of a lawsuit is interpreted differently in these two societies.

By comparison, for trade officials and other stakeholders from non-litigious countries, the process of participating in dispute resolution under the WTO DSM framework is vastly different from their past experiences. Having invested heavily in domestic norms against litigation, the officials' non-litigious predispositions naturally persist after they begin to interact with officials from other countries in the new setting. Though the WTO DSM provides a formal adjudicatory institution for resolving disputes, non-litigious officials will try to avoid it. When disputes occur, a non-litigious state will more likely insist on a non-judicial resolution. As in their domestic settings, lawsuits are filed only to signal hostility, to terminate cooperative relationships, or to resolve disputes of great importance when less confrontational solutions are unavailable. Put differently, while all member states may prefer settlement to litigation, as the former tends to be more cost-efficient and timely than the latter,[44] trade officials and other relevant stakeholders from non-litigious countries will make more of an effort to settle than those from litigious countries.[45] Such preference for settlement reflects not only systemic inadequacy of the non-litigious countries' capacity to litigate complicated cases, but also their long-formed predispositions against formal dispute resolution.[46] Though the non-litigious norms and predispositions are generally static, they are subject to change if exposed to conflicting information and incentives.[47] But during the early period of participation in the WTO DSM, non-litigious trade officials treated all other member states similarly, considering them as trade partners and not distinguishing the litigious from the non-litigious. As a result, very few non-litigious states would initiate lawsuits soon after their participation in the WTO DSM.

In contrast, officials from litigious countries are not bound by the same non-litigious normative constraints, so they file lawsuits more frequently and do so without regard for the defendant's non-litigious predispositions. When a litigious state files a lawsuit against a non-litigious state, trade officials and other stakeholders in the latter naturally perceive such behaviour as a signal of hostility, lack of commitment to cooperation, or interests of great importance at stake. Their natural reaction would be retaliation for the former and concessions for the latter, or a mixture of both (eg, making

[44] Li, 'From See You in Court—To See You in Geneva' (n 10) 492; Amelia Porges, 'Settling WTO Disputes: What Do Litigation Models Tell Us' (2003) 19 *Ohio State Journal on Dispute Resolution* 141, 145.

[45] Li (n 10).

[46] ibid.

[47] Chong, *Rational Lives Norms and Values in Politics and Society* (n 36).

concessions on the specific trade issue but threatening retaliation on other bilateral matters). Such reactions may have prevented litigation if targeted at a non-litigious state, but not when the other party is from a litigious society and is immune to retaliation. Officials from litigious states interpret excessive concessions not as a virtuous gesture signalling goodwill, but as a sign of weakness in legal position or capacity. Such interpretation will only trigger more lawsuits from litigious states. And the 'unexpected' frequent filings of lawsuits by litigious states challenge the pre-existing non-litigious norms and dispositions. As the conflict translates into high costs, receivers of the non-litigious predispositions will adapt.

As discussed at the beginning of this section, individuals exposed to new incentives and information that contradict their pre-existing predispositions may adapt to new norms if the cost is otherwise too high. However, if past investment in their value and norm systems is significant, the individuals will adapt in a way that minimises the cost. So instead of adopting litigious norms wholesale and completely rejecting their non-litigious norms, they will likely differentiate the litigious states and apply subsets of their existing norms to resolving disputes with them. Every country has in place a full range of institutions for dispute resolution, from informal mediation to formal judicial tribunals. Litigation is socially approved in limited situations even in non-litigious countries.

Non-litigious states, once having identified and distinguished litigious states from non-litigious states, will apply differentiated treatments. Non-litigious norms no longer constrain the non-litigious states, nor do they expect the litigious states to misinterpret the filing of lawsuits. They will behave in ways similar to litigious states, making their choice of dispute resolution method based on material cost-benefit analysis. To most observers, the non-litigious states have become 'legally aggressive'. But what the observers have missed is the differentiation of litigious states from non-litigious states. While suing the 'outsiders' is approved of, suing your 'neighbours' is still frowned upon. The 'newly aggressive' non-litigious states are expected by other non-litigious states to refrain from litigation when resolving disputes among them. Thus, disputes between two non-litigious states continue to be governed by shared norms against litigation.

The causal relationship between domestic social norms governing dispute resolution and state's behaviour under the WTO DSM framework is described in the two-by-two table (see Table 1). Everything else being equal, when both disputing parties are litigious states, ie, under their domestic social norms, the filing of lawsuits are not associated with hostility or lack of commitment to cooperative relationship, trade disputes are more likely to escalate. Not bound by non-litigious norms, litigious states do not hesitate to sue non-litigious states, which, at different stages of learning and differentiation, may offer excessive concessions to avoid

Table 1: The Effect of Disputing State's Domestic Social Norms on Litigation Frequency

<table>
<tr><td colspan="2" rowspan="2"></td><th colspan="2">Complaining State's Domestic Social Norm</th></tr>
<tr><th>Non-litigious</th><th>Litigious</th></tr>
<tr><th rowspan="2">Responding State's Domestic Social Norm</th><th>Non-litigious</th><td>Low
(static)</td><td>Medium
(unstable)</td></tr>
<tr><th>Litigious</th><td>Medium to High
(unstable)</td><td>High
(static)</td></tr>
</table>

litigation. Therefore, we will likely observe medium frequency of disputes escalating into lawsuits when litigious states complain against non-litigious states. The frequency should vary according to changes in legal capacity and other case-specific factors.

In contrast, two non-litigious states share the same norm against formal dispute resolution. Between them, the filing of lawsuits is interpreted as a signal of hostility, and a lack of commitment to cooperative relationships, or substantial interests at stake. The sharing of the norm exhibits the feature of what economists call 'common knowledge'. That is, non-litigious state A knows that non-litigious state B knows that A will perceive a filing of lawsuit by B as a show of hostility, and vice versa. Therefore, B should avoid suing unless it intends to show hostility, and the normal reaction by A to such a show of hostility is retaliation. Thus, barring serious deterioration of diplomatic relations, two non-litigious states will avoid litigating trade disputes under the WTO DSM. Hence, low frequency of dispute escalation as noted in the up-left cell of Table 1. Because of the shared expectation, no single party is incentivised to deviate from the pattern of behaviour, so the frequency of litigation should remain low and relatively steady.

In comparison, when a non-litigious state enters into a dispute with a litigious state, the former is not subject to the same normative constraint governing disputes between two non-litigious states. In other words, officials from non-litigious states view the litigious states as belonging to a different category, excluded from the communal norm. Based on past experience and observation as third parties, they understand that to litigious states, lawsuits are not interpreted as hostility, nor are concessions for the sake of settlement viewed as tokens of goodwill. Litigation decisions are based on routine cost-benefit analysis. Therefore, non-litigious states will be more inclined to sue litigious states, and the decision is affected more by capacity, if any, than by the sense of appropriateness. As a result, we observe medium or even high frequency of dispute escalation when a non-litigious state complains against a litigious state (see lower-left cell of Table 1).[48]

One may argue that the prediction reflects the effect of nothing more than varying legal capacity of the member states. It is reasonable to expect high correlation between the level of litigiousness and legal capacity. However, if legal capacity is the only explanation, we should observe more cases where non-litigious states have become 'legally aggressive' and are suing other non-litigious states to take advantage of their relative superior legal capacity. But as will be discussed in a moment, what we have generally observed is that newly aggressive states focus their fight on the traditional litigious states.

Another alternative explanation of the litigation pattern described above is retaliation. A member state will more likely file a lawsuit if previously sued by the responding state. As a result, we observe frequent litigation between litigious states, and a litigious state and a non-litigious state, but not between two non-litigious states. Retaliation and the threat of it are no doubt critical factors in maintaining liberal trade order without litigation. But it is important to note that the forms, meanings, and conditions of retaliations vary according to different domestic social norms of the retaliating states. As will be discussed in more detail, Korea, a traditionally non-litigious state, began to sue the United States actively because its officials learned to understand that the US government viewed litigations under the WTO DSM as a routine matter and would not retaliate. In comparison, Japan refrained from suing China because of the expectation that a lawsuit would cause retaliation and serious damages to their diplomatic relations. The idea of retaliation, I argue, has limited predicting power if separated from the understanding of domestic social norms.

An important question of relevance is how non-litigious states maintain a liberal trade order without frequently resorting to a formal dispute resolution mechanism under the WTO. Order may be achieved without litigation, as demonstrated by our experience with international trade before the WTO DSM was established. The long-term gains of free trade, plus the threat of retaliation for violating liberal trade principles, had induced compliance and cooperation. The formal legal regime under the WTO DSM was partially intended to protect those countries without sufficient power to retaliate.

Before proceeding to the empirical case-study section, I would like to pause and clarify the goal of this chapter. The proposed norm-based perspective over international trade dispute resolution is not to supplant

[48] Although, everything else equal, the two types of mixed configurations of the disputants both result in medium frequency of litigation, I do not mean the two will be exactly equal. Suffice it to say the two posit in between the frequencies of dispute escalation when two non-litigious states or two litigious states quarrel.

extant theories, but to supplement them. The study is to demonstrate that without understanding varying domestic norms of WTO member states, scholars have missed important aspects of the operation and development of the WTO DSM.

IV. EMPIRICAL CASE STUDIES

To evaluate the new theoretical approach, I conducted interviews with trade officials of selected countries and collected secondary materials on how they resolved trade disputes. When a trade dispute arises, the complaining state typically has three options: (1) to not take any action (absorbing the loss without protesting); (2) to protest and then settle it outside the WTO DSM or during the mandatory consultation stage in the WTO DSM, or (3) to resort to the formal dispute resolution mechanism, ie, filing a request for panel adjudication.[49] As I will demonstrate in this section, domestic norms governing dispute resolution of *both* disputing states exert significant impact, in an inter-subjective manner, on the states' choice.

For the following reasons, four countries (Japan, Korea, China, and the United States) were chosen for the empirical case-study. First, trade among these countries is of high volume (see Figure 1), which generates a sizable pool of disputes that may escalate to lawsuits under the WTO DSM. Second, because I hypothesise that a non-judicial dispute resolution mechanism is preferred by non-litigious countries in resolving disputes between them, I need at least two of such states to test the proposition. Moreover, the United States is included in the study as a litigious state to illustrate what happens when domestic norms of two disputing states diverge. I will also briefly discuss disputes between the United States and the European Union as an illustration of how two litigious states resolve trade disputes.[50] Below is a brief description of the trade relations and the domestic norms of these selected countries, as necessary background for the discussion.

Relatively speaking, on the social norm spectrum, Japan, China, and Korea are non-litigious, and the United States is litigious. The three countries in East Asia have developed norms that discourage litigation and elevate the importance of compromise and harmony. Striving to resolve disputes through negotiation is viewed as an expression of goodwill, whereas litigation is a signal of hostility and the end of a cooperative relationship,

[49] The parties may still negotiate a settlement during the formal adjudicatory process.

[50] Yet dispute resolution between 'the two elephants' is not the focus of this chapter because scholars have thoroughly studied the subject.

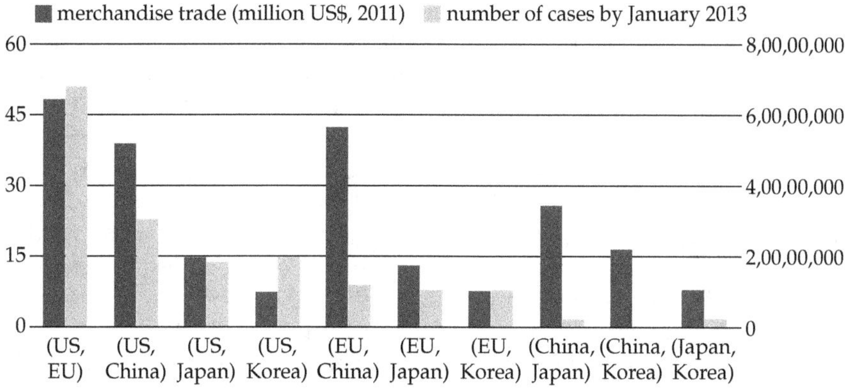

Figure 1: Trade Volume and Number of Cases

set aside for use in only extreme situations.[51] Granted, litigation is also an unpleasant experience in the United States, but it is not necessarily a strong signal of hostility. Though there are communities within the United States that have adopted norms against litigation, such as diamond traders in New York City,[52] ranchers from Shasta County in California,[53] or members of the Amish community,[54] the American domestic social norm in general does not associate litigation with hostility *to the same degree* as one will find it does in China, Japan, or Korea.[55] The position of the European Union on the continuum of litigiousness is likely in-between the United States on one end and Japan, China, and Korea on the other, but closer to the former than the latter. For example, the weighted average lawyer population ratio of the European Union is slightly more than half of the US ratio, but more than 10 times that of Japan, and 17 times that of Korea and China.[56]

[51] See Ugo Mattei, 'Three Patterns of Law: Taxonomy and Change in the World's Legal System' (1997) 45 *American Journal of Comparative Law* 5, 39; Phillip J McConnaughay, 'Rethinking the Role of Law and Contracts in East-West Commercial Relationships' (2001) 41 *Virginia Journal of International Law* 427, 479.

[52] Lisa Bernstein, 'Opting Out of the Legal System: Extralegal Contractual Relations in the Diamond Industry' (1992) 21 *Journal of legal Studies* 115.

[53] Ellickson, *Order Without Law How Neighbors Settle Disputes* (n 40).

[54] Bruce Bonta, 'Conflict Resolution among Peaceful Societies: The Culture of Peacefulness' (1996) 33 *Journal of Peace Research* 403.

[55] There have been movements in the United States to curb social litigiousness. Litigants are encouraged to use alternative mechanisms, and not courts, to resolve disputes. Setting aside the degree of success of such programs, the general recognition of the pathological level of litigation is by itself a clear sign that the society is litigious relative to most other countries.

[56] Li (n 10) 514.

As indicated in Table 1, everything else equal, the norm-based theory described herein predicts high frequency of trade disputes between litigious countries escalating to lawsuits. This paragraph is a brief case-study of trade dispute resolution between two litigious states, the United States and the European Union. Trade disputes between the two are resolved regularly through litigation, and officials on both sides treat litigation as a routine matter.[57] Filing a panel request is considered business as usual.[58] Legal professionals decide on the preferred mechanism for dispute resolution based on cost-benefit analysis. Settlement is preferred not because it is considered appropriate or it signals goodwill, but because litigation is time-consuming and costly.[59] Even if a trade dispute escalates to a lawsuit, neither side will view the panel request as expressing hostility or lack of commitment to the cooperative relationship, not to say a personal offence. By the end of 2012, the two parties had filed 51 cases against each other under the WTO DSM, by far the most active litigants in the system (see Figure 1). And there has not been clear evidence that such active use of the WTO DSM has negatively impacted their diplomatic relations.

The theory also predicts that when disputing states have diverging social norms regarding the 'proper' way to resolve disputes, the states will more likely adjudicate their trade disputes, though the frequency is usually lower than if both states were litigious. Also, in their historical dealings over trade disputes, the litigious state tends to be the first one to file a lawsuit, 'surprising' the non-litigious state. The case studied below involves the United States and China. The US government filed two complaints at the WTO DSM against China in April 2007. In one of the two cases, the US government alleged that China failed to meet its obligations to protect intellectual property rights under the WTO.[60] In the other, the allegation was that the Chinese government violated the WTO law by restricting the access of US companies to the Chinese market of audio-visual products.[61]

If the respondent had been the European Union, the filing of the panel requests might have just been viewed as business as usual. But because it was targeted at China, a non-litigious state, the response of Chinese officials was dramatically different. Immediately after the filing, the Chinese

[57] Conti (n 30).

[58] ibid.

[59] ibid.

[60] Information about the case from the official website of the WTO is available at: www.wto.org/english/tratop_e/dispu_e/cases_e/ds363_e.htm.

[61] Information about the case from the official website of the WTO is available at: www.wto.org/english/tratop_e/dispu_e/cases_e/ds362_e.htm.

government 'expressed deep regret and strong dissatisfaction'.[62] The spokesman for the Ministry of Trade commented that 'the American decision to complain [at the WTO DMS] will seriously undermine the cooperative relations the two nations have established in the field and will adversely affect bilateral trade'.[63] Not having expected the strong reaction and the association of the filing with hostility, ranking US officials travelled to China in an effort to convince the Chinese leaders that the filing was not a sign of hostility indicating lack of commitment to long-term cooperative relationships, but rather a common practice in resolving international trade disputes. The US officials stressed that their government 'utilizes trade dispute settlement mechanisms with our closest allies and trading partners'. They noted that '[t]his is not a sign of hostility toward the country in question. In fact, it is often a sign of the deepening of the overall economic relationship between the United States and its trade partners',[64] and litigation against China at the WTO DSM 'were not acts of aggression but a normal recourse to legitimate grievance procedures'.[65] Their Chinese counterparts were reported to have 'understood that the United States was more accustomed to litigating disputes'.[66] However, the US officials 'were not sure they had entirely convinced the Chinese side that legal challenges were not personal insults'.[67]

On another occasion, in response to the complaint filed by the United States over weak IP protection in China, the Chinese vice premier in charge of foreign trade stressed that the filing of a formal complaint against China at the WTO DSM was not only against the mutual understanding built by leaders of the two states, but also seriously affecting cooperation in the field of IP protection. She emphasised that the Chinese government would react affirmatively according to the legal framework of the WTO.[68] Immediately after the US government filed the complaint, the Chinese government ceased all negotiations with the United States on the protection of IP rights, apparently to express the ranking officials' anger at the perceived show of hostility. Soon after, China filed a complaint against the

[62] Keith Bradsher, 'China Conveys Regret Over US Trade Complaints' (*The New York Times*, 11 April 2007).

[63] ibid.

[64] Thomas J Christensen, Deputy Assistant Secretary for East Asian and Pacific Affairs, Remarks Before the US China Economic and Security Review Commission (delivered by John Norris, Director of the Office of Chinese and Mongolian Affairs on Mr Christensen's behalf) Washington, DC, 2 Feb 2007, available at: http://2001-2009.state.gov/p/eap/rls/rm/2007/79866.htm.

[65] Steven R Weisman, 'Little Headway with China on Finance' (*The New York Times*, 13 Dec 2007).

[66] ibid.

[67] ibid.

[68] 'Zhongmei Kaitan Zhishichanquan; Meifang Zhishaohui Shudiao Yi'an' ('China and US Began IP Talk; US Will Lose At Least One Case') (*Shanghai Securities*, 5 June 2007).

United States in the WTO DSM.[69] As discussed earlier, the non-litigious social norm allows retaliation in the form of litigation once a cooperative relationship has been terminated by a lawsuit. In addition to retaliations, Chinese officials also responded to litigation threats by making concessions that were deemed excessive from a legal perspective.[70]

Because of their size and power, the United States and the European Union are relatively immune to retaliations. Nor did excessive concessions, interpreted not as tokens of goodwill but as signs of legal weakness, appear to have any positive effect. After being sued repeatedly by the United States and the European Union and observing how they resolved disputes with other member states, Chinese officials adapted by categorising them in a different group from the non-litigious states. By the end of 2012, China has filed eight suits against the United States and three against the European Union, which has been cited by scholars as evidence for becoming more 'legally aggressive' in the use of the WTO DSM system (see Figure 1).

Similarly, the experience of Korea illustrates how a non-litigious country changes its dispute resolution behaviour in response to more frequent litigation. As a member of the GATT, Korea rarely utilised the international dispute resolution institution, partially because of its domestic social norm that treats 'legal confrontation as the demise of diplomatic or normal relations'.[71] Like China, in the early years of the WTO, Korea acted mostly on the responding side of trade complaints, and the complainants were either the United States or the European Union.[72] Repeated conflicts between Korea's non-litigious norms and legal challenges under the WTO DSM resulted in a normative adaptation. In 1997, with the assistance of foreign lawyers, the Korean government brought a dispute to the DSM over certain anti-dumping measures adopted by the US government.[73] Thoroughly prepared, the Korean government won the case, and the anti-dumping measure at issue was subsequently revoked. The US government did not perceive the lawsuit as 'demise of diplomatic relations', nor did it take any retaliatory action. Having recognised the fact that litigation is largely detached from hostility in litigious countries, trade officials and other stakeholders in Korea have adapted and been making decisions

[69] Information from the official website of the WTO is available at: www.wto.org/english/tratop_e/dispu_e/cases_e/ds368_e.htm.

[70] Li (n 10).

[71] Dukgeun Ahn, 'Korea in the GATT/WTO Dispute Settlement System: Legal Battle for Economic Development' (2003) 6 *Journal of International Economic Law* 597.

[72] By the time of this research, Korea was sued 7 times before its first panel request. In the 7 cases, 4 were filed by the United States, 2 by the European Union, and 1 by Canada.

[73] Junsok Yang, 'Learning by Doing: The Impact of a Trade Remedy Case in Korea', available at: www.wto.org/english/res_e/booksp_e/casestudies_e/case21_e.htm.

about trade disputes in accordance with material cost-benefit analysis.[74] Consequently, Korea has become an active user of the WTO DSM when the other party is known not to associate litigation with hostility. In the 15 cases Korea had filed with the WTO DSM by the end of 2012, nine were targeted at the United States, and three at the European Union.[75]

Though non-litigious states such as Korea and China have become more 'legally aggressive', in contrast to other scholars, I argue that fewer disputes will be resolved formally between non-litigious countries because of the shared norm denigrating litigation. Evidence of the trade relations between China and Korea is consistent with my argument. As shown in Figure 1 above, China has grown to be Korea's largest export market, yet the Korean government has not filed a single panel request to resolve a trade dispute with China. This is not due to absence of trade quarrels, or China's strict compliance with the WTO rules.[76] Liberal trade order has been maintained through a limited tit-for-tat strategy for violations; not litigation under the WTO DSM. For instance, in 1999 when Sino-ROK bilateral trade amounted to $25 billion and Korea enjoyed a substantial trade surplus with China,[77] a 'trade war' broke out between these two non-litigious countries. On 1 June 1999, the Korean government increased tariffs on garlic imported from China to 315 per cent in an effort to protect Korean farmers. The Chinese government immediately retaliated by temporarily banning importation of Korean mobile phones and polyethylene. Soon after the conflict arose, both governments began to actively negotiate a solution.[78] By August, an agreement had been reached. The settlement reflected a compromise of interests on both sides, and immediately thereafter normal bilateral trade resumed.[79] The dispute over the garlic tariffs appeared not to have any lasting negative impact, as the Sino-ROK bilateral trade have continued to grow at a high rate.

Trade disputes may occur unexpectedly. Claiming food safety concerns, South Korea imposed restrictions over 'kimchi' products imported from China in October 2005. Following the limited tit-for-tat strategy, the Chinese government announced the finding of the same problem in food

[74] Email interview with a legal professional working for the Korean government on international trade matters (New Haven, 3 May 2007). (The interview reflects only personal opinions of the interviewee; not the official view of the Korean government.)

[75] Data from the official website of the WTO, available at: www.wto.org/english/tratop_e/dispu_e/dispu_by_country_e.htm.

[76] eg, Japan's Ministry of Economy, Trade and Industry (METI) published 2006 Report on the WTO Consistency of Trade Policies by Major Trading Partners, which 'devotes 75 pages to explain China's policies whose WTO consistency are at least problematic'. Junji Nakagawa, 'No More Negotiated Deals?: Settlement of Trade and Investment Disputes in East Asia' (2007) 10 *Journal of International Economic Law* 837, 844.

[77] 'Sino-ROK Trade Dispute: Not Worth It' (*People's Daily*, 10 Aug 2000).

[78] 'China, Korea Discuss Garlic Trade Dispute' (*People's Daily*, 30 June 2000).

[79] See ibid.

imported from Korea and imposed similar restrictions. Once again, ranking officials from both states investigated the issue and publicly expressed the belief that the general cooperative relationship between China and Korea would not be affected.[80] Meanwhile, food safety agencies of the two countries established a consultation and cooperation mechanism to resolve the problem. Import of kimchi made in China was resumed and the random testing rate was eventually lowered to the pre-crisis level.[81] Though Korea has become 'legally aggressive' and filed 15 suits under the WTO DSM, it has refrained from suing China, its biggest trade partner that is not known for perfect compliance with the WTO rules. In an interview with a Korean trade official who had extensive experience dealing with WTO issues, I asked his view about the influence of social norms on trade dispute resolution with China. The official believes that with a shared social norm against litigation, the Korean government will not resolve disputes with China in the same way as it does with the United States, even when the disputes are the same in all other aspects.[82]

Though my theory predicts that non-litigious states will avoid suing each other to resolve trade disputes, it does not completely rule out the possibility of a lawsuit. It only predicts that under the shared non-litigious norms, when a lawsuit is filed, the complaining party intends to send a signal of hostility or of the fact that interests of great importance are at stake, yet less confrontational solutions are unavailable, and the responding non-litigious state will interpret, and is expected to interpret, such filing as a signal of hostility or an action deriving from extreme situations, as evidenced by the next case between Korea and Japan. High volume of bilateral trade between the two inevitably generates disputes. Trade officials and other stakeholders in Japan are guided by non-litigious norms and adopt them as the default standard to evaluate different options for resolving international dispute resolution.[83] Everything else being equal, Japanese officials make more effort to resolve disputes through negotiation and believe that countries sharing similar norms will do the same.[84]

Korea filed its first panel request against a non-litigious state, Japan, in February 2005. The case was triggered by an investigation conducted

[80] 'Hanguo Wanzhang Biaoshi Bunengrang Paocai Wenti Yingxiang Hanzhong Maoyi' ('Korean Foreign Minister Vowed no Influence from the Kimchi Problem') (*Xinhuanet*, 2 Nov 2005) available at: http://news.xinhuanet.com/fortune/2005-11/02/content_3720526.htm.

[81] 'Han Zaijiang Rujing Choujian Bili, Zhonghan Paocai Shijian Jiejue' ('Korea Again Lowered Testing Rate, Kimchi Incident Resolved') (*Xinhua Daily Telegraph*, 11 Jan 2008) available at: http://news.xinhuanet.com/mrdx/2008-01/11/content_7406768.htm.

[82] See data from the official website of the WTO, available at: www.wto.org/english/tratop_e/dispu_e/dispu_by_country_e.htm.

[83] Interview with a former senior WTO official of Japan (New Haven, 12 Feb 2006) (the statements represent only the official's personal opinions, and not the official view of the Japanese government).

[84] ibid.

under the Provisional Investigation Rules of 2002 by the Chinese government against Japan's laver import quota allocated exclusively to Korea.[85] As my theory would have predicted, Japan and China resolved the issue through negotiation, and Japan agreed to allocate a certain quota to China. The Korean government, however, filed a complaint at the WTO DSM, alleging that Japan's quota violates Article XI.1 of the GATT 1994, and Article 4.2 of the WTO Agreement on Agriculture.[86] Instead of agreeing to settle during the mandatory consultation stage, Korea took the dispute to the panel.[87] The interviewed Japanese trade official expressed his surprise at the Korean government's move and his belief that the Korean officials were aiming at something other than resolving the dispute.[88] As discussed in section III, filing a lawsuit over a trade dispute was perceived by officials adopting non-litigious social norms not as a routine technical move, but as a signal carrying greater meaning, for example, hostility or diminishing commitment to cooperation. Records show that at the time of the trade dispute, Korea and Japan experienced difficulties in their diplomatic relations. It was reported that an internal memorandum by the Japanese Foreign Ministry expressed its official view that politicians in Korea were stimulating anti-Japan sentiments among Korean voters to boost their political support.[89] Thus, the persistence in litigating the trade dispute was likely interpreted as a sign of hostility and demise of diplomatic relations.

Japan's panel requests against China were filed in a similar diplomatic context. Given shared non-litigious norms, Japanese officials had avoided adjudicating trade disputes with China. When the US government filed the formal complaint against China's IP protection, Japan was invited to join as a co-complainant. The Japanese government declined the invitation, though its review of China's compliance with the WTO rules cited numerous violations. The decision was made shortly before the Chinese Prime Minister's visit to Japan.[90] Interviews with industry leaders and government officials in Japan indicate that their concern with possible damages to diplomatic relations was a major reason for their abstaining

[85] Nakagawa, 'No More Negotiated Deals?' (n 76).

[86] ibid.

[87] More details on the case are available at the official website for the WTO. WTO, Dispute Settlement: Dispute DS323, available at: www.wto.org/english/tratop_e/dispu_e/cases_e/ds323_e.htm.

[88] See Interview with a former senior WTO official of Japan (New Haven, 12 Feb 2006) (the statements represent only the official's personal opinions, and not the official view of the Japanese government).

[89] 'Ri Waiwusheng Neibu Baogao Renao Hanguo Rihan Waijiao Chongtu Yichu Jifa' ('Internal Report of Japanese Foreign Ministry Angers Korea Japan-Korea Diplomatic Conflict Ready') *China Youth Daily* (Beijing, 6 April 2006).

[90] Nakagawa (n 76).

from suing China at the WTO DSM.[91] Because of the non-litigious social norm, Japanese officials and industry leaders anticipated that the filing of a lawsuit would be interpreted by Chinese officials as an insult, and jeopardise diplomatic relations. When bilateral relations were improving, the Japanese officials declined to send such signals to their Chinese counterparts.

The normative restraint, however, does not prevent Japan from filing a panel request when diplomatic relations with China have reached a nadir that blocks all less confrontational solutions to a trade dispute of great importance to Japan's core interests, as evidenced by the suits filed by Japan against China over its control of rare earth export quota. The backdrop of the cases was deteriorating bilateral relations ignited by a territorial dispute. In September 2010, a Chinese captain was detained by Japan after his fishing ship collided into Japanese coastguard vessels in disputed waters.[92] As Japan refused to release the captain, Chinese officials blocked the export of rare earth to Japan, causing a surge of its market price. China had a near monopoly of the international supply of rare earth, and Japan's industry relied heavily on the material.[93] The Japanese government eventually released the captain, a move considered political humiliation.[94] Since the incident, diplomatic relations between the two states have further deteriorated. Anti-Japan protests erupted in major Chinese cities and high-level meetings were cancelled. Against this backdrop, settlement of the trade dispute over the ban of rare earth export would be politically costly on both sides. Hence, Japan filed its first panel request against China at the WTO DSM.[95]

To recapitulate, by studying selected cases, this section evaluates and substantiates my theory, ie, in the inter-subjective process of dispute resolution, the norms of *both* disputing parties matter. Everything else being equal, disputes are more likely to escalate when the two parties are both litigious, treating litigation as a matter of routine (eg, United States v European Union). The WTO DSM allows litigious states to force non-litigious states into using formal procedures to resolve trade disputes,

[91] Davis and Shirato, 'Firms, Governments, and WTO Adjudication' (n 14).

[92] Mure Dickie and Kathrin Hille, 'Japan's Arrest of Captain Angers Beijing' (*Financial Times*, 8 Sept 2010) available at: www.ft.com/cms/s/0/a09e651a-bb04-11df-9e1d-00144feab49a.html#axzz2J7vUL9tP.

[93] James T Areddy, David Fickling, and Norihiko Shirouzu, 'China Denies Halting Rare-Earth Exports to Japan' (*Wall Street Journal*, 23 Sept 2012), available at: http://online.wsj.com/article/SB10001424052748704062804575509640345070222.html; Keith Bradsher, 'China Still Bans Rare Earth to Japan' (*The New York Times*, 10 Nov 2010), available at: www.nytimes.com/2010/11/11/business/global/11rare.html?pagewanted=all&_r=0.

[94] Martin Fackler and Ian Johnson, 'Japan Retreats With Release of Chinese Boat Captain' (*The New York Times*, 24 Sept 2010) A1.

[95] The only other Panel request was filed in Dec 2012, when there was no sign of improving diplomatic relations.

and exerts pressure on them to adapt their norms to the new legalistic institutional context (eg, United States v Korea or China). Non-litigious states subsequently become legally aggressive and learn to file more panel requests (eg, Korea or China v United States or European Union). Such aggressiveness, however, is selectively targeted. The newly-aggressive states continue to refrain from suing other non-litigious states since the latter (non-litigious) states expect the former states to retain the shared norm against formal dispute resolution (eg, Korea or Japan v China). As a result, very few trade disputes between non-litigious states escalate to lawsuits, and only when perceived hostility is intended or substantial interests are at stake with no alternative resolutions.

The empirical case-study also demonstrates the inadequacy of extant theories focusing on objective and structural factors. Take power as an example. Though the United States is by any measure more powerful than China, Korea sues the former frequently but has avoided litigating against the latter. As to trade volume, China has long surpassed the United States as Korea's largest trade partner, yet Korea has not filed a single panel request against China. Nor do political regimes fully explain the differences. China has refrained from suing Japan and Korea, both liberal democracies, but has been more inclined to take the United States to court. And given the wide range of trade disputes between the studied countries, varying transaction costs alone cannot explain the different choices of dispute resolution mechanism. In short, besides structural and objective factors, the configuration of domestic social norms—in particular, norms regarding the selection of dispute resolution mechanism—play a significant role in determining how states resolve trade disputes. Though the non-litigious states studied herein are selected from East Asia, the theory is not limited in application to that region.[96]

V. CONCLUSION

Extant studies of international trade dispute resolution under the WTO DSM pay scant attention to domestic social norms. The few that have considered country or region-specific cultures that are inconsistent with the legalistic structure of the WTO DSM advocate and predict a linear transformation that will result in non-litigious states becoming more 'legally

[96] Social norms are contagious, so states of similar normative systems tend to cluster geographically. Still, I expect to see significant cross-country variation in the level of litigiousness, and other non-litigious countries outside East Asia. A more comprehensive quantitative study incorporating a measure of litigiousness will be able to test the hypothesis about the importance of social norms in shaping trade dispute resolution under the WTO DSM regime.

aggressive'.[97] And the few that adopt a constructivist's perspective over the WTO DSM offer theories that are either of limited predictive power[98] or indistinguishable from the literature on legal capacity.[99] This chapter provides an alternative norm-based theory about how domestic social norms governing dispute resolution affect the inter-subjective discourse over international trade disputes and their resolution against the backdrop of the WTO DSM. I argue that even if non-litigious states have substantially strengthened their legal capacity, they may continue to refrain from suing each other. Because of the shared norms against litigation, the 'newly aggressive' non-litigious states will continue to behave in ways consistent with the common expectation and settle most of their trade disputes.

Counter-intuitively, the non-litigious states' legal aggressiveness towards litigious states and enhanced legal capacity to litigate under the WTO DSM may actually facilitate the settling of disputes between non-litigious states because it strengthens the positive signalling function of litigation avoidance.[100] In other words, with sufficient legal capacity to litigate, a state may better signal goodwill to a non-litigious state by refraining from litigation. A good example is Korea. Having sued the United States and won numerous times, the government has demonstrated ample capacity to play the legal game in the WTO DSM. Thus, its efforts in settling all trade disputes with China will not be misinterpreted as a lack of capacity, but respect and commitment to long-term cooperative relations. And the more frequently Korea sues the United States, the more Chinese officials will appreciate its restraint from filing a lawsuit against China.

Though the equilibrium for dispute resolution among non-litigious states is relatively stable, substantial changes in domestic social norms, if they occur simultaneously, may change it. After years of interaction with litigious states in the WTO DSM, many non-litigious states have developed enough capacity to legally resolve trade disputes. If trade officials and other stakeholders of these countries all agree at certain moment to forget the normative association between litigation and hostility, there will be a surge of panel requests. Such simultaneous change in domestic social norms, however, rarely occurs spontaneously. For instance, while

[97] Henry Gao, 'Aggressive Legalism: the East Asian Experience and Lessons for China' in Henry Gao and Donald Lewis (ed), *China's Participation in the WTO* (London, Cameron May Ltd, 2005) 322.

[98] Cho, 'Beyond Rationality: A Sociological Construction of the World Trade Organization' (n 29).

[99] Joseph A Conti, 'Producing Legitimacy at the World Trade Organization: the Role of Expertise and Legal Capacity' (2010) 8 *Socio-Economic Review* 131.

[100] For a more detailed discussion of the application of signaling games to social norms, see See Eric A Posner, *Law and Social Norms* (Cambridge, Mass, Harvard University Press, 2000).

evidence indicates that certain aspects of domestic Japanese norms are moving towards the US model,[101] China has in the past few years turned against judicial dispute resolution.[102]

One should not confuse changes of the values and dispositions of the trade officials stationed in Geneva with those of other stakeholders. Individuals invested heavily in the legal profession, eg, trade lawyers, tend to adapt to the WTO rules quickly. Evidence shows that most trade officials recognise the regime as legitimate.[103] Such professionals, however, are not the only actors in the process. Important decision-makers and stakeholders in international trade disputes are deeply imbedded in domestic normative contexts. Heavily invested in non-litigious norms, these actors are reluctant to adapt.

Because of the historical dominance of diplomacy in resolving trade disputes, certain legalisation that provides certainty and order is long overdue and beneficial to all member states. The WTO DSM enables non-litigious states to resolve trade disputes between each other when their diplomatic relations break down, foreclosing informal resolution channels. However, scholars have pointed out that litigation is not the best solution for all trade disputes,[104] and litigious states have exploited the formal system by over-lawyering, which renders the system more complex, costly, and time-consuming.[105] Though every state will benefit from a less litigious WTO DSM environment that is free of 'legal trickeries', rational pursuit of the litigious states and subsequent reactions from the non-litigious states create a prisoner's dilemma problem that results in a suboptimal collective outcome.

The trend further disadvantages non-litigious states.[106] While litigious states such as the United States are pulling countries that posit close to the non-litigious end on the litigiousness continuum, major non-litigious states are dragging them back by retaliation. Though litigious states such as the United States and the European Union are largely immune to the

[101] By increasing the bar, reforming its legal education system, and introducing jury trials to criminal cases. See Nicholas C Howson and Mark D West, 'Law, Norms and Legal Change: Global and Local in China and Japan' (2006) 27 *Michigan Journal of International Law* 687, 690; Takao Tanase, 'Global Markets and the Evolution of Law in China and Japan' (2006) 27 *Michigan Journal of International Law* 873, 875.

[102] Carl Minzner, 'China's Turn Against Law' (2011) 59 *American Journal of Comparative Law* 935.

[103] Conti, 'Producing Legitimacy at the World Trade Organization (n 99) 133.

[104] Susan Esserman and Robert Howse, 'The WTO on Trial' (2003) 82 *Foreign Affairs* 130, 140.

[105] Joseph A Conti, 'The Good Case: Decisions to Litigate at the World Trade Organization' (2008) 42 *Law & Society Review* 145, 167.

[106] Karen J Alter, 'Resolving or Exacerbating Disputes? The WTO's New Dispute Resolution System' (2003) 79 *International Affairs* 783, 790.

threat of retaliations from non-litigious states, smaller states that are moving towards the litigious end of the continuum may be deterred. When asked which country China may sue next other than the United States and the European Union, a former WTO legal advisor suggested Mexico, for it had litigated against China without showing sufficient faith in reaching a settlement first.[107] Mexico, as a litigious state, probably sees its filings as reflecting a 'mature' attitude that should 'never been considered a hostile act warranting any type of reprisals'.[108] If reactions from non-litigious states pose substantial conflicts with existing norms adopted by officials and relevant stakeholders in Mexico, they will likely learn to separate the non-litigious countries from the litigious ones.

Non-litigious states have made efforts to curb the use of the system by litigious states. For instance, China has officially proposed to reform the WTO DSM to limit the number of lawsuits developed countries could file each year against a developing country.[109] To gain support from other members, the proposal has to borrow the widely-accepted concept of equity, not diverging social norms governing dispute resolution. What it fails to recognise is that many litigious states are developing countries benefiting substantially from the formal dispute resolution regime.[110] It is unlikely that such proposals therefore will receive enough support. Less dramatic measures, however, should be taken to reform the system in order to prevent the lawyering 'race to the bottom'. The remedies provided by the WTO for victims of any violation of the WTO rules should include monetary compensation for past damages. Thus, the defending state will bear part of the costs for delays, which will force it to reconsider the benefits from engaging in time-consuming 'legal trickeries'.[111]

Scholars recognising the legal capacity shortage of developing countries have long recommended reforms that will strengthen negotiated settlement of trade disputes rather than litigation. Mediation and arbitration under current the rules of DSU 5 and DSU 25, respectively, should be put into active use.[112] This chapter provides additional support to such proposals. I argue that the reform should also take into account the normative preference of non-litigious states and strengthen the mediation

[107] Interview in Beijing with an anonymous Chinese lawyer who worked as legal counsel for China's WTO mission (17 Sept 2012).

[108] Torres, 'Use of the WTO Trade Dispute Settlement Mechanism by the Latin American Countries' (n 5) 12.

[109] Georgiev and Borght, *Reform and Development of the WTO Dispute Settlement System* (n 2) 23.

[110] Torres (n 5).

[111] Porges, 'Settling WTO Disputes' (n 44) 145.

[112] Busch and Reinhardt, 'Developing Countries and General Agreement on Tariffs and Trade/World Trade Organization Dispute Settlement' (2003) 37 *Journal of World Trade* 733.

and the consultation mechanisms of the WTO DSM. Because of its heavy reliance on diplomatic relations, the WTO DSB may play a vital role in maintaining liberal trade order by acting as impartial mediators when the diplomatic relations between non-litigious states break down.

The study has broader implications. Without effective independent tribunals, international rule of law, widely or narrowly defined, will remain an illusion that vanishes upon the change of heart of powerful participating states.[113] As one of the most frequently used international adjudicatory institutions, the WTO DSM provides the best showcase of how such institutions operate and facilitate the implementation of agree-upon international rules. The study finds two clusters of states with diverging normative inclinations for judicial dispute resolution. Non-litigious states prefer mediation in the shadow of the law, and leaving judicial resolution of disputes to extreme situations, whereas litigious states are inclined to litigate and push the boundary of the law. The former risks the disuse of international tribunals, hence lack of opportunities to establish sufficient jurisprudence and to strengthen the institutional authority. Yet the latter raises the concern of over-lawyering, which results in unnecessarily complex adjudicatory procedures and more disadvantages for less litigious states.

Both results harm the institution's legitimacy, and the development of international rule of law. Viewed under the framework of the interfaces between the national and international rule of law, broadly defined, the avoidance of non-litigious states to use formal international adjudication constitutes a de facto contestation to the regime modelled on the norms and institutions of litigious states. Lack of positive response to the contestation will inevitably damage the long-term prospect of international rule of law. Going forward, in designing substantive and procedural rules for international adjudicatory tribunals, scholars and practitioners should be more sensitive to the diversity of domestic social norms governing dispute resolution. Institutional mechanisms should be put in place so that contracting states would resort to judicial resolution when and only when their disputes concern genuine issues of material domestic or international law and interests.

[113] For a discussion of international law as an instrumental tool for the powerful, see Jack L Goldsmith and Eric A Posner, *The Limits of International Law* (Oxford, Oxford University Press, 2005).

Part II

International Deference to the National Legal Order

8

The Rule of Law Dimensions of Dialogues Between National Courts and Strasbourg

BIRGIT PETERS

I. INTRODUCTION

IT IS WELL known that national courts have long since maintained a transjudicial dialogue with the European Court of Human Rights (ECtHR).[1] This concept refers to the formal and informal conversations of the ECtHR with the national constitutional and highest courts on the implementation and interpretation of the European Convention on Human Rights (ECHR). Those conversations are conducted in various fora and in manifold ways. Informal dialogues start as corridor conversations between the judges at Strasbourg, Karlsruhe, London, or Moscow, and continue as conversations between national and ECtHR judges in more formalised settings such as in Strasbourg's annual seminar series called 'dialogues between judges'; in these fora, some of the fundamental aspects on the interpretation of the Convention are debated and discussed.[2] Moreover, several national constitutional courts, such as the German Bundesverfassungsgericht or the French Cour Constitutionnel, organise similar seminars to which Strasbourg's judges eagerly contribute.[3] At the

[1] cp Anne-Marie Slaughter, 'A Typology of Transjudicial Communication' (1994) 29 *University of Richmond Law Review* 99; Christopher McCrudden, 'Common Law of Human Rights?: Transnational Judicial Conversations on Constitutional Rights' (2000) 20 *Oxford Journal of Legal Studies* 499; Monica Claes and Maartje De Visser, 'Are You Networked Yet? On Dialogues in European Judicial Networks' (2012) 8 *Utrecht Law Review* 100.

[2] On the 'Dialogue between Judges', see: www.echr.coe.int/Pages/home.aspx?p=court/events&c=#n14338512935024058350598_pointer. For the interaction of the ECtHR with national constitutional courts, cp, esp, the 2007 seminar: ECtHR, *Dialogue between Judges* (Strasbourg, European Court of Human Rights, 2007) available at: http://echr.coe.int/Documents/Dialogue_2007_ENG.pdf.

[3] cp, eg, the visits of the German Constitutional Court (Bundesverfassungsgericht, BVerfG) to other Supreme Courts and the ECtHR in 2012: BVerfG, Press Release no 41/2012,

same time, the transjudicial dialogue also takes place in a formal setting through judgments delivered at the national or the international levels concerning the interpretation of the fundamental rights of the ECHR. The formal dialogue, which is facilitated by the great number of decisions rendered regarding the Convention, is deeply intertwined with the informal dialogue. Informal dialogue may initiate or facilitate formal dialogue and create encouraging atmospheres for sharing ideas or raising disagreements. Still, it is mostly the formal dialogues between Strasbourg and the domestic courts that form the major part of the reception and contestation processes on the interpretation and development of the ECHR.[4] They constitute part of the state and international judicial practice relevant to the (dynamic) interpretation of the ECHR,[5] to considerations concerning the exercise of international (and national) judicial authority,[6] and to considerations on their interplay.[7]

There exists an extensive body of literature about particular national and international interactions, which has contributed to the interpretation and evolution of ECHR law.[8] Moreover, research has been undertaken on the legitimising effect of transjudicial dialogues,[9] on the socio-scientific[10] and legal explanations of its origins.[11] Yet, we still lack assessments on the actual processes constituting that dialogue. In which situations do national courts contest particular judgments from Strasburg, and how does the ECtHR respond?[12]

14 June 2012, *Constitutional Court of Turkey visits Bundesverfassungsgericht*; ibid, Press Release no 20/2012, 23 March 2012, *Slovenian Constitutional Court visits Bundesverfassungsgericht*; ibid, Press Release no 5/2012, 24 Jan 2012, *Bundesverfassungsgericht visits the European Court of Human Rights*.

[4] Helen Keller and Alec Stone Sweet, *A Europe of Rights: The Impact of the ECHR on National Legal Systems* (Oxford; New York, Oxford University Press, 2008).

[5] Vienna Convention on the Law of Treaties, 23 May 1969, 1155 UNTS 311 (entered into force 27 Jan 1980) (1969) Art 31(3)(b).

[6] *cf* Armin von Bogdandy and Ingo Venzke, 'In Whose Name? An Investigation of International Courts' Public Authority and Its Democratic Justification' (2012) 23 *European Journal of International Law* 7, 8.

[7] See ch 1 (Kanetake) of this volume.

[8] Of the many treatises on this matter, consider above all Keller and Stone Sweet, *A Europe of Rights* (n 4). See also Giuseppe Martinico, 'Is the European Convention Going to Be "Supreme"? A Comparative-Constitutional Overview of ECHR and EU Law before National Courts' (2012) 23 *European Journal of International Law* 401, 407. See also ch 10 (Legg) of this volume.

[9] Merris Amos, 'The Dialogue Between United Kingdom Courts and the European Court of Human Rights' (2012) 61 *International & Comparative Law Quarterly* 557, 575ff.

[10] Laurence R Helfer and Anne-Marie Slaughter, 'Toward a Theory of Effective Supranational Adjudication' (1997) 107 *Yale Law Journal* 273; Slaughter, 'Typology' (n 1) 99; Claes and Visser, 'Are You Networked Yet?' (n 1) 100–14; McCrudden, 'Common Law of Human Rights' (n 1) 449–532.

[11] Keller and Stone Sweet (n 4).

[12] For the UK, see Amos, 'Dialogue' (n 9) 557–84.

In this chapter, I will investigate the transjudicial dialogues between the national courts of the member states to the ECHR and the ECtHR. I will concentrate on the formal interactions which take place as a form of 'genuine' transjudicial dialogue in which national judgments provoked a reaction from Strasbourg and vice versa. I will argue that national courts have formalised and methodised contestations of Strasbourg's case law by defining criteria or situations in which a rejection of Strasbourg's interpretations could be justified. I will identify three different types of national contestations: (1) the 'constitutional core' exception; (2) the 'rule of law' exception, and (3) the 'incompatible methods of interpretation' exception (section III(B) below). I will demonstrate that Strasbourg has responded to those national contestations in three ways: namely, (1) by accepting the constitutional core and the rule of law exception; (2) by deference to the national levels on applying the margin of appreciation doctrine; and (3) by safeguarding the further development of ECHR rights via its consensus doctrine (section III(C) below). Taken as a whole, these elements eventually define a framework for the interactions between the ECtHR and national courts on matters of substantive human rights, thus contributing to the further development of the rule of law in the wider European realm.

II. TRANSJUDICIAL DIALOGUE

The notion of a transjudicial dialogue between the judges of highest national courts and the ECtHR is not new. Broadly understood, it describes the interactions of the ECtHR with national constitutional or supreme courts.[13] The interactions may be formal, in the sense that they represent official pronouncements of the courts, such as judgments and decisions rendered upon individual complaints,[14] or they may be informal, in the sense that they take place through joint meetings, such as joint seminars, conferences, and corridor conversations.[15] The difference between formal and informal is often one of kind and not of importance. As stated in the introduction to this chapter, formal and informal aspects of dialogue are often intertwined; informal conversations may precede, facilitate, or prepare a formal outcome and vice versa.

[13] Slaughter (n 1) 105; Joël Andriantsimbazovina, *L'autorité des décisions de justice constitutionelles et européennes sur le juge administratif francais* (Paris, Bibliothèque de droit public, 1998) 460, 503; Joël Andriantsimbazovina, 'Le modèle juridictionnel de la cour européenne des droits de l'homme et la réforme de la Cour de justice des Communautés européennes' (2000) 10(4) *Revue des affaires européennes* 410.

[14] This was assessed in Slaughter (n 1) 99.

[15] *cf* Claes and Visser (n 1) 105; Anne-Marie Slaughter, 'A Global Community of Courts' (2003) 44 *Harvard International Law Journal* 191, 192.

The above definition of judicial dialogue differs from the common dictionary definition of a dialogue as conversation between two individuals or groups[16] conducted without a particular aim[17] in that the definition used this chapter includes intentional conversations and interactions. The formal interactions between national and international courts take place with the aim of pronouncing upon concrete legal questions or interpretations of the law and build on punctual contestations of final authority[18] or agreed values,[19] and the reactions thereto. A good example for such a formal interaction is the *Horncastle* case, in which the UK Supreme Court established that there could be cases in which it could decline to follow the Strasbourg decisions, 'giv[ing] the Strasbourg Court the opportunity to reconsider the particular aspect of the decision that is in issue, so that there takes place what may prove to be a valuable dialogue between this court and the Strasbourg Court'.[20] This chapter is about those intentional and formal transjudicial dialogues.

Concerning the normative implications of the intentional, formal transjudicial dialogues between national courts and Strasbourg, previous research has shown that the reactions and contestations expressed by formal transjudicial dialogues are conducted via a certain framework.[21] Both Slaughter and Claes and Visser showed that dialogues led to structured interactions between the different levels,[22] but also noted that the dialogues were also preconditioned by the procedures in which they were conducted. In the case of the Court of Justice of the European Union (CJEU), for instance, inter-judicial dialogues are usually comprised of the preliminary reference procedure, which is formally ended by a dictum of the CJEU, after which no further judgment of a national court follows.[23]

While previous studies addressed certain normative implications of formal transjudicial dialogues, they did so in a rather piecemeal fashion. Authors have either looked at just one partner of the dialogue, or described a broad effect of dialogues as the formulation of 'structured'

[16] Oxford Dictionaries, '*Dialogue*' (Oxford University Press). Available at: http://oxforddictionaries.com/definition/english/dialogue?q=dialogue.

[17] Luc B Tremblay, 'The Legitimacy of Judicial Review: The Limits of Dialogue Between Courts and Legislatures' (2005) 3 *International Journal of Constitutional Law* 617, 630–31.

[18] André Nollkaemper, 'Contestation of Decisions of International Human Rights Courts' (2012) Draft Presented to the Multirights Annual Conference, Oslo 30 May–1 June 2012, on file with the author, 1, 2f.

[19] *cf* Slaughter (n 1) 129–32; Amos (n 9) 575.

[20] *R v Horncastle and Others* [2009] UKSC 14 (UK Supreme Court, Judgment of 9 December 2009) [11].

[21] cp Martinico, 'Is the European Convention Going to Be "Supreme"?' (n 8) 419 who argued that the dialogues between the national courts and the ECtHR nowadays develop along the lines of the principles established for the interaction of national courts with the CJEU.

[22] Slaughter (n 1) 129–32; Claes and Visser (n 1) 113.

[23] Claes and Visser (n 1) 105.

interactions.[24] This chapter, albeit scrutinising only a fraction of the possible formal transjudicial interactions, attempts to overcome the piecemeal approach by encompassing multiple cases of dialogues between the ECtHR and national courts. Moreover, this chapter considers the normative implications of the formal interactions from the perspective of the rule of law. The concept of the international rule of law is concerned primarily with procedures, which generate acceptance and respect, as well as elements of control (checks and balances) between institutions.[25] It thus may be worthwhile to consider whether and how formal transjudicial dialogues contribute to the rule of law. Yet, the rule of law is a complex and contested concept. There exist manifold understandings of it, both in common and civil law jurisdictions.[26] Therefore, I will, in this chapter, turn to those accepted elements of the international rule of law, which the framework of this book characterises as 'thin' and formalistic,[27] and which Waldron describes as setting constraints on the exercise of authority; those elements include the clarity of decisions, judicial control, and legal equality.[28]

III. TRANSJUDICIAL DIALOGUES IN THE ECHR

I will now consider particular elements of the formal transjudicial dialogue which has taken place between the highest and constitutional courts of member states and the ECtHR on the interpretation of the ECHR. I will first turn to the legal framework of that dialogue set by the ECHR and national constitutions. I will then turn to the actual framework of contestations formulated in the national courts of member states, and, thereafter, to the responses by the ECtHR.

A. The Legal Framework Established by the ECHR and National Constitutions

The rules which determine the framework of formal interactions between member states' courts and the ECtHR may be found, on the one hand, in

[24] Slaughter (n 1) 129–32; Claes and Visser (n 1) 113.

[25] *cf* Andreas Føllesdal, *PluriCourts: The Legitimate Roles of the Judiciary in the Global Order, Research Plan* (2013) 4, 8, available at: www.jus.uio.no/ior/english/research/projects/pluricourts/doc/project-plan.pdf.

[26] Simon Chesterman, 'An International Rule of Law?' (2008) 56 *American Journal of Comparative Law* 340.

[27] See chapter 1 (Kanetake) of this volume.

[28] Jeremy Waldron, 'Are Sovereigns Entitled to the Benefit of the International Rule of Law' (2011) 22(2) *European Journal of International Law* 315, 317.

the national constitutions and national laws of the member states and, on the other hand, in the ECHR. They are well known and a general overview suffices here.

From the viewpoint of the member states, their relations to the ECtHR are primarily determined by their national constitutions and national laws. Even though the traditional differentiation between monism and dualism may still be the primary perspective to characterise national approaches toward international law, it is trite to appeal to these formal distinctions with view to the ECHR.[29] Whether monist or dualist, most member states have accommodated the ECHR in their national legal order, or consider ECHR rights to have a direct effect at the national levels. Additionally, the Convention usually occupies a supra-legislative rank in the hierarchy of national laws, ie, it ranks above ordinary national laws and below the constitution.[30] Sometimes, national adherence to the ECHR and the ECtHR case law is corroborated by a provision or case law that calls for an interpretation of constitutional rights provisions 'in light of' international law.[31] On the other hand, this adherence may also be limited in case of a violation of (core) constitutional rights. Sometimes, this is supported by a so-called eternity clause, which exempts certain fundamental rights provisions of the constitution from later amendment, thus expressing their overriding importance in the hierarchy of laws.[32]

At the same time, the ECHR itself sets some general rules on the relation of national courts with the ECtHR. Article 1 of the ECHR affirms and demands that it is the obligation of the member states to respect and ensure the enjoyment of the rights enshrined in the Convention. Member states are obliged to give effect to the rights of the ECHR, pursuant to Article 46(1) of the ECHR. The principle of subsidiarity and the margin of appreciation doctrine, which have been developed by the case law of the Court, also structure the relations of the ECtHR with the member states on matters of substantive ECHR law. Both principles will become new elements of the ECHR preamble upon the entry into force of Protocol 16 to

[29] Constance Grewe, 'La question de l'effet direct de la Convention et les resistances nationales. La situation dans les autres pays' in P Tavernier, *Quelle Europe pour les droits de l'homme? La cour de Strasbourg et la realization d'une 'union plus étroite'* (Brussels, Bruylant, 1996) 149. For a similar view on the general relation of international law and constitutional law, see Armin von Bogdandy, 'Pluralism, Direct Effect and the Ultimate Say: On the Relationship between International and Domestic Constitutional Law' (2008) 6 *Journal of International Constitutional Law* 397, 400.

[30] See Alec Stone Sweet, 'A Cosmopolitan Legal Order: Constitutional Pluralism and Rights Adjudication in Europe' SSRN eLibrary (2011) 21. But there are differences with regard to individual provisions. *cf* the assessment of the Belgian Conseil Constitutionnel in *N v MJ*, Appeal in cassation, Case no C 09 0236 F, ILDC 1624 (BE 2010) (11 June 2010).

[31] *cf* Spanish Constitution, Art 10(2).

[32] *cf* German Basic Law, Art 79(3); Turkish Constitution, Art 4.

the ECHR.[33] The principle of subsidiarity is concerned, on the one hand, with a delimitation of competences, preventing unnecessary encroachment upon competences distributed among different entities and, on the other hand, with a positive right to assume competences by one entity in case the agreed competences are not met by the other.[34] The margin of appreciation concerns the deference of the ECtHR to national interpretations of ECHR rights.[35] Furthermore, judgments of the ECtHR exhibit a precedential character and are considered by member state courts not only in cases where courts are asked to enforce the judgment against the respective defendant state. This is, in part, expressed by Article 46(3) of the ECHR, which focuses on the interpretive authority of the Court in conflicts over diverging interpretations of the rights of the Convention and allows for the Committee of Ministers to refer the matter back to the Court if execution of a judgment by a member state is 'hindered by a problem of interpretation of the judgment'.[36]

The most important article for the present purposes is, however, Article 53 of the ECHR. It acknowledges and reaffirms the diversity and independence of the member states' constitutional orders. The article provides that nothing in the ECHR may be understood 'as limiting or derogating from any of the human rights and fundamental freedoms which may be ensured under the laws of any High Contracting Party or under any other agreement to which it is a party'. As the provision is yet to be successfully invoked before the ECtHR, various interpretations exist as to its normative scope and content. On the one hand, some contend that it describes a minimum standard of protection of the Convention system[37]

[33] CoE Treaty Series No 214, Strasbourg, 2 Oct 2013. As of 27 October 2015, the protocol has been signed by 11 and ratified by 5 member states of the Council of Europe. It will enter into force upon the 10th ratification. Available at: www.coe.int/en/web/conventions/full-list/-/conventions/treaty/214/signatures?p_auth=uXphUCut.

[34] Ottfried Höffe, 'Subsidiarität als staatsphilosophisches Prinzip' in Knut Wolfgang Nörr and Thomas Oppermann (eds), *Subsidiarität: Idee und Wirklichkeit: Zur Reichweite eines Prinzips in Deutschland und Europa* (Tübingen, Mohr Siebeck, 1997) 49–68. On the importance of subsidiarity in guiding the interactions between domestic and international courts on the matter of immunity, see ch 3 (Platiše) of this volume.

[35] There is an abundant literature on the principle of the margin of appreciation. For one of the latest contributions see Yutaka Arai-Takahashi, 'The Margin of Appreciation Doctrine' in A Føllesdal, B Peters and G Ulfstein (eds), *Constituting Europe: The European Court of Human Rights in a National, European, and Global Context* (Cambridge, Cambridge University Press, 2013) 62. On the margin of appreciation, see further ch 10 (Legg) of this volume.

[36] The interpretative authority of the ECtHR is further supported by Art 47(1) of the ECHR, which establishes the competence of the ECtHR to give Advisory Opinions at the request of the Committee of Ministers 'concerning the interpretation of the Convention and the protocols thereto'.

[37] The exact framework of the article does not yet seem to be clear. Jan de Meyer, 'Brèves réflexions à propos de l'article 60 de la Convention européenne des Droits de l'Homme' in Fritz Matscher and Herbert Petzold (eds), *Protecting Human Rights: The European Dimension* (Cologne, Carl Heymanns, 1988) 125 regards Art 53 as a 'most favourite protection principle', whereas Louis-Edmond Pettiti, Pierre-Henri Imbert, and Emmanuel Decaux, *La Convention*

and thereby expresses a prohibition for the member states to fall below the standard of protection provided by the ECHR. On the other hand, the article may also be understood in a positive manner, providing a right of the member states and a corresponding duty of the Strasbourg Court to respect the national constitutional identity of the member states and protect them from disproportionate infringements. Both the positive and the negative understanding correspond to the interpretation which exists in the EU for Article 4(2) of the Treaty on European Union (TEU), which has a similar content as Article 53 of the ECHR. Article 4(2) of TEU reminds the Union to 'respect the equality of Member States before the Treaties as well as their national identities, inherent in their fundamental structures, political and constitutional, inclusive of regional and local self-government', thus standardising the right and the corresponding duty of the Union to respect the constitutional core of the member states and protect it from disproportionate violations.[38] The positive and the negative right emanating from Article 4(2) of the TEU have already been discussed in two cases before the CJEU. In a case against Austria, the CJEU followed the positive definition of constitutional identity and affirmed that carrying titles of nobility was part of the national identity of Austria.[39] In another case, the CJEU invoked the negative concept of constitutional identity and considered linguistic interests as part of the national identity of Union member states and as a legitimate interest justifying restrictions to the free movement of workers.[40]

The negative and the positive understandings of Article 53 of the ECHR have also been highlighted by those who consider Article 53 as an expression of the principle of subsidiarity.[41] However, the subsidiarity principle is mainly concerned with the allocation of competence. It may provide an answer where, in a multilevelled order, decisions should preferably be located, but has not yet been developed into a concept of positive and negative rights and corresponding duties towards safeguarding a particular standard of legal protection. Thus, Article 53 of the ECHR has an

européene des droits de l'homme: commentaire article par article (Paris, Economica, 1999) at 900 conclude that the article's main proposition (the supremacy of the national constitutional order) contains a mere ritual declaration, without any practical effect.

[38] Armin von Bogdandy and Stephan Schill, 'Die Achtung der nationalen Identität unter dem reformierten Verfassungsvertrag' (2010) 70 *Heidelberg Journal of International Law* (ZaörV) 702, 725f. Some, however, contend that Art 4(2) of the TEU stipulates an ultimate limit, thus neglecting the application of the proportionality principle. See Adelheid Puttler and Wolfgang Kahl 'Art 4' in Christian Calliess and Matthias Ruffert (eds), *EUV/AEUV, Commentary* (4th edn, München, CH Beck, 2011) note 22.

[39] Case C-208/09 *Ilonka Sayn-Wittgenstein v Landeshauptmann von Wien* (Court of Justice, 22 Dec 2010).

[40] Case C-202/11 *Anton Las v PSA Antwerp NV* (Court of Justice, 16 April 2013) notes 29 and 33.

[41] Robert Spano, 'Universality or Diversity of Human Rights? Strasbourg in the Age of Subsidiarity' (2014) 14(3) *Human Rights Law Review* 493.

individual meaning beyond the idea of subsidiarity: the provision safeguards national interests by granting member states a right to invoke such interests against ECHR organs, while, at the same time, allowing those organs, in particular the ECtHR, to interpret ECHR provisions in a manner which is proportionate to national constitutional interests, safeguarding a minimum standard of protection of the ECHR. Since Article 53 of the ECHR is concerned with protecting this substantive, minimum standard of protection, it goes beyond the formal considerations of subsidiarity.

After all, constitutional provisions or constitutional practice allowing for the interpretation of national constitutions 'in light of the ECHR' as well as Article 53 of the ECHR, the subsidiarity principle, and the margin of appreciation doctrines appear as the major gate-openers for transjudicial dialogues between national constitutional courts and the ECtHR. These provisions and principles open the ECHR to national constitutions and vice versa, and allow for national as well as international interactions. Nonetheless, this primary framework for the relations of the ECtHR with member state courts is still rudimentary. It may be insufficient to capture the variety of interactions between national courts and the ECtHR and the multitude of open questions which have ensued. Are there cases in which member state courts may legitimately deviate from judgments of the ECtHR? Shall member state courts apply the same methods of interpretation as the ECtHR? In the following part of this chapter, I will therefore turn to the normative dimensions of the transjudicial interactions developed by member state courts and the ECtHR and address whether it captures some of those additional concerns.

B. The Framework of National Contestations

As pointed out above, the formal dialogue of national courts with Strasbourg emanates from the rejections of interpretive or legal authority by national courts, on the one hand, and the responses by Strasbourg to these rejections, on the other. In this part, I will first turn to the contestations of ECHR law and ECtHR jurisprudence by the national constitutional and highest courts. Considering selected cases from national courts of Belgium, France, Germany, Italy, Norway, and Slovakia, it is striking that these courts have adopted similar strategies for contesting an ECtHR judgment or ECHR interpretation in a particular case.[42] I identify three situations in which national courts found it justified not to apply ECHR law

[42] The case selection is based on the list of entries tackling the relationship between domestic courts and the ECtHR in the ILDC database until December 2014, available at: www.oxfordlawreports.com. It has been supplemented with cases from France and Norway.

and jurisprudence: (1) the constitutional core exception; (2) the rule of law exception, and (3) the incompatible methods of interpretation exception.

i. The Constitutional Core Exception

The constitutional core exception refers to the situations described by Article 53 of the ECHR; namely, the right of the ECtHR to guarantee a minimum standard of protection, on the one hand, and the right of member state courts to safeguard national constitutional particularities and human rights standards, on the other. The ECtHR will usually consider whether and how national constitutions do indeed provide a higher level of protection than does the ECHR, whereas contestations at the national levels will mostly invoke the right to safeguard a higher standard of constitutional protection. Article 53 of the ECHR thus opens significant interpretive space for the ECtHR, as well as a corresponding room for contestations for member state courts, as it may be debatable in a particular case at hand, whether or not the ECHR guarantees a particular standard of rights or whether national constitutional rights provide indeed a higher standard of protection.

Several cases before national supreme and constitutional courts deliberate whether member states may exceed ECHR standards, invoking a higher standard of constitutional rights protection. For example, the UK House of Lords held in *Ullah,* a case concerning asylum claims based on the fear of prosecution, that it was open to member states to provide standards more generous than those granted by the Convention.[43] Similarly, the German Constitutional Court emphasised in its recent case on the practice of preventive detention that it will consider ECHR law as well as interpretations by the ECtHR only as long as this did not lead to a restriction of or reduction in the strength of constitutional protection at the national level.[44] And the Slovak Supreme Court highlighted that the ECHR was not to be taken into account by the Court if the Constitution offered some wider protection than the ECHR.[45] However, national courts have also accepted the corresponding consideration that where ECHR rights provide a higher standard of protection, this higher standard of protection should be provided at the national level. This has been argued, for example, by the Italian Constitutional Court, which underlined in a decision of 2009 concerning the right to appeal against a conviction in absentia that the national constitutional provisions had to be interpreted to include the higher standard of protection of the ECHR.[46]

[43] *R v Special Adjudicator, ex parte Ullah (FC)* [2004] UKHL 26, [20] (UK House of Lords, Judgment of 17 June 2004).

[44] BVerfG, *Preventive Detention,* No 2 BvR 2365/09 (Judgment of 4 May 2011).

[45] Slovak Supreme Court, II ÚS 129/08, (Judgment of 22 April 2008), ILDC 1206 (SK 2008).

[46] Italian Constitutional Court, No 317/2009 (Judgment of 4 Dec 2009) [7].

Sometimes, however, the minimum standard of protection rule is employed in such a manner as to exclude further review by the ECtHR. For example, in a case concerning the appropriate amount of compensation for an expropriation, the Italian Constitutional Court emphasised that it was for the Constitutional Court to determine whether the ECHR or the interpretations of ECHR rights by the ECtHR provided for a protection of fundamental rights equivalent to the Constitution.[47] Such interpretations are problematic from the perspective of Article 53 of the ECHR. The provision does not exclude the jurisdiction of the ECtHR in constitutional matters. To the contrary, as highlighted before, Article 53 of the ECHR opens a corresponding interpretive space at the international level and allows for the ECtHR to assess whether or not the ECHR sets a minimum standard in comparison to constitutional provisions. Moreover, the minimum standard of protection rule functions only as long as the domestic level takes the necessary steps domestically to give effect to international fundamental rights. The rule may therefore not be applicable where the national level of fundamental rights protection is poor, defunct,[48] or violates ECHR rights. Hence, the ECtHR may also examine whether or not national constitutional provisions, or aspects which belong to the constitutional core of the member states, may justify infringements of ECHR rights.

The 'constitutional core' and the corresponding right enshrined in Article 53 of the ECHR to protect constitutional particularities has long featured in French scholarly discussions as a concept allowing for a disregard of the ECHR or Strasbourg's case law.[49] German scholars have also discussed similar ideas: Voßkule and Kaufhold argued that the implementation of the ECHR or the case law of the ECtHR, must not conflict with the eternity clause of Article 79(3) of the German Basic Law.[50] Cases from France exemplify how this argument on the constitutional core may come into action. It surfaced lately in a series of judgments on the French system of police detention. Several cases of the ECHR, amongst others, *Salduz v Turkey*, *Dayanan v Turkey*, and *Brusco v France*, had clarified that the detained, at least in cases where the arrest had been ordered by a judge prior to his arrest, had the right to be assisted by a lawyer during the

[47] Italian Constitutional Court, No 349/2007 (Judgment of 22 Oct 2007) [6.2].

[48] *cf* Helen Keller, Andreas Fischer and Daniela Kühne, 'Debating the Future of the European Court of Human Rights after the Interlaken Conference: Two Innovative Proposals' (2010) 21(4) *European Journal of International Law* 1025, 1032.

[49] Joël Andriantsimbazovina, *L'autorité des décisions de justice constitutionelles et européennes sur le juge administratif francais* (n 17) 460, 503. Andriantsimbazovina, 'Le modèle juridictionnel de la cour européenne des droits de l'homme et la réforme de la Cour de justice des Communautés européennes' (n 17) 410. *cf* Nico Krisch, 'The Open Architecture of European Human Rights Law' (2008) 71 *Modern Law Review* 183, 196.

[50] Ann-Kathrin Kaufhold and Andreas Voßkule, 'Grundwissen: Offene Staatlichkeit' (2013) 4 *JuS: Juristische Schulung* 309, 310.

beginning of the arrest as well as during the following interrogations.[51] In 2010, the Conseil Constitutionnel found the system to be in violation of the Constitution. This applied, the Court added, as far as police detention was generally allowed for the prosecutor to prolong detention after 48 hours, irrespective of the gravity of the crime committed,[52] as long as it denied the detained access to their lawyer, and, unless *cogent reasons provided by the French Constitution* demanded otherwise.[53]

The core exception also appears in the case law of the Cour Constitutionnel and the Conseil d'Etat on France's relations to the EU. In several decisions of 2004 and 2006, the Cour Constitutionnel had emphasised that even though it was a constitutional duty to implement EU directives at the national level, an exception to this duty could be made on the basis of the principle of constitutional identity.[54] The Conseil d'Etat, in its *Arcelor* decision of 2007, further refined this approach and found that the invocation of this exception required an assessment whether there was a principle at the Community law level, which, in its current nature and range, corresponded to national constitutional principles and provisions.[55] Nonetheless, only few national constitutional principles might miss out on a counterpart at the EU level, such as the principle of *laïcité*, or the definition of the electorate. Even though it is not entirely clear whether the *Arcelor* solution may be a viable way of understanding France's relationship with the ECtHR,[56] it may offer an understanding of how 'cogent constitutional reasons' could be understood in the future, and on ECHR matters.

Following this assessment of the case law on the contestations of the highest national courts, the constitutional core exception has been invoked

[51] *Brusco v France* App no 1466/07 (ECtHR, 14 Oct 2010) [45]; *Salduz v Turkey* App no 36391/02 (ECtHR, 27 Nov 2008) [50]–[62]; *Dayanan v Turkey* App no 7377/03 (ECtHR, 13 Oct 2009) [30]–[34].

[52] Case no 2010-14/22 QPC (Conseil Constitutionnel, 30 July 2010) [26].

[53] ibid [28].

[54] Case no 2006-540 DC (Conseil Constitutionnel, 27 July 2006) [18]–[20]. *cf* Case no 2004-496 (Conseil Constitutionnel, 10 June 2004) [7].

[55] Conseil d'Etat, *Societé Arcelor Atlantique et Lorraine et autres*, No 287110 (Judgment, Plenary, 27 Jan 2007).

[56] After the decision of the Conseil Constitutionnel, the Cour de Cassation declared the law in force prior to the assessment by the Conseil to be in violation of Art 6(1) of the ECHR, in so far as it did not allow for the detained to be able to consult with a lawyer in the first hour after his or her detention (Cour de Cassation, No 5699 (10–82.902), 19 Oct 2010). Subsequently, an amended law on preliminary detention was promulgated (No 2011-392, entered into force 1 July 2011). Shortly thereafter, the Cour de Cassation was called to adjudicate again on the conformity of the new law with the ECHR and reiterated that the *Salduz and Dayanan v Turkey* judgments of the ECtHR had unmistakably stated that as a general rule a detained person had the right of access to a lawyer from the first hours of detention (Cour de Cassation, No 592 (10–30.316), 15 April 2011, decision, plenary session). Thus, there is significant disagreement between the two courts on the application of Art 6 of the ECHR and on the constitutional core exception.

in cases involving three kinds of questions: first, on whether the national level of constitutional rights provides a higher level protection than does the ECHR; second, whether national constitutional traditions may provide limitations to ECHR standards; and third, whether or not national courts have the exclusive competence to determine whether the first two cases apply.

ii. The Rule of Law Exception

Another category of national contestations of ECtHR jurisprudence concerns alleged violations of the principles of clarity and consistency, which constitute the elements of the national and international rule of law. Two recent decisions invoking this rule of law objection are the *Horncastle* and *Cadder* decisions of the UK Supreme Court. In *Horncastle*, the Supreme Court established that the requirement of the ECHR to take into account the jurisprudence of the ECtHR would normally result in 'applying principles that are *clearly* established by the Strasbourg Court'.[57] Yet, the UK Supreme Court continued, there could be rare circumstances where it was in doubt whether Strasbourg 'appreciates or accommodates particular aspects of [the UK] … domestic process'. In those cases, the Court held, it was open to the Supreme Court to decline to follow the Strasbourg decisions giving reasons for adopting this course.[58] The UK Supreme Court thought this was the case in *Horncastle*, since Strasbourg's case law on hearsay evidence lacked clarity and had not sufficiently taken into account the particularities of the English common law system.[59]

Cadder, the decision following *Horncastle*, further refined the preconditions, under which national courts could refrain from applying ECHR law under the rule of law exception. First, it formulated in reverse that national courts should follow the interpretations of the ECtHR if the latter provided a clear and consistent interpretation of the rights enshrined in the ECHR. Second, the Supreme Court Justices further specified that Strasbourg's jurisprudence had to be considered as clear and consistent and therefore in line with elements of the rule of law if it was unanimous, followed repeatedly, and if it included review of other legal systems supporting the ECtHR's interpretation.[60] Moreover, the Supreme Court referred to two main cases, in which it might be possible not to apply the case law and interpretations of the ECtHR. First, national courts might ignore ECtHR case law if it departed from previous case law. Second, they

[57] *Horncastle* (n 20) [11] (emphasis added).
[58] ibid [11].
[59] ibid [14], [107]–[08].
[60] *Cadder v Her Majesty's Advocate (Scotland)* [2010] UKSC 43 (UK Supreme Court, Judgment of 26 Oct 2010) [45]–[49].

could disregard ECtHR jurisprudence if it laid down a new principle that had not been established before.[61] The *Cadder* decision establishes some higher thresholds than the previous *Horncastle* decision; yet, the problems which might ensue from this approach are obvious: taken literally, the exception gives the UK Supreme Court a veto right in all cases where Strasbourg establishes a new interpretation of the ECHR for the first time.

UK courts were not the only national courts to allow themselves to consider whether Strasbourg complied with certain rule of law standards; in particular, aspects of clarity and consistency, before applying its decisions in their national legal systems. Before the adoption of the Norwegian Human Rights Act in 1999, also the case law of the Norwegian Supreme Court built upon this 'rule of law review' of the ECtHR's findings. It considered clarity and non-ambiguity as conditions for the interpretation of national law in light of international law.[62] This jurisprudence was later abandoned.[63] Today, the Supreme Court safeguards an interpretation of national laws in line with Norway's international obligations via a balancing test. In this it may, however, be relevant whether the rights interpreted by the ECtHR appear sufficiently clear.[64] Yet, this has not yet been formulated as an exception allowing for contestations.[65]

iii. The Incompatible Methods of Interpretation Exception

Even if national, constitutional, and supreme courts have increasingly resorted to the ECtHR's methods of interpreting ECHR rights in their constitutional practice,[66] they have also contested Strasbourg's interpretations on the basis of the interpretive methodology employed at the national level. One example exhibiting this approach is Germany. Here, the question of a methodologically sound statutory interpretation arose in the *Görgülü* judgment of 1994. In this case, the German Constitutional Court found that 'German courts must observe and apply the Convention within the limits of *methodically* justifiable interpretation like other statute law of the Federal Government'.[67] The *Preventive Detention* decision of 2011 then extended this exception to constitutional interpretation, explaining that a consistent interpretation of the German Basic Law in light of the ECHR and the ECtHR's judgments must end where it can no

[61] ibid [59].
[62] Norwegian Supreme Court, Rt 1995, 1922 (18 Dec 1995).
[63] Norwegian Supreme Court, Rt 2000, 996 (23 June 2000).
[64] Norwegian Supreme Court, Rt 2011, 1118 (1 June 2011).
[65] Against this idea, see Mads Andenæs and Eirik BjørgeD, 'Norske Domstoler Og Utviklingen Av Menneskerettene' (2011) 46 *Jussens Venner* 251, 251–86, 254.
[66] Françoise Tulkens, 'The European Convention on Human Rights between International Law and Constitutional Law' (2007) *Dialogue between Judges* 8, 13.
[67] BVerfG, *Görgülü* Case no 2 BvR 1481/04 (14 Oct 2004) [32] (emphasis added).

longer be methodologically justified. The German Constitutional Court found that a consistent interpretation should not be employed where the rights of various right holders needed to be balanced against each other[68] or where the ECHR guarantees, in their 'autonomous interpretation by the ECtHR', did not match the corresponding interpretation of a textually similar constitutional guarantee under the Basic Law.[69] In any case, the German Constitutional Court found that the jurisprudence of the ECtHR had to be adjusted very carefully to the existing dogmatic framework of national constitutional interpretation.[70] Somewhat similar to the German Constitutional Court, the Spanish Supreme Court considered that the ECHR and the ECtHR's interpretations must always be interpreted as narrowly as possible, textually and functionally, thus restricting the national effects of application of the ECHR by the means of interpretation.[71]

Compared to the exception of core constitutional provisions, as suggested by Article 53 of the ECHR, the incompatible methods of interpretation exception provide a very wide exception for the implementation of ECHR rights. Constitutional rights provisions may often be formulated and interpreted differently from the ECHR. The ECHR does not contain a duty to employ the ECtHR's methods for the interpretation of the constitution. As a supranational regime with its own text, the ECHR will always be interpreted in its own right; the ECtHR has emphasised this on many occasions.[72] Therefore, the incompatible methods of interpretation exception allows, in theory, for the exclusion of virtually every interpretation by the ECtHR. This may on occasion conflict with the direct effect which ECHR rights enjoy at the national levels and the corresponding duty of the member states to effectively implement ECHR rights in their national jurisdictions. Member states may thus not circumvent their obligations under Article 1 and 13 of the ECHR by virtue of the incompatible interpretation exception.

C. International Reception

The ECtHR has responded to the above challenges in a twofold manner. On the one hand, a genuine formal dialogue has been created between Strasbourg and the national courts. The Strasbourg Court took up the

[68] BVerfG, *Preventive Detention* (n 44) [93].

[69] ibid [93].

[70] ibid [94]. For a more detailed account of the dialogue of the Constitutional Court with the ECtHR, see Birgit Peters, 'Germany's Dialogue with Strasbourg: Extrapolating the Bundesverfassungsgericht's Relationship with the European Court of Human Rights in the Preventive Detention Decision' (2012) 13 *German Law Journal* 757.

[71] Spanish Constitutional Court, José Luis PM (3 Feb 2002) [7].

[72] *Engel and others v The Netherlands* App nos 5100/71; 5101/71; 5102/71; 5354/72; 5370/72 (ECtHR, 8 June 1976) [80]–[81].

national arguments based on the constitutional core, the rule of law, and on the incompatible interpretative methods, and responded to the individual national contestations in the respective follow-up decisions. This concerns, for example, the *Lautsi* case against Italy, the *Al Khawaja and Tahery* case against the UK, and the *von Hannover* cases against Germany, as will be discussed below. Yet, the case law of the ECtHR is not confined to those immediate reactions to individual contestations. The Court formulated responses to national contestations also in further cases, either against the member states in question or against other member states, expressing general responses to some of the questions raised before, building on the quasi *erga omnes* effect on its decisions—which requires that national courts consider, not only a relevant single case, but also the general lines of Strasbourg's case law developed in cases against other member states. Those cases rely on the principle of subsidiarity, the margin of appreciation doctrine, and the consensus argument.

i. On the Constitutional Core: Legitimate Interference with ECHR Rights and the Margin of Appreciation

The ECtHR has responded to member state court challenges based upon Article 53 of the ECHR in a twofold manner. First, by engaging with the arguments brought forward on the basis of that very article; and second, by resorting to its doctrine on the margin of appreciation.

Concerning the application of Article 53 of the ECHR, the ECtHR has not yet accepted arguments turning to the constitutional core as a legitimate basis for national contestations.[73] Rather, the Court has emphasised that national measures implementing a higher standard of national constitutional rights still needed to comply with the restriction clauses of the ECHR and must be proportionate.[74] For example, in the case of *Open Door and Dublin Well Woman v Ireland*, the ECtHR dismissed the arguments made by Ireland that the right to life granted by the Irish Constitution would guarantee a higher level of protection and therefore justify legislation that prohibited the distribution of counselling material on abortion facilities outside Ireland to women of child-bearing age. The Court held that a higher constitutional level of protection of the right to life could not justify infringements of conflicting rights, such as the freedom of expression. National measures considered as infringements of ECHR rights still

[73] See section II(B)(i) of this chapter above.

[74] The ECtHR's position resembles the jurisprudence of the CJEU on Art 4(2) of the TEU; the CJEU established that measures based on this article could be considered as justified interferences with the fundamental freedoms of the TEU, but still needed to comply with the proportionality principle. See Case C-208/09 *Ilonka Sayn-Wittgenstein v Landeshauptmann von Wien* (CJEU, Judgment of 22 Dec 2010); Case C-202/11, *Anton Las v PSA Antwerp NV* (CJEU, Judgment of 12 July 2012).

needed to be in accordance with the provisions of the ECHR on restrictions of ECHR rights and proportionate.[75] Another case, *Leempoel & SA ed Cine Revue* against Belgium, concerned measures taken against the editors of a periodical who in an article had published extracts from court files delivered to a commission of parliamentary inquiry. In this case, the Court dismissed the complainants' argument that the measures taken against the editors violated provisions of the Belgian Constitution, which provided a higher level of protection than Article 10 of the ECHR. The Court argued that it had already considered the legality of the measure when considering whether it was 'prescribed by law', according to Article 10(2) of the ECHR, thus making it unnecessary to turn to Article 53.[76] Even though the respondent states were unsuccessful in invoking Article 53 of the ECHR in the cases above, this does not exclude that they may not and have not in other cases invoked proportionate measures based on the protection of core constitutional provisions as legitimate restrictions of ECHR rights.

The *Lautsi* case can be considered as a case that responded to a national contestation based on arguments, which by their nature and quality may be considered as falling into the general scope of Article 53 of the ECHR on the constitutional core. In this case, the Court adjudicated upon the Italian tradition of displaying crucifixes in the classrooms of public schools under Article 2(1) of Protocol 1 to the ECHR. The Second Section of the Court had initially not considered the Italian arguments that states, in fulfilling their obligations under Article 2(1) of Protocol 1 to the Convention, enjoyed a wide margin of appreciation with regard to cultural and historical particularities linked to religious education.[77] In contrast, the Grand Chamber found that states enjoyed a wide margin of appreciation 'in their efforts to reconcile the religious beliefs of parents when organising the curriculum and the further conditions of school education'.[78] In so holding, the Court paid regard to the cultural and historical particularities governing education in Italy.

The *Lautsi* case demonstrates that arguments belonging to the scope of Article 53 of the ECHR on the protection of the constitutional core may be considered and recognised by the Court in the application of the margin of appreciation doctrine.[79] The doctrine lends deference to national decisions and interpretations of ECHR rights.[80] Recent case law of the Court

[75] *Case of Open Door and Dublin Well Woman v Ireland* App nos 14234/88; 14235/88, No A246-A (ECtHR, 29 Oct 1992) [69].

[76] *Leempoel & SA ed Cine Revue v Belgique* App no 64772/01 (ECtHR, 9 Nov 2006) [87].

[77] *Lautsi v Italy* App no 30814/06 (Second Section, 3 Nov 2009) note 38.

[78] *Lautsi v Italy* App no 30814/06 (Grand Chamber, 3 March 2011) note 69.

[79] For a late example on this, see *SAS v France* App No 43835/11 (Grand Chamber, 1 July 2014) [129].

[80] For this distinction, *cf* George Letsas, 'Two Concepts of the Margin of Appreciation' (2006) 26(4) *Oxford Journal of Legal Studies* 705.

has emphasised that all three powers, executive, judiciary, and legislative, enjoy the margin of appreciation.[81] The concept has also been understood as an expression of the notion of subsidiarity.[82] Concerning decisions of the judiciary, in particular, the margin of appreciation doctrine must be viewed together with the so-called fourth instance doctrine, which the ECtHR applies to the review of the findings of domestic courts. This doctrine provides that, as a general rule, the Court will only reassess or call into question national courts findings on the facts if there are 'cogent reasons',[83] ie, where the assessment of the national courts was so arbitrary and unreasonable that it amounts to a breach of Article 6 of the Convention.[84] Thus, both the fourth instance and the margin of appreciation doctrines are able to embrace arguments made with regard to the protection of national rights and particularities protected by core constitutional provisions in the member states.

ii. Rule of Law Arguments Limited by European Consensus

Responses based on certain elements of the international rule of law have long found recognition in the general jurisprudence of the ECtHR. The Court has acknowledged in various cases that it is bound by rule of law standards, emphasising that

> while it is not formally bound to follow any of its previous judgments, it is in the interests of legal certainty, foreseeability and equality before the law that it should not depart, without good reason, from precedents laid down in previous cases.[85]

The application of rule of law standards, in particular, of the requirements of legal certainty, consistency, and foreseeability in the relations of the ECtHR with member state courts, is illustrated by the *Al Khawaja and Tahery* case. In this case, the Grand Chamber of the ECtHR took the findings of *Horncastle* and *Cadder* seriously, which had criticised the consistency and clarity of the 'sole and decisive rule'. This rule established that a defendant in a criminal case will suffer an infringement of his right to an

[81] References omitted; *Axel Springer Ag v Germany* App no 39954/08 (ECtHR, Grand Chamber, 7 Feb 2012) [87]; *cf Von Hannover v Germany (No 2)* App nos 40660 and 60641/08 (ECtHR, Grand Chamber, 7 Feb 2012) [107]; *MGN Limited v the United Kingdom* App no 39401/04 (ECtHR, 18 Jan 2011) [150] and [155]; *Petrenco v Moldova* App no 20928/05 (ECtHR, 30 March 2010) [54]; *Polanco Torres and Movilla Polanco v Spain* App no 34147/06 (ECtHR, 21 Sept 2010) [41]; *Petrov v Bulgaria* App no 27103/04 (ECtHR, 2 Nov 2010).

[82] Arai-Takahashi, 'The Margin of Appreciation Doctrine' (n 36) 93–94.

[83] See, eg, *Tanli v Turkey* App no 26129/95 (ECtHR, 10 April 2001) [110].

[84] *Sentürk v Turkey* App no 27577/04 (ECtHR, 24 Nov 2009) [17].

[85] *Herrman v Germany* App no 9300/07 (ECtHR, Grand Chamber, 26 June 2012) note 78 (concerning the obligation of small landowners to become members of hunting organisations following provisions of the German Hunting Law).

effective defence if the evidence in the trial is not available for challenge by the defendant.[86] In *Al Khawaja and Tahery*, the ECtHR addressed virtually every objection raised by the Supreme Court in *Horncastle*.[87] The Court considered, on the one hand, that while it must have due regard for the differences in the common and civil law systems, this must not lead to the application of different standards as to whether there is a violation of Article 6(1) of the Convention.[88] On the other hand, the Court defined the criteria of 'sole' and 'decisive', leaving no further room for the argument that they were imprecise.[89] Finally, the Court considered the further objections on the practical application of the rule, arguing that even considering the peculiarities of UK criminal procedure, it was possible to apply and execute the rule in the UK. Thus, the Court considered the rule of law, in particular, the requirements of consistency and certainty, not violated. It concluded: '[f]or these reasons, the Court has *consistently* assessed the impact that the defendant's inability to examine a witness has had on the overall fairness of his trial'.[90]

However, the Court recently emphasised that adherence to standards of consistency and coherence is not a means without ends and cannot lead to a standstill in the substantive development of ECHR rights according to present-day conditions. In *Herman v Germany*, the Court found with regard to the standards of consistency and clarity:

> it is in the interests of legal certainty, foreseeability and equality before the law that it should not depart, without good reason, from precedents laid down in previous cases. However, since the Convention is first and foremost a system for the protection of human rights, the Court must have regard to the changing conditions in Contracting States and respond, for example, to any evolving convergence as to the standards to be achieved.[91]

The existence or emergence of a European consensus on matters concerning the Convention arguing for the dynamic evolution of substantive ECHR law may therefore require a turn in the Court's case law, despite arguments in favour of consistency and clarity.

Yet, this latter consensus argument does not restrict further transjudicial dialogues. On the contrary, it encourages them: the existence of a European consensus is one of the prerequisites for the Court to establish and justify the further development of ECHR rights in the light of

[86] *Al Khawaja and Tahery v UK* App nos 26766/05 and 22228/06 (ECtHR, Grand Chamber, 15 Dec 2011) note 128.

[87] ibid note 129ff.

[88] ibid note 130.

[89] ibid note 131.

[90] ibid note 143 (emphasis added).

[91] *Herrman v Germany* (n 85) note 78. *cf Bayatyan v Armenia* App no 23459/03 (Grand Chamber, 7 July 2011) note 102.

its dynamic interpretation doctrine. And the absence of a consensus on a particular interpretation of the ECHR establishes a rebuttable presumption for the application of the margin of appreciation doctrine by the Court.[92] Consensus therefore provides another procedure by which national contestations and reactions to the ECHR may be taken up in the case law of the Court.

Still, the consensus doctrine is not uncontested. Using consensus as an aid to interpret the Convention establishes a certain dependence on the opinions and views held at the member state level about the scope and content of particular ECHR rights and their limitations. Hence, the argument is prone to expose the problem which is known as counter-majoritarian difficulty, or, more generally, as the tyranny of the majority.[93] In particular, if state consensus alone is used to develop the material content and core of Convention rights, reliance upon it supports a view on ECHR rights of the majority without protection for those most in need of human rights: vulnerable groups and minorities. As Benvenisti argued, this would not befit the ECtHR's role as an independent arbitrator and guardian of the international rights enshrined in the ECHR.[94]

However, the different types of consensuses that the Court may refer to must be considered more closely. Above all, the tyranny argument concerns the consensus derived from state practice. Yet, even considering state practice alone, the consensus approach may be defendable if the state practice leading to a consensus reflected a 'subsequent agreement between the parties regarding the interpretation of the … [ECHR] or the application of its provisions'; or 'subsequent practice in the application of the … [ECHR] which establishes the agreement of the parties regarding its interpretation' in the sense of Article 31(3)(a) and (b) of the Vienna Convention on the Law of Treaties (VCLT). Consensus then corroborates an interpretation of the ECHR in light of its context. Moreover, conclusions about the permissible scope of limitations, ie, for what may be 'necessary in a democratic society' or what may constitute a state's morals cannot be made without reference to state practice. In *Stübing v Germany* or in *Ireland v UK*, the Court used the consensus approach to substantiate what may permissibly constitute state morals. A similar case in point is the

[92] Kanstantsin Dzehtsiarou, 'Comparative Law in the Reasoning of the European Court of Human Rights' (2010) 10 *UCD Law Review* 109, 113; Eva Brems, *Human Rights: Universality and Diversity* (Leiden, Kluwer, 2001) 420. Yet, as demonstrated, the national measures still need to be proportionate, strike a fair balance with other affected rights, and remain within the framework of its permissible limitations.

[93] Eyal Benvenisti, 'Margin of Appreciation, Consensus, and Universal Standards' (1999) 31 *New York University Journal of International Law and Politics* 843, 852; Arai-Takahashi (n 35) 96.

[94] Benvenisti, 'Margin of Appreciation, Consensus, and Universal Standards' (n 93) 852.

fulfilment of positive obligations under the Convention, as these leave the exact choice of methods and means required to conform with the standard set by the ECHR to the state.[95] For example, in the above cited *Lautsi v Italy* judgment, the Grand Chamber found that as long as there was no European consensus on the question whether or not a crucifix could be displayed in public school classrooms and as long as Italy's school system and curricula were in line with the requirements of Article 2(1) of Additional Protocol 1 to the ECHR and the proportionality principle, and complied, in particular, with the requirements of pluralism, democracy, and tolerance, states could take measures to comply with the right to education, taking into account their cultural and historical peculiarities.[96]

In addition, evidence of a 'practice' establishing an 'agreement between the parties', pursuant to Article 31(3)(b) of the VCLT may be derived from a variety of sources evidencing the change of present-day conditions beyond the individual member state. The Court has relied on international agreements and instruments,[97] social consensus,[98] and expert consensus[99] in its findings on interpretation of the Convention. Finally, if practice is derived from international treaties and agreements—thus reflecting an international consensus—the approach can be covered by Article 31(3)(c) of the VCLT. *Demir and Baykara v Turkey* and subsequent decisions relying on international instruments demonstrate this.[100] Reliance upon an international consensus also establishes a common understanding of the rights and values enshrined in the ECHR beyond and above the individual level of the member states.[101]

After all, the ECtHR has reacted to national contestations of its interpretive authority either by invoking standards of the international rule of law—ie, standards of consistency and clarity—or by relying on the emergence of a European consensus. The consensus argument remains problematic in cases where it hinges on interpretations of the ECHR formulated at the domestic levels of the member states. Yet, there are viable ways of employing consensus in the framework of the ECHR. On the

[95] Birgit Peters, 'Kruzifixe Im Klassenraum: EGMR (GK) 18.03.2011, 30814/06 (Lautsi/It)' (2012) 67(3) *Zeitschrift für Öffentliches Recht—Austrian Journal for Public and International Law* 573, 583.

[96] *Lautsi v Italy* App no 30814/06 (n 79) [26]–[28].

[97] *Demir and Baykara v Turkey* App no 34503/97 (2008) ECHR 1345 [76]; *Saadi v The United Kingdom* App no 13229/03 (ECtHR, Grand Chamber, 27 Sept 2005) [63].

[98] *Sheffield and Horsham v The United Kingdom* App nos 22885/93, 23390/94 1998-V ECHR (Grand Chamber, 30 July 1998), [60].

[99] *X and others v Austria* App no 19010/07 (Grand Chamber, 19 February 2013) [67].

[100] *Demir and Baykara v Turkey* (n 98) [76]. *cf* George Letsas, 'The ECHR as a Living Instrument' in A Føllesdal, B Peters, and G Ulfstein (eds), *Constituting Europe: The European Court of Human Rights in a Global, European and National Context* (Cambridge, Cambridge University Press, 2013) 106, 115ff for further reference.

[101] Letsas, 'Living Instrument' (n 100) 122.

one hand, the consensus argument may corroborate the preconditions for the dynamic interpretation of the ECHR; for example, pursuant to Article 31(3)(c) of the VCLT. On the other hand, it may corroborate the interpretation of the ECHR in other cases, such as in the determination of what constitutes 'public morals'. In any case, it allows for reactions to and the recognition of affirmations as well as contestations at the national and international levels.

iii. Incompatible Interpretations and Proportionate Balancing

A final mode of response of the Court to contestations raised by national courts is illustrated by the *von Hannover* saga against Germany. This concerns a series of ECtHR judgments,[102] which considered arguments raised by German courts falling into the general scope of the incompatible methods of interpretation exception discussed above.[103] Dealing with press photos published in several tabloid newspapers of Princess Caroline von Hannover, the *von Hannover* cases gave rise to the issue of the balancing of the right to private enjoyment of family life and the freedom of expression under Articles 8 and 10 of the ECHR. Upon consideration of the ECtHR's jurisprudence, the German Constitutional Court had argued that an interpretation of the provisions of the Basic Law in light of the ECHR should not result in a lowering of the standard of constitutional protection, thus combining both arguments on methodological compatibility and on the constitutional core exception.[104] In the follow-up case, *von Hannover No 2*, the ECtHR conceded to some of these arguments. First, it pointed out that national courts enjoyed a margin of appreciation on balancing the particular rights involved in the case. Second, the Strasbourg court established that it could reconsider this balancing only in cases where the balancing that had resulted was artificial and arbitrary.[105] The ECtHR concluded that both the German Constitutional Court and the German Federal Court of Justice, which took detailed account of Strasbourg's case law and revised previous decisions on the criteria developed for the balancing of rights, had

> carefully balanced the right of the publishing companies to freedom of expression against the right of the applicants to respect for their private life. In doing so, they attached fundamental importance to the question whether the photos,

[102] See *Von Hannover v Germany (No 2)* App no 40660/08 (ECtHR, 7 Feb 2012); *Von Hannover v Germany (No 3)* App no 8772/10 (ECtHR, 19 Sept 2013).

[103] See section III(B)(iii) of this chapter.

[104] BVerfG, Case no 1 BvR 1602/07, 26 Feb 2008, [52].

[105] *Von Hannover v Germany (No 2)* (n 102) note 93; *Von Hannover v Germany (No 3)* (n 102) note 50.

considered in the light of the accompanying articles, had contributed to a debate of general interest.[106]

Following those findings, the ECtHR will not consider member states to be in violation of the Convention if domestic courts carefully balanced the individual human rights at stake, taking due account of the case law of the Court. Therefore, both the elements of proportionate balancing and the margin of appreciation leave room for taking up national contestations at the ECHR level, thus allowing the ECtHR to respond to such contestations.

IV. CONCLUSION: THE RULE OF LAW DIMENSIONS OF TRANSJUDICIAL DIALOGUES

Having elaborated on the framework of the formal transjudicial dialogues between national courts and Strasbourg, I now turn to the rule of law dimensions of such formal dialogues. Two major impacts may be identified. On the one hand, from a substantial point of view, transjudicial dialogues may be held to *reaffirm* standards of the international rule of law in the relations of the ECtHR and national supreme and constitutional courts. Second, the conduct of transjudicial dialogues along the lines of a certain framework demonstrates *compliance* with standards of the international rule of law.

On the first issue, the assessment demonstrated that the rule of law is a standard which is reaffirmed by formal transjudicial dialogues. This is sustained by the cases from the UK and Norway, which have scrutinised ECtHR case law according to the requirements of the rule of law. Moreover, also the ECtHR has underlined the importance of adhering to standards of clarity, foreseeability, and coherence. In doing so, it has not only reaffirmed those standards of the national rule of law; it also affirmed their belonging to the concept of the international rule of law.[107] As rule of law aspects develop into a constant, governing the transjudicial, multilevelled dialogues on the ECHR, traditional distinctions between the national and the international rule of law become less significant.

Second, the conduct of formal transjudicial dialogues along the lines of a certain framework demonstrates compliance with (international) rule of law standards, particularly with coherence, foreseeability, and clarity. As the assessment demonstrated, dialogues of national courts with Strasbourg evolve along three major strands: they invoke arguments concerning the constitutional core, as reflected in Article 53 of the ECHR; they are concerned with rule of law guarantees proper; or they concern the

[106] *Von Hannover v Germany* (No 2) (n 102) notes 124–26.
[107] ch 1 (Kanetake) of this volume.

methodological compatibility of the rules of constitutional and ECHR interpretation. Replying to those contestations, Strasbourg demonstrated and affirmed that there is such a thing as a formal transjudicial dialogue in the ECHR. Moreover, Strasbourg reaffirmed the basic lines along which the dialogue is constructed: it accepted arguments on the constitutional core, either on consideration of Article 53 of the ECHR or on application of the margin of appreciation doctrine, concerning the interpretation of substantive rights enshrined in the ECHR. Strasbourg also reacted to the rule of law queries, reaffirming the importance of this principle for the ECHR system and particularly for its relations with the member states. Finally, Strasbourg pointed to the fact that rule of law considerations cannot turn the further development of ECHR rights into a stalemate. Thus, contestations based on the rule of law will not be successful where they encounter a European or international consensus arguing in favour of a further development of ECHR provisions.

Bearing in mind the legal framework of the dialogue foreseen by the ECHR and national constitutions, it is striking that many of the arguments raised remain within that framework: national contestations concern arguments covered by Article 53 of the ECHR; parallel national provisions concerned with the protection of the core rights of the constitution; or raise concerns under the rule of law proper. The application of Article 53 of the ECHR, in particular, will possibly gain further importance in the ECHR, considering the development of the parallel provision of Article 4(2) of the TEU in the EU. Reactions of the ECtHR, on the other hand, remain within the standards of subsidiarity and the margin of appreciation doctrine, which are soon to be part of the ECHR preamble. Finally, the limitation concerning the further development of ECHR rights building upon a European consensus resonates—in part—in the preconditions for a dynamic interpretation of international law, following Articles 31(3)(b) and (c) of the VCLT.

Despite the foregoing, some arguments made in favour of the international rule of law rest outside this legal framework guiding the formal dialogue. At the national levels, this concerns the arguments presented on the methodologically sound interpretation, as well as those making the domestic application of Strasbourg's judgments contingent upon whether or not it presented a new principle or where it departed from previous case law. At the level of the ECHR, the use of domestic consensus continues to be problematic. Lacking a formal (legal) recognition, these arguments must therefore primarily be considered to politically influence the transjudicial dialogues.[108]

[108] Jürgen Habermas, *Faktizität und Geltung* (Heidelberg, Suhrkamp, 1994) 449.

Ultimately, in the present chapter I presented only a fraction of the general framework of judicial interactions between Strasbourg and national supreme and constitutional courts and of its rule of law effects. More research is needed to flesh out the impact and effects of informal dialogues and of the general influence of the latter on the formal dialogues assessed here. In addition, further research is needed to elaborate on if and how formal and informal dialogues contribute to the substantive development of a shared understanding of ECHR rights and common European values. The international rule of law seems a promising concept to facilitate further elaborations on those matters.

9

Three Interpretive Constraints on the European Court of Human Rights

SHAI DOTHAN

I. INTRODUCTION

THE EUROPEAN COURT of Human Rights (ECtHR) operates under three interpretive constraints. According to the Court's established doctrine, it is supposed to: render judgments that are consistent with the scope of the obligations that states took upon themselves by ratifying the Convention for the Protection of Human Rights and Fundamental Freedoms (the Convention); show deference to the policies of the state whose behaviour it is evaluating;[1] and follow the consensual view on the issue within Europe, the so-called 'emerging consensus'.[2]

These constraints on the ECtHR's interpretive discretion often conflict with one another. For example, the consensual view in Europe may require greater human rights protections than granted by the text of the convention. Yet the Court has not adopted a consistent approach for weighing one constraint over the others. This chapter argues that when these constraints conflict, the Court should look to the normative underpinnings of each constraint to determine which is most salient in the instant case. It then develops a framework to assist courts in making this determination.

The framework suggests that in cases of contradiction between the constraints, the ECtHR should follow constraints that would render its decision normatively legitimate. Only after assuring that the Court's judgments are normatively legitimate can the Court try to follow constraints

[1] Convention for the Protection of Human Rights and Fundamental Freedoms, 4 Nov 1950, 213 UNTS 221, Art 23.

[2] On these interpretive constraints, see also ch 8 (Peters) of this volume, which demonstrates that the ECtHR's responses to domestic contestations have been incrementally formalised and methodised.

that are likely to lead to substantively good decisions. If the ECtHR would apply the interpretive constraints in this manner, it would serve the values of the international rule of law.

The international rule of law mandates that the ECtHR as an unelected body ought to show deference to the treaty obligations and the policy choices of states so long as these properly represent all the individuals affected by the states' actions. Democratic states that adhere to the national rule of law are usually the best available representatives of individuals, who are, in turn, the ultimate bearers of rights recognised by the international rule of law.[3] Yet there are situations, some of which are examined in this chapter, when states' treaty obligations and policies do not adequately represent the interests of all affected individuals. In these cases, deference is not merited. The ECtHR's judgments are normatively legitimate if they show the proper deference to the states so long as such deference is merited.

This chapter starts by describing the doctrines that constrain and direct the ECtHR and their normative justifications (section II). It then explains when the ECtHR can interpret the Convention expansively without damaging its normative legitimacy and when it should narrow the states' margin of appreciation (section III). The chapter then describes when allowing states a margin of appreciation is likely to lead to good results, and conversely when it would be better to follow the emerging consensus (section IV). It concludes by arguing that applying the aforementioned doctrines can help the ECtHR make good and legitimate decisions, but highlights the fact that the ECtHR is also subject to political constraints that might limit its discretion (section V).

II. THE DOCTRINES CONSTRAINING THE ECtHR

The ECtHR is not formally constrained to follow its prior judgments by the Convention. Yet the ECtHR has stressed its commitment not to digress from its previous decisions without good reason.[4] The ECtHR is especially committed to certain doctrines that it regularly and consistently uses in its

[3] See Armin von Bogdandy and Ingo Venzke, 'In Whose Name? An Investigation of International Courts' Public Authority and Its Democratic Justification' (2012) 23 *European Journal of International Law* 7, 41 (arguing that in the Kantian tradition, the ultimate democratic justification is always the freedom of individuals).

[4] See *Christine Goodwin v the United Kingdom* App no 28957/95, ECHR 2002-VI (ECtHR, Grand Chamber, 11 July 2002) 26. However, the ECtHR also noted there that it will respond to changing conditions in states parties in order to effectively protect the rights enshrined in the Convention.

judgments. Such doctrines are the commitment to the text of the Convention, the margin of appreciation,[5] and emerging consensus.

While these doctrines constrain the ECtHR's discretion, they do not eliminate it. The Court can use its interpretive discretion to determine how these doctrines are applied and what results they will lead to.[6] For example, while the Court is constrained to grant some margin of appreciation to the states, the boundaries of the latitude given to the states may vary with the judges' discretion. In some situations, the judges may reason that a state's actions do not merit a finding of violation because the state deserves a wide margin of appreciation and in different situations the Court may find a similar action in violation of the Convention because the margin of appreciation given to the state should be limited.[7]

The ECtHR developed the constraints on its discretion for a host of historical reasons,[8] and to trace the historical development is not the main concern of this chapter. Instead, this chapter studies possible normative justifications for these doctrines. This chapter addresses two types of normative justifications: following a constraint is normatively legitimate because it serves the basic value of democracy—allowing all individuals affected by the decision a fair share in making it; and following a constraint is likely, in general, to lead to substantively good results.

This chapter argues that under conditions in which the normative justifications for a constraint do not apply, the Court should not adhere to this constraint. The Court's interpretive discretion is broad enough to allow it to ignore certain constraints when there is no good reason to follow them. If the Court were to follow constraints only when it is normatively justified to do so, it would maximise its chances to make legitimate and substantively correct decisions.

[5] On the margin of appreciation, see also ch 10 (Legg) of this volume.

[6] Aharon Barak, *Judicial Discretion* (Tel Aviv, Papyrus, 1987) (Hebrew) 58–66 (arguing that in some judicial decisions, the so-called 'hard cases', judges exercise judicial discretion).

[7] The Court listed a series of considerations that determine the width of the margin of appreciation granted to the state. These considerations include the type of rights infringed upon, the aims that the state pursued when it infringed upon the rights, and the interests at stake. Furthermore, if there were no consensus in Europe on how the right should be protected, the margin of appreciation would be wider. See *Dickson v The United Kingdom* App no 44362/04, ECHR 2007-V (ECtHR, Grand Chamber, 4 Dec 2007) [77]–[78]; *Evans v the United Kingdom* App no 6339/05, ECHR 2007-I (ECtHR, Grand Chamber, 10 April 2007) [77]; Dean Spielmann, 'Allowing the Right Margin the European Court of Human Rights and the National Margin of Appreciation Doctrine: Waiver or Subsidiarity of European Review?' (2012) CELS Working Paper Series, 9–23.

[8] See Eyal Benvenisti, 'Margin of Appreciation, Consensus, and Universal Standards' (1999) 31 *New York University Journal of International Law and Politics* 843, 845–46 (arguing that the margin of appreciation doctrine was initially developed to alleviate the fears of states that international intervention would jeopardise their national security. The doctrine later developed to other issues based on considerations of subsidiarity—allowing states to preserve their democratic decisions and unique identities—and as a result of judicial politics).

A. Commitment to the Text of the Convention

The first constraint on the ECtHR's discretion is its commitment to the text of the Convention. The ECtHR is tasked with interpreting the Convention. It is not allowed to change the Convention or to bend it at will. However, the Court can use a variety of interpretive techniques to expand the obligations of the states beyond the text of the Convention without changing the text.[9] The ECtHR often relies on the so-called 'principle of effectiveness'—according to which the rights enshrined in the Convention must be protected effectively—to expand the obligations of states.[10] Over the years, the Court has rejected formalistic interpretations that limit Convention rights in favour of interpretations that fulfil the purpose of protecting the rights in the Convention.[11] The Court has read into the Convention rights that do not appear clearly in the text[12] and required states to provide practical safeguards for the protections of rights protected in the Convention.[13] The Court has read Convention rights as implying positive obligations on the part of the states to protect these rights,[14] even from other individuals.[15] The Court has also interpreted narrowly derogations and exceptions from Convention rights[16] and prevented states from evading responsibility by delegating responsibilities to other actors.[17]

But expansive interpretation raises a potential problem for the normative legitimacy of the ECtHR because it overrides the decisions of democratically accountable states on what treaty obligations to assume.[18] This problem arises because the obligations within the Convention are a result of negotiations between democratic states that usually, at least in theory, represent the public within them. Democratically accountable state representatives also make the decision whether or not to join additional protocols to the Convention and assume further obligations. In contrast, the ECtHR is not an elected body. While each of the 47 states in Europe has

[9] See Shai Dothan, 'In Defence of Expansive Interpretation in the European Court of Human Rights' (2014) 3 *Cambridge Journal of International and Comparative Law* 508.

[10] Pieter Van Dijk and Godefridus JH Van Hoof, *Theory and Practice of the European Convention on Human Rights* (3rd edn, The Hague, Kluwer Law International, 1998) 74–76; G Merrills, *The Development Of International Law by the European Court of Human Rights* (2nd edn, Manchester, Manchester University Press, 1993) 98–124.

[11] *Minelli v Switzerland* App no 8660/79, Ser A no 62 (ECtHR, 25 March 1983).

[12] *Soering v the United Kingdom* App no 14038/88, Series A no 161 (ECtHR, 7 July 1989) 34.

[13] *Artico v Italy* App no 6694/74, Series A no 37 (ECtHR, 13 May 1980); *Airey v Ireland* App no 6289/73, Series A no 32 (ECtHR, 9 October 1979).

[14] *Marckx v Belgium* App no 6833/74, Series A no 31 (ECtHR, 13 June 1979); *Mehemi v France (No 2)* App no 53470/99, ECHR 2003-IV (ECtHR, 10 April 2003) 311, 325.

[15] *X and Y v the Netherlands* App no 8978/80, Series A no 91 (ECtHR, 26 March 1985).

[16] *Klass and Others v Germany* App no 5029/71, Ser A no 28 (ECtHR, 6 Sept 1978) 21.

[17] *Van Der Mussele v Belgium* App no 8919/80, Ser A no 70 (ECtHR, 23 Nov 1983) 15.

[18] See Jeffrey L Dunoff and Joel P Trachtman, 'The Law and Economics of Humanitarian law Violations in Internal Conflict' (1999) 93 *American Journal of International Law* 394, 399.

one judge on the Court, the significant differences in the populations of the states in Europe prevent the Court from giving any fair representation of the European public.[19] The ECtHR, as an unelected and unrepresentative body, should usually show deference to the states' decisions not to assume further human rights obligations.[20]

B. Margin of Appreciation

The margin of appreciation doctrine directs the ECtHR to defer to the state's policies unless they significantly digress from what the Court views as permitted conduct under the Convention.[21] This chapter develops two normative justifications for this doctrine: it usually directs the ECtHR to make decisions that are normatively legitimate, and it usually directs the ECtHR to make decisions that are substantively good.

The ECtHR is tasked with monitoring the behaviour of democratic states in the Council of Europe. Usually the behaviour of these states is directed by elected institutions that represent the will of the majority of the population and give each member of the state a fair share of the political power. If the state clearly digresses from its commitments under the Convention, the ECtHR is justified in finding a violation, since the state freely assumed its treaty obligations and showed a willingness to be bound by them, even if in the future its government would want to digress from these commitments.[22] If, however, the digression from the standards set in the Convention is not substantial and the Court has discretion whether or not to find a violation, then finding a violation and not allowing the state a margin of appreciation is sometimes normatively illegitimate, as such a decision would not give the proper deference to the will of elected bodies that represent the general public.[23]

Allowing a margin of appreciation to the state can also be justified because the state is likely to make good decisions more often than is the

[19] See Yuval Shany, 'Toward a General Margin of Appreciation Doctrine in International Law?' (2005) 16 *European Journal of International Law* 907, 919–21. See also James Slack, 'Social Ties Keep Rapists in Britain' (*Mail Online*, 21 Sept 2011), available at: www.dailymail.co.uk/debate/article-2039657/Akindoyin-Akinshipe-Social-ties-rapists-Britain.html.

[20] *cf* Vijay M Padmanabhan, 'The Human Rights Justification for Consent' (2013) 35 *University of Pennsylvania Journal of International Law* 1, 50 (arguing that states' decisions not to undertake human rights obligations should be respected to protect the right of the people within the state to self-determination).

[21] Benvenisti, 'Margin of Appreciation, Consensus, and Universal Standards' (n 8) 843–44.

[22] See Andrew Moravcsik, 'The Origins of Human Rights Regimes: Democratic Delegation in Postwar Europe' (2000) 54 *International Organization* 217 (arguing that states joined the European Convention system deliberately in order to commit to democratic values and institutions and to prevent future governments from digressing from them).

[23] See Padmanabhan, 'The Human Rights Justification for Consent' (n 20) 50–51.

ECtHR. Issues relating to the balancing of human rights involve questions of fact as well as questions of morality; finding the answers to both of these questions is necessary to determine if a decision is good.[24] Take, for example, the question of whether prisoners should be allowed to vote in national elections.[25] Many considerations can determine the answer to this question: will preventing prisoners from voting increase the deterrence of crime? Is the prevention of prisoners from voting likely to affect the elections result, and how? And is it morally legitimate to deny citizens their voting rights if they breached the law? Reasonable people may disagree about the answers to these questions. Yet research can help to find better answers to the factual questions and a reasoned argument can improve the chances of making a moral decision.

The decision-making bodies within the state have the knowledge of the state's unique situation. They have the expertise, the time, and the resources to uncover the facts and to argue through the relevant moral issues. This increases the chances that the state will reach a good decision. The ECtHR does not enjoy these advantages. Most of its judges are not familiar with the special conditions of each state and the Court does not have the resources necessary to make as informed and sophisticated a decision as the state.[26]

C. Emerging Consensus

The doctrine of emerging consensus directs the ECtHR to take into account the policies adopted by European states as it interprets the states' treaty obligations. While there are several possible interpretations of this

[24] Eric A Posner and Cass R Sunstein, 'The Law of Other States' (2006) 59 *Stanford Law Review* 131, 142–43.

[25] This question was raised in the *Hirst* case (*Hirst v the United Kingdom (No 2)* App no 74025/01, 2005-IX, 187 (ECtHR, 6 Oct 2005), where applicants argued that the United Kingdom's complete disenfranchisement of all prisoners violated their right to vote under the Convention. The judgment found the United Kingdom in violation. The majority opinion stressed that only a minority of European states indiscriminately prevent prisoners from voting, although many states restrict prisoners' voting rights in certain ways ([81]) and that, in any case, this does not determine the result as the indiscriminate ban lies out of the states' margin of appreciation ([82]). In contrast, 5 dissenting judges (Wildhaber, Costa, Lorenzen, Kovler, and Jebens, [6]) called attention to the fact that though only a minority of European states have a blanket ban on prisoners' voting rights, most of the states in Europe have some restriction of prisoners' ability to vote. The dissenting judges warned that the majority's judgment does not explain what restriction on prisoners' voting rights are allowed and would consequently cause problems in most of the states in Europe, which restrict prisoners' voting rights in some way.

[26] See Shany, 'Toward a General Margin of Appreciation Doctrine in International Law? (n 19) 918–19; Andrew Legg, *The Margin of Appreciation in International Human Rights Law: Deference and Proportionality* (Oxford, Oxford University Press, 2012) 26.

doctrine,[27] the ECtHR tends to find a state in violation of the Convention when that state transgresses against rights that are protected by the majority of the other states in Europe.[28]

Following emerging consensus allows the ECtHR to continually progress the human rights protections granted to individuals in Europe, while learning from the experience of European states.[29] At the same time, the ECtHR must give states some leeway to make their own policies and defer to some of their choices according to the margin of appreciation doctrine. The greater the consensus among European states that a certain right should be protected, the more the ECtHR is willing to narrow the margin of appreciation granted to a state that infringes upon this right and find it in violation of the Convention.[30]

The doctrine of emerging consensus can lead the ECtHR to make good decisions. If all states are assumed to make an informed and independent decision on what legal rules to adopt, then according to the Jury Theorem—a simple mathematical model developed by the eighteenth century French philosopher Nicolas de Condorcet—following the majority of states is likely to lead to good legal rules. The Jury Theorem argues that increasing the pool of decisions-makers reduces the chances of error since any additional decision-maker is more likely to push the majority's decision in the right direction than in the wrong direction. This argument was presented to support the practice of using comparative law that directs national courts to follow the laws of the majority of the other states in the world.[31] Yet if all national courts try to follow the majority of other national courts, their decision is no longer independent and they may fall prey to information cascades. That is, courts would follow courts that did not make an independent decision and the results they reach may be determined arbitrarily by the order in which other courts made their decision. In contrast, when states decide independently and the ECtHR uses emerging consensus, information cascades are prevented and the benefits of the Jury Theorem are fully realised.[32]

[27] See Laurence R Helfer, 'Consensus, Coherence and the European Convention on Human Rights' (1993) 26 *Cornell International Law Journal* 133, 138–39 (arguing that the ECtHR can look for a consensus in the laws of different states; it can follow the consensus of experts or the prevailing views within the public).

[28] Laurence R Helfer and Erik Voeten, 'International Courts as Agents of Legal Change: Evidence from LGBT Rights in Europe' (2014) 68 *International Organization* 77, 106.

[29] *Tyrer v the United Kingdom* App no 5856/72, Ser A no 26 (ECtHR, 25 April 1978) [31]; Helfer, 'Consensus, Coherence and the European Convention on Human Rights' (n 27) 134.

[30] See ibid 140; Benvenisti (n 8) 851.

[31] Posner and Sunstein, 'The Law of Other States' (n 24).

[32] See Shai Dothan, 'The Optimal Use of Comparative Law' (2014) 43 *Denver Journal of International Law and Policy* 21.

III. PROTECTING THE COURT'S NORMATIVE LEGITIMACY

In order to protect its normative legitimacy, the ECtHR must exercise its judicial discretion to choose only between options that are normatively legitimate. To issue legitimate judgments, the Court should usually show deference to states' decisions whether or not to assume treaty obligations and to states' human rights practices. But the Court should show this deference only under conditions that make deference normatively justified. If deference to the state's treaty obligations is justified, the Court should not require the state to grant protections beyond the treaty obligations the state has assumed. If deference to the state's actions is normatively justified, the Court should not require the state to improve its human rights protections. However, under certain conditions, deference is not normatively justified and the Court should not be similarly constrained. It should be allowed to extend further the protections of rights within the states.

A. When the Court Can Use Expansive Interpretation

The decision to assume international human rights obligations, such as the ones contained in the Convention and its protocols, is a decision made by states' democratically accountable bodies. Therefore, states' decisions not to undertake human rights obligations should usually be deferred to by the ECtHR.

Yet states' treaty obligations are not determined by a state in isolation, and are subject to collective decisions that expose each state to strategic behaviour by other states. The Convention was first drafted more than 60 years ago by a fraction of the states that are today subject to it. These states used mechanisms of coercion and persuasion to shape the treaty to suit their interest in a process that did not necessarily give equal representation to all the states involved.[33] The many states that joined the Convention afterwards certainly had no real ability to renegotiate its provisions, and consequently may have failed to assume obligations that suit the interests of their citizens. Furthermore, the states that shaped

[33] See Posner and Sunstein (n 24) 165–66 (presenting this argument); Moravcsik, 'The Origins of Human Rights Regimes' (n 22) 231 (describing the historical process of negotiation). See also Ed Bates, *The Evolution of the European Convention on Human Rights—From its Inception to the Creation of a Permanent Court of Human Rights* (Oxford, Oxford University Press, 2010) 92–93, 95, 100 (showing how the attempt of the states that drafted the Convention to secure the agreement of all drafting states gave a minority of states who were especially concerned to preserve their sovereignty, primarily the United Kingdom, a disproportionally large power in the negotiation. This power allowed this minority to impose a weak and partial Convention on the majority of the states).

the Convention could not foresee the far-reaching political and cultural changes that have occurred since. Consequently, they may have neglected to assume obligations that became essential at a later point in time. These states were also constrained by the need to define human rights protections succinctly within a brief document, leading to ambiguous provisions that do not cover all aspects of the rights they wished to protect and every possible future eventuality.

States can amend the Convention by ratifying amending protocols. These protocols must be ratified by all the contracting states to enter into force—subjecting all states to strategic behaviour by other states that can deliberately withhold their ratification. Such was the case with Protocol No 14,[34] which, until January 2010, was ratified by all European counties other than Russia. Only after delaying ratification for years, Russia finally agreed to ratify the protocol. By its persistent refusal to ratify, Russia prevented the Council of Europe from reforming and strengthening the ECtHR.[35]

The need to secure the unanimous agreement of all states to amending protocols means that a state may be prevented from assuming further obligations by the strategic behaviour of other states. As a result, the Convention does not represent the will of the state's government, and by implication it does not represent the will of the public within the state. In such situations, when the ECtHR expands a state's obligations by interpretation, it does not necessarily contradict the will of the public within that state or even within a majority of the states in Europe. This makes the use of expansive interpretation legitimate.

Yet states can also extend their human rights obligations by the process of ratifying additional protocols to the Convention. The states that draft an additional protocol can set a number of ratifications; for example the ten that are required for the protocol to enter into force. The additional protocol only applies to states that have ratified it. Once an additional protocol enters into force, every state that wishes to undertake the obligations within it only has to ratify it. In that case, the state's choice is not subject to substantial strategic behaviour. Therefore, when an additional protocol exists and a state deliberately decides not to ratify it, the ECtHR should be constrained to respect the state's decision, at least to the extent that the state represents all individuals affected by its decision to assume human rights obligations. Judge Borrego Borrego of the ECtHR shared this premise when he criticised, in his concurring opinion in the *Stec* case, the Court's willingness to subject states that did not sign additional Protocol 12

[34] Protocol no 14 to the Convention for the Protection of Human Rights and Fundamental Freedoms, amending the control system of the Convention, CETS no 194.

[35] See Shai Dothan, 'Judicial Tactics in the European Court of Human Rights' (2011) 12 *Chicago Journal of International Law* 115, 136.

to the obligation to protect a general right to equality included in this protocol.[36]

But some individuals who are affected by the state's decision to undertake treaty obligations are not properly represented by the state. As an example, consider the situation of foreigners and prisoners. In many European countries, foreigners who reside within the state[37] and prisoners, or even former prisoners,[38] cannot vote. Individuals who belong to these groups are certainly affected by the practices of the state, perhaps even to a greater extent than ordinary citizens, yet they have no share of the political power. Some may argue that foreigners and prisoners are properly excluded from the political process;[39] but this does not mean that their rights can be freely abused.[40]

Some individuals can vote but nevertheless possess a systematically inferior political position because of a prevailing prejudice and hostility towards their social group. Such groups are often termed 'discrete and insular minorities'. The prejudice against these groups prevents them from engaging in political logrolling and from forming coalitions with other social groups and causes them to have minimal political influence.[41]

[36] *Stec and Others v the United Kingdom* App nos 65731/01 and 65900/01, ECHR 2006-VI (ECtHR, 12 April 2006).

[37] Citizens who are not residents are also excluded in many states, formally or in practice, from voting. See Rainer Bauböck, 'Expansive Citizenship: Voting beyond Territory and Membership' (2005) 38 *Political Science and Politics* 683, 683–85 (presenting data on the rights of non-resident citizens and non-citizen residents to vote in several countries).

[38] See *Hirst (No 2)* (n 25) at [81].

[39] See Reuven Ruvi Ziegler, 'Legal Outlier, Again? US Felon Suffrage, Comparative and International Human Rights Perspectives' (2011) 29 *Boston University International Law Journal* 197, 203–10 (discussing arguments and counter arguments on the issue of prisoners' right to vote).

[40] The ECtHR has often protected the rights of foreigners and prisoners, even against strong public criticism in European countries and by this corrected a deficit in the regular democratic processes. In *Hirst (No 2)* (n 25), the ECtHR decided that the United Kingdom's general ban on prisoners' right to vote violated the Convention. After the United Kingdom failed to comply, the ECtHR issued a Pilot Judgment, requiring it to amend its laws within 6 months to comply with the *Hirst* Judgment: *Greens and MT v United Kingdom* App nos 60041/08 and 60054/08 (ECtHR, 23 Nov 2010). The period allotted for compliance was later extended in *Scoppola v Italy (No 3)* App no 126/05 (22 May 2012), where the United Kingdom served as a third party. In another case, the ECtHR suspended the extradition of an extremist Muslim cleric suspected of terrorist crimes to Jordan, where he was about to face trials for his alleged crimes, because the trial might rely on testimonies of individuals who were tortured. The cleric was finally deported only on July 2013 after 8 years of legal struggle. See *Othman (Abu Qatada) v the United Kingdom* App no 8139/09 (ECtHR, 17 Jan 2012). These cases caused severe public criticism of the ECtHR in the United Kingdom. See Erik Voeten, 'Public Opinion and the Legitimacy of International Courts' (2013) 14 *Theoretical Inquiries in Law* 411, 418–19.

[41] *United States v Carolene Products Co*, 304 US 144 (1938); John Hart Ely, *Democracy And Distrust: A Theory Of Judicial Review* (Cambridge, Mass, Harvard University Press, 1980) 181–83 (justifying judicial review by the need to protect such discrete and insular minorities).

Even if individuals are not part of a discrete and insular minority they may possess very little political power compared to small interest groups that can capture the political process and divert their state's authorities towards setting policies that suit their interests.[42] Some small interest groups are especially powerful because they can prevent free-riding among their members due to the high utility that each member gains from cooperation and to the low costs of monitoring their members.[43] Some small groups can more easily inform their members about the actions of their representatives and can therefore respond collectively to the actions of elected politicians.[44] For these reasons, some lobbies of farmers in developed countries hold disproportionate power against their government and receive special benefits as a result.[45] Some small groups can more easily exit their countries in search of other markets, a fact which gives them a potent threat against their government and increases their power.[46] Such groups include owners of international companies that can easily establish branches in other countries. Individuals whose political power is diminished because their government is captured by such small interest groups may be abused by their states.

If states do not represent all of the individuals affected by their decisions, their collective treaty obligations may not take into account the interests of these individuals. In these cases it is therefore normatively legitimate for the Court to use expansive interpretation to extend the state's obligations over and above what they agreed to in the Convention and in the protocols that they ratified.

B. The Proper Boundaries of the Margin of Appreciation

A possible justification for constraining the ECtHR to grant states a margin of appreciation is that democratic states tend, at least in theory, to represent the views of all their citizens. Since states' decisions on human rights issues, such as the ones dealt with by the ECtHR, usually do not create harmful externalities for individuals outside their territory, states often represent all individuals affected by their practices.[47]

[42] Eyal Benvenisti, 'Exit and Voice in the Age of Globalization' (1999) 98 *Michigan Law Review* 167, 170–75 (analysing the mechanisms discussed below that give small interest groups substantial political power).

[43] See Mancur Olson, *The Logic of Collective Action* (Cambridge, Mass, Harvard University Press, 1965) 33–34.

[44] See Susanne Lohmann, 'An Information Rationale for the Power of Special Interests' (1998) 92 *American Political Science Review* 809, 812.

[45] See ibid 809.

[46] On the power of exit, see Albert O Hirschman, *Exit, Voice, And Loyalty: Responses To Decline In Firms, Organizations, and States* (Cambridge, Mass, Harvard University Press, 1970) 55.

[47] See Shany (n 19) 920.

Yet, as highlighted above, under certain conditions states might not properly represent all the individuals whose interests are involved. States rely on democratic processes to make decisions and these processes may sometimes fail to give a fair share of the political power to certain individuals and groups. When individuals are politically powerless and the ECtHR suspects that their rights have been abused, there is no justification to grant a margin of appreciation to the state because the state does not properly represent these individuals' interests. It is therefore normatively legitimate for the ECtHR to intervene and set the standard of human rights it deems appropriate without showing deference to the state.

The same democratic failures that afflict the states' decision to assume treaty obligations are also relevant to the states' policies that are covered by the margin of appreciation doctrine. Accordingly, groups who are denied the ability to vote, discrete and insular minorities, and groups whose rights are abused by small interest groups all lack a fair share of the political power. The policies that impinge on the rights of these groups are not based on a process that properly represents all individuals concerned. Consequently, they do not deserve the Court's deference. Such policies should receive only a narrow margin of appreciation by the ECtHR.

Based on similar arguments, scholars have argued that the ECtHR should narrow the margin of appreciation granted to the states when their practices impinge on the rights of minorities.[48] Some scholars have argued that the ECtHR does in fact grant states varying degrees of deference based on how well the state's internal democratic processes operate.[49]

IV. STRIVING TO REACH GOOD RESULTS

The constraints discussed in the previous section are intended to prevent the ECtHR from acting in a way that is normatively illegitimate. If these constraints do not apply, or if the Court can digress from them without damaging its normative legitimacy, the Court has the discretion to reach what it views as a good result. Some doctrines of the Court can be justified as attempts to guide the Court towards reaching better results.

[48] See Benvenisti (n 8) 849 (arguing that the ECHR should not grant a margin of appreciation to states when they are likely to take advantage of their national minorities).

[49] See Andreas von Staden, 'The Democratic Legitimacy of Judicial Review Beyond the State: Normative Subsidiarity and Judicial Standards of Review' (2012) 10 *International Journal of Constitutional Law* 1023, 1042 (arguing that the ECtHR does in fact grant greater deference to the states when their democratic processes seem to operate well); Legg, *The Margin of Appreciation in International Human Rights Law: Deference and Proportionality* (n 26) 27–31 (arguing that the ECtHR considers the quality of a state's decision-making when it determines the boundaries of the state's margin of appreciation).

The Court is a guardian of the rights of individuals under its jurisdiction and its goal is to reach results that serve the interests of these individuals. As mentioned above, what constitutes a good result depends on questions of both facts and morality. It is reasonable to assume that individuals who make an independent and informed decision on a factual issue are more likely to be right than those who make a random decision. Similarly, provided that complete moral scepticism is rejected, it is reasonable to assume that individuals who make a rational decision are more likely to make a morally correct decision than those who choose a policy randomly. According to the Condorcet Jury Theorem, under these assumptions, the larger the pool of independent decision-makers, the more likely it is that the decision of a majority within the group would be a good one.[50]

The doctrines of margin of appreciation and emerging consensus can both be justified on the basis of the Jury Theorem logic as mechanisms to reach good results. These doctrines often pull in opposite directions.[51] Setting the boundaries of margin of appreciation and emerging consensus in light of their relative advantages can guide the ECtHR towards making better decisions.

A. When a State Can Make Good Decisions on its Own

One of the justifications for the margin of appreciation is that states can often make good decisions for their own citizens. State bureaucracies can form good policies because of their experience and their expertise. But the best way to reach good decisions based on the Jury Theorem logic is to open a decision to the entire population of the state by the use of democratic institutions. Democratic institutions are primarily majoritarian and the Jury Theorem implies that following the majority's decision in a large group is an excellent method to reach good decisions. It is therefore plausible to assume that democracies make better decisions than non-democracies and should therefore be granted a wide margin of appreciation.[52]

Yet not all democracies have the same abilities to reach good decisions. Some democracies have a free and robust media that can lead to an informed public; such an informed public is likely to reach good results. Some states have an independent judiciary that can correct democratic failures, such as the abuse of minorities, political corruption, or capture of the government by interest groups, and consequently lead to better results. Therefore, even among democracies, those countries that excel in terms of the protection of the rule of law should be granted a wider margin

[50] See Posner and Sunstein (n 24) 142–43.
[51] See (n 30).
[52] See Posner and Sunstein (n 24) 158–59.

of appreciation. Furthermore, because the Jury Theorem implies that the larger the group of decision-makers, the more likely it is that the result will be correct, states with large populations may be more likely than states with small populations to make good laws. States with large populations may therefore deserve an especially wide margin of appreciation.

The public within a state does not view all decisions equally. The public views some decisions as salient and makes them after careful deliberation, while the public views other decisions as politically insignificant and is therefore less involved in making them. If the public is involved and interested in a decision, the chances that a good policy will be chosen are higher. Such decisions should therefore receive a wide margin of appreciation. Moreover, if a decision is supported by a substantial majority, it is more likely to be a good decision than a decision that won by an insignificant margin and should therefore receive a wider margin of appreciation.[53]

If the ECtHR allows certain states a narrower margin of appreciation than it allows to other states, it may face accusations of bias by the states that face stricter scrutiny. Despite fearing similar accusations of bias, research suggests that the ECtHR treats states with good reputations for protecting human rights—states that usually comply with its judgments—with greater deference than it treats states with bad reputations.[54] In such situations in which the Court strategically decides to discriminate between European countries, the Court may hide this practice by the use of doctrinal and rhetorical tools. The Court can use its interpretive discretion to distinguish between similar cases in order to convey that it does not treat equal cases differently.

B. When Emerging Consensus Works Best

The Jury Theorem implies that if a majority of European states favours a certain policy of protecting human rights, then this is likely to be a good policy and therefore a policy worth following. But for this argument to work, three conditions must hold: the decisions of states must sincerely reflect their private information on the matter, the states must

[53] Posner and Sunstein suggest that it is possible to assess the likelihood of states making good decisions based on the standards of living they provide to their citizens, with the states that provide better living conditions presumed more likely to reach good results. See ibid at 174–75. While this measure is intuitive and may sometimes be helpful by providing an empirical metric to assess the outcomes of states' decision-making it raises many problems. The primary issue is how to define the success of the state. There are many contending options such as economic strength, economic growth, the happiness of the populations, public health, and many others.

[54] See Dothan, 'Judicial Tactics in the European Court of Human Rights' (n 35); Shai Dothan, *Reputation and Judicial Tactics: A Theory of National and International Courts* (New York; Cambridge, Cambridge University Press, 2015).

be sufficiently similar, and the states must decide independently.[55] The analysis below focuses on the two later conditions.[56]

The condition of similarity implies that if the states in Europe differ substantially from one another, across a dimension that is relevant for the decision, then a consensus among the states does not suggest that the majority favours a good policy. If each state is different from the others, then its policy choices may be right for itself, but not for the other states. Therefore, the court should be less willing to rely on emerging consensus.

Furthermore, if most of the states in Europe are similar to one another, but the state whose conduct is brought before the court is different from all the other states, then the majority of the states may adopt a policy that is not good for the state in question. In contrast, the government of the state in question may be familiar with the unique situation within this state and make good policy on its own. Therefore, when the state under review is fundamentally different from other European states, the ECtHR should be less willing to follow the emerging consensus and more willing to grant the state a margin of appreciation.[57]

The *Sahin case*[58] demonstrates the Court's willingness to defer to the practices of states that are fundamentally different from the rest of Europe even when their policies contrast with the European consensual view. This case concerned a practicing Muslim female student who was prevented from wearing a headscarf by a Turkish University. The applicant argued that Turkey violated her freedom of religion and that an emerging consensus exists against Turkey's policy since Turkey is the only European country that forbids the wearing of headscarves at a university. Despite the overwhelming consensus against Turkey's practices the ECtHR granted Turkey a margin of appreciation and deferred to its policies, arguing that Turkey is significantly different from all other European states. Among the qualities that make Turkey different from the other states are the facts that most of Turkey's citizens are Muslims and that Turkey's special history and fear of Muslim extremism strongly commit it to secularism.[59] Because Turkey is different from other European states, the policies that suit it may be different from those that suit other European countries.

[55] See Posner and Sunstein (n 24) 144. The condition that states are making their decisions based on private information makes the use of comparative law beneficial, since other countries cannot know the underlying reasons behind the policies the state chose. This condition also implies that states are making a decision based on facts or values and not only because they were pressured to do so by internal political dynamics that may not reflect a reasoned judgment. See ibid at 146–48.

[56] See Dothan, 'The Optimal Use of Comparative Law' (n 32) (expanding on this analysis).

[57] Shai Dothan, 'Why Granting States a Margin of Appreciation Supports the Formation of a Genuine European Consensus' (unpublished draft).

[58] *Leyla Şahin v Turkey* App no 44774/98, ECHR 2005-XI (ECtHR, Grand Chamber, 10 Nov 2005).

[59] See ibid [114]–[24]. Judge Tulkens criticised this decision in [3] of his dissenting opinion.

Consequently, in this and in similar situations the Court should grant states a wide margin of appreciation even when their policies contradict a clear European consensus.[60]

The condition requiring states to decide independently highlights the benefit of the emerging consensus doctrine over the use of comparative law by the states themselves. If states try to follow the majority of other states, as the use of comparative law implies, their decision will no longer be independent. In contrast, it is possible for all states to decide independently and for the ECtHR to apply emerging consensus—setting a standard that can then be followed by all other states.

But sometimes states may choose not to decide independently even when a system of emerging consensus exists. A possible reason is that states wish to make the correct decision quickly, without waiting for the ECtHR to intervene. States may reason that they can make better decisions if they learn from the experience of other states than if they decide independently. The more states make this calculation, the less independent will be their decision and consequently, the informational advantages of emerging consensus would decline. However, if the states are convinced that the ECtHR will apply emerging consensus correctly and reach its decision quickly enough, the states may be willing to decide independently, knowing that the ECtHR will soon amend their policy for the better.

Another reason states may be reluctant to decide independently is that they fear being found in violation of the Convention because of their policies; they fear a judgment against them may damage their reputation. If states want to prevent judgments against them, they may try to follow what they believe to be the policy adopted by the majority of states in Europe. But if all states make this calculation, they will not follow the policy that most states would adopt independently, but instead, the policy that the majority thinks that the majority thinks (etc) is a good policy. This guessing game, known in game theory terms as a *Beauty Contest*, can easily lead to results disfavoured by the majority of states, only because they are somehow a focal point and states believe they can coordinate around them.[61] The best way for the ECtHR to prevent states from falling into

[60] Another possible explanation mentioned in the judgment (ibid [109]) for this decision relies not only on the fact that Turkey is different from the rest of Europe, but also on the fact that attitudes regarding religious symbols are diverse across Europe generally. In this respect, all European states may be different from one another, therefore limiting the ability of an emerging consensus to lead to good policies and supporting a greater role for the margin of appreciation doctrine.

[61] See John Maynard Keynes, *The General Theory of Employment, Interest and Money* (New Delhi, Atlantic Publishers & Distributors, 2008) 140 (for an explanation of a Beauty Contest); Thomas C Schelling, *The Strategy of Conflict* (Cambridge, Mass, Harvard University Press, 1960) 94 (for an explanation of focal points).

a beauty contest is to alleviate the fear of states of being found in violation. The Court can achieve that by warning states, when it finds an emerging consensus, that their policies may lead to a finding of violation in the future. If the states know they will not suffer a reputational penalty before they are warned and allowed time to change their policies, they are likely to decide independently, allowing the Court to establish a genuine emerging consensus, which the states can then conform to, following the Court's recommendation. The willingness of the Court to warn the United Kingdom for over 15 years that its policies regarding transsexuals contradict the European consensus and may become unacceptable in the future, before an actual violation was found, may have been such an attempt not to frighten states into changing their policies prematurely in anticipation of the Court's judgments.[62]

The Court can use the margin of appreciation doctrine as an instrument to warn states that they are out of step with the emerging consensus without finding them in violation. The margin of appreciation protects the state's policies from a violation ruling, while allowing the Court to indicate that they contradict the emerging consensus. More generally speaking, the Court can sometimes employ the margin of appreciation strategically, preserving policies that are inferior, at least according to Jury Theorem logic underlying emerging consensus, in order to give states an incentive to decide independently. Guaranteeing the independence of the states' decision is, in turn, vital for the emergence of a genuine European consensus.

There may be other cases in which the Court can employ a similar strategic calculation to give states an incentive to decide independently. For example, when the Court fears a substantial backlash against a judgment mandated by the emerging consensus, it can indicate the emerging consensus while using the margin of appreciation to defer to the state and to avoid a ruling of violation. Such a strategy would disarm the state of the ability not to comply with the judgment and reduce its incentive to damage the Court's interests. At the same time, it does not grant a stamp of approval to the state policies by misconstruing the emerging consensus to imply that that the state's policies are legitimate. Instead, it lets all states know what is the true emerging consensus. Using the margin of appreciation in such cases is also superior to trying to delay the decision or avoid it; for example, by declaring that the Court does not have jurisdiction.

[62] The ECHR criticised the United Kingdom's policies in the following judgments: *Rees v the United Kingdom* App no 9532/81, Ser A no 106 (ECtHR, 17 Oct 1986); *Cossey v the United Kingdom* App no 10843/84, Ser A no 184 (ECtHR, 27 Sept 1990) at 17; *Sheffield and Horsham v the United Kingdom* App nos 22985/93 and 23390/94, ECHR 1998-V (30 July 1998) 2011, 2029, before finally finding the United Kingdom in violation of the Convention in the *Goodwin* case (n 4).

The advantage of issuing a judgment quickly, even though the margin of appreciation immunises the state from a finding of violation, is that the states are receiving the guidance of the ECtHR and are therefore less likely to try to learn from what the other states are doing, which would inevitably lead to information cascades.[63]

Recent empirical evidence suggests that states are likely to change their policy following a judgment by the ECtHR, instead of following what seems to be the majority of states before the ECtHR makes its decision.[64] This implies that states may be deciding independently, and consequently, that emerging consensus can lead to good results. The more evidence there is that states are deciding independently, the greater should be the Court's willingness to use emerging consensus.

V. CONCLUSION

This chapter argues that the ECtHR should strive to apply its doctrines in ways that ensure its normative legitimacy and can also help it make good decisions. Preserving the Court's normative legitimacy is crucial to protecting the international rule of law. It allows the Court to give the proper deference to democratic bodies within states and thereby to remain loyal to the national rule of law. The ability of the Court to ratchet the margin of appreciation given to the states based on the normative legitimacy of the state's decisions and the state's propensity to make good decisions allows for the proper level of flexibility and pluralism within the European legal system. This flexibility minimises the chances that the ECtHR will replace good policy decisions of the states with bad policy decisions, as well as the chances that the Court will illegitimately encroach on decisions that were accepted according to the prescriptions of the national rule of law.

But what if the ECtHR does not apply the doctrines correctly? For example, what if the judges claim to be applying emerging consensus but instead misconstrue the laws of the states they refer to in order to reach the result that suits their preferences? In that case, the Court's decision would not enjoy the advantages mentioned in this chapter and may lead to bad policy outcomes. The doctrines of the Court can try to constrain judicial discretion in a way that minimises judges' ability to misapply doctrines in the future. While the ECtHR is not formally bound by its precedents, judges usually follow them and therefore if doctrines are entrenched and clear, the ability of future judges to misconstrue them is limited.

[63] See Dothan, 'Why Granting States a Margin of Appreciation Supports the Formation of a Genuine European Consensus' (n 57).

[64] Helfer and Voeten, 'International Courts as Agents of Legal Change: Evidence from LGBT Rights in Europe' (n 28) 100.

Yet even if the Court faithfully applies the doctrines, this cannot guarantee that it would always adopt good policies. Doctrines such as emerging consensus are imperfect tools with which to search for good results; sometimes the majority of states in Europe are wrong and violate important human rights. At other times, well-functioning democratic states, that would ordinarily deserve a margin of appreciation, are nevertheless abusive of human rights. Fortunately, the ECtHR judges are not automatons; while they are committed to applying the doctrines mentioned in this chapter, they can use their judicial discretion to prevent results they view as contradicting the effective protection of the rights enshrined in the Convention.

While judicial discretion is sometimes essential, the judges' discretion is not absolute. A fuller picture of judicial decision-making must take into account that judges are limited by the text of the treaty and by the need to conform to the major doctrines and practices of the Court. Furthermore, judges must also be attentive to the political constraints on the ECtHR. If the Court's decisions contradict the interest of states, they may fail to comply with the Court, criticise it, or damage its budget.[65] To avert the danger of these harmful responses, judges may sometimes have to use their discretion to compromise on the result they view as legally correct and issue slightly different decisions to protect the Court's interest.

Besides trying to protect the interests of the Court, judges must also be concerned about the treaty system generally and try not to give states perverse incentives. For example, if states realise that the Court uses, more then they intended, expansive interpretation to read into the obligations they took upon themselves, states may be less willing to undertake treaty obligations. The result may be that states would not ratify protocols they view as beneficial to their interests, if they are strictly construed, from fear that the Court would interpret them expansively.[66] The judges should consider such problems as they make their decisions, and use their discretion, when possible, to avert them.

[65] See Dothan (n 54) ch 3.

[66] See Dothan, 'In Defence of Expansive Interpretation in the ECHR' (n 9) (suggesting a possible example—the refusal of the United Kingdom to ratify Protocol 12, which protects a general right to equality, from fear that this protocol would be interpreted expansively to include a right to the equal enjoyment of rights protected by international human rights instruments and not only to rights protected by national law, as a strict interpretation of the protocol would imply).

10

Human Rights, the Margin of Appreciation, and the International Rule of Law

ANDREW LEGG

I. INTRODUCTION

THE DOCTRINE OF the margin of appreciation operates at the interface of international and national legal orders. It is a doctrine of deference according to which international human rights tribunals grant a degree of latitude to a respondent state's conception of its international human rights obligations in a particular case.[1] Where a tribunal accepts that there can be a margin of appreciation, it signals that it proceeds from the premise that human rights obligations can, in certain circumstances, be implemented in different ways in different places. This raises the question of whether the judicial acceptance of such 'variable geometry'[2] of human rights protection would in some way undermine the rule of law in the practice of international human rights law.[3] This chapter

[1] See generally Andrew Legg, *The Margin of Appreciation in International Human Rights Law Deference and Proportionality* (Oxford, Oxford University Press, 2012). See also Yutaka Arai-Takahashi, *The Margin of Appreciation Doctrine and the Principle of Proportionality in the Jurisprudence of the ECHR* (Antwerp; New York, Intersentia, 2002); Howard Yourow, *The Margin of Appreciation Doctrine in the Dynamics of European Human Rights Jurisprudence* (Dordrecht, Martinus Nijhoff Publishers, 1996). As Birgit Peters discusses, the margin of appreciation doctrine is one of the means of creating a dialogue between national entities and international judges: see ch 8 (Peters) of this volume and Legg, *The Margin of Appreciation in International Human Rights Law* (n 1) 106. The doctrine is also part of the interpretative constraints discussed by Shai Dothan: see ch 9 (Dothan) of this volume.

[2] Lord Lester of Herne Hill, QC, 'The European Convention on Human Rights in the New Architecture of Europe: General Report', 'Proceedings of the 8th International Colloquy on the European Convention on Human Rights' (Council of Europe, 1995) at 236–37, cited in Paul Mahoney, 'Marvellous Richness of Diversity or Invidious Cultural Relativism?' (1998) 19 *Human Rights Law Journal* 1, 1.

[3] Ch 1 of this volume describes the 'international' rule of law as concerning how *international law and institutions* regulate states, international organisations, and other non-state

discusses how the concept of the 'international' rule of law can accommodate the margin of appreciation as it applies in international human rights law.

As discussed in greater detail in the next section, there are two different approaches to the concept of the rule of law, as developed traditionally at the national level. First, there is a 'formal' conception[4] of the rule of law, containing such criteria as, for example, the requirement that laws should be able to guide behaviour and be impartially and effectively enforced. From the perspective of the 'formal' concept, it might be argued that the margin of appreciation, which permits a degree of varied application of human rights, results in uncertainty in international human rights law and therefore is in tension with the formal conception of the rule of law. Secondly, a 'substantive' conception of the rule of law requires that certain values or rights be part of a legal system, and may require that human rights be protected in the same way by all states. From the standpoint of the 'substantive' conception, therefore, it might be said that human rights standards, if they are to be protected in conformity with the rule of law, must be uniformly applied and upheld. Since the margin of appreciation permits international human rights standards to be applied differently in different states and contexts, one may argue that this would also undermine a substantive conception of the rule of law in international human rights law.

This chapter advances an alternative approach, however. It argues that the margin of appreciation doctrine is an integral part of the rule of law in international human rights law, whether that is understood as a formal or substantive conception. The chapter starts by reviewing the two conceptions of the rule of law (section II). The chapter moves on to introduce the margin of appreciation (section III) and then considers how that doctrine affects our understanding of the rule of law in the context of international human rights law (section IV).

II. PREFATORY REMARKS ABOUT THE RULE OF LAW AND THE INTERNATIONAL RULE OF LAW

This section seeks, without being comprehensive, to set out the broad parameters of the aforementioned two conceptions of the rule of law, which were traditionally developed at the national level: namely, the

actors. International human rights law is noted there as one of the areas of international law that is subject to the 'international' rule of law.

[4] The dichotomy between 'concept' and 'conception' is adopted and discussed, eg, in Ronald Dworkin, *Law's Empire* (Oxford, Hart Publishing, 1998) 70–72.

formal (or 'thin') and the substantive (or 'thick') conceptions.[5] These two conceptions can be used as a framework for discussing the rule of law at the 'international' level.

A. The Formal and Substantive Conceptions of the Rule of Law

Proponents of the formal conception of the rule of law tend to argue that there are certain qualities that a legal system needs to possess in order to be 'legally in good shape'.[6] These qualities of a legal system, like the sharpness of a knife,[7] can be present whether or not the system itself is used for good or evil or if the content of the laws is good or bad, although this is not to say that any corrupt or evil legal system has the same likelihood of complying with the qualities of this conception of the rule of law.[8] The formal conception of the rule of law requires laws to meet two categories of requirements: (1) the requirement that laws can guide behaviour; this means, *inter alia,* that laws should be prospective, clear, stable, promulgated, and coherent; (2) the requirement that laws can be effectively enforced; this commonly refers to the requirement for an independent judiciary, accessible courts, fair hearings, the existence of law enforcement agencies, and the accountability of those people who have authority to make, apply, and enforce the law.[9]

Proponents of the substantive conception of the rule of law argue that the law should include fundamental rights of individuals and that these rights should be upheld by courts and law enforcement agencies. On this view, not only should there be a system of justice that enforces the laws, but the laws themselves should be 'good laws'.[10] In respect of human rights law, substantive conceptions of the rule of law may require that interpretations of human rights treaty provisions are given the 'right' interpretation uniformly by all states.

There is opposition to the substantive concept of the rule of law. For instance, a powerful response to the substantive conception of the rule of law is provided by Raz:

> If the rule of law is the rule of the good law then to explain its nature is to propound a complete social philosophy. But if so the term lacks any useful function.

[5] Paul Craig, 'Formal and Substantive Conceptions of the Rule of Law: An Analytical Framework' (1997) *Public Law* 467. For the distinction between formal and substantive, see also 'Framework Paper', ch 1 (Kanetake) of this volume, s II(B)(ii).

[6] John Finnis, *Natural Law and Natural Rights* (Oxford, Clarendon Press, 1980) 270.

[7] Joseph Raz, *The Authority of Law: Essays on Law and Morality* (Oxford, Clarendon Press, Oxford University Press, 1979) 225.

[8] Finnis, *Natural Law and Natural Rights* (n 6) 273–74.

[9] eg, Raz, *The Authority of Law* (n 7) 214; Finnis (n 6) 270–71.

[10] Ronald Dworkin, *A Matter of Principle* (Cambridge, Mass, Harvard University Press, 1985) 11–13. See further those accounts referred to in Paul Craig, 'Formal and Substantive Conceptions of the Rule of Law' (n 5) 477–84.

> We have no need to be converted to the rule of law just in order to discover that to believe it is to believe that good should triumph.[11]

In this quote, Raz suggests that a substantive conception of the rule of law is another way of saying that the law should be good, which in itself requires a comprehensive philosophy of what 'good' looks like, and how that 'good' would be implemented in law. Such a comprehensive theory would render a separate concept of the rule of law otiose. It is for this reason that the formal conception of the rule of law is in this author's view preferable to a substantive conception. People can debate what justice requires whilst sharing the view that there is inherent value in living in a society that complies with the requirements of the formal conception of the rule of law; namely, that laws guide behaviour and are enforced.

B. The International Rule of Law

There is a rich discussion in the literature as to the meaning of an *international* rule of law.[12] The rule of law in international law can be used differently depending on the relationships that are under observation.[13] First, in a 'narrow' sense, the rule of law in international law could be used for the relationships between states and other international actors, such as international organisations. Secondly, in a 'broad' sense, the rule of law in international law could be used for the relationships between states (and other international actors) and individuals. This conceptual distinction broadly corresponds with what Jeremy Waldron has described as the 'conventional' and the 'new' approach to articulating the application of

[11] Raz (n 7) 211.

[12] See, eg, Elihu Lauterpacht, 'Review of The International Rule of Law by Arthur Larson' (1962) 56 *American Journal of International Law* 851; William Bishop, 'The International Rule of Law' (1961) 59(4) *Michigan Law Review* 553; Jeremy Waldron, 'The Rule of International Law' (2006) 30 *Harvard Journal of Law and Public Policy* 15; Simon Chesterman 'An International Rule of Law?' (2008) 56(2) *American Journal of Comparative Law* 331. See also the European Journal of International Law's Symposium on 'Are Sovereigns Entitled to the Benefit to the International Rule of Law?': Nehal Bhuta, 'Are Sovereigns Entitled to the Benefit of the International Rule of Law? An Introduction' (2011) 22 *European Journal of International Law* 313; Jeremy Waldron, 'Are Sovereigns Entitled to the Benefit of the International Rule of Law?' (2011) 22 *European Journal of International Law* 315; Alexander Somek, 'A Bureaucratic Turn?' (2011) 22 *European Journal of International Law* 345; Thomas Poole, 'Sovereign Indignities: International Law as Public Law' (2011) 22 *European Journal of International Law* 351; David Dyzenhaus, 'Positivism and the Pesky Sovereign' (2011) 22 *European Journal of International Law* 363; Samantha Besson, 'Sovereignty, International Law and Democracy' (2011) 22 *European Journal of International Law* 373; Jeremy Waldron, 'Response: The Perils of Exaggeration' (2011) 22 *European Journal of International Law* 389.

[13] On multiple relationships regulated by the international rule of law, see 'Framework Paper' ch 1 (Kanetake) of this volume, s II(A).

the rule of law in international law.[14] This has particular relevance in the context of international human rights law where individuals are subjects of the law and in a variety of contexts have standing to bring international claims.

This chapter accepts that it is not possible simply to analogise the concept of the rule of law as it has existed in relation to domestic law and apply it to the international context. Both the formal and substantive conception of the rule of law should be modified to reflect the differences between domestic and the international legal orders. For instance, the two categories of requirements that constitute the formal conception of the rule of law (namely, (1) that laws should guide behaviour; and (2) that those laws should be effectively enforced) would have a different meaning at the international level from that of the domestic legal order, as will be further discussed in section IV of this chapter. There is obviously no court system of universal jurisdiction or global law enforcement agency and it is necessary to rethink the details of the rule of law for the international arena. Traditionally, the lack of enforcement mechanisms has given rise to the Austinian complaint that there is no such thing as international law, which in turn has led to the response that international law exists because it is habitually obeyed.[15] Whilst matters are of course more complex than this, the mere lack of global courts and law enforcement mechanisms is insufficient to lead to the conclusion that international law is not complied with,[16] and thus insufficient to lead to the conclusion that the formal concept of the rule of law does not exist at the international level.

III. THE MARGIN OF APPRECIATION

The margin of appreciation, which is the focus of this chapter, provides a good illustration of the characteristics of the rule of law in the context of international human rights law. The remainder of this chapter discusses how the margin of appreciation elucidates the nature of the rule of law at the international level. This section provides a brief description of the doctrine of the margin of appreciation[17] before returning, in the next section, to considering the international rule of law through the prism of the margin of appreciation.

[14] Jeremy Waldron, 'Are Sovereigns Entitled to the Benefit of the International Rule of Law?' (n 12) 329.

[15] James Brierly, *The Law of Nations: An Introduction to the International Law of Peace* (6th edn, Oxford, Clarendon Press, 1963) 68–76.

[16] Vaughan Lowe, *International Law* (Oxford, Oxford University Press, 2007) 18–24.

[17] A more detailed analysis by this author is found in Legg (n 1). This section is based on the matters discussed therein.

A. Describing the Concept

The margin of appreciation is a judicial creation that was developed by the European Court of Human Rights (ECtHR). There is no express textual peg on which to hang the doctrine in the European Convention on Human Rights. Its origins have been traced to analogous concepts of judicial deference in the administrative law of a number of European countries.[18] Given that the doctrine of the margin of appreciation is a judicial creation, it is unsurprising that a theory of deference has not been set out comprehensively in the decisions themselves, which are confined to their specific facts. Since the doctrine's early use,[19] it has featured in hundreds of decisions, and continues to be of huge importance today. Many commentators have written about the doctrine; some supportively, which has involved explaining its ramifications and impact in European human rights law;[20] and others critically,[21] preferring that it be banished as a concept in international human rights law.

Although the doctrine of the margin of appreciation is most well developed in the European Convention system, it also finds expression in the

[18] eg, the *marge d'appréciation* in French Administrative law, and similar concepts in German Constitutional law: see Yutaka Arai-Takahashi, *The Margin of Appreciation Doctrine* (n 1) 2–3; Howard Yourow, *The Margin of Appreciation Doctrine* (n 1) 14–15. For an overview of similar concepts in France, Germany, Spain, and the UK, see Benjamin Goold, Liora Lazarus and Gabriel Swiney, 'Public Protection, Proportionality and the Search for Balance' 10/07 (September) Ministry of Justice Research Series.

[19] eg, *Handyside v United Kingdom* App no 5493/72, (1979–80) 1 EHRR 737 (ECtHR, 7 Dec 1976).

[20] eg, Ronald Macdonald, 'The Margin of Appreciation' in Ronald Macdonald, Franz Matscher and Herbert Petzold (eds), *The European System for the Protection of Human Rights* (Dordrecht; London, Martinus Nijhoff, 1993) 123; John Merrills, *The Development of International Law by the European Court of Human Rights* (2nd edn, Manchester, Manchester University Press, 1993) 174–75; Paul Mahoney, 'Marvellous Richness of Diversity or Invidious Cultural Relativism?' (n 2); Humphrey Waldock, 'The Effectiveness of the System Set up by the European Convention on Human Rights' (1980) 1 *Human Rights Law Journal* 1, 9; David Harris and others, *Harris, O'Boyle & Warbrick: Law of the European Convention on Human Rights* (2nd edn, Oxford, Oxford University Press, 2009) 11–14, Alastair Mowbray, *Cases and Materials on the European Convention on Human Rights* (2nd edn, Oxford, Oxford University Press, 2007) 629–33; Mark Janis and others, *European Human Rights Law: Text and Materials* (3rd edn, Oxford, Oxford University Press, 2008) 242–44; Philip Leach, *Taking a Case to the European Court of Human Rights* (2nd edn, Oxford, Oxford University Press, 2005) 163–64, 284; Yutaka Arai-Takahashi (n 1); Pieter van Dijk and others (eds), *Theory and Practice of the European Convention on Human Rights* (3rd edn, The Hague; London, Kluwer Law International, 1998) 82; Janneke Gerards, 'Pluralism, Deference and the Margin of Appreciation Doctrine' (2011) 17 *European Law Journal* 80.

[21] eg, Lord Lester describes the margin of appreciation doctrine as 'slippery and elusive as an eel': Anthony Lester, 'Universality versus Subsidiarity: A Reply' (1998) 1 *European Human Rights Law Review* 73, 75. See also Eyal Benvenisti, 'Margin of Appreciation, Consensus, and Universal Standards' (1999) 31 *New York University Journal of International Law and Politics* 843, 844; George Letsas, 'Two Concepts of the Margin of Appreciation' (2006) 26 *Oxford Journal of Legal Studies* 705; George Letsas, *A Theory of Interpretation of the European Convention on Human Rights* (Oxford, Oxford University Press, 2007).

American Convention on Human Rights system and the Inter-American Court of Human Rights as well as the UN Human Rights Committee.[22] The concept also appears in other international human rights contexts,[23] although it may bear a different label.[24]

The concept of the margin of appreciation can be helpfully clarified by drawing on a distinction between two different types of reasons that are employed in the judicial decision-making process.[25] So-called 'first-order reasons' are the direct pros and cons of any particular dispute; for example, a dispute's impact on the individuals concerned, the facts of the dispute, and the particular justifications for the respondent state's approach. So-called 'second-order reasons' are the external factors that influence how one assesses these direct pros and cons of the dispute. In the context of the margin of appreciation, such external factors include an assessment of the democratic credentials of the respondent state's justification (the 'democratic legitimacy' factor),[26] whether the state has any particular expertise which deserves deference (the 'expertise' factor),[27] and whether the state's approach is representative of how other states deal with the same issue (or whether state practice, through lack of consensus, signifies that state parties have a broader discretion in interpreting the content of international human rights obligations) (the 'consensus' factor).[28] The margin of appreciation is a result of the judicial application of these different factors, which explains why international human rights laws can be applied differently from place to place and at different times, as will be further elaborated on in section IV(A) below.

Other factors that routinely affect the margin of appreciation in practice are the nature of the right or the type of case.[29] These are not the factors

[22] The doctrine is less well developed in the Inter-American system, and in the communication to the UN Human Rights Committee, but it is nevertheless possible to observe it in practice. See further, Legg (n 1) 3–6, 31–36.

[23] See, eg, the Maastricht Guidelines on Violations of Economic, Social and Cultural Rights, Maastricht, 22–26 January 1997 at para 8, which reads as follows:

> Margin of discretion
>
> 8. As in the case of civil and political rights, States enjoy a margin of discretion in selecting the means for implementing their respective obligations. State practice and the application of legal norms to concrete cases and situations by international treaty monitoring bodies as well as by domestic courts have contributed to the development of universal minimum standards and the common understanding of the scope, nature and limitation of economic, social and cultural rights.

[24] It is argued that the label given to the concept is less important than that the concept itself is well understood: see Legg (n 1) 224–25.

[25] This distinction finds its origins in the philosophy of practical reasoning. A more detailed exploration of the application of first and second order reasoning is found in Legg (n 1) ch 2.

[26] The 'democratic legitimacy' factor is discussed further in Legg (n 1) ch 4.

[27] The 'expertise' factor is discussed further in Legg (n 1) ch 6.

[28] The 'consensus' factor is discussed further in Legg (n 1) ch 5.

[29] The nature of the right or the type of case are both discussed further in Legg (n 1) ch 8.

directly relevant to the determination of a margin of appreciation in that they do not provide second-order reasons to give deference to (or heighten scrutiny of) the respondent state's approach to its human rights obligations. Yet the nature of the right is still related to the first-order reasons for a decision. For instance, when the right at issue is the right to life or the right to be free from torture, this clearly affects the level of justification needed by the state before any interference can be permitted, when compared, for example, to the right to peaceful enjoyment of property rights for which there is greater room for intervention by states. Judges are likely to show greater deference to states when the cases involve those rights which are expressly subject to various limits for, for example, public safety, health, and morals.[30] This is not to say that judges do not allow the margin of appreciation in cases involving so-called absolute rights (to life, to freedom from torture)[31] or so-called strong rights (to a fair trial or liberty).[32] Yet the level of justification required for a margin of appreciation would have to be much stronger if the cases involve such fundamental rights as the right to life and the right not to be tortured.

B. The Margin of Appreciation and Proportionality

In understanding the margin of appreciation, one also needs to refer to proportionality, as these concepts work together in the determination of international human rights law cases.[33] The relationship between proportionality and the margin of appreciation is especially relevant to the analysis of whether the judicial process permits a measure of diversity in human rights standards, and to our understanding of the meaning of the international rule of law, as will be further elaborated on in section IV.

The proportionality assessment is not required in all cases; for example, if the facts reveal a deliberate use of lethal force by the state without legal justification, there is a clear violation of the right to life and any analysis of the proportionality of the state conduct may not be called for. However, many human rights cases involve the difficult analysis of conflicting justifications and interests presented by the state and the individual claimants. In such cases, human rights courts must undertake a careful assessment of all the relevant reasons in the case. The courts initially consider the first-order reasons (ie, the direct pros and cons relevant to the dispute) and apply to them the second-order reasons (ie, external matters such as level of state consensus or democratic legitimacy) which may cancel out,

[30] eg, ECHR, Arts 8–11.
[31] As discussed further in Legg (n 1) 204–10.
[32] See, eg, Legg (n 1) ch 6.5 on fair trial rights.
[33] This section is largely taken from Legg (n 1) ch 8, esp 194–99.

strengthen or reduce the ordinary weighting based upon first-order reasons. The proportionality assessment is the final analysis in the courts' decision-making process after they identify the relevant factors. Once the courts have considered the composite effect of all the reasons in the case, they must make a judgement about what the guiding rationale is for their decision. This process is the assessment of proportionality, and can be described as balancing, understood as a heuristic device to illustrate the practical reasoning of the tribunal. Thus, the proportionality assessment may result in a measure of diversity in the application of international human rights, which is of particular interest when considering both formal and substantive conceptions of the international rule of law (see section IV below).

Such a process of reasoning involving proportionality can be seen in many cases of the ECtHR, in which the language of proportionality and the margin of appreciation are employed. In *Odièvre v France*,[34] for instance, France set out the first-order reasons[35] and second-order reasons[36] side-by-side in a paragraph that was meant to discuss the 'proportionality of the interference'.[37] Having identified and weighed the relevant factors, both first-order reasons[38] and second-order reasons,[39] the Court observed that France sought to 'strike a balance and to ensure sufficient proportion between the competing interests'[40] and concluded that 'France has not overstepped the margin of appreciation'.[41]

The ECtHR's reasoning in *Odièvre* shows that the Court considers both first-order and second-order reasons in assessing proportionality for the matters with regard to which member states have the margin of appreciation. Other cases also show the same structure of judicial reasoning. In

[34] *Odièvre v France* App no 42326/98 (ECtHR, Grand Chamber, 13 Feb 2003).

[35] The first-order reasons invoked by France involved the importance to women of the ability to decline giving their identity following birth: see ibid.

[36] The second-order reasons invoked by France involved the international consensus of the state: see ibid.

[37] ibid [37], which addressed arguments related both to the child's right to know information about its identity as against the mother's right to anonymity, but also to such matters as the level of European consensus on the way states deal with this tension.

[38] The Court set out the importance under Art 8 of knowing one's origins and a mother's interest in anonymity, the impact on the wider adoptive family, as well as the aim of preventing illegal abortions and unofficial child abandonment, and thus pursued the right to life: ibid [44]–[45]. The Court also discussed the non-identifying information given to the applicant about her mother, and the new legislation in France: ibid [48]–[49].

[39] ibid [46]–[47] (mentioning both the legislative aspect of the case and the role of international consensus).

[40] ibid [49].

[41] ibid [49]. The Court found the second-order reasons to have significance in leading to a finding in favour of the state: 'Overall, the Court considers that France has not overstepped the margin of appreciation which it must be afforded in view of the complex and sensitive nature of the issue of access to information about one's origins, an issue that concerns the right to know one's personal history, the choices of the natural parents, the existing family ties and the adoptive parents' (ibid [49]).

Cumpana and Mazare v Romania,[42] the ECtHR found that the state had a margin of appreciation with regard to the limitations on the freedom of speech in Article 10 ECHR.[43] On this basis, the Court moved on to assess the severity of the punishment by considering and weighing both first-order[44] and second-order reasons,[45] leading to the conclusion that the state's action was 'manifestly disproportionate'.[46] Overall, as indicated by these examples, the ECtHR weighs both case-specific facts and external considerations in assessing proportionality with regard to the issues for which the ECtHR grants the margin of appreciation to states. This can result in a measure of diversity in the application of international human rights law, which, as already noted, can raise questions about the compatibility of the margin of appreciation with the international rule of law. It is to this matter that the next section turns.

IV. THE MARGIN OF APPRECIATION AND THE INTERNATIONAL RULE OF LAW

Having summarised the doctrine of the margin of appreciation, this section considers the question posed at the outset of the chapter: how we can understand the international rule of law through the concept and practice of the margin of appreciation in the international legal order. It will be recalled that the two main conceptions of the rule of law are the formal and substantive conceptions, and that the international rule of law can be understood in a narrow and broad sense, depending on which relationships are under consideration.[47] This section considers the margin of appreciation for the purpose of enhancing our understanding about the formal and substantive conception of the international rule of law.

[42] *Cumpana and Mazare v Romania* App no 33348/96 (ECtHR, Grand Chamber, 17 Dec 2004). In this case, two journalists wrote an article strongly accusing a judge and politician of corruption for giving contractual rights to a car parking company on council property. It was claimed that the council had authorised one company, but that the officials granted the rights to an entirely different company who caused damage to cars and yet who received assistance from officials and the police. The national court punished the journalists by barring them from journalism and with imprisonment. Whilst neither punishment was enforced and pardons were granted, the domestic decisions were nevertheless challenged at the ECtHR.

[43] ibid [110].

[44] ibid [111]–[14].

[45] ibid [115]. In this case, the second-order reasons strengthened first-order reasons in favour of the state, but nevertheless, the first-order reasons in favour of the applicant outweighed these combined considerations.

[46] ibid [120].

[47] See ss II(A) and (B) above.

A. The Margin of Appreciation and the Formal Conception of the International Rule of Law

As noted in section II(A) of this chapter, the formal conception of the rule of law developed at the domestic level generally requires laws to guide behaviour and to be effectively enforced. On the face of it, the margin of appreciation appears to undermine these elements of the formal rule of law at the international level. It could be argued that, first, the margin of appreciation results in human rights law that, because it is not uniformly applied, does not properly guide the behaviour of states in their relations with other states (the narrow version of the formal conception of the rule of law)[48] or of governments in their relation to individuals (the broader version), and second, human rights laws are not properly enforced on the basis that international judges will at times leave the matter within the states' margin of appreciation. Nevertheless, as will be observed below, these observations do not adequately take into account the unique way in which the margin of appreciation doctrine may uphold the international rule of law.

i. Laws' Ability to Guide Behaviour

With regard to the first requirement, it might be said that finding a margin of appreciation results in human rights law that, because it is not uniformly applied, does not properly guide the behaviour, and whose meaning is thus obscure or incoherent. For example, in the case of *Handyside v UK*,[49] the ECtHR found that due to the margin of appreciation, the prosecution of the applicant under obscenity legislation did not violate the freedom of expression, albeit that there were no such restrictions on the publication in other European countries. Accordingly, it might be said that the lack of uniformity entailed by the margin of appreciation means that European human rights law in relation to Article 10 is not sufficiently clear or coherent to be able to guide conduct.

There is, of course, some undeniable truth in such a view. The provisions of international human rights treaties are by their nature broad and general and they do contain an inherent vagueness. This is sometimes referred to as the open-textured[50] nature of such provisions. At the same time, it would be too simplistic to conclude that because the provisions are

[48] See s II(B) of this chapter about the broad and narrow versions of the international rule of law.

[49] *Handyside v United Kingdom* (n 19).

[50] See Timothy Endicott, *Vagueness in Law* (Oxford, Oxford University Press, 2000) 31 and 37 (for definitions of 'vague' and 'open-texture', respectively).

vague there is necessarily a deficit in the rule of law with regard to international human rights law. The vagueness in human rights standards does not prevent them from being a helpful guide, particularly in light of case law that can elucidate their content. On the contrary, there are two ways in which the margin of appreciation rather sustains this aspect of a formal conception of the rule of law in international human rights law.

First, in international human rights law, it can be argued that it is not possible or desirable to set out exhaustive definitions of general rules; in such a context, these general rules suffice from a rule of law perspective in relation to their ability to guide conduct. International human rights law, in accordance with the principle of subsidiarity, gives states a primary role in the protection of human rights.[51] It is from this background that the margin of appreciation emerges in international human rights law.[52] Subsidiarity as a general concept involves a complex tension designed to enhance the freedom of smaller groupings of people to act (down to individuals). It operates as a presumptive theory, described by Finnis as a principle that 'larger associations should not assume functions which can be performed efficiently by smaller associations'.[53] For this reason, it cannot be regarded as a significant rule of law failing for international human rights law to have developed a concept of the margin of appreciation to reflect the subsidiary nature of the international protection of human rights.

The founders of international human rights treaties did not intend that those treaties encompass the application of detailed articulations of uniform standards for peoples everywhere. As Jacques Maritain, the influential French philosopher-diplomat involved in the negotiation of the Universal Declaration of Human Rights, which along with the International Covenant on Civil and Political Rights forms part of what is commonly referred to as an International Bill of Rights, said of that treaty,

[51] eg, ICCPR 1966, Art 2; ECHR 1950, Art 1; ACHR 1969, Art 1. See Dominic McGoldrick, *The Human Rights Committee: its Role in the Development of the International Covenant on Civil and Political Rights* (Oxford, Clarendon Press, 1991) 13: 'There was general agreement during the drafting that the primary obligation under the ICCPR would be implementation at the national level'.

[52] Paolo Carozza similarly sees the margin of appreciation as reflective of subsidiarity (see Paolo Carozza, 'Subsidiarity as a Structural Principle of International Human Rights Law' (2003) 97 *American Journal of International Law* 38, 40):

> The principle of subsidiarity provides an analytically descriptive way to make sense of a variety of disparate features of the existing structure of international human rights law … [I]t is not surprising to find in the development of human rights law that other doctrines and ideas have arisen that function at least in part as analogues to subsidiarity in addressing the pervasive dialectic between universal human rights norms and legitimate claims to pluralism. The doctrine of the 'margin of appreciation'", first developed by the European Court of Human Rights (ECHR), is the most notable example.

[53] Finnis (n 6) 146–47.

'many different kinds of music can be played on the document's thirty strings'.[54]

Second, the margin of appreciation demonstrates what is and what is not within the discretion of states when implementing human rights standards, which is in itself a form of guidance. In this respect, there is a close interface between the international and domestic legal systems. International human rights courts and tribunals are thus fora for the contestation of sovereignty in the field of human rights.[55] In making decisions involving the margin of appreciation, the tribunals set out where sovereign freedom to protect human rights is limited, and where it is not. This is a form of guidance, as envisaged by formal conceptions of the rule of law (though perhaps this is one of the aspects of the formal conception of the rule of law that is reserved for the *international* rule of law).

In summary, the first scepticism that might be raised from the perspective of the formal conception of the rule of law (that the margin of appreciation might prevent human rights law from guiding conduct) is overstated. Any latent ambiguity in the vague and open-textured nature of human rights treaty obligations is unavoidable in the absence of an international government that plays a very intrusive role in the affairs of peoples everywhere. The absence of such a body is no bad thing. Indeed, the existence of the margin of appreciation entitles international tribunals to navigate a course through troubled waters—to identify where there is a sufficiently clear international norm that is not likely to be affected by arguments for a wide margin of appreciation. In this respect, the doctrine in fact contributes to a more vibrant international rule of law.

ii. Effective Enforcement of Laws

The second criticism that could be made from the perspective of a formal conception of the rule of law is that the margin of appreciation results in a situation where courts themselves are not entertaining the complaints of applicants because they prefer to give a margin of appreciation, and thus human rights are not properly enforced in the courts.

It is a not uncommon misconception that arguments for deference or the margin of appreciation are tantamount to non-justiciability arguments and attempts to achieve an abdication of the international court's responsibility to decide the case,[56] and consequently are a threat to the

[54] See Mary Ann Glendon, *A World Made New: Eleanor Roosevelt and the Universal Declaration of Human Rights* (New York, Random House, 2001) 230 at note 21. See also Mary Ann Glendon, 'The Rule of Law in the Universal Declaration of Human Rights' (2004) 2 *Northwestern Journal of International Human Rights* 67.

[55] This idea is discussed further in Legg (n 1) 58–60.

[56] Trevor RS Allan, 'Human Rights and Judicial Review: a Critique of "Due Deference"' (2006) 65 *Cambridge Law Journal* 671, 689 opines: 'Due deference turns out, on close inspection,

rule of law. Non-justiciability is a doctrine that operates as a substantive bar on adjudication, which means that the tribunal does not make a decision because it is not competent to adjudicate on the subject matter of the dispute. This is, in principle, different from the margin of appreciation;[57] the margin does not prevent the courts from making a decision. Yet critics still argue that where arguments about deference hold sway, the margin of appreciation is tantamount to non-justiciability in the sense that the court does not make its own assessment of the appropriate standard and simply adopts the approach of the domestic authorities.

The critics' arguments can be either empirical or conceptual. Empirical versions of the argument would claim that particular decisions do not adequately, or at all; assess the first-order reasons relevant to a case; and instead, adopt wholesale the approach of the agency or state seeking deference. This claim is true on occasion. There are certainly cases in international human rights law where the tribunal's reasoning has either not taken account of the first-order reasons or has been deficient in this regard.[58] But this is not an argument that the margin of appreciation entails non-justiciability, but rather it is an argument that the tribunal has failed to provide an adequate explanation for its decision.

Conceptual versions of the argument are not persuasive either. Critics claim that the margin of appreciation necessarily means that the tribunal fails to make a decision on the basis of the direct pros and cons of a case. Yet this claim holds true neither as a matter of theory or as a matter of practice.[59] Tribunals can and do consider the direct pros and cons of

to be non-justiciability dressed in pastel colours'. The argument is made at the international level, eg, by Benvenisti, who claims that international courts undermine their role by using the doctrine: see Benvenisti, 'Margin of Appreciation, Consensus, and Universal Standards' (n 21) 844, 852, and 854. See also Cora Feingold, 'The Doctrine of Margin of Appreciation and the European Convention on Human Rights' (1977) 53 *Notre Dame Lawyer* 90, 95. In relation to the terminology of margin of appreciation, see Murray Hunt, 'Sovereignty's Blight: Why Contemporary Public Law Needs the Concept of "Due Deference"' in Nicholas Bamforth and Peter Leyland (eds), *Public Law in a Multi-Layered Constitution* (Oxford, Hart Publishing, 2003) 344–49; Timothy Jones, 'The Devaluation of Human Rights under the European Convention' (1995) *Public Law* 430, 732.

[57] Some of this discussion is taken from Legg (n 1) 26–27.

[58] eg, *Ominayak v Canada* CCPR/C/38/D/167/1984 (UN Human Rights Committee, 26 March 1990). In *Ominayak*, 27 pages of relevant factual information were set out, leading to a decision that was a matter of lines long and failed to articulate which aspects of the factual details were relevant or why, finding only that the life and culture of an indigenous Canadian tribe was endangered by the commercial activities at issue, and thus there was a violation of Art 27 of the ICCPR. This decision gives little guidance about when Art 27 would apply in future cases.

[59] States have made requests for such deference, but they have received short shrift from the tribunals. See, eg, *Open Door and Dublin Well Woman v Ireland* App no 14234/88 (ECtHR, 29 Oct 1992). In this case, Ireland argued that applying the necessity standard of proportionality was inappropriate in cases involving the sensitive moral issue of counselling women

a case whilst also considering factors for a margin of appreciation. The case law of the ECtHR demonstrates time after time that arguments about the margin of appreciation appear alongside a full consideration of the relevant factors, and that no such abandonment of the judicial function takes place.[60] Sometimes the arguments for a margin of appreciation are strong, but the state nevertheless loses the case because they have failed to comply with the principle of proportionality—in other words, the first-order reasons against the state outweigh those in favour of the state, even where the state's logic is supported by strong second-order reasons (such as a high level of expertise or a lack of international consensus as to how to deal with the matter).

The criticism that the margin of appreciation results in damage to the enforcement of human rights laws is thus based on the misconception that in considering arguments for a margin of appreciation, the international tribunal is failing to consider all the relevant factors and failing to make a decision. On the contrary, a decision *is* made. Sometimes the decision is in favour of an individual, and sometimes it is in favour of a state. When states succeed, they do not do so on the basis that they are permitted to violate human rights because they are within the margin of appreciation. Instead, the court or tribunal makes a finding that there was no violation of their treaty obligations, and that the state action was consistent with those obligations.

In any event, complaints that the margin of appreciation offends the rule of law on the basis that it undermines the enforcement of international law ring hollow when one steps back to consider enforcement more broadly. For the purposes of the rule of law, the enforcement of international human rights laws includes a range of factors, such as the existence of a domestic police force and a judiciary that upholds the law and applies it impartially and fairly. The widespread and systematic failure of many domestic public justice systems[61] puts into perspective the comparative importance of any alleged impact of the margin of appreciation on the enforcement of international human rights laws.

about how to get an abortion overseas and publishing information about where to receive an abortion in Great Britain. The Court responded strongly: 'The Court cannot agree that the State's discretion in the field of the protection of morals is unfettered and unreviewable': ibid [68]; 'To accept the Government's pleading on this point would amount to an abdication of the Court's responsibility under Article 19 (art. 19) "to ensure the observance of the engagements undertaken by the High Contracting Parties"': ibid [69]. The Court went on to find that the injunction was disproportionate.

[60] See generally the discussion of the relevant cases in Legg (n 1) chs 4–6.

[61] See Gary A Haugen and Victor Boutros, *The Locust Effect: Why the End of Poverty Requires the End of Violence* (Oxford; New York, Oxford University Press, 2014).

B. The Margin of Appreciation and the Substantive Conception of the International Rule of Law

On a substantive conception of the international rule of law,[62] the role of international human rights courts is to develop a uniform meaning for each human rights treaty provision.[63] On this view, because the margin of appreciation permits a level of variation in the application of human rights treaty provisions, one may argue that the margin undermines the universality of human rights and the rule of law in international human rights law.

However, it is a mistake to consider that human rights should be applied uniformly. The margin of appreciation is conceptually consistent with the universality of human rights which, as discussed further below, requires human rights to be locally embedded, and necessarily entails a level of differentiation. It would be highly undesirable to impose the same interpretation of universally shared values on all peoples. It would also be problematic to insist on a uniform protection of such rights in all the world's many different legal systems. Accordingly, if any particular substantive conception of the international rule of law fails to take into account the fact that human rights will necessarily (at a conceptual, normative, and pragmatic level) entail a level of differentiation, such a conception should be rejected.

The accounts that designate the margin of appreciation a retreat into relativism are not persuasively argued. For instance, Eyal Benvenisti states, '[m]argin of appreciation, with its principled recognition of moral relativism, is at odds with the concept of the universality of human rights'.[64] He goes on to state that he is not 'entering into the well-trodden general debate on universalism versus relativism in human rights jurisprudence', and is instead focusing on institutional arguments about the margin of appreciation, especially arguments concerning 'the inherent deficiencies of the democratic systems'.[65] His initial claim, that the margin of appreciation involves a 'principled recognition of moral relativism', does not appear to have any sufficient supporting argument. Indeed, by going on to discuss institutional considerations relevant to the margin of appreciation, Benvenisti may have unwittingly accepted that in fact there are

[62] The discussion in this section is largely taken and adapted from Legg (n 1) ch 3.

[63] The following authors argue that human rights within Europe, eg, should be harmonised rather than permit diversity: see Letsas, *A Theory of Interpretation of the European Convention on Human Rights* (n 21); Neil Walker, 'Human Rights in a Postnational Order: Reconciling Political and Constitutional Pluralism' in Tom Campbell, Keith Ewing and Adam Tomkins (eds), *Sceptical Essays on Human Rights* (Oxford, Oxford University Press, 2001) 138, 138–40; Steven C Greer, *The European Convention on Human Rights: Achievements, Problems and Prospects* (Cambridge, Cambridge University Press, 2006); Legg (n 1) ch 3, 50–55.

[64] Benvenisti (n 21) 844.

[65] ibid 847.

reasons for the doctrine other than (and not reliant upon) the entrenching of moral relativism. Likewise, James Sweeney refers to arguments that suggest the margin of appreciation has a 'perceived culturally relativist bias',[66] but relies only on a dated, partly dissenting opinion of Judge De Meyer in the case of *Z v Finland*:

> In the present judgment the Court once again relies on the national authorities' 'margin of appreciation'. I believe that it is high time for the Court to banish that concept from its reasoning. It has already delayed too long in abandoning this hackneyed phrase and *recanting the relativism it implies*.[67]

It is important to consider what universality means in the context of fundamental values and human rights in order to assess whether universality requires uniformity or is otherwise compatible with a margin of appreciation. It is only when the meaning of universality has been clarified that it is possible to ascertain whether the margin of appreciation is relativist or whether it is compatible with the universality of human rights and also substantive conceptions of the rule of law.

Joseph Raz's account of universality is persuasive in overcoming the claim that the margin of appreciation succumbs to moral relativism. Raz explains that whilst maintaining a commitment to the universality of values, one can also expect these values to be articulated differently according to time and context. Raz' explanation of universality can be paraphrased as follows. The fact that something is of value to us requires that that which is of value can be identified and extrapolated and then applied to something else outside of those specific circumstances. This extrapolation objectifies the value making it in a 'thin' sense universalisable. Furthermore, the universalisability of values is what makes them intelligible as values. For example, saying a movie is good today but yesterday was terrible obviously lacks intelligibility. This is because we are entitled to assume that any change of value can be explained, and that value explanations depend on universal characteristics: factors such as time and location do not account for varied explanations.[68]

The mistaken understandings of universality and how it operates in moral discourse have caused significant confusion regarding the doctrine

[66] James A Sweeney, 'Margins of Appreciation: Cultural Relativity and the European Court of Human Rights in the Post-Cold War Era' (2005) 54 *International & Comparative Law Quarterly* 459, 459. Sweeney's aim is to discount such views and show that the margin of appreciation is based upon institutional subsidiarity.

[67] *Z v Finland* App no 22009/93, (1998) 25 EHRR 371 (ECtHR, 25 Feb 1997), partly dissenting opinion of Judge De Meyer (Translation), Part III (emphasis added). Cited in Sweeney, ibid 463. See also the footnote to his separate concurring opinion in *Ahmed v UK* App no 22954/93, (2000) 29 EHRR 1 (ECtHR, 2 Sept 1998), and the cases cited at Sweeney, ibid 463 note 21. See further Marie-Bénédicte Dembour, *Who Believes in Human Rights? Reflections on the European Convention* (Cambridge, Cambridge University Press, 2006) 159–65.

[68] Dembour, ibid 47–54.

of the margin of appreciation. The argument that the universality of values entails their legitimate differential instantiation from place to place means that where a state interprets a human right standard differently within its margin of appreciation this is not necessarily a reflection of moral relativism. Why should, for example, there be only one right way for a state to decide what a fair trial requires with respect to the anonymity of particular classes of offender, whether they are rapists or children? Why should a uniform approach to free speech be imposed on states that operate in radically different contexts?

The legitimacy of different approaches from state to state can be illustrated in the margin of appreciation context by looking again at the landmark case of *Handyside v UK*.[69] Despite the fact that some countries allowed the publication of 'The Schoolbook',[70] the Court held that,

> The Contracting States have each fashioned their approach in the light of the situation obtaining in their respective territories; they have had regard, inter alia, to the different views prevailing there about the demands of the protection of morals in a democratic society. The fact that most of them decided to allow the work to be distributed does not mean that the contrary decision of the Inner London Quarter Sessions was a breach of Article 10.[71]

Universal human rights thus depend on social factors to find expression and realisation, and this necessarily differs from place to place and over time. It is also necessary to consider the importance of legal differences from place to place.

In different legal systems decisions on the articulation of rights may vary in a way that is consistent with sharing the same values. Raz discusses an example that shows how laws translated from universal moral principles may differ between legal systems and over time:[72]

> The moral wrong committed by rape may involve the violation of a universal moral principle. But the legal regulation of rape may rightly vary from place to place and time to time. To go no further, it is far from a universal principle that rape should constitute a separate offence rather than be assimilated to serious assault … Whether and when a sexual motive should determine the character of the offence, rather than be relevant to sentence only, whether or when penetration should single out some sex offences from others, whether or when violence matters or not (it is not a necessary ingredient of rape, according to most jurisdictions)—*all these are questions sensitive to social conditions, to perceived social*

[69] *Handyside v United Kingdom* (n 19).

[70] ibid [11].

[71] ibid [57].

[72] Joseph Raz, 'On the Authority and Interpretation of Constitutions: Some Preliminaries' in L Alexander (ed), *Constitutionalism: Philosophical Foundations* (Cambridge, Cambridge University Press, 1998) 166.

> *meanings, to the informal consequences of criminal convictions, and to many other factors that are as variable as any.*[73]

It is this last emphasised part of the above quotation that is most relevant. Building on the above argument that expressions of moral value are socially contingent in a way that does not jeopardise their universality, this contingency is augmented when considering the social implications within a particular community's *legal* system. Thus, sharing a belief in the universal moral wrong of rape and in the desirability of protection against rape in human rights law is compatible with accepting the legitimacy of differentiation within different societies' human rights laws. Such differentiation does not reject the universal nature of the human right, but does reject an unnatural uniformity of legal expression.

It is important not to take this too far or to draw hasty conclusions from this discussion. Legal differentiation from place to place *may* rightly vary; the argument is not that it must vary, but simply that uniformity between legal systems ought not to be forced. Such uniformity may lead to injustice and a failure to implement human rights, rather than their proper protection.[74] Consequently, there are reasons to consider the external factors for deference because they provide the tribunals with the opportunity to recognise legitimate diversity. At the same time, there may not be strong reasons to defer in a particular case, it being better to rely on a more uniform legal solution, perhaps based on a common trend among states.[75]

The connection between laws and the nature of the society in which they exist has attracted debate. Some writers emphasise the transplantability of laws into different contexts[76] whilst others have emphasised the uniqueness of law to their own systems based on their history and culture.[77] The scope for any legal 'transplantation' must be exercised with caution and skill. Hasty comparisons will fail in the allotted aim,[78] but nevertheless, legal systems do often deal with similar questions. Foreign case law cannot be transplanted blindly, nor is this the experience of courts dealing with human rights. As Chris McCrudden says, '[m]ost judges using comparative judicial decisions recognize, indeed insist, on the constructed and (to some extent) contingent nature of decision-making on issues of contemporary human rights'.[79] Such judicial practice is consistent with the

[73] ibid 166 (emphasis added).

[74] See further the UNESCO Universal Declaration on Cultural Diversity (2 Nov 2001), esp Art 4.

[75] Legg (n 1) ch 5.

[76] eg, Alan Watson, 'Comparative Law and Legal Change' (1978) 37 *Cambridge Law Journal* 313.

[77] eg, Pierre Legrand, 'How to Compare Now' (1996) 16 *Legal Studies* 232.

[78] ibid 236.

[79] Christopher McCrudden, 'A Common Law of Human Rights?: Transnational Judicial Conversations on Constitutional Rights' (2000) 20 *Oxford Journal of Legal Studies* 499, 528.

arguments made above that notwithstanding the universality of human rights, there is a justifiable moral and, even more so, legal differentiation of these rights from place to place.

In addition to being theoretically robust, this broader approach to the universality of human rights is reflected in the practice of the tribunals.[80] As Judge Tulkens put this idea in one case, 'the Court must seek to reconcile universality and diversity'.[81]

Overall, any substantive conception of the international rule of law should be mindful of the importance of permitting diversity of the legal protection of human rights where appropriate. The margin of appreciation is the legal doctrine that guides the international courts in this endeavour. There may be commentators who disagree with this approach, and would argue that human rights within Europe, for instance, should be harmonised rather than allow for diversity.[82] However, it is possible that adherents to a substantive conception of the rule of law might nevertheless accept a measure of diversity on the basis that to do otherwise would lead to wrong results that offend justice and the rule of law in particular places. There are good reasons for this. Whereas the margin of appreciation has most impact in complex cases of interpretation of human rights obligations, human rights treaties nevertheless provide a wide and diverse range of standards that enjoy broad support from the international community.

V. CONCLUSION

This chapter has considered how the margin of appreciation doctrine affects our understanding of the international rule of law in the context of human rights law. Substantive conceptions of the rule of law that argue that human rights should be uniform to be universal, and that international human rights treaty systems should produce the 'right' answers, argue wrongly that the margin of appreciation undermines the rule of law because it permits a measure of diversity. The concept of the universality of value itself entails contextual application, particularly in relation to law. After all, diversity was always envisaged to be part of the international human rights law system.

Focusing on the formal conceptions of the rule of law, it might be said that the margin of appreciation renders human rights laws a poor guide

[80] See further the discussion of relevant cases in Legg (n 1) 47–49.

[81] Judge Tulkens *Leyla Şahin v Turkey* (2007) 44 EHRR 5 (ECtHR, Grand Chamber, 10 Nov 2005) dissenting opinion of Judge Tulkens (trans) [2] (agreeing on this point with the majority).

[82] See (n 63).

to behaviour and undermines the enforcement of human rights. In relation to the former, there is no failing in the fact that there is some inherent vagueness in human rights laws that permits states a measure of liberty and discretion in the implementation of those treaty standards. Indeed, the margin of appreciation provides guidance as to where that discretion does and does not exist. In relation to the argument about enforcement, this is based on the misconception that the margin of appreciation stops international courts from reaching a decision based on all relevant factors—it does not do this at all. The enforcement of international human rights laws, as part of formal conceptions of the rule of law, is jeopardised instead by such matters as inadequate police provision and under-resourced and unfair judicial systems.

The doctrine of the margin of appreciation, which lies at the interface between domestic and international legal orders, guides international courts in making determinations about the scope of any room for states to have sovereign freedom of action in human rights. The doctrine demonstrates how courts are able to commit to the protection of universal human rights whilst permitting a measure of local variation in their implementation. This is consistent with the rule of law. Substantive conceptions of the rule of law ought to take into account that international human rights norms inherently require a measure of diversity of application given the requirement to apply those shared universal norms in different contexts. Formal conceptions of the rule of law likewise benefit from guidance as to the scope of any discretion in implementing human rights standards. In these ways, the doctrine of the margin of appreciation elucidates the meaning of the rule of law in the context of international human rights law.

11

Subsidiarity in the Practice of International Courts

MACHIKO KANETAKE

I. INTRODUCTION

SUBSIDIARITY AS AN idea about the allocation of competence has two inseparable facets. On one side of the coin, it signifies that decision-making ought to be taken primarily at a lower level of governance. On the other side of the same coin, subsidiarity allows a shift of competence to a higher level of governance when a matter is not appropriately dealt with at the lower level. By prima facie favouring local decision-making, subsidiarity makes a particular normative claim that the protection of autonomy, diversity, and individual liberty should be prioritised over effectiveness, coherence, and unity that demand centralised decision-making at a higher level of governance.[1] While subsidiarity is a relatively unfamiliar lexicon in international law, the idea is already embedded in the decentralised structure of international law which is based on the principle of sovereign equality, the autonomy of each state, and its consent to be bound by a rule without any higher centralised law-maker.

The idea of subsidiarity has gained renewed significance since the mid-twentieth century due to incremental change in the decentralised processes in which states make, apply, and enforce international law. One of the most visible changes is the presence of international courts and tribunals in the international legal order. International courts have not only increased in number[2] but have also assumed the multiple functions

[1] See George A Bermann, 'Taking Subsidiarity Seriously: Federalism in the European Community and the United States' (1994) 94 *Columbia Law Review* 331, 339–44; Augusto Zimmermann, 'Subsidiarity, Democracy and Individual Liberty in Brazil' in M Evans and A Zimmermann (eds), *Global Perspectives on Subsidiarity* (Dordrecht, Springer, 2014) 85, 88–89.

[2] See Cesare PR Romano, 'The Proliferation of International Judicial Bodies: The Pieces of the Puzzle' (1999) 31 *New York University Journal of International Law and Politics* 709, 709–23; Yuval Shany, *The Competing Jurisdictions of International Courts and Tribunals* (Oxford, Oxford

to apply the rules of international law and progressively develop them.[3] The visible presence of international courts in the development of international law renewed the question of competence allocation between states and international courts.

This chapter aims at examining the idea of subsidiarity in the practices of international courts. Just as the notion of subsidiarity itself, this inquiry has two facets. First, the chapter analyses how international courts preserve a state's decision-making competence. Second, it considers how a shift of competence to international courts is justified in practice. Among a wide range of international courts and tribunals, this chapter puts a special focus on the jurisprudence of the European Court of Human Rights (ECtHR) which has encountered, especially during the last decade, the question of competence allocation between member states and the Court. Subsidiarity in this chapter is about favouring national 'decision-making'; this means that subsidiarity here does not prioritise domestic 'law' over international 'law'.[4]

The question examined in this chapter is not merely a theoretical interest. The inquiry has been gaining practical relevance since international judicial decisions have met confrontational responses from national authorities. A well-known example is a response to the ECtHR decision in *Hirst v UK (No 2)*[5] over the prisoners' voting entitlement. The UK Parliament disagreed with the ECtHR on the basis that the decisions on the prisoners' right to vote 'should be a matter for democratically-elected lawmakers'.[6] In addition to the widely discussed human rights examples, Prabhash Ranjan in this edited volume exposed non-judicial national

University Press, 2003) 3–7. Before the 1990s, the active international and regional courts included: the ICJ, the ECJ, the Court of Justice of The Andean Community (established in 1979), the Court of Justice of the Benelux Economic Union (in 1958), the European Court of Human Rights (in 1959), and Inter-American Court of Human Rights (in 1979). Since the 1990s, many other international courts and tribunals have been established: eg, International Tribunal for the Law of the Sea (established in 1982), the Appellate Body of the World Trade Organization (in 1995), International Criminal Court (in 1998), and African Court on Human and Peoples' Rights (in 1998). See Shany, ibid 5–7.

[3] See Armin von Bogdandy and Ingo Venzke (eds), *International Judicial Lawmaking: On Public Authority and Democratic Legitimation in Global Governance* (Berlin; New York, Springer, 2012); Armin von Bogdandy and Ingo Venzke, 'In Whose Name? An Investigation of International Courts' Public Authority and Its Democratic Justification' (2012) 23 *European Journal of International Law* 7.

[4] *cf* Leonard FM Besselink, 'Entrapped by the Maximum Standard: On Fundamental Rights, Pluralism and Subsidiarity in the European Union' (1998) 35 *Common Market Law Review* 629, (discussing subsidiarity primarily as a matter of the relationships between EU law, human rights treaties, and national law in the context of fundamental rights protection).

[5] *Hirst v United Kingdom (No 2)* App no 74025/01, ECHR 2005-IX (ECtHR, Grand Chamber, 6 Oct 2005).

[6] House of Commons Votes and Proceedings, Sessions 2010–11, No 115, 10 Feb 2011 (234 in favour, 22 against) available at: www.publications.parliament.uk/pa/cm201011/cmvote/110210v01.htm.

contestations against international investment arbitration,[7] and Shotaro Hamamoto provided an insight into the reasoning of the *Metalclad* case in which the British Columbia Supreme Court partially set aside an arbitral award.[8] Given the confrontational national reception, it is worth examining the extent to which international courts preserve a state's autonomous decision-making process.

This chapter starts with overviewing the different historical contexts to which the idea of subsidiarity has been invoked (section II). It then moves on to examine how international courts resolve the question of competence allocation. International courts preserve a state's autonomy in multiple phases of their decisions (section III). This is combined with a shift of competence to international courts when a state's decisions are of such a quality that, among others, they deny justice, exclude involvement of the legislature, or suffer from systematic problems (section IV). An analysis of the idea of subsidiarity in the practices of international courts sheds light on the kind of normative values upheld by international law and the rule of law at the international level (section V and conclusion).

II. A HISTORICAL OVERVIEW OF SUBSIDIARITY

Historically, the idea of subsidiarity has been employed in several different social and political contexts.[9] This section outlines three major contexts which nurtured the notion of subsidiarity and thereby provides a background to the analysis of competence allocation between states and international courts.

Subsidiarity was first articulated as a 'principle' as part of Catholic social thought. Pope Pius XI coined the term 'principle of "subsidiary function"' in *Quadragesimo Anno* in 1931[10] as a principle of social pluralism which acknowledges diversity and yet still assumes each society's contribution

[7] Ch 5 (Ranjan) of this volume.

[8] Ch 4 (Hamamoto) of this volume.

[9] See Gerald Neuman, 'Subsidiarity' in D Shelton (ed), *The Oxford Handbook of International Human Rights Law* (1st edn, Oxford, Oxford University Press, 2013) 360, 360–63; Isabel Feichtner, 'Subsidiarity' in R Wolfrum (ed), *Max Planck Encyclopedia of Public International Law* (Online, New York, Oxford University Press, 2008).

[10] Pope Pius XI , 'Quadragesimo Anno, On Reconstruction of the Social Order', Encyclica of Pope Pius XI (15 May 1931) available at: www.papalencyclicals.net/Pius11/P11QUADR.HTM, paras 78, 80. While it was Pope Pius XI that employed the term 'subsidiary' as a principle, Pope Leo XIII's earlier encyclical in 1891 already regarded the protection of workers' dignity as the duty of state and, at the same time, called for the limits of state intervention. See Pope Leo XIII, 'Rerum Novarum, on Capital and Labor', Encyclica of Pope Leo XIII (15 May 1891) available at: www.papalencyclicals.net/Leo13/l13rerum.htm, paras esp 33, 35–36.

to the common good.[11] The Catholic version of subsidiarity is close to the etymological origin of the term; subsidiarity is the paraphrase of 'subsidiary' which comes from the Latin word *subsidium*, meaning 'help' or 'aid'.[12] A higher community performs a 'subsidiary' function, or more appropriately, an 'auxiliary' role, in order to support a lower community.[13] In the Catholic social thought, the principle of subsidiarity ultimately serves human flourishing, and one's immediate human communities were considered as a best site for achieving it.[14]

Second, subsidiarity has been employed in the context of federal states as an idea for the allocation of powers between a federal government and constituent states.[15] In the US, subsidiarity is arguably implicit in the allocation of powers between the federal and state governments,[16] although the principle of subsidiarity has been invoked in the political processes rather than in legal practices.[17] The idea is also adopted in Germany[18] as part of the wider attempts to divide the powers within the state that had experienced the totalitarian regime.[19] In Italy, the Constitution contains an explicit reference to subsidiarity regarding the allocation of administrative functions between the municipalities and other larger institutions.[20]

[11] Patrick McKinley Brennan, 'Subsidiarity in the Tradition of Catholic Social Doctrine' in M Evans and A Zimmermann (eds), *Global Perspectives on Subsidiarity* (Dordrecht, Springer, 2014) 29, 34–41.

[12] See Jonathan Chaplin, 'Subsidiarity: the Concept and the Connections' (1997) 4 *Ethical Perspectives* 117, 118–19.

[13] See ibid 118.

[14] ibid 118–19; Brennan, 'Subsidiarity in the Tradition of Catholic Social Doctrine' (n 11).

[15] Johannes Althusius (1557–1630) has developed a theory of subsidiarity as part of the modern federalist thought: see further Ken Endo, 'The Principle of Subsidiarity: From Johannes Althusius to Jacques Delors' (1994) 44 *Hokkaido Law Review* 2064, 2043–33 (the largest page number comes first in descending order); Andreas Føllesdal, 'Survey Article: Subsidiarity' (1998) 6 *Journal of Political Philosophy* 190, 200–03.

[16] See Alex Mills, 'Federalism in the European Union and the United States: Subsidiarity, Private Law, and the Conflict of Laws' (2010) 32 *University of Pennsylvania Journal of International Law* 369, 431–35; David P Currie, 'Subsidiarity' (1998) 1 *Green Bag 2d* 359.

[17] George A Bermann, 'Subsidiarity as a Principle of US Constitutional Law' (1994) 42 *American Journal of Comparative Law Supplement* 555. The US Constitution does not expressly provide subsidiarity, although the constitutional provisions express the idea that those powers not conferred to the federal authorities are reserved to the states: ibid 555–58.

[18] Art 72(2) of the German Basic Law embodies the notion of subsidiarity: 'The Federation shall have the right to legislate … if and to the extent that the establishment of equivalent living conditions throughout the federal territory or the maintenance of legal or economic unity renders federal regulation necessary in the national interest' (Basic Law for the Federal Republic of Germany, in the revised version published in the Federal Law Gazette Part III, classification no 100-1, as last amended by the Act of 21 July 2010 (Federal Law Gazette I, 944)).

[19] Endo, 'The Principle of Subsidiarity' (n 15) 2051.

[20] Constitution of the Italian Republic, Art 118(1).

Finally, subsidiarity has been a principle of EU law, most notably by the Maastricht Treaty,[21] which explicitly included the principle of subsidiarity in order to give assurance to member states that the Union (then Community) would respect democratic self-governance and cultural diversity.[22] The principle of subsidiarity was adopted in conjunction with the expansion of the powers of European institutions under the Maastricht Treaty in an attempt to safeguard the powers of member states.[23]

As contrasted with EU law, international law did not, traditionally, give rise to the strong need for discussing and invoking the idea of subsidiarity. The unfamiliarity is not because of the absence of the idea itself in international law. Rather, as noted at the beginning of this chapter, the decentralised structure of international law, which preserves the autonomy of each state's decision-making, almost took the idea of subsidiarity for granted. The issue of competence allocation nevertheless gained renewed importance by the growing presence of international courts whose internationally binding decisions direct the manner in which the states exercise their authority against individuals and private entities.

III. PRESERVING A STATE'S COMPETENCE

The idea of subsidiarity appears to play a role in various stages of international judicial decision-making. At the stage of admissibility, international courts often favour letting domestic authorities first deal with an application submitted to the courts (A). At the level of merits, international courts may preserve a state's autonomous decision-making by adjusting the intensity of review (B) and the extent to which the courts specify remedial measures (C).

[21] Treaty on European Union, Treaty of Maastricht, 7 February 1992, 1992 OJ (C191) 1; 31 ILM 253 (1992). See Consolidated Versions of the Treaty on European Union (2010) OJ C83/13 Art 5. Art 5(3) provides: '3. Under the principle of subsidiarity, in areas which do not fall within its exclusive competence, the Union shall act only if and in so far as the objectives of the proposed action cannot be sufficiently achieved by the Member States, either at central level or at regional and local level, but can rather, by reason of the scale or effects of the proposed action, be better achieved at Union level'.

[22] See Bermann, 'Taking Subsidiarity Seriously' (n 1) 334.

[23] Mills, 'Federalism in the European Union and the United States' (n 16) 392–93. Nevertheless, it is argued that the principle of subsidiarity was supported by relevant actors for opposite reasons; the UK regarded it as an antidote to federalism, while Germany regarded it as a step towards the development of federalism: Alessandro Colombo, *The Principle of Subsidiarity and European Citizenship* (Milan, Vita e Pensiero, 2004) 9–10. There are obviously a large number of studies regarding subsidiarity in EU law and governance: see, eg, Bermann (n 1); Theodor Schilling, 'A New Dimension of Subsidiarity: Subsidiarity as a Rule and a Principle' (1994) 14 *Yearbook of European Law* 203; Graínne de Búrca, 'Proportionality and Subsidiarity as General Principles of Law' in U Bernitz and J Nergelius (eds), *General Principles of European Community Law* (The Hague, Kluwer Law International, 2000) 95.

A. Rule of Exhaustion of Local Remedies and the Principle of Complementarity

At the phase of admissibility, one of the mechanisms through which an international court safeguards national competence is a rule of exhaustion of local remedies. It is a rule of customary international law that local remedies must be exhausted before the institution of international proceedings,[24] and the non-exhaustion of local remedies renders inadmissible a claim of state responsibility.[25] While the rule of exhaustion of local remedies had originally developed in the context of diplomatic protection,[26] the rule has been adopted by the major human rights treaties as one of the criteria according to which human rights courts (and treaty-monitoring bodies) assess the admissibility of complaints.[27]

The rule on the exhaustion of national remedies reflects the idea that 'in some situations, domestic courts ought to be viewed as more appropriate fora' for taking a first look at international legal claims.[28] A linkage

[24] *Interhandel* [1959] ICJ Reports 6, (Preliminary Objection, Judgment of 21 March 1959), 27; 'Draft Articles on Diplomatic Protection with Commentaries' ILC Report UN Doc A/61/10 (2006) 71 (Art 14, commentary, para 1). The exhaustion rule applies insofar as a state's claim originates from private claims, even if the case concerns a violation of a treaty and injuries to the state itself: see *Elettronica Sicula S.pA (ELSI)* [1989] ICJ Reports 15 (Judgment of 20 July 1989); Matthew H Adler, 'The Exhaustion of the Local Remedies Rule after the International Court of Justice's Decision in ELSI' (1990) 39 *The International and Comparative Law Quarterly* 641. Amerasinghe noted in 1990 that the issue is not whether the rule is a part of customary international law, but how and when it applies to different situations: Chittharanjan F Amerasinghe, *Local Remedies in International Law* (Cambridge, Grotius Publications Limited, 1990) 29.

[25] See 'Draft Articles on Responsibility of States for Internationally Wrongful Acts' (2001) II 2 Yearbook of the International Law Commission 26 Art 44(b) (concerning the admissibility of claims); James R Crawford and Thomas D Grant, 'Exhaustion of Local Remedies' in Wolfrum (ed), *The Max Planck Encyclopedia of Public International Law* (n 9) para 5. In this sense, the exhaustion rule is generally treated by international courts as a procedural (admissibility) rule, although the denial of local remedies can separately constitute a wrongful act: see ibid paras 35–41.

[26] See generally, eg, Edwin M Borchard, 'The Local Remedy Rule' (1934) 28 *The American Journal of International Law* 729; Theodor Meron, 'Incidence of the Rule of Exhaustion of Local Remedies, The' (1959) 35 *British Year Book of International Law* 83; Chittharanjan F Amerasinghe, *Local Remedies in International Law* (2nd edn, Cambridge; New York, Cambridge University Press, 2004).

[27] Convention for the Protection of Human Rights and Fundamental Freedoms, 4 Nov 1950, ETS 5, 213 UNTS 221 (1950) Art 35 (1) ('The Court may only deal with the matter after all domestic remedies have been exhausted, according to the generally recognised rules of international law'); International Covenant on Civil and Political Rights, 16 Dec 1966, 999 UNTS 171 (1966) Art 41(1)(c) (inter-state complaints); Optional Protocol to the International Covenant on Civil and Political Rights, 16 Dec 1966, 999 UNTS 302 Arts 2, 5(2)(b) (individual complaints); American Convention on Human Rights, 22 Nov 1969, 1144 UNTS 123, OAS Treaty Series No 36 (1969) Art 46(1)(a); African Charter on Human and Peoples' Rights, 27 June 1981, 1520 UNTS 217; 21 ILM 58 (1982) Arts 50, 56(5).

[28] Yuval Shany, *Regulating Jurisdictional Relations Between National and International Courts* (Oxford, Oxford University Press, 2007) 178. See also ibid 16, 28, 128.

between the idea of subsidiarity and the rule of exhaustion of remedies is particularly evident in the jurisprudence of the ECtHR, which has, from the early stage of its life, emphasised the subsidiary character of the conventional mechanism.[29] The ECtHR in *Vučković v Serbia* acknowledged an indispensable role of the rule of exhaustion of domestic remedies in the system of the European Convention of Human Rights (ECHR), which is subsidiary to the national systems and assumes an effective remedy at the national level.[30]

Not all international courts operate based on the idea of leaving domestic courts to decide matters first. A case in point is an investor-state arbitration based on investment treaties which expressly waive the exhaustion rule.[31] One of the main purposes of investment arbitration is precisely 'to avoid the use of domestic courts'.[32] National courts are not an attractive forum from the perspective of investors, who are often concerned about the lack of judicial independence and the political obstacles to enforcing judgments at the domestic level.[33] In the context of investment arbitration, demand for avoiding domestic proceedings thus, in general, outweighs a need for preserving national decision-making competence.

Albeit in a specific and extraordinary circumstance, another principle which favours national decision-making at the stage of admissibility is the principle of complementarity provided in the Statute of the International Criminal Court (ICC).[34] Domestic justice is given priority on the basis that

[29] eg, *Case 'Relating to Certain Aspects of the Laws on the Use of Languages in Education in Belgium' v Belgium (Merits)* App nos 1474/62 et al (1968), Ser A No 6 (ECtHR, Judgment of 23 July 1968) [10]; *Handyside v United Kingdom* App no 5493/72, (1976) 1 EHRR 737, (1979) 1 EHRR 737 (ECtHR, 7 Dec 1976) [48]. The principle of subsidiarity was explicitly adopted by Protocol No 15 to the ECHR: see (n 45) below.

[30] *Vučković and Others v Serbia* App nos 17153/11 et al (ECtHR, Grand Chamber, 25 March 2014, Preliminary Objection) [69]. See also, eg, *Selmouni v France* App no 25803/94 (ECtHR, 28 July 1999) [74] ('rule is based on the assumption, reflected in Article 13 of the Convention … that there is an effective remedy available in respect of the alleged breach in the domestic system'); *Kudła v Poland* App no 30210/96 (ECtHR, Grand Chamber, 26 Oct 2000) [152].

[31] The exhaustion requirement is waived by ICSID Convention, which is referred to by many investment treaties: see Convention on the Settlement of Investment Disputes Between States and Nationals of Other States, 18 March 1965, 17 UST 1270, 575 UNTS 159, Art 26; *Emilio Agustín Maffezini v The Kingdom of Spain* ICSID ARB/97/7, Decision of the Tribunal on Objections to Jurisdiction, 25 Jan 2000, para 22. For non-ICSID arbitration, see, eg, SCC Arbitration V079/2005 *RosInvestCo UK Ltd v The Russian Federation* (Arbitration Institute of the Stockholm Chamber of Commerce, Award on Jurisdiction, Oct 2007) para 153. The exhaustion rule cannot be tacitly dispensed: *Elettronica Sicula S.p.A (ELSI)* (n 24) para 50. Nevertheless, in non-ICSID cases, the consent to investor-state arbitration is considered as a waiver of the principle of exhaustion of local remedies: see, eg, *RosInvestCo UK Ltd v The Russian Federation* para 153.

[32] Christoph Schreuer, 'Interaction Of International Tribunals And Domestic Courts In Investment Law' in A W Rovine (ed), *Contemporary Issues in International Arbitration and Mediation: The Fordham Papers (2010)* (Leiden, Brill Academic Publishers, 2011) 71, 71.

[33] See ibid 71–72.

[34] See Rome Statute of the International Criminal Court, 37 ILM 1002 (1998); 2187 UNTS 90 pre-para 10, Art 1. In principle, the ICC's complementarity is contrasted with the International

it is 'the duty of every State to exercise its criminal jurisdiction over those responsible for international crimes'.[35] Just as in the case of the rule of exhaustion of domestic remedies, the principle of complementarity preserves decision-making at the national level with regard to the investigation and prosecution of certain international crimes.[36]

B. Margin of Appreciation

At the phase of merits, the idea of subsidiarity is precisely embodied in the margin of appreciation developed by the ECtHR as a judicial doctrine.[37] It adjusts the intensity of review by the Court and thereby preserves space for a state's autonomous decision-making. According to the jurisprudence of the ECtHR, a certain margin of appreciation is accorded to national authorities who make an initial assessment as to whether a fair balance between competing interests is struck in a particular case involving human rights.[38] In general, the margin would be wide if there were no European consensus and if the cases raised 'complex issues and choices of social strategy'.[39] For instance, with regard to certain sensitive issues such as euthanasia,[40] incest,[41] and the display of religious symbols in public

Criminal Tribunal for the Former Yugoslavia (ICRY) and the International Criminal Tribunal for Rwanda (ICTR). These ad hoc international criminal tribunals and national courts have concurrent jurisdiction, and the former has primacy over the latter: Statute of the International Criminal Tribunal for the Former Yugoslavia, adopted by 25 May 1993 by Security Council Resolution 827 (last amended by Resolution 1877 of 7 July 2009) Art 9; Statute of the International Criminal Tribunal for Rwanda UN Doc S/Res/955 (1994); 33 ILM 1598 (1994) Art 8. At the same time, the ICTY's 'Completion Strategy' can be understood as one materialisation of the idea of subsidiarity: see Fausto Pocar, 'Completion or Continuation Strategy? Appraising Problems and Possible Developments in Building the Legacy of the ICTY' (2008) 6 *Journal of International Criminal Justice* 655.

[35] Rome Statute of the International Criminal Court (n 34) para 6 of the preamble.

[36] William A Schabas, *An Introduction to the International Criminal Court* (4th edn, Cambridge, Cambridge University Press, 2011) 191.

[37] The ECtHR observed that: the Court 'cannot assume the role of the competent national authorities, for it would thereby lose sight of the subsidiary nature of the international machinery of collective enforcement established by the Convention': *Case 'Relating to Certain Aspects of the Laws on the Use of Languages in Education in Belgium' v Belgium (Merits)* (n 29) [I.B.10]. This paragraph is referred to in *Handyside*, a seminal case for the margin of appreciation doctrine: *Handyside v United Kingdom* (n 29) [48]. The comparable practices may still exist in other international courts: Yuval Shany, 'Toward a General Margin of Appreciation Doctrine in International Law?' (2005) 16 *European Journal of International Law* 907.

[38] See, eg, *Dickson v The United Kingdom* App no 44362/04, ECHR 2007-V (ECtHR, Grand Chamber, 4 Dec 2007) [77].

[39] ibid [78].

[40] eg, *Pretty v The United Kingdom* App no 2346/02, ECHR 2002-III (ECtHR, 29 April 2002); *Haas v Switzerland* App no 31322/07 (ECtHR, 20 Jan 2011). In *Pretty*, Ms Pretty was refused governmental assurance that her husband would not face prosecution if he assisted her suicide. The ECtHR did not find a violation on the basis of the UK's margin of appreciation for this issue. The Court reached the similar conclusion in *Haas*.

[41] eg, *Stübing v Germany* App no 43547/08 (ECtHR, 12 April 2012).

places,[42] the ECtHR assumes that the national authorities have better knowledge of what is in the public interest.[43] A further analysis on the margin of appreciation is provided in the present volume by Birgit Peters, Shai Dothan, and Andrew Legg.[44]

It is noteworthy that both the margin of appreciation and the principle of subsidiarity are gaining importance in the system of the ECHR. Protocol No 15 to the ECHR made an explicit reference to the principle and doctrine[45] for the purposes of enhancing the protection of human rights at the domestic level and alleviating the huge workload of the Strasbourg mechanism.[46] The ECtHR's Judge Robert Spano, in his lecture in 2014, characterised the Strasbourg Court's next phase as 'the age of subsidiarity'[47] in which the Court engages with 'empowering the Member States to truly "bring rights home"'.[48] The augmented importance of the principle of subsidiarity may represent the ECtHR's response to a call for an increased diversity in the protection of human rights.[49]

C. Non-Specified Remedial Measures

At the stage of merits, the idea of subsidiarity is further reflected in the practice of remedial measures as a consequence of finding a violation. The ECtHR's basic approach is that the Court's judgments are essentially declaratory, and they leave a state with 'the choice of the means to be utilised in its domestic legal system' in order for the state to abide by the final

[42] eg, in *Lautsi v Italy* (2011), the Court decided in favour of the Italian government, observing that the Court has a duty in principle to respect the contracting states' decisions with respect to the presence of religious symbols in public schools: *Lautsi and Others v Italy* App no 30814/06 (ECtHR, Grand Chamber, Judgment of 18 March 2011) [69]. The Court has also noted the lack of European consensus on this issue: ibid [70].

[43] See *Dickson v The United Kingdom* (n 38) [78].

[44] Chs 8 (Peters), 9 (Dothan), 10 (Legg) of this volume.

[45] Protocol No 15 amending the Convention on the Protection of Human Rights and Fundamental Freedoms, CETS 213, 24.VI.2013, Art 1. Protocol No 15 was adopted following the Interlaken discussions in 2010, the declarations at Izmir in 2011, and the Brighton Declaration in 2012.

[46] See Dean Spielmann, 'Allowing the Right Margin: the European Court of Human Rights and the National Margin of Appreciation Doctrine: Waiver or Subsidiarity of European Review?', Speech at the Max Planck Institute for Comparative Public Law and International Law, Heidelberg (13 Dec 2013) available at: www.echr.coe.int/Documents/Speech_20140113_Heidelberg_ENG.pdf, at 8.

[47] Robert Spano, 'Universality or Diversity of Human Rights? Strasbourg in the Age of Subsidiarity' (2014) 14 *Human Rights Law Review* 487.

[48] ibid 491. Judge Robert Spano observes that *Animal Defenders* and some other cases around 2009–14 already: 'demonstrate … that the Strasbourg Court is currently in the process of reformulating the substantive and procedural criteria that regulate the appropriate level of deference to be afforded to the Member States so as to implement a more robust and coherent concept of subsidiarity in conformity with Brighton and Protocol 15': ibid 498.

[49] See ibid 491.

judgment of the Court.[50] By not directing states how to remedy a violation, the ECtHR can further safeguard a state's competence.

The same level of trust in the domestic legal system might not have been built by the Latin American counterpart. Compared with the ECtHR, the Inter-American Court of Human Rights (IACtHR) has been known for its proactive approach to remedial measures that purport to restrict a state's autonomous decision-making.[51] The IACtHR has been conducting a so-called 'quasi-criminal review' by ordering the specific modalities of national criminal prosecutions.[52] Insofar as the remedial measures are concerned, the IACtHR thus appears to be less amenable to the idea of subsidiarity than the ECtHR.

At the same time, a gap between the ECtHR and IACtHR has been narrowed down as the Strasbourg Court has likewise begun to issue both general and individual remedial measures for the implementation of the Court's judgment.[53] Since the *Broniowski v Poland* case in 2004,[54] the ECtHR has adopted a 'pilot judgment' procedure,[55] in which the Court orders 'general' measures for the purpose of addressing systemic problems in the interests of other possibly affected persons.[56] The procedure aimed at effectively resolving in the national legal order a systemic problem underlying large numbers of repetitive cases, offering individuals more rapid

[50] *Marckx v Belgium* App no 6833/74, Ser A No 31 (ECtHR, 13 June 1979) [58]; ECHR (n 27) Art 46(1).

[51] Alexandra Huneeus, 'International Criminal Law by Other Means: The Quasi-Criminal Jurisdiction of the Human Rights Courts' (2013) 107 *American Journal of International Law* 1. See also Neuman, 'Subsidiarity' (n 9) 372–73.

[52] Huneeus, 'International Criminal Law by Other Means' (n 51).

[53] Jannika Jahn, 'Ruling (In)directly through Individual Measures?: Effect and Legitimacy of the ECtHR's New Remedial Power' (2014) 74 *Zeitschrift für ausländisches öffentliches Recht und Völkerrecht (ZaöRV)* 1 (analysing the practices of ordering spefici 'individual' measures, which are relatively less known); Nino Tsereteli, 'The Relevance of the Principle of Subsidiarity for the Evolvement of Remedial Regimes of Regional Human Rights Courts (ECtHR and IACtHR)' paper presented at the Workshop on Subsidiarity in Global Governance (19–20 June 2014) (extensively analysing the relevant decisions of the ECtHR and the IACtHR).

[54] *Broniowski v Poland* App no 31443/96, ECHR 2004-V (ECtHR, Grand Chamber, 22 June 2004). In *Broniowski*, the Court held that the Polish government breached the applicant's right to the peaceful enjoyment of his possessions by failing to provide compensatory property to which the applicant was entitled under the Polish legislation. The applicant was one of the so-called 'Bug River' claimants, who had to abandon their properties which, before the Second World War, had been located within the Polish borders. The Court accepted that a wide margin of appreciation had to be accorded to the Polish state (ibid [182]). Nevertheless, the Court found a violation on the ground that the applicant's disproportionate and excessive burden could not be justified by the legitimate general community interest (ibid [187]).

[55] Steering Committee for Human Rights (CDDH), the Council of Europe, 'Guaranteeing the Long-Term Effectiveness of the Control System of the European Convention on Human Rights', Addendum to the Final Report containing CDDH Proposals, CDDH(2003)006 Addendum Final (9 April 2003). On the pilot judgment procedure, see further Dominik Haider, *The Pilot-Judgement Procedure of the European Court of Human Rights* (Leiden, Martinus Nijhoff Publishers, 2013).

[56] See (nn 91–93) below and corresponding text.

redress, and easing the Court's increasing caseload. The degree of specificity varies among general measures; they have been formulated both in a broad term[57] and in a much more specified manner.[58] The somewhat indeterminate jurisprudence of the ECtHR about remedial practices illustrates that the regional human rights court is trying to maintain its basic position to refrain from specifying appropriate remedial measures while responding to the need to address a systemic problem in the domestic legal order.[59]

In addition to these general measures, since *Assanidze v Georgia*,[60] the ECtHR has developed the practices of ordering specific 'individual' measures that direct the manner according to which a state ought to implement the judgment.[61] In *Assanidze v Georgia*, the Strasbourg Court, while reiterating the primary competence of the state to decide the manner of execution of a judgment, moved on to order the imprisoned applicant's release at the earliest possible date.[62] By ordering these general and individual

[57] See, eg, *Hutten-Czapska v Poland* App no 35014/97, ECHR 2006-VIII (ECtHR, Grand Chamber, 19 June 2006) op [4]. In *Hutten*, the ECtHR directed Poland to secure in its domestic legal order 'a mechanism maintaining a fair balance' between the competing interests involved: ibid.

[58] eg, in *Suljagić v Bosnia and Herzegovina* on the treatment of bank deposits before the dissolution of the Socialist Federal Republic of Yugoslavia (SFRY), the ECtHR specifically directed the state to issue government bonds and pay outstanding instalments within 6 months: *Suljagić v Bosnia and Herzegovina* App no 27912/02 (ECtHR, 3 Nov2009) [64], op [4]. *cf Ališić and Others v Bosnia and Herzegovina, Croatia, Serbia, Slovenia and the Former Yugoslav Republic of Macedonia* App no 60642/08 (ECtHR, Grand Chamber, 16 July 2014). In *Ališić*, the Court ordered the similar general measures, albeit in a less specific manner: see *Ališić*, ibid, op [10]–[11].

[59] eg, the ECtHR in *Hutten, after* having directed a state to take the general measures to remedy the systemic human rights violations, still noted that '[i]t is not for the Court to specify what would be the most appropriate way', while, at the same time, suggesting 'in passing' several options open to the state: see *Hutten-Czapska v Poland* (n 57) [239]. The delicate balance is also illustrated by the cases in which the ECtHR made 'suggestions' regarding the kind of remedial measures. For instance, in *Atanasiu v Romania*, the Court, while holding that the state must take general measures, merely 'suggest[ed], on a purely indicative basis' the types of general measures that the state 'might take': *Maria Atanasiu and Others v Romania* App nos 30767/05, 33800/06 (ECtHR, 12 Oct 2010) [228], [230], op [6].

[60] *Assanidze v Georgia* App no 71503/01, ECHR 2004-II (ECtHR, Grand Chamber, 8 April 2004). In this case, the Court found the violations of the rights of the applicant who had been imprisoned despite the acquittal by the Georgian Supreme Court.

[61] See further Jahn, 'Ruling (In)directly through Individual Measures?' (n 53).

[62] *Assanidze v Georgia* (n 60) op [14(a)]. *cf Papamichalopoulos and Others v Greece (article 50)* App no 14556/89 (ECtHR, 31 Oct 1995), op [2]–[3] (requiring the state to return to the applicant the land occupied by the military, yet, at the same time, allowing the monetary payment as an alternative remedy). Likewise, the Court in *Ilaşcu* ordered the measures to secure the 'immediate release' of the imprisoned applicants: *Ilaşcu and Others v Moldova and Russia* App no 48787/99, ECHR 2004-VII (ECtHR, Grand Chamber, 8 July 2004) op [22]. The Court in *Slawomir Musical v Poland* also ordered the transfer of the mentally ill detained persons to a suitable psychiatric hospital or an equivalent place: see *Sławomir Musiał v Poland* App no 28300/06 (ECtHR, 20 Jan 2009), op [4(a)] ('the respondent State is to secure at the earliest possible date adequate conditions of the applicant's detention in a specialised institution capable of providing him with necessary psychiatric treatment and constant medical supervision'); Jahn (n 53) 8–9.

measures, the ECtHR seems to have limited space for a state's autonomous decision-making with regard to a remedy for a violation of the ECHR.

In sum, this limited analysis suggests that the idea of favouring local autonomy subsists in the practices of international courts. At the level of admissibility, a state's competence is internationally preserved by the rule of exhaustion of local remedies under customary international law and by the principle of complementarity under the specific international treaty. At the stage of reviewing the states' acts or omissions, the margin of appreciation under the ECtHR's jurisprudence materialises the idea of subsidiarity, and, at the stage of ordering remedial measures, the regional human rights courts, to a varying degree, leave the choice of means to state parties.

IV. SHIFTING COMPETENCE TO INTERNATIONAL COURTS

As noted at the beginning of this chapter, subsidiarity is inseparable from an idea that international courts would step in should a state be no longer seen as an appropriate forum. This section elucidates, with particular reference to the ECtHR, some of the noteworthy criteria under international law, which justify a shift of competence to international courts. Such criteria illuminate some of the normative values that are respected in international law when it interacts with the national legal order, as will be later discussed in section V.

A. Denial of Justice and Ineffectiveness

At the level of admissibility, a shift of competence is justified by a range of criteria which render the rule of exhaustion of local remedies satisfied or inapplicable. In general, domestic authorities are no longer seen as appropriate fora if domestic proceedings are of 'undue delay'[63] or 'futility'.[64] There are also regime-specific criteria which justify a shift of competence from the national level to the international one. For instance, the American Convention on Human Rights explicitly provides the lack of due process of law, the denial of access to remedies, and unwarranted delay as exceptions to the exhaustion rule.[65] These conditions can be seen as part of the

[63] See 'Draft Articles on Diplomatic Protection with Commentaries' (n 24) Art 15(b).
[64] See ibid Art 15(a), (d).
[65] American Convention on Human Rights (n 27) Art 46(2)(a)–(c). For an overview of treaty provisions, see, eg, AO Adede, 'A Survey of Treaty Provisions on the Rule of Exhaustion of Local Remedies' (1977) 18 *Harvard International Law Journal* 1.

somewhat outdated, yet still relevant, notion of a 'denial of justice', which is a traditional limit to the exhaustion of local remedies.[66]

Apart from the traditional yardsticks such as undue delay and futility, the jurisprudence of the ECtHR[67] developed the additional criteria of the accessibility, effectiveness,[68] and sufficient certainty of domestic remedies.[69] In *Vučković and Others v Serbia*, the ECtHR held that the existence of remedies in question must be 'sufficiently certain not only in theory but in practice' in order to meet 'the requisite accessibility and effectiveness'.[70] In other words, a competence may shift to the international level if domestic proceedings are not accessible and effective. The ECtHR and IACtHR also take into account the personal circumstances of the individual applicants in deciding whether claims ought to be dealt with at the domestic level.[71]

With regard to the principle of complementarity under the ICC Statute, one of the criteria that justify a shift of competence is the 'unwilling or unable' test.[72] Under Article 17(2) of the ICC Statute, 'unwillingness' is defined as a national decision for the purpose of shielding the person from criminal responsibility, an unjustified delay, or non-independent or non-impartial proceedings.[73] Under Article 17(3), 'inability' is due to 'a total or

[66] On the denial of justice, see Adede, 'A Survey of Treaty Provisions on the Rule of Exhaustion of Local Remedies' (n 65) 9–12.

[67] In principle, the exhaustion of domestic remedies under the ECHR is supposed to be 'according to the generally recognised rules of international law': ECHR (n 27) Art 35(1). Yet the rule has been applied more flexibly before the ECtHR: see, eg, *Cardot v France* App no 11069/84 (ECtHR, 19 March 1991) [34]; *Lehtinen v Finland* App no 39076/97 (Admissibility Decision, 14 Oct 1999).

[68] *Vučković and Others v Serbia* (n 30) [71], [73].

[69] See, eg, *Vernillo v France* App no 11889/85 (ECtHR, 20 Feb 1991) [27]. In *Vučković*, the ECtHR held that the obligation to exhaust domestic remedies 'requires an applicant to make normal use of remedies which are available and sufficient … The existence of the remedies in question must be sufficiently certain not only in theory but in practice, failing which they will lack the requisite accessibility and effectiveness': *Vučković and Others v Serbia* (n 30) [71].

[70] *Vučković and Others v Serbia* (n 30) [71].

[71] For the ECtHR, see *Akdivar and Others v Turkey* App no 21893/93 (ECtHR, Grand Chamber, 16 Sept 1996) [69]. The IACtHR also accepted, as exceptions to the rule of exhaustion of domestic remedies, an individual complainant's indigency and a general fear in the legal community to represent the individual: *Exceptions to the Exhaustion of Domestic Remedies (Arts 46(1), 46(2)(a) and 46(2)(b) of the American Convention on Human Rights)* Inter-Am Ct HR (Ser A) No 11 (1990) (Advisory Opinion, 10 Aug 1990).

[72] Under Art 17(1)(a) and (b) of the ICC Statute, the ICC first inquires whether a state with jurisdiction has investigated and either prosecuted or decided not to prosecute. If such investigation or prosecution exists, the ICC then decides whether the state is unwilling or unable genuinely to carry out the investigation or prosecution: Rome Statute of the International Criminal Court (n 34) Art 17(1)(a) and (b). The unwillingness and inability is assessed by the Prosecutor in deciding whether to initiate an investigation (Art 53(1)(b)) and whether to proceed to prosecution (Art 53(2)(b)) before the admissibility is ultimately determined by the Court.

[73] ibid Art 17(2)(a)–(c). See Mohamed M El Zeidy, 'The Principle of Complementarity: A New Machinery to Implement International Criminal Law' (2002) 23 *Michigan Journal of International Law* 869, 899–902.

substantial collapse or unavailability of its national judicial system'.[74] As in the aforementioned case of the rule of exhaustion of domestic remedies, the 'unwilling or unable' test could be understood as originating in the classic concept of a denial of justice.[75]

B. Non-Involvement of the Legislature

At the level of merits, one of the noteworthy criteria in the ECtHR's jurisprudence on the margin of appreciation is that the Strasbourg Court takes into account the involvement of a *legislative* body in assessing whether the impugned measures fall within the margin of appreciation and whether they meet the requirement of proportionality.[76] The crux is that the ECtHR differentiates between various branches of the state in deciding whether the Court should respect a state's autonomous decision.[77]

For instance, the Grand Chamber in *Dickson v UK*[78] observed that the Court generally respects the 'legislature's policy choice' in cases where the wide margin is accorded to a state.[79] In finding a violation of Article 8 of the ECHR, the Grand Chamber took into account the fact that Parliament did not get involved in weighting competing interests and assessing the proportionality.[80] In a similar vein, in *Hirst v UK (No 2)* concerning the prisoners' voting,[81] the ECtHR decided against the UK by observing that 'it cannot be said that there was any substantive debate by members of the legislature on the continued justification' for maintaining the restriction.[82]

[74] Rome Statute of the International Criminal Court (n 34) Art 17(3). See Zeidy, 'Principle of Complementarity' (n 73) 902–04.

[75] Frédéric Mégret, 'Qu'est-ce qu'une juridiction « incapable » ou « manquant de volonté » au sens de l'article 17 du Traité de Rome? Quelques enseignements tirés des théories du déni de justice en droit international' (2004) 17 *Revue québécoise de droit international* 185.

[76] See, eg, *Shindler v The United Kingdom* App no 19840/09 (ECtHR, 7 May 2013) [118] ('the margin of appreciation available to the domestic legislature in regulating parliamentary elections'); *Alajos Kiss v Hungary* App no 38832/06 (ECtHR, 20 May 2010) [41] ('a wide margin of appreciation should be granted to the national legislature in determining whether restrictions … can be justified … and, if so, how a fair balance is to be struck').

[77] In the *Handyside* case, the Strasbourg Court already noted that the margin is 'given both to the domestic legislator … and to the bodies, judicial amongst others, that are called upon to interpret and apply the laws': *Handyside v United Kingdom* (n 29) [48].

[78] *Dickson v The United Kingdom* (n 38). In *Dickson*, the Grand Chamber decided whether the UK breached Art 8 (right to respect for private and family life) by refusing the prisoners' access to artificial insemination facilities. The Court found a breach on the basis that a fair balance had not been struck between the conflicting individual and public interests involved.

[79] ibid [78].

[80] ibid [83].

[81] *Hirst v United Kingdom (No 2)* (n 5).

[82] ibid [79]. The fact that Parliament voted for the relevant legislation was not satisfactory; the Strasbourg Court noted that 'there is no evidence that Parliament has ever sought to weigh the competing interests or to assess the proportionality': ibid.

The involvement of the legislative body was also considered in several cases after *Hirst (No 2)*. In finding this time in favour of the UK, the ECtHR in *Doyle v UK* found merit in parliamentary scrutiny into the voting restriction on non-residents.[83] Likewise, the ECtHR put emphasis on the existence of parliamentary scrutiny in *Shindler v UK*[84] and in *Alajos Kiss v Hungary*.[85] In *Animal Defenders International*[86] concerning the right to freedom of expression, the Strasbourg Court, in assessing the proportionality of the impugned ban on political advertising, observed that '[t]he quality of the parliamentary and judicial review of the necessity of the measure is of particular importance' including 'to the operation of the relevant margin of appreciation'.[87] In finding that the measure was not a disproportionate interference with the right to freedom of expression, the ECtHR attached considerable weight to the extensive pre-legislative review by Parliament and subsequent domestic judicial scrutiny.[88] The ECtHR in *Evans* also made a particular reference to Parliament, noting that the key question was 'whether Parliament exceeded the margin of appreciation afforded to it'.[89]

Overall, a series of Strasbourg cases illustrate that a shift of competence to the ECtHR can be justified according to the deliberative involvement of a legislative body. The ECtHR considered whether and how the national legislature was involved in weighting the competing interests and striking a fair balance with regard to the issues for which the state has the wide margin of appreciation.

[83] *Doyle v The United Kingdom* App no 30158/06 (ECtHR, Admissibility Decision of 6 Feb 2007) 4.

[84] *Shindler v The United Kingdom* (n 76). In this case, the ECtHR decided whether or not the UK violated the right to vote by preventing British citizens residing overseas for more than 15 years from voting. The Court decided in favour of the UK. The request for referral to the Grand Chamber was rejected. The ECtHR referred to the existence of parliamentary scrutiny as a relevant factor in holding that the restriction on non-residents' voting rights, about which the member state has the wide margin of appreciation, may be proportionate to the legitimate aim pursued: ibid [102], [117].

[85] *Alajos Kiss v Hungary* (n 76). In this case, the Court found that Hungary's blanket restriction on franchise of those under partial guardianship violated the right to vote. The Strasbourg Court, in finding a violation on the right to vote, noted the ostensible absence of legislative scrutiny in weighing the competing interests and assessing the proportionality of the restrictions on the right to vote, for which the national legislature has a wide margin of appreciation: ibid [41].

[86] *Animal Defenders International v The United Kingdom* App no 48876/08 (ECtHR, Grand Chamber, 22 April 2013). The Court decided whether or not the ban on political advertising in the UK violated the right to freedom of expression. The dispute concerned whether the interface with the rights was 'necessary in a democratic society' (Art 10(2) of the ECHR). The Court upheld the compatibility of the ban with Art 10 of the ECHR.

[87] ibid [108]. According to the Court, the core issue is whether 'in adopting the general measure [on political advertising] and striking the balance it did, the legislature acted within the margin of appreciation afforded to it': ibid [110].

[88] See *Animal Defenders International v The United Kingdom* (n 86) [114]–[116].

[89] *Evans v The United Kingdom* App no 6339/05 (ECtHR 2007, 10 April 2007) [91].

C. Systematic Problems

Finally, with regard to the remedial measures, the existence of systematic problems in the domestic legal mechanisms has driven both the IACtHR and ECtHR to take an interventionist approach to their remedial measures. From the outset, the IACtHR has been encountering the cases involving mass state-sponsored violations of fundamental rights. The need to alleviate the systematic human rights violations existing in the member states has presumably led the Court to take a proactive step to issue specific remedial measures.

The existence of a 'systemic problem' has also been one of the key criteria for the ECtHR to issue general measures.[90] In *Broniowski*, the ECtHR, while reiterating the traditional position that it is, in principle, not for the Court to determine appropriate remedial measures,[91] moved on to identify in its operative paragraphs a 'systemic problem' connected with the 'malfunctioning of domestic legislation and practice',[92] requesting that Poland take legal measures not only with regard to the applicant, but also a whole class of individuals who had similar property claims.[93]

With regard to individual measures, the ECtHR's proactive approach has been justified by a wide variety of grounds. In *Assanidze v Georgia*,[94] in which the ECtHR for the first time issued an unconditional specific order for restitution in the operative part of its judgment,[95] the ECtHR justified it by the lack of other remedial measures, the particular circumstances of the case, and the urgent need to end the violation.[96] In *Oleksandr Volkov v Ukraine*,[97] the Chamber of the ECtHR ordered the reinstatement of the former Supreme Court judge, who had been dismissed in violation of his

[90] See, eg, *Hutten-Czapska v Poland* (n 57) [235]–[37], op [3]; *Suljagić v Bosnia and Herzegovina* (n 58) [64], op [3]; *Oleksandr Volkov v Ukraine* App no 21722/11, ECHR 2013 (ECtHR, 9 Jan 2013) [199] (albeit not in the operative paragraphs); *Ališić and Others v Bosnia and Herzegovina, Croatia, Serbia, Slovenia and the Former Yugoslav Republic of Macedonia* (n 58) op [9].

[91] *Broniowski v Poland* (n 54) [193].

[92] ibid op [3]. In this case, the Court made it clear that 'general measures at national level are undoubtedly called for' in execution of the judgment and to remedy the systemic defect underlying the Court's finding of a violation: ibid [193].

[93] See *Broniowski v Poland* (n 54) op [4]. The Court then adjourned its consideration of applications deriving from the same general course: see *Broniowski*, ibid [198]; *EG v Poland and 175 Other Bug River Applications* App no 50425/99 (ECtHR, 23 Sept 2008). *cf Sejdovic v Italy* App no 56581/00, ECRH 2006-II (ECtHR, Grand Chamber, 1 March 2006). In *Sejdovic*, the Grand Chamber did not find it necessary to indicate any general measures at the national level, given that Italy implemented various legislative reforms which have yet to be applied by domestic courts: see *Sejdovic*, ibid [122]–[24].

[94] *Assanidze v Georgia* (n 60).

[95] Jahn (n 53) 5.

[96] See *Assanidze v Georgia* (n 60) [202]–[03].

[97] *Oleksandr Volkov v Ukraine* (n 90). In this case, the Chamber decided that Ukraine violated the right to a fair trial of the applicant, who had been dismissed from the post of judge of the Supreme Court.

right to a fair trial.[98] *Oleksandr Volkov* went further than *Assanidze*, in that the Court justified such a specific 'individual' measure by the Ukrainian judiciary's systemic problems which led the Court to suggest 'general' measures as well.[99] Namely, the lack of judicial independence and the judiciary's systemic problems justified both individual and general remedial measures.

V. NORMATIVE VALUES OF SUBSIDIARITY

As demonstrated in section III, these are principles, rules, and practices which preserve a state's decision-making competence. As discussed in section IV, such principles, rules, and practices are accompanied by a series of criteria under international law, with which to confer competence to international courts. The study of these two facets of the idea then leads us to consider a normative value underlying the idea of subsidiary in the context of allocation of competence between states and international courts. While such values may vary depending on specific treaties, courts, and cases, this section draws attention to the following four normative values which can be ascertained from the practices analysed in this chapter.

First, the idea of subsidiarity must have traditionally served to safeguard *state sovereignty*. The exhaustion of local remedies was indeed meant to protect the sovereignty of the host state and to prevent excessive intervention from other states' attempts to resort to international judicial procedures.[100] From this normative value, the criteria such as 'undue delay' and 'futility' should be construed in such a way as to prevent, as far as possible, international courts from deciding on a matter. At the same time, if subsidiarity simply serves to safeguard state sovereignty, it may not add much to the traditional mechanisms, such as the formal separation of legal orders and the decentralised structure of the international legal order, that, albeit in an unsatisfactory manner, serve to counterbalance the authority exercised by international courts.

Second, the protection of sovereignty has then been counterbalanced by the protection of *individuals' rights and interests* as another normative value underlying the practice of international courts which materialise the idea of subsidiarity. The protection of the sovereignty as a rationale for the idea of subsidiarity is particularly problematic for human rights cases which are meant to safeguard individuals' rights from a state's exercise

[98] ibid op [9] ('Ukraine shall secure the applicant's reinstatement in the post of judge of the Supreme Court at the earliest possible date').

[99] See Jahn' (n 53) 9; *Oleksandr Volkov v Ukraine* (n 90) 199–202 (general measures) [207]–[208].

[100] See Shany, *Regulating Jurisdictional Relations Between National and International Courts* (n 28) 28.

of authority. The greater emphasis on individuals' interests is therefore reflected in the conditions on the basis of which human rights courts find the exhaustion rule being inapplicable or already satisfied. Human rights courts apply the exhaustion rule differently from the cases of diplomatic protection, apparently because the interests of individuals should enjoy greater emphasis than the case of traditional diplomatic protection.[101]

Third, the jurisprudence of the ECtHR with regard to the margin of appreciation suggests that *democracy* is one of the normative values accommodated in the practice concerning the idea of subsidiarity. As analysed in the previous section, the jurisprudence of the ECtHR has been taking into account the involvement of the legislature as one of the criteria for justifying a shift of competence to the international judicial venue. The consideration to the legislature's involvement is consistent with a justification for the doctrine of the margin of appreciation, which is to promote and respect democratic decisions within local communities unless the issues concern the protection of minorities.[102] The Strasbourg Court's respect for national democracy is combined with the recognition of the lack of democratic legitimacy on the part of the international court itself.[103] According to Judge Spano, the Court has thus been adopting its 'qualitative, democracy-enhancing approach'[104] as a criterion in the application of the margin of appreciation and the subsidiarity principle. If the margin of appreciation can be seen as judicial deference to democratic legitimacy, it is not surprising that the Court occasionally makes a special reference to the legislator.

Finally, subsidiarity serves to safeguard the *legitimacy of international courts* themselves. The margin of appreciation, for instance, is understood as one way in which the ECtHR sustains the states' propensity for compliance and ultimately upholds judicial legitimacy.[105] If the Strasbourg Court exercises judicial discretion for sensitive issues which lack consensus, the Court is likely be criticised for imposing obligations which are not agreed upon by member states, and is giving them a political excuse for not complying with the judgment.[106] By employing the margin, the ECtHR can

[101] See Amerasinghe, *Local Remedies in International Law* (n 24) 83–86.

[102] Eyal Benvenisti, 'Margin of Appreciation, Consensus, and Universal Standards' (1999) 31 *New York University Journal of International Law and Politics* 843, 849. As the former president of the ECtHR observed, national authorities enjoy an area of discretion owing to their role in 'the expression of the democratic will of their people': Luzius Wildhaber, *The European Court of Human Rights, 1998–2006: History, Achievements, Reform* (Kehl, NP Engel, 2006) 95.

[103] See Yutaka Arai-Takahashi, *The Margin of Appreciation Doctrine and the Principle of Proportionality in the Jurisprudence of the ECHR* (Antwerp; New York, Intersentia, 2002) 239–41.

[104] Spano, 'Universality or Diversity of Human Rights?' (n 47) 499 (original emphasis omitted).

[105] See Yuval Shany, *Assessing the Effectiveness of International Courts* (Oxford, Oxford University Press, 2014) 155–56.

[106] See ibid 155–57.

be indeterminate on the sensitive issues while still subjecting them to the future assessment of the Convention.

VI. CONCLUSION

As contrasted with EU law, international law has been relatively unaccustomed to the language of subsidiarity. The relative unfamiliarity is due to the fundamentally decentralised structure of the international legal order, which did not give rise to the pressing need for introducing the idea of subsidiarity and counterbalancing the presence of higher authority. The traditional assumption was that international law is prescribed and enforced horizontally between states. This horizontal model has been, however, incrementally mismatched with an active role played by international courts in deciding on states' compliance with international law. Domestic confrontations against some of the decisions of international courts have shed new light on the idea of subsidiarity as a possible framework that guides the allocation of competence between states and international courts.

The present study cannot lead us to any general conclusion about the extent to which the idea guides a wide range of international courts and tribunals. This chapter makes a limited observation that there are certain principles, rules, and practices which favour decision-making at a lower level of governance. The rule of exhaustion of local remedies safeguards national competence; the ECtHR's margin of appreciation preserves space for a state's autonomous decision-making; and the ECtHR generally refrains from specifying the modalities of appropriate remedies. These practices develop side-by-side with the yardsticks under international law according to which international courts may regard domestic authorities as no longer appropriate.

While multiple normative values sustain the two facets of the idea of subsidiarity in the context of competence allocation between states and international courts, such normative values can be contradictory to each other. A tension between the protection of state sovereignty and the respect for individuals' rights is one of such contradictions. A traditional value of international law, and thus the idea of subsidiarity therein, is to protect state sovereignty and avoid interference from an external body. The prevention of international judicial supervision is, however, problematic especially for human rights courts which scrutinise a state's conduct for the benefit of individuals' fundamental rights. The rule of exhaustion of local remedies has therefore been applied more flexibly in the jurisprudence of the ECtHR which takes into account the interests of individual claimants. In the practice of the margin of appreciation, the ECtHR no longer treats a state as a single voice and places greater weight on the legislature among domestic organs which benefit from the idea of subsidiarity. The consideration of the involvement of the legislature is, after all, a regime-specific trend. Nevertheless, it is noteworthy that an influential regional human rights court unpacks the state which is generally treated as a monolithic entity at the international level and employs the quality of decision-making processes as one of the criteria with which to decide to what extent national decisions ought to be preserved.

Overall, a study of the idea of subsidiarity in the context of international courts presents us with a nuanced picture about how international courts, which formally operate in the international legal order, interact with the national legal order. While the need for ensuring a state's compliance with international law calls for a shift of competence to international courts, as long as an application is submitted, international law has developed certain flexible criteria which both secure each state's autonomy and simultaneously allow international judicial supervision of domestic decision-making. Such a duality inherent in the idea of subsidiarity enriches our understanding about the rule of law at the international level which, as this chapter attempted to illustrate, preserves national autonomy while expecting it to be within international criteria about national decision-making.

12

Revisiting the Reservations Dialogue: Negotiating Diversity while Preserving Universality Through Human Rights Law

EKATERINA YAHYAOUI KRIVENKO*

I. INTRODUCTION

THE RULE OF law and human rights are two notions widely accepted as having positive values in both national and international law. However, the understanding of the contents and meaning of these two notions, including their relationship, is still a work in progress within international law scholarship. The diversity of states' legal cultures, societal structures, and social practices makes it challenging to gain a better understanding about, and a more precise definition of, both the rule of law and human rights. The difficulty in understanding the relationships between the two concepts arises precisely because human rights often encounter two ostensibly contrasting demands of universality and diversity. To meet these two demands may appear to undermine the elements of the rule of law, such as certainty and foreseeability. This chapter addresses this conceptual difficulty by proposing a new perspective with which to examine human rights and the rule of law. The chapter develops the perspective through the specific analysis on the reservations to human rights treaties. I choose to examine the reservations to human rights treaties as the cornerstone of the analysis because what can be observed within the context of states' reservations practice illuminates our understanding about the above described difficulty. Similarly, the reservations' practice

* This chapter is based on the author's previous works, including: Yahyaoui Krivenko, 'The "Reservations Dialogue" as a Constitution-Making Process' (2013) 15 *International Community Law Review* 381.

illustrates the interactive processes through which universality and diversity are negotiated, and further provides us with the new understanding about the rule of law in human rights practices.

This chapter aims at furthering our understanding of the rule of law in the context of international human rights law. More specifically, it examines the question of how the value of relative uniformity and certainty, which may be seen as intrinsic in the rule of law, is balanced with the value of diversity while maintaining the universality of human rights.[1] In answering these questions, I propose a specific concept of the rule of law at the 'international' level, in a way which is not built upon a parallel notion at the domestic level. By so doing, this chapter also contributes to enhancing our understanding of the relationship between the rule of law in the national and international legal orders.

In order to address the above questions, the chapter analyses reservations to human rights treaties from the perspective of the dialogical understanding of the international rule of law. As will be demonstrated below, the issue of reservations highlights the tension between diversity and the universality of international human rights law. The reservation dialogue accommodates the tension, and, through this process, develops international human rights law and the international rule of law. Given that treaties are the major instruments to guarantee human rights, the very possibility of making reservations to human rights treaties, combined with the status attributed to human rights within the theories of the international rule of law, poses a question as to whether the rule of law can be reserved or 'opted out' of at the international level by a state's reservations.

I will address the relationship between the rule of law and international human rights law by using the notion of the 'reservations dialogue' developed initially by the International Law Commission's (ILC) Special Rapporteur on Reservations to Treaties, Alain Pellet.[2] Building on his initial notion, I adopt a broader view and definition of the reservations dialogue. The broader view encompasses a fuller recognition of the role of various actors participating in the dialogue, multiple forms of the dialogue, and their effects. The broader view adopted in this chapter better allows us to reconcile human rights, on the one hand, which are among the core elements of the international rule of law (as will be described in section II below),

[1] On the question of universality and diversity in human rights law, see also chs 10 (Legg), 13 (Donders and Vleugel) of this volume.

[2] ILC, 'Seventeenth Report on Reservations to Treaties, by Alain Pellet, Special Rapporteur' UN Doc A/CN.4/647 (26 May 2011). See also Report of the International Law Commission, 'Guide to Practice on Reservations to Treaties, Adopted by the Commission at Its Sixty-Third Session' UN Doc A/66/10 (2011). The conclusions reached based on the reports of the Special Rapporteur are summarised in this report.

and the regime of reservations, on the other hand, which permits states to limit and circumvent human rights and the international rule of law. In defining this broader vision of reservations dialogue and its functions within the international rule of law, I draw upon the actual practices of states and human rights treaty-monitoring bodies.

The broader vision of the reservations dialogue helps us understand its dynamics beyond the confines, not only of the Vienna Convention on the Law of Treaties,[3] but also of the law of treaties in general, and allows us to take into consideration some non-legal elements that play out in the dynamics of the reservations dialogue. I will argue that the adoption of the broader vision of the reservations dialogue matters because the view allows for a constructive and productive negotiation of inscription of the national diversity into the international rule of law. The broader vision of the reservations dialogue allows for more intensive input from domestic constituencies, and ultimately enhances the legitimacy of the international rule of law. I will also submit that the international rule of law cannot exist independently from these negotiative practices developing within the framework of the reservations regime. In fact, the very substance of today's international rule of law consists of these negotiative practices and their outcomes at any given point in time. These negotiative practices shall never stop; and indeed, 'there is no place at which we could finally arrive'.[4] However, as this chapter will demonstrate, this does not necessarily mean uncertainty and the absence of universality.

This chapter starts with a discussion of the notion of the rule of law especially as it has been interpreted in its application to law's regulation of international relations (section II). After a brief overview of the traditional vision of the reservations regime and the reservations dialogue, I will analyse the examples from state practice and demonstrate how the reservations regime and the reservations dialogue have been used by states for purposes beyond the traditional understanding of these notions (sections III–IV). Finally, I will provide the assessment of how these developments in state practice have impact on our understanding of the relationship between the domestic and international rule of law, and of some unique features of the 'international' rule of law. The chapter will also suggest how the reservations regime itself could be revised in order to become more conductive towards negotiative and dialogical practices, which are evaluated positively within the context of this chapter's reading of the rule of law.

[3] Vienna Convention on the Law of Treaties, 23 May 1969, 1155 UNTS 311 (entered into force 27 Jan 1980) (1969).

[4] Katharine T Bartlett, 'Feminist Legal Methods' (1990) 103 *Harvard Law Review* 885.

II. THE RELATIONSHIP BETWEEN THE RULE OF LAW CONCEPT, HUMAN RIGHTS, AND UNIVERSALITY

The relationships between the rule of law and human rights are controversial both in theory and practice. Rule of law has diverse meanings and interpretations depending on both time and space. Here, I attempt to present some existing dominant definitions of the concept of the rule of law, which are of particular importance to the arguments formulated in this chapter. Specific attention will be paid to the relationship between the rule of law and human rights. It is important to be aware of different connotations and meanings which we allude to when using the term 'rule of law'.

The general support for the rule of law is often motivated by the desire to place constraints on the arbitrary exercise of power and to prevent any arbitrary use of public power. From this point of view, the first important distinction we need to bear in mind is between the concept of the 'rule by law' and the concept of the 'rule of law'.[5] As one author noted in relation to the development of the rule of law in the early period, '[t]hroughout this early period, … law continued to be seen largely as a means by which to rule rather than a constraint on the rule as such'.[6]

Summarising some generally accepted requirements of the rule of law, Jeremy Waldron enumerates the following:

1. a requirement that people in positions of authority should exercise their power within a constraining framework of public norms …;
2. a requirement that there be general rules laid down clearly in advance …;
3. a requirement that there be court, which operate according to recognized standards of procedural due process or natural justice …;
4. a principle of legal equality[7]

Within this context it is important to understand the goals pursued by the rule of law by considering why exactly we value this notion, what we intend to achieve, and for whose benefit the rule of law is established. Arguably, one of the ultimate goals pursued by the rule of law is the protection of individual freedom. As one author observed regarding the rule of

[5] See, eg, Simon Chesterman, 'An International Rule of Law?' (2008) 56 *American Journal of Comparative Law* 331, 333. According to the concept of the rule by law, a ruler agrees to exercise power in a non-arbitrary fashion, whereas the rule of law signifies that the ruler him/herself is bound by law (limited government). For the formal elements of the rule of law, see also ch 1 (Machiko Kanetake) of this volume.

[6] ibid 334.

[7] Jeremy Waldron, 'Are Sovereigns Entitled to the Benefit of the International Rule of Law?' (2011) 22 *European Journal of International Law* 315, 316–17.

law's objectives, 'the whole point of the rule of law is to secure individual freedom by providing a predictable environment in which individuals can act freely, plan their affairs, and make their decisions'.[8]

If this is one of the goals of the rule of law, on which the majority of, if not all, lawyers may agree, the above four components of the rule of law may appear too formalistic and procedural in nature. They seem to overlook the quality and nature of the 'law' component of the rule of law. For example, in a particular national setting, some of the aforementioned requirements (such as the principle of legal equality) can be readily met by very strict and intrusive laws which, at the same time, excessively limit the individual's freedom of action and decision-making. Individuals can still be discontented with those laws which apply to everyone equally, have a clear content, and are enforced by independent courts. Given that such laws frustrate one of the key objectives of the rule of law, at least certain substantive standards—such as 'constitutional rights' within domestic legal systems and 'human rights' at the international arena—should form an integral part of our understanding of the rule of law.

At the same time, the precise relationship between human rights and the rule of law remains unsettled. To some extent, human rights law has been discussed only as an instrument of guaranteeing, protecting, and promoting some rights associated with the traditional vision of the components of the rule of law, such as equality before the law or the right to a fair trial by independent and impartial tribunals.[9]

The UN's position on the rule of law is indeterminate about whether and to what extent human rights are intrinsic to it. This is illustrated by, for instance, the Declaration of the High-Level Meeting of the UN General Assembly on the Rule of Law at the National and International Levels adopted in 2012.[10] The Declaration states that '[w]e reaffirm that human rights, the rule of law and democracy are interlinked and mutually reinforcing and that they belong to the universal and indivisible core values and principles of the United Nations'.[11] While this statement makes clear that human rights and the rule of law cannot be separated, it continues to portray them as different and distinct notions. Also, while this statement

[8] Jeremy Waldron, 'The Rule of International Law' (2007) 30 *Harvard Journal of Law and Public Policy* 15, 17.

[9] See, eg, Chesterman, 'An International Rule of Law?' (n 5) 344–45; Randall Peerenboom, 'Human Rights and Rule of Law: What's the Relationship?' (2005) 36 *Georgetown Journal of International Law* 809.

[10] UN GA Res adopted on 24 Sept 2012, 'Declaration of the High-level Meeting of the General Assembly on the Rule of Law at the National and International Levels' UN Doc A/RES/67/1 (30 Nov 2012).

[11] ibid para 5.

puts the rule of law within a triad, the resolution devotes one separate paragraph to human rights,[12] which may be a further indication that the rule of law and human rights are considered separately.

The unresolved question about the relationships between the rule of law and human rights also arises with regard to *international* human rights law. This is, for instance, illustrated by the UN Secretary-General's report that defined the rule of law in the following way:

> [The rule of law] refers to a principle of governance in which all persons, institutions and entities, public and private, including the State itself, are accountable to laws that are publicly promulgated, equally enforced and independently adjudicated, *and which are consistent with international human rights norms and standards*. It requires, as well, measures to ensure adherence to the principles of supremacy of law, equality before the law, accountability to the law, fairness in the application of the law, separation of powers, participation in decision-making, legal certainty, avoidance of arbitrariness and procedural and legal transparency.[13]

The UN Secretary-General's definition seems to suggest an intrinsic link between international human rights and the rule of law. One could also interpret the above definition as finding a value-dictating quality in human rights placing them above the rule of law. While it is not entirely clear whether the definition given in this report applies to any rule of law or only to the domestic rule of law as promoted by the UN, it would, at any rate, be difficult to imagine an international rule of law without the requirement of consistency with human rights norms and standards, especially if the same is required from the domestic rule of law.

The relationship between international human rights and the rule of law is further complicated by the following statement in the preamble of the Universal Declaration of Human Rights: 'it is essential, if man is not to be compelled to have recourse, as a last resort, to rebellion against tyranny and oppression, that human rights should be protected by the rule of law'.[14] If the aforementioned statement by the UN Secretary-General suggested that the rule of law needs human rights in order to function adequately, this statement reverses the assumption and affirms that human rights cannot exist and be guaranteed without the rule of law.

Thus, while these statements indicate that protection of individual rights and freedoms should form part of the substantive core of any rule

[12] ibid para 6: 'We reaffirm the solemn commitment of our States to fulfil their obligations to promote universal respect for, and the observance and protection of, all human rights and fundamental freedoms'. Two other paragraphs are devoted to women's rights (ibid para 16) and children's rights (ibid para 17).

[13] Report of the Secretary-General, 'The Rule of Law and Transitional Justice in Conflict and Post-Conflict Societies' UN Doc S/2004/616 (23 Aug 2004) para 6 (emphasis added).

[14] 'Universal Declaration of Human Rights', GA Res 217A (III) UN Doc A/810 (1948) 71, para 3 of the preamble.

of law, they do not provide any guidance to a range of relevant questions. For example, they contain no indication about the content and definition of these rights and values which should form the substantive core of the rule of law. Most importantly, if we leave the definition of this substantive core of the rule of law to each individual state, the actual implementation of international human rights in the domestic legal orders does not lend much support to the universality in international human rights law or ultimately the international rule of law.

The regime of reservations and the reservations dialogue provide an instructive insight into the relationships between the rule of law, international human rights law, universality, and diversity. Universality and equality are cornerstones of human rights protection as an ideal. The very idea behind the promotion and protection of human rights is that human beings should be equally protected in their dignity irrespective of their place of residence, their citizenship, etc. Yet universality is often a difficult issue for international human rights. Human rights treaties often allow for selective application, not only because states can choose to remain outside of the treaty regime, but also because states can tailor application of a particular treaty to their territory by entering reservations. Assuming that human rights form an integral part of the international rule of law, does the very possibility of making reservations mean that states can opt out of the international rule of law? Is an international rule of law at all possible under these conditions? We can observe here that the tension between universality and diversity so characteristic of the human rights law, but also of the reservations regime,[15] starts haunting the rule of law too.

As will be argued in the following sections of this chapter, universality and diversity are not exclusionary terms but inform each other. Following the deconstructionist and radical feminist critique of the binary thinking of the modern Western culture,[16] the opposition between universality and diversity within the rule of law, human rights, and the reservations regime

[15] Within the reservations regime, this tension is usually described as the necessity to strike a balance between the universality of participation and the integrity of a treaty: see, eg, Second Report on Reservations to Treaties UN Doc A/CN.4/477/Add 1, para 90, p 16. To some extent, we can see here a primary tension between two unifying and universalising tendencies which are regarded as not achievable simultaneously: *one* text for *all* states. However, this recognition of the impossibility to achieve these two goals simultaneously points out that in fact we need somehow to recognise and accept diversity. This becomes clearer in the following description of the balance between universality and integrity within the context of human rights treaties as a balance between 'the legitimate role of States to protect their sovereign interests and the legitimate role of the treaty bodies to promote the effective guarantee of human rights' (Rosalyn Higgins, 'Introduction' in JP Gardner (ed), *Human Rights as General Norms and a State's Rights to Opt Out: Reservations and Objections to Human Rights Conventions* (London, British Institute of International and Comparative Law, 1997) xv.

[16] See, eg, Hilary Charlesworth, Christine Chinkin and Shelly Wright, 'Feminist Approaches to International Law' (1991) 85 *American Journal of International Law* 613.

is reviewed and rethought. The central notion, which allows for a rethinking of these binary terms as oppositionary, is the reservations dialogue. In order to allow for a full development of the interconnectedness between these apparently opposed poles, the reservations dialogue is read and understood beyond the meaning attributed to it in the report of the Special Rapporteur and the Guide to Practice on Reservations to Treaties.[17]

As I noted above, human rights is intertwined with the rule of law at the *international* level; yet this does not mean that all the rule of law principles and requirements developed within the domestic legal system can be readily transposed to the level of international law and without affecting the function of such requirements. Despite the very strong affirmation of the UN General Assembly that 'the rule of law applies to all States equally, and to international organizations, including the United Nations and its principal organs',[18] there are still numerous doubts and uncertainties surrounding the meaning of the rule of law at the international level.

The ambiguity of the international rule of law comes to the surface especially when we attempt to clarify how international and domestic legal systems interact, and what influence the domestic rule of law has on the international rule of law. This effort at clarification brings about a view of the international and the domestic rule of law as interrelated and interdependent concepts. The specific analysis conducted in this chapter on the functioning of the reservations regime and dialogue provides a very good tool for the clearer understanding of mechanisms and dynamics at play in developing the international rule of law.

III. THE RESERVATIONS REGIME AND THE RESERVATIONS DIALOGUE

After having considered the meanings of the rule of law and its relationship to international human rights, the following section provides a brief introduction to the reservations regime before analysing the relevant examples from the practice developed by states within the context of the reservations dialogue.

[17] In the remainder of the chapter, I will refer on a few occasions to the narrow and insufficiently open approach of the Special Rapporteur. I would like to emphasise that I fully acknowledge the variety of constraints under which his work on the topic was performed. I also admit that most probably the final product of his 18 years of work (the Guide to Practice) was the best possible balance one could achieve under these constraints. However, now when the work is finished, there is a need to go further and use this work as creatively as possible. I hope that criticism expressed in this chapter will be regarded as a constructive engagement with and a tribute to the difficult work performed by the Special Rapporteur under a variety of constraints so vividly presented in Alain Pellet, 'The ILC Guide to Practice on Reservations to Treaties: A General Presentation by the Special Rapporteur' (2013) 24 *European Journal of International Law* 1061.

[18] UN GA Res adopted on 24 Sept 2012 High-level Meeting Declaration on the Rule of Law (2012) (n 10) para 2.

A. Basics of the Reservations Regime

When a state becomes a party to a treaty with a reservation, it is because the state is either unwilling or unable to respect all the obligations imposed on it by the treaty. In order to accommodate such states into the treaty, the current reservations regime[19] allows them, when they become parties to a treaty, 'to exclude or to modify the legal effect of certain provisions of the treaty in their application to that State'.[20] Obviously, the state can become a party with the reservation only if at least one other state party to the treaty agrees to this modification or exclusion either expressly or tacitly.[21] Moreover, states are not permitted to make reservations which would deprive the treaty of its object and purpose.[22] States that do not agree with the modification or exclusion are given the chance to express their objections during a 12-month period.[23] In objecting, the states are given the choice of either simply objecting—in which case, the provision to which the reservation relates does not apply between the reserving and the objection state while the rest of the treaty does—or objecting to the entry into force of the treaty in its entirety.[24] The states who wish to object shall be very attentive to the 12-month period; if they do nothing during this period, they are considered as having accepted the reservation and have no other chance to lodge a formal objection.[25] The accepted reservation thus enters into force and modifies the treaty relationships between the reserving and the accepting state to the extent of the reservation.[26]

This brief and formal description of the reservations regime demonstrates that within the reservations regime itself, states have only limited opportunities for interaction pre-set by the regime. In addition, there are several difficulties and uncertainties with regard to the application of the reservation regime, including the consequences of incompatible reservations,[27] effects of objections to excluding as opposed to modifying

[19] For a more detailed general discussion of the reservations regime, see, eg, Frank Horn, *Reservations and Interpretative Declarations to Multilateral Treaties* (North-Holland, TMC Asser Instituut, 1988); Alexander Behnsen, *Das Vorbehaltsrecht völkerrechtlicher Verträge: Vorschlag einer Reform* (Berlin, Duncker & Humblot, 2007); Donald W Greig, 'Reservations: Equity as a Balancing Factor' (1995) 16 *Australian Year Book of International Law* 21; José Maria Ruda, 'Reservations to Treaties' (1975) 146 *Recueil des Cours* 11. For more recent literature, see Edward T Swaine, 'Reserving' (2006) 31 *Yale Journal of International Law* 307; Laurence R Helfer, 'Not Fully Committed? Reservations, Risk, and Treaty Design' (2006) 31 *Yale Journal of International Law* 367.

[20] Vienna Convention on the Law of Treaties (n 3) Art 2(1)(d).

[21] ibid Arts 20(4)(a), 20(4)(c), 20(5).

[22] ibid Art 19(c).

[23] ibid Art 20(5).

[24] ibid Arts 20(4)(b) and 21(3).

[25] ibid Art 20(5).

[26] ibid Art 21(1).

[27] See, eg, Roberto Baratta, 'Should Invalid Reservations to Human Rights Treaties be Disregarded?' (2000) 11 *European Journal of International Law* 423; Curtis A Bradley and

reservations,[28] and insufficiency of the 12-month period.[29] While the limited occasions may still allow substantively meaningful interaction between states, procedural limitations imposed by the regime combined with these difficulties, undermine the quality of interaction among states. However, as will be shown below, these limitations and difficulties have led to a significant degree of creativity in state practice. This creativity was named by the Special Rapporteur 'the reservations dialogue'.[30]

B. The Reservations Dialogue

In the practices of reservations, I investigated the reservations dialogue which took many different forms. The dialogue has often been initiated by states who desired to discourage reservations in terms of their number as well as their extent. Being faced with general or imprecise reservations, the states request clarifications and precision from the states which made reservations. In response to apparently incompatible reservations, non-reserving states invite the reserving states to reconsider their reservations. In response to the inflexibility of the 12-month rule, the non-reserving states still send their opinions on reservations to the depositary so that the reserving state and other states parties can be informed about their position. In their attempt to invite the reserving state to reconsider the reservation or provide clarifications, the non-reserving states at times omit to formally object to the reservation. As will be demonstrated later, in some instances, the analysis of surrounding circumstances allows us to affirm that the so-called objecting states intentionally omit to formally object to reservations in order to avoid the inflexibility of the reservations regime. This nuanced and flexible attitude of non-reserving states is one of the key

Jack L Goldsmith, 'Treaties, Human Rights and Conditional Consent' (2000) 149 *University of Pennsylvania Law Review* 399; Ryan Goodman, 'Human Rights Treaties, Invalid Reservations, and State Consent' (2002) 96 *American Journal of International Law* 531; Lisbeth Lijnzaad, *Reservations to UN Human Rights Treaties: Ratify and Ruin?* (Dordrecht, M Nijhoff, 1995); Eric Neumayer, 'Qualified Ratifications: Explaining Reservations to International Human Rights Treaties' (2007) 36 *Journal of Legal Studies* 397; Catherine Redgwell, 'Reservations to Treaties and Human Rights Committee General Comment no 24 (52)' (1997) 46 *International and Comparative Law Quarterly* 245; Brunno Simma and Gleider I Hernández, 'Legal Consequences of an Impermissible Reservation to a Human Rights Treaty: Where Do We Stand' in E Cannizzaro (ed), *The Law of Treaties Beyond the Vienna Convention* (Oxford, Oxford University Press, 2011) 60.

[28] Massimo Coccia, 'Reservations to Multilateral Treaties on Human Rights' (1985) 15 *California Western International Law Journal* 34; Rebecca J Cook, 'Reservations to the Convention on the Elimination of All Forms of Discrimination Against Women' (1990) 30 *Virginia Journal of International Law* 656; Horn, *Reservations and Interpretative Declarations to Multilateral Treaties* (n 19) 182; Ruda, 'Reservations to Treaties' (n 19) 199–200.

[29] Greig, 'Reservations' (n 19) 118–35; Horn (n 19) 206–9; Swaine, 'Reserving' (n 19) 319.

[30] ILC Seventeenth Report (2011) (n 2).

features of the reservations dialogue, as will be discussed further below. In response to the nuanced 'objection', the reserving states do not always remain silent and passive. They sometimes respond with clarifications, provide additional information, or even reconsider their reservations by modifying or partly withdrawing them. In turn, the objecting states respond creatively not only by re-expressing their objection in a nuanced way, but also by welcoming the effort made by the reserving states and by indicating that more effort would be desirable. An important role has been played in this context by some human rights treaty-monitoring bodies which utilise their diplomacy in enquiring about states' reasons for making reservations, exchanging views with the reserving states on different possibilities for reform, and eventually leading to a partial or total withdrawal of the reservations.[31]

The questions then arise as to the relationship between the reservations dialogue and the reservations regime under the Vienna Convention, and what this relationship instructs us about the reservations regime and human rights treaties and standards. In Alain Pellet's Seventeenth Report, the first part of which is devoted to the reservations dialogue, it appears clear from the outset that he tried to keep the traditional vision of the reservations regime intact. As will be demonstrated in section IV, many developments taking place in relation to the reservations dialogue challenge the traditional framework and can be interpreted as qualitatively new practices. However, the official vision of the reservations dialogue as it appears from the Seventeenth Report and the Guide to Practice underplays many of these developments.

Pellet starts by defining borders within which he will then keep his description of the reservations dialogue: 'The reservations regime instituted by the Vienna Convention does not impose static solutions on contracting States or contracting organizations; rather, it leaves room for dialogue among the key players'.[32] The report contains two separate parts: one about the reservations dialogue *within* the Vienna Convention's regime (paras 8 to 27) (explained in section C below) and another about the reservations dialogue *outside* the Vienna system (paras 28 to 53) (section D).

[31] Unfortunately, the limited space of the chapter does not allow for a detailed consideration of the particular role played by treaty-monitoring bodies in the reservations dialogue. However, the internal dynamics of the reservations dialogue as it takes place with participation of the treaty-monitoring bodies is very similar to that of the reservations dialogue between states which is analysed below. Some of the most important examples will be introduced. For an interesting analysis of the role played by the CEDAW with regard to reservations, see Ekaterina Yahyaoui Krivenko, *Women, Islam and International Law Within the Context of the Convention on the Elimination of All Forms of Discrimination Against Women* (The Hague, Brill, 2009) 199–208.

[32] ILC Seventeenth Report (2011) (n 2) 2, para 2.

C. Reservations Dialogue within the Vienna Convention

According to Pellet, the two reactions to reservations recognised by the Vienna Convention, namely, acceptance and objection, are the means of conducting the reservations dialogue. His report affirms that consequences of objections are not limited to the effects attributed to them by the Vienna Convention. The states' objections also 'may mark the beginning of cooperation between the key players'.[33] Pellet continues describing how some objecting states invited the reserving state to reconsider its reservation and to provide additional information on the reservation, and how the objecting states could thereby initiate the reserving state's reflection on the reservation. In some cases, the objections may result in the withdrawal or reformulation of the reservation, although, as the Special Rapporteur himself notes, it is not always possible to establish the link between the reactions of the objecting states and the withdrawal or modification of the reservation.[34]

Pellet also observes that a similar effect (ie, to encourage the reserving states to react to the objections, comment on them, and possibly withdraw reservations) can be produced by other reactions which do not formally qualify as objections under the Vienna Convention but which, according to him, still fall *within* the Vienna Convention regime. Such reactions include: objections formulated by non-contracting states, conditional objections to specified but potential or future reservations, late objections formulated after the end of the time period, and objections to incompatible reservations.[35]

Pellet's description of the reservations dialogue within the Vienna Convention regime makes clear that any positive effects of the reservations dialogue within the Vienna Convention are achieved, not because of the legal effects attributed to various reactions of states by the Vienna Convention, but for other incidental reasons that are not examined in detail in the report. The Special Rapporteur simply notes that number and consistency of objections would play a significant role,[36] as does the concerted way of expressing opinion on reservations.[37] I will examine some of these incidental reasons later, using examples from state practice (section IV(B)) I will demonstrate that the understanding of these reasons and motivations is

[33] ibid 5 para 9.

[34] See, eg, his observation with regard to Malaysia's partial withdrawal of its reservations to Convention on the Elimination of All Forms of Discrimination Against Women: 'Although the link cannot been clearly established' (ibid 5 para 9) or his note with regard to Chile's withdrawal of a reservation to the Convention Against Torture: 'The political changes that took place in Chile in the early 1990s probably encouraged withdrawal of the reservation formulated in 1988' (ibid 11 note 37).

[35] ILC Seventeenth Report (2011) (n 2) 7 paras 14ff.

[36] ibid 13 para 22.

[37] ibid 14 para 25.

fundamental for the potential creation of enhanced efficiency of the reservations dialogue within the context of promotion of the rule of law.

D. Reservations Dialogue Outside the Vienna Convention

Pellet discussed two groups of reactions which, according to him, fall *outside* the Vienna Convention regime: (1) contracting states/orgnisations' reactions *other than* objections and acceptance;[38] and (2) reactions of treaty-monitoring bodies and international organisations.[39] The placing of this latter type of reservations dialogue outside the Vienna Convention regime is not contested: the Vienna Convention does not envisage either the existence of treaty-monitoring bodies or the interventions from international organisations. However, the reasons for situating the former group of reactions outside the Vienna Convention regime are less straightforward. This is because the effect and role of the reactions in the former group would be, in fact, very similar to those of 'other reactions' (eg, objections formulated by non-contracting states) discussed above in section C which are placed *within* the Vienna Convention regime.

For example, the Special Rapporteur places outside the Vienna Convention regime 'undefined reactions which do not reveal their purpose and complaints about reservations'.[40] He even affirms that these undefined reactions and complaints 'serve little purpose'.[41] Yet, at least in terms of legal effect, it is difficult to distinguish these imprecise reactions from, for instance, the late objections which are categorised by Pellet as the reservations dialogue *within* the Vienna Convention regime. Also, the practical effects of the imprecise statements are exactly the same as that of late objections: partial or total withdrawals of reservations. It seems that the distinction between inside and outside of the Vienna Convention regime serves the purpose of preparing the ground for maintenance of the status quo and avoiding any modifications to the Vienna Convention regime. The relatively conservative attitude of the Special Rapporteur is confirmed by his conclusions and proposals. Although he insists that the reservations dialogue is a valuable practice, he abstains from proposing any specific draft guideline on the reservations dialogue. He simply recalls that some previously adopted draft guidelines recommending that states

[38] ibid paras 30–38.

[39] ibid paras 39–53. This second aspect of the reservations dialogue outside of the Vienna Convention is not discussed further because, as stated previously (n 31), the limited space of the chapter does not allow for consideration of the role of treaty-monitoring bodies in the reservations dialogue.

[40] ibid para 31. Pellet puts into this group all reactions to reservations that do not express an objection to a reservation *stricto sensu*. The examples are discussed in paras 30–38 of the report.

[41] ibid.

adopt certain practices with regard to reservations and objections are sufficient indicators of the ILC's support of the reservations dialogue.[42] Pellet also formulates draft recommendations or conclusions on the reservations dialogue which use language different from the language used in the main text of the draft guidelines. These conclusions do not form part of the Guide to Practice itself but are included as an annex to it. Overall, despite ILC's 'welcoming the efforts … to encourage such a dialogue',[43] the dialogue appears to have been pushed into its periphery, rather than into the core of the reservations regime.

IV. RE-IMAGINING THE RESERVATIONS DIALOGUE

The previous section presented the dynamics of the reservations dialogue in general, as they appear through the reading of the report presented by the Special Rapporteur and reflected in the Guide to Practice. The present section aims at putting the practices of the reservations dialogue into a new light. For this purpose, I will present the context within which the reservations dialogue has been developing, and demonstrate the prevalence of human rights treaties in the development of the reservations dialogue (section A). I will then analyse in detail the practice of the reservation dialogue as it developed within the context of the Convention on the Elimination of All Forms of Discrimination Against Women (ICEDAW) (section B).[44] This convention is chosen because, as will be demonstrated below, it is a single treaty that produced the majority of instances of the reservation dialogue.

A. Context of the Reservations Dialogue

The distinguishing feature of the reservations dialogue is obviously its dialogical nature. Such a feature is significant and unique, especially given that the Vienna Convention regime, in the context of which the reservations dialogue develops, is characterised by preference for definite and statist solutions. As explained above, under the Vienna Convention, the reservations regime was designed in quite a formalistic way. Despite the Special Rapporteur's affirmation that the Vienna Convention does not

[42] Thus, he points out the draft guidelines 2.1.9 (became 2.1.2) encouraging states to indicate reasons for their reservations (ibid para 58); the draft guideline 2.6.10 (became 2.6.9) encouraging states to do the same with regard to their objections (para 59); the draft guideline 4.5.3 (became 4.5.2, paragraph 2) encouraging states to formulate objections to invalid reservations (para 60); and finally, the draft guideline 2.5.3 encouraging periodic review of reservations with a view of withdrawing them either partially or totally (para 61).

[43] Report of the International Law Commission Guide to Practice (2011) (n 2) Annex, last para of the preamble.

[44] Convention on the Elimination of All Forms of Discrimination against Women, 18 Dec 1979, 1249 UNTS 13.

impose 'static solutions',[45] the drafters of the Vienna Convention may not have envisaged the reservations regime as a dialogue. The reservations regime was conceived as a means of allowing as many states as possible to become parties to a treaty while preserving the centrality of the notion of state consent and the appearance that all parties to a treaty (whether reserving or not) are bound only by what they consented to.

Yet the formalistic traditional logic of the reservations regime is often unable to account for the dynamics of the reservations dialogue. For instance, the traditional framework may not appropriately account for why an objecting state should engage in any discussions about the extent and nature of a particular reservation if this objecting state's position and interests can be preserved by simply formulating an objection. The reservations regime of the Vienna Convention allows any objecting state desiring to preserve its interests to go as far as to exclude any treaty relationships between itself and the reserving state; yet the reality is that many states still prefer other types of reactions not envisaged by the Vienna Convention to this extreme form of objection. Also, the traditional logic does not sufficiently explain why states, which complain about the lack of resources and insufficiency of time limit rule should, first, formulate such detailed objections and engage in any dialogue; second, from the point of view of reserving states, respond to these objections; and, finally, again from the point of view of objecting states, continue to respond to modified reservations, knowing that all this has no legal effects *stricto sensu*.

In order to understand these dynamics and motives of states, we need first to take a closer look at the context within which the reservations dialogue takes place in practice. As is already evident from the practices referred to by the Seventeenth Report of the Special Rapporteur, the majority of instances of the reservations dialogue take place within the framework of *human rights treaties*. The table below contains the number of instances relating to reservations dialogue[46] for different types of treaties mentioned in the report. I distinguish three types of treaties: human rights treaties, non-human rights treaties, and an intermediate category of treaties related to human rights and humanitarian affairs. The category of human rights treaties is based on the contents of the Chapter IV of the Collection of Multilateral Treaties Deposited with the Secretary General as of May 2013.[47] The meaning of each abbreviation is provided in footnotes.

[45] See (n 32) and accompanying text.

[46] In this context, the 'instances' refer to any occurrence identified by the Special Rapporteur as an example of the reservations dialogue. Such instances include a particular objection, reservation, or other reaction. The objection, reservation, and other reactions are counted as different 'instances' if they concern different treaties; on the other hand, they are counted as one 'instance' if they concern different states within the same treaty.

[47] An online version is available at: http://treaties.un.org/Pages/ParticipationStatus.aspx. The only human rights treaty not mentioned in this Chapter IV but included in the table is the European Convention on Human Rights. However, the 'human rights' nature of this regional treaty is undisputed.

I created the intermediate category for those treaties which are not contained in Chapter IV of the Collection but still concern human rights and humanitarian affairs.[48] Finally, while some treaties do not deal with human rights and are thus included in the category of non-human rights treaties, they may still contain provisions of humanitarian or human rights spirit and the reservations dialogue could be developing around these provisions.

Table 1: Types of Treaties Used as Examples in the Seventeenth Report

Type of Treaties	Number of Instances	Percentage
Human Rights	26	62%
ICEDAW[49]	10	
CRC[50]	4	
CERD[51]	1	
CESCR[52]	2	
CCPR[53]	4	
ECHR[54]	1	
CAT[55]	3	
CRD[56]	1	
Humanitarian/human rights-related	9	21%
Non-human rights[57]	7	17%
Total	42	100%

[48] The following treaties used in the Seventeenth Report are included into this category (the number in parenthesis indicates the number of instances for each particular treaty): UN Convention against Illicit Trafficking in Narcotic Drugs and Psychotropic Substances, 20 Dec 1988, 1582 UNTS 95 (1); International Convention for the Suppression of Terrorist Bombings, 15 Dec 1997, 2149 UNTS 256 (1); International Convention for the Suppression of the Financing of Terrorism, 9 Dec 1999, 2178 UNTS 197 (2); Convention on the Environmental Impact Assessment in a Transboundary Context, 25 February 1991, 1989 UNTS 309 (1); Protocol III to the Convention on Prohibitions or Restrictions on the Use of Certain Conventional Weapons Which May Be Deemed to be Excessively Injurious or to Have Indiscriminate Effect, 10 Oct 1980, 1342 UNTS 137 (2); Rome Statute of the International Criminal Court, 17 July 1998, 2187 UNTS 3 (1); Additional Protocol III to the Geneva Conventions of 1949, 8 Dec 2005, Notification of the Federal Department of Foreign Affairs of Switzerland, Bern, 4 Jan 2006 (1).

[49] Convention on Discrimination against Women (n 44).

[50] Convention on the Rights of the Child, 20 Nov 1989, 1577 UNTS 3.

[51] International Convention on the Elimination of All Forms of Racial Discrimination, 21 Dec 1965, 660 UNTS 195.

[52] International Covenant on Economic, Social and Cultural Rights, 16 Decr 1966, 993 UNTS 31.

[53] International Covenant on Civil and Political Rights, 16 Dec 1966, 999 UNTS 171 (1966).

[54] Convention for the Protection of Human Rights and Fundamental Freedoms, 4 Nov 1950, ETS 5, 213 UNTS 221 (1950).

[55] Convention against Torture and Other Cruel, Inhuman or Degrading Treatment or Punishment, 10 Dec 1984, 1465 UNTS 85.

[56] Convention on the Rights of Persons with Disabilities, 13 Dec 2006, 2515 UNTS 3.

[57] The following treaties are concerned (the number in parenthesis indicates the number of instances for each particular treaty): Inter-American Treaty of Reciprocal Assistance,

This table clearly demonstrates that the reservations dialogue is the most active within the context of human rights treaties (ie, 62 per cent of the practices).

One of the possible reasons human rights treaties predominate in the practice of the reservations dialogue is that the reservations dialogue develops when states are faced with most serious challenges to human rights standards. The review of the examples used in the Seventeenth Report reveals the interesting pattern that the majority of instances of the reservations dialogue involve Muslim majority states and discussion around reservations linked to various degrees to application of Islamic laws in these countries. The reservations dialogue has been utilised as a tool to address the core difficulties surrounding the international rule of law and its relationship with international human rights as well as the relationship between divergent understandings of the rule of law emerging within the domestic and the international spheres.

Among human rights treaties, ICEDAW[58] has generated more instances of the reservations dialogue than all other treaties, which makes it worth elaborating further on the practice developed by states within the context of this treaty.

B. Substance of the Reservations Dialogue

When taking a closer look at the state practice with regard to reservations, a broader view of 'reservations dialogue' is emerging. The view helps us to realise, not only the artificial character of the distinction between 'inside' and 'outside' of the Vienna Convention, but also the significance of non-legal consequences of reactions that, according to the Seventeenth Report, 'serve little purpose'.[59] We also understand the importance of the role played by treaty-monitoring bodies. In order to demonstrate these

2 Sept 1947, OAS Treaty Series nos 8 and 61 (1); Charter of the Organization of American States, 30 April 1948, OAS Treaty Series, nos 1C and 61 (1); Agreement on the International Carriage of Perishable Foodstuffs and on the Special Equipment, 1 Sept 1970, 1028 UNTS 121 (1); Vienna Convention on the Law of Treaties, 25 May 1969, 1155 UNTS 331 (1); Geneva Convention on the Territorial Sea and the Contiguous Zone, 29 April 1958, 516 UNTS 205 and the Geneva Convention on the Continental Shelf, 29 April 1958, 499 UNTS 311 (1: both Conventions are mentioned as one instance in the Seventeenth Report because they concern an identical reservation made by the same state); Vienna Convention on Consular Relations, 24 April 1963, 596 UNTS 261 (1); Vienna Convention on Diplomatic Relations, 18 April 1961, 500 UNTS 95 (1).

[58] Convention on Discrimination against Women (n 41). All reservations, objections, and other reactions to reservations discussed here are at the corresponding page of the UN Treaty Collection website, available at: http://treaties.un.org/pages/ViewDetails.aspx?src=TREATY&mtdsg_no=IV-8&chapter=4&lang=en. The latest official printed version dates 2009: UN, 'Multilateral Treaties Deposited With the Secretary-General' ST/LEG/SER.E/26 (status as at 1 April 2009).

[59] See (n 41) above.

implications of state practice that support the broader view of the reservations regime, I will draw on the practices relating to the ICEDAW. The practices are divided into four groups: (1) reactions to reservations which states deemed incompatible; (2) reactions dealing with the impact of reservations on reserving states' human rights obligations; (3) reactions to reservations expressed after the expiry of the 12-month time limit, and (4) responses of reserving states to objections and other reactions to their reservations. The first two groups are based on the substance of issues addressed by states, while the two next groups are based on particular types of reactions that do not fit into the categories of the Vienna Convention regime. The third and fourth group of reactions will be analysed together because of the close links they entertain.

It is important to emphasise the following preliminary observation: in all groups of practices that will be discussed below, states express their views on reservations and clarify some aspects of the reservations regime without really objecting to reservations. This is a very peculiar stance, taking into account the often expressed contention that the 12-month period is insufficient for many states for formulating objections. What happens in the series of examples presented below is that even when states react within the 12-month period, they find it more important to express their views on the reservations and uncertainties of the reservations regime than to express a formal objection.

i. Reactions to Reservations Deemed Incompatible

States are not always certain as to whether a particular reservation is compatible with the object and purpose of the treaty. The uncertainty is augmented by the fact that the Vienna Convention regime left unresolved the issue of consequences of incompatible reservations.[60] When reacting to reservations, states tend to use the objections as an opportunity to clarify the nature of the reservation and the legal consequences of this reservation, should it be considered incompatible.

For instance, Denmark made the following statement with regard to the Libyan initial reservation. This statement was included by the depositary in the text of objections:

> The Government of Denmark has taken note of the reservation made by the Libyan Arab Jamahiriya when acceding [to the said Convention]. In the view of the Government of Denmark this reservation is subject to the general principle of treaty interpretation according to which a party may not invoke the provisions of its internal law as justification for failure to perform a treaty.[61]

[60] For discussions on this issue, see references in (n 27) above.
[61] UN Multilateral Treaties (2009) (n 58) 309.

This statement simply acknowledges the existence of the reservation and reminds the reserving state about a general rule of treaty law that is supposed to be known by all states. However, this statement does not constitute a formal objection. It could rather be interpreted as an indirect expression of the state's opinion about the nature of the reservation. Other reactions of states to reservations would also contain explanations about why a particular state regards a specific reservation as potentially incompatible with the object and purpose of the treaty without, however, making a final authoritative statement. They would rather suggest that the reservation 'creates doubts' as to the commitment of the reserving state.[62] Alternatively, some objecting states would invite the reserving state either to provide additional information or proof through subsequent practice that the reservation is not incompatible.[63]

As far as uncertain consequences of incompatible reservations are concerned, many states choose to express their opinion on this issue in their reactions to reservations (be they formal objections or other types of statements). Many states emphasised that the particular reservation deemed to be incompatible 'cannot alter or modify in any respect the obligations arising from the Convention for any State Party thereto'.[64]

ii. Reactions Dealing with Impact of Reservations on Reserving States' Human Rights Obligations

Another interesting group of reactions to reservations is constituted by objections and other statements which clarify one or another aspect of the relationship between the reservations regime and existing human rights treaty obligations. Several states included statements indicating that the reserving state is already a party to human rights conventions protecting rights similar to those it attempts to reserve. Moreover, they also stress that these rights are also protected in virtue of customary law. Therefore, the reserving state is not entitled to make the reservation.[65]

[62] See objections of Norway to the reservations by the Maldives, Kuwait, and Pakistan. For some reasons, the objections of Norway are not listed in the latest 2009 edition of Multilateral Treaties; for an official reference, see the 2006 edition ST/LEG/SER.E/25 (31 Dec 2006) 278. See also Austria's objection to the reservation of Pakistan: UN Multilateral Treaties (2009), ibid 306.

[63] Austria's objection to the reservation by Pakistan: ibid.

[64] See statements made by Austria with regard to the reservation of the Maldives (UN Multilateral Treaties (2009), ibid 305); Finland with regard to reservations of Bahrain, Kuwait, Malaysia, Mauritania, Niger, Pakistan, Saudi Arabia, and Syria (ibid 312–14); Norway with regard to reservations of Niger, Mauritania, Saudi Arabia; Portugal with regard to reservations of the Maldives (ibid 326–27); and Sweden with regard to reservations of Bahrain, Mauritania, Saudi Arabia, and Syria (ibid 331–33).

[65] See statements made by Mexico with regard to reservations of Bangladesh, Egypt, Iraq, and Libya (Multilateral Treaties (2009), ibid 322); Sweden with regard to reservations of Bahrain, Bangladesh, Tunisia, Egypt, Iraq, Libya, Jordan, the Maldives, Kuwait, and Syria (ibid 331–32); and Denmark with regard to the reservation of Syria (ibid 310).

In order to understand these types of statements, the Vienna Convention regime on its own is insufficient. The Vienna Convention regime was designed to bring into the international treaty law the balance between the universality of participation and integrity of a treaty by preserving at the same time the fundamental principle that states cannot be bound without their consent.[66] The drafters of the Vienna Convention could not have imagined that states in reacting to reservations would express their opinions on the reservations regime itself or discuss the nature of the reservation with the reserving state. In attempting to subsume these statements under the Vienna Convention regime, the Special Rapporteur missed the opportunity to favour a more innovative and far-reaching development. The mandate of the Special Rapporteur was defined quite broadly[67] and allowed him to engage in both a broader reading of the Vienna Convention regime itself and development of a reading of the reservations regime going beyond the confines of the Vienna Convention. According to my interpretation of the part of his report related to the reservations dialogue, he has taken neither of these routes.

Before analysing further the implications of such statements beyond the Vienna Convention regime, it is important to recall two other practices relevant to the reservations dialogue: reactions after the expiry of the 12-month period and responses of reserving states.

iii. Reactions to Reservations after the Expiry of the 12-Month Period and Responses of Reserving States

Many states reacted to reservations after the expiration of the 12-month period. These reactions can be divided into two groups. First, some of these reactions can be regarded as motivated by the desire of states to catch up the missed time because they were not able to object within the prescribed 12-month time limit.[68] This type of late reactions is less significant for the

[66] See, eg, Second Report of Alain Pellet UN Doc A/CN.4/477/Add 1 (13 June 1996) 16–18, paras 90–98. A similar view was also expressed by the International Court of Justice already in 1951: *Reservations to the Convention on Genocide* [1951] ICJ Reports 15 (Advisory Opinion of 28 May 1951) esp 24–26.

[67] See the title of the mandate: 'Law and Practice Relating to Reservations to Treaties' and the way this topic was introduced into the ILC's work: Report of the International Law Commission on the Work of its Forty-Fifth Session (1993) *Yearbook of the International Law Commission*, vol 2, pt 2, at 96, paras 428–30.

[68] These types of reactions will contain such words as 'objection', 'object', etc. See, eg, the French communication sent in response to the reservation of Niger where the French government even attempted to persuade the depositary that the time limit did not yet elapse: UN Multilateral Treaties (2009) (n 58) 344. See also communications by Denmark to the reservation of Kuwait (Multilateral Treaties (2009), ibid note 30, 340–41), communication of Portugal to the reservation of Pakistan (Multilateral Treaties (2009), ibid 344, note 49). It should be noted that when the reaction of the state is submitted after the time limit but does not have as its primary purpose to object to the reservation, simply making a statement about the reservation, the depositary labels it 'notification'.

purposes of present analysis, but demonstrates that the 12-month time limit rule presents a real problem for some states. More significant is the second group of reactions where states reacting to reservations are not at all concerned with the 12-month time limit rule. The only real motivation for them was the desire to express their view on the reservations. As with the previously mentioned reactions to reservations made within the prescribed time limit but without containing a formal objection, these statements are even less subsumable under the reservations regime. In order to understand their real implications, we need to analyse them from a broader perspective.

At the following stage of the reservations dialogue some reserving states provide responses to the requests they received from reacting states. Although direct responses to concrete inquiries are relatively rare, they do exist and evidence the emergence of a new trend.[69] In other instances the responses are more indirect and take the form of partial withdrawals or reformulations of reservations. Within this category of responses, the 'dialogical' nature can be easily established in some cases, while in other cases there is little evidence as to the precise reasons for withdrawal or modification.

For example, the sequence of events which led to the first partial withdrawal of Malaysia's initial reservation described below clearly indicates the role which objections played in the process as well as the fact that Malaysia acted 'in response' to these objections.

Finally, in some cases, the dialogue continues and states react even to these modified or partially withdrawn reservations. These reactions can never fit into the framework of the reservations regime because it does not provide for the possibility to object to a partially withdrawn reservation.[70] However, they are fundamental for a deeper understanding of the reservations dialogue and its reading articulated below. Therefore, I will reproduce the full text of the two of these reactions.

In response to the proposed partial withdrawal and modification of the reservation by Malaysia, the government of The Netherlands declared:

> The Government of the Kingdom of the Netherlands has examined the modification of the reservations made by Malaysia to article 5(a) and 16.1. (a) and

[69] See, eg, response of Syria to the objection of Germany provided on 6 May 1996 within the context of the Convention on the Rights of the Child (n 50) 3. The response is contained in the note 52 of the status of the Convention, available at: http://treaties.un.org/pages/ViewDetails.aspx?src=TREATY&mtdsg_no=IV-11&chapter=4&lang=en#EndDec.

[70] This situation is maintained in the Guide to Practice: Rule 2.5.7 and 2.5.11. I emphasised the illogical nature of this solution, especially as far as states which objected to the initial reservations are concerned. States that objected to the initial reservation might legitimately still have some objections to the partially withdrawn reservation, but the Vienna Convention regime does not allow for expression of objections or any other reactions at this stage. See Yahyaoui Krivenko, *Women, Islam and International Law* (n 31) 93–94.

> paragraph 2 of the [Convention]. The Government of the Kingdom of the Netherlands acknowledges that Malaysia has specified these reservations, made at the time of its accession to the Convention. Nevertheless the Government of the Kingdom of the Netherlands wishes to declare that it assumes that Malaysia will ensure implementation of the rights enshrined in the above articles and will strive to bring its relevant national legislation into conformity with the obligations imposed by the Convention. This declaration shall not preclude the entry into force of the Convention between the Kingdom of the Netherlands and Malaysia.[71]

Very similar in nature was the reaction of Finland to the proposed modification of the reservation by Maldives:

> The Government of Finland welcomes with satisfaction that the Government of the Republic of Maldives has specified the reservations made at the time of its accession to the Convention. However, the reservations to Article 7 (a) and Article 16 still include elements which are objectionable. The Government of Finland therefore wishes to declare that it assumes that the Government of the Republic of Maldives will ensure the implementation of the rights recognised in the Convention and will do its utmost to bring its national legislation into compliance with obligations under the Convention with a view to withdrawing the reservation. This declaration does not preclude the entry into force of the Convention between the Maldives and Finland.[72]

These two statements adopt a very cautious language: they emphasise the positive aspects of the effort made by governments in attempting to revise the reservation and express faith in the fact that the government will respect the Convention. While they note that additional efforts are required to bring the situation in these states into full conformity with the provisions of the Convention, they do not formally object to any part of the modified reservations. Finland's reaction simply states that there are still 'elements which are objectionable'. The Netherlands indicates the same idea by using 'nevertheless' after acknowledging the effort made by the Malaysian government. However, they also use the opportunity to remind reserving states about their expectations (and expectations of many other states) concerning the fulfilment of international obligations.

What clearly emerges from this brief description of the reservations dialogue as it took place within the context of the ICEDAW is its broader scope going clearly beyond the reservations regime. In order to discover its full potential and significance, it is necessary to read this exchange between states that are party to a convention beyond the Vienna Convention regime. One such reading is proposed below.

[71] UN Multilateral Treaties (2009) (n 58) 342, note 35.
[72] ibid 342, note 36.

V. THE RESERVATIONS DIALOGUE AS AN INTERFACE BETWEEN THE DOMESTIC AND THE INTERNATIONAL RULE OF LAW

The exchange taking place within the framework of the reservations dialogue has a distinct negotiative nature. The subject matter of the negotiation is not always obvious. The apparent subject matter of the reservation is not always the only issue negotiated. The dialogue could also have an impact on related but unstated matters.

Within the context of the ICEDAW, the dialogue broadly raises three main issues: first, the rules of the reservations regime itself; second, the nature of the states' human rights obligations, including the relationship between various types of obligations; and, third, the substantive content of states' human rights obligations, especially from the point of view of each particular state's domestic laws. At first sight, the latter set of issues appears as the most important for the purposes of understanding the relationship between domestic and international rule of law. However, the overall attitude of states with regard to all issues is equally significant.

In this negotiative process, brought into being by the reservations dialogue, a particular image of international law emerges. International law appears as an arena where values proposed as candidates for universal acceptance are negotiated, where mechanisms to assist states with implementation of these newly negotiated values are created. It is important to realise that, although the text of adopted human rights treaties contains some rules and definitions pretending to have a universal validity, the reality is that many of these rules and values are too general to be interpreted uniformly. Moreover, far from being universal, they are often an expression of a consensus reached by states participating in the drafting process only. The reservations dialogue and the following discussion, also mediated by a treaty-monitoring body, allow not only the clarification of the content of the rules, but also the taking into account of opinions and positions of a variety of states and other actors (NGOs), thus universalising a particular rule or value and conveying to it a required degree of legitimacy. The input from domestic law of various countries plays a crucial role in this process. While the domestic law as such does not become a part of the international law and does not modify the text or wording of the rule, it leaves a mark on the international law which will influence the operation of the international rule and allow it, in turn, to be more demanding on non-compliant domestic law.

A. Impact of the Domestic Law on the Negotiation of Universal Values

In order to illustrate this point, I will turn to some examples related to the discussion of various Islamic family laws within the context of the

ICEDAW. The fact that many Muslim states entered several general reservations to the ICEDAW in order to protect the application of Islam-inspired family laws has often been viewed as one of the major negative trends in the implementation of the ICEDAW.[73] The reservations dialogue evolved very actively around this issue between states and the Committee on the Elimination of Discrimination against Women (CEDAW), which has so far adopted a particular attitude toward state reports.

The Committee would normally ask many questions for clarification in an attempt to understand the operation of domestic law in the relevant states.[74] It also uses the insights gained during the examination of a state's reports as a tool for suggesting possible ways of improvement for other states.[75] For example, during the examination of the initial report of Libya, one of the members stated that 'she did not see why those reservations should be upheld out of respect for Shari'a, when the report had emphasised the pioneering role the Shari'a had played in promoting women's rights'.[76] This attitude of the Committee prompted Libya to give more explanations about the precise operation of Islamic law, thus demonstrating how its domestic law confirms to the rights codified in the

[73] This concern has been voiced very early and only with regard to reservations based on Islam, although other states also entered similar reservations motivated by their culture/tradition. See, eg, Michele Brandt and Jeffery A Kaplan, 'The Tension Between Women's Rights and Religious Rights: Reservations to CEDAW by Egypt, Bangladesh and Tunisia' (1995) 12 *Journal of Law and Religion* 105; Rebecca J Cook, 'Reservations to the Convention on the Elimination of All Forms of Discrimination against Women' (1990) 30 *Virginia Journal of International Law* 643.

[74] eg, during the discussion about a particular type of divorce which appears to be discriminatory against women and thus to be an obstacle to the withdrawal of Egypt's reservation but which is presented as constituting an advancement in the field of women's rights by Egyptian representatives, one member of the Committee said that 'It would be helpful to see documentation of exactly how khula divorce was administered in practice'. Committee on the Elimination of Discrimination Against Women, Forty-fifth session, Summary records of the 919th meeting, CEDAW/C/SR.919 (2010) 6, para 31.

[75] See, eg, the following observation made by one of the Committee members during the examination of combined third and fourth periodic reports of Kuwait: 'she suggested that the approaches adopted by other Arab nations that had succeeded in withdrawing sharia-based reservations might be studied for guidance.' Committee on the Elimination of Discrimination Against Women, Fiftieth Session, Summary records of the 1011th meeting, CEDAW/C/SR.1011, para 6, p 2; or the statement made during the examination of the combined sixth and seventh periodic report of Egypt in relation to this country's reservations: 'She was aware of the complexities involved; similar issues arose in her own country with regard to Jewish law. The Committee had heard from a neighbouring Middle Eastern country of a very interesting review of family and personal status laws, which was being conducted in cooperation with the Grand Mufti and women's non-governmental organizations'. Committee on the Elimination of Discrimination Against Women, Forty-fifth Session, Summary records of the 918th meeting, CEDAW/C/SR.918 (2010) 3–4, para 19.

[76] Consideration of the initial report by Libya, Committee on the Elimination of Discrimination Against Women, Thirteenth Session, Summary records of the 237th meeting, CEDAW/C/SR.237 (1994) para 52.

Convention. These explanations, in turn, give the Committee members a better understanding of the operation of international human rights standards in particular domestic contexts and also a sense of how these rules are interpreted by particular states, thus allowing it to develop an interpretation which is as inclusive possible.

The example of interactions between Libya and the Committee suggests that the reservation dialogue could become a channel through which diversity is negotiated, and ultimately absorbed into universal values protected by human rights treaties. The universal values will, in turn, shape the international and the domestic rule of law. The reservations dialogue and the reservations regime generally are there to strike a balance between universality and diversity but not in the traditionally conceived way. What occurs within the reservations dialogue and the reservations regime is not a static phenomenon, but a process in which the making of the reservation is just the starting point. The process does not end with the expiration of the 12-month time limit. It continues all the way forward. Whether or not this process would contain meaningful interactions between a reserving state and the Committee would also determine whether there is a mutually beneficial interaction between the domestic and international rule of law. The success is understood as a capacity of the negotiative process to generate consensus at given point in time (substantive aspect) as well as an always-open possibility for further constructive interaction and dialogue to renegotiate the previously established consensus (procedural aspect).

B. Conditions for Constructive Dialogue

In order for this success to transpire, there is a need to sustain appropriate conditions for constructive dialogue. The reservations dialogue should be understood and interpreted more broadly than what is presented in the report of the Special Rapporteur. The value of exchanges taking place outside of the Vienna Convention regime should be recognised and supported. Possibility for reaction beyond 12 months, especially if there is a suspicion that the reservation might be incompatible with the object and purpose should be offered. Similarly, states should be able and encouraged to react to proposed modifications of reservations without running a danger of preventing the entry into force of a positive modification. The reservations dialogue should also promote replies from reserving states.

One of the most important aspects of the reservations dialogue which needs to be preserved and cultivated is an open and dialogical attitude of all participants. In order to understand how this can achieved, I use the following example analysed through the prism of a theory formulated in the context of understanding the constitution-making processes. John Elster, writing about constitution-making processes, observes:

> There is one particular passion that has, somewhat surprisingly, played a considerable role in constitution-making. This is vanity or self-love, *amour-propre,* which many moralists from La Rochefoucauld onwards have considered the most powerful human emotion.[77]

Thus, public discussion or debates, especially if they involve commitment, tend to encourage stubbornness because vanity might prevent states from changing their minds. Once a state has adopted a particular stance, representing itself as a state protecting certain cultural, religious, or other values, it is difficult to persuade this state to change its position based on the critique of its values except when a state's self-identification with particular values changes, which is not a very common phenomenon.[78] In the context of the reservations dialogue all discussion is public. Therefore, the aim of bringing about a change or a modification in the position of reserving states can only be successful if it attempts to constructively engage with the values a particular state attempts to protect through the reservation, rather than criticising the values and the stance of the state. In this sense, the formalities of the Vienna Convention reservation regime do not encourage constructive dialogue and negotiation but tend to produce more stubbornness. The flexible nature of the reservations dialogue as reflected in the state practice opens ways for such a constructive discussion which will not deter states from changing their positions. The danger in attempting to put the reservations dialogue back into the framework of the reservations regime is that opportunities for such an open and constructive public discussion will become almost non-existent. A very telling example in this regard is the situation around Malaysia's attempted modification of its initial reservation.

When accessing to the ICEDAW on 5 July 1995, Malaysia formulated a reservation.[79] This reservation attracted a few reactions and objections

[77] Jon Elster, 'Forces and Mechanisms in the Constitution-Making Process' (1995) 45 *Duke Law Journal* 364, 384. This issue is also discussed in Jon Elster, 'Ways of Constitution-Making' in A Hadenius (ed), *Democracy's Victory and Crisis* (Cambridge, Cambridge University Press, 1997) 123, 131ff. For analysis of the reservations dialogue from a constitution-making perspective, see Ekaterina Yahyaoui Krivenko, 'The "Reservations Dialogue" as a Constitution-Making Process' (2013) 15 *International Community Law Review* 381.

[78] This change in the self-identification of the state is not impossible. The examples include regime change and change in foreign policy orientations, in the importance of values for states' international relations.

[79] This reservation reads as follows: 'The Government of Malaysia declares that Malaysia's accession is subject to the understanding that the provisions of the Convention do not conflict with the provisions of the Islamic Sharia' law and the Federal Constitution of Malaysia. With regards thereto, further, the Government of Malaysia does not consider itself bound by the provisions of articles 2(f), 5(a), 7(b), 9 and 16 of the aforesaid Convention. In relation to

from other states parties.[80] These reactions emphasised, among others, the general and unspecified nature of the reservation, which does not allow other states parties to understand the degree of Malaysia's commitment to the Convention. They also criticised a general and unqualified reference to national laws without any further information as well as reference to some central articles of the ICEDAW. On 6 February 1998, relatively rapidly for the treaty-related context, the government of Malaysia responded to these comments made by objecting states and proposed to partially withdraw the reservation while providing a clarification for remaining reservations.[81] The depositary of the ICEDAW, for some reason, did not regard this act of the Malaysian government as a partial withdrawal of reservations but as a modification comparable to a late formulation of a reservation. One of the explanations for this confusion could be the details provided by Malaysia on some of the pre-existing reservations. This wrong qualification of the Malaysian proposal led the depositary to ask other states whether they had any objections to the deposit of the Malaysian modified reservation or to the procedure envisaged by the depositary and to communicate any objections by 20 July 1998. The depositary also specified that Malaysia's intended withdrawal would be effective only if no objection was received by this date.[82] On 20 July 1998, France submitted the following reaction:

> France considers that the reservation made by Malaysia, as expressed in the partial withdrawal and modifications made by Malaysia on 6 February 1998, is incompatible with the object and purpose of the Convention. France therefore objects to the [reservation]. This objection shall not otherwise affect the entry into force of the Convention between France and Malaysia. Consequently, the

article 11, Malaysia interprets the provisions of this article as a reference to the prohibition of discrimination on the basis of equality between men and women only'. Multilateral Treaties (n 58) 290–91.

[80] Finland, Germany, Netherlands, Norway and Sweden formulated objections within 12 months: UN Multilateral Treaties (2009) (n 58) 312, 317, 323. Denmark submitted a communication after the expiration of the 12-month period: ibid 341, note 29.

[81] The government declared that it withdrew its reservation in respect of Arts 2(f), 9(1), 16(b), 16(d), 16(e), and 16(h). It also provided explanations on its remaining reservations. With respect to Article 5(a) of the Convention, the government of Malaysia declared that the provision was subject to the Syariah law on the division of inherited property. With respect to Art 7(b) of the Convention, the government of Malaysia declared that the application of said Art 7(b) would not affect appointment to certain public offices, such as the Mufti Syariah Court Judges, and the Imam which was in accordance with the provisions of the Islamic Shariah law. With respect to Art 9, para 2 of the Convention, the government of Malaysia declared that its reservation would be reviewed if the government amended the relevant law. With respect to Art 16.1 (a) and para 2, the government of Malaysia declared that under the Syariah law and the laws of Malaysia, the age limit for marriage for women was 16, and for men, was 18. See UN Multilateral Treaties (2009) (n 58) 341, note 35.

[82] ibid.

modification in question is not accepted, the Government of France having objected thereto.[83]

As a consequence, confusion arose. For quite a long period of time, the depositary, Malaysia, and the ICEDAW Committee could not determine what was the situation with regard to Malaysia's reservations.[84] The most adverse impact of this situation was the virtual retreat of Malaysia from the ICEDAW for about eight years. Malaysia resumed its active participation in the ICEDAW by submitting its initial report only in 2006, once consensus was reached and reflected in the UN documents that the withdrawal did take place.

The reaction of France should be compared to the reaction of the Netherlands to the very same proposed withdrawal by Malaysia. The Netherlands has a very consistent and regular record of objections to reservations based on Islam. It objected to almost all reservations invoking Islam, contrary to France, which did so only on a few occasions. Despite this regularity and respect for the 12-month period, when the Netherlands reacted to the proposed withdrawal of Malaysia, it submitted its reaction was on 21 July 1998, one day after the expiry of the time limit prescribed by the depositary.[85] It is hardly possible that this is just a coincidence. Contrary to France, which has very limited experience in objecting to the reservations based on Islam and in conducting reservations dialogue, the government of the Netherlands is very skilful in this field. The reaction was comprised of a welcoming of the government's efforts and expressed the belief in Malaysia's respect of the reserved articles.[86]

[83] ibid 342, note 35. The last sentence of the French statement no longer appears in the text of the official printed collection of multilateral treaties since the acceptance of Malaysia's partial withdrawal was decided. However, this last sentence appears in the version published on the website (see above n 58).

[84] The confusion can be illustrated by the following. In the CEDAW official document 'Declarations, reservations, objections and notifications of withdrawal of reservations relating to the CEDAW', its Annex I contains a comprehensive table of states parties that maintain their reservations. This table has, among others, two separate columns: one for reservations made and another for reservations withdrawn. This document in its 2000 edition contains no information on reservations withdrawn by Malaysia: see Declarations, reservations, objections and notifications of withdrawal of reservations relating to the CEDAW, 20 July 2000, CEDAW/SP/2000/2. The corresponding space in the column 'withdrawn' is empty (see ibid 93). In the 2002 edition (Declarations, reservations, objections and notifications of withdrawal of reservations relating to the CEDAW, 26 July 2002, CEDAW/SP/2002/2), the situation is different. All the reservations intended by Malaysia for withdrawal are indicated as withdrawn (see ibid 77). In 2004 (CEDAW/SP/2004/2), surprisingly, only one reservation appears as withdrawn; namely, that to Art 2(f) (see ibid 28). In the document prepared in 2006 (CEDAW/SP/2006/2) all the reservations intended by Malaysia for withdrawal are again indicated as withdrawn (see ibid 51).

[85] UN Multilateral Treaties (2009) (n 58) 342, note 35.

[86] The text of the reaction is reproduced above (n 71) and in the accompanying text.

While the reaction of France perfectly fits into the Vienna Convention regime and ensures that the Vienna Convention regime's consequences are produced, it does nothing but impede positive developments in the field of human rights. The reaction of the Netherlands is less straightforward. It is so careful that it does not even qualify the remaining reservations as incompatible with the object and purpose of the ICEDAW, although this idea is implied in its declaration that 'it assumes that Malaysia will ensure implementation of the rights enshrined in the above articles'. However, it engages in a dialogical conversation, provides space for the expression of views by the reserving state, and is respectful of the culture and efforts of this reserving state. The very similar open, respectful, and dialogical attitude of the majority of states participating in the reservations dialogue allowed for withdrawal of many problematic reservations and thus improvement of the situation of women. The important aspect of this process for our purposes is that this withdrawal, and thus the change in the attitude of reserving states, occurs from inside their own culture and religion. As a result, they accept the newly negotiated rights as reflecting also their own values and adhere to them sincerely. This fact is very important for the success of the future of human rights as international constitutional rights and as a part of the substantive international rule of law.

In a public discussion, if a participant makes an apparent effort to improve his or her compliance with the mainstream vision, responses similar to that made by France will only offend this participant. The reaction of the offended participant will be stubbornness and refusal to continue negotiation, as happened with Malaysia. The Netherlands' reaction produces the contrary effect. Conducted in a public discussion, it even pushes the participant to continue its efforts by presenting it as a member of the human rights complying group.

Finally, some observations on certainty and predictability are required to clarify the nature of the international rule of law as shaped by the domestic experiences and values. First, since with regard to its human rights component, the international rule of law has only procedural significance, certainty and predictability are not as central to its successful operation as they would be for a substantive rule of law. However, since international human rights standards are important components of negotiation, which takes place between the domestic and the international rule of law, some level of certainty and predictability would be expected by all participants. In this regard, it should be recalled that domestic constitutional laws are also often formulated in very general terms. Interpretation and understanding of these terms evolves and changes over time without complaints about lack of certainty and predictability. All participants of this constant negotiative process taking place within the procedural international rule of law are able to know at all times how to adapt and model their behaviour so as not to infringe upon the existing rules: states submit reports and adopt legislation; committees examine these reports and give advice to states, but also issue decisions on complaints submitted by individuals.

VI. CONCLUSIONS

This chapter started with the thesis that substantive human rights guarantees form an integral part of any rule of law worthy of its name. I also pointed out that the understanding of the place of human rights within the international rule of law is insufficient and unclear, especially if we consider the uneasy relationship between internationally formulated human rights standards and their domestic implementation. I proposed to shed more light on this issue by reflecting on the relationship between the international and the domestic rule of law within the context of the reservations dialogue.

The reservations dialogue, which is born out of uncertainties of the reservations regime as codified in the Vienna Convention, provided space and opportunities for interesting developments that reinforce the legitimacy of the international rule of law through negotiative practices involving the domestic rule of law of several states. Paradoxically, the very uncertainties which may be understood by some as contradictory to the rule of law in part facilitate the dialogue, which allows constant negotiation about the content of human rights obligations and more broadly, the substance of the international rule of law.

The examples of states' engagements in the reservation dialogue analysed above demonstrate the readiness of states to use the space provided by international law (in this case, the context of reservations to treaties) to engage in negotiations of the most complex but also the most important issues around the relationship between universal human rights and their domestic interpretation, the domestic and the international rule of law, universality, and diversity. The practices analysed also demonstrate an urgent need for broadening our view of the reservations dialogue beyond the confines of the Vienna Convention regime. In order to give full recognition to the negotiative processes taking place within the framework of the reservations dialogue, we need to recognise the value not only of legal effects of various reactions, but also their political, ethical, and interactive effects. We also need to realise the importance of the role played by actors not envisaged by the Vienna Convention regime, especially by treaty-monitoring bodies. I do not argue for the creation of new rules or regimes. It is more important to fully understand these dynamics, acknowledge their significance and various roles played, and be able to create conditions favourable to these valuable constructive engagements.

The above analysis of the reservations dialogue illuminates the following aspect of the interface between the domestic and the international rule of law. At this stage of the development of the international rule of law, it is difficult to speak about substance of the rule of law: the contours and content of human rights that are part of the international rule of law are quite obscure. However, we can clearly identify important negotiative or dialogical aspects of this relationship. While the domestic rule of law requires today an input from the international law (at least its human rights component) the international rule of law is also shaped by the constant contribution of the national legal orders. At this stage of development of the international rule of law it functions rather as an arena, a relatively neutral and open space where substantive values can be negotiated and renegotiated. This ability of the international law to create and sustain this space is the most valuable contribution of the international rule of law which also sustains its legitimacy. It should also be observed that without this input from the domestic rule of law experience, no international rule of law, even as a procedural mechanism, would arise. Theoretically, the conundrum which emerges is the fact that the arena where substantive rule of law values are negotiated and then absorbed by various domestic versions of the rule of law does not seem to have itself any substantive values except those linked to the regulation of interactions taking place within it. Paradoxically, while today's understanding of the domestic rule of law seems to suggest that it must comply with international human rights standards, there are no such fixed standards. These standards emerge only though a constant and on-going negotiation within the space provided by the international rule of law. The circular negotiative process which involves mutual influence and interaction between various domestic rules of law and the international rule of law is the only substance we can identify today within the international rule of law.

Perhaps the time will come when we will be able to speak of the international rule of law in a substantive sense; but we should be aware of the aspirational nature of any such substantive definition. Today, the ability of the international rule of law to provide and keep this open negotiative space is more important than the substantive values of the international rule of law themselves. And if we agree that international law should not mutate into a super-state, then this international rule of law will always remain something qualitatively different from the domestic rule of law and its emphasis on a series of defined standards.

13

Universality, Diversity, and Legal Certainty: Cultural Diversity in the Dialogue Between the CEDAW and States Parties

YVONNE DONDERS AND VINCENT VLEUGEL

I. INTRODUCTION

IT IS BROADLY accepted that the universal value and application of international human rights norms does not imply a uniform implementation of these rights, thereby leaving room for local and culture specific implementation at the national level. The question remains, however, what the precise scope of that room is or should be. A common criticism of allowing for cultural diversity in the implementation of international human rights law is that it leads to relativism and to a lack of sufficient clarity and predictability of the norms, undermining legal certainty as a constitutive element of the rule of law. It could, however, also be argued that a certain amount of flexibility allowing for cultural diversity is inherent in the international legal human rights system and is not detrimental to legal certainty.

This chapter analyses the room for variation in implementation based on cultural differences, as well as the process of determining this room by states parties and the treaty-monitoring bodies. It analyses the dialogue as regards the elaboration of the normative content of the provisions, and the process of the dialogue itself. Both dimensions of content and process are linked to the principle of legal certainty.

States interpret and implement international human rights treaties in a way that fits their culture, history, and local settings. International monitoring bodies, including UN treaty bodies, are set up to supervise the implementation of these treaties, including determining whether or not states comply with their obligations. Treaty bodies have various mechanisms at their disposal to carry out this task whereby states are involved to a greater or lesser extent. The periodic state reporting procedure, for instance, includes a dialogue with the states parties before the adoption of Concluding Observations by the Committees. The individual communications procedure involves states as party to the case on which the Committees express their 'Views' or Opinions.

This chapter focuses on the Committee on the Elimination of All Forms of Discrimination against Women (CEDAW) and the states parties to the International Convention on the Elimination of All Forms of Discrimination against Women (ICEDAW). The ICEDAW was selected because it is one of the most ratified human rights treaties, while at the same time containing provisions, for instance on equality between men and women in family matters, that have strong cultural connotations. Divergent views on some of the principal matters in the ICEDAW are also reflected in the large number of reservations to this treaty.

Aiming to clarify the implications of the interaction between states and the CEDAW for the development of the international rule of law, the following issues are addressed below: to what extent and how does the dialogue between the CEDAW and states parties enable states to reiterate, revisit, or be challenged on the value of particular cultural norms and practices in relation to universal human rights? How does this dialogue relate to the development of consensus and certainty over the meaning of these rights? How does the interaction between states parties and the CEDAW take place and to what extent can it truly be spoken of as a dialogue? How does this process contribute to the possible conjuncture between legal certainty and (cultural) flexibility?

First, we introduce the concepts of cultural diversity and legal certainty (section II). Then we provide an overview of the substantive issues of cultural diversity that come to the fore in the implementation of the ICEDAW (section III). We then analyse how these issues generate a dialogue in the state reporting procedure and the individual complaints procedure of the CEDAW, and how such a dialogue affects the meaning of conventional rights and the room for the culture-specific implementation (section IV). We end with concluding remarks on the role of dialogue in mediating cultural diversity and legal certainty (section V).

II. TWO CONCEPTUAL ISSUES ON CULTURAL DIVERSITY IN INTERNATIONAL HUMAN RIGHTS LAW

A. Universality and Cultural Diversity

Cultural diversity is defined in Article 2 of the UNESCO Convention on the Protection and Promotion of the Diversity of Cultural Expressions as 'the manifold ways in which the cultures of groups and societies find expression. These expressions are passed on within and among groups and societies'.[1] In this chapter, 'cultural diversity' denotes the factual situation of cultural differences existing between and within states, whereby the term 'cultural' can refer to many things, including ethnicity, history, language, religion, customs, and so forth.[2] Cultural diversity can operate at different levels: *between* states, regions, communities, and individuals, but also *within* states, regions, and communities.

Human rights and cultural diversity have been discussed extensively in the context of universalism and cultural relativism.[3] In an attempt to reconcile universalism and cultural relativism, the predominant view now suggests that respect for cultural diversity can very well be consistent with the notion of the universality of human rights.[4] Cultural relativism and universality do not have to mutually exclude each other if the former is understood as respect for cultural diversity as opposed to a challenge to the legitimacy of international human rights norms. The dichotomy can be overcome, for instance, by making a distinction between the universality of the subjects to whom international human rights apply (beneficiaries) and the universality of the normative content of the rights.

The idea that human rights should be universally enjoyed—by all persons on the basis of equality—is not controversial. In general, the universality of the subjects of human rights is widely accepted, and international human rights instruments clearly endorse this approach. The Universal Declaration of Human Rights (UDHR)[5] as well as international human rights treaties speak of 'everyone' or 'all persons', affirming that *all* human beings have these rights and freedoms, no matter where they were born or to which community they belong.

[1] Convention on the Protection and Promotion of the Diversity of Cultural Expressions, adopted by the General Conference of UNESCO on 20 Oct 2005, entry into force on 18 March 2007.

[2] UNESCO uses the following definition of 'culture': 'the set of distinctive spiritual, material, intellectual and emotional features of society or a social group, and that it encompasses, in addition to art and literature, lifestyles, ways of living together, value systems, traditions and beliefs', Universal Declaration on Cultural Diversity, 2001.

[3] 'Statement on Human Rights' (1947) 49 *American Anthropologist* 539, 542, submitted to the UN Human Rights Commission drafting the Universal Declaration of Human Rights. On universalism and cultural relativism, see *inter alia*, Jack Donnelly, *Universal Human Rights in Theory and Practice* (Ithaca, Cornell University Press, 1989) 107–60; Douglas Lee Donoho, 'Relativism versus Universalism in Human Rights: The Search for Meaningful Standards' (1991) 27 *Stanford Journal of International Law* 345, 345–91; Fernand de Varennes, 'The Fallacies in the Universalism Versus Cultural Relativism Debate in Human Rights Law' (2006) 7 *Asia-Pacific Journal on Human Rights and the Law* 67, 67–84; Eibe Riedel, 'Universality of Human Rights and Cultural Pluralism' in C Starck (ed), *Constitutionalism, Universalism and Democracy: A Comparative Analysis: The German Contributions to the Fifth World Congress of the International Association of Constitutional Law* (Baden-Baden, Nomos, 1999) 25–52; Ann-Belinda S Preis, 'Human Rights as Cultural Practice: An Anthropological Critique' (1996) 18 *Human Rights Quarterly* 286, 286–315.

[4] See ch 10 (Legg) of this volume.

[5] 'Universal Declaration of Human Rights' UN GA Res 217A (III) (10 Dec 1948).

The universality of the normative *content* of human rights at the level of *specific national implementation* is, however, a different matter. It is increasingly agreed that the universal value and application of human rights does not necessarily imply the *uniform implementation* of these rights. In other words, while human rights apply universally to everyone on the basis of their human dignity, the implementation of these rights does not have to be uniform.[6] The UDHR, for instance, was meant to be a common standard of achievement without fully uniform practices.[7] This process has been given various names: the 'universalisation of human rights',[8] the 'relative universality of human rights',[9] or 'inclusive universality'.[10] In other words, universal human rights do not have to be implemented in a uniform way, thereby leaving room for variation at the national level.

B. Legal Certainty

Legal certainty is often considered as one of the central elements of the rule of law, which is mainly developed at the national level.[11] Legal

[6] The European Court of Human Rights has adopted this approach by stating that, while the purpose of the European Convention on Human Rights was to lay down international standards, 'this does not mean that absolute uniformity is required'. See *Sunday Times v United Kingdom* App no 13166/87 (ECtHR, 26 Nov 1991) [61].

[7] Mary Ann Glendon, 'The Rule of Law in the Universal Declaration of Human Rights' (2004) 2 *Northwestern University Journal of International Human Rights* 1, 15.

[8] Advisory Council on International Affairs, *Universality of Human Rights. Principles, Practice and Prospects*, Advice no 63 (The Hague, Nov 2008) 19.

[9] Jack Donnelly, 'The Relative Universality of Human Rights' (2007) 29 *Human Rights Quarterly* 281, 281, 300. Donnelly argues that 'universal human rights, properly understood, leave considerable space for national, regional, cultural particularity and other forms of diversity and relativity'.

[10] Eva Brems, 'Reconciling Universality and Diversity in International Human Rights: A Theoretical and Methodological Framework and Its Application in the Context of Islam' (2004) 5 *Human Rights Review* 5, 11–12; Eva Brems, 'Reconciling Universality and Diversity in International Human Rights Law' in A Sajó (ed), *Human Rights with Modesty: the Problem of Universalism* (Leiden; Boston, M Nijhoff Publishers, 2004) 213, 223–25. Other authors agree that the international human rights system should be or is flexible enough to integrate cultural differences: Niels Petersen, 'International Law, Cultural Diversity, and Democratic Rule: Beyond the Divide Between Universalism and Relativism' (2011) 1 *Asian Journal of International Law* 149, 149–50; David Kinley, 'Bendable Rules: The Development Implications of Human Rights Pluralism' in BZ Tamanaha, CM Sage and MJV Woolcock (eds), *Legal Pluralism and Development: Scholars and Practitioners in Dialogue* (Cambridge; New York, Cambridge University Press, 2012) 50, 50–65. Other authors, however, also emphasise the need for a flexible and dynamic approach of cultures; see Preis, 'Human Rights as Cultural Practice' (n 3) 296–97; Brems, 'Reconciling Universality and Diversity in International Human Rights Law' (n 10) 226–27.

[11] Jeremy Waldron, 'The Rule of International Law' (2006) 30 *Harvard Journal of Law and Public Policy* 15, 17; Jeremy Waldron, 'Are Sovereigns Entitled to the Benefit of the International Rule of Law?' (2011) 22 *European Journal of International Law* 315, 316–17; James R Maxeiner, 'Some Realism about Legal Certainty in the Globalization of the Rule of Law' (2008) 31 *Houston Journal of International Law* 27, 28; Ofer Raban, 'The Fallacy of Legal Certainty: Why Vague Legal Standards May Be Better for Capitalism and Liberalism' (2010) 19

certainty serves to provide individuals with a predictable environment, which guides them in complying with the law and protects them from arbitrary government action by controlling government power to make and apply the law. Legal certainty concerns how the law is made, how it is interpreted, and how it is applied.[12] According to the European Court of Human Rights, legal certainty, in particular the aspect of foreseeability, 'requires that all law be sufficiently precise to allow the person—if need be, with appropriate advice—to foresee, to a degree that is reasonable in the circumstances, the consequences which a given action may entail'.[13] Consequently, laws and decisions must be made public; they must be definite and clear; and the retroactivity of laws and decisions must be strictly limited.[14]

To what extent can the legal certainty principle be transposed to the international level as part of an international rule of law? The precise scope, meaning, and implications of the concept of the rule of law at the international level remain debated.[15] In this chapter, the concept of the rule of law at international level refers to the so-called rule of law 'internationalised', meaning the externalisation and application of rule of law values within the international legal order.[16] The UN also adheres to this meaning of the international rule of law, whereby the principles of the rule of law provide a regulatory framework for international institutions, international normativity, and international adjudication.[17]

Boston University Public interest Law Journal 175, 177–78; Report of the Secretary-General, 'The Rule of Law and Transitional Justice in Conflict and Post-conflict Societies' UN Doc S/2004/616 (23 Aug 2004) para 6. Also, G8 Foreign Ministers Declaration on the Rule of Law (2007) described the rule of law as including the principles of supremacy of law, equality before the law, accountability to the law, legal certainty, procedural and legal transparency, equal and open access to justice for all, irrespective of gender, race, religion, age, class, creed, or other status, avoidance of arbitrary application of the law, and eradication of corruption.

[12] Maxeiner, 'Some Realism about Legal Certainty' (n 11) 36, 38; Paul Heinrich Neuhaus, 'Legal Certainty versus Equity in the Conflict of Laws' (1963) 28 *Law and Contemporary Problems* 795, 802–03.

[13] *Korchuganova v Russia* App no 75039/01 (ECtHR, 8 June 2006) [47].

[14] Maxeiner (n 11) 32, 36, 38; Waldron, 'The Rule of International Law' (n 11) 17. Legal certainty is also often linked to criminal punishment, such as is laid down in Art 7 of the ECHR, including the prohibition of being convicted retroactively or increasing the penalty retroactively. A person can only be convicted for an act or omission which constituted a criminal offence under national or international law at the time when it was committed.

[15] See ch 1 (Kanetake) of this volume.

[16] This idea is taken from Stéphane Beaulac, 'Lost in Transition? Domestic Courts, International Law and Rule of Law "À la Carte"' in E Kristjánsdóttir, A Nollkaemper and C Ryngaert (eds), *International Law in Domestic Courts: Rule of Law Reform in Post-Conflict States* (Cambridge, Intersentia, 2012) 17, 20. Beaulac distinguishes this from the 'internationalisation' of the rule of law, which refers to the exportation of the rule of law at the national level, via the international plane, to other domestic levels, mainly in relation to conflict, post-conflict situations, and long-term development situations.

[17] Beaulac, ibid; Randall Peerenboom, Michael Zürn and André Nollkaemper, 'Conclusion: From Rule of Law Promotion to Rule of Law Dynamics' in M Zürn, A Nollkaemper and R Peerenboom (eds), *Rule of Law Dynamics: In an Era of International and Transnational*

Legal certainty as part of an international rule of law would imply that treaties and treaty provisions should be sufficiently clear and precise to be predictable and foreseeable. It seems that achieving legal certainty at the international level is more difficult than at the national level.[18] Since international human rights law is primarily formed by states that have different historical, political, and cultural backgrounds and interests, one may question how legal certainty is understood and materialised in the practice of international human rights law. Although applying the rule of law element of legal certainty at the international level should force states to create international human rights law in the clearest and most foreseeable way, it appears that international human rights treaties are, *par excellence*, characterised by the use of broad and vague language and open-ended concepts. Human rights treaties are the products of long negotiations and political compromise among a variety of states; a process that does not do well for clarity and unambiguous language. This vagueness may be problematic for legal certainty. At the same time, it could be argued that the subject matter—human rights—is so multidimensional and complex that it does not lend itself to being reduced to clear and unambiguous language.[19] Moreover, states may keep international human rights law deliberately vague, because it provides them with a framework with certain flexibility to implement and apply human rights at the national level.

Some have called predictability, including clarity and stability, of laws and adjudication 'formal' legal certainty, distinguishing it from 'substantive' legal certainty, which refers to the rational acceptability of laws and adjudication. Acceptability implies that decisions are justified, using arguments that are not only clear, but also persuasive.[20] This distinction draws on the fact that even if laws are sufficiently clear and predictable, fulfilling the criteria of formal legal certainty, their application in concrete situations cannot and perhaps should not be fully predictable. This situation highlights the importance of argumentation and justification by supervisory bodies in order to achieve rational acceptability; in other words, substantive legal certainty.[21] The context sensitivity, flexibility, and thereby possible unpredictability in the application and implementation of norms, as well as the importance of clear and consistent argumentation

Governance (Cambridge, Cambridge University Press, 2012) 305, 314–15; Simon Chesterman, 'An International Rule of Law?' (2008) 56 *American Journal of Comparative Law* 331, 341, 355–56.

[18] Waldron argues that because of the absence of an overarching sovereign at the international level, the rule of law principles, including legal certainty, are more difficult to realise. Waldron, 'Are Sovereigns Entitled to the Benefit of the International Rule of Law?' (n 11) 320.

[19] Raban, 'Fallacy of Legal Certainty' (n 11) 188, 191.

[20] Elina Paunio, 'Beyond Predictability—Reflections on legal Certainty and the Discourse Theory of Law in the EU Legal Order' (2009) 10 *German Law Journal* 1469, 1484–86. The author follows legal theorists such as Habermas, Aulius Aarnio and Alexander Peczenik in drawing this distinction.

[21] ibid 1473–75.

by international supervisory bodies are highly relevant for international human rights law.

International monitoring bodies[22] provide a procedural safeguard related to formal legal certainty and they play an important role in promoting substantive legal certainty; in other words, the acceptability of the outcome of the procedures, for instance, by providing clear and well-justified arguments.[23] This is all the more necessary in an international context, where language, concepts and principles may differ widely. Indeed, international law is not homogenous in terms of content and application.[24] Treaties often need to balance certainty and reliability against flexibility.[25] Treaty provisions should be, in principle, defined as clearly as possible, but flexibility is needed for the individual application of the treaty provisions. A certain amount of flexibility is not necessarily a weakness; it could also be a strength, because the 'application of the norm occasions, frames and facilitates a certain process of reflection and argumentation', which is an important process.[26]

With regard to UN human rights treaties, not only states but also treaty bodies play an important role in this balancing process. Treaty bodies supervise the application and implementation by states parties and thereby play a crucial role in the interpretation of the scope, content, and application of treaty norms. The outcome of this process in terms of determining the scope and content of international norms, as well as the process itself, could be an important element in creating or improving legal certainty.

III. CULTURAL DIVERSITY IN THE IMPLEMENTATION OF THE ICEDAW

The aforementioned process of balancing between cultural diversity and legal certainty comes to the fore in the implementation of the ICEDAW. This comes as no surprise, because gender-based differentiation is often justified with religious, cultural, and historical arguments.[27] This section

[22] We use the term 'monitoring' or 'supervision', since the procedures of the treaty bodies are quasi-judicial and cannot be truly called 'adjudication'.

[23] Paunio, 'Beyond Predictability' (n 20) 1475–76.

[24] Stephan calls the assumption that international law is homogenous the 'homogeneity fallacy'. Paul B Stephan, 'Rethinking the International Rule of Law: The Homogeneity Fallacy and International Law's Threat to Itself' (2012) 4 *Jerusalem Review of Legal Studies* 19, 19–41.

[25] See Joseph Raz, 'Legal Principles and the Limits of Law' (1972) 81 *Yale Law Journal* 823, 842. See also Waldron, 'Are Sovereigns Entitled to the Benefit of the International Rule of Law?' (n 11) 336.

[26] Waldron, 'Are Sovereigns Entitled to the Benefit of the International Rule of Law?' (n 11) 336; Neuhaus, 'Legal Certainty versus Equity in the Conflict of Laws' (n 12) 804.

[27] Christine Chinkin, 'Reservations and Objections to the Convention on the Elimination of All Forms of Discrimination Against Women' in JP Gardner (ed), *Human Rights as General*

focuses on the question how much room and flexibility the Committee leaves to states parties that interpret and apply the treaty provisions in conformity with their cultural background, and the question to what extent the Committee is consistent and clear in its approach towards the cultural diversity argument.

A. Cultural Diversity and Non-Discrimination

The core principle of all human rights treaties, and the ICEDAW in particular, is the obligation of states to ensure equal enjoyment of human rights and to prevent and put an end to all forms of discrimination. This may imply taking special measures to promote and protect inclusion and participation of *all* women, including those from ethnic, racial, and sexual minority groups. Discrimination against women often not only concerns their sex, but also their ethnic or cultural background. Women often suffer from what the Committee calls *intersectional discrimination*, *multiple forms of discrimination*, or *compounded discrimination*, and the state is called upon by the Committee to protect and promote the rights of these groups.[28]

The equality principle, however, also implies the right to be different. The ICEDAW also creates obligations of states to recognise the special situation of certain groups of women and to take special measures to sustain diversity. This follows from the recognition that respect for cultural differences can be fully in line with the principle of equality. Having equal rights is not the same as being treated equally. Indeed, equality and non-discrimination not only imply that equal situations should be treated equally, but also that unequal situations should be treated unequally. At the international level, it is understood that 'the enjoyment of rights and freedoms on an equal footing … does not mean identical treatment

Norms and a State's Right to Opt Out: Reservations and Objections to Human Rights Conventions (London, BIICL, 1997) 77; Eric Neumayer, 'Qualified Ratification: Explaining Reservations to International Human Rights Treaties' (2007) 36(2) *Journal of Legal Studies* 397, 404.

[28] The Committee's recommendations to states parties may vary from negative obligations ('respect the Bedouin population's right to their ancestral land and their traditional livelihood', Concluding Observations Israel) to positive obligations ('improve access to health services for all women and in particular for the most vulnerable groups of women, such as indigenous, Afro- and Asian-descendant women', Concluding Observations Panama). The recommendations of the Committee tend to be very general, such as its recommendation to 'address the disparities that disadvantaged women face', to 'intensify its efforts to eliminate discrimination against disadvantaged groups of women', to 'adopt proactive measures, including temporary special measures, to eliminate such discrimination', to 'implement effective measures to eliminate discrimination and violence against women belonging to religious minorities', to 'conduct regular and comprehensive studies on discrimination against disadvantaged groups of women', or to 'provide information on specific measures taken by the State party to ensure gender equality for women, who experience intersectional discrimination based on factors such as ethnicity, religion … and sexual orientation, in all areas covered under the Convention'.

in every instance'.[29] Consequently, not all difference in treatment constitutes discrimination, as long as the criteria for differentiation are reasonable and objective and serve a legitimate aim.[30] Difference in treatment may also involve affirmative or positive action to remedy historical injustices, social discrimination or to create diversity and proportional group representation.[31]

Culture may also function as an underlying cause of discrimination against women, or its practices may be considered discriminatory in themselves. Many discriminatory practices are grounded in custom and stereotyping. The ICEDAW combats both these (cultural) practices and the underlying (cultural) beliefs.[32] The Convention requires states parties to abandon the defence of such harmful custom and to promote new attitudes.[33] As the analysis below shows, the Committee actively supervises this requirement without leaving much room, if at all, for the cultural diversity argument.

B. Cultural Stereotypes, Attitudes, and Practices

The CEDAW has on many occasions expressed its concern about cultural or traditional stereotypes, attitudes, and practices that determine the roles and responsibilities of women and men in the family and society and that

[29] Human Rights Committee, 'General Comment No. 18, Non-Discrimination' (10 Nov 1989) para 8. The European Court of Human Rights has reaffirmed this in many cases, including the following cases: *Thlimmenos v Greece* App no 34369/97 (ECtHR, 6 April 2000) [44]; *DH and others v the Czech Republic* App no 57325/00 (ECtHR, 7 February 2006) [44].

[30] Legal doctrine generally distinguishes between differentiation, distinction, and discrimination. Differentiation is difference in treatment that is lawful; distinction is a neutral term which is used when it has not yet been determined whether difference in treatment is lawful or not; and discrimination is difference in treatment that is arbitrary and unlawful. Consequently, only treatment that results in discrimination is prohibited. See Marc Bossuyt, 'Prevention of Discrimination: The Concept and Practice of Affirmative Action' UN Doc E/CN 4/Sub 2/2002/21 (17 June 2002) para 91 at 20.

[31] See also International Convention on the Elimination of Racial Discrimination, 21 Dec 1965, 660 UNTS 195, Art 1(4): 'Special measures taken for the sole purpose of securing adequate advancement of certain racial or ethnic groups or individuals requiring such protection as may be necessary in order to ensure such groups or individuals equal enjoyment or exercise of human rights and fundamental freedoms shall not be deemed racial discrimination, provided, however, that such measures do not, as a consequence, lead to the maintenance of separate rights for different racial groups and that they shall not be continued after the objectives for which they were taken have been achieved'. The Human Rights Committee has further stated that the principle of equality under Art 26 of the International Covenant on Civil and Political Rights (ICCPR) may sometimes require states parties to take affirmative action to diminish or eliminate conditions which cause or help to perpetuate discrimination prohibited by the ICCPR. Human Rights Committee, 'General Comment No. 18, Non-Discrimination' (10 Nov 1989) para 10.

[32] Marsha A Freeman, Christine Chinkin and Beate Rudolf (eds), *The UN Convention on the Elimination of All Forms of Discrimination against Women: A Commentary* (Oxford, Oxford University Press, 2012) 156.

[33] ibid 161.

may pose obstacles to the enjoyment of the rights or cause violations of these rights. This concern is linked to Article 5(a) of the ICEDAW, which secures that

> States Parties shall take all appropriate measures … to modify the social and cultural patterns of conduct of men and women, with a view to achieving the elimination of prejudices and customary and all other practices which are based on the idea of the inferiority or the superiority of either of the sexes or on stereotyped roles for men and women.[34]

According to the CEDAW, cultural practices and beliefs under the scope of Article 5 may range from traditional harmful practices and beliefs—such as female genital mutilation, forced and early marriages, levirate, sororate, and polygamy (eg, in Côte d'Ivoire)[35]—to other forms of practices and beliefs, such as machismo culture (eg, in Nicaragua),[36] overemphasis on the traditional roles of women as mothers and spouses (eg, in Belarus),[37] segregation of the labour market and in educational choices (eg, in Brazil),[38] portraying immigrant and migrant women and men as being backward (eg, in The Netherlands),[39] and the stereotyping of women as sex objects and in traditional roles in the media (eg, in Italy).[40] In other words, Article 5 covers practices and beliefs in all possible cultures and contexts.

The Committee discusses the issue of cultural or traditional stereotypes, attitudes, and practices in relation to different topics. The Committee, for instance, critically considers *violence against women* as 'socially legitimized'[41] or being linked to 'the persistence of socio-cultural attitudes condoning such violence'.[42] Such violence may be underreported due to

[34] Convention on the Elimination of All Forms of Discrimination against Women, 18 December 1979, 1249 UNTS 13 Art 5(a).

[35] CEDAW, 'Concluding Observations of the Committee on the Elimination of Discrimination against Women: Cote d'Ivoire' CEDAW/C/CIV/CO/1-3 (8 Nov 2011) para 26.

[36] CEDAW, 'Concluding Observations of the Committee on the Elimination of Discrimination against Women: Nicaragua' A/56/38 (1 Jan 2001) para 294; although CEDAW no longer uses the word 'machismo'; see Summary Records Bolivia CEDAW/C/SR 811 (20 Feb 2008) para 55.

[37] CEDAW, 'Concluding Observations of the Committee on the Elimination of Discrimination against Women: Belarus' CEDAW/C/BLR/CO/7 (4 Feb 2011) para 17.

[38] CEDAW, 'Concluding Observations of the Committee on the Elimination of Discrimination against Women: Brazil' CEDAW/C/BRA/CO/7 (23 March 2012) para 27.

[39] CEDAW, 'Concluding Observations of the Committee on the Elimination of Discrimination against Women: The Netherlands' CEDAW/C/NLD/CO/5 (5 Feb 2010) para 24.

[40] CEDAW, 'Concluding Observations of the Committee on the Elimination of Discrimination against Women: Italy' CEDAW/C/ITA/CO/6 (26 July 2011) paras 24–25.

[41] See, eg, CEDAW, 'Concluding Observations of the Committee on the Elimination of Discrimination against Women: Uganda' CEDAW/C/UGA/CO/7 (22 Oct 2010) para 23; CEDAW, 'Concluding Observations of the Committee on the Elimination of Discrimination against Women: Turkmenistan' CEDAW/C/TKM/CO/3-4 (24 Oct 2012) para 22.

[42] See, eg, CEDAW, 'Concluding Observations of the Committee on the Elimination of Discrimination against Women: Italy' CEDAW/C/ITA/CO/6 (26 July 2011) para 26; CEDAW, 'Concluding Observations of the Committee on the Elimination of Discrimination against Women: Bulgaria' CEDAW/C/BGR/CO/4-7 (27 July 2012) para 25.

'the prevalence of discriminatory social and cultural norms'[43] or 'cultural taboos'.[44] In its General Recommendation on violence against women, the Committee also addresses its cultural dimensions, arguing that 'traditional attitudes by which women are regarded as subordinate to men or as having stereotyped roles perpetuate widespread practices involving violence or coercion, such as family violence and abuse, forced marriage, dowry deaths, acid attacks and female circumcision'.[45]

According to the CEDAW, socio-cultural factors may also prevent women from accessing *healthcare* services.[46] Women may face difficulties in accessing family planning services due to stigmatisation of abortion and contraception.[47] Sometimes women need the consent from their husband or a male guardian to undergo medical treatment.[48] Socio-cultural factors may form obstacles to access by women from minority groups to healthcare services,[49] or there may be discrimination against lesbian, bisexual, transgender, and intersex women in the provision of healthcare services.[50] In its General Recommendation on women and health, the Committee requests that states demonstrate 'that health legislation, plans and policies are based on … assessment of the health status and needs of women in that country and take into account any ethnic, regional or community variations or practices based on religion, tradition or culture'.[51]

The Committee further recognises the cultural dimension in *marriage and family relations*. The dissolution of marriage, inheritance, property rights, custody, and guardianship of children are often subject to customary

[43] See, eg, CEDAW, 'Concluding Observations of the Committee on the Elimination of Discrimination against Women: Greece' CEDAW/C/GRC/CO/7 (1 March 2013) para 20; CEDAW, 'Concluding Observations of the Committee on the Elimination of Discrimination against Women: Jamaica' CEDAW/C/JAM/CO/6–7 (27 July 2012) para 21.

[44] See, eg, CEDAW, 'Concluding Observations of the Committee on the Elimination of Discrimination against Women: Chad' CEDAW/C/TCD/CO/1–4 (21 Oct 2011) para 22.

[45] CEDAW, 'General Recommendation No. 19' UN Doc A/47/38 (1992) para 11.

[46] See, eg, CEDAW, 'Concluding Observations of the Committee on the Elimination of Discrimination against Women: Angola' CEDAW/C/AGO/CO/6 (27 March 2013) para 31; CEDAW, 'Concluding Observations of the Committee on the Elimination of Discrimination against Women: Togo' CEDAW/C/TGO/CO/6–7 (8 Nov 2012) para 34.

[47] See, eg, CEDAW, 'Concluding Observations of the Committee on the Elimination of Discrimination against Women: Hungary' CEDAW/C/HUN/CO/7–8 (25 March 2013) para 30.

[48] See, eg, CEDAW, 'Concluding Observations of the Committee on the Elimination of Discrimination against Women: Indonesia' CEDAW/C/IDN/CO/6–7 (7 Aug 2012) para 41; CEDAW, 'Concluding Observations of the Committee on the Elimination of Discrimination against Women: Kuwait' CEDAW/C/KWT/CO/3–4 (8 Nov 2011) para 42.

[49] See, eg, CEDAW, 'Concluding Observations of the Committee on the Elimination of Discrimination against Women: Congo' CEDAW/C/COG/CO/6 (22 March 2012) para 35; CEDAW, 'Concluding Observations of the Committee on the Elimination of Discrimination against Women: Norway' CEDAW/C/NOR/CO/8 (22 March 2012) para 31.

[50] See, eg, CEDAW, 'Concluding Observations of the Committee on the Elimination of Discrimination against Women: Norway' CEDAW/C/NOR/CO/8 (22 March 2012) para 33.

[51] CEDAW, 'General Recommendation No. 24' UN Doc A/54/38/Rev 1 (1999) para 9.

and religious laws and practices. Acknowledging that there are various forms and concepts of the family between and within states, the Committee submits that 'whatever the legal system, religion, custom or tradition within the country, the treatment of women in the family both at law and in private must accord with the principles of equality and justice for all people'.[52] The Committee further notes the potential difference between laws and practice: 'while most countries report that national constitutions and laws comply with the Convention, custom, tradition and failure to enforce these laws in reality contravene the Convention'.[53] The Committee often expresses concerns about the prevalence of traditional stereotypes of women in relation to their role in the family,[54] or discriminatory legal provisions and negative customary practices related to marriage and family relations.[55] In its General Recommendation on equality in marriage and family relations, the Committee, for instance, 'notes with concern that some states parties, whose constitutions guarantee equal rights, permit polygamous marriage in accordance with personal or customary law'.[56] As regards the division of marital property, the Committee argues that

> any discrimination in the division of property that rests on the premise that the man alone is responsible for the support of the women and children of his family and that he can and will honourably discharge this responsibility is clearly unrealistic.[57]

With regard to *participation in political and public life*, the Committee expressed concerns that systematic barriers, such as negative cultural attitudes, impede women's equal participation in political life.[58] In its General Recommendation on political and public life, the Committee considers that 'in all nations, the most significant factors inhibiting women's ability to participate in public life have been the cultural framework of values and religious beliefs', and that 'in all nations, cultural traditions and religious beliefs have played a part in confining women to the private spheres of activity and excluding them from active participation in public

[52] ibid para 13.
[53] ibid para 15.
[54] See, eg, CEDAW, 'Concluding Observations of the Committee on the Elimination of Discrimination against Women: Jamaica' CEDAW/C/JAM/CO/6-7 (7 Aug 2012) para 37.
[55] See, eg, CEDAW, 'Concluding Observations of the Committee on the Elimination of Discrimination against Women: Congo' CEDAW/C/COG/CO/6 (22 March 2012) para 43.
[56] CEDAW, 'General Recommendation No. 21: Equality in Marriage and Family Relations' (1994) para 14.
[57] ibid para 28.
[58] See, eg, CEDAW, 'Concluding Observations of the Committee on the Elimination of Discrimination against Women: Turkmenistan' CEDAW/C/TKM/CO/3-4 (9 Nov 2012) para 26; CEDAW, 'Concluding Observations of the Committee on the Elimination of Discrimination against Women: Greece' CEDAW/C/GRC/CO/7 (25 March 2013) para 24; CEDAW, 'Concluding Observations of the Committee on the Elimination of Discrimination against Women: Zimbabwe' CEDAW/C/ZWE/CO/2-5 (22 March 2012) para 27.

life'.[59] When reporting, states parties are requested to provide details of any restrictions to those rights, 'whether arising from legal provisions or from traditional, religious or cultural practices'.[60]

Access to *education* may also be affected by cultural considerations, according to the Committee. Harmful practices, such as early and forced marriages, are identified as barriers to girls' education,[61] as are negative cultural attitudes and excessive domestic duties.[62] The Committee also regularly expresses concerns regarding stereotyped educational choices[63] and persistent inequalities in the access to education for girls on the basis of race, ethnicity, and socio-economic background.[64] According to the Committee, women's subordinate roles[65] and child-rearing responsibilities[66] within the family contribute to their lower level of education. At the same time, education is often discussed by the Committee as a vehicle or means to change those very same negative cultural practices and attitudes. The Committee, for instance, regularly recommends that states adopt education and information programmes which will help eliminate prejudices and change attitudes concerning the roles and statuses of men and women.[67]

These examples show that, at least when it comes to the implementation of the ICEDAW, culture is not the flexibility tool that it is sometimes held out to be. The Committee is very critical of cultural arguments that undermine the working of the treaty, and broadly prefers universality over flexibility. It should, however, be noted that the analysis above is based on issues that were raised by the Committee. A full insight into the possible flexibility left to states parties could only be gained by also exploring the issues *not* raised by the Committee. For example, why does the Committee decide to express its concerns on discrimination of lesbian, bisexual,

[59] CEDAW, 'General Recommendation No. 23: Political and Public Life' UN Doc A/52/38 (1997) para 10.

[60] ibid para 48(b).

[61] See, eg, CEDAW, 'Concluding Observations of the Committee on the Elimination of Discrimination against Women: Togo' CEDAW/C/TGO/CO/6–7 (8 Nov 2012) para 30; 'Concluding Observations of the Committee on the Elimination of Discrimination against Women: Zimbabwe' CEDAW/C/ZWE/CO/2–5 (22 March 2012) para 29.

[62] See, eg, CEDAW, 'Concluding Observations of the Committee on the Elimination of Discrimination against Women: Turkmenistan' CEDAW/C/TKM/CO/3–4 (9 Nov 2012) para 31.

[63] See, eg, CEDAW, 'Concluding Observations of the Committee on the Elimination of Discrimination against Women: Turkey' CEDAW/C/TUR/CO/6 (16 Aug 2010) para 30.

[64] See, eg, CEDAW, 'Concluding Observations of the Committee on the Elimination of Discrimination against Women: Brazil' CEDAW/C/BRA/CO/7 (22 March 2012) para 24.

[65] CEDAW, 'General Recommendation No. 19: Violence against Women' (1992) para 11.

[66] CEDAW, 'General Recommendation No. 21: Equality in Marriage and Family Relations' UN Doc A/49/38 (1994) para 21.

[67] CEDAW, 'General Recommendation No. 3: Education and Public Information Campaigns' UN Doc A/42/38 (1987); CEDAW, 'General Recommendation No. 19: Violence against Women' (1992) para 24(t)(ii).

transgender, and intersex women in Norway,[68] while it is silent on the issue in Uganda,[69] a country where, at the time, an 'anti-homosexuality bill' was pending,[70] with life imprisonment as the minimum punishment for anyone convicted of having gay sex.[71] Is this a sign of cultural sensitivity? Or a sign of double standards? Or are there too many other, more pressing issues that need to be raised? In other words, determining the room for cultural diversity is a very complex process involving many factors. While it is important to keep this complexity in mind, the aforementioned examples lead us to conclude that the Committee leaves states parties little to no room for cultural variation in the implementation of the Convention.

IV. THE PROCESSES OF DIALOGUE BETWEEN THE COMMITTEE AND STATES PARTIES

Having established that the Committee is very critical and restrictive when it comes to accepting cultural variation in the implementation of the Convention, the question arises to what extent states parties still engage in a dialogue with the Committee. This section analyses the processes of dialogue between the Committee and states parties on issues of cultural diversity. It considers procedures through which the Committee and states interact, the extent to which states accept the critical and restrictive stance of the Committee, and whether and how states use the opportunity to explain their views on specific cultural norms and practices. This also leads us to the question of how 'constructive' the dialogue is in practice.

A. Fora for Interaction Between the Committee and States Parties

The Committee monitors compliance by states with their obligations under the ICEDAW. The procedures at its disposal—the periodic state reporting procedure and the individual communications procedure—have different levels of state involvement and thereby of interaction or dialogue between

[68] See, eg, CEDAW, 'Concluding Observations of the Committee on the Elimination of Discrimination against Women: Norway' CEDAW/C/NOR/CO/8 (22 March 2012) para 33.

[69] See, eg, CEDAW, 'Concluding Observations of the Committee on the Elimination of Discrimination against Women: Uganda' CEDAW/C/UGA/CO/7 (4 Nov 2010).

[70] The Bill can be read in full, available at: www.scribd.com/doc/208846690/The-Anti-Homosexuality-Bill-2009-in-full.

[71] Xan Rice, 'Uganda considers death sentence for gay sex in bill before parliament' (*The Guardian*, 29 Nov 2009) available at: www.theguardian.com/world/2009/nov/29/uganda-death-sentence-gay-sex; on 24 Feb 2014, a revised version of the law was signed by Ugandan President Museveni. See, eg, Faith Karimi and Nick Thompson, 'Uganda's President Museveni Signs Controversial Anti-Gay Bill into Law' (*CNN International Edition*, 25 Feb 2014) available at: http://edition.cnn.com/2014/02/24/world/africa/uganda-anti-gay-bill/.

the Committee and states. With regard to the state reporting procedure, *initial reports* should 'outline any distinctions, exclusions or restrictions made on the basis of sex and gender … imposed by law, practice or tradition, or in any other manner on women's enjoyment of each provision of the Convention'.[72] Subsequent *periodic reports* should contain information on the implementation of recommendations (Concluding Observations) to the previous report and explanations for the non-implementation or difficulties encountered as well as information on any remaining or emerging obstacles to the exercise and enjoyment by women of their human rights, and on measures envisaged to overcome these obstacles.[73]

A pre-session working group of the Committee then drafts a short *list of issues and questions*, indicating the main points it wants to discuss with the state. Then a 'constructive dialogue' takes place. The Committee takes two (open) meetings each of three hours for consideration of initial and periodic reports. Representatives of the state party may make introductory comments for a maximum of 30 minutes, followed by several rounds of questions and answers, until all articles have been covered.[74] The minutes of the meeting are laid down in an official document, called *Summary Records*. The dialogue leads to the adoption of *Concluding Observations* by the Committee, which include only issues and concerns raised during the constructive dialogue.[75] In other words, states are actively involved in this process and can take the opportunity to explain their views, even though the Concluding Observations are adopted by the Committee as an independent supervisor. The Concluding Observations are not shared in advance with the state party and only afterwards can be commented upon by the state party. At the same time, the observations are meant as recommendations or practical advice for improving implementation of treaty rights, and do not have legally binding force.[76] Even though the Committee strives 'to formulate detailed Concluding Observations, with concrete, achievable, but non-prescriptive recommendations',[77] in reality, the Concluding Observations generally concern broad recommendations about legislative and other measures states parties should take. Rather than making recommendations on an article-by-article basis, the

[72] Compilation of Guidelines on the Form and Content of Reports to be Submitted by States Parties to the International Human Rights Treaties, HRI/GEN/2/Rev 5 (29 May 2008) ch V, para D.3

[73] ibid ch V.

[74] ibid paras 11–12.

[75] ibid para 18.

[76] Daniel Moeckli, Sangeeta Shah and Sandesh Sivakumaran (eds), *International Human Rights Law* (Oxford, Oxford University Press, 2010) 407.

[77] Compilation of Guidelines on the Form and Content of Reports to be Submitted by States Parties to the International Human Rights Treaties, HRI/GEN/2/Rev 5 (29 May 2008) ch V, para 21.

Concluding Observations use subject headings, which are used flexibly.[78] No explicit reference is made to the articles of the Convention. The Concluding Observations consequently provide limited insight into the scope and normative content of specific Convention articles.

While the reporting procedure is compulsory for each state party, the individual communications procedure needs to be specifically accepted by states, via an Optional Protocol.[79] The cases are initiated and brought by individuals after national remedies are exhausted.[80] After a communication has been received, the Committee brings it confidentially to the attention of the state party, with a request to submit, within six months, a written reply concerning the admissibility of the communication and its merits.[81] The Committee then transmits to each party the submissions made by the other party and affords them an opportunity to comment.[82] The whole procedure is written and confidential; no oral hearings take place. The Committee finally presents its Views on the case, concluding whether or not a violation of the treaty provision has taken place.[83] Although a simple majority is sufficient,[84] Committees generally adopt their views by consensus. Occasionally, individual members of the Committee attach separate (and dissenting) opinions. In case of a violation, the Committee may suggest remedies or compensation to the state party. The Views are not legally binding.[85] The state party is involved in the communication procedure, but more as respondent and less as active participant, as with the reporting procedure.

After the Committee has adopted its Views, the state party is requested to submit, within six months, a written response including information on the action taken following the Committee's recommendations. One member of the Committee is appointed as rapporteur for follow-up on the Views. The Committee periodically decides whether further action is required and until the case is closed, it reports to the General Assembly that 'the dialogue is on-going'.[86] Although the meetings that rapporteurs

[78] Overview of the working methods of the Committee on the Elimination of Discrimination against Women in relation to the reporting process, CEDAW/C/2009/II/4, para 21.

[79] Optional Protocol to the Convention on the Elimination of All Forms of Discrimination against Women, 6 Oct 1999, 2131 UNTS 83.

[80] ibid Art 4.

[81] ibid Art 6.

[82] Rules of Procedure for the Optional Protocol to CEDAW, A/56/38, r 69(9).

[83] Optional Protocol to the Convention on the Elimination of All Forms of Discrimination against Women (n 79) Art 7.

[84] Rules of Procedure for the Optional Protocol to CEDAW, A/56/38, r 72(5).

[85] Moeckli, Shah and Sivakumaran (eds), *International Human Rights Law* (n 76) 412–13.

[86] CEDAW, Annual Report to GA, UN Doc A/64/38 (2009) at 111; Rules of Procedure of the CEDAW (UN Doc A/56/38 (SUPP), as amended by UN Doc A/62/38 (SUPP) ch V) r 73 on 'Follow-up to the views of the Committee'.

on follow-up have with states parties are considered as some form of continuing dialogue between the Committee and the state party, it should be noted that this dialogue takes place only *after* the View has been adopted. This means that the treaty norm interpretation (and thus the development of the general jurisprudence) has already been shaped.

The practice and experience of the Committee is laid down in General Recommendations, in which it comments on specific treaty provisions or elaborates on the relationship between the Convention and specific themes or issues.[87] States parties play a limited and more indirect role in the adoption of these Recommendations. They are drafted and adopted by consensus by the Committee, whereby states parties are invited to comment on the draft texts.[88]

B. State Reporting Procedure: Three Modes of (Non-)Engagement

In order to unveil the practice of dialogue between the Committee and states parties regarding the room for cultural diversity, we have analysed the state reporting procedure of 30 states which took place between January 2010 and July 2013, including state periodic reports, (replies to) lists of issues, and Concluding Observations. We selected the states on the basis of their geographic spread.[89] The analysis of the state reporting procedure is necessarily an intricate one, because states parties and the Committee categorise their reports differently.

Since June 2008, the Committee includes subject headings—such as *stereotypes and harmful practices*, *violence against women*, *health*, or *education*— in its Concluding Observations, which are to be used 'flexibly and as appropriate for the State party concerned'.[90] By contrast, states parties usually categorise their reports according to the provisions of the Convention. This makes it methodologically difficult to identify which part of the Committee's observations addresses which part of the state's report. For

[87] Report on the Working Methods of the Human Rights Treaty Bodies relating to the State Party Reporting Process, UN Doc HRI/MC/2005/4 (25 May 2005) 28, para 105.

[88] Nisuke Ando, 'General Comments/Recommendations' in R Wolfrum (ed), *The Max Planck Encyclopedia of Public International Law* (Oxford, Oxford University Press, 2008), online edn, available at: www.mpepil.com.

[89] Selection criteria: 6 countries from each of the 5 regions as identified by the UN: Africa Region; Americas Region; Asia Pacific Region; Europe, North America and Central Asia Region; Middle East and North Africa Region, available at: www.ohchr.org/EN/Countries/Pages/HumanRightsintheWorld.aspx.

[90] 'Overview of the working methods of the Committee on the Elimination of Discrimination against Women in relation to the reporting process', CEDAW/C/2009/II/4, para 21.

example, the subject of *violence against women* has been linked to Articles 2, 3, 5, 6, 10, 11, 12, 14, and 16 of the Convention.[91] At the same time, the practice of early marriage has not only been discussed under this subject, but also under *legislative framework*, *stereotypes and harmful practices*, *education*, *health*, and *marriage and family life*, linking it to many different articles of the Convention. It is not uncommon that one issue is discussed under different articles or subjects throughout one reporting cycle. For example, in the reporting procedure of Bangladesh, the Committee requested information about early marriages under *stereotypes and harmful traditional practices*[92] and *health*[93] in its list of issues and questions, while it addressed early marriages in its Concluding Observations under *education*[94] and *marriage and family relations*.[95] The Committee does this consciously, for reasons of flexibility, but it complicates the analysis of a dialogue on any one particular topic.

Among a wide range of issues on cultural diversity, we focused specifically on the practice of dialogue concerning Articles 5 (stereotyping and prejudice),[96] 12 (the right to health), and 16 (rights related to marriage and family relations) of the Convention. The most intensive discussion between the Committee and states parties took place on these rights, including on the (in)compatibility of certain (traditional) cultural practices and beliefs with the implementation of the Convention. Not coincidentally, these include provisions of the Convention with a large number of reservations by states.[97]

States responses to the Committee's interpretations of cultural diversity issues can broadly be categorised into three groups. First, states may *accept* the Committee's interpretations and recommendations (section i, below). Second, states may also *reject* the Committee's interpretations and recommendations, and put their own interpretation forward (section ii). The state justifies its actions in an attempt to convince the Committee. Finally, states may *ignore* their non-compliance and avoid a dialogue on the issue (section iii); namely, the state rejects the Committee's interpretations and recommendations, but does not (consider it necessary to) defend its actions or policies.

[91] CEDAW, 'General Recommendation No. 19: Violence against Women' (1992) paras 10–23.

[92] CEDAW, 'List of issues and questions: Bangladesh' CEDAW/C/BGD/Q/7 (6 Sept 2010) para 8.

[93] CEDAW, 'List of issues and questions: Bangladesh' CEDAW/C/BGD/Q/7 (6 Sept 2010) para 18.

[94] CEDAW, 'Concluding Observations of the Committee on the Elimination of Discrimination against Women: Bangladesh' CEDAW/C/BGD/CO/7 (21 March 2011) para 27.

[95] ibid paras 39–40.

[96] See (n 34) above.

[97] On reservations and cultural diversity, see further Yvonne Donders, 'Cultural Pluralism in International Human Rights Law: The Role of Reservations' in A Vrdoljak (ed), *The Cultural Dimension of Human Rights* (Oxford, Oxford University Press, 2013) 205.

i. Accepting the Committee's Interpretation and Recommendations

States parties may accommodate the Committee's critical remarks. For instance, when considering the combined fifth and sixth periodic report of Kenya (2007), the Committee commented on 'the persistence of adverse cultural norms, practices and traditions as well as patriarchal attitudes and deep-rooted stereotypes regarding the roles, responsibilities and identities of women and men in all spheres of life'.[98] It considered the cultural norms, practices, and traditions obstacles to implementation of the Convention, and requested that the state party 'view its cultures as dynamic aspects of the country's life and social fabric and as subject, therefore, to change'.[99] In response, in its seventh periodic report, Kenya conceded that

> one of the biggest challenges to women's equality with men on matters concerning marriage and the family is cultural construction of women's roles vis-à-vis that of men, cultural attitudes and belief about women and their traditional roles, which lead to women's subjugation and, in many cases, retrogressive cultural practices[100]

and submitted that measures were being taken for modification of social and cultural patterns of conduct.[101] In the subsequent Concluding Observations, the Committee, 'while noting some efforts made by the state party', reiterated its concerns.[102]

Likewise, in the dialogue with Bangladesh, the Committee expressed concern that 'strong stereotypical attitudes persist with respect to the roles and responsibilities of women in the family and society, negatively affecting women's enjoyment of their rights and impeding the full implementation of the Convention'.[103] Bangladesh responded to the Committee by observing that the country had been implementing 'programs that include awareness raising activities to change stereotype attitude and norms about the roles and responsibilities of women and men in the family and society'[104] and carried out 'activities as measures to address sex roles and stereotyping towards eliminating prejudices and biases'.[105] In the Concluding Observations, the Committee recognised Bangladesh's efforts to

[98] CEDAW, 'Concluding Observations of the Committee on the Elimination of Discrimination against Women: Kenya' CEDAW/C/KEN/CO/6 (15 Aug 2007) para 21.

[99] ibid para 22.

[100] CEDAW, 'Seventh periodic report of Kenya' CEDAW/C/KEN/7 (24 March 2010) para 265.

[101] ibid paras 74–96.

[102] CEDAW, 'Concluding Observations of the Committee on the Elimination of Discrimination against Women: Kenya' CEDAW/C/KEN/CO/7 (5 April 2011) para 17.

[103] CEDAW, 'Concluding Comments of the Committee on the Elimination of Discrimination against Women: Bangladesh' A/59/38 Part II (23 July 2004) para 246.

[104] CEDAW, 'Combined sixth and seventh periodic report of Bangladesh' CEDAW/C/BGD/6-7 (24 March 2010) para 110.

[105] ibid para 232.

promote changes in the stereotypical roles of women, albeit still expressing its remaining concern.[106]

In these situations where the state party agrees and accepts (or at least pays lip service to) the Committee's recommendations, the 'interaction' usually follows some general format of pre-established lines. The Committee's recommendations to the state party are quite broad and vague: the Committee 'urges' or 'calls upon' the state party to 'strengthen its efforts', or to 'accelerate efforts', or to 'put in place a comprehensive strategy' to modify or eliminate harmful practices and stereotypes that discriminate against women. The Committee does not specify these strategies, efforts, or measures; it merely stipulates what they should accomplish.

In several cases, the state party accepted the Committee's concerns, but argued that it faced obstacles or resistance in addressing these concerns. For example, in the dialogue with Indonesia, the Committee expressed concerns about the persistence of entrenched patriarchal attitudes and stereotypes about the roles and responsibilities of women and men in the family and society. Indonesia, although sharing these concerns, argued that 'values and cultural practices, especially when framed in a justification stemming from narrow religious interpretations, are difficult to address', and observed that a common understanding, also among policy-makers, is often difficult to achieve.[107] An example is the practice of female genital mutilation (FGM). The Committee was concerned about the incidence of FGM in Indonesia, the reported medicalisation of FGM, and the lack of legislation prohibiting or penalising it.[108] Indonesia replied that 'efforts to eradicate female circumcision constitute an uphill challenge as the custom is still practiced widely and reinforced by entrenched beliefs and religious interpretations',[109] while stressing that it 'continuously supports the efforts to combat violence against women in all forms, including FGM'.[110] In 2008, the influential Indonesian Ulema Council issued a fatwa to the effect that the abolition of female circumcision was against sharia provisions. In light of that development, the state party issued a new regulation providing a set of safeguards for medical personnel in performing female circumcision. The state stressed, however, that 'this regulation should not in any way be construed as encouraging or promoting the practice of

[106] CEDAW, 'Concluding Observations of the Committee on the Elimination of Discrimination against Women: Bangladesh' CEDAW/C/BGD/CO/7 (21 March 2011) para 17.

[107] CEDAW, 'Combined sixth and seventh periodic reports of the Republic of Indonesia' CEDAW/C/IDN/6–7 (7 Jan 2011) para 31.

[108] CEDAW, 'Concluding Observations of the Committee on the Elimination of Discrimination against Women: Indonesia' CEDAW/C/IDN/CO/5 (15 Aug 2007) para 20.

[109] CEDAW, 'Combined sixth and seventh periodic reports of the Republic of Indonesia' CEDAW/C/IDN/6–7 (7 Jan 2011) para 131.

[110] CEDAW, 'Responses to the list of issues and questions: Indonesia' CEDAW/C/IDN/Q/6-7/Add 1 (19 Jan 2012) para 35.

female circumcision'.[111] Indonesia justified its policy by referring to 'the dynamic of the implementation of rights and freedoms of its citizens, particularly with regards to the freedom to practice their religion and beliefs in a democratic society'.[112] Nevertheless, the Committee expressed its concern about the serious regression with regard to FGM, and, in particular, the state party's authorisation of certain medical practitioners to conduct it. It urged Indonesia to withdraw the regulation authorising female circumcision when performed by medical practitioners, to restore the ban on the practice of female circumcision, and to adopt robust legislation criminalizing the practice.[113]

ii. Justifying Different Interpretation and Implementation

States do not always respond to the Committee in an accommodating manner. The Committee may also be confronted with a state party rejecting its interpretations, while explaining and justifying its own interpretation of certain provisions.

In the dialogue with South Africa, for instance, the Committee was concerned about the continuing recognition of customary and religious laws,[114] and recommended that the state prepare a uniform family code in conformity with the Convention, with the aim of abolishing (among others) polygamy.[115] In its periodic report, South Africa replied that it would retain a combination of marital regimes, including civil, customary, and religious laws.[116] It explained that the Constitution recognises the protection of customary laws and institutions, which 'automatically allows for polygamy because it is a customary practice'.[117] Accordingly, the Recognition of Customary Marriages Act recognises customary marriages, including polygamy, as 'inspired by the dignity and equality rights entrenched in the Constitution and normative value system it establishes and necessitated by the country's international treaty obligations'.[118] South Africa considers the proprietary rights of women in customary marriages sufficiently protected, since the Act provides that a husband in a customary

[111] CEDAW, 'Responses to the list of issues and questions: Indonesia' CEDAW/C/IDN/Q/6-7/Add 1 (19 Jan 2012) para 36.

[112] ibid para 37.

[113] CEDAW, 'Concluding Observations of the Committee on the Elimination of Discrimination against Women: Indonesia' CEDAW/C/IDN/CO/6–7 (7 Aug 2012) para 22.

[114] CEDAW, 'Concluding Comments of the Committee on the Elimination of Discrimination against Women: South Africa' A/53/38/Rev 1 (SUPP) (1 Jan 1998) para 117.

[115] ibid para 118.

[116] CEDAW, 'Combined second, third and fourth periodic report of South Africa' CEDAW/C/ZAF/2–4 (24 March 2010) para 16.1.

[117] CEDAW, 'Responses to the list of issues and questions: South Africa' CEDAW/C/ZAF/Q/4/Add.1 (10 Jan 2011) paras 36–37.

[118] ibid para 49.

marriage, who wants to marry a second or subsequent wife, must apply to the High Court for the division of the estate and submit a contract that will govern the new proprietary regime.[119] The state party further stated in its periodic report that for women (already) living in polygamous marriages, 'their livelihood would be threatened if polygamy was not recognized'.[120] Nevertheless, in its Concluding Observations, the Committee remained concerned that the state party upheld customary and religious laws and civil, customary, and religious marital regimes that discriminate against women in the field of marriage and family relations, including polygamy[121] and—again—urged South Africa to adopt a unified family law in conformity with the Convention, with the aim of abolishing (among others) polygamy.[122]

In the dialogue with Tunisia, the Committee asked to provide information on steps taken to ensure equality between women and men in matters of personal status; among others, regarding dowry (Article 16 of the Convention).[123] Tunisia explained that in the case of dowries, Article 3 of the Personal Status Code states that 'marriage shall be constituted only with the consent of both spouses. The presence of two reputable witnesses and the payment of a dowry for the bride are also conditions for the validity of the marriage'. 'The dowry in this context has been reduced to a symbolic sum of one dinar (approximately 0.7 US dollars), and is therefore not discriminatory'.[124] In its Concluding Observations, the Committee did not accommodate such a 'symbolic dowry': 'While noting the efforts of the State party to reduce the value of the dowry to one dinar, the Committee is concerned that it remains a condition for the validity of the marriage'.[125] The Committee urged Tunisia to amend without delay discriminatory provisions or regulations relating to dowry.[126]

The dialogue between the United Arab Emirates (UAE) and the Committee addressed equality between women and men in respect to inheritance. The UAE submitted in their report to the CEDAW that

> the Personal Status Act includes provisions governing questions of … inheritance. The sharia is the basic source for the provisions of the Act, inasmuch as it

[119] CEDAW, 'Combined second, third and fourth periodic report of South Africa', CEDAW/C/ZAF/2-4 (24 March 2010) para 16.7.

[120] ibid para 16.8 (textbox 31: *Polygamy and Women's Rights*).

[121] CEDAW, 'Concluding Observations of the Committee on the Elimination of Discrimination against Women: South Africa' CEDAW/C/ZAF/CO/4 (5 April 2011) para 41.

[122] ibid para 42.

[123] CEDAW, 'List of issues and questions: Tunisia' CEDAW/C/TUN/Q/6 (29 March 2010) para 31.

[124] CEDAW, 'Responses to the list of issues and questions: Tunisia' CEDAW/C/TUN/Q/6/Add 1 (18 Aug 2010) para 366.

[125] CEDAW, 'Concluding Observations of the Committee on the Elimination of Discrimination against Women: Tunisia' CEDAW/C/TUN/CO/6 (4 Nov 2010) para 60.

[126] ibid para 61.

> relates to matters clearly spelled out by the religion concerning which no debate is permissible.[127]

It explained that the provisions of the Islamic sharia are the principal reference with regard to the distribution of inheritance.[128] Acknowledging that different shares are allocated to male and female inheritors, it argued that gender was not the dictating factor, but the financial burden which, in accordance with the sharia, is placed on the inheritor to fulfil the responsibilities towards others.[129] The UAE further defended this practice, arguing that the differentiation does not lead to any wrong or unfairness towards the female, as follows:

> it is a man's responsibility to support the female, his wife and his children, whereas a female inheritor has in her brother someone who must support her and her children, she receives less than her brother, who receives twice as much as she does, but is more fortunate in respect of the inheritance because she is not obliged to support anyone else: that money is hers alone and is intended to provide a form of insurance for her.[130]

In the Concluding Observations, the Committee nevertheless noted with concern that the legal provisions relating to personal status, including inheritance, in particular under the Personal Status Act, do not provide for equal rights of women and men. It called upon the UAE to introduce legislative reforms to provide women with equal rights in the field of inheritance.[131]

iii. Rejecting the Committee's Interpretation and Recommendations

Some states parties expressly avoid a dialogue on a particular subject by ignoring the Committee's questions or recommendations on a certain subject. It thereby implicitly rejects the Committee's interpretation of certain provisions. This 'tactic' can be recognised, for example, in situations where the state party's underlying 'worldview' is fundamentally different from that of the Committee, and the state party apparently does not believe that a dialogue can bridge this.

An example of this can be found in the dialogue between the Committee and Kuwait concerning the minimum age of marriage. After the Committee urged Kuwait to raise the minimum age of marriage for women and

[127] CEDAW, 'Initial periodic report of United Arab Emirates' CEDAW/C/ARE/1 (17 Sept 2008) 58.

[128] CEDAW, 'Responses to the list of issues and questions: United Arab Emirates' CEDAW/C/ARE/Q/1/Add.1 (19 October 2009) answer to question no 29.

[129] ibid.

[130] ibid.

[131] CEDAW, 'Concluding Observations of the Committee on the Elimination of Discrimination against Women: United Arab Emirates' CEDAW/C/ARE/CO/1 (5 Feb 2010) para 48.

men to 18 years,[132] it replied that 'the official registration or certification of a marriage is prohibited if the girl is under 15 years of age and the young man is under 17 years of age at the time of registration',[133] thus ignoring the Committee's recommendation, and maintaining its own position. In the list of issues and questions in another round of reporting, the Committee asked Kuwait whether it was taking steps to bring discriminatory provisions contained in its Personal Status Act into conformity with the Convention,[134] including the raising of the minimum age of marriage for women and men from 15 and 17 years to 18 years, 'as recommended by the Committee'.[135] Kuwait's short reply was that 'matters relating to personal status, marriage, divorce and inheritance are governed by Islamic law, as clarified in the combined third and fourth report of the State of Kuwait'.[136] The Committee, absent any explanation or justification by the state party, again expressed its concern about the absence of information on any steps taken by the state party to raise the minimum age of marriage for women and men to 18[137] and reiterated its previous recommendations.[138]

The Committee has occasionally tried to resolve such a deadlock, in particular regarding countries with an Islamic background, by pointing at countries with a similar background. For example, in the Concluding Observations on Kuwait, the Committee urged the state party to adopt specific legislation, 'seeking inspiration from other countries with similar cultural specificities which have taken steps in this regard',[139] however, without specifying which countries could serve this purpose.

The recommendations in the state reporting procedure, unlike those in the individual communications procedure, do not deal with specific provisions and do not conclude violations. Consequently, Concluding Observations are vaguer with regard to the content of the norms.

C. Individual Communications Procedure ('Views')

In the individual communications procedure, the Committee, through concrete dispute resolution, gives abstract rights a concrete meaning,

[132] CEDAW, 'Concluding Comments of the Committee on the Elimination of Discrimination against Women: Kuwait' A/59/38 Part I (18 March 2004) para 67.

[133] CEDAW, 'Combined third and fourth periodic report of Kuwait' CEDAW/C/KWT/3–4 (12 Aug 2010) para 110.

[134] CEDAW, 'List of issues and questions: Kuwait' CEDAW/C/KWT/Q/3–4 (8 March 2011) para 29.

[135] ibid para 31.

[136] CEDAW, 'Responses to the list of issues and questions: Kuwait' CEDAW/C/KWT/Q/3–4/Add.1 (9 May 2011) para 82.

[137] CEDAW, 'Concluding Observations of the Committee on the Elimination of Discrimination against Women: Kuwait' CEDAW/C/KWT/CO/3–4 (8 Nov 2011) para 50.

[138] ibid para 51.

[139] ibid para 31. The Committee does not specify which other countries.

while striking a balance between the universal application of human rights and the reality of their implementation in diverse cultural contexts. This section discusses several individual complaints—in terms of content and process—where cultural diversity played a role in order to show what role the individual communications procedure plays in the interaction between the CEDAW and the state party. From the Committee jurisprudence,[140] the cases selected for review are those where culture functioned as an underlying cause of discrimination, or was considered discriminatory in itself.[141]

In all selected cases, Article 5, containing the elimination of prejudices, stereotypes, and traditional attitudes that are discriminatory towards women, was invoked.[142] The cases concern diverse contexts. For example, in a rape case against the Philippines, the domestic court's decision was found to be grounded in gender-based myths and misconceptions about rape and rape victims in violation of Article 5. The Committee in its Views stressed that 'stereotyping affects women's right to a fair and just trial'.[143] The Committee came to similar conclusions in a domestic violence case against Bulgaria, where it not only stressed that stereotyping affects women's right to a fair trial, but also stated that 'traditional attitudes by which women are regarded as subordinate to men contribute to violence against them'.[144] It considered that the (domestic) courts interpreted domestic violence in a too stereotyped and overly narrow way.[145] In another domestic violence case against Hungary, the Committee noted that the facts of the communication reflected earlier observations in the state party's periodic report about attitudes towards women in the country as a whole. Recalling that at that time it was concerned about the 'persistence of entrenched

[140] OHCHR website, available at: www2.ohchr.org/english/law/jurisprudence.htm.

[141] Thus, not discussed are the two cases of *intersectional discrimination*, where discrimination against women is linked with other (cultural) factors that affect (inclusion and participation of) women, such as race, ethnicity, religion or belief, sexual orientation, etc. In *Cecilia Kell v Canada* (Comm no 19/2008), the Committee found that the author was a victim of intersectional discrimination based on her status as 'an aboriginal woman victim of domestic violence' (para 10.2). The Committee recommended that Canada compensate the author, and recommended recruiting and training more aboriginal women to provide legal aid to women from their communities, and reviewing the legal aid system to ensure aboriginal women who are victims of domestic violence have effective access to justice. In *Maria de Lourdes da Silva Pimentel v Brazil* (Comm no 17/2008), the Committee concluded that the author was discriminated against, not only on the basis of her sex, but also on the basis of her status as a woman of African descent and her socio-economic background. The Committee recommended to provide 'appropriate reparation', to the author, and to 'ensure women's right to safe motherhood and affordable access for *all* women to adequate emergency obstetric care' (para 8).

[142] For an analysis of Art 5 of the ICEDAW, see Rikki Holtmaat, 'Article 5' in Freeman, Chinkin and Rudolf (n 32) 141, 141–67.

[143] *Karen Tayag Vertido v Philippines* (Comm no 18/2008) para 8.4.

[144] *Ms VK v Bulgaria* (Comm no 20/2008) para 9.11.

[145] ibid para 9.12.

traditional stereotypes regarding the role and responsibilities of women and men in the family',[146] the Committee concluded a violation, and recommended the state party to 'implement expeditiously and without delay the Committee's concluding comments of August 2002 on the combined fourth and fifth periodic report of Hungary in respect of violence against women and girls'.[147]

As in the cases of state reporting procedures, states responded differently to the allegations concerning prejudices, stereotypes, and traditional attitudes. Hungary, for instance, admitted that it had failed to comply with its obligations.[148] Bulgaria and the Philippines, however, ignored[149] and Turkey denied[150] a link between the facts and the existence of certain stereotypes or cultural patterns. In all these cases, the Committee found that the state party had failed to fulfil its obligations under Article 5. Its recommendations to the state party always included specific measures concerning the author of the communication, usually in the form of appropriate reparation, including adequate compensation.[151] The Committee also added recommendations on measures of a more general character, which in the case of Article 5 violations, are measures to modify cultural patterns and stereotypes, such as providing regular, appropriate, and mandatory training on the Convention, its Optional Protocol, and its

[146] *Ms AT v Hungary* (Comm no 2/2003) para 9.4.

[147] ibid para 9.6.

[148] ibid para 5.7: 'Having realized that the system of remedies against domestic violence is incomplete in Hungarian law and that the effectiveness of the existing procedures is not sufficient, the State party states that it has instituted a comprehensive action programme against domestic violence in 2003. … These actions include: … requesting the judiciary to organize training for judges and to find a way to ensure that cases relating to violence within the family are given priority; and *launching a nationwide campaign to address indifference to violence within the family and the perception of domestic violence as a private matter and to raise awareness of State, municipal and social organs and journalists*'; paras 7.3–7.4: 'The State party admits that the experience of the Office and the information it has shows that domestic violence cases as such do not enjoy high priority in court proceedings. … *it is conceded that the legal and institutional system in Hungary is not ready yet to ensure the internationally expected, coordinated, comprehensive and effective protection and support for the victims of domestic violence*' (emphasis added by authors).

[149] *Ms VK v Bulgaria*; *Karen Tayag Vertido v Philippines*. Although in the latter case, the state party noted that 'it would consider developing trainings on gender responsiveness for the judiciary' (Comm no 18/2008, para. 7.2).

[150] *RKB v Turkey*, para 4.3: 'The State party also submits that the claim of a violation of article 5, paragraph (a), of the Convention is incompatible with the provisions of the Convention, manifestly ill-founded and not sufficiently substantiated, as *the author does not refer to any social and cultural pattern that the State party would have failed to take appropriate measures to modify*. Therefore, there is *no clear link between the author's dismissal and a social and cultural pattern*'; para 6.8: 'Likewise, it would not be possible to link the fact that access to a therapeutic abortion was denied to the *alleged existence of a certain stereotype* against women' (emphasis added by authors).

[151] *Ms AT v Hungary*, para 9.6; *Ms VK v Bulgaria*, para 9.16(a); *Karen Tayag Vertido v Philippines*, para 8.9(a); *RKB v Turkey*, para 8.10(a).

general recommendations for judges, lawyers, law enforcement personnel, and medical personnel in a gender-sensitive manner.[152]

The above shows that in these cases, cultural (diversity) arguments are not accepted by the Committee as a justification for perpetuating inequality and the infringement of women's human rights. In fact, it is the other way around: the Committee considers cultures as dynamic and subject to change. Actors (judges, lawyers, law enforcement personnel, medical personnel, and so on) should be informed and trained by the state in order to ensure that their decision-making is in line with universal norms.

D. Constructive Dialogue?

In the introductory paragraphs of its Concluding Observations, the Committee usually notes that it appreciates the 'constructive dialogue' that took place between the delegation and the members of the Committee.[153] How constructive are these dialogues between Committee and states parties really? Arguably, the interaction between Committee and states parties falls short of deserving the label 'constructive dialogue'. To call it a 'dialogue', there should be more *exchange* of ideas or opinions. To call it 'constructive', there needs to be more *argumentation* and *motivation*.

Taking a closer look at the reporting procedure reveals that the interaction does not really go both ways. The state, in its periodic report, in its written replies to the list of issues and questions, and during the open sessions, is afforded considerable opportunity to explain its (culture-specific) views on the implementation of the Convention. Nevertheless, what seems to be missing is *discussion*. The Committee sometimes 'notes'

[152] Specifically, the Committee made (among others) the following recommendations to the state parties: 'Provide for appropriate and regular training on the Convention, its Optional Protocol and its general recommendations for judges, lawyers and law enforcement personnel in a gender-sensitive manner, so as to ensure that stereotypical prejudices and values do not affect decision-making' (*RKB v Turkey*, para 8.10(b)(ii)); 'Provide mandatory training for judges, lawyers and law enforcement personnel on the application of the Law on Protection against Domestic Violence, including on the definition of domestic violence and on gender stereotypes, as well as appropriate training on the Convention, its Optional Protocol and the Committee's general recommendations, in particular general recommendation No. 19' (*Ms VK v Bulgaria*, para 9.16(b)(iv)); 'Ensure that all legal procedures in cases involving crimes of rape and other sexual offences are impartial and fair, and not affected by prejudices or stereotypical gender notions. … Concrete measures include: … Appropriate training for judges, lawyers, law enforcement officers and medical personnel in understanding crimes of rape and other sexual offences in a gender-sensitive manner so as to avoid revictimization of women having reported rape cases and to ensure that personal mores and values do not affect decision-making' (*Karen Tayag Vertido v Philippines*, para 8.9(b)).

[153] The CEDAW uses this term mainly in direct relation to the meeting with the state party in Geneva. For this chapter, however, we consider the whole process of state reporting, including the submission of state periodic reports, the preparation by the Committee of lists of issues and questions, the written replies by states parties, and the meeting between the Committee and states parties, as being part of the constructive dialogue.

or 'welcomes' measures taken by the state, but other than that, the Committee does not show much responsiveness to the explanations or input from the state. The Committee, time and again, reiterates its concerns and recommendations, no matter what efforts or measures the state party has employed. There is not much motivation or reasoning behind the Committee's observations and recommendations to the state party, or at least these are not explicitly mentioned. For example, in the discussed example of 'symbolic dowry' in the dialogue with Tunisia, the Committee only observed, very briefly: 'while noting the efforts of the State party to reduce the value of the dowry to one dinar, the Committee is concerned that it remains a condition for the validity of the marriage'.[154]

Presumably, the Committee is of the opinion that even a purely symbolic dowry condones the underlying cultural beliefs and attitudes, but it does not say so. In a *constructive* dialogue, should the Committee not explicitly substantiate its decision and explain its reasoning and motivation to the state party? It may be self-evident to the Committee, but the state party may genuinely believe that lowering the amount of the dowry (and thus the barrier to equality) while maintaining the dowry as a tradition or folklore is the optimal implementation of its international obligations, bearing in mind the (local) circumstances.

Another case in point is the example of FGM in Indonesia, discussed above. The Committee urged the state party to withdraw the regulation and restore the circular letter, thereby ignoring explanations of the state party that it supports efforts to combat FGM, and that the regulation was adopted in light of the fatwa, with a view to preventing parents from opting for illegal and often more harmful FGM by traditional medical practitioners. The Committee could be more constructive in this situation. It is understandable that the Committee does not accept a deviation from the state's international obligations; in fact, it is a clear violation of the Convention. But the Committee could enhance the acceptability of its decision by responding to the state party's struggles and explanations. It could well be that following up on the Committee's recommendations may lead to a rise in female circumcisions by (non-medical) traditional practitioners, performing more harmful forms of circumcision. Bearing in mind these considerations and (local) circumstances, is withdrawing the regulation and restoring the circular letter still in the best interests of women? The Committee could be more responsive towards states argumentation and more constructive through sharing its motivations and reasoning in greater detail.

Another point is that the Committee is not very specific in its recommendations. Recommendations such as 'to put in place a comprehensive

[154] CEDAW, 'Concluding Observations of the Committee on the Elimination of Discrimination against Women: Tunisia' CEDAW/C/TUN/CO/6 (4 Nov 2010) para 60.

strategy',[155] 'to educate and raise awareness',[156] or 'to address' certain practices[157] are rather broad and vague. Such measures lack clear indicators and benchmarks. In fact, the Committee leaves the formulation of indicators and benchmarks to the state, making recommendations such as to 'undertake an assessment of the impact of those measures in order to identify shortcomings, and improve them accordingly in a clear timeframe'.[158] Even though the Committee has a subsidiary role, leaving the final choice of measures of implementation to the states parties, it could aim for more concrete and measurable recommendations. This would allow the Committee to monitor progress between reporting cycles and it would also contribute to a better understanding and thereby acceptability of the recommendations.

Often it is just as important to read what is *not* incorporated in the Concluding Observations. What does it mean when previous recommendations are not 'reiterated' in the new Concluding Observations? One can assume that these recommendations have been sufficiently implemented. One can also conclude that the issue is no longer 'requiring the priority attention of the state party'. Again, this indicates a point for improvement in argumentation and reasoning on behalf of the Committee. In this regard, the relatively new[159] follow-up mechanism is a significant step forward. Under the follow-up mechanism, the Committee requests the state party to provide, usually within two years, further information regarding some

[155] See, eg, CEDAW, 'Concluding Observations of the Committee on the Elimination of Discrimination against Women: Congo' CEDAW/C/COG/CO/6 (22 March 2012) para 22(a); CEDAW, 'Concluding Observations of the Committee on the Elimination of Discrimination against Women: South Africa' CEDAW/C/ZAF/CO/4 (5 April 2011) para 21(a); CEDAW, 'Concluding Observations of the Committee on the Elimination of Discrimination against Women: Mexico' CEDAW/C/MEX/CO/7–8 (7 August 2012) para 35(c); CEDAW, 'Concluding Observations of the Committee on the Elimination of Discrimination against Women: Egypt' CEDAW/C/EGY/CO/7 (3 February 2010) para 22.

[156] See, eg, CEDAW, 'Concluding Observations of the Committee on the Elimination of Discrimination against Women: Congo' CEDAW/C/COG/CO/6 (22 March 2012) para 22(a); CEDAW, 'Concluding Observations of the Committee on the Elimination of Discrimination against Women: Kenya' CEDAW/C/KEN/CO/7 (5 April 2011) para 18(a); CEDAW, 'Concluding Observations of the Committee on the Elimination of Discrimination against Women: Singapore' CEDAW/C/SGP/CO/4/Rev 1 (10 Aug 2011) para 22(a); CEDAW, 'Concluding Observations of the Committee on the Elimination of Discrimination against Women: Côte d'Ivoire' CEDAW/C/CIV/CO/1–3 (8 Nov 2011) para 27(a).

[157] See, eg, CEDAW, 'Concluding Observations of the Committee on the Elimination of Discrimination against Women: Mexico' CEDAW/C/MEX/CO/7–8 (7 Aug 2012) para 35(b), CEDAW, 'Concluding Observations of the Committee on the Elimination of Discrimination against Women: The Netherlands' CEDAW/C/NLD/CO/5 (5 Feb 2010) para 11; CEDAW, 'Concluding Observations of the Committee on the Elimination of Discrimination against Women: Jamaica' CEDAW/C/JAM/CO/6–7 (7 Aug 2012) para 20; CEDAW, 'Concluding Observations of the Committee on the Elimination of Discrimination against Women: Norway' CEDAW/C/NOR/CO/8 (22 March 2012) para 36(d).

[158] See, eg, CEDAW, 'Concluding Observations of the Committee on the Elimination of Discrimination against Women: Congo' CEDAW/C/COG/CO/6 (22 March 2012) para 22(c).

[159] Implemented since 2010.

specific recommendations or 'areas of concern' identified by the Committee. In a letter by the Rapporteur for Follow-up on Concluding Observations, progress on each of these recommendations is examined and the Committee adopts an assessment on each one of them. A recommendation can be considered '(fully) implemented', 'partially implemented', or 'not implemented'. In its annual report to the General Assembly, the CEDAW reported that 'the follow-up procedure is achieving its stated goal of acting as a tool of implementation of the Convention and more specifically the recommendations set out in selected concluding observations'. Moreover, 'this procedure ... enables the Committee to monitor progress achieved between reporting cycles'.[160] Although probably not feasible in terms of (financial) resources, it would be a considerable improvement if it were applied, not only to one or two selected 'areas of concern', but to *all* recommendations by the Committee.

V. CONCLUDING REMARKS: ROLE OF DIALOGUE IN MEDIATING CULTURAL DIVERSITY AND LEGAL CERTAINTY

The ICEDAW is no exception to the fact that international human rights provisions are often formulated in rather broad and ambiguous language. This makes it possible for universal principles to be applied in diverse cultural contexts. At the same time, the vagueness of treaty terms increases the importance of the processes of interpreting treaty provisions for determining their scope and normative content. Such processes involve dialogues between states and the treaty bodies.

This chapter aimed to illustrate to what extent the dialogue between states parties to the ICEDAW and its monitoring committee enable states parties to reiterate, revisit, or be challenged on the value of particular cultural norms and practices in relation to the implementation of the ICEDAW, and how this dialogue informs the development of consensus and certainty over the meaning of the norms in the Convention. This chapter also addressed the question as to what extent this dialogue between the CEDAW and the states parties strengthens legal certainty in formal and substantive terms; in other words, in terms of clarity and predictability of the norms and procedures, and in terms of acceptability of these norms and procedures.

Our starting point was that legal certainty serves a purpose in relation to international human rights law. Clarity and determinacy provide states with a clear framework for action, and individuals and communities with insight on their rights and the rights of others. At the same time, legal certainty should not be reduced to predictability alone.

[160] CEDAW Annual Report to GA, A/67/38 (2012), 43.

Flexibility is needed to be able to apply the norm in different specific contexts. Universal human rights norms should be flexible enough to be implementable in a large variety of situations without losing their universal validity. Treaty bodies have an important role in advancing legal certainty, both from a formal perspective (predictability) and a substantive perspective (acceptability).[161] This implies balancing predictability of the norms (through clear formulation, consistency, and unity) with a certain flexibility to implement the norms in different contexts and to argue as clearly and consistently as possible in order to be acceptable.

The analysis of the dialogue on cultural diversity issues between the CEDAW and states parties shows that the Committee does not, generally speaking, leave much room for cultural diversity in the implementation of the treaty provisions. The Committee seems not very open or receptive to states cultural (diversity) arguments concerning the implementation of the Convention. On the contrary, the Committee considers cultures as 'dynamic' and therefore, 'subject to change'. It is the culture that should change; not the interpretation of the (scope of the) norms or obligations of states parties.

In the determination of the room for cultural diversity, the Committee mainly relies on its own understanding of the specific content of the norms, in which states parties play a very limited role. Others have already observed that the dialogue between treaty bodies and states parties often reflects the Committee's understanding of the specific content of rights whereby states are pressed to explain practices.[162] The present analysis, especially in the context of the state reporting procedure,[163] supports this observation. It shows that the Committee's interpretation of the content of the rights hardly depends on an understanding resulting from the dialogue with states parties. The Committee rather follows its own, independent, understanding.

In the practice of the CEDAW, limited constructive interaction with the states parties takes place. Other than (sometimes) 'noting' or 'welcoming' some efforts by the state party, the Committee and the state party do not fully engage in a two-way dialogue; the Committee, for instance, neither gives reasons for its observations nor shares its reasoning. Arguably, this has implications for the acceptability of the procedure and its outcome, or what was called substantive legal certainty. While the Committee, to some extent, succeeds in contributing to formal legal certainty by creating predictability and commonality in its interpretation of treaty norms, the

[161] For the definition of formal and substantive legal certainty, see section II(B) above.

[162] Douglas Lee Donoho, 'Autonomy, Self-Governance, and the Margin of Appreciation: Developing a Jurisprudence of Diversity within Universal Human Rights' (2001) 15 *Emory International Law Review* 391, 436.

[163] But also in the individual communications procedure, the Committee opted for its own interpretation of Art 5 and the obligations it imposes on states.

lack of a real dialogue implies that the interpretation of treaty norms by the Committee may not always be acceptable to states. It seems that the Committee mainly promotes formal legal certainty, even to the extent that it may be at the expense of substantive legal certainty. States that demonstrate a willing and constructive attitude in the reporting procedure, and use the opportunity to explain their cultural beliefs and practices in relation to the CEDAW norms, may become frustrated by the lack of motivation on the side of the Committee. This could eventually cause states to refuse to engage in a dialogue.

In order to promote the acceptability of its work, the CEDAW should not only be more clear in its argumentation and open to dialogue, but it should also better align the different mechanisms—state reports and individual communications. References to other cases or Concluding Observations could enhance consistency and show the commonality in the application of the norms. The CEDAW does this regularly,[164] but not consistently. Likewise, the Committee could work on improving coherence and consistency between its own reporting format, based on a thematic categorisation, and the one used by states parties, who categorise their obligations and implementation measures along the articles of the Convention. At the same time, alignment is no guarantee of acceptability and convincingness. It is therefore important to improve the dialogue—in particular its constructiveness—between the Committee and the states parties. This would, in turn, contribute to a better balance between universality, diversity, and legal certainty.

[164] Occasionally, the Committee refers in its individual communications to concerns expressed earlier in the Concluding Observations as part of the state's periodic reporting process. Eg, as discussed above in *AT v Hungary*, para 9.4. Sometimes, the Committee refers to the periodic reporting procedure in general, such as in the case of *Karen Tayag Vertido v Philippines*, para 8.7. While the Committee in individual communications regularly refers to the state reporting procedure, the other way around is rare. In the selected case law, one example was found. In the Concluding Observations of Norway, the Committee urged the state party to 'adopt a legal definition of rape in the Penal Code … in line with the Committee's general recommendation No. 19, and the *Vertido case*' (*Karen Tayag Vertido v Philippines*, para 24).

14

Domestic Courts Under Scrutiny: The Rule of Law as a Standard (of Deference) in Investor-State Arbitration

HEGE ELISABETH KJOS*

I. INTRODUCTION

THE TERM 'RULE of law' is interconnected with courts by definition and in practice. First, the concept contains governance criteria applicable to courts;[1] and it stipulates that the judiciary—like any state organ—is accountable under law.[2] Second, courts and tribunals play an important contribution in advancing the rule of law at the national and international levels.[3] This chapter looks at the role played in that regard by arbitral tribunals settling disputes between foreign investors and host states. Its focus is on the accountability of domestic courts under international investment agreements (IIAs); in particular the provisions on fair and equitable treatment (FET), expropriation, and the duty to provide 'effective means' of asserting claims and enforcing rights.

Two main arguments are made. First, international investment law reflects and elucidates the meaning of the rule of law, and investment arbitration can facilitate synergy between the national and international dimensions of the concept. Second, investors must meet a high threshold to demonstrate that the host state, through acts or omissions of its courts,

* This research forms part of the project 'International Law through the Prism of National Law: the Impact of Judicial Dialogue', funded by the European Science Foundation as a European Collaborative Research Project in the Social Sciences.

[1] Report of the Secretary-General K Annan, 23 Aug 2004 UN Doc S/2004/616 (2004).

[2] Simon Chesterman, 'An International Rule of Law?' (2008) 56(2) *American Journal of Comparative Law* 331, 343.

[3] André Nollkaemper, *National Courts and the International Rule of Law* (Oxford, Oxford University Press, 2011) 1; 'Declaration of the High-level Meeting of the General Assembly on the Rule of Law at the National and International Levels' ('GA Declaration') UN Doc A/RES/67/1 (30 Nov 2012) para 32.

has violated an IIA. The wide latitude for the judiciary is best viewed as stemming from the substantive treaty provisions, and these may provide lower protection than domestic rule of law criteria. At the same time, there is evidence of arbitrators applying a degree of institutional/procedural deference to domestic courts, which further reduces the likelihood of liability.[4]

The link between investor-state arbitration and the rule of law is not merely a conceptual issue. A positive correlation has been made between the rule of law and economic growth, and between IIAs and the rule of law.[5] From this perspective, international investment law and arbitration may also contribute to the rule of law at a more concrete level.[6] Lately, however, the link between international investment law and arbitration on the one hand, and the rule of law on the other, has been questioned. As Schill observes, '[n]umerous critics question the legitimacy of international investment law and investor-state arbitration, arguing that this field of law and dispute resolution presents a threat to foundational principles of domestic public law, including democracy and the rule of law'.[7] It is not the aim of this chapter to offer solutions to the larger 'legitimacy' controversy.[8] Yet, our findings on the degree of latitude enjoyed by courts under IIAs do offer nuancing perspectives to negative portrayals of the regime, for instance that treaty provisions 'have been given unduly pro-investor

[4] 'Deference' has been given different labels and interpretations in investor-state arbitration. In this chapter, the term 'latitude' implies that host state behaviour must reach a certain threshold for a breach to be found, and that this threshold is provided by the normative content of the claim at hand. 'Institutional/procedural deference' relates to the division of interpretative powers between the tribunal and the respondent state, ie who is better placed to make a certain assessment. For literature, see, eg, Johannes Fahner, 'The Margin of Appreciation in Investor-State Arbitration' (2014) 26 *Hague Yearbook of International Law* 2013; Gus Van Harten, *Sovereign Choices and Sovereign Constraints* (Oxford, Oxford University Press, 2014); Valentina Vadi and Lukasz Gruszczynski, 'Standards of Review in International Investment Law and Arbitration' (2013) 16 *Journal of International Economic Law* 613; Stephan W Schill, 'Deference in Investment Treaty Arbitration' (2012) 3 *Journal of International Dispute Settlement* 577.

[5] Kenneth J Vandevelde, *Bilateral Investment Treaties* (Oxford, Oxford University Press, 2010) para 3.5.2; GA Declaration (n 3) para 7; Bruno Simma, 'Foreign Investment Arbitration: A Place for Human Rights?' (2011) 60(3) *International & Comparative Law Quarterly* 573, 576; Matthias Herdegen, *Principles of International Economic Law* (Oxford, Oxford University Press, 2013) 55.

[6] Thomas W Wälde, 'Denial of Justice: A Review Comment on Jan Paulsson, Denial of Justice in International Law' (2006) 21(2) *ICSID Review* 449, 485; Thomas Schultz and Cedric G Dupont, 'Investment Arbitration: Promoting the Rule of Law or Over-Empowering Investors?' (2015) 25(4) *European Journal of International Law* 1147.

[7] Stephan W Schill, 'Enhancing International Investment Law's Legitimacy (2011) 52(1) *Virginia Journal of International Law* 57. *cf* Michael Waibel and others (eds), *The Backlash Against Investment Arbitration* (Alphen aan den Rijn, Kluwer, 2010); ch 5 (Ranjan) of this volume.

[8] According to Schultz and Dupont, the discussion between actors outside and within the system can be likened to 'ships … passing in the night': Schultz and Dupont, 'Investment Arbitration' (n 6) 1148.

interpretation at the expense of states, their governments, and those on whose behalf they act'.[9]

The chapter is structured as follows. We start by briefly discussing the concept of the rule of law and its relation to domestic courts (section II). Then we focus on international investment law and arbitration, examining a selection of awards involving domestic court proceedings (section III). In section IV, we consider the possibility for tribunals to rely on national rule of law criteria when solving the case at hand, after which conclusions are drawn in section V.

II. THE CONCEPT 'RULE OF LAW' AND THE ROLE OF DOMESTIC COURTS

Although there is no universally accepted definition of the concept of the rule of law at either the national or the international level,[10] the judiciary is often seen to hold a central position. Stated Lord Bingham of Cornhill in a decision of the United Kingdom House of Lords:

> It is also of course true … that Parliament, the executive, and the courts have different functions. But the function of independent judges charged to interpret and apply the law is universally recognised as a cardinal feature of the modern democratic state, a cornerstone of the rule of law itself.[11]

Relatedly, the General Assembly of the United Nations (UN) has pointed out that 'the independence of the judicial system, together with its impartiality and integrity, is an essential prerequisite for upholding the rule of law'.[12]

Several definitions of the rule of law give criteria that also apply to courts; and in addition to a procedural dimension, these may contain a substantive core of human rights.[13] A prominent example, encompassing the rule of law at both the national and the international level, is contained in a report of former UN Secretary-General Annan:

> The 'rule of law' … refers to a principle of governance in which … [also] the State itself … [is] accountable to laws that are publicly promulgated, equally

[9] Public Statement on the International Investment Regime, 31 Aug 2010, para 5, available at: www.osgoode.yorku.ca/public-statement-international-investment-regime-31-august-2010/.

[10] Brian Z Tamanaha, *On the Rule of Law* (Cambridge, Cambridge University Press, 2004) 3; Mattias Kumm, 'International Law in National Courts' (2003) 44(1) *Virginia Journal of International Law* 19, 22.

[11] *A (FC) and others (FC) v Secretary of State for the Home Department* [2004] UKHL 56 (UK House of Lords, Judgment of 16 Dec 2004) (per Lord Bingham of Cornhill) [42]. *cf* 'Declaration of the High-level Meeting of the General Assembly on the Rule of Law at the National and International Levels', 19 Sept 2012, para 13.

[12] Meeting of the General Assembly on the Rule of Law at the National and International Levels, 19 Sept 2012, para 13.

[13] Nollkaemper, *National Courts and the International Rule of Law* (n 3) 4–5.

> enforced and independently adjudicated, and which are consistent with international human rights norms and standards.[14]

According to the same report, the rule of law is dependent on *inter alia* adherence to the principles of supremacy of law, equality before the law, fairness in the application of the law, separation of powers, legal certainty, avoidance of arbitrariness, and procedural and legal transparency.[15] The World Justice Project gives a related description of the term. Similar to the UN Secretary-General's report it refers to fundamental rights, yet specifies that these include security of persons and property.[16] Moreover, it requires that '[j]ustice is delivered timely by competent, ethical, and independent representatives and neutrals who are of a sufficient number [and] have adequate resources'.[17]

Our discussion does not require us to decide on the precise scope of the term 'rule of law'. Rather, the criteria put forth by the UN Secretary-General and the World Justice Project will be used as standards against which arbitral practice involving domestic court proceedings will be assessed.

III. ASSESSING DOMESTIC COURT PROCEEDINGS THROUGH THE LENS OF INVESTMENT TREATY STANDARDS

When doing business in a foreign country, investors are protected by various sources of law. In addition to the domestic law of the host state,[18] customary international law sets out a minimum standard of treatment of aliens.[19] Further, there are now more than 2900 bilateral investment treaties (BITs) and several hundred other IIAs, including investment chapters in free trade agreements.[20] The substantive IIA provisions are generally bolstered by the procedural right of investors to arbitrate against the host state in case of an investment dispute.[21] Often, domestic court proceedings

[14] Report of the Secretary-General K Annan (n 1) para 6.

[15] ibid.

[16] The World Justice Project, 'What is the Rule of Law?' available at: http://worldjusticeproject.org/what-rule-law.

[17] ibid.

[18] Jeswald W Salacuse, *The Three Laws of International Investment* (Oxford, Oxford University Press, 2013); Hege E Kjos, *Applicable Law in Investor-State Arbitration* (Oxford, Oxford University Press, 2013).

[19] Hollin Dickerson, 'Minimum Standards' in R Wolfrum (ed), *Max Planck Encyclopedia of Public International Law* (Oct 2010) available at: http://mpepil.com.

[20] UNCTAD, *World Investment Report 2014* (2014) 114. Friendship, commerce, and navigation treaties also provide protection.

[21] Charles N Brower and Lee A Steven, 'Who then should Judge?' (2001) 2 *Chicago Journal of International Law* 193, 196 (The major reason for including arbitration is that 'domestic courts are often in fact, and, just as important, usually are perceived to be, biased against alien investors, especially when those courts must evaluate and pronounce upon acts of their own governments').

precede arbitration, and these proceedings may give rise to, or at least form part of, the investment dispute.[22] In such disputes, the investor may argue that the host state, through its judiciary, violated one of the substantive standards set out in the IIA.

In this section, we examine how arbitral tribunals have ruled on allegations that acts or omissions of the host state's judiciary constitute a breach of the IIA entered into with the investor's home state. The three most commonly invoked IIA provisions in such cases are those concerning fair and equitable treatment, expropriation, and the obligation to provide 'effective means' of asserting claims and enforcing rights. The number of awards that can be analysed is necessarily limited. While the possibility exists that unpublished awards may modify our conclusions, it is believed that the selection made enables us to draw relevant conclusions.[23]

In brief, we will see that all three treaty provisions have been interpreted in a way that reflects rule of law criteria set out in the previous section. From this perspective, investor-state arbitration tribunals can be seen not only to perform an 'institutional' rule of law function in that they may sanction law violations; their awards on the merits may also indicate whether the host state, through its courts, acted in accordance with the rule of law. The following discussion per treaty standard is structured according to whether a violation was found or not, and the cases are presented in a chronological manner.

A. Fair and Equitable Treatment

The treaty standard most frequently invoked in arbitrations concerning acts or omissions of courts is fair and equitable treatment.[24] In fact, scholars have referred to FET as 'an embodiment of the rule of law'[25] and this

[22] Van Harten, *Sovereign Choices and Sovereign Constraints* (n 4) 15, fn 34 ('Of the 162 cases, 71 were found to have involved a domestic court decision including 21 that involved a decision by a supreme or constitutional court'); ibid 120. Unlike diplomatic protection, the principle of the exhaustion of local remedies does not apply in investment arbitration unless the consent of the host state stipulates this. ibid 119.

[23] *cf* Charles N Brower and Sadie Blanchard, 'What's in a Meme? The Truth about Investor-State Arbitration: Why It Need Not, and Must Not, Be Repossessed by States' (2014) 52 *Columbia Journal of Transnational Law* 689, 716 ('Investor-State treaty arbitration ceased to be hidden from public view long ago. Most awards are public and readily found on the internet and, increasingly, so are hearings, party submissions, and other data from proceedings'.).

[24] Christoph Liebscher, 'Monitoring of Domestic Courts in BIT Arbitrations' in Christina Binder and others (eds), *International Investment Law for the 21st Century* (Oxford, Oxford University Press, 2009) 105, 122.

[25] Alexandra Diehl, *The Core Standard of International Investment Protection* (Alphen aan den Rijn, Kluwer, 2012) 335. *cf* Stephan W Schill, 'Fair and Equitable Treatment under Investment Treaties as an Embodiment of the Rule of Law' (2006) 6 IILJ Working Paper; Nicolas Angelet, 'Fair and Equitable Treatment' in R Wolfrum (ed), Max Planck Encyclopedia of Public International Law (March 2011) para 13, available at: http://mpepil.com.

also explains the relatively richer jurisprudence for the purposes of this chapter.[26] The FET clause is found in the vast majority of IIAs;[27] yet the treaties differ as to the precise formulation of the standard. There is the unqualified obligation to accord FET;[28] or FET is linked to international law[29] or to the minimum standard of treatment of aliens under customary international law.[30] We also note an emerging trend to add substantive content to FET clauses.[31]

The FET standard has been found to include the following acts or omissions, which may also involve the judiciary: lack of due process, transparency, and predictability; ambiguity and inconsistency in judicial and administrative decisions; bias and prejudice; and bad faith and arbitrariness.[32] In addition, and as we will see below, FET embraces protection from denial of justice, which is a cause of action under customary international law that is intrinsically linked to the rule of law.[33] Tribunals confirm that denial of justice is a high standard to meet, also because of the requirement to exhaust domestic remedies.[34]

i. Awards Where a Violation was Found

A violation of the FET standard was identified, for instance, in *Petrobart v Kyrgyzstan* which concerned a dispute between a UK company and Kyrgyzgazmunaizat (KGM), an oil and gas company owned by the Kyrgyz Republic.[35] Following non-payment of goods delivered under a contract, Petrobart sued KGM before Kyrgyz courts and obtained a favourable

[26] Next to those referenced below, relevant cases include *Waste Management v Mexico*, Award, ICSID ARB(AF)/00/3, Award 30 April 2004, IIC 270 (2004) (no violation); *Frontier v Czech Republic*, Award 12 Nov 2010, IIC 465 (2010) (no violation); *Alps Finance v Slovakia*, Award 5 March 2011, IIC 489 (2011) (failing prima facie test for jurisdiction); *Bosh v Ukraine*, ICSID ARB/08/11, Award 22 Oct 2012, IIC 565 (2012) (no violation); *Iberdrola v Guatemala*, ICSID ARB/09/15, Award 17 Aug 2012, IIC 559 (2012) (no violation); *Vannessa Ventures v Venezuela*, ICSID ARB(AF)04/6, Award 16 Jan 2013, IIC 572 (2013) (no violation).

[27] Patrick Dumberry, 'The Prohibition against Arbitrary Conduct and the Fair and Equitable Treatment Standard under NAFTA Article 1105' (2014) 15(1–2) *The Journal of World Investment & Trade* 117, 118.

[28] eg, Italy Model Investment Treaty (2003) Art 3(2).

[29] eg, France Model Investment Treaty (2006) Art 3.

[30] eg, Canada Model Investment Treaty (2004) Art 5.

[31] UNCTAD, 'Fair and Equitable Treatment: A Sequel', UNCTAD Series on Issues in International Investment Agreements II (2012) 29; Draft Consolidated CETA Text, 26 Sept 2014, Art 10.X.9(2), available at: www.international.gc.ca/ceta; Columbia Model Investment Treaty (2007) Art III.

[32] Liebscher, 'Monitoring of Domestic Courts in BIT Arbitrations' (n 24) 123; Dumberry, 'The Prohibition against Arbitrary Conduct and the Fair and Equitable Treatment Standard under NAFTA Article 1105' (n 27) 119.

[33] Francesco Francioni, 'Access to Justice, Denial of Justice and International Investment Law' (2009) 20(3) *European Journal of International Law* 729, 730.

[34] Carlo Focarelli, 'Denial of Justice' in R Wolfrum (ed), *Max Planck Encyclopedia of Public International Law* (Jan 2009) paras 29–30, available at: http://mpepil.com.

[35] *Petrobart v Kyrgyzstan*, SCC 126/2003, Award 29 March 2005, IIC 184 (2005).

judgment. The Vice Prime Minister of Kyrgyzstan, Mr Silayev, wrote to the Chairman of the country's Bishkek Court asking his assistance in granting a deferral of enforcement. A few days later, the Court granted a request by KGM for a stay of execution for three months. KGM was then declared bankrupt, which meant that enforcement of the judgment was no longer possible.

In ruling that the host state had violated the FET provision in the Energy Charter Treaty, the arbitral tribunal found significant the government's interference in the domestic proceedings:

> Minister Silayev's letter must be regarded as an attempt by the Government to influence a judicial decision to the detriment of Petrobart … [T]he fact that the Court, in its decision, specifically referred to the Government's intervention indicates that the Court attached some weight to Mr. Silayev's letter … The Arbitral Tribunal considers that such Government intervention in judicial proceedings is not in conformity with the rule of law in a democratic society and that it shows a lack of respect for Petrobart's rights as an investor having an investment under the Treaty.[36]

A violation of the FET standard was also found in *ATA v Jordan*.[37] In 1998, ATA Construction, Industrial and Trading Company (ATA) entered into a contract with the state-owned Arab Potash Company (APC) to build a dike by the Dead Sea. A dispute arose under the contract. APC commenced commercial arbitration proceedings, which resulted in an award in favour of ATA's counterclaim. APC obtained an annulment of the award by the Jordanian Court of Appeal, which ruled that the arbitration agreement in the 1998 contract had been extinguished by the 2001 Arbitration Act. This judgment was upheld by the Jordanian Court of Cassation, after which ATA brought arbitration proceedings alleging that Jordan had violated the Turkey-Jordan BIT.

The arbitral tribunal observed first that the actions of the Jordanian courts in adjudicating the grounds for annulment of the arbitration award could hardly be said to have constituted abusive conduct, bad faith, or a denial of justice.[38] Yet, the tribunal did find a breach of the BIT on the basis that the Jordanian Court of Cassation retroactively applied the 2001 Arbitration Law when extinguishing the 1998 arbitration agreement. To the tribunal, this agreement was 'a valuable asset' to ATA considering that in state courts 'Jordan would have been both litigant and judge'.[39]

Another award in which domestic court proceedings were evaluated against the FET standard is *Deutsche Bank v Sri Lanka*, a case that concerned

[36] ibid para 414.

[37] *ATA v Jordan*, ICSID ARB/08/2, Award 12 May 2010, IIC 430 (2010).

[38] ibid para 123. The claims regarding the annulment of the award would also have failed on jurisdictional grounds. ibid paras 95, 103.

[39] ibid paras 124–28.

a hedging agreement entered into between the German bank and Ceylon Petroleum Corporation (CPC), Sri Lanka's national oil company.[40] When oil prices dropped, CPC owed Deutsche Bank a large sum of money and there was growing public concern. The Supreme Court of Sri Lanka issued interim orders barring further payments to Deutsche Bank and called for an investigation of corruption. In addition, the Central Bank of Sri Lanka requested several banks not to proceed with the transactions. While the interim orders were revoked, the country's Central Bank reiterated in a public statement that the hedging transactions should not be given effect.

The arbitral tribunal found that Sri Lanka had breached the FET provision in the German-Sri-Lanka BIT.[41] As for the Supreme Court's interim order issued within less than 48 hours of the request, the tribunal concluded that 'without a proper examination and without giving the banks involved an opportunity to respond', the order constituted a 'serious due process violation'.[42] In so holding, the tribunal relied on statements made by Sri Lanka's Chief Justice Silva who presided over the hearing:

> In those public statements the Chief Justice confirmed that the decision was issued for political reasons. He indeed declared that '*the Government was forced to comply with the hedging agreements. We will stop that on a judicial order, just pass on to benefit to the people. The Government said you stop the hedging agreements we won't pass on the benefit*'. The Chief Justice further recognized that internationally, Sri Lanka had no defence to present in the arbitration proceedings, that it was a difficult fight.[43]

Arbitrator Khan wrote a dissenting opinion in which he reproached the majority for adopting 'the role of an appellate court sitting in judgment on the Supreme Court's [interim] order' and for determining its propriety 'in a legal and contextual vacuum'.[44] To Khan:

> There is no doubt that certain actions by domestic courts can constitute a breach of the FET standard, but an international tribunal should not be quick to reach such a conclusion without clear evidence to that effect. The judiciary of a host State is entitled to a 'high measure of deference' and there should be a presumption that it has acted in a proper manner. To hold that an interim order passed by the Supreme Court of a host State on the first day of hearing breaches the international FET standard is a finding which needs to be supported by more than the subjective view of the majority that the evidence before the Supreme Court did not warrant the making of such an order.[45]

As for statements 'allegedly' made by the Chief Justice of the host state, Khan noted that Sri Lanka had 'vehemently denied these allegations but

[40] *Deutsche Bank v Sri Lanka*, ICSID ARB/09/02, Award 31 Oct 2012, IIC 578 (2012).
[41] ibid para 474.
[42] ibid paras 478, 480.
[43] ibid para 479 (emphasis in original).
[44] ibid, dissenting opinion by MA Khan, 23 Oct 2012, para 105.
[45] ibid para 107 (citing *SD Myers v Canada*, Award 13 Nov 2000, para 236).

had also pointed out that these statements only appeared in an internet newspaper run by a person wanted in Sri Lanka for fraud and for whom a red warrant had been issued by Interpol'.[46] In his view:

> [R]elying solely on such contested evidence to impute bad faith to the highest court of a country does not meet the standard for rigorous analysis and reasoning that should be the *sine qua non* for any international tribunal recording such a damaging finding about the Supreme Court of a Sovereign State.[47]

Khan was unable to conclude that the Court had 'acted in an improper or discreditable manner' or that the conduct of the judges or the content of their orders were 'arbitrary, grossly unfair, unjust, idiosyncratic or discriminatory. They did not act in a manner or pass such orders which shock or surprise a sense of judicial propriety'.[48]

In this regard, it is also interesting to refer to the *Arif v Moldova* case.[49] The claimant, Mr Arif, argued that the annulment by Moldovan courts of agreements relating to the operation of duty free stores in Moldova constituted denial of justice in violation of the France-Moldova BIT's FET provision. In addressing this claim, the arbitral tribunal first rejected the notion that domestic courts were entitled to more deference than the legislative and executive branches of government:

> International law has evolved in recent decades and the previous conviction as expressed in the *Chattin* award [of 1927] that acts of the judiciary had to be judged with more 'delicacy' and circumscription than acts committed by the other branches of government, is obsolete. The Tribunal shares the modern opinion according to which the State has to be seen as a unity and the acts of any of its organs, including the judiciary, may violate international law.[50]

It then made two *caveats*, the first being that 'international tribunals must refrain from playing the role of ultimate appellate courts'.[51] To the arbitral tribunal:

> It would blur the necessary distinction between the hierarchy of instances within the national judiciary and the role of international tribunals if '*[a] simple difference of opinion on the part of the tribunal is enough*' to allow a finding that a national court has violated international law.[52]

[46] ibid para 107.
[47] ibid para 113. See also ibid para 114.
[48] ibid para 117 (citing *Mondev v US*, ICSID ARB(AF)99/2, Award 11 Oct 2002, para 127).
[49] *Arif v Moldova*, ICSID ARB/11/23, Award 8 April 2013, IIC 585 (2013).
[50] ibid para 439 (citing *BE Chattin (US) v Mexico*, Award 23 July 1927, paras 10–11; Jan Paulsson, *Denial of Justice in International Law* (Cambridge, Cambridge University Press, 2005) 72.
[51] ibid para 440 (citing *Loewen v US*, ICSID ARB(AF)98/3, Award 25 June 2003, IIC 254 (2003) para 242).
[52] ibid para 441 (citing Paulsson, *Denial of Justice in International Law* (n 50) 72; emphasis in original).

The tribunal's second *caveat* concerned the requirement of exhaustion of local remedies: since 'the respondent State must be put in a position to redress the wrongdoings of its judiciary', responsibility for a denial of justice may only be engaged 'if and when the judiciary has rendered final and binding decisions after fundamentally unfair and biased proceedings or which misapplied the law in such an egregiously wrong way, that no honest, competent court could have possibly done so'.[53]

Mr Arif claimed that the Moldovan courts had ordered provisional measures in collusion with his competitors and without any basis in the Moldova Civil Procedure Code.[54] The arbitral tribunal did not find a violation on this ground: the procedural errors committed by the Moldovan judiciary did not amount to such a 'manifest disrespect of due process that they offend a sense of judicial propriety'.[55] The tribunal noted that the delays of the local proceedings were not excessive; that the claimant's company was never prevented from lodging appeals, from accessing the courts and from presenting its arguments; and that 'as a system, the judiciary devoted the necessary time to the applications and gave overall reasoned decisions'.[56] The arbitrators were also not convinced that 'the judiciary acted in collusion with outside plaintiffs, that it was guided by a spirit of bias and partiality and that it was grossly incompetent as a system'.[57]

Yet, after the tribunal had considered also the behaviour of other branches of the government, the claimant prevailed on its FET claim. The arbitrators found significant the 'direct inconsistency between the attitudes of different organs of the State to the investment' in that Moldova's Airport State Enterprise and the State Administration of Civil Aviation endorsed and encouraged the investment, as contrasted with the courts that found the same investment to be illegal.[58]

In sum, examples can be given of arbitral tribunals that have found a violation of the FET provision based on acts or omissions of the host state judiciary. Further, we can conclude that the threshold for such breach is quite high, and may require evidence of wrongdoing also by other branches of government or by the domestic justice system as a whole. This conclusion is strengthened by the following analysis of cases in which no FET breach was found.

[53] ibid paras 442–45 (citing *Jan de Nul v Egypt*, ICSID ARB/04/13, Award 24 Oct 2008, IIC 356 (2008) paras 258–60).
[54] ibid paras 446, 449.
[55] ibid para 447.
[56] ibid.
[57] ibid para 448.
[58] ibid para 547.

ii. Awards Where No Violation was Found

One example of an award where the arbitral tribunal did not find that the domestic court proceedings ran afoul of the FET provision is *Azinian v Mexico*.[59] The claimants, US citizens and shareholders of a Mexican company, alleged denial of justice contrary to the North American Free Trade Agreement (NAFTA) following an annulment by the Naucalpan City Council of a concession contract relating to waste collection and disposal. This annulment was upheld by three levels of Mexican courts.

The tribunal in *Azinian* reasoned that state responsibility for domestic courts conduct may result from three different types of judicial decision:

> The first is a decision of a municipal court *clearly incompatible with a rule of international law*. The second is what it known traditionally as a *'denial of justice.'* The third occurs when, in certain exceptional and well–defined circumstances, a State is responsible for a judicial decision contrary to municipal law.[60]

The tribunal specified that this does not entitle the claimants to seek international review of domestic court decisions 'as though the international jurisdiction seised has plenary appellate jurisdiction. This is not true generally, and it is not true for NAFTA'.[61] Rather, stated the arbitrators, '[w]hat must be shown is that the court decision itself constitutes a violation of the treaty … either a denial of justice, or a pretence of form to achieve an internationally unlawful end'.[62]

The claimants were unsuccessful in this regard, as the arbitral tribunal did not find that the Mexican courts had refused to entertain a suit, subjected the investor to undue delay, or administered justice in a seriously inadequate way.[63] There was also no 'clear and malicious misapplication of the law,' a wrong that 'overlaps with the notion of "pretence of form" to mask a violation of international law'.[64] To the arbitrators, the evidence was 'sufficient to dispel any shadow over the *bona fides* of the Mexican judgments. Their findings cannot possibly be said to have been arbitrary, let alone malicious'.[65]

Denial of justice was also alleged in *Loewen v United States*.[66] This case arose out of a commercial dispute between the US company O'Keefe and the Canadian company Loewen, which were competitors in the funeral home and funeral insurance business in Mississippi. The Mississippi jury

[59] Azinian v Mexico, ICSID ARB(AF)/97/2, Award 18 Oct 1999, IIC 22 (1999).

[60] ibid para 98 (emphasis in original; relying on Eduardo Jiménez de Aréchaga, 'International Law in the Past Third of a Century', 159–1 *Recueil des cours* (The Hague, 1978)).

[61] ibid para 99.

[62] ibid.

[63] ibid para 102.

[64] ibid para 103.

[65] ibid.

[66] *Loewen* (n 51) para 3.

awarded O'Keefe $500 million in damages, including $75 million in damages for emotional distress and $400 million in punitive damages, the largest in Mississippi history. Loewen sought to appeal, but was confronted with the application of a bond requirement of $625 million that had to be posted within seven days without facing immediate execution of the judgment. In the arbitration proceedings that ensued, the Canadian company alleged that the Mississippi trial court, by admitting extensive anti-Canadian and pro-American testimony and prejudicial counsel comment, violated NAFTA.

Ultimately, the arbitral tribunal dismissed the claims for lack of jurisdiction.[67] However, it still examined the claimant's allegation of denial of justice. Obiter dictum, the tribunal observed that domestic courts have the responsibility to 'ensure that litigation is free from discrimination against a foreign litigant and that the foreign litigant should not become the victim of sectional or local prejudice'.[68] The tribunal's assessment of the domestic court proceedings was more than negative: '[b]y any standard of measurement, the trial [in the US] involving O'Keefe and Loewen was a disgrace'; 'the [Mississippi] trial court permitted the jury to be influenced by persistent appeals to local favouritism as against a foreign litigant'; '[t]he methods employed by the jury and countenanced by the judge were the antithesis of due process'; the judge failed 'to discharge his paramount duty to ensure that Loewen received a fair trial'; and 'the whole trial and its resultant verdict were clearly improper and discreditable and cannot be squared with minimum standards of international law and fair and equitable treatment'.[69] Still, the tribunal found that even if it had been vested with jurisdiction, the claim for denial of justice would have failed, as Loewen had not exhausted local remedies.[70]

Another noteworthy case is *Amto v Ukraine*.[71] The claimant corporation had invested in a Ukrainian company that provided services to Zaporozhskaya AES (ZAES), Ukraine's largest nuclear power plant and a division of the National Nuclear Power Generating Company (Energoatom) owned by Ukraine. The claimant successfully obtained domestic judgments in relation to debts owned by ZAES/Energoatom, but these were stayed due to bankruptcy proceedings pending against Energoatom. Eventually, Amto turned to arbitration pursuant to the Energy Charter Treaty, alleging that the handling of its attempt to enforce its claims before the Ukrainian courts amounted to a denial of justice.

On the meaning of denial of justice, the arbitral tribunal quoted from the *Mondev v US* award of 2002:

[67] ibid para 240.
[68] ibid para 123.
[69] ibid paras 119, 122, 136–38.
[70] ibid para 217.
[71] *Amto v Ukraine*, SCC 080/2005, Award 26 March 2008, IIC 346 (2008).

> The test is not whether a particular result is surprising, but whether the shock or surprise occasioned to an impartial tribunal leads, on reflection, to justified concerns as to the judicial propriety of the outcome, bearing in mind on one hand that international tribunals are not courts of appeal, and on the other hand [IIAs are] intended to provide a real measure of protection. In the end the question is whether, at an international level and having regard to generally accepted standards of the administration of justice, a tribunal can conclude in the light of all the available facts that the impugned decision was clearly improper and discreditable, with the result that the investment has been subjected to unfair and inequitable treatment. This is admittedly a somewhat open-ended standard, but it may be that in practice no more precise formula can be offered to cover the range of possibilities.[72]

By applying the test of *Mondev* to the present case, the arbitral tribunal rejected the aforementioned claim raised by Amto. There was no indication that the courts had been improperly influenced by the executive branch, that the decisions were delivered without undue delay, or that the parties had not been properly heard.[73] To the tribunal,

> Claimant's objection to these decisions is simply that they are wrong in law. Tribunal is not a court of appeal for the decisions of the Ukrainian courts and, in any event, the Tribunal does not accept that these decisions are wrong in law.[74]

A claim of FET breach was also rejected in *Liman v Kazakhstan* which concerned a licence to explore and extract hydrocarbons, whose assignment to another party Kazakhstani courts had invalidated.[75] The claimants argued that they had thereby been denied justice, contrary to the Energy Charter Treaty's FET provision. The tribunal in this case stressed that 'an international arbitration tribunal is not an appellate body and its function is not to correct errors of domestic procedural or substantive law which may have been committed by the national courts'.[76] It also emphasised that 'the threshold of the international delict of denial of justice is high and goes far beyond the mere misapplication of domestic law'.[77] In fact, it continued, 'Respondent can only be held liable for denial of justice if Claimants are able to prove that the court system fundamentally failed'.[78]

On this basis and on the facts of the case, the investor's complaints about the Kazakh court proceedings failed on the merits. The *Liman* tribunal reasoned that even if the procedural treatment and substantive outcome of the proceedings 'could be considered surprising', they were not 'arbitrary, grossly unfair, unjust or idiosyncratic or involving lack of due

[72] ibid para 75 (citing *Mondev* (n 48) para 127).
[73] ibid para 80.
[74] ibid. *cf Jan de Nul* (n 53) paras 258–60.
[75] *Liman Caspian Oil v Kazakhstan*, ICSID ARB/07/14, Award 22 June 2010, IIC 590 (2010).
[76] ibid para 274. See also ibid paras 276 (citing Paulsson (n 50) 289, 325, 346–47, 364, 383).
[77] ibid para 274.
[78] ibid para 279.

process'.[79] As for the allegation of corruption, the arbitrators noted that this is 'a serious allegation, especially in the context of the judiciary'.[80] Since 'the standard of proof in this respect is a high one', it was not 'sufficient to present evidence which could possibly indicate that there might have been or even *probably* was corruption'.[81]

Lack of FET was also alleged in the case *White Industries v India*.[82] White Industries, an Australian company, had obtained a commercial arbitration award in a contractual dispute with the state-owned company Coal India. When White Industries started arbitration proceedings pursuant to the Australia-India BIT, enforcement proceedings had been pending before Indian courts for over nine years.[83]

The arbitral tribunal did not agree that the judicial delays were grave enough to constitute a FET violation. It first dismissed the argument that the delays were contrary to claimant's legitimate expectations:

> [A]n investor must generally take a host State (including its court system) as it finds it ... White [Industries] ... either knew or ought to have known at the time it entered into the Contract that the domestic court structure in India was overburdened.[84]

The tribunal also rejected White Industry's denial of justice claim:

> [w]hile the most recent delay is regrettable, there being no suggestion of bad faith, it does not amount in the Tribunal's mind to 'a particularly serious shortcoming' or egregious conduct that 'shocks or at least surprises, a sense of judicial proprietary'.[85]

The arbitrators considered it relevant 'to bear in mind that India is a developing country with a population of over 1.2 billion people with a seriously overstretched judiciary'.[86] They concluded that while the duration of the proceedings 'is certainly unsatisfactory in terms of efficient administration of justice, neither has yet reached the stage of constituting a denial of justice'.[87]

By way of conclusion, we have seen that the FET provision has been applied in cases involving *inter alia* allegations of lack of due process, retroactive applications of laws, judicial delays, and improper interference by other government branches in domestic court proceedings. Such conduct may also run afoul with rule of law criteria stipulated by the UN

[79] ibid para 348.
[80] ibid para 422.
[81] ibid paras 422–24 (emphasis added).
[82] *White Industries v India*, Award 30 Nov 2011, IIC 529 (2011).
[83] ibid para 10.4.4.
[84] ibid para 10.3.15.
[85] ibid para 10.4.23 (citing *Chevron and Texaco Petroleum v Ecuador*, Award 30 March 2010, IIC 421 (2010) para 244).
[86] ibid para 10.4.18.
[87] ibid para 10.4.22.

Secretary-General and World Justice Project. At the same time, we observe that arbitrators have interpreted the FET standard in a way that give considerable, although not unlimited, latitude to host state courts; and investors must meet a relatively high threshold for a violation to be found.

B. Expropriation

Besides the FET standard, international investment agreements generally include a provision obliging the host state not to directly or indirectly expropriate investments unless several conditions are satisfied: the measures must be non-discriminatory and taken in the public interest, under due process of law, and against compensation.[88] In the following, examples are given of awards in which domestic court proceedings have led to a finding of (non-)violation of such provisions.

i. Awards Where a Violation was Found

A noteworthy instance of a tribunal finding a breach of the expropriation provision is *Saipem v Bangladesh*.[89] This case arose from a contractual dispute between the Italian company Saipem and the Bangladeshi state-owned energy company Petrobangla. The dispute resulted in arbitration proceedings under the Arbitration Rules of the International Chamber of Commerce. During the proceedings, Bangladeshi courts issued injunctions against the continuation of the arbitration. Also, the First Court of the Subordinate Judge of Dhaka issued a decision revoking the authority of the arbitral tribunal. When the arbitrators issued an award in Saipem's favour, Petrobangla applied for an annulment; yet the High Court Division of the Supreme Court of Bangladesh denied the application because it was 'misconceived and incompetent inasmuch as there is no Award in the eye of the law, which can be set aside'.[90] Saipem brought arbitration proceedings pursuant to the Italy-Bangladesh BIT, alleging expropriation.

In the arbitral award, the investor prevailed on the ground that the actions of the Bangladeshi courts substantially deprived Saipem of its residual contractual rights under the investment as crystallised already in the earlier award of the International Chamber of Commerce tribunal.[91] The present arbitral tribunal specified that for an expropriation to be found, the court must have acted 'illegally'; otherwise every annulment of an award could found a claim for an expropriation.[92] Partly because the

[88] eg Netherlands Model BIT (2004) Art 6.
[89] *Saipem v Bangladesh*, ICSID ARB/05/7, Award 30 June 2009, IIC 378 (2009).
[90] ibid para 50. The ICC arbitration (unpublished) is discussed in paras 18–34.
[91] ibid paras 128–29.
[92] ibid paras 133–34.

courts refused the orders sought by Petrobangla on at least two occasions, the tribunal was not satisfied that the Bangladeshi courts acted in collusion or conspired with Petrobangla.[93] It did, however, accept Saipem's argument that the Dhaka High Court decision in Bangladesh violated international law as the Court applied a 'spurious standard' and the decision was rendered 'without making any proper investigation whether Petrobangla's accusation were founded'.[94] To the tribunal, Bangladesh had not even attempted to show that the International Chamber of Commerce tribunal had committed any misconduct that could reasonably justify the revocation of the arbitration; and it could not 'but agree with Saipem that the "judge simply took as granted what Petrobangla falsely presented"'.[95]

As such, the arbitrators in *Saipem* concluded that the standard for revocation used by the Bangladesh courts and the manner in which the judge applied that standard to the facts constituted an abuse of right in violation of international law.[96] In so holding, they dismissed Bangladesh' argument that by agreeing to arbitrate in Dhaka, Saipem had accepted the risk of interference by local courts: 'such an argument is self-serving. It cannot be disputed that "the supervision of the courts of the seat must be exercised in good faith, in accordance with the rule of law, and with generally accepted principles of international arbitration"'.[97]

Another case in which domestic court proceedings formed part of the factual background of an expropriation claim is *RosInvest v Russia*, which was brought by former shareholders of the Russian oil company Yukos under the UK-Russia BIT.[98] The claimants alleged that their investment had been expropriated following abusive tax enforcement proceedings resulting in liquidation of the company. The arbitral tribunal stressed that 'the threshold of the international delict of denial of justice is high and goes far beyond the mere misapplication of domestic law'.[99] It further observed that Russia could only be held liable for denial of justice by the Russian courts if 'Claimants are able to prove that the court system fundamentally failed. Such failure is mainly to be adopted in cases of major procedural errors such as lack of due process'.[100] The tribunal refrained from reaching a firm conclusion on this point.[101] Rather, it assessed the totality of the host state's measures in their cumulative effect, including the conduct of

[93] ibid paras 146–47.
[94] ibid para 151.
[95] ibid paras 156–57 (references omitted).
[96] ibid para 159. See also ibid para 170.
[97] ibid para 186 (references omitted).
[98] *RosInvest v Russia*, SCC V (079/2005), Award 12 Sept 2010, IIC 471 (2010).
[99] ibid paras 275–78.
[100] ibid para 279 (citing *Mondev* (n 48) para 127; *Loewen* (n 51) para 132).
[101] ibid paras 498, 525, 557, 568, 575, 581, 612.

the Russian courts; and finding them *mala fide* and discriminatory, it ruled in favour of RosInvest.[102]

The facts relevant to *RosInvest* have led to another case involving an expropriation claim, *Renta 4 v Russia*.[103] This time, the claimants were Spanish former shareholders invoking the Spain-Russia BIT. Yukos, the Russian oil company, had previously brought a case before the European Court of Human Rights which found a violation by Russia of the right to a fair trial and the right to property set out in Article 6 of the European Convention on Human Rights (ECHR) and Article 1 of Protocol No 1.[104] Other claims brought under Articles 1 of Protocol No 1, taken alone and in conjunction with the Articles 1, 7, 13, 14, and 18, were rejected in light of the high threshold to be met under those provisions.[105]

While paying 'respectful heed' to the earlier analysis and conclusions of the European Court of Human Rights, the arbitrators in *Renta 4* pointed to the need to distinguish the ECHR from the BIT at hand:

> [H]uman rights conventions establish minimum standards to which all individuals are entitled irrespective of any act of volition on their part, whereas investment-protection treaties contain undertakings which are explicitly designed to induce foreigners to make investments in reliance upon them.[106]

For this reason, the arbitral tribunal did not find it 'extraordinary' that under a BIT, foreigners can invoke a higher standard of protection than that received by nationals.[107] To the tribunal, the difference in nature between the ECHR and the BIT also extended to the degree of deference granted the respondent state: the reliability of an IIA should not be 'diluted' by a margin of appreciation.[108] On this basis, the tribunal held that the totality of measures taken by Russia against Yukos amounted to an expropriation: the tax delinquency was a pretext for transferring Yukos' assets to the state-owned Russian oil company Rosneft or one of its affiliates.[109]

In sum, we have seen that a violation of the expropriation provision has been found where the domestic court applied a 'spurious standard' to factual allegations that were accepted without independent review. Also, and even though the IIA at hand is said to offer higher protection than the ECHR, a successful claim might require evidence of inappropriate conduct also of non-judicial government branches.

[102] ibid para 633.

[103] *Quasar de Valores v Russia*, SCC V (024/2007), Award 20 July 2012, IIC 557 (2012). The award is commonly named after the first original claimant that was denied standing by the tribunal in a preliminary award: *Renta 4 v Russia*, SCC V (024/2007) Award 20 March 2009.

[104] *Yukos v Russia* App no 14902/04 (ECtHR, Judgment 20 Sept 2011). The judgment was rectified on 17 January 2012. The final decision was rendered on 8 March 2012.

[105] ibid.

[106] *Renta 4* (n 103) para 22.

[107] ibid para 21. *cf Roussalis v Romania*, ICSID ARB/06/1, Award 7 Dec 2011, IIC 516 (2011) para 312.

[108] ibid para 22.

[109] ibid paras 133, 159–60, 177, 184–86.

ii. Awards Where No Violation was Found

The aforementioned cases notwithstanding, foreign investors are more often than not unsuccessful when arguing that conduct by the host state's judiciary violates the IIA expropriation provision. By way of illustration, we refer to the case *GEA v Ukraine* which arose from a contractual dispute between a German company and Oriana, a Ukrainian state-owned oil refinery.[110] The claimant's predecessor had obtained a favourable arbitration award, but enforcement had been denied by Ukrainian courts on the ground that the underlying agreement should have been signed by the president of the company.

The arbitral tribunal did not agree with the claimant that the refusal to enforce the award constituted an expropriation under the Germany-Ukraine BIT: there was 'no reason to believe that the courts of Ukraine were "applying a discriminatory law," only that the Ukrainian courts came to a conclusion different to that which GEA had hoped'.[111] Moreover, there was no evidence that the actions taken by the Ukrainian courts were 'egregious' in any way; that they amounted to anything other than the application of Ukrainian law; or that they were somehow deliberately taken to thwart GEA's ability to recover on the arbitration award.[112]

Another example is *Arif v Moldova*. As we saw above, the claimant in this case was successful in arguing that Moldova had violated the FET provision in the France-Moldova BIT. Yet, the arbitral tribunal rejected Mr Arif's expropriation claim.[113] It noted first that the agreements had been declared invalid under Moldovan law by the whole of the Moldovan judicial system, including the country's Supreme Court.[114] The tribunal was not persuaded that there had been 'collusion between the courts and the investor's competitors in the proceedings before the Moldovan courts over these agreements or that the Moldovan courts have acted in denial of justice in any way'.[115] Moreover, there was no evidence that the judiciary had not applied Moldovan law legitimately and in good faith.[116] The arbitrators also found it significant that the investor had had 'a fair opportunity to defend its position under Moldovan law before Moldovan courts'.[117] In conclusion, no wrongful taking could have resulted from 'the legitimate application of Moldova's legal system (which the Tribunal

[110] *GEA v Ukraine*, ICSID ARB/08/16, Award 31 March 2011, IIC 487 (2011).

[111] ibid para 236. See also ibid para 231 (the claim would still have failed, since the award did not constitute an investment under the BIT).

[112] ibid.

[113] *Arif* (n 49).

[114] ibid para 415.

[115] ibid.

[116] ibid para 415 (references omitted).

[117] ibid para 416.

notes has not changed since the time the investment was made) and the subsequent invalidity of the rights at stake'.[118]

Based on the foregoing, we can conclude that tribunals have assessed domestic court proceedings against the expropriation standard in cases involving the application of 'spurious standards' to allegations accepted as true; and where the investor has alleged that the court acted in bad faith, in collusion, and/or without observing the right to due process. If true, such conduct would be contrary to the rule of law as defined by the UN Secretary-General and the World Justice Project. Still, arbitrators impose a high burden for an expropriation to be found, requiring, for example, that the conduct must be 'egregious' or constitute an abuse of right. Tribunals may also consider behaviour of other state organs next to that of the judiciary.

C. Effective Means of Asserting Claims and Enforcing Rights

Apart from treaty provisions on FET and expropriation, another relevant provision stipulates that '[e]ach Party shall provide effective means of asserting claims and enforcing rights with respect to investment, investment agreements, and investment authorizations'. Vandevelde explains that such 'effective means' provisions are intended to create a separate obligation 'to develop an effective judicial system and in that to promote the rule of law'.[119] They are not as prevalent in IIAs as the other standards;[120] hence, there is also less jurisprudence.

i. *Awards Where a Violation was Found*

Starting with awards where the tribunal found a violation of the 'effective means' provision, we first refer to *Chevron v Ecuador*.[121] This is a useful example also because the tribunal clarifies how the provision relates to other treaty standards involving domestic court proceedings. In this case, the claimants, Chevron Corporation and Texaco Petroleum Company, brought arbitration proceedings alleging no 'effective means' as well as denial of justice following a series of disputes related to oil exploration

[118] ibid para 417.

[119] Kenneth J Vandevelde, *U.S. International Investment Agreements* (New York; Oxford, Oxford University Press, 2009) 581. *cf Chevron* (n 85), expert opinion DD Caron, 3 Sept 2010 paras 65–66.

[120] *Chevron* (n 85) para 241 ('BIT provisions such as this one are relatively rare. They appear only in U.S. BITs, the Energy Charter Treaty, and a handful of other BITs').

[121] ibid.

agreements that had been pending before Ecuadorian courts for up to 15 years.

The arbitral tribunal first noted that while there is a significant overlap between the two causes of action, the effective means clause 'constitutes a *lex specialis* and not a mere restatement of the law on denial of justice'.[122] Referring to Vandevelde, it found that 'a distinct and potentially less-demanding test is applicable under this provision as compared to denial of justice under international law'.[123] It further noted that the threshold of 'effectiveness' requires that 'a measure of deference be afforded to the domestic justice system; the Tribunal is not empowered by this provision to act as a court of appeal reviewing every individual alleged failure of the local judicial system *de novo*'.[124]

On the merits, Ecuador was found in breach of the effective means clause, making it unnecessary to decide on the denial of justice claim:

> [I]t is the nature of the delay, and the apparent unwillingness of the Ecuadorian courts to allow the cases to proceed that makes the delay in the seven cases undue and amounts to a breach of the BIT by the Respondent for failure to provide 'effective means' … In particular, the Tribunal finds the existence of long delays, even after official acknowledgements by the courts that they were ready to decide the cases, to be a decisive factor demonstrating that the delays experienced by TexPet [Texaco Petroleum Company] are sufficient to breach the BIT.[125]

The tribunal dismissed Ecuador's argument concerning judicial backlogs: the fact that congestion applied from the filing of the claimants' cases in the early-1990s and continued unabated through the end of that decade, made the tribunal conclude that the backlogs could not be considered temporary enough to provide justification for otherwise undue delay.[126]

A second example is the aforementioned case of *White Industries v India*.[127] While we recall that the tribunal found that the delays by Indian courts did not constitute a lack of FET, the effective means clause offered a remedy also for this claimant. The arbitrators had 'no difficulty' in concluding the Indian judicial system's inability to deal with White Industries' jurisdictional claim in over nine years and the Indian Supreme Court's inability to hear White Industries' appeal for over five years constituted a breach of India's obligation to provide the claimant with 'effective means' of asserting claims and enforcing rights.[128]

[122] ibid para 242.

[123] ibid paras 243–44 (citing Kenneth J Vandevelde, *United States International Investment Agreements* (Boston, Kluwer, 1992) 112, and ibid (n 119) 411, 415)).

[124] ibid para 247.

[125] ibid para 262.

[126] ibid paras 263–65.

[127] *White Industries* (n 82).

[128] ibid para 262 (applying India-Kuwait BIT, Art 4(5)). A violation of the effective means clause was also found in *Petrobart* (n 35).

In summary, the less prevalent 'effective means' provision in IIAs may offer protection to investors having suffered extensive judicial delays, including where such delays were not found to have violated the FET provision.

ii. Awards Where No Violation was Found

Turning to awards where the investor failed to establish a violation of the 'effective means' clause, we can refer to the aforementioned case *Amto v Ukraine* in which the tribunal dismissed the denial of justice claim.[129] The claimant had also alleged a breach of the 'effective means' clause in Article 10(12) of the Energy Charter Treaty, and the tribunal interpreted this clause as follows:

> The fundamental criteria of an 'effective means' for the assertion of claims and the enforcement of rights within the meaning of Article 10(12) is law and the rule of law. There must be legislation for the recognition and enforcement of property and contractual rights. This legislation must be made in accordance with the constitution, and be publicly available. An effective means of the assertion of claims and the enforcement of rights also requires secondary rules of procedure so that the principles and objectives of the legislation can be translated by the investor into effective action in the domestic tribunals.[130]

The tribunal also observed that the provision 'does not offer guarantees in individual cases. Individual failures might be evidence of systematic inadequacies, but are not themselves a breach of Article 10(12)'.[131]

On the facts of the case, the arbitrators recognised that there were 'some problems' with the modern Ukrainian Bankruptcy Law; that 'the customs of thought of its lawyers and judges have not succeeded in finding solutions to these problems'; and that the claimant 'has had a frustrating experience in the collection of its debts from Energoatom'.[132] Still, they were not convinced that the Law did not provide an effective means to enforce a creditor's rights in the Ukraine.[133]

In conclusion, the 'effective means' provision is relatively rare and there is therefore also less arbitral practice. Yet, we have seen that it can offer protection in cases where the investor may fail to satisfy the higher threshold required by the FET and expropriation standards, especially where he or she has been subjected to extensive delays in the domestic court system of the host state. Also this provision can be linked to the rule of

[129] *Amto* (n 71).
[130] ibid para 87.
[131] ibid para 88.
[132] ibid para 89.
[133] ibid.

law definitions examined above in section II, particularly that of the World Justice Protect which requires that '[j]ustice is delivered timely'.[134]

IV. THE ROLE OF DOMESTIC LAW CRITERIA WHEN ASSESSING DOMESTIC COURT PROCEEDINGS

We have seen that when applying treaty provisions on FET, expropriation, or 'effective means' in cases involving the host state judiciary, arbitration tribunals interpret the relevant provisions in a way that mirrors rule of law criteria as defined by the UN Secretary-General and the World Justice Project. Among the requirements distilled by arbitrators, we find independent and impartial judges, due process, and avoidance of arbitrariness, discrimination, undue delay, and legality (non-retroactivity). These criteria have a parallel in, and sometimes even originate from, other sources: domestic law[135] and international human rights,[136] the latter which are often part and parcel of domestic law. Rule of law criteria are therefore a good example of what has been coined 'consubstantial' norms.[137]

In this section, we will see that the normative overlap between international and domestic law creates opportunities for the disputing parties and the arbitral tribunals to draw from and/or apply domestic law and jurisprudence in disputes concerning the host state judiciary. Some of these possibilities are inherent to international norms in general; others flow from special features of the field of international investment law and arbitration. Such practice not only illustrates the relationship between international and domestic rule of law norms; the simultaneous reliance of both sources may also strengthen the interpretation and hence application of IIA standards with a rule of law dimension.

Taking Article 38(1) of the Statute of the International Court of Justice (ICJ) as our starting point, it is uncontroversial that domestic sources can constitute elements in the formation and identification of international law. A *first* possibility for arbitrators to draw from these sources is when determining customary international law.[138] The IIA provision invoked by

[134] World Justice Protect, 'What is the Rule of Law?' (n 16).

[135] Schill, 'Fair and Equitable Treatment under Investment Treaties as an Embodiment of the Rule of Law' (n 25) 9. *cf* Giorgio Gaja, 'General Principles of Law' in R Wolfrum (ed), *Max Planck Encyclopedia of Public International Law* (May 2013) para 8.

[136] Liebscher (n 24) 124–27.

[137] International Law Association (ILA) Study Group on Principles on the Engagement of Domestic Courts with International Law, Preliminary Report by Co-Rapporteur A Tzanakopoulos, para 29. See also Hege E Kjos, 'International Law through the National Prism: the Role of Domestic Law and Jurisprudence in Shaping International Investment Law' in Christina Binder, August Reinisch and Mary Footer (eds), *ESIL Conference Proceedings 2014* (Oxford, Hart Publishing, forthcoming).

[138] Statute of the International Court of Justice, 26 June 1945, 33 UNTS 993, Art 38(1)(b).

the investor may reflect custom; and custom can also constitute a separate cause of action depending on the dispute settlement clause.[139] It is generally accepted that domestic legislation and jurisprudence can be consulted for evidence of state practice and *opinio juris*.[140]

Second, treaty provisions may find a parallel in general principles of law. FET, for instance, has been stated to constitute such principle applicable to the investor-state relationship:

> The notions of FET form core elements of any legal system—of any legal 'family' or 'tradition' ... As most developed and developing countries recognize in their domestic laws that FET ought to be applied to foreign investments and investors, one has to conclude that FET is a general principle of law in the realm of foreign investment. This is the case, even though the term FET itself may not be applied as such, but the content of FET, namely the absence of arbitrary action of courts and governmental agencies, is found in national provisions.[141]

Since general principles of law derive from 'the consistent provisions of the various municipal legal systems',[142] arbitration tribunals can rely on domestic law and jurisprudence when interpreting IIA provisions.[143] In fact, it is likely that such reliance was envisaged by drafters of some IIAs. For example, the US Model BIT (2012) includes in the definition of FET 'the obligation not to deny justice in criminal, civil, or administrative adjudicatory proceedings in accordance with the principle of due process embodied in the principal legal systems of the world'.[144]

Third, Article 38(1)(d) stipulates that judicial decisions may be considered as subsidiary means for the determination of rules of law.[145] Hence, it could for instance be possible for a tribunal to inform the meaning of an IIA provision by looking to a decision by a domestic court applying an international norm on due process or by interpreting domestic legislation on due process in light of international law.

Leaving aside Article 38 of the ICJ Statute, the Vienna Convention on the Law of Treaties (VCLT) may provide other avenues for tribunals to consider domestic court decisions. First, they can be viewed as 'subsequent practice' providing evidence of how states parties understand their

[139] cf *Chevron* (n 85) para 209.

[140] Tullio Treves, 'Customary International Law' in R Wolfrum (ed), *Max Planck Encyclopedia of Public International Law* (Nov 2006) para 26, available at: http://mpepil.com.

[141] Diehl, *The Core Standard of International Investment Protection* (n 25) 173–74.

[142] Hugh Thirlway, *The Law and Procedure of the International Court of Justice*, vol I (Oxford, Oxford University Press, 2013) 233. *cf* ICJ Statute (n 138) Art 38(1)(c).

[143] Jeswald W Salacuse and Nicholas P Sullivan, 'Do BITs Really Work?' in Karl P Sauvant and Lisa E Sachs (eds), *The Effect of Treaties on Foreign Direct Investment* (Oxford, Oxford University Press, 2009) 109, 159.

[144] US Model BIT (2012), Art 5(2)(a). *cf* Liebscher (n 24) 122–23.

[145] ICJ Statute (n 138) Art 38(1)(d); Hugh Thirlway, *The Sources of International Law* (Oxford, Oxford University Press, 2014) 124–26.

treaty obligations.[146] Yet, this might be difficult, as the conduct must be 'concordant', ie, the treaty parties have done essentially the same thing expressly in pursuance of the treaty; and for unilateral conduct, it must reveal the agreement of the other party or parties.[147] A second, and more promising possibility is Article 31(1)(3)(c) of the VCLT which provides that when interpreting a treaty, account shall be taken of 'any relevant rule of international law applicable in the relations between the parties'.[148] As noted by Simma and Kill, human rights law can qualify as 'relevant rules' within the meaning of this article.[149] In light of the foregoing discussion of Article 38(1) of the ICJ Statute, it would seem that tribunals may consider domestic (human rights) jurisprudence in this context.

Further, the IIA itself may provide reasons for relying on domestic law and jurisprudence on the rule of law. Many IIAs explicitly allow the investor to invoke the norm—national or international—that offers the best protection.[150] For example, the Greece-Romania BIT stipulates:

> If the provisions of law of either Contracting Party or obligations under international law existing at present or established hereafter between the Contracting Parties in addition to this Agreement, contain a regulation, whether general or specific, entitling investments by investors of the other Contracting Party to a treatment more favourable than is provided for by this Agreement, such regulation shall to the extent that it is more favourable, prevail over this Agreement.[151]

In *Middle East Cement v Egypt*, the arbitral tribunal considered that an identical clause in the Egypt-Greece BIT 'requires the application of additional provisions … if more favourable for the investor', and even when they are not more favourable, such provisions can be 'taken into account' in order to 'supplement' the rules set out in the BIT.[152] The fact that domestic law may impose higher standards of protection was pointed out by the ICJ in the *ELSI* case: it does not 'follow from a finding by a municipal court that an act was unjustified, or unreasonable, or arbitrary, that that act is necessarily to be classed as arbitrary in international law'.[153] Accordingly, another possibility for arbitrators to 'take into account' or even apply

[146] Vienna Convention on the Law of Treaties (VCLT) (adopted 23 May 1969, entered into force 27 Jan 1980) 1155 UNTS 331, Art 31(3); Richard Gardiner, *Treaty Interpretation* 228–30 (Oxford, Oxford University Press, 2008) (Practice may consist of executive, legislative, and judicial acts.).

[147] Gardiner, ibid, 227.

[148] VCLT (n 146) Art 31(1)(3)(c).

[149] Bruno Simma and Theodore Kill, 'Harmonizing Investment Protection and International Human Rights' in Binder and others (eds), *International Investment Law for the 21st Century* (n 24) 678, 695–70.

[150] Kjos, *Applicable Law in Investor-State Arbitration* (n 18) 300–01.

[151] Greece-Romania BIT, Art 10.

[152] Middle East Cement v Egypt, ICSID ARB/99/6, Award 12 April 2002, IIC 169 (2002).

[153] *Elettronica Sicula (ELSI)* (*US v Italy*) [1989] ICJ Reports 15 (Judgment 20 July 1989) para 124. *cf* Paulsson (n 50) 231; Nollkaemper (n 3) 44.

domestic law[154] is when it provides more protection than, for example, the minimum standard of treatment.

Last, but not least, IIAs often lists domestic law as part of the applicable substantive law,[155] and this offers another reason for looking to domestic rule of law criteria. These criteria can also be relied upon in cases where the IIA does not stipulate the applicable law, for instance by virtue of Article 42(1) of the ICSID Convention which provides for the application of domestic law and international law in the absence of party agreement.[156]

Arbitrators may thus draw from domestic law and jurisprudence. In fact, there are many examples of tribunals emphasising normative convergence between national and international law; and they often refer to domestic law in support of their findings on the merits.[157] Yet, only one of the tribunals in the cases examined above expressly relied on domestic jurisprudence when assessing domestic court proceedings. Stated the Tribunal in *Loewen*:

> In the United States and in other jurisdictions, advocacy which tends to create an atmosphere of hostility to a party because it appeals to sectional or local prejudice, has been consistently condemned and is a ground for holding that there has been a mistrial, at least where the conduct amounts to an irreparable injustice.[158]

Other tribunals, while not explicitly citing domestic law, have supported a comparative approach. In *Total v Argentina*, it was observed:

> In determining the scope of a right or obligation, Tribunals have often looked as a benchmark to international or comparative standards. Indeed, as is often the case for general standards applicable in any legal system (such as 'due process'), a comparative analysis of what is considered generally fair or unfair conduct by domestic public authorities in respect of private firms and investors in domestic law may also be relevant to identify the legal standards under BITs. Such an approach is justified because, factually, the situations and conduct to be evaluated under a BIT occur within the legal system and social, economic and business environment of the host State. Moreover, legally, the fair and equitable treatment standard is derived from the requirement of good faith which is undoubtedly a general principle of law under Article 38(1) of the Statute of the International Court of Justice.[159]

[154] Kjos (n 18) 268–69.
[155] ibid 6–7. See, eg, UK-Argentina BIT, Art 8(4).
[156] ICSID Convention, Art 42(1). See also UNCITRAL Arbitration Rules (2010) Art 35(1). This may depend on the scope of the arbitration agreement. Kjos (n 18) 118–27.
[157] Kjos (n 18) 271–93.
[158] *Loewen* (n 51) para 123 (citing 7 US cases).
[159] *Total v Argentina*, ICSID ARB/04/1, Decision on Liability 21 Dec 2010, IIC 484 (2010) para 111. *cf Mobil Corporation v Venezuela*, ICSID ARB/07/27, Decision on Jurisdiction 10 June 2010, IIC 435 (2010) para 169; *Toto v Lebanon*, ICSID ARB/07/12, Award 30 May 2012, IIC 545 (2012) para 166.

This approach has been encouraged by scholars as a means to give substance and meaning to IIA provisions. To Schill, for instance, '[w]hile the arbitral jurisprudence continuously develops a more precise meaning of fair and equitable treatment, it nevertheless meanders around without any clear conceptual vision of the principle's function'.[160] He therefore suggests that 'tribunals should draw—in a comparative approach—on the jurisprudence of domestic and international courts on rule of law standards in order to further concretize fair and equitable treatment'.[161] Montt also favours a comparative methodology.[162] To him, the best perspective is '*BITs-as-developed-countries-constitutional-law-and-no-more*' and this can ensure that IIAs positively influence domestic laws of developing countries and increase the rule of law not only for foreign investors, but more generally.[163]

Relatedly, and in light of the consubstantial nature of rule of law criteria, reliance by tribunals on domestic law, as well as human rights law, can have both a progressive development and defragmenting effect. Wälde explains:

> [T]erms and concepts used in investment law (eg fair and equitable treatment, indirect expropriation, denial of justice, due process) should reflect the progress of law in the specialized fields of international, but also national law. The concept of 'general principles of law recognized by civilized nations' of Article 38(1)(c) of the ICJ statute allows us to take into account not just significant progress in special areas of international law (eg the guarantees of a fair judicial procedure under Article 6 of the ECHR), but also, identified through a comparative public law approach, common approaches to due process and good governance, indirect expropriation, scope of anti-avoidance measures in tax law, or mine reclamation standards, to name but a few.[164]

Moreover, awards that reference both domestic and international law may also be considered more persuasive and legitimate, especially for the party who is unsuccessful on the merits.[165]

While it was brought under a national investment code rather than an IIA, the case *Lahoud v Democratic Republic of the Congo* illustrates the interrelationship between domestic and international law as concerns rule of law criteria pertaining to the investor-state relationship.[166] It is also instructive

[160] Schill (n 25) 37. *cf* Benedict Kingsbury and Stephan Schill, 'Investor-State Arbitration as Governance' (2009) Public Law and Legal Theory Research Paper Series: Working Paper No 09-46, 19–20.

[161] ibid.

[162] Santiago Montt, *State Liability in Investment Treaty Arbitration* (Oxford, Hart Publishing, 2009) 21–23, 75, 165–67.

[163] ibid para 369 (emphasis in original); ibid 80–82.

[164] Thomas W Wälde, 'Interpreting Investment Treaties' in Binder and others (eds) (n 24) 724, 774 (references omitted).

[165] Jan Paulsson, 'Unlawful Laws and the Authority of International Tribunals' (2008) 23(2) *ICSID Review* 215, 230; Kjos (n 18) 273–74.

[166] *Lahoud v DRC*, ICSID ARB/10/4, Award 7 Feb 2014, IIC 637 (2014) (in French).

in that it offers a reason why tribunals do not look to domestic law when assessing court behaviour: lack of reliance on and failure to substantiate such law by the disputing parties.

The arbitration was initiated by a Lebanese couple following a dispute about rental premises and the couple's eviction and subsequent folding of their wood and electricity business. The DRC Investment Code provided for FET 'in conformity with the principles of international law' and included criteria for expropriation, without an explicit reference to international law.[167] The tribunal observed that the parties had offered little argumentation concerning the applicable law in the written and oral pleadings.[168] Thereafter, and at the request of the tribunal, the claimants gave reasons for the application of international law and relied on international law sources;[169] while the DRC pleaded the application of its domestic law.[170] As there was no agreement, the tribunal held that it would apply both DRC law and international law, in accordance with Article 42(1) of the ICSID Convention.[171]

Still, the award in favour of Lahoud was rendered by reference to international law. While it quoted from the DRC Constitution's provision on expropriation,[172] the tribunal justified the lack of reference to domestic law by noting that apart from the copy of the Constitution, neither party had submitted any authority on Congolese law as concerned FET and expropriation.[173]

While arbitrators could conduct their own investigation of domestic law, tribunals generally do not have a duty to go beyond requesting relevant material.[174] Thus, it would have been possible for the Tribunal in *Azinian*, for instance, to refer to the provisions cited by the respondent in its Counter-Memorial. Here, the host state argued that its courts had acted in accordance with fundamental rights embedded in the Mexican Constitution, namely: 'the right to be heard; the observance of due process; the obligation of authorities to set forth the rationale for their acts and cite applicable law; and the prohibition of taking justice into one's own hands'.[175] If no such material is brought forward and substantiated, it is difficult to see how arbitrators should be required to draw on domestic

[167] ibid paras 359, 362 (referring to DRC Investment Code, Arts 25–26).

[168] ibid para 305.

[169] ibid paras 351–53.

[170] ibid paras 354–55.

[171] ibid paras 358, 364.

[172] ibid para 492 (referring to Transitional Constitution, Art 37).

[173] ibid paras 365, 437, 476, 491. *cf Biloune v Ghana Investments Centre and the Government of Ghana*, Award 27 Oct 1989, 95 ILR 183, s VI.

[174] Hege E Kjos, 'Knowing the Law: A Power or a Duty? The Role of Arbitrators and Counsel in Ascertaining the Applicable Law in Investor-State Arbitration' Amsterdam, ESIL Research Forum, 25 May 2013.

[175] *Azinian* (n 59) Counter-Memorial of Mexico, para 240, available at: www.economia.gob.mx/files/comunidad_negocios/solucion_controversias/inversionista-estado/casos_concluidos/Azinian/Counter_Memorial_Azinian_et_al__Mexico.pdf.

law and jurisprudence to further concretise IIA provisions. Keeping in mind the difficulties involved in comparative law research,[176] this observation applies with greater force to the proposition that arbitrators should draw not only from the law of the respondent state but from a multitude of jurisdictions.

The award in *Saar Papier v Poland* stands out in this respect, as the arbitrators looked to domestic law without much assistance by the parties.[177] It is also noteworthy in that it illustrates the consubstantial nature of foreign investment law. The case concerned the claim by the German company Saar Papier that the prohibition on importation of raw material for its production of tissue rolls and toilet paper constituted indirect expropriation in violation of the Germany-Poland BIT. While the facts were not disputed, the parties disagreed on the law.[178] The tribunal asked the parties to discuss at the hearing '"the law of expropriation matérielle" and "Vertrauensschutz im Verwaltungsrecht [legitimate expectations in administrative law]", under the laws of Poland and Germany, and in comparative law, including the [ICSID] Convention and ICSID awards'.[179] Despite repeated requests, the arbitrators received little help from the parties on domestic law.[180] Thus, they relied on their own understanding of general administrative law and the principle of good faith when interpreting the BIT, and drew from German and Swiss law and jurisprudence before concluding that Poland was liable for expropriation.[181]

V. CONCLUDING OBSERVATIONS

As has been seen, IIAs contain standards which have been interpreted to require court behaviour that mirrors several of the rule of law criteria set out by UN Secretary-General and the World Justice Project. We therefore agree with Crawford's observation that in investment disputes, 'if the applicable law is international law, the criterion of liability is a set of standards more or less indistinguishable from the standards of the rule of law—absence of arbitrary conduct, judicial independence, non-retrospectivity'.[182] Furthermore, by applying these criteria to concrete disputes, arbitration

[176] Valentina S Vadi, 'Critical Comparisons' (2010) 39(1) *Denver Journal of International Law and Policy* 67.

[177] *Saar Papier v Poland*, Award 16 Oct 1995, available at: http://italaw.com/.

[178] ibid paras 23–24.

[179] ibid para 15.

[180] ibid paras 16, 79.

[181] ibid paras 79–92.

[182] James Crawford, 'International Law and the Rule of Law' (2003) 24 *Adelaide Law Review* 3, 9.

tribunals give them practical meaning, and at times sanction their breach. Ideally, international investment agreements thereby inspire States to act in accordance with the rule of law.[183] According to Schreuer, this is already the case.[184]

Still, we have seen that IIAs have been interpreted to provide states with a high degree of latitude as concerns domestic court proceedings. Leaving aside cases involving the less prevalent 'effective means' clause which offers more protection, misconduct was only found in cases involving undue influence by other government branches;[185] retroactive application of laws;[186] and decisions based on 'spurious standards', lacking reasoning, and constituting an abuse of right.[187]

The high threshold is consistent with and can also explain statistics showing that states prevail in the majority of investment arbitrations in general.[188] Rather than reflecting institutional or procedural deference vis-à-vis domestic decision-making, we suggest that the wide latitude is best considered as stemming from the IIA provisions themselves.[189] Nonetheless, it may be more difficult to succeed when alleging wrongful behaviour by courts as compared to other branches of government.[190] Although the tribunal in *Renta 4*, for instance, expressly rejected the application of a 'margin of appreciation'[191] and other tribunals characterised as outdated the notion that courts are entitled to more deference than other branches of government,[192] the observation that some degree of procedural or institutional deference has been applied in addition to and beyond substantive latitude is supported by Wälde. To him, judicial misconduct is more frequent than indications in most arbitral awards would indicate:

> Tribunals, even with evidence of corruption and political interference, will prefer to rest their reasoning on other, less sensitive and problematic, facts and claims even if the findings in an award will be indirectly influenced by evidence of judicial misconduct. But there is—and probably has to be—a certain

[183] René Gayle, 'Investment Treaty Arbitration' (2013) 1(1) *Latin American Journal of International Trade Law* 481, 484, 491.

[184] Christoph H Schreuer, 'Do We Need Investment Arbitration?' (2014) 11(1) *Transnational Dispute Management* 4. *cf* Wälde, 'Denial of Justice' (n 6) 478–79; Kingsbury and Schill, 'Investor-State Arbitration as Governance' (n 160) 16–17. But see Benjamin K Guthrie, 'Beyond Investment Protection' (2013) 45 *NYU Journal of International Law & Politics* 1151, 1153 (The question whether BITs help or harm the quality of domestic rule of law depends heavily on the specific legal, political, and social contexts of individual countries).

[185] *Petrobart* (n 35); *Deutsche Bank* (n 40).

[186] *ATA* (n 37).

[187] *Saipem* (n 89).

[188] Schultz and Dupont (n 6) 16; ICSID, *The ICSID Caseload—Statistics* (Issue 2015-1) 13–14, 27–28.

[189] Fahner (n 4). *cf Whaling in the Antarctic* (Australia v Japan: New Zealand Intervening) [2014] ICJ Reports (Judgment, 31 March 2014) paras 59, 65–67.

[190] Van Harten (n 4) 130.

[191] *Renta 4* (n 103) para 22.

[192] *Arif* (n 49) para 439; *Azinian* (n 59) para 89.

element of 'taboo' in having an international tribunal condemning the conduct of a national court.[193]

Indeed, in *Arif* and the *Yukos* cases, the arbitrators found a violation based on a cumulative assessment of the behaviour of several state organs including, but not limited to, the judiciary.[194]

With this high threshold and possible additional deference in mind, investors and their counsel might consider invoking domestic rule of law criteria next to treaty provisions on FET, expropriation, and 'effective means'. These could set out higher standards of protection; but perhaps more importantly, there may be less of a 'taboo' when tribunals sanction court behaviour by reference to the 'law of the land'. When adopting this approach, arbitrators may not only play a part 'in advancing the rule of law at the international and national levels';[195] they also enhance the legitimacy of the award for the respondent state and its population. Notes Paulsson:

> [W]hen a government has overreached, when it has cowed legislators or judges, when it has followed a practice of weakening the judiciary, even citizens of the country whose law is in question may come to see the international tribunal as a defender of enduring national values.[196]

From the perspective of the larger theme examined in this edited volume, such practice also illustrates a 'pendulum effect' with respect to the national and international dimensions of the rule of law: IIA provisions may originate in domestic law and when applying these provisions, tribunals may inform their interpretation by reference to domestic law.

[193] Wälde (n 6) 445–46. *cf Deutsche Bank* (n 40), dissenting opinion Khan, para 107.

[194] *Arif* (n 49) para 547; *RosInvest* (n 98); *Renta 4* (n 103). See also *Deutsche Bank* (n 40) paras 520–24 (the 'coordinated actions of the Supreme Court and the Central Bank' amounted to a 'financially motivated and illegitimate regulatory expropriation by a regulator lacking in independence'); *Swisslion v Macedonia*, ICSID ARB/09/16, Award 6 July 2012, IIC 558 (2012) paras 275, 300; *Rumeli v Kazakhstan*, ICSID ARB/05/16, Award 21 July 2008, IIC 344 (2008) para 708.

[195] GA Declaration (n 3) para 32.

[196] Paulsson, 'Unlawful Laws and the Authority of International Tribunals' (n 165) 232.

15

The Rule of Law at the National and International Levels in Post-Conflict Peace Agreements

JENNIFER EASTERDAY

I. INTRODUCTION

PEACE AGREEMENTS CREATE a framework for the transition from war to peace and serve as a context-specific opportunity to study the rule of law in post-conflict settings.[1] They develop a new political order for the future, devising norms that are meant to foster sustainable peace. Peace agreements are inherently political, negotiated between parties to the conflict, often with international input and mediation.

Constitutional peace agreements—those agreements that act as constitutions or analogous documents—also serve as an interface between national and international law. They are a mechanism through which national and international law can develop the rule of law in an interactive manner. Constitutional peace agreements create the laws and institutions through which conflicts can be politically mediated and establish the laws that will govern newly peaceful societies. They become the vehicle for rule of law—nationally and internationally—by embedding international norms into the social contract between the people and the state and creating connections between individuals and international law. The unique aspects of constitutional peace agreements, such as their conceptual and legal hybridity; their various levels of inclusion of international interlocutors and exclusion of domestic constituents; and their reliance on a process of contentious bargaining complicates this process and requires careful consideration.

[1] This chapter adopts the definition of 'rule of law' set forth in ch 1 (Kanetake) of this volume. Moreover, this chapter discusses the theoretical potential of constitutional peace agreements, acknowledging that many peace agreements fail and many of their aspirations are frequently unrealised.

This chapter will discuss how peace agreements serve as an interface between international law and national law in post-conflict settings, where establishing the rule of law is often a priority of peacebuilders. Although examining substantive norms in constitutional peace agreements is important from a rule of law perspective, this chapter will argue that the *process* of incorporating international norms and laws is particularly important for the study of international rule of law. The study of constitutional peace agreements demonstrates the importance of striking a delicate balance between international and national interests through a process of dialogue between the national and international and adherence to the principle of qualified deference to national law. Constitutional peace agreements show that, in some situations, dialogue and qualified deference might foster increased compliance with international law and in some respects also might serve the international rule law of law.

Section II of this chapter first introduces distinct features of constitutional peace agreements. Section III goes on to explore how constitutional peace agreements embody conceptual and legal hybridity and are crafted with constructive ambiguity through a process of contentious bargaining that changes significantly depending on who gets a seat at the negotiation table. Section IV addresses constitutional peace agreements as an interface between domestic and international law, and discusses how international law shapes—and is shaped by—constitutional peace agreements. Section IV also analyses the mutually reinforcing legitimising relationship between international law and constitutional peace agreements through dialogue and qualified deference. The chapter concludes in section V by arguing that the study of constitutional peace agreements shows that flexible norms of dialogue and qualified deference should be applied by international actors in post-conflict situations in order to better foster peace and the rule of law.

II. PEACE AGREEMENTS AS CONSTITUTIONS

Peace agreements are documents created with the aim to end a violent military conflict through discussion with parties to the conflict.[2] They are transformative documents in the life of a conflict, setting out a new 'power map' for the state, establishing organs of government and societal institutions, and redefining the relationship between the state and the citizen.[3]

[2] Christine Bell, *On the Law of Peace: Peace Agreements and the Lex Pacificatoria* (Oxford, Oxford University Press, 2008) 53.

[3] Christine Bell, *Peace Agreements and Human Rights* (Oxford, Oxford University Press, 2000) 304–05.

Successful or not, they provide a 'snap-shot' of an agreed-upon framework for moving from conflict to peace. They indicate the types of trade-offs parties to a conflict, the international community, and others who sit at the negotiating table will make in the interests of peace. They provide a list of 'ingredients' for a possible peaceful solution to the conflict.[4]

Peace agreements create linkages between the international and domestic spheres, the state and individuals, and politics and law. The agreements are a site of convergence for these dyads, and, within each area, they also bring together different actors (such as the state, military, non-state armed groups, civil society, and the general public) and areas of law (such as domestic, international human rights, and international humanitarian law). One way that peace agreements manage these relationships and utilise them as a tool for peace is through their constitutional nature.[5] The constitutional characteristics of a peace agreement determine how the aforementioned dyads are intertwined in post-conflict peace management.

Peace agreements pave the way for more in-depth negotiation and constitution-making in the future. They are, fundamentally and by definition, driven by the transformation from conflict to peace. Bell and O'Rourke write that 'peace agreements offer an example of the type of structures which can emerge when radical change is viewed not just as possible, but as necessary: peace agreements constitute a site of experimentation on which democratic renewal efforts can draw'.[6]

Peace agreements can be broadly classified into pre-negotiation agreements (agreements about the negotiations), substantive or framework agreements (agreements about the substantive aspects of the peace process and post-conflict governance), and implementation agreements (agreements about the process and details of implementing the substantive agreements).[7] These different types of agreements appear at different stages or phases of peace negotiations. The focus of this chapter is on substantive or framework agreements, which provide a legal framework for governance and aim to permanently end the conflict. They typically involve processes to end military violence, such as demilitarisation and demobilisation. They also include constitutional provisions to address

[4] Kirsti Samuels, 'Postwar Constitution Building: Opportunities and Challenges' in R Paris and TD Sisk (eds), *The Dilemmas of Statebuilding: Conflicting the Contradiction of Postwar Peace Operations* (London and New York, Routledge, 2009) 173, 174.

[5] Bell, *Lex Pacificatoria* (n 2) 142–49, 151–52. Bell acknowledges downsides to characterising peace agreements as constitutions, including the tensions of translating between law and politics vis-à-vis a constitution in post-conflict societies, as well as challenges with compliance due to the relationship of the agreement with the previous constitutional order.

[6] Christine Bell and Catherine O'Rourke, 'The People's Peace? Peace Agreements, Civil Society, and Participatory Democracy' (2007) 28 *International Political Science Review* 293, 296.

[7] Classification involves its own problems and dilemmas, but is a useful tool for comparison and study of peace agreements. Bell (n 2) 64–65.

issues of governance, elections, justice institutions, and human rights.[8] They link the ceasefire to new political and legal structures, creating governance institutions for the transition to peace.[9]

Among these substantive or framework agreements, this chapter explores those agreements that serve as surrogate or interim constitutions and those that are explicitly drafted as constitutions. Substantive peace agreements approximate the definition of a 'constitution', but differ from traditional constitutions in both form and substance.[10] Many substantive agreements explicitly include a constitution or provisions for drafting a constitution. Other agreements might not, but rather might set out guiding principles as a basis for a constitution, or detailed proposals for constitutional amendments or revision.[11] Some peace agreements are explicitly structured like constitutions or include constitutional provisions.

Those substantive peace agreements that closely resemble or include a constitution are termed 'constitutional peace agreements' for the sake of this chapter. The South African Interim Constitution,[12] the Bosnia-Herzegovina Constitution, which was included as an annex in the Dayton Accords,[13] the failed Rambouillet Accords[14] in Kosovo, and the Bougainville Peace Agreement[15] are some examples of constitutional peace agreements. Constitutional peace agreements arise in part out of a push to establish 'constitutionalism' in post-conflict societies.[16] They act as transformative constitutional moments, engaging a process of constitutional change brought on by the signing of the peace agreement. The description of 'constitutional peace agreements' is intended to capture the transformative power of substantive peace agreements that shape the future governance structure and legal system of post-conflict states. It is also used here to show the relationship between levels of governance at national and international levels, including the relationship of international law to individuals in post-conflict states.

[8] Bell (n 2) 60.

[9] Bell and O'Rourke, 'The People's Peace' (n 6).

[10] Bell (n 2) 150. A government that includes democratic institutions, a bill of rights, and judicial oversight is considered 'constitutional'. ibid.

[11] Michele Brandt, Jill Cottrell, Yash Ghai and Anthony Regan, *Constitution-Making and Reform: Options for the Process* (Geneva, Interpeace, 2011) 258.

[12] Constitution of the Republic of South Africa, Act no 200 of 1993.

[13] General Framework Agreement for Peace in Bosnia and Herzegovina ('Dayton Peace Agreement') 14 Dec 1995, 35 ILM 75 (1996).

[14] Interim Agreement for Peace and Self-Government in Kosovo (Rambouillet, 23 Feb 1999).

[15] Bougainville Peace Agreement (Arawa, 30 Aug 2001).

[16] See, eg, Samuels, 'Postwar Constitution Building' (n 4); see also Ruti Teitel, 'Transitional Jurisprudence: The Role of Law in Political Transformation' (1997) 106 *Yale Law Journal* 2009, 2076.

III. CONSTITUTIONAL PEACE AGREEMENTS AS 'HYBRID' INSTRUMENTS

Constitutional peace agreements are hybrid, negotiated documents. They create the institutional framework that will guide the application of international law within a legal setting that has traditionally been conceived of as a 'social contract' between the state and its peoples. They shape the environment in which international law operates in the domestic context in states that are undergoing significant transition. Constitutional peace agreements frequently reference or incorporate international law—sometimes as a superior source of constitutional law—and use international states or organisations as enforcers. Because of their hybridity, they do not just relate to the domestic rule of law or the international rule of law. They are a unique interface of both, and the extent to which they can serve either depends on how well they balance the international/domestic dyad.

This section describes unique 'hybrid' characteristics of constitutional peace agreements and their drafting process. It first discusses their conceptual and legal hybridity. The legal nature of peace agreements exists in a 'middle space', outside traditional notions of international law as between states, but at the same time outside the realm of the purely domestic law. It then turns to the drafting process and potential result. Multiple actors are involved in a process of contentious bargaining in drafting constitutional peace agreements. Due to the post-conflict context, this process might exclude important constituents and lead to constructive ambiguity in the final text. In the following section, this chapter argues that because of this hybridity and unique process, to successfully support the rule of domestic and international law, the constitutional peace agreement process must carefully balance dialogue and qualified deference to local initiatives with the delicate process and priority of establishing peace.[17]

A. Conceptual and Legal Hybridity

Because constitutional peace agreements are conflict-driven, they forge and manage multiple relationships beyond those between the state and individual. They display a 'conceptual hybridity', mediating between war/peace; past/future; old state/new state; and international/national law, and by shaping future politics through a quasi-legal document drafted through a conflict-driven political process.[18] Constitutional peace

[17] See further section IV of this chapter.
[18] See Bell (n 2) 200.

agreements also display a 'legal hybridity'. They create a new and detailed power map for the post-conflict state. This power map redefines the state, disaggregating and dislocating power.[19] These power relations are central to the peace agreement debate and can be more important than, for example, a bill of rights.[20] They involve state, non-state, and international actors, creating questions over the legal nature of peace agreements and taking them outside of traditional notions of international law as between states. However, the 'internationalisation' of the agreements also takes them outside of the realm of the purely domestic 'social contract'.[21]

It is in this 'hybrid' context that the relationship between international and domestic law is mediated. Constitutional peace agreements reflect an international/domestic hybridity. For example, they may acknowledge the international status of some non-state entities or establish a role for international actors in their domestic implementation. This 'internationalises' future domestic power arrangements.[22] Constitutional peace agreements frequently refer to international law and use international states or organisations as enforcers.[23] This hybridity allows peace agreements to resolve classic constitutional law dilemmas and function in a weakened post-conflict state.[24] It embeds international law into the relationship between the state and the people.

The relationship between international and national law in constitutional peace agreements is not one-directional. The use of international law in constitutional peace agreements has the potential to influence the development of international law. For example, this could arise through the creation of a general practice for the negotiation and drafting of future peace agreements, what Christine Bell terms a '*lex pacificatoria*'. International law captured in constitutional peace agreements can also shape the setting for the application of international legal norms during the transition from conflict to peace, also known as *jus post bellum*.[25] It could also be through domestic judicial interpretation of international norms captured in the constitution, which can lend to the development of customary international law as evidence of state practice and *opinio juris*. In addition, constitutional peace agreements can more subtly influence international

[19] ibid 122.

[20] Sujit Choudry, 'After the Rights Revolution: Bills of Rights in the Postconflict State' (2010) 6 *Annual Review of Law and Social Science* 301, 303.

[21] Bell (n 2) 122–23.

[22] Bell, *Human Rights* (n 3) 305.

[23] Bell (n 2) 151.

[24] ibid 200.

[25] 'Peace Agreements as a Framework for *Jus Post Bellum*' in C Stahn, J Easterday, and J Iverson, *Jus Post Bellum: Mapping the Normative Foundations* (Oxford, Oxford University Press, 2014) 379.

legal norms; for example, by providing greater protection of rights than does international law and forcing a normative shift in the application of international law.[26]

Bell argues that 'precisely because of the peace agreement's hybrid nature, international law's assumptions of a separate international and domestic sphere do not fit. [...] Peace agreements are constitutive of international law, even as international law attempts to regulate their content'.[27] She argues that peace agreements shape international law by both underwriting its moral claims and notions of ideal institutions. Peace agreements go further than what international law requires by addressing wider notions of justice. For example, because peace agreements reflect micro-bargains over the meta-conflict, peace agreements might provide for ethnic balance in institutions, while international soft law standards about institutional best practices do not deal with the question of ethnic balance. Other specific areas where international law could learn from peace agreements include: balancing human rights institutions according to ethnic make-up; goals for dealing with the past that move beyond the accountability/impunity dyad to include notions of restorative justice and reconciliation; inclusion of a structural place for civil society in peace negotiations; and the impact of peacebuilding operations on civil society.[28]

Constitutional peace agreements are both shaped by, and shape, international law, and have potentially far-reaching influence on the constituencies in the states that adopt them. Thus, the inclusion of international law in constitutional peace agreements, which are drafted as negotiated documents and intended to bring sustainable peace, presents a unique interface between international and domestic law. In order to mutually reinforce the two in post-conflict states, the correct balance between them must be struck during the processes of negotiation and drafting.

B. Multiplicity of Actors Involved

The hybridity of constitutional peace agreements is often a reflection of the multiplicity of actors involved in the negotiation process. The dynamics and results of the negotiation process are driven by who sits at the table. Peace agreement negotiations are often exclusionary when it comes to members of civil society or representatives of the broader population. They are frequently drafted with international involvement. This exclusion/inclusion of domestic and international factors becomes a site

26 Bell (n 3) 314; Bell (n 2) 218.
27 Bell (n 2) 218–19.
28 Bell (n 3) 229–30, 314–17.

of tension when the constitution is viewed as the manifestation of the will of the people. The exclusion of 'the people' in the negotiating process can delegitimise the resulting constitution, a document which purports to reflect the democratic principles of a state but which was created in the absence of the democratic value of inclusion and participation of the people.[29] The role of international arbitrators and technicians can both support and detract from the perceived legitimacy of the constitutional peace agreement, as it can be seen as reflecting international values of rule of law or, alternatively, as imposed from an external intervener.

In terms of substance, international law is often included as neutral language that can both add legitimacy to the agreement internationally and domestically as well as constrain the future actions of politicians.[30] This constraint can reassure signatories and constituents during the post-conflict phase, when the future of the state seems precarious. However, international law then becomes part of the primary laws of the state, again resting on the assumption that those international laws reflect values that are accurate representations of the will of the domestic people the constitution purports to reflect.

i. Inclusion and Exclusion of Local Constituents

Traditionally, it has been understood that the *pouvoir constituent*, or the people of a nation as a political body, is the only entity with the force to create a new political order vis-à-vis a constitution.[31] The power of the *pouvoir constituent* is rooted in the individual.[32] Therefore, the multiplicity of actors at the peace negotiation table—few of which are likely to adequately represent 'the people'—presents a unique problem when a constitution arises out of a peace agreement. Can these actors legitimately create a constitution that binds the (largely unrepresented) people to a new social contract?

Peace agreement scholars have found that peace agreement negotiation processes generally exclude members of society at large and only include parties to the conflict and the other stakeholders that are seen as

[29] Participation can come in the form of oversight, direct input, or ratification. They might be different conceptions of involvement, but constitute involvement nevertheless. Zachary Elkins, Tom Ginsburg and Justin Blount, 'The Citizen as Founder: Public Participation in Constitutional Approval' (2008) 81 *Temple Law Review* 361, 363.

[30] See, eg, ibid 363.

[31] Philipp Dann and Zaid Al-Ali, 'The Internationalized Pouvoir Constituant—Constitution-Making Under External Influence in Iraq, Sudan and East Timor' (2006) 10 *Max Planck Yearbook of United Nations Law* 423, 426.

[32] ibid 426.

critical for reaching a peace settlement.[33] In spite of moral imperatives to allow the broader public to have a voice in constitutional peace agreement processes,[34] practical considerations—namely, bringing a stop to the fighting—limit their inclusion.[35] Introducing members of civil society, interest groups, or human rights groups can complicate and detract from this goal.[36]

Peace agreement data also suggests that the agreements may not be as inclusive as might be ideal. For example, only 9 per cent of peace agreements in a UN peace agreement database provided for national dialogue or consultation mechanisms as part of the implementation arrangements. Twenty-two per cent provide for military monitors of implementation, but only 11 per cent include civilian monitors. Moreover, in terms of supporting actors, only 13 per cent of peace agreements include provisions related to civil society, whereas 40 per cent include provisions related to the United Nations.[37] While this data is not conclusive about the inclusion or exclusion of different groups in peace agreement negotiation and drafting processes, it does suggest that provisions about the inclusion of broad segments of society are not frequently included in peace agreements.

Exclusion and inclusion of 'the people' can directly impact the success of the constitutional peace agreement. According to one study, durable peace agreements involved direct participation by civil society in the peace negotiations. This was especially the case when the negotiations also involved undemocratic elites.[38] The exclusion of certain groups, especially

[33] Bell (n 3) 231; Vivien Hart, *Democratic Constitution Making* (United States Institute of Peace, 2003) 4; Vivien Hart, 'Constitution-Making and the Transformation of Conflict' (2001) 26 *Peace and Change* 153, 160; David Lanz, 'Who Gets a Seat at the Table? A Framework for Understanding the Dynamics of Inclusion and Exclusion in Peace Negotiations' (2011) 16 *International Negotiation* 275, 277. See also Samuels (n 4) 177.

[34] Hart, *Democratic Constitution Making* (n 33) 4; Hart, 'Constitution-Making and Transformation' (n 33) 160.

[35] Lanz, 'Who Gets a Seat at the Table? (n 33) 277; Anonymous, 'Human Rights in Peace Negotiations' (1996) 18 *Human Rights Quarterly* 249; Anthony Wanis-St John and Darren Kew, 'Civil Society and Peace Negotiations: Confronting Exclusion' (2008) 13 *International Negotiation* 11, 12–13.

[36] Anonymous, 'Human Rights in Peace Negotiations' (n 35); Lanz (n 33); Wanis-St John and Kew, 'Civil Society and Peace Negotiations' (n 35) 13.

[37] These numbers were gleaned from an examination of the UN database on peace agreements. The UN Peacemaker Database of Peace Agreements is a reference tool with over 750 documents broadly considered as peace agreements and related material. The data has been coded by the UN Peacemaker project. The information was downloaded and analysed by the frequency of particular codes. More detailed information, about how the coding was done or according to what criteria, is available at: http://peacemaker.un.org/document-search. Moreover, numerical evaluations should be treated with caution, given the complexity of how peace agreements are drafted, categorised, and developed. See, eg, Bell and O'Rourke (n 6) 297.

[38] Wanis-St John and Kew (n 35) 14.

in ethnic conflicts, can lead to an outbreak of violence.[39] One way to bring the view of the people into peace negotiations is to include members of civil society in the negotiation, drafting, and implementation processes.[40] Inclusion seems to be even more critical when the peace process results in a constitution, which will form the basis of a new pact between the government and society and a continuous conversation about how to sustain peace. Indeed, there appears to be an emerging consensus that legitimate constitution-making processes require public participation and consent,[41] and constitution-drafting norms advocate an open, transparent, and participatory drafting process with input from citizens at all stages of the process.[42]

This suggests the critical need for broad dialogue and consultation in the constitutional peace agreement process, and a consideration of the views of the wider population of the relevant state. The dialogue will also include international interveners, who, as discussed below in section IV, will need to show openness and qualified deference to domestic views in their interventions.

ii. International Involvement

Various international actors can exercise influence at various stages of the constitutional peace agreement drafting process. The United Nations, foreign occupying powers, regional organisations, groups of states, and individual actors can all be involved.[43] These actors can play a variety of roles: instigating and setting a framework for the constitutional process but leaving the details to domestic actors (as in East Timor);[44] intervening throughout the process, such as by determining the composition of drafting bodies and procedural frameworks or influencing how constitutional committees undertake their work (as in Iraq);[45] and by brokering a peace agreement that becomes the basis for the constitution (as in Sudan).[46] Typically, the external influence is provided through expert technical

[39] Clive Baldwin, Chris Chapman and Zoë Gray, 'Minority Rights: The Key to Conflict Prevention' (Minority Rights Group International Report 2007) 5, noting that excluding minorities may push them to resort to violence in order to obtain their needs; Hallie Ludsin, 'Peacemaking and Constitution-Drafting: A Dysfunctional Marriage' (2011) 33 *University of Pennsylvania Journal of International Law* 239, 281.

[40] Wanis-St John and Kew (n 35) 13.

[41] Hart, *Democratic Constitution Making* (n 33) 12.

[42] Donald Horowitz, 'Conciliatory Institutions and Constitutional Processes in Post-Conflict States' (2008) 49 *William & Mary Law Review* 1213, 1231–32.

[43] Dann and Al-Ali, 'The Internationalized Pouvoir Constituant' (n 31) 430.

[44] ibid 434.

[45] ibid 442.

[46] ibid 448.

assistance in the drafting process.[47] International organisations, foreign states, academic institutions, and NGOs deploy legal technicians to help draft provisions of the constitution, which can influence the inclusion of international law.[48] There might also be international involvement as a 'check' on domestic drafting processes in order to 'guarantee' protection of different minority groups.[49] In the case of brokering peace agreements, the international influence can again vary by degree, actors, and role.[50] It can also vary over time: when this influence or attention to the process wanes, local powerful elites can push for relaxing or rolling back terms of the peace agreement.[51]

International involvement can impact the substance and process of the constitution, and can have a negative impact on the legitimacy of the constitution.[52] First, international actors bring an external group of interests and concerns to the table, some of which might detract from the legitimacy and effectiveness of the resultant constitution. For example, in constitutional negotiations between Sudan and South Sudan, the United States and Norway reportedly pressured international mediators to tilt the agreement in favour of the South in order to serve their respective Christian communities and move away from the application of Islamic sharia law. This caused a negative reaction from the Sudanese delegate, criticism of the international mediators, and relegation of the international mediators and experts to a more background role.[53]

Furthermore, international actors' timetables and agendas, which usually focus on conflict resolution over constitution drafting, often dominate—and detract from—the process.[54] International actors may place short time frames on constitutional drafters, who face pressure to

[47] ibid 455.

[48] Vicki C Jackson, 'What's in a Name? Reflections on Timing, Naming and Constitution-Making' (2008) 49 *William & Mary Law Review* 1249, 1296; Dann and Al-Ali (n 31) 424, 427; Vijayashri Sripati, 'UN Constitutional Assistance Projects in Comprehensive Peace Missions: An Inventory 1989–2011' (2012) 19 *International Peacekeeping* 93 (noting that 'since 1989, the UN Security Council has mandated peace missions to assist 12 states in writing new constitutions: Burundi, Namibia, Rwanda, Somalia, Sudan, South Sudan, Afghanistan, Cambodia, East Timor, Nepal, Kosovo and Iraq. It has mandated peace missions to assist states such as Sierra Leone and Liberia in reforming their existing constitutions. The UN Development Program (UNDP) has offered constitutional support to Bhutan, Ecuador, Eritrea, Gambia, Guyana, Malawi, Maldives, Nauru, Solomon Islands, Tokelau, Zambia and Zimbabwe. In 2011 the UN extended its offer of constitutional assistance to new Arab governments in Egypt, Tunisia and Libya'. Internal citations omitted.).

[49] Jackson, 'What's in a Name?' (n 48) 1298.

[50] Dann and Al-Ali (n 31) 448.

[51] Alvaro De Soto and Graciana del Castillo, 'Implementation of Comprehensive Peace Agreements: Staying the Course in El Salvador' (1995) 1 *Global Governance* 190.

[52] Dann and Al-Ali (n 31) 456–57.

[53] Dann and Al-Ali (n 31) 446.

[54] Brandt and others, *Constitution-Making and Reform* (n 11) 260.

adopt a constitution with limited resources of time and expertise. In Iraq, for example, a short timeline imposed by the US pressured the transitional Iraqi government to move ahead with a constitution even though it had not first established a ceasefire with Sunni groups. This posed a serious disadvantage for the success of the constitution, making it less inclusive of Sunni participation and therefore lacking in legitimacy. Some have argued that Sunni exclusion from the process may have fuelled an insurgency that has plagued peace in Iraq.[55]

Additionally, international actors can also directly influence who is included and excluded from the drafting process. Bell has observed that civil society tends to be involved in negotiation processes when the process is primarily internal. Internationally mediated processes, however, tend to approach the problem from an 'international relations and violence-focused' paradigm and do not tend to include civil society. She notes,

> Internally driven processes by their nature must preserve the link between politicians and their constituents. Internationally facilitated processes often focus on bringing together those who have directly waged the war, often in secret and isolated locations, while the skills of those who have waged peace through churches, voluntary associations, women's groups, and trade unions are left at home.[56]

This suggests that in order to preserve democratic principles in negotiating constitutional peace agreements, international facilitators should strive to include a broad range of local constituents.

The scope of international influence appears to be increasing. Over time, the UN has begun to explicitly recognise constitution drafting as a conflict resolution and prevention mechanism. Its influence is more than just technical, as the UN pushes for particular substantive norms to be included in peace agreements[57] and post-conflict constitutions. The UN position emphasises open and participatory processes, human rights, accountability, and anti-corruption measures. Increasingly, the UN is also concerned with protecting the rights of women and minorities. It has developed outreach, consultation, and education programs so that citizens are informed about the new norms of constitutionalism and can

[55] Ludsin, 'Peacemaking and Constitution-Drafting' (n 39) 256, 270.

[56] Bell (n 3) 231. Roland Paris has also noted that participatory constitution-making processes that have emerged in the past few decades arose of out largely internal processes without international involvement. Samuels (n 4) 177.

[57] eg, the Sierra Leone Lomé Peace Accord included a blanket and unconditional amnesty for all participants to the conflict. The United Nations Special Representative added a disclaimer to the agreement, stating that the amnesty would not apply to crimes against humanity, war crimes, genocide, or other serious violations of international law. Seventh Report of the Secretary-General on the United Nations Mission in Sierra Leone UN Doc S/1999/836, 30 July 1999, para 7.

comment on draft provisions.[58] The UN has also educated drafters on issues such as human rights, gender, and equality, and has pushed the 'Paris Principles'—best practices and guidelines on national human rights institutions.[59] The UN will also audit draft constitutions.[60]

The UN Secretary-General has explicitly outlined 'Guiding Principles' for its assistance in constitution drafting.[61] A key principle is to encourage compliance with international norms and standards. The Secretary-General has explicitly called for the UN to

> [C]onsistently promote compliance of constitutions with international human rights and other norms and standards. Thus, it should speak out when a draft constitution does not comply with these standards, especially as they relate to the administration of justice, transitional justice, electoral systems and a range of other constitutional issues. The UN should be the advocate of the standards it has helped to develop. Accordingly, the UN should engage national actors in a dialogue over substantive issues, and explain the country's obligations under international law and the ways in which they could be met in the constitution.[62]

Ensuring national ownership and inclusivity are also key parts of the UN principles. The Secretary-General specifically calls for dialogue with national actors in order to foster compliance with international norms. The UN position also seems to promote the concept of a 'qualified' deference (explained further in section IV), as it seeks to find mutually acceptable ways for the post-conflict state to meet its international obligations through constitutional revision.

Combined, international efforts arguably have a significant impact on the outcome of the drafting process.[63] However, in practice, the international influence can be marred by a number of factors, such as a lack of genuine public participation, in spite of claims that such participation is critical; engaging primarily with political elites and warring factions; stressing narrow solutions to problems of representation and legitimacy; and a failure to develop the capacity of national actors and promote national ownership.[64]

[58] Sripati, 'UN Constitutional Assistance Projects in Comprehensive Peace Missions' (n 48) 94–95.

[59] UN Doc A/RES/48/134, 4 March 1994.

[60] Sripati (n 48) 94–95.

[61] UN Secretary-General, 'Guidance Note of the Secretary-General: United Nations Assistance to Constitution-making Processes' (UN Rule of Law, 2009) 3, available at: http://unrol.org/files/Guidance_Note_United_Nations_Assistance_to_Constitution-making_Processes_FINAL.pdf.

[62] ibid 4.

[63] Sripati (n 48) 94–95.

[64] Brandt and others (n 11) 322–27.

International interveners turn to the constitution as a place to shift and develop the social mores of the post-conflict society through basic democratic education of the population.[65] However, as previously mentioned, this is a complicated task and one that has not always been undertaken successfully.[66] Assuming that law can impact and change social behaviour, the inclusion of international norms, then, could also play a significant role both in the sustainability of peace as well as in shaping the social mores of the society. For example, it is possible that the inclusion of human rights norms in constitutional peace agreements could foster a more rights-respecting society, and a polity that understands and demands that its rights are protected by the government. However, it is also possible that the inclusion of human rights norms, if not undertaken carefully or if 'tacked on' to the agreement, could create future unanticipated problems and reduce the potential impact of these norms on the post-conflict society.[67] This again underscores the importance of process, and not just content.

Peacebuilding initiatives that focus on the creation and reformation of institutions and legal codes in the hope that the conflict will be transformed into the peaceful arena of politics wrongly assume that such changes will naturally lead to a commitment to the rule of law; and fail to recognise that the creation of democratic constitutions will not automatically embed democratic ideals into the population.[68] Kim Lane Scheppele argues that predicting the success of a constitution does not only turn on how it is initially designed or the rights it contains, but may actually depend more on the development of 'constitutional culture'. She argues that '[t]he most important element of 'constitutional culture' is the willingness of a population battered by recent political turbulence to treat the newly designed constitutional institutions as real from the start'.[69]

The population might fail to consider new institutions and mechanisms as means of conflict resolution, especially if the government is absent, weak, perceived as illegitimate, or if there is restricted access to justice for parts of the population. Often, these factors exist in post-conflict situations

[65] Samuels (n 4) 173, 177 (pointing to participatory constitution-making processes in Uganda, Colombia, Guatemala, South Africa, and Rwanda as examples of constitution drafting that involved extensive education programs in addition to widespread national consultation and discussion).

[66] See, eg, Roland Paris, *At War's End: Building Peace after Civil Conflict* (Kindle edn, 2004).

[67] See, eg, Bell (n 3).

[68] Jane Stromseth, 'Post-Conflict Rule of Law Building: The Need for A Multi-Layered, Synergistic Approach' (2008) 49 *William & Mary Law Review* 1443, 1450–51.

[69] Kim Lane Scheppele, 'A Constitution Between Past and Future' (2008) 49 *William & Mary Law Review* 1377, 1406. See also Samuels (n 4) 173.

and can reflect causes of the violent conflict.[70] Moreover, peacebuilding assumptions also frequently disregard the cultural context of a given situation, where courts and constitutional institutions might be irrelevant to the interests and practices of the population or parts thereof.[71] For example, in Sierra Leone, a significant majority of the population has little access to formal justice mechanisms, especially in rural areas.[72] The focus of international actors should be broadened to consider how their intervention and institutional and legal reforms interact with the larger political and cultural context in which they operate. In particular, interveners should avoid entrenching pre-existing inequalities or perpetuate limited access to justice amongst historically marginalised segments of the population or those who have been most drastically impacted by the conflict. As Jane Stromseth argues, interveners should focus on the 'demand side' of legal institutions—including marginalised groups such as women, minorities, and un/under-employed youth—in addition to their normal focus on the 'supply side'—such as judges, lawyers, and politicians.[73] This is an important consideration during all phases of peacebuilding, from inclusion of such groups at the negotiating table, inclusion of their concerns in peace agreements, and considering their needs during the implementation of the peace agreements and constitutional reforms.[74] Failing to do so could pose a significant threat to the sustainability of peace and the rule of law.

These factors mean that the inclusion of international law in constitutional peace agreements could have little or no impact on the actual implementation of those laws in the domestic system or on creating a culture of constitutionalism—which is meant to defuse future conflict and promote the rule of law—in the domestic society. This demonstrates that perhaps more than the substantive international law provisions included, the bargaining process and inclusion of local constituents is important for fostering peace and the rule of law.

[70] See, eg, Cindy Daase, 'The Redistribution of Resources in Internationalized Intra-State Peace Processes by Comprehensive Peace Agreements and Security Council Resolutions' (2011) 3 *Goettingen Journal of International Law* 23, 62 (arguing that 'more often than not, the state and the government themselves are *de facto* of a dubious democratic legitimacy in [post-conflict] situations despite their *de iure* status').

[71] Stromseth, 'Post-Conflict Rule of Law Building' (n 68) 1452.

[72] Chandra Lekha Sriram, '(Re)building the Rule of Law in Sierra Leone' in C Lekha Sriram, O Martin-Ortega, and J Herman (eds) *Peacebuilding and Rule of Law in Africa: Just Peace?* (London, Routledge, 2011) 127, 128. Some estimate that as many as 70–80% of the population in rural areas rely on informal or traditional forms of justice, such as customary courts located at the chiefdom level.

[73] Stromseth (n 68) 1453, 1457–59.

[74] See, eg, Rama Mani and Jana Krause, 'Democratic Governance' in V Chetail (ed), *Post-Conflict Peace-Building: A Lexicon* (Oxford, Oxford University Press, 2009) 105, 111 (arguing that the exclusion of the local stakeholders other than the elite is detrimental to the legitimacy and sustainability of post-conflict democratic reforms).

C. Contentious Bargaining

International law provisions in constitutional peace agreements have the potential to directly influence the domestic rule of law as well as the legal rights and responsibilities of individuals living in the post-conflict society. However, the inclusion of international law must be considered against the backdrop of peace agreements as negotiated documents that are intended to create peace in a post-conflict society. Therefore, it is important to understand the contentious bargaining process and how this influences the particular international norms in constitutional peace agreements and the strength of the resulting agreement.

Constitutions are generally meant to represent a social contract between the people and the state. However, negotiation processes can lead to individuals contracting between themselves rather than creating a contract between society and the state.[75] The institutions that are created through the peace agreement process are a direct result of a political bargaining process rather than principled design, even if they might be guided by international law.

The institutions created as a result of the negotiation dynamic can be unsound and incapable of effecting real change, advancing the rule of law or fostering a sustainable peace.[76] The parties at the negotiating table often have different reasons for including certain provisions or institutions in their peace agreement, and also have different ideas about how those provisions and institutions will function in the future. Rather than engage in coherent institutional design, parties define institutions based on strategic negotiation. Haggling over detailed provisions about, for example, who is appointed to an institution, can become a micro-version of the meta-conflict. Moreover, peace negotiations might involve a narrow range of issues of immediate concern to the parties of the conflict, which could mean that larger issues important to a constitution are left unaddressed.

[75] Christine Bell, 'Peace Agreements: Their Nature and Legal Status' (2006) 100 *American Journal of International Law* 373, 398. This self-interested negotiation between parties can lead to extremely detailed agreements, as parties seek to predict and eradicate future threats to their power. eg, in ethnic conflicts, agreements reflect specific details about ethnic representation in new state institutions and their relative power. This can be seen in agreements in Burundi, Northern Ireland, and Bosnia-Herzegovina. ibid. Another possibility is that parties will seek to entrench their power in new constitutional roles, such as the military or certain rebel groups. Brandt and others (n 11) 260. If not all ethnic groups are present at the negotiation or do not wield the same bargaining power, the agreement might not adequately reflect an agreement with the society at large.

[76] Bell (n 3) 229, 231. eg, Bell argues that human rights institutions, which are secondary priorities for negotiators, can be 'almost hastily tacked on to an agreement without the institutional detail which would make them effective'. ibid 231. She points to human rights institutions included in the Dayton Peace Agreement for Bosnia-Herzegovina as an example.

This lack of balance could undermine the broader legitimacy of the constitutional peace agreement.[77]

Bargaining can also lead to incoherent constitutional peace agreements, as it creates a trade-off between negotiation and coherence.[78] Coordination among politically powerful groups is most difficult in post-conflict situations where no one has 'won' and the international community is involved in constitution drafting. In such situations, coherent political visions can be sacrificed in the name of the bargain.[79] In post-conflict societies, the coherence of the constitutional agreement is important; they need an agreement that establishes strong, well-designed, and mutually reinforcing institutions that are meant to peacefully absorb and resolve the conflict. In practice, however, the agreement resulting from a negotiated process often fails to establish such institutions. Instead, negotiation can lead to the creation of institutions that detract from or stymie the settlement.[80]

Bargaining over constitutional provisions in these circumstances can also affect the negotiation and drafting processes and further augment the incoherence of the agreement. On the one hand, the legal form of the constitution and its hierarchy in the national legal system can promote greater compliance amongst parties to the conflict and provide them with incentives to try to make it succeed. Getting combatants to engage in constitutional debate and consider constitutional change can create space for political discussion, improve understanding of competing positions, and help parties redefine their grievances.[81] On the other hand, the constitutional nature of the agreement might make parties hesitate to bargain over a document that establishes such overarching legal provisions. For example, minority groups might fear that the process will lead to further entrenchment of majority power, and powerful elites might fear the embedded loss of power.[82]

Another bargaining paradox relates to the types of norms included in constitutional peace agreements. The negotiated process might detract from the substantive norms and development of institutions designed to

[77] Brandt and others (n 11) 260. eg, privileged parties to the negotiation, such as rebel armed forces who pose a threat to a return to violence, can narrow the constitutional agenda to reflect their specific interests. This might result in an agreement that does not take into consideration broader society needs or interests. If a society feels less vested in the resulting constitutional peace agreement, it might see the agreement as illegitimate.

[78] Horowitz, 'Conciliatory Institutions' (n 42) 1235 (pointing to Fiji as an example).

[79] Nehal Bhuta, 'New Modes and Orders: The Difficulties of a Jus Post Bellum of Constitutional Transformation' (2010) 60 *University of Toronto Law Journal* 799, 844; Horowitz (n 42) 1230.

[80] Horowitz (n 42) 1235, 1238.

[81] Brandt and others (n 11) 257 (pointing to South Sudan as an example).

[82] Jackson (n 48) 1251–52 (pointing to Northern Ireland and South Africa as examples).

foster reconciliation or goals of transitional justice.[83] However, peace processes can be useful for fostering a commitment to principles of justice, human rights, and reconciliation, and can provide an opportunity to include related international norms in the constitutional peace agreement.

Lurking in the background is the threat of a return to violence, creating heightened stakes for both domestic and international drafters. The drafters will have to balance long-term and short-term goals. Peacemakers might need to act immediately to solve emerging crises,[84] whereas constitution-makers need more time to allow for deliberate, inclusive procedures. Moreover, the conflict could drive—and therefore narrow—the constitutional agenda, leaving other critical societal issues un- or under-addressed.[85] Compromises favouring conflict resolution can result in weak settlements and weak states.[86] There might also be genuine conflicts between short-term interests (such as the immediate cessation of violence) that require cooperation with warlords or potential spoilers, which could ultimately empower them to later derail the peacebuilding project.[87] Different parties to the bargain might also have different reasons for including norms in the constitutional peace agreement.

International legal norms may be included as a form of pre-commitment in an effort to bind future domestic actors[88] or as a signal of legitimacy.[89] International legal norms might also be included as the result of norm diffusion[90] or the particular expertise of negotiators. A country might

[83] Andrea Armstrong and Gloria Ntegeye, 'The Devil is in the Details: The Challenges of Transitional Justice in Recent African Peace Agreements' (2006) 6 *African Human Rights Journal* 1, 23.

[84] Ludsin (n 39) 271; Roland Paris and Timothy D Sisk, *Managing Contradictions: The Inherent Dilemmas of Postwar Statebuilding* (New York, International Peace Academy, 2007) 4–5.

[85] Ludsin (n 39) 271. See also Fionnuala Ní Aoláin, 'The Fractured Soul of the Dayton Peace Agreement: A Legal Analysis' (1998) 19 *Michigan Journal of International Law* 957, 964; Armstrong and Ntegeye, 'The Devil is in the Details' (n 83) 23 (arguing that 'Negotiations focused on the primary purpose of bringing violent conflict to an end are not conducive to designing an inclusive process that takes into consideration the full range of needs society has for reconciliation and justice'.).

[86] Ní Aoláin, 'Fractured Soul' (n 85) 964–65.

[87] Stromseth (n 68) 1449; Paris and Sisk, 'Managing Contradictions: The Inherent Dilemmas of Postwar Statebuilding' (n 84) 4–5; Bell, 'Peace Agreements: Their Nature and Legal Status' (n 75) 399 (discussing the relative value of drafting precision in peace agreements for the short-term, and its limitations for the long-term).

[88] Tom Ginsburg, 'Locking in Democracy: Constitutions, Commitment and International Law' (2006) 38 *NYU Journal of International Law and Policy* 707; Tom Ginsburg, Svitlana Chernykh, and Zachary Elkins, 'Commitment and Diffusion: How and Why National Constitutions Incorporate International Law' (2007) 2008 *University of Illinois Law Review* 201, 202–03.

[89] Michael Riegner, 'The Two Faces of the Internationalized pouvoir constituent: Independence and Constitution-Making Under External Influence in Kosovo' (2010) 2 *Goettingen Journal of International Law* 1035, 1062. eg, the Kosovo Constitution gained legitimacy by relying on widely accepted international human rights treaties in a constitution that was otherwise very heavily influenced by external powers.

[90] Ginsburg and others, 'Commitment and Diffusion' (n 88) 203.

adopt a constitutional model based on a bias for constitutional models adopted by other countries in their regional or cultural zone or the model used by a former colonial power.[91] There might be a bias for a constitutional model proposed by an influential advisor, who might propose a model familiar to her but unfamiliar to the domestic drafters. A historical bias might prompt a constitution designed to avoid problems from the country's past, or based on past constitutional models, the effects of which might be misunderstood by the drafters. Pre-existing institutional capacity might make certain models, such as federal systems, more difficult to implement.[92] Moreover, new formal institutions will have to be able to co-exist and not interfere with informal institutions.[93] However, diffusion might be outweighed in some circumstances by 'imposition' or 'persuasion' by external mediators and technical assistance, detracting from the perceived legitimacy of the constitutional peace agreement. These reasons, and the nature of the bargain, will impact exactly how norms are written into constitutional peace agreements, setting the stage for the future application and interpretation of these norms during the transition to peace.

D. Constructive Ambiguity

The constitutional peace agreement is not intended to resolve the origins of the conflict, but to defer it until it can be resolved through peaceful political means.[94] The conflict will continue to be negotiated through the political and legal institutions designed by the drafters. Constitutional peace agreements are by design intended to allow possible future change and amendment. The incorporation of international legal norms should be understood in this context; namely, that the conflict would continue to be negotiated. The language and norms of international law serve the mediation of conflicts, providing a neutral terminology and displacing the power of interpretation to external authorities. International law can thus provide the language of conflict (resolution) and simultaneously create the legal framework in which this (now political) conflict is played out.

Due to their conflict-driven nature, constitutional peace agreements often employ 'constructive ambiguity' in the drafting process. This type of language is frequently used when dealing with the most contentious issues, including strong disagreements over constitutional vision. Using intentionally ambiguous language is an overt attempt to capture, and

[91] Horowitz (n 42) 1227–28. See also Ginsburg and others (n 88).

[92] Horowitz (n 42) 1227–28.

[93] Kirsti Samuels, 'Post-Conflict Peace-Building and Constitution-Making' (2006) 6 *Chicago Journal of International Law* 663, 9.

[94] Bell (n 2) 205.

thereby move beyond, the parties' lack of agreement over a common constitutional project. Constructive ambiguity in constitutional peace agreements can also bridge fundamentally opposed constitutional positions and forge unity through a legalised constitutional discourse by building disagreement into the agreement.[95] Constructive ambiguity and deferral of resolving core disagreements can create time and space that could be conducive to future negotiation when the stakes are not as high and tensions have lowered.[96] By using the language of international norms in this constructive ambiguity, drafters can also shift contentious language and discord over the meta-conflict into the broader realm of international law.

However, using constructively ambiguous language in the agreement simply means that the disagreement will have to be resolved, and the language clarified, later. Undertaking significant political change and engaging in state-building activities through constitutional peace agreements risks the creation of instability, weakness, and/or corruption in the state institutions if the proper balance between international and domestic laws is not carefully managed.[97] Because a constitutional peace agreement defers the resolution of the conflict until it can be mediated through these institutions, the creation of weak institutions that are perceived as imposed or illegitimate could cause a resurgence of the conflict, or the subversion of the international norms by future power holders.

Moreover, by displacing the immediacy of the conflict and building the disagreement into the agreement, how the agreement is implemented becomes more critical. For example, the inclusion of international human rights norms in a constitutional peace agreement might be necessary to reach agreement and peace, but the impact of these norms on society and their ability to absorb and resolve the meta-conflict will still depend on the extent of access to justice and the interpretation of the norms by the domestic judiciary. Depending on the context, the norms could either become meaningless or could be used to adopt the veneer of legitimacy and conflict resolution while the conflict continues to boil beneath the surface. They could also be the site of future contestation by national courts against the international norms, or could simply be written out of future constitutions. To the same extent as they can foster peace, using international legal norms in the creation of this constructive ambiguity also makes international law a potential vehicle and site of future conflict.

[95] Bell (n 2) 174.

[96] Brandt and others (n 11) 67.

[97] Samuels (n 4) 173 (pointing to Haiti, Liberia, and East Timor as examples of where this risk has been realised).

IV. DIALOGUE AND DEFERENCE IN CONSTITUTIONAL PEACE AGREEMENTS

As discussed above, the process of negotiation and drafting constitutional peace agreements results in multiple layers of hybridity: legal, conceptual, temporal, and a hybridity of actors and influences. Their hybridity often leads to ambiguity and incoherence in constitutional peace agreements. At the same time, however, this hybridity in turn situates peace agreements as potential tools for facilitating the accountability of *both* domestic organs and international organisations. The process of negotiating and drafting constitutional peace agreements fosters dialogue between international and national interests as well as between various domestic constituencies that have been in conflict. The process is contentious and often reflects bargains that can either strengthen or weaken the rule of law. However, constitutional peace agreement processes that involve international actors may be seen as illegitimate or imposed, which can in turn weaken the rule of law that their involvement attempted to foster.[98] By engaging in constitutional peace agreement processes that prioritise dialogue and adopt the principle of qualified deference, international actors can harness the hybridity of constitutional peace agreements to foster the international and domestic rule of law.

A. Dialogue

As discussed above, the hybrid nature of constitutional peace agreements creates unique connections that influence the future relationship among the post-conflict state, its people, and international law and organisations. The inclusion of international laws and norms in constitutional peace agreements creates a subject matter overlap[99] and dialogue between national and international law at the highest domestic level. International law becomes a part of the authority of domestic governments over individuals and non-state actors (the 'B' level described by Kanetake) and strengthens the connection between international law and the individual (at the 'C' level of interaction).[100] The influence of international actors helps shape domestic law. At the same time, constitutional peace agreements influence the development of international law and the best

[98] Brandt and others (n 11) 321.
[99] See ch 1 (Kanetake) of this volume.
[100] ibid.

practices and norms of international organisations, as seen by the development of peacebuilding practices and evolving approaches of the UN.[101]

The inclusion of international law in post-conflict constitutions may reflect pre-commitments of those sitting at the negotiating table, committing their future counterparts to international obligations and oversight. At the same time, the inclusion of particular norms may reflect a process of diffusion or adaption from similar systems or based on the experience/expertise of international interlocutors. They are drafted with constructive ambiguity, and may include intentionally broad norms reached through a process of contentious bargaining. Sometimes this results in weak institutions, which can risk the return of violent conflict. Therefore, the constitutional peace agreement cannot be considered as static, but rather is a starting point for an evolving relationship between national and international rule of law.

Keeping this dialogue open and fluid is important for the legitimacy of both international and national law in post-conflict states. If the negotiating process of the constitutional peace agreement is seen as imposed, illegitimate or lacking inclusion, it could detract from compliance with international law and national rule of law as it is implemented during the transition to peace. Therefore, drafters and interveners should approach the negotiation and bargaining process with an understanding of the hybrid nature of the constitutional peace agreement and be committed to flexibility and dialogue. This is manifested in practice by an inclusive process of broad dialogue and showing qualified deference to domestic law.

B. Qualified Deference

The hybridity in constitutional peace agreements not only creates the opportunities for dialogue. This chapter argues that it also makes it necessary for international interlocutors involved in the processes to maintain flexibility and to allow for national diversity and pluralism. Deference to national interests and normative values is very often critical to ensuring the successful negotiation and implementation of constitutional peace agreements.

However, deference in this context should be a 'qualified' or 'bounded' one, as opposed to complete deference. Based on the concepts of the

[101] Bell (n 2) 243. This can be seen in the evolving attitudes about the balance between accountability and amnesty in peace agreements. The influence of international law and actors combined with the self-interest of constitutional peace agreements has led to a new norm of requiring some type of accountability but also permit a level of amnesty. Bell describes this process as a 'regime merge'.

margin of appreciation and subsidiarity,[102] qualified deference could help mitigate tensions over 'imposed' international norms and the vertical relationship between international and national law. It reduces the democratic deficit that arises with intensive international influence over national constitutions and the lack of the broader society in the negotiation and drafting process.[103] Moreover, it allows for constitutional peace agreements that will be credible and enforceable in the specific contexts appropriate for diverse communities. Kristen Boon argues that this would allow a degree of freedom in approaches to peacebuilding and for context-specific and culturally relevant post-conflict constitutional orders.[104]

'Qualified deference' allocates authority over peace agreements and constitutional norms to domestic authorities. However, it does not allow for derogation from certain fundamental norms, and protects against the subversion of international norms by domestic elites in the implementation of the constitutional peace agreement.[105] In exploring domestic accountability process for international crimes, Mark Drumbl also argues in favour of applying 'qualified deference':

> Qualified deference does not involve a blind retreat to national or local institutions. Such a retreat would be problematic. In some postconflict societies, juridical institutions are devastated, illegitimate, corrupt, manipulable, complicit in violence, or in the service of repressive social control; not all postconflict societies move toward democracy or peace, some trend in the direction of authoritarianism; some postconflict societies look more like societies between conflicts. [...] [Q]ualified deference meets important utilitarian objectives in promoting legitimacy [...] and in minimizing unrealistic expectations of local legitimacy upon which subsidiarity is predicated.[106]

Drumbl, in exploring how 'qualified deference' should be interpreted, puts forth a number of indicia that could be used to evaluate whether a state's initiatives should be shown deference or not. A re-working of his test to make it relevant to the discussion of constitutional peace agreements would include the following factors: good faith; the democratic legitimacy of the national initiative; the specific characteristics of the conflict and the current political context; the effect of the state's initiative on universal substantive norms; and the protection of human rights.

[102] On the margin of appreciation and subsidiarity within the context of the European Convention on Human Rights, see chs 8 (Peters), 9 (Dothan), and 10 (Legg) of this volume.

[103] See, eg, George A Bermann, 'Taking Subsidiarity Seriously: Federalism in the European Union and United States' (1994) 94 *Columbia Law Review* 331, 343.

[104] Kristen Boon, 'The Application of *Jus Post Bellum* in Non-International Armed Conflicts' in Stahn, Easterday and Iverson, *Jus Post Bellum* (n 25) 259.

[105] See, eg, Eyal Benvenisti, 'Margin of Appreciation, Consensus and Universal Standards' (1998) 31 *New York University Journal of International Law and Politics* 843.

[106] Mark Drumbl, *Atrocity, Punishment, and International Law* (Cambridge, Cambridge University Press 2007) 188–89.

These indicia help balance between international actors' policy of promoting and implementing international legal norms, such as international human rights law, while also showing deference to national processes and laws, which may not always adhere to international law. For example, domestic laws may violate fundamental human rights standards, such as Taliban laws in Afghanistan that denied women basic rights.[107] Existing domestic laws may also be outdated or have significant gaps that do not adhere to contemporary social realities, such as property and inheritance rights for women in Sierra Leone.[108] It would also help balance the inclusion of norms that are established in good faith, based on the context of the conflict, with those that are suggested as attempts for one of the warring parties to entrench their power or policies.[109]

Qualified deference is an important concept to apply when internationals intervene in the drafting of constitutional peace agreements. It would mitigate the risks and challenges associated with implementing constitutional peace agreements, such as bad faith interpretations of their constructive ambiguity, the influence of spoilers, distrust of the state based on a history of abuse, or the lack of resources or expertise in devastated institutions. Applying the principle of 'qualified deference' to the process of negotiating and drafting constitutional peace agreements can both ensure the protection of fundamental values in international law as well as help foster national rule of law in post-conflict states.[110] There are many questions that remain about the exact application of this norm, but utilising such a 'qualified deference' test for constitutional peace agreements might better foster sustainable peace and the rule of law.[111]

[107] Jane Stromseth, David Wippman and Rosa Brooks, *Can Might Make Rights?* (Cambridge, Cambridge University Press, Kindle Edition, 2007) 194.

[108] ibid.

[109] eg, different policies regulating reparations and return of internally displaced persons in Bosnia-Herzegovina were seen both as a remedy of past abuse (a policy focusing on return) and as an entrenchment of ethnic cleansing policies that characterised the conflict (a policy focusing on financial reparations and no return). Barbara McCallin, 'The Role of Restitution in Post-Conflict Situations' in J Unruh and RC Williams (eds), *Land and Post-Conflict Peacebuilding* (London, Earthscan, 2013) 99, 103.

[110] The peace process in Afghanistan is a good example of why deference should be qualified or bounded. See Marieke Wierda, 'The Positive Role of International Law in Peace Negotiations: Implementing Transitional Justice in Afghanistan and Uganda' in M Bergsmo and P Kalmanovitz (eds), *Law in Peace Negotiations* (2d edn, FICHL Publication Series no 5, 2010) 281. The debate about amnesties is also a useful example of how 'bounded' discretion is important. See, eg, Claus Kreß and Leena Grover, 'International Criminal Law Restraints in Peace Talks to End Armed Conflicts of a Non-International Character' in Bergsmo and Kalmanovitz (ibid) (arguing that there are limited exceptions to a customary international law duty to prosecute grave international crimes); and 'The Belfast Guidelines on Amnesty and Accountability' (Transitional Justice Institute at the University of Ulster, 2013) 9, 10, and 13, available at: http://transitionaljustice.ulster.ac.uk/documents/TheBelfastGuidelinesonAmnestyandAccountability.pdf.

[111] Drumbl, *Atrocity, Punishment, and International Law* (n 106) 189.

C. Legitimacy

Dialogue and qualified deference can ultimately contribute to the legitimacy of constitutional peace agreements. The process by which constitutional peace agreements are negotiated and drafted can impact their perceived legitimacy, especially when they are drafted with heavy outside influence. Vivien Hart argues that non-participatory, elite-made constitutions will be seen as lacking a cultural element of legitimacy because the process, and not just the final document, is seen as flawed.[112] Widespread consultation and participation of the larger society can increase the perceived legitimacy of the constitution.[113] International involvement can also have a negative impact on the legitimacy of the constitution. It seems that the risk of illegitimacy is tied to the extent to which international interveners undermine local ownership over the process.[114] However, if international interveners are perceived as legitimate and legal, which Jane Stromseth argues can happen if international actors themselves adhere to international legal norms and collaborate with broad sectors of society, they have more likelihood of success in long-term rule of law development.[115] This shows one way that the constitutional peace agreement process can influence the practices of international actors involved in these processes. It also adds further support to the argument that international interveners should show qualified deference to national interests in the drafting process.

V. CONCLUSION

This chapter suggests that the hybridity and other unique features of constitutional peace negotiations and agreements require international law and institutions to make a compromise with, engage in dialogue with, and defer to other actors. The hybridity of peace agreements is a unique one, in that the multiplicity is not simply of the traditional actors (judges, courts, legislators, petitioners, and so forth) that normally operate in the realm of international rule of law. The level of inclusion, influence of external interveners, and the peace agreement bargain are important aspects

[112] Hart, *Democratic Constitution Making* (n 33) 3; Hart, 'Constitution-Making and the Transformation of Conflict' (n 33) 161.

[113] Samuels (n 4) 175. Samuels describes the 'pacted' constitutions that arose out of democratic transitions in Latin America. These constitutions were created by pacts formed between members of the elite with the result of creating social and economic inequity and further empowering already powerful actors.

[114] Bhuta, 'New Modes and Orders' (n 79) 803.

[115] Stromseth (n 68) 1448, 1455–56 (pointing to Iraq as an example).

of constitutional peace agreements that change the nature of the relationship between international and domestic law. National rule of law is strengthened through the legitimising effects of international legal norms, the development of a culture of constitutionalism, and the creation of strong domestic institutions that can mediate the conflict. International rule of law is in turn strengthened by the increased ability and motive of the national institutions to comply with international law commitments and by constitutional peace agreements underwriting its moral claims and norms of ideal institutions. Examining the role of international law in constitutions that arise out of negotiated bargains over peace shows that this interface needs to be delicately constructed through a process of dialogue and qualified deference in order to foster compliance with both national and international rule of law.

Applying flexible norms of dialogue and qualified deference at the stage of the peace negotiations might later result in increased compliance with international law as the post-conflict society resolves the root causes of the conflict through political means. First, as the conflict is resolved, the state will be better able to comply with its international legal obligations, especially the protection of fundamental human rights. Second, applying these norms during the contentious negotiating process could increase perceived legitimacy of the resulting constitution and thereby strengthen the 'culture of constitutionality' and the impetus to adhere to the international norms embedded in the constitution. Third, dialogue and qualified deference will lead to the creation of stronger post-conflict institutions that will be better able to absorb the conflict and correctly interpret and apply international law. Fourth, by engaging in dialogue and showing qualified deference to national laws and interests, international law is itself strengthened, developed, and made more relevant to the individuals' lives that it impacts through constitutional peace agreements.

16

The Rule of Law and the Division of Labour Between National and International Law: The Case of International Energy Relations

STEPHAN W SCHILL*

I. INTRODUCTION

PARALLEL TO THE view that national and international law are two separate legal orders, the concept of the rule of law is often separated into a national and an international rule of law. Since the content of both may differ, this separation can lead to a confrontational perspective on the relationship between the international and the national rule of law that focuses on which legal order—national or international—is supreme over the other. From the perspective of international law, the notion of the international rule of law is often used to mean merely compliance of national law with international law. This understanding underlies, for instance, the recommendations made by the UN Secretary-General in his March 2012 report on *Delivering Justice*.[1] For the report, strengthening the international rule of law primarily means 'increasing compliance with international law' by states, including 'national implementation' of international law, and 'strengthening international dispute resolution'.[2] Viewed from this perspective, national contestation is necessarily contrary to the international rule of law. By contrast, from a national perspective,

* This chapter was written with the support of a European Research Council Starting Grant on 'Transnational Private-Public Arbitration as Global Regulatory Governance: Charting and Codifying the Lex Mercatoria Publica' (LexMercPub, Grant agreement no: 313355).

[1] Report of the Secretary General, 'Delivering Justice: Programme of Action to Strengthen the Rule of Law at the National and International Levels' UN Doc A/66/749 (16 March 2012).

[2] ibid paras 11–17. Similarly, the recommendations made in this report turn on strengthening domestic institutions, the economy, and civil society, and enhancing processes of cooperation between national and international institutions, in order to better implement international law: see ibid paras 18–34.

the national rule of law comes along with its own, usually constitutionally embedded, yardstick to which the action of national institutions, including their implementation of international law and national acceptance of the decisions of international institutions, has to conform. In fact, by invoking the primacy of national law over international law, national contestation may have the function, as various examples discussed in the present book show,[3] to bring to bear the national rule of law as a limit on the primacy of international law and its compliance-based understanding of the rule of law.

The present chapter aims to overcome this focus on conflict in understanding what the rule of law means in the context of global governance as a concept that guides the exercise of public authority either at the national or international level. Instead, this chapter argues that, in conceiving the concept of the rule of law, one should take account of and internalise the fact that the separation between national and international law and between national and international public authority becomes increasingly blurred. Many areas of social relations in today's globalised world are governed by a combination of both national and international law, with national and international actors and instruments standing in a relationship of division of labour that is put into practice through a number of different interfaces. This division of labour between national and international law should also be reflected in our understanding of the rule of law. As a consequence, neither a purely national, nor a purely international understanding of the rule of law can be supreme. National law and national authorities need to be receptive to international law and accommodate its normative demands, including its idea of the rule of law, just as international law and international institutions need to accommodate demands stemming from national laws and their understandings of the rule of law.

Interfaces between national and international law, in turn, assume an important function in operationalising the rule of law in global governance in this context. Understanding interactions between national and international actors and instruments as a division of labour leads us to revise the compliance-based understanding about the international rule of law and to see it, not as the rule of international law, but as part of an overarching concept of the global rule of law. This overarching concept is formed through interactive processes of mutual control and cross-fertilisation between national and international law and between national and international actors, and their partly diverging understandings of the rule of law. The key, in other words, for developing a fuller understanding of the meaning of the rule of law in global governance is a reassessment of

[3] See, eg, chs 2 (Fikfak) and 3 (Platiše) of this volume.

the relationship between international and national law from a confrontational to an interdependent and complementary perspective.

For this purpose, it is necessary, in my view, to overcome the traditional hierarchy-based theories on the relationship between national and international law, ie, monism and dualism, and replace them with a less static concept that does not operate on the basis of either/or-solutions. Adopting the concept of 'interfaces', understood as the 'points where the actors, norms and procedures belonging to respective legal orders interact with one another',[4] seems much more sensible, as it allows for nuanced and dynamic solutions according to different factual contexts and circumstances that may return a variety of solutions for the relationship between national and international law and their potentially diverging understandings of the meaning of the rule of law. The concept of interfaces also helps to shift focus towards analysing the mutual interpenetration of national and international law in terms of their complementarity in jointly governing trans-border social relations rather than putting mutual conflicts and tensions centre stage.[5]

In order to illustrate the idea of division of labour between national and international law and its contribution to the understanding of the rule of law in global governance, this chapter takes the way international energy relations are governed as an example. Energy law is understood as 'the allocation of rights and duties concerning the exploitation of all energy resources between individuals, between individuals and the government, between governments and between states'.[6] It covers all sources of energy, including oil, gas, coal, nuclear power, hydro power, and renewable energy resources;[7] all phases of energy production, transport, and distribution, both through networks and other means of transportation, such as the shipping of oil; and all possible legal relationships, that is, between energy companies and governments, among energy companies, between energy companies and consumers, and between states. Energy law is therefore not only a field that cuts across different legal fields, including private and public law. It is also a transnational legal field, in which both national

[4] Machiko Kanetake, 'The Interfaces between the National and International Rule of Law: The Case of UN Targeted Sanctions' (2012) 9 *International Organizations Law Review* 267, 268.

[5] *cf* already Luigi Ferrari-Bravo, 'International and Municipal Law: The Complementarity of Legal Systems' in RS Macdonald and DM Johnston (eds), *The Structure and Process of International Law* (The Hague, Martinus Nijhoff, 1983) 715.

[6] Adrian Bradbrook, 'Energy Law as an Academic Discipline' (1996) 14 *Journal of Energy & Natural Resources Law* 193, 194.

[7] Treating energy law as a field that encompasses all energy resources, instead of looking at different energy resources separately, is preferable in my view because, even though there are differences in the regulation of different energy resources and forms of energy, energy sources are, in principle, substitutable. It is mainly a political decision how the energy demand of a political economy is met, for example, by coal-powered or nuclear power plants, by relying on domestic energy sources or imports from abroad, etc.

and international law play an important role in governing the increasing amount of trans-border relations, including exploration, exploitation, transport and distribution of oil and gas, the regulation of trans-border electricity networks and gas pipelines, and the effects of energy markets on the environment and the global climate. This structure illustrates that pursuing and achieving policy goals in the energy sector involves balancing different national and international interests against each other and requires a comprehensive understanding of the relationship between national and international energy law and the interactions between actors at the national and the international level. It is therefore no wonder that the interplay between national and international law has been designated as 'the real cutting edge of energy law at the present time'.[8]

In the present context, I choose energy law for multiple reasons. Energy law concerns the regulation of a primary sector of the economy that is crucial for any more advanced economic activity in the secondary or tertiary sector (goods and services) and hence for economic growth and development; energy is a public good that is nowadays to a large extent supplied across borders and is no longer a purely domestic concern; it is an area of law where both national and international legal instruments intervene to achieve public policy objectives; the transition from national to international energy markets is rather recent and can be studied fairly well parallel to how the governing legal framework developed in response to changes of the social reality in the energy context; and, finally, energy law covers relations between multiple actors, including state-state, private-public, and private-private. Energy law is thus a good example for building and testing theories about the relationship between international and national law that are not built on a conflict-centred perspective. In fact, in energy law, international and national law are mostly complementary

[8] Bradbrook, 'Energy Law as an Academic Discipline' (n 6) 203. EU law is not dealt with separately in the present contribution, primarily in order to simplify the illustration of how different legal orders interact with each other. This is because EU law assumes a hybrid position in between national and international law. From the perspective of national law, EU law shares functional similarities with both international but also constitutional law; from the perspective of international law, EU law shares similarities with both national law and other international regional regimes, depending on the circumstances. This is also the case in the area of energy law, where EU law assumes partly the function of national law, and partly the function of international law. On EU energy law, see Thomas Wälde, 'The International Dimension of EU Energy Law and Policy' in M Fitzmaurice and M Szuniewicz (eds), *Exploitation of Natural Resources in the 21st Century* (The Hague, London, Kluwer Law International, 2003) 9; Peter D Cameron (ed), *Legal Aspects of EU Energy Regulation* (Oxford, Oxford University Press, 2005); Christopher W Jones (ed), *EU Energy Law*, vol 2 (2nd edn, Leuven, Claeys & Casteels, 2007); Sanam S Haghighi, *Energy Security—The External Relations of the European Union with Major Oil- and Gas-Supplying Countries* (Oxford, Portland, OR, Hart Publishing, 2007); Dirk Buschle, Simon Hirsbrunner, and Christine Kaddous (eds), *European Energy Law/Droit européen de l'énergie* (Basel, Helbing Lichtenhahn, 2011); Angus Johnston and Guy Block, *EU Energy Law* (Oxford, Oxford University Press, 2012); Kim Talus, *EU Energy Law and Policy: A Critical Account* (Oxford, Oxford University Press, 2013).

to each other in achieving the goals of energy policy; hence only viewing national and international law together gives a complete picture of the national law-international law relationship. All of this makes energy law a good example for studying the interfaces between national and international law and how these interfaces relate to the rule of law in global governance.

In a first step, this chapter highlights the need for a new conceptual framework to think about the relationship between national and international law in the energy sector that goes beyond the traditional theories of monism and dualism (section II). Based on a functional analysis of national and international energy law, it then suggests conceptualising the relationship between national and international energy law not primarily in light of potential conflicts, but in terms of its complementarity in achieving policy goals in the regulation of the energy sector. In this context, it proposes the division of labour between different legal orders as a guiding concept (section III). Subsequently, the chapter zooms in on different types of interfaces that structure the division of labour beyond managing conflicts between the two legal orders (section IV). Understanding interfaces in this perspective shows that, today, neither national nor international law is able to achieve the goals of transnational energy policy independently. Instead, cooperation of actors and instruments across legal orders is necessary, but also, to a certain extent, contestation in order to bind the pursuance of transnational public policies to the principle of the rule of law. Ultimately, the distinction between national and international law, and between national and international actors, and their potentially diverging understandings of the rule of law, may be understood as an important factor in achieving one of the core goals of the rule of law, that is, to limit the exercise of public authority and to avoid despotism in global governance (section V).

II. THE NEED FOR NEW THEORIES TO CONCEPTUALISE THE RELATIONS BETWEEN NATIONAL AND INTERNATIONAL ENERGY LAW

Developing theories about the relationship between national and international law and its impact on the understanding of the concept of the rule of law must start with an analysis of today's increasingly globalised energy markets and the emergence of international, in addition to national, energy law (A). The complex interactions between national and international law that result from this reality contrast with the relatively crude and schematic theories of monism and dualism that are traditionally used to conceptualise the interfaces between national and international law and that focus primarily on normative conflict between both legal orders. Instead, as the law governing international energy markets shows, alternative approaches, or new theories, are needed for understanding the relationship between national and international law (B).

A. The Emergence of International Energy Markets and International Energy Law

The interaction between national and international legal instruments in the field of energy is closely connected to the structure and scope of the energy industry and its governance structure.[9] Initially, the generation and supply of energy took place almost exclusively within the confines of nation-states. In fact, in many countries, the energy industry was even organised as a state monopoly that did not function based on market operations, but which rendered a public service. The paradigm in this phase was (national) energy autarky or energy autonomy. With the exception of the oil industry, which has always involved, at its core, cross-border energy production, the supply with energy, and accordingly energy law, was largely a domestic matter. Hence, as the late Thomas Wälde stated, '[i]n 1970, there was no international energy law'[10] in the modern sense.

There was, of course, some international law that also affected actors in the energy industry. Yet, this was a rather negligible amount of law that was not discussed as being constitutive of an independent legal field. Relevant international law was restricted to a few rules regarding the involvement of foreign investors in the exploitation of energy resources and in the generation of energy, and some international legal rules regarding the transport of oil.[11] Yet, there was no social need for international energy law and no epistemic community that would self-identify as constituting a community of international energy lawyers.

International law relating to energy, however, grew and a proper international energy law developed in tandem with the emergence of truly international energy markets. These markets developed following two severe oil crises (between 1973 and 1981) and several wars with an impact on the oil industry (above all, the 1973 Arab-Israeli war, the Iran-Iraq war, and the Gulf wars). The markets came to fruition in particular since the late-1990s, when cross-border electricity networks and cross-border supply of oil and gas through pipelines became more and more widespread. Liberalisation of the former state monopolies also played a key role, as did market liberalisation and increased trans-border trade and investment in

[9] See on this and the following, Thomas W Wälde, 'International Energy Law: An Introduction to Modern Concepts, Context, Policy and Players' in JP Schneider and C Theobald (eds), *Handbuch zum Recht der Energiewirtschaft: die Grundsätze der neuen Rechtslage* (Munich, CH Beck, 2003) 1127ff.

[10] ibid 1129.

[11] ibid 1129–30.

the energy sector. The reason for these developments was that states pursued the goal of energy security, that is, the 'uninterrupted availability of energy resources at an affordable price',[12] no longer within the confines of a domestically autarkic framework, but in cooperation with energy producers outside their borders through international energy markets.

The scarcity and uneven distribution of energy resources was a driving factor in the creation of those markets. At the same time, increased exploitation, production, transportation, and consumption of energy started raising concerns about environmental and social impacts, not only domestically, but with worldwide consequences, above all as regards climate change. All of this led to a thinking about energy security and the social implications of the energy industry in global rather than domestic terms. Already in 2003 Thomas Wälde described this as a paradigm shift:

> New 'paradigms', i.e. ways of perceiving and valuing the industry and its relations to society, have entered, namely the move from state to market, from pursuit of public objectives by public ownership to pursuit of such objectives by economic regulation, from monopoly to competition, from public ownership to privatisation. Concern for the environment was largely non-existent in 1969; it is now, in particular with respect to global climate change, a key theme for corporate strategy and governmental policy in the energy industries ... But most of all, the various energy industries (oil & gas development; electricity production; gas and electricity transportation and distribution) organised primarily on a national level have started to converge into an increasingly global and integrated energy industries [sic], a trend we can observe as, possibly, pointing towards one global energy industry.[13]

With the transition from segregated national energy markets to internationalised, or even globally integrated, energy markets also came the increased need for international legal rules. In fact, international energy markets started demanding that

> rights and duties in the energy sector ... be allocated by law between states. This, of course, raises a consideration of the application of principles of international law in the context of energy. This area has evolved and continues to evolve very rapidly and ... represents the real cutting edge of energy law at the present time. Until comparatively recently, energy was seen to be very much a national issue and one that required little, if any, international legal intervention. In recent years, however, world concern for the environment and the restriction of trade barriers has led to a realisation that international law has a significant role to play in this domain.[14]

Today, the international regulation of energy activities by public international law covers a number of issues relevant for the implementation

[12] See the definition of the International Energy Agency at: www.iea.org/topics/energysecurity/.

[13] Wälde, 'International Energy Law' (n 9) 1139.

[14] Bradbrook (n 6) 203.

and regulation of international energy markets and attracts increasing attention in legal scholarship.[15] Subject matter-wise, there is a significant amount of international law concerning the exploration and exploitation of oil and gas, including off-shore;[16] rules regarding maritime transport of petroleum, in particular, rules on the prevention of maritime pollution from oil tankers and rules on liability and compensation for oil pollution damage;[17] rules ensuring the civil and safe use of nuclear energy;[18] rules regarding the protection of the environment, including the regulation of air pollution and climate change;[19] rules on energy trade, transfer and transit, including through networks and pipelines;[20] rules on investment promotion and protection in the energy industry;[21] and also human rights

[15] For an overview, see Catherine Redgwell, 'International Regulation of Energy Activities' in MM Roggenkamp, A Rønne, C Redgwell and I del Guayo (eds), *Energy Law in Europe* (Oxford, Oxford University Press, 2001) 13.

[16] See, eg, the contributions in Geoffrey Picton-Turbervill (ed), *Oil and Gas: A Practical Handbook* (London, Globe Law and Business, 2009); Hazel Fox (ed), *Joint Development of Off-shore Oil and Gas: A Model Agreement for States for Joint Development with Explanatory Commentary* (London, British Institute of International and Comparative Law, 1989); Hazel Fox (ed), *Joint Development of Offshore Oil and Gas: The Australia/Indonesia Zone of Co-Operation Treaty, 1989 vol 2* (London, British Institute of International and Comparative Law, 1990). See also Edward Reiter, *Selective Bibliography on Oil and Gas: International Law Bibliography* (New York, Oceana Publications, 1985).

[17] See Douglas Brubaker, *Marine Pollution and International Law: Principles and Practice* (London, Belhaven Press, 1993); David W Abecassis and Richard L Jarashaw, *Oil Pollution from Ships: International, United Kingdom, and United States Law and Practice* (2nd edn, London, Stevens, 1985); Sergei V Vinogradov and Jay Paul Wagner, 'International Legal Regime for the Protection of the Marine Environment Against Operational Pollution from Offshore Petroleum Activities' in Zhiguo Gao (ed), *Environmental Regulation of Oil and Gas* (The Hague, London, Kluwer Law International, 1998) 93–142; Gotthard Gauci, *Oil Pollution at Sea: Civil Liability and Compensation for Damage* (Chichester, New York, Wiley, 1997); Z Oya Özcayir, *Liability for Oil Pollution and Collision* (London, LLP Reference Pub, 1997); Colin M de la Rue (ed), *Liability for Damage to the Marine Environment* (London, LLP, 1993); Colin M de la Rue and Charles B Anderson, *Shipping and the Environment: Law and Practice* (London, LLP, 1998).

[18] See the extensive basic documents collection Mohamed M ElBaradei, Edwin I Nwogugu, and John M Rames (eds), *The International Law of Nuclear Energy: Basic Documents* (Dordrecht, M Nijhoff, 1993); Fabrizio Nocera, *The Legal Regime of Nuclear Energy: A Comprehensive Guide to International and European Union Law* (Antwerp, Intersentia, 2005). See also Nathalie LJT Horbach (ed), *Contemporary Developments in Nuclear Energy Law: Harmonising Legislation in CEEC/NIS* (The Hague, Kluwer Law International, 1999); Norbert Pelzer (ed), *Die Internationalisierung des Atomrechts/Internationalizing Atomic Energy Law* (Baden-Baden, Nomos, 2005).

[19] See Adrian J Bradbrook, 'Energy Law: The Neglected Aspect of Environmental Law' (1993) 19 *Melbourne University Law Review* 1; Rosemary Lyster and Adrian J Bradbrook (eds), *Energy Law and the Environment* (Cambridge, Cambridge University Press, 2006) 34ff. See also the contributions in Adrian J Bradbrook and Richard L Ottinger (eds), *Energy Law and Sustainable Development*, IUCN Environmental Policy and Law Paper No 47 (2003).

[20] See, eg, the contributions in Yulia Selivanova (ed), *Regulation of Energy in International Trade Law: WTO, NAFTA, and Energy Charter* (Alphen aan den Rijn, Kluwer Law International, 2011). On pipelines see Danae Azaria, *Treaties on Transit of Energy via Pipelines and Countermeasures* (Oxford, Oxford University Press, 2015).

[21] Clarisse Ribeiro (ed), *Investment Arbitration and the Energy Charter Treaty* (Huntington, NY, JurisNet, 2006); Graham Coop and Clarisse Ribeiro (eds), *Investment Protection and the Energy Charter Treaty* (Huntington, NY, JurisNet, 2008); Peter D Cameron, *International Energy*

norms that are relevant for the energy industry.[22] Beyond public international law rules, scholars, such as Wälde, also include the international commercial practice developed for contractual transactions in the energy industry among the ambit of international energy law.[23]

All in all, public international law today therefore regulates crucial factors that are necessary for international energy markets to function and to avoid harm to globally protected concerns. Yet, international energy law is not contained in a single international instrument and does not form the subject matter of a specific international legal regime. Its rules and principles are dispersed over many different areas of international law, including international environmental law, international investment law, international trade law, international human rights law, law of the sea, and so on.

Similarly, actors generating and implementing energy law are no longer only domestic legislators, domestic administrative agencies, and domestic courts, but also international actors, including international organisations that both legislate (or provide a forum for inter-state legislation by treaty, such as the International Atomic Energy Agency or the International Energy Agency (IEA)) and administer certain aspects of international energy markets,[24] as well as international courts and tribunals that settle energy-related disputes and may have different views on the relationship of national and international energy law as compared to their domestic counterparts. Today, for example, disputes between energy companies and host governments are regularly settled not in domestic courts, but before international arbitral tribunals, either because the contracts between both parties provide for recourse to arbitration or because an international investment treaty does.[25] Similarly, disputes about energy trade may be resolved under the WTO Dispute Settlement Understanding or panels established under free trade agreements. Finally, there may be

Investment Law: The Pursuit of Stability (Oxford, Oxford University Press, 2010); Crina Baltag, *The Energy Charter Treaty: The Notion of Investor* (Alphen aan den Rijn, Kluwer Law International, 2012).

[22] See Adrian J Bradbrook and Judith G Gardam, 'Placing Access to Energy Services within a Human Rights Framework' (2006) 28 *Human Rights Quarterly* 389; Jenny Sin-Hang Ngai, 'Energy as a Human Right in Armed Conflict: A Question of Universal Need, Survival, and Human Dignity' (2012) 37 *Brooklyn Journal of International Law* 579.

[23] See Wälde (n 9) 1137.

[24] See Catherine Redgwell, 'International Organizations and their Activities in the Energy Sector' in Roggenkamp and others, *Energy Law in Europe* (n 15) 97ff; Thomas W Wälde, 'The Role of Selected International Agencies in the Formation of International Energy Law and Policy Towards Sustainable Development' in Bradbrook and Ottinger, *Energy Law and Sustainable Development* (n 19) 171.

[25] See Thomas Roe and Matthew Happold, *Settlement of Investment Disputes under the Energy Charter Treaty* (Cambridge, Cambridge University Press, 2011); Graham Coop (ed), *Energy Dispute Resolution: Investment Protection, Transit and the Energy Charter Treaty* (Huntington, NY, JurisNet, 2011).

disputes between energy companies and their contracting partners that are settled not in domestic courts but through international commercial arbitration.[26]

All of these rules and actors together, as they are engaged in the regulation of international energy markets, make up international energy law. This body of law, in turn, interacts through different sources and different means of application, interpretation, and enforcement with domestic energy law. Yet, in contrast to the complex reality of these interactions, the theories to conceptualise the relationship between national and international law have remained limited.

B. Overcoming Traditional Theories on the National-International Law Divide

Traditionally, when considering the relationship between national and international law, textbooks and scholarship primarily discuss monism and dualism as theories to manage that relationship.[27] While monism assumes that national and international law form part of one legal order, dualism perceives national and international law as separate. What is more, the main focus in the application of these theories is often on conflicting normative commands coming from the two legal orders, and hence on ideas of precedence, supremacy, and hierarchy as a way to structure the relationship. As put by Ian Brownlie,

> the theoretical issue is normally presented as a clash between dualism (or pluralism) and monism. Both these schools of thought assume that there is a common field in which the international and municipal legal orders can operate simultaneously in regard to the same subject-matter, and the problem then is, which is to be master?[28]

Picking up on this hierarchy-based framework, international law textbooks primarily focus on how international law is implemented in the municipal legal order based on the consideration that '*most* international rules, to become operative, need to be applied by State officials or individuals within domestic legal systems'.[29] International law commands compliance of states, disallows reliance on municipal law as a justification for

[26] Comprehensively on international commercial arbitration, see Gary Born, *International Commercial Arbitration* (3rd edn, Alphen aan den Rijn, Kluwer Law International, 2009).

[27] See, eg, Ian Brownlie, *Principles of Public International Law* (7th edn, Oxford, Oxford University Press, 2008) 31ff; Antonio Cassese, *International Law* (2nd edn, Oxford, Oxford University Press, 2005) 213ff; Malcolm Shaw, *International Law* (6th edn, Cambridge, Cambridge University Press, 2008) 129ff.

[28] Brownlie, *Principles of Public International Law* (n 27) 31.

[29] Cassese, *International Law* (n 27) 217 (emphasis in the original).

breach,[30] and imposes responsibility for internationally wrongful behaviour. This focus grounds international law's claim to supremacy. Conversely, from the perspective of domestic law, the relationship between national and international law is framed in terms of how international law is integrated in, and interacts with, domestic law according to the rules and principles established by domestic constitutional law and the practice of domestic courts.[31] Controlling which value international law has within the domestic legal order (as regards direct effect and relation to other domestic law), and the idea that external action of the state is subject to constitutional law limitations, grounds domestic law's claim to supremacy.

As a consequence, both international law's and domestic law's claim to be 'master' over the other, the resulting doctrines of monism and dualism, and the landmark cases on this point, are conflict-centred. Just consider the practice regarding the relationship between European Union (EU) law and domestic constitutional law, the conflicts between the International Court of Justice and the US Supreme Court in *Avena* and *Medellín*, or the relationship between the World Trade Organization (WTO) Appellate Body and the Court of Justice of the European Union (CJEU), and the theoretical reflections these types of cases have produced.[32] In all of these instances, actors at both the national and international levels treat each other as potential predators to their own claim to supremacy. Likewise, the central benefit of classical theories about the relationship between international and national law, such as monism and dualism, is their contribution to resolve conflicts of applicable law in a specific forum by giving 'either-or' answers, that is, declaring that either national or international law, and the values they further, have primacy.

From the perspective of legal certainty, predictability, and the rule of law, such conflicts are problematic because they create uncertainty as to which normative command is applicable and should be followed. Moreover, such clashes constitute an impediment to the effective implementation of

[30] *cf* Art 27 of the Vienna Convention on the Law of Treaties, 1155 UNTS 331 (1980) (adopted 23 May 1969; entered into force 27 Jan 1980); Art 32 of the ILC Articles on Responsibility of States for Internationally Wrongful Acts, 53rd Session UN Doc A/56/10 (2001).

[31] For an analysis of the relationship from a comparative constitutional law perspective, see Antonio Cassese, 'Modern Constitutions and International Law' (1985-III) 192 *Recueil des Cours* 331; Thomas M Franck and Arun K Thiruvengadam, 'International Law and Constitution-Making' (2003) 2 *Chinese Journal of International Law* 467–518; Attila Tanzi, 'Remarques sur le droit international dans une perspective constitutionnelle' in *Studi in onore di Umberto Leanza* (Naples, Editoriale scientifica, 2008) 761–84; Markus Kotzur, 'Overcoming Dichotomies: A Functional Approach to the Constitutional Paradigm in Public International Law' (2012) 4 *Göttingen Journal of International Law* 585–97; for a focus on the practice of domestic courts and their view on international law see Shaw, *International Law* (n 27) 138–79.

[32] These and other examples are discussed, eg, in Niels Petersen, 'Determining the Domestic Effect of International Law through the Prism of Legitimacy' (2012) 72 *ZaöRV/Heidelberg Journal of International Law* 223 (with further references).

international law. At the same time, non-compliance does not necessarily equal defiance vis-à-vis international obligations or the values furthered by international law. Occasionally, non-compliance may also be a way for domestic actors and domestic law to ensure that international law is in line with farther-reaching rule of law standards contained in domestic law (mostly at the constitutional level).[33] This suggests that different perspectives on the relationship between national and international law by different actors, and competing claims for supremacy, and hence the rejection of theories that provide 'either-or' answers, may not be that problematic. Instead, the mutual control actors at both levels exercise in relation to each other may be thought of as a constructive element of an emerging concept of the global rule of law that impacts today's global political, social, economic, and legal space in a manner that overarches national and international law. This consideration, however, requires rethinking the relationship between national and international law as presented by hierarchy-based theories, such as monism and dualism.

In fact, like many others,[34] I doubt whether, today, the relationship between national and international law can still be conceptualised fruitfully by binary theories. Monism and dualism are historically contingent and responded to the specific political context of the inter-war period, which was characterised, as compared to today, by a much more rigorous opposition between the nation-state, on the one hand, and universalism under international law, on the other, and their differing conceptions of the rule of law, of the power of the state, and of individual freedom.[35] Monism and dualism developed in a world that was not only much less interconnected, socially and economically, but also in terms of international law, international institutions, and international politics, and their interaction with domestic law. Meanwhile, the expansion of international law in

[33] The CJEU's *Kadi* case (Case C-402/05 P and C 415/05 P, *Kadi & Al Barakaat Int'l Found v Council of the EU & Commission of the EC (Kadi I)*, ECR 2008, I-6351) is often read in this fashion. See on this reading, but offering a positive outlook, Juliane Kokott and Christoph Sobotta, 'The Kadi Case: Constitutional Core Values and International Law. Finding the Balance?' (2012) 23 *European Journal of International Law* 1015, 1017ff.

[34] See only the contributions in Janne Nijman and André Nollkaemper (eds), *New Perspectives on the Divide Between National and International Law* (Oxford, Oxford University Press, 2007).

[35] It bears noting that the debate about monism versus dualism in the writings of Triepel, Kelsen, Scelle, and others has also been driven by the concern for the rule of law. Those supporting monism and the primacy of international law were concerned about authoritarian state power that would act contrary to the rule of law and individual freedoms, whereas those supporting dualism and the primacy of domestic law saw domestic law and its understanding of the rule of law as potentially threatened by international law's intrusion. *cf* Janne Nijman and André Nollkaemper, 'Introduction' in Nijman and Nollkaemper, *New Perspectives on the Divide Between National and International Law* (n 34) 1, 6–10 (discussing the historical politico-philosophical background of the doctrines of dualism and monism and their relation to values of the rule of law).

terms of subject matter and its functional differentiation into various specialised legal regimes,[36] its deformalisation coupled with the increasing importance of private authority,[37] the deterritorialisation of governance,[38] and the spread of the idea of international law as both the law of the international community and a universal value system,[39] all account for a deeper penetration of international law into the domestic sphere.[40] This is matched by an equally impressive adaptation and opening of national law, including constitutional law and the practice of domestic courts, vis-à-vis international law.[41]

Yet, the penetration of international law into the domestic realm also shows the need to rethink the relationship between national and international law more generally. Unlike in Triepel's view, national and international law today are no longer 'two spheres that at best touch one another, but never intersect';[42] they are deeply interconnected. Indeed, what is characteristic for the relationship between international law and national law today is much less occasional conflict but rather the

> increasing interpenetration of international law and domestic law across a number of fields, such as human rights, environmental and international investment law, where at the least the same topic is subject to regulation at both the domestic and the international level.[43]

Still couching the debate about national and international law in terms of monism and dualism is therefore questionable and arguably of little use to confront the reality of today's multifaceted interactions between national and international law. In fact, as Brownlie stated, these theories have 'probably done much to obscure realities'.[44] What is needed instead is a

[36] On the increasing importance of subject matter orientation rather than legal order-oriented classification as a factor in dissolving the traditional national-international law divide, see Christian Walter, 'International Law in a Process of Constitutionalization' in Nijman and Nollkaemper (n 34) 191.

[37] See Christine Chinkin, 'Monism and Dualism: The Impact of Private Authority on the Dichotomy Between National and International Law' in Nijman and Nollkaemper (n 34) 134; Mayo Moran, 'Shifting Boundaries: The Authority of International Law' in Nijman and Nollkaemper (n 34) 163.

[38] See Catherine Brölmann, 'Deterritorialization in International Law: Moving Away from the Divide between National and International Law' in Nijman and Nollkaemper (n 34) 84.

[39] See Philip Allot, 'The Emerging Universal Legal System' in Nijman and Nollkaemper (n 34) 63; Andreas Paulus, 'The Emergence of the International Community and the Divide Between International and Domestic Law' in Nijman and Nollkaemper (n 34) 216.

[40] For a summary of the structural changes affecting the national-international law divide, see Janne Nijman and André Nollkaemper, 'Beyond the Divide' in Nijman and Nollkaemper (n 34) 341.

[41] See Anne Peters, 'The Globalization of State Constitutions' in Nijman and Nollkaemper (n 34) 251; Anne-Marie Slaughter and William Burke-White, 'The Future of International Law is Domestic (or, The European Way of Law)' in Nijman and Nollkaemper (n 34) 110.

[42] Heinrich Triepel, *Völkerrecht und Landesrecht* (Leipzig, CL Hirschfeld, 1899) 111 ('zwei Kreise, die sich höchstens berühren, niemals schneiden'—translation by the author).

[43] Shaw (n 27) 129–30.

[44] Brownlie (n 27) 53.

concept that allows grasping the dynamic interrelations between national and international law and the different perspectives on that relationship by different institutions and actors. The concept of 'interfaces'[45] is well-suited for that purpose.

Moreover, to conceptualise the 'interpenetration' of national and international law and the role of interfaces, I suggest understanding the overarching relationship between international and national law in terms of the division of labour in achieving public policy objectives that are shared by those actors that enter into international legal obligations (ie, primarily states, but also international organisations). International law, in this view, is used strategically as an instrument to achieve, together with domestic law, policy objectives that are initially set domestically and then coordinated internationally.[46] While not ignoring or normatively negating the possibility and, in fact, the reality of conflicts, international law and national law are not analysed with a focus on competing commands they may create, but functionally in terms of how they contribute to pursuing policy objectives in governing trans-border, or even global legal problems as part of a scheme of division of labour. Conceptually, this perspective is inspired by debates in EU law, where the idea of understanding both domestic and EU legal orders as part of a composite structure (*Verbund*), in which national and supranational law closely interpenetrate in governing the European legal space and in which jurisprudential conflicts have been understood as a form of separation of power, has helped overcome traditional, and somewhat simplistic, notions of 'supra-' and 'subordination', similar to those of monism and dualism.[47] This idea, which was first

[45] Kanetake, 'The Interfaces between the National and International Rule of Law' (n 4) 268.

[46] This perspective does not deny that international law and international institutions, once created, assume a life and dynamic of their own and become actors participating in global policy-making in their own right. Initially, however, international law and international institutions were purely tools of domestic policy-making and hence can be analysed in terms of their contribution to policy goals laid down by states.

[47] The characteristic feature of a *Verbund* is the intertwining of cooperation and hierarchy as ordering paradigms for the conduct of actors. The *Verbund*-concept highlights the autonomy of actors at the international and the national levels, and their mutual dependence in aiming to achieve common policy goals. On the *Verbund*-concept in the European legal space, see Eberhard Schmidt-Aßmann, 'Einleitung: Der Europäische Verwaltungsverbund und die Rolle des Europäischen Verwaltungsrechts' in E Schmidt-Aßmann and B Schöndorf-Haubold (eds), *Der Europäische Verwaltungsverbund* (Tübingen, Mohr Siebeck, 2005) 1, 6ff.; Andreas Voßkuhle, 'Multilevel Cooperation of the European Constitutional Courts: Der Europäische Verfassungsgerichtsverbund' (2010) 6 *European Constitutional Law Review* 175, 183–84; Ingolf Pernice, 'Theorie und Praxis des Europäischen Verfassungsverbundes' in C Calliess (ed), *Verfassungswandel im europäischen Staaten- und Verfassungsverbund* (Tübingen, Mohr Siebeck, 2007); Ingolf Pernice, 'Multilevel Constitutionalism in the European Union' (2002) 5 *European Law Review* 511. See now also the related idea of interlocking constitutions in Luis I Gordillo, *Interlocking Constitutions: Towards an Interordinal Theory of National, European and UN Law* (Oxford, Hart Publishing, 2012). On the separation of power across legal orders, see Armin von Bogdandy and Stephan W Schill, 'Overcoming Absolute Primacy: Respect for National Identity under the Lisbon Treaty' (2010) 48 *Common Market Law Review* 1417, 1452–53.

developed in EU law, can arguably also be applied fruitfully to conceptualise the relations between national and international energy law.

III. THE DIVISION OF LABOUR BETWEEN NATIONAL AND INTERNATIONAL ENERGY LAW

The emergence of international energy law responded primarily to the inability of domestic law and domestic actors to provide the necessary legal institutions for the functioning of international energy markets. Such markets require uniform rules for the coordination of the behaviour of all actors and institutions, including states, which can implement those rules without any distortion by national interests.[48] The emergence of international energy law, however, does not mean a displacement of national law. On the contrary, domestic law and domestic actors fulfil an equally important function in governing and regulating international energy markets. Yet, domestic law does not do so independently, but together with international law. In fact, both national energy law (A) and international energy law (B) perform specific functions that the respective other is unable to fulfil. Similarly, interfaces between the two have a specific function in allowing national and international energy law to engage in a division of labour in providing the legal infrastructure that is necessary for international energy markets to work (C).

A. The Functions of National Energy Law

National energy law is the primary source of rights and obligations for all actors engaged in conduct that is relevant for the energy industry.[49] National law governs virtually all contracts concluded in the area of

[48] Just consider cross-border electricity networks or gas pipelines, which only function when the supply and consumption of electricity and gas is coordinated among energy suppliers and consumers across borders. On the challenges for the legal regulation of electricity networks, see Hamilcar Knops, *A Functional Legal Design for Reliable Electricity Supply* (Cambridge, Intersentia, 2008). Similarly, international energy markets require legal rules that establish a level playing field that can incentivise efficient trans-border production and distribution of energy. The emergence of international energy law therefore responded to the social need for such an area of international law.

[49] On national energy law, see the contributions on various European countries in Roggenkamp and others (n 15). For a comparative overview over various domestic laws, see also Catherine Redgwell, Martha M Roggenkamp, Anita Rønne and Iñigo del Guayo, 'Energy Law in Europe: Comparisons and Conclusions' in Roggenkamp and others (n 15) 975. See further the contributions on various issues of energy law from a comparative perspective in Martha M Roggenkamp, Lila Barrera-Hernández, Donald N Zillman and Iñigo del Guayo (eds), *Energy Networks and the Law: Innovative Solutions in Changing Markets* (Oxford, Oxford University Press, 2012).

energy law (between energy companies and consumers and also between energy companies and governments) and also the public law relations between energy companies and governments. Most issues concerning the production, transportation, and distribution of energy are thus governed by domestic law. This includes ownership issues and property regimes relevant for the exploitation of energy sources, statutory regulation of the energy industries, licensing systems, taxation, subsidies, competition and antitrust law, unbundling, tariff regulation, treatment of nuclear waste, construction, operation and decommissioning of plants, but also environmental protection or labour issues. In addition, domestic law sets up a large part of the institutional framework for the implementation of energy law, namely, domestic agencies and domestic courts, and governs the procedures these institutions apply. Domestic law and domestic political processes also define the objectives of energy law. These are (1) energy security, a factor that is important for the functioning of the economy; (2) closely connected to that, the aim of energy efficiency; (3) the avoidance of harm to third parties; and (4) the avoidance of negative impact of energy activities on the environment.[50] National law, finally, also defines the means for achieving these goals.

From a functional perspective, national law is therefore of primary importance for the operation of energy markets. Indeed, in a world where the provision of energy was achieved, following the goal of energy autarky, within nation-states (and often through state monopolies), national energy law was the only type of energy law needed to achieve energy policy goals. At most, it needed to be complemented in some countries by some international legal rules in light of, for example, the import of energy sources and products, such as oil and gas. Yet, in today's international energy markets, international energy law assumes a much more important and complementary function to national energy law in achieving energy policy goals.

B. The Functions of International Energy Law

The shift in paradigm for achieving energy security and energy efficiency from that of a public service in a domestic framework to the idea of an international energy market is responsible for the increased amount and importance of international energy law understood as the law governing the emergence and regulation of the trans-border aspects of the energy industry. In fact, international energy law became an instrument for those states that participated in the creation and operation of international

[50] See, eg, Christian Koenig, Jürgen Kühling and Winfried Rasbach, *Energierecht* (Frankfurt am Main, Verlag Recht und Wirtschaft, 2006) 21.

energy markets in order to achieve their domestic energy policy goals, including, above all, energy security and security of supply through international cooperation. At the same time, while pursuing their respective national interests, the policy goals states shared concerning international energy markets emerged as guiding principles of international energy law.

In governing the trans-border aspects of international energy markets, international law performs a number of important functions that national law is not at all, or only insufficiently, able to perform. First, public international law has an important function for the allocation of claims for territorial sovereignty and for the exercise of jurisdiction among different states (*jurisdictional function*).[51] This helps distribute power horizontally among different states and other internationally relevant actors, such as international organisations. Public international law clarifies the respective jurisdiction of states to legislate, administer, and adjudicate in respect of issues relevant for the functioning of international energy markets, including avoidance of harm to third parties and the environment (so-called jurisdictions to prescribe and to adjudicate). This function of public international law is crucial for international energy markets because it allows, for example, for the establishment of clear property regimes for the exploration and exploitation of energy resources (such as oil and gas).[52] Moreover, public international law clarifies that states have the power to redistribute ownership over natural resources under the principle of permanent sovereignty over natural resources.[53] Furthermore, the allocation of sovereignty or sovereign rights is also important for clarifying the jurisdiction of states to regulate other issues that are relevant for energy production and distribution. This holds true, for example, as regards the allocation of sovereign rights in the sea under the UN Convention on the Law of the Sea (UNCLOS), which provides for different rules regarding jurisdiction over activities in different maritime zones, or regulation on energy exploitation in the global commons.[54] Finally, the horizontal allocation of power also clarifies who is responsible for enforcing international law and international standards (so-called jurisdiction to enforce).

Second, public international law has a crucial function in providing the institutional infrastructure, including formal organisations and legal instruments, necessary for inter-state cooperation, above all, in the form of

[51] See generally Bernard H Oxman, 'Jurisdiction of States' in R Wolfrum (ed), *Max Planck Encyclopedia of Public International Law*, vol VI (Oxford, Oxford University Press, 2012) 546.

[52] On the importance of property law and its interconnections with energy law, see also Aileen Mcharg, Barry Barton, Adrian Bradbrook and Lee Godden (eds), *Property and the Law in Energy and Natural Resources* (Oxford, Oxford University Press, 2010).

[53] See Nico Schrijver, *Sovereignty over Natural Resources* (Cambridge, Cambridge University Press, 1997) 258ff.

[54] The jurisdictional rules regarding the sea, the Arctic, the Antarctic, and extraterrestrial areas are discussed in Rex J Zedalis, *International Energy Law: Rules Governing Future Exploration, Exploitation, and Use of Renewable Resources* (Farnham, Surrey, Ashgate, 2000).

international treaties (*institutional function*). This function plays an important role for inter-state cooperation, bilaterally as well as multilaterally, and for establishing international institutions to administer and adjudicate energy-related issues. An example of bilateral cross-border energy production based on an international treaty is Itaipú Binacional, one of the largest hydro-electric power plants worldwide, operated jointly by Paraguay and Brazil at the Paraná river.[55] Examples of multi-party projects include pipelines to transport oil or gas across borders, such as the Baku-Tblisi-Ceyhan (BTC) Oil Pipeline[56] or the Nabucco Pipeline Project.[57] Yet, public international law is also used by states as an instrument to cooperate on other subject matter in the area of energy law, such as providing rules on energy trade, energy investment, or environmental protection. Furthermore, public international law is used by states to create international organisations in the field, such as the International Atomic Energy Agency, whose objective it is to 'seek to accelerate and enlarge the contribution of atomic energy to peace, health and prosperity throughout the world'.[58] Another example is the IEA, an intergovernmental organisation originally set up to help member countries coordinate a collective response to major disruptions in oil supply through the release of emergency oil stocks to the markets; today, the Agency has much wider objectives, including providing authoritative and unbiased research, statistics, analysis, and recommendations on energy-related topics, such as energy security, economic development, and environmental awareness.[59] In addition to such institutions of a more administrative nature, international

[55] Treaty Between the Federative Republic of Brazil and the Republic of Paraguay Concerning the Hydroelectric Utilization of the Water Resources of the Parana River Owned in Condominium by the Two Countries, from and including the Salto Grande de Sete Quedas or Salto del Guaira, to the Mouth of the Iguassu River, signed 26 April 1973, 923 UNTS 57 (1981).

[56] Agreement among the Azerbaijan Republic, Georgia and the Republic of Turkey relating to Transportation of Petroleum via the Territories of the Azerbaijan Republic, Georgia and the Republic of Turkey through the Baku-Tbilisi-Ceyhan Main Export Pipeline, signed 18 Nov 1999, available at: http://subsites.bp.com/caspian/BTC/Eng/agmt4/agmt4.PDF.

[57] Agreement among the Republic of Austria, the Republic of Bulgaria, the Republic of Hungary, Romania and the Republic of Turkey regarding the Nabucco Project, signed 13 July 2009, entered into force 1 Aug 2010, available at: http://treaties.un.org/doc/Publication/UNTS/No%20Volume/48457/Part/I-48457-08000002802d4b2c.pdf. See further Johannes Fuchs, 'Kooperative Erdgassicherheit—Energietransit im Völkerrecht unter besonderer Berücksichtigung des Nabucco-Abkommens vom 13.7.2009' (2011) 71 *ZaöRV/Heidelberg Journal of International Law* 103.

[58] See Art II of the Statute of the International Atomic Energy Agency, concluded 26 Oct 1956, entered into force 29 July 1957, 276 UNTS 3 (1957).

[59] Agreement on an International Energy Program, concluded 18 Nov 1974, entered into force 19 Jan 1976, 1040 UNTS 271 (1977). Its members are most EU member states, plus Australia, Canada, Japan, Switzerland, Norway, New Zealand, South Korea, Turkey, and the United States.

law is also used to establish international dispute settlement institutions for both inter-state and investor-state disputes relating to international energy markets.[60]

Third, and turning to the subject matter of international energy law, public international law has an important role in enabling, facilitating, and stabilising the functioning of international energy markets (*market function*). Through rules on trade in energy and energy transit (including under the WTO,[61] free trade agreements such as the North-American Free Trade Agreement (NAFTA),[62] the Energy Community,[63] and the Energy Charter Treaty (ECT)),[64] international law ensures that energy and energy resources can be traded across borders.[65] In addition, bilateral investment treaties (BITs), as well as the investment protection provisions in the ECT, stabilise the relations between foreign-owned energy companies and host governments.[66] Rules on energy investments ensure that foreign-owned energy companies are not expropriated without compensation, have a right to be treated fairly and equitably and in accordance with the treatment that other nationals or third-party nationals receive. In addition, treaties protecting energy investments provide that investor-state disputes can be settled by arbitration and not in domestic courts, which would normally be competent in such matters.[67] All of these international rules stabilise investor-state relations in the energy sector and protect and promote energy investments. Without such rules, host states would only be constrained by domestic law and domestic institutions and could change the original terms of an energy investment unilaterally, thus upsetting the basic prerequisites for the functioning of markets in the energy field.

[60] See nn 21 and 25 and accompanying text.

[61] See further Thomas Cottier, Garba Malumfashi, Sofya Matteotti-Berkutova, Olga Nartova, Joëlle De Sépibus and Sadeq Z Bigdeli, 'Energy in WTO Law and Policy' in Thomas Cottier and Panagiotis Delimatsis (eds), *The Prospects of International Trade Regulation* (Cambridge, Cambridge University Press, 2011) 211.

[62] North American Free Trade Agreement (NAFTA), signed 17 Dec 1992, entered into force 1 Jan 1994, 32 ILM 289 and 605 (1993). See further Roberto Rios Herrán and Pietro Poretti, 'Energy Trade and Investment under the North American Free Trade Agreement' in Selivanova, *Regulation of Energy in International Trade Law: WTO, NAFTA, and Energy Charter* (n 20) 335.

[63] Treaty Establishing the Energy Community, signed 25 Oct 2005, OJ L 198, 20 July 2006, 18. See further Roman Petrov, 'Energy Community as a Promoter of the European Union's "Energy Acquis" to Its Neighborhood' (2012) 39 *Legal Issues of Economic Integration* 331.

[64] Energy Charter Treaty (ECT) (Annex I of the Final Act of the European Energy Charter Conference) (ECT), signed 17 Dec 1994, 34 ILM 373 (1995). See further on the ECT Thomas W Wälde (ed), *The Energy Charter Treaty: An East-West Gateway for Investment and Trade* (Alphen aan den Rijn, Kluwer Law International, 1996), as well as the literature cited in nn 21 and 25.

[65] See also the contributions in Selivanova (n 20).

[66] See the literature cited in n 21. In the literature on international investment law more generally, see Stephan W Schill, 'W(h)ither Fragmentation? On the Literature and Sociology of International Investment Law' (2011) 22 *European Journal of International Law* 875.

[67] See further the literature cited in nn 21 and 25.

Fourth, public international law has the function of preventing and mitigating harm to third parties and public goods, such as the environment, that results from energy production and distribution (*public policy function*). In international energy markets, the existence of such rules under international law is crucial to address a collective action problem in avoiding externalities. Individually, no state would have an incentive to impose rules for the protection of the environment, as this would impose costs on some but not all energy producers, and thereby potentially lead to a market distortion. Only collective agreements on environmental standards remove such an obstacle to protecting the environment in the context of energy relations. The environmental rules under UNCLOS,[68] multilateral environmental agreements,[69] or international instruments and initiatives to promote renewable energy and to limit carbon emissions,[70] are examples of this, as are conventions regarding obligations in case of oil spills.[71] Likewise, public international law ensures that no harm to another state's interests occurs when producing and distributing energy. Rules on nuclear safety are one example of such international rules.[72] Similarly, the international human rights framework[73] and international law concerning the rights of indigenous populations[74] ensure that states do not distort the functioning of international energy markets by allowing costs of energy producers or distributors to be imposed on certain, usually vulnerable groups.

Finally, public international law serves an important role in ensuring that domestic law complies with its own energy policy objectives (*constitutional function*). This is the case if we consider that international law serves a function similar to constitutional law in locking domestic law and policy-making in the energy sector to objectives and principles once set, such as the goal of achieving energy security through international energy

[68] See United Nations Convention on the Law of the Sea, adopted 10 Dec 1982, entered into force 16 Nov 1994, 1833 UNTS 3 (1994). James L Kateka, 'Protection and Preservation of the Marine Environment in the Area under UNCLOS' in HP Hestermeyer, D König, N Matz-Lück, V Röben, A Seibert-Fohr, P-T Stoll and S Vöneky (eds), *Coexistence, Cooperation and Solidarity*, vol 1 (Leiden, Martinus Nijhoff, 2012) 919; John ED Larkin, 'UNCLOS and the Balance of Environmental and Economic Resources in the Arctic' (2009/10) 22 *Georgetown International Environmental Law Review* 307; Erik Franckx, 'Regional Marime Environment Protection Regimes in the Context of UNCLOS' (1998) 13 *International Journal of Marine and Coastal Law* 307.

[69] See Tullio Treves (ed), *Non-Compliance Procedures and Mechanisms and the Effectiveness of International Environmental Agreements* (The Hague, TMC Asser Press, 2009).

[70] See Elena Blanco and Jona Razzaque, *Globalisation and Natural Resources Law* (Cheltenham, Edward Elgar, 2011) 328ff.

[71] See the literature cited in n 17.

[72] See the literature cited in n 18.

[73] See the literature cited in n 19.

[74] For an overview, see Benedict Kingsbury, 'Indigenous Peoples' in Wolfrum, *Max Planck Encyclopedia of Public International Law* (n 50) vol V, 116, paras 8ff.

markets. International law, in this context, prevents states from later taking measures that counteract policy goals set earlier.

While all these functions are important for international energy markets to operate properly, it is important to recognise that international law cannot and does not replace domestic law; it has a more limited ambit in governing certain trans-border aspects of international energy markets only. International law in the field, in fact, cannot replace domestic law because of the amount and diversity of legal rules necessary to govern all aspects of energy markets. In addition, international law should not be all-encompassing, given that domestic law in many cases has superior institutional expertise and capacity, and a greater democratic potential. Instead, what is crucial is international energy law's interaction with domestic law in making international energy markets function. As the next section shows, the interfaces between national and international energy law themselves can be analysed in terms of their functions for international energy markets.

C. Functions of Interfaces

In light of the above, it seems that, from a functional perspective, national and international energy law can be separated neatly in relation to different subject matter. However, the functions of interfaces between national and international law in the energy sector itself are of crucial importance for understanding how national and international law relate to each other in governing international energy markets.

First, from an enforcement and compliance perspective, national law and national actors have an important function for implementing international energy law. This is the case with domestic legislation implementing international energy law, national courts enforcing claims under international law and using international law to interpret domestic energy law, and domestic administrations applying international energy law. In this regard, interfaces between national and international law serve to enforce the international rule of law.

Second, from the perspective of international actors, international law and international institutions can function to ensure that the exercise of public authority at the domestic level in the energy sector accords with international law standards. International investment arbitrations or international trade disputes, for example, can have the objective of determining the legality of state conduct under international law and determining whether international rule of law standards have been met by domestic actors in the energy sector. In this regard, interfaces between national and international law serve to control domestic actors' compliance with international law.

Third, national law and national actors also exercise important functions in concretising the meaning of international energy law. Thus, national law and national actors, in particular, domestic courts, can contribute to concretising what the often abstract and ambiguous rules and principles of international law mean for specific circumstances in the energy sector. Furthermore, national actors, by applying an international law concept, actively contribute to the normative clarification of that very concept. Together with national courts in other domestic jurisdictions that pursue similar jurisprudential strategies, domestic courts do not simply apply concepts of international energy law, but further develop and shape them.[75] The interaction between national actors and international law, in other words, can contribute to international energy law-making.

Fourth, national law and national actors can also exercise a function in controlling that international institutions meet rule of law standards by reviewing, if only incidentally, the legality of the conduct of international institutions. These cases, for example the *Kadi* decision of the CJEU,[76] or the *Nada* judgment of the European Court of Human Rights,[77] are often conceptualised as cases where international and national law collide and conflict. Yet, instead of viewing such cases as challenging the validity of international law, or the desirability of international cooperation, such cases of (more or less open) contestation can also be viewed as ensuring compliance of international actors with rule of law standards that either already exist elsewhere under international law, for example in international human rights law,[78] or that reflect values that are essential for predictable and fair international cooperation, including in the energy sector. One can thus perceive the possibility of contestation of national actors invoking national law, when reviewing or opposing acts of an international institution, as an act that reflects the separation of powers across the national law-international law divide. It accords with the principle that no act of public authority shall go without appropriate judicial review. From that perspective, in appropriate cases, national law and national

[75] For the dual function of domestic courts as enforcers and makers or international law, see Anthea Roberts, 'Comparative International Law? The Role of National Courts in Creating and Enforcing International Law' (2011) 60 *International & Comparative Law Quarterly* 57.

[76] See n 33.

[77] *Nada v Switzerland*, App no 10593/08 (ECtHR, Grand Chamber, 12 Sept 2012).

[78] Such an argument underlies, for example, the argument that the UN Security Council is bound by general principles of law that stem from widely ratified human rights instruments, such as the International Covenant on Civil and Political Rights. See, eg, *Prosecutor v Dusko Tadic a/k/a 'Dule'*, Decision on the Defence Motion for Interlocutory Appeal on Jurisdiction (2 Oct 1995) paras 41ff. Note that the argument here is not that the validity of international law itself is challenged, but rather that international law demands different conduct from that actually undertaken by the UN Security Council.

actors, and their review and control of acts of international institutions, can be seen as part and parcel of a system of international governance that is programmed to meet rule of law standards by distributing control functions across national and international actors and institutions.[79]

In sum, interfaces between national and international law not only serve the important function of making the interaction between national and international law in governing international energy markets operational. Interfaces can also ensure that the governance of those markets, and the actors engaged in that governance, effectively behave according to rule of law standards that are common to international and national legal orders. Even conflicts between national and international actors and between national and international law can then have a productive function for the effective and fair implementation of international cooperation in the energy sector. Even in cases of conflict, national and international law can be understood to function complementarily in ensuring compliance of public authorities, whether domestic or international, with the concept of the rule of law and in striking an appropriate balance between private and public interests in energy markets underlying that concept. The close interaction between international law and national law also shows that the concept of the rule of law in global governance cannot be equated with the rule of international law, but is a concept that constrains the exercise of public authority more generally and is implemented through the various interfaces between national and international law.

IV. INTERFACES STRUCTURING THE DIVISION OF LABOUR

The complementary function, or the division of labour, of national and international energy law is put into practice through a number of interfaces. Structurally, these can be found at the level of the different instruments that play a role in governing international energy relations (norm-interfaces) (A), at the level of actors that apply domestic and international energy law (actor-interfaces), and, closely connected to the latter, at the level of procedures applied by those actors (procedure-interfaces) (B). This structure captures the interlocking nature of national and international law in the energy sector.

[79] In fact, without the possibility of control by domestic actors, the rule of law would suffer in cases where no international court reviewing the conduct in question is available. National actors exercising control of international actors in such circumstances can then be seen as functioning as agents not only of their national law, but also of the international rule of law and international law more generally.

A. Legal Instruments as Norm-Interfaces

Interfaces between national and international law can be found in different legal instruments. These interfaces can be understood as norm-interfaces. They encompass cases where international legal instruments make reference to domestic law (i), but also where domestic law makes reference to, incorporates, or implements norms of international energy law (ii). In addition, contracts between energy companies and governments can serve as norm-interfaces (iii).

i. Treaties as Interfaces

Many international treaties that govern aspects of international energy markets contain provisions that connect international law to domestic legal orders. This can be the case, for example, with international legal obligations requiring that domestic law be structured in a certain way, such as the requirement under international environmental law that environmental impact assessments be conducted under domestic law, including in the context of energy projects.[80]

Another example of norm-interfaces can be found in clauses in BITs that expressly provide that investments, including in the energy sector, are protected under the treaty only when made 'in accordance with host State law'.[81] A typical example of such as clause is Article 1(1) of the Italy-Morocco BIT, which provides that the notion of protected investments comprises

> all categories of assets invested, after the coming into force of the present agreement, by a natural or legal person, including the Government of a Contracting Party, on the territory of the other Contracting Party, in accordance with the laws and regulations of the aforementioned party.[82]

Here, an international treaty makes express reference to domestic law, in a way that is well known in private international law as a renvoi.

[80] See Convention on Environmental Impact Assessment in a Transboundary Context (Espoo Convention), adopted 25 Feb 1991, entered into force 10 Sept 1997, 1989 UNTS 309 (1997); see also *Pulp Mills on the River Uruguay (Argentina v Uruguay)* [2010] ICJ Reports (Judgment 20 April 2010) 14, 82–83, para 204 (stating that 'it may now be considered a requirement under general international law to undertake an environmental impact assessment where there is a risk that the proposed industrial activity may have a significant adverse impact in a transboundary context, in particular, on a shared resource').

[81] See Christina Knahr, 'Investments "In Accordance with Host State Law"' (2007) 4(5) *Transnational Dispute Management*; Andrea Carlevaris, 'The Conformity of Investments with the Law of the Host State and the Jurisdiction of International Tribunals' (2008) 9 *Journal of World Investment & Trade* 35; Stephan W Schill, 'Illegal Investments in Investment Treaty Arbitration' (2012) 11 *Law and Practice of International Courts and Tribunals* 281.

[82] See *Salini Costruttori SpA and Italstrade SpA v Morocco*, ICSID ARB/00/4, Decision on Jurisdiction 23 July 2001, 42 ILM 609 (2003) para 45.

There are numerous other examples of such norm-interfaces. The ECT, for example, refers to domestic law in order to determine the nationality of natural and judicial persons as protected investors.[83] National law is further mentioned explicitly in the context of the transfer provision of the ECT. Article 14(4) of the ECT permits, that

> a Contracting Party may protect the rights of creditors, or ensure compliance with laws on the issuing, trading and dealing in securities and the satisfaction of judgements in civil, administrative and criminal adjudicatory proceedings, through the equitable, nondiscriminatory, and good faith application of its laws and regulations.

Article 18(2) of the ECT, in turn, clarifies that the treaty shall not 'prejudice the rules in Contracting Parties governing the system of property ownership of energy resources'. Domestic law, finally, is explicitly mentioned in Article 45(1) of the ECT in the context of the provisional application of the treaty, which states that such application depends on whether the respective state's constitution, laws, or regulations so permit.[84]

Yet, norm-interfaces in international treaties do not need to be explicit. It is equally possible that, because of its subject matter, a certain question is governed by domestic law and not by international law. The determination of nationality, if relevant for an international treaty, is such an example.[85] Similarly, the question of whether a contract between an energy investor and a host government was validly formed, which is a question that could become relevant as a preliminary question for the operation of umbrella clauses in investment treaties, is one to be determined according to the applicable domestic law.[86] Through such norm-interfaces, international and national law divide the task of governing international energy markets.

[83] See ECT, Art 1(7). The connection between domestic law and the determination of nationality of corporations is also reinforced in declarations of states parties to the ECT, namely the Russian Federation, the European Communities and their member states, in which these contracting parties reaffirm the importance of national legislation in regard of ECT, Art 1(6) (regarding the definition of investment) and ECT, Art 25 (regarding economic integration agreements). See Declaration of the Parties Nos 1 and 5.

[84] Beyond these issues, the relation between the ECT and domestic law is further mentioned explicitly in a number of provisions contained in the 'Understandings of Contracting Parties when signing the ECT'.

[85] *cf Nottebohm Case* (second phase) [1955] ICJ Reports (Judgment, 6 April 1955) 4, 20. For further examples in the context of international investment law, see Monique Sasson, *Substantive Law in Investment Treaty Arbitration—The Unsettled Relationship between International and Municipal Law* (Alphen aan den Rijn, Kluwer Law International, 2010).

[86] See Stephan W Schill, 'Enabling Private Ordering: Function, Scope and Effect of Umbrella Clauses in International Investment Treaties' (2009) 18 *Minnesota Journal of International Law* 1, 59–62.

ii. Domestic Laws as Interfaces

The division of labour between international law and national law can be seen not only in international treaty provisions that make reference to domestic law, but also at the level of domestic law. While direct references of domestic law to international norms are rare,[87] domestic law often mirrors international legal norms, when implementing international legal obligations. This is the case, for example, when EU member states implement EU directives in the energy sector into their domestic law, such as Directive 2009/72/EC concerning common rules for the internal market in electricity[88] or Directive 2009/73/EC concerning common rules for the internal market in natural gas.[89] These directives, *inter alia*, require EU member states to implement rules regarding consumer protection, environmental protection, and competition among energy producers. Domestic law can therefore link international and national law and integrate requirements of international energy law into domestic law. This brings about the coordination of different domestic legal orders and ensures the effective division of labour among the different legal orders.

iii. Contracts as Interfaces

Finally, even contracts between energy companies and governments, such as concession contracts or production sharing agreements, which concern the exploitation of energy resources, or Build-Operate-Transfer contracts concerning the generation of electricity, often serve as norm-interfaces. This is the case, for example, when considering contractual provisions aiming to mitigate the political risk inherent in long-term projects involving significant upfront investments, that is, the risk that the sovereign party to the contract will unilaterally modify or terminate the contract by amending the governing domestic law in order to extract additional value from the original bargain or by expropriating foreign investors without adequate compensation.[90]

[87] An example from outside energy law would be the US Alien Tort Claims Act (28 USC § 1350; ATS) which provides that '[t]he district courts shall have original jurisdiction of any civil action by an alien for a tort only, committed in violation of the law of nations or a treaty of the United States'.

[88] Directive 2009/72/EC of the European Parliament and of the Council of 13 July 2009 concerning common rules for the internal market in electricity and repealing Directive 2003/54/EC, OJ L 211, 14 Aug 2009, 55.

[89] Directive 2009/73/EC of the European Parliament and of the Council of 13 July 2009 concerning common rules for the internal market in natural gas and repealing Directive 2003/55/EC, OJ L 211, 14 Aug 2009, 94.

[90] On the notion of political risk, see Noah Rubins and Stephan N Kinsella, *International Investment, Political Risk and Dispute Resolution: A Practitioner's Guide* (Dobbs Ferry, NY, Oceana Publications, 2005) 2–3.

While such contracts are normally governed by the domestic law of the state that is party to the contract, various contract provisions have emerged in practice to internationalise private-public contracts, including in the energy sector.[91] Thus, through specific choice of law clauses, a private-public contract can be subjected to public international law or general principles of law.[92] Other internationalisation techniques are the inclusion of so-called stabilisation clauses that freeze the governing domestic law and exempt an investor-state contract from certain subsequently enacted laws[93] and renegotiation clauses that require to negotiate adaptations of investor-state contracts to unforeseen changes in circumstances.[94] Most importantly, investor-state contracts regularly contain forum selection and arbitration clauses. These ensure that disputes do not fall prey to problems with litigation in the state party's domestic courts, such as lengthy and inefficient court proceedings or exposure to the real or perceived bias of domestic courts in favour of their government.

All of these clauses decouple investor-state contracts from domestic law and subject them to the international legal order. Hence, such contracts serve as norm-interfaces between national and international law by subjecting the exercise of power by host governments to international law. Similar to treaties and domestic laws, contracts, in such cases, serve as norm-interfaces that create a close interconnectedness between national and international law, thus putting the division of labour between both legal orders in governing international energy markets into practice.

B. Actor-Interfaces and Procedure-Interfaces

The division of labour between national and international energy law does not only play out at the level of legal norms and instruments, it also plays out when focusing on the actors applying and implementing energy law, and the procedures they use when doing so. Accordingly, one can

[91] See Rudolf Dolzer and Christoph Schreuer, *Principles of International Investment Law* (2nd edn, Oxford, Oxford University Press, 2012) 79–86; Cameron, *International Energy Investment Law* (n 21) 59ff.

[92] This was the case with many of the early oil concession agreements. See André von Walter, 'Oil Concession Disputes, Arbitration on' in Wolfrum (n 50) vol VII, 948, paras 24–27.

[93] See Cameron (n 21) 68ff; Hanno Merkt, *Investitionsschutz durch Stabilisierungsklauseln* (Heidelberg, Verlag Recht und Wirtschaft, 1990). On the problems of states' regulatory freedom arising out of such clauses, see Jorge Viñuales, *Foreign Investment and the Environment in International Law* (Cambridge, Cambridge University Press, 2012) 337ff (with further references).

[94] See Cameron (n 21) 83ff; Klaus Peter Berger, 'Renegotiation and Adaptation of International Investment Contracts: The Role of Contract Drafters and Arbitrators' (2003) 36 *Vanderbilt Journal of Transnational Law* 1347; Stefan Kröll, 'The Renegotiation and Adaptation of Investment Contracts' in N Horn and S Kröll (eds), *Arbitrating Foreign Investment Disputes* (Alphen aan den Rijn, Kluwer Law International, 2004) 425.

understand both domestic and international public actors, and their procedures, as interfaces between national and international energy law. This holds true as regards the exercise of public authority by administrations through administrative proceedings (i), dispute settlement institutions in adjudicative procedures (ii), and in negotiations between private and public actors (iii).

i. Administration as Interface

Administrations are an important point where international law and national law interact. Notably, in the area of energy law, administrations that draw connections between national and international energy law do not only exist at the domestic level. On the contrary, administrative agencies applying international and domestic energy law have also emerged at the international level. This makes it necessary to understand administrations as interfaces on both the national and the international level. While there is a range of different national and international administrations one could draw on, I will here only address two examples of a specifically close interaction between domestic and international law: first, an example where a domestic administrative agency applies norms originating from the international level; and second, an example of an international administration dealing with domestic law. These examples show how administrations and administrative proceedings function as interfaces of national and international energy law.

First, in many instances, domestic agencies, when engaging in governing the energy industry, not only apply domestic standards, but also implement, or act according to, international standards. One example is the way the Convention on Access to Information, Public Participation in Decision-Making and Access to Justice in Environmental Matters (the so-called Aarhus Convention) has transformed administrative law and procedure by granting the public rights to information, public participation, and access to justice regarding decision-making processes concerning the environment.[95] In the context of energy-related projects, the international environmental standards of the Aarhus Convention affect how domestic agencies conduct, for example, the procedure for the issuance of a construction or operating licence for an electric power plant.[96] In this context, domestic administrations can be viewed as actor-interfaces, and the procedures they apply as procedure-interfaces, that make the interaction between national and international law operational.

[95] See Convention on Access to Information, Public Participation in Decision-Making and Access to Justice in Environmental Matters, opened for signature 25 June 1998, 2161 UNTS 447.

[96] On the Convention's effect on domestic administrative law, see Andreas Fischer-Lescano, 'Transnationales Verwaltungsrecht' (2008) 63 *Juristenzeitung* 373.

Second, an example of an international institution exercising partly administrative functions (in a wide sense) is the IEA.[97] It conducts, *inter alia*, country policy reviews according to IEA Standards and issues recommendations to deal with deficiencies in the respective country's energy law and policy framework. Recommendations may address a wide variety of energy-related subjects and, if implemented, may have a deep impact on how domestic energy law is structured and applied. Recommendations can refer, *inter alia*, to the establishment and functioning of a national regulatory authority, the restructuring of the energy-related economy or the methodology of pricing of energy-related products.[98] Such reviews are not binding, but nevertheless are often implemented under domestic law.[99] This exemplifies how international administrations and their administrative procedures can function as actor- and procedure-interfaces that implement the interaction between international and national law.

ii. Dispute Settlement as Interface

Not only administrations function as interfaces. Also dispute settlement institutions—that is, courts and arbitral tribunals—play an important role in making national and international energy law interact. As is the case with administrative agencies, dispute settlement institutions applying energy law exist both at the domestic and the international levels. We can therefore observe both domestic courts applying rules of international law and international dispute settlement organs applying domestic law functioning as actor interfaces. In doing so, domestic and international courts and tribunals engage in a division of labour in settling energy-related disputes and thereby contribute to governing international energy markets.

As an example of a domestic court applying and reconsidering international law, consider the domestic court review and enforcement of awards of international arbitral tribunals resolving disputes between energy

[97] Agreement on an International Energy Program, concluded 18 Nov 1974, entered into force 19 Jan 1976, 1040 UNTS 271 (1977). Its members are most EU member states, plus Australia, Canada, Japan, Switzerland, Norway, New Zealand, South Korea, Turkey and the United States. On the classification of such activities of international organisations as administration, see Benedict Kingsbury, Nico Krisch and Richard B Stewart, 'The Emergence of Global Administrative Law' (2005) 68 *Law & Contemporary Problems* 15.

[98] See the list of country reviews conducted by the IEA available at: www.iea.org/publications/countryreviews.

[99] Despite their non-bindingness, such reviews should be regarded as instances of international public authority. On the notion of international public authority, see Armin von Bogdandy, Philipp Dann and Matthias Goldmann, 'Developing the Publicness of Public International Law: Towards a Legal Framework for Global Governance Activities' in A von Bogdandy, R Wolfrum, J von Bernstorff, P Dann and Matthias Goldmann (eds), *The Exercise of Public Authority by International Institutions: Advancing International Institutional Law* (Heidelberg, Springer, 2009) 3, 11–16.

investors and host governments. For example, disputes about whether the host government has breached the rights of energy investors under the ECT can be submitted, pursuant to Article 26(4)(c) of the ECT, to arbitration under the rules of the Arbitration Institute of the Stockholm Chamber of Commerce. Provided the seat of such an arbitration is Sweden, the domestic courts in Sweden exercise a supervisory function in relation to the arbitral proceedings and can, under certain circumstances—in particular, in case the arbitral tribunal exceeded its powers or breached fundamental rules of procedure—review and set aside any resulting arbitral award; they can also perform other supporting functions for the conduct of an arbitration; for example, regarding collection of evidence or the issuance of interim measures.[100] This illustrates how a domestic court controls and supports dispute settlement proceedings under international law.

Similarly, domestic courts in countries where enforcement of an arbitral award is sought under the rules of the 1958 United Nations Convention on the Recognition and Enforcement of Foreign Arbitral Awards (the so-called New York Convention)[101] can refuse recognition and enforcement pursuant to Article V of the Convention. This includes a review of the arbitral award for compliance with the parties' agreement to arbitrate, fundamental rules of procedure, and conformity with the enforcement state's rules on arbitrability and *ordre public*. Again, domestic courts in this context act as supervisory bodies that can review whether international dispute settlement bodies complied with requirements, not only of international law, but also of fundamental principles of domestic law. Domestic courts in these cases act as interfaces in processing the interrelationship between international and national law.

As an example of the second category (ie, an international tribunal applying domestic law), one may consider how international arbitral tribunals apply domestic law concerning the legality of an investment in the energy sector. Thus, even though the ECT does not contain an explicit clause providing that investments protected by the Treaty need to comply with domestic law, an ECT tribunal in *Plama Consortium v Bulgaria*[102] found that the claimant had misled the host state as to the identity of the members of the participating bidder in the privatisation process of a state-owned oil refinery, because the bidder did not consist, as represented to

[100] See Marie Öhrström, 'SCC Rules' in RA Schütze (ed), *Institutional Arbitration: A Commentary* (Oxford, Hart Publishing, 2013) 815, paras 5, 62, 93, 121, 140, 141, 149, 166, 171, 184, 202.

[101] United Nations Convention on the Recognition and Enforcement of Foreign Arbitral Awards, done in New York on 10 June 1958 (New York Convention) 330 UNTS 38.

[102] *Plama Consortium Limited v Republic of Bulgaria*, ICSID ARB/03/24, Decision on Jurisdiction 8 Feb 2005; *Plama Consortium Limited v Republic of Bulgaria*, ICSID ARB/03/24, Award 27 Aug 2008.

Bulgaria, of a consortium of major companies with substantial assets, but of an individual without significant financial resources who was acting under the guise of a consortium.[103] The Tribunal held that the illegality in the form of a misrepresentation deprived the investment of the substantive protection of the ECT because the claimant's behaviour was contrary to both domestic and international law.[104] The Tribunal considered, even though it was established by an international legal instrument, that domestic law was relevant for the question of whether the ECT protected the investment in question; accordingly, it applied domestic law in addition to international norms. The Tribunal therefore served as an actor-interface, and its adjudicative procedure as a procedure-interface, between national and international law.

iii. Negotiations as Interfaces

Both public administration and dispute settlement are decision-making procedures in which one actor, an administrative agency or adjudicatory body, is given authority to make decisions unilaterally, including on the relationship between international law and national law. Yet, not all procedures that constitute interfaces between international and national law involve an exercise of public authority. Negotiations leading to contractually agreed solutions between actors, too, can serve as interfaces between national and international law. This is the case, for example, when energy investors and host governments negotiate agreements regarding the operation of oil exploration and exploitation ventures or the construction and operation of energy facilities, and include in such agreements as discussed above internationalisation, stabilisation, or forum selection clauses that regulate the relationship between dispute resolution in domestic courts and dispute settlement before an investment-treaty based tribunal.[105] Likewise, settlement negotiations after an alleged breach of an international investment treaty by the host state, or breach of an environmental treaty by the investor that dispose of both a domestic and an international dispute, would qualify as procedure-interfaces between international and national law.

[103] *Plama*, Award (n 102) para 133.

[104] ibid para 135 (observing that '[t]he investment in Nova Plama was, therefore, the result of a deliberate concealment amounting to fraud, calculated to induce the Bulgarian authorities to authorise the transfer of shares to an entity that did not have the financial and managerial capacities required to resume operation of the Refinery … the Tribunal is of the view that this behavior is contrary to … Bulgarian law and to international law and that it, therefore, precludes the application of the protections of the ECT').

[105] See nn 91–94 and accompanying text.

V. CONCLUSION: THE RULE OF LAW AS INTERFACE BETWEEN INTERNATIONAL AND NATIONAL LAW

Certainly, in terms of formal sources, national and international energy law remain separable. Likewise, each legal order and its institutions determine independently which value they accord to norms of the respective other legal order. Yet, in international energy markets, as in many other transnational contexts, national and international law can no longer be neatly separated in regard to different social relations or subject matters that the two bodies of law govern. Stressing the different underlying social relations, a consideration that allowed the fathers of modern international law positivism, such as Triepel or Oppenheim, to differentiate between both legal orders, is no longer viable in the present context because international energy relations (just as many other areas of modern economic activities) can no longer be separated into purely domestic and purely international aspects. Instead, the economic and social reality of increasingly close-knit global interactions, such as in the context of global energy markets, demand different theoretical conceptions to structure and analyse the relations between national and international law. Energy markets today are trans-border, globalised markets that are governed by both domestic and international legal instruments, and involve the activity of institutional actors and processes at both the domestic and the international level. Furthermore, energy relations create externalities, such as harm to the environment or public health, which cannot be confined to domestic settings and hence require regulation under international law. It is because of the increasing globalisation of the energy market, as is the case with other global markets, that only national and international legal instruments together can provide the framework required by that market to function, and address the concerns of third parties or global goods arising in connection with such a market.

For this purpose, national and international energy law interact closely and, as has been argued in this chapter, functionally stand in a relationship of division of labour. Likewise, institutions at the domestic and the international level exist that apply and implement domestic and international energy law in order to make the division of labour of national and international legal instruments operative. In fact, the interaction between national and international law, and national and international institutions, is so wide-spread and intensive that it goes beyond punctual interactions. National and international law and institutions form a regulatory complex of interlocking legal orders that function to stabilise and govern international energy markets. National and international law are therefore not normatively autonomous or factually capable of governing the social reality of national energy markets on their own. Accordingly, perspectives, such as those of monism and dualism, that seek to reduce the relationship between national and international law to the question of who is to be master at specific junctures and instances are too limited. Instead, the interactions between national and international law in the context of energy relations are so numerous in terms of issues, instruments, and actors, who all have their specific vision on how national and international energy law interrelate, that binary models fail to reflect the full picture of the national law-international law interface in the field. Instead, national and international legal instruments in combination, that is, as part of a regulatory complex functioning in a relationship of division of labour, make up the framework for regulating international energy markets.

The division of labour between national and international law also impacts the concept, content, and implementation of the rule of law. Instead of understanding the rule of law as a concept that exists independently at the national and the international level, depending on whether the exercise of domestic or international public authority is at stake, one should adopt an integrated perspective on the concept of the rule of law that is applied by and binds both national and international actors. Under this conceptualisation, the rule of law itself constitutes a norm-interface because its content fuses (1) ideas about primacy of international law and compliance of national law with international legal requirements and (2) the constitutional law concept that authority which is delegated from the national to the international level still needs to abide by constitutional standards of the rule of law. In this context, clear normative hierarchies cannot be established; instead, the rule of law in global governance requires international law to be open vis-à-vis national rule of law standards and integrate them in its understanding of the rule of law just as it demands of national law and its concept of the rule of law to be receptive to international legal norms and to international law's demand for compliance. All in all, one should therefore abandon the idea of compartmentalised notions of the rule of law that depend on whether domestic or international public authority is at stake. Instead, one should understand the concept of the rule of law as a norm-interface and develop an encompassing notion of the rule of law that constrains the exercise of public authority as such; its content, in turn, is fed by both international and national ideas about the rule of law.

While divergences between the content of the international and the national rule of law may exist at the fringes, there is arguably a large common core of both notions. As argued by André Nollkaemper, both the national and the international rule of law encompass at least four common elements: first, the idea that 'the exercise of public powers should be based upon authority conferred by law and must be controlled by law'; second, the idea that 'public powers cannot set or change the law at will'; third, the idea that 'the exercise of powers, including the change of existing law, conforms to fundamental civil and political human rights'; and fourth, the idea that 'public powers that contravene their legal obligations, whether international or national, are accountable on the basis of the law'.[106] Yet, how this common core translates in specific situations, and whether international or national considerations may prevail in the way public authority is exercised and controlled, is a matter for different actor and process interfaces to work out. The exercise of national public authority may be controlled under the concept of the international rule of law by international actors, but also the exercise of international public authority may be controlled by national actors under the concept of the national rule of law. The rule of law in global governance is therefore both a norm-interface as well as an actor- and procedure-interface in controlling the exercise of public authority by national and international actors.

What is more, understanding the rule of law as an interface between national and international law can be connected to one of the core goals of the very idea of the rule of law, namely, that the exercise of public power can never be without limits and needs to be subject to control mechanisms. In the domestic context, this is achieved through the separation of powers and the interplay between administration, legislator, and courts, and through the distinction between the constitution and ordinary law. The judiciary ensures that administrations apply, and are accountable to, the law set by the legislator; and the judiciary, and particularly its law-making function, is controlled by the legislator. The legislator, in turn, is constrained by the constitution and, as the case may be, by a constitutional court; effects of decisions of that court, in turn, can be modified by the constitution-making power.

The international context, of course, is very different from the domestic one, in particular, as regards the incompleteness of governance institutions. There is no centralised legislator, and international courts for the control of international administration are often missing. Yet, these functions can be performed at the national level. As a consequence, controlling the way national and international actors exercise public authorities can be achieved through the allocation of control mechanisms across the divide of national and international law and across national and international authorities. Ultimately, the distinction between national and international law, and between national and international actors and their potentially diverging understandings of the rule of law, may therefore be understood as an important factor in achieving one of the core goals of the rule of law, that is, to limit the exercise of public authority and to avoid despotism in global governance, no matter whether this authority is exercised at the national or the international level.

[106] See André Nollkaemper, *National Courts and the International Rule of Law* (Oxford, Oxford University Press, 2011) 3–5.

Conclusion

17

The International Rule of Law in the Cycle of Contestations and Deference

MACHIKO KANETAKE AND ANDRÉ NOLLKAEMPER

THE REQUIREMENT OF the 'rule by law'[1] is commonly considered as one of the integral elements of the rule of law.[2] This formalistic requirement is arguably constitutive, not only of the rule of law in the national legal order, but also of the rule of law which has been developing in the international legal order. This is in part illustrated by the fact that the discourse concerning the rule of law at the 'international' level[3] tends to underline the primary importance of *compliance*, as an extension of the 'rule by law' concept, with international law by states and other subjects of international law. For instance, UN Secretary-General Annan in his 2012 report prepared for the high-level meeting of the General Assembly[4] foremost referred to 'compliance' with international law as a step to strengthen the international rule of law.[5] The invigoration of international courts and tribunals[6] has arguably heightened the significance of

[1] Albert Venn Dicey, *Introduction to the Study of the Law of the Constitution* (Indianapolis, Liberty Fund, 1982) 110–13 (first requirement). See Simon Chesterman, 'An International Rule of Law?' (2008) 56 *American Journal of Comparative Law* 331, 342 (a 'government of laws' as the first core definition of the rule of law).

[2] See ch 1 (Kanetake) s II(B).

[3] As noted in various contributions of this volume, the UN General Assembly has given recognition not only to the rule of law at the national level, but also to the rule of law at the 'international' level: eg, 2005 World Summit Outcome UN Doc A/RES/60/1 (24 Oct 2005) para 134; UN Doc A/RES/61/39 (18 Dec 2006).

[4] See UN GA Res adopted on 24 Sept 2012, 'Declaration of the High-level Meeting of the General Assembly on the Rule of Law at the National and International Levels' UN Doc A/RES/67/1 (30 Nov 2012).

[5] See Report of the Secretary-General, 'Delivering Justice: Programme of Action to Strengthen the Rule of Law at the National and International Levels' UN Doc A/66/749 (16 March 2012) s II.A.1.

[6] On the political and judicial impact of international courts, see, eg, Karen J Alter, *The New Terrain of International Law: Courts, Politics, Rights* (Princeton, New Jersey, Princeton University Press, 2014); Armin von Bogdandy and Ingo Venzke (eds), *International Judicial Lawmaking: On Public Authority and Democratic Legitimation in Global Governance* (Berlin; New York, Springer, 2012); Armin Von Bogdandy and Ingo Venzke, *In Whose Name? A Public Law Theory of International Adjudication* (Oxford, Oxford University Press, 2014). Kingsbury notes that

compliance[7] which is indeed regarded as the core element of legality and the rule of law.[8]

Contestations in the national legal order discussed in this volume would be considered problematic if one assimilates the international rule of law with national compliance. Part I of the present volume exposed the proliferation of national practices that avoid, re-interpret, review, and reject international law or (especially in a dualist state in which treaties have no automatic domestic validity) national regulation that implements international law. As demonstrated by the chapters of Veronika Fikfak, Mateja Steinbrück Platiše, Shotaro Hamamoto, and Prabhash Ranjan, various signs of disagreement extend to international security law, international immunity law, international investment law, and international human rights law.[9] Their chapters also showed that contestations emanate from multiple branches of states and have been justified on the basis of both constitutional *and* international law. National contestations immediately or cumulatively lead to a state of discrepancy between the actual conduct of state institutions on the one hand, and international obligations as interpreted and applied by international organisations, international courts, and treaty-monitoring bodies, on the other hand.

At the same time, part II of this volume informed us that such a discrepancy needs not be understood as being in opposition to the idea of the rule of law, but can be the source of dynamic interactions and mutual learning between relevant actors, and thereby between the two legal orders as such. National contestations can encourage international organisations and their member states to reflect on, and improve, decision-making processes within the organisations. Confrontational practices also motivate international courts and treaty-monitoring bodies to revise the extent to which they leave the margin to national decision-makers. The enduring cycles of national resistance and international adjustment, despite many

the growth in the activities of international courts and tribunals posed the problem of the connection between these international bodies and national law and institutions: Benedict Kingsbury, 'Foreword: Is the Proliferation of International Courts and Tribunals a Systemic Problem' (1998) 31 *New York University Journal of International Law and Politics* 679, 694.

[7] For empirical analyses on compliance with international judicial decisions, see, eg, Constanze Schulte, *Compliance with Decisions of the International Court of Justice* (Oxford; New York, Oxford University Press, 2004); Sara McLaughlin Mitchell and Paul R Hensel, 'International Institutions and Compliance with Agreements' (2007) 51 *American Journal of Political Science* 721; Courtney Hillebrecht, 'Rethinking Compliance: The Challenges and Prospects of Measuring Compliance with International Human Rights Tribunals' (2009) 1 *Journal of Human Rights Practice* 362. As Shany observes, however, compliance is not always the reliable indicator in understanding the effectiveness of international courts: see Yuval Shany, *Assessing the Effectiveness of International Courts* (Oxford, Oxford University Press, 2014).

[8] See Alexandra Huneeus, 'Compliance with Judgments and Decisions' in C Romano, KJ Alter and Y Shany (eds), *Oxford Handbook of International Adjudication* (Oxford, Oxford University Press, 2013) 437, 440.

[9] Chs 2 (Fikfak), 3 (Platiše), 4 (Hamamoto), 5 (Ranjan) of the present volume.

shortcomings, present us with a complex picture on the rule of law in the international legal order which continues to value compliance yet simultaneously respects diversity, self-determination, and the democratic legitimacy of decision-making in national legal orders.

I. NATIONAL CONTESTATIONS

There is nothing novel in the practices of states that avoid and resist the domestic application of treaties and the internationally binding decisions of international organisations and international courts. To name a few well-known instances, South Africa under the apartheid regime rejected the UN Security Council's economic sanctions for many years;[10] the US government dismissed the judgments of the International Court of Justice (ICJ) in *Nicaragua*;[11] and Iran rejected the ICJ's judgment in the *Hostage* case.[12] In addition, each state's general amenability to international law is conditioned by many long- and short-term factors—such as the state's (dis)connection with the historical genesis of international law, languages, education of lawyers regarding international law, monist-dualist traditions on the domestic validity of treaties, and specific governmental policies.

However, the materials discussed in part I of this volume allowed us to capture some patters of national contestations in a more systematic way. The main confrontational practices analysed in this volume and the wider literature can be organised in terms of the diversity of sources of international law that are being contested (A), the variety of national organs that engage in contestations (B), and the standards of review (C).

[10] The UN Security Council imposed a mandatory arms embargo under Resolution 418: UN Doc S/RES/418 (4 Nov 1977). South Africa defied the sanctions for many years: see, eg, UN Doc A/RES/40/64 (10 Dec 1985) para 3 ('Condemns the South African racist regime for defying resolutions of the United Nations'). On South Africa's approaches to international law, see Robert Kolb, *Interprétation et création du droit international: Esquisses d'une herméneutique juridique moderne pour le droit international public* (Brussels, Bruylant, 2006) 68–69; John Dugard, *International Law: A South African Perspective* (4th edn, Cape Town, Juta, 2011).

[11] *Military and Paramilitary Activities in and against Nicaragua (Nicaragua v United States of America), Jurisdiction and Admissibility* [1984] ICJ Reports 392 (Judgment of 26 Nov 1984); *Military and Paramilitary Activities in and against Nicaragua (Nicaragua v United States of America)* [1986] ICJ Reports 14 (Merits, Judgment of 27 June 1986). On the US' approaches to the ICJ decisions, see Andreas L Paulus, 'From Neglect to Defiance? The United States and International Adjudication' (2004) 15 *European Journal of International Law* 783.

[12] *United States Diplomatic and Consular Staff in Tehran (United States of America v Iran) (Provisional Measures)* [1979] ICJ Reports 7 (Provisional Measures, Order of 15 December 1979); *United States Diplomatic and Consular Staff in Tehran (United States of America v Iran)* [1980] ICJ Reports 3 (Merits, Judgment of 24 May 1980).

A. Contested International Law and Decisions

The contributions to this volume demonstrated that the scope of potentially resistible international law and decisions has enlarged, not only by the expansion of the subject matter overlap between national and international law,[13] but also by the invigoration of international institutions, especially the UN Security Council,[14] and international courts.[15] First, the political decisions of international organisations have been subject to direct or indirect contestations at the domestic level. In this volume, Veronika Fikfak recalled that this is most notably illustrated by *Kadi*[16] and related judicial contestations regarding the human rights (in)compatibility of the regulation implementing the decisions of the UN Security Council and its sanctions committees to designate certain individuals and entities for the purpose of the UN's targeted sanctions regimes.[17]

Second, the judicial decisions of international courts have been subject to critical scrutiny at the domestic level. In international human rights law, the decisions of the Inter-American Court of Human Rights (IACtHR) have been constantly avoided and rejected at the national level.[18] While national compliance is much more secured with regard to the ECtHR's decisions, national judges still utilise their interpretive discretion in giving effect to ECtHR judgments in domestic law,[19] and also explicitly contradict them, as the UK Supreme Court's decision in *Horncastle*[20] declined to

[13] International treaties and customary international law prescribe principles and rules concerning, eg, human rights, criminal justice, environment, development, investment, and intellectual property, which are likewise regulated by constitutional law and other domestic laws: see, eg, Anne-Marie Slaughter and William Burke-White, 'The Future of International Law Is Domestic (or, the European Way of Law)' (2006) 47 *Harvard International Law Journal* 327.

[14] On the invigoration of the UN Security Council and its impact on individuals, see, eg, Erika De Wet, *The Chapter VII Powers of the United Nations Security Council* (Oxford; Portland Oregon, Hart Publishing, 2004).

[15] On the political and judicial impact of international courts, see, eg, Alter, *The New Terrain of International Law* (n 6); Bogdandy and Venzke, *International Judicial Lawmaking: On Public Authority and Democratic Legitimation in Global Governance* (n 6); Bogdandy and Venzke, *In Whose Name?* (n 6).

[16] See (nn 57, 59) below.

[17] See ch 2 (Fikfak) of this volume.

[18] See Alexandra Huneeus, 'Rejecting the Inter-American Court: Judicialization, National Courts, and Regional Human Rights' in J Couso, A Huneeus and R Sieder (eds), *Cultures of Legality: Judicialization and Political Activism in Latin America* (New York, Cambridge University Press, 2010) 112; Alexandra Huneeus, 'Courts Resisting Courts: Lessons from the Inter-American Court's Struggle to Enforce Human Rights' (2011) 44 *Cornell International Law Journal* 493.

[19] See Nico Krisch, 'The Open Architecture of European Human Rights Law' (2008) 71 *Modern Law Review* 183.

[20] *R v Horncastle and Others* [2009] UKSC 14 (UK Supreme Court, Judgment of 9 Dec 2009). Lord Phillips observed (as agreed upon by all judges) that it is 'open to [the] court to decline to follow the Strasbourg decision' if it fails to sufficiently accommodate particular aspects of the UK's domestic process: ibid [11]. Similarly, ibid [107]–[08] (Lord Phillips), [117]–[21] (Lord Brown).

follow *Al-Khawaja and Tahery v UK*[21] regarding the compatibility of hearsay evidence with the right to a fair trial under the European Convention on Human Rights (ECHR).[22] As elaborated on in this volume by Hamamoto, in the field of international investment law, the British Columbia Supreme Court in *Mexico v Metalclad Corporation* set aside part of an award under the North American Free Trade Agreement (NAFTA) Chapter 11.[23]

Third, national contestations can be seen even with regard to formally non-binding instruments adopted by treaty-monitoring bodies, such as those for UN human rights treaties.[24] Despite the lack of formal binding force,[25] the bodies' documents inform the domestic interpretation of human rights treaties and of constitutional and statutory human rights provisions.[26] However, domestic courts occasionally reject and contest the monitoring bodies' findings explicitly through their reasoning or implicitly by the consequences of their decisions, as illustrated by *Jones v Saudi Arabia*, in which the UK judges apparently disagreed with the treaty interpretation put forward by the Committee against Torture's Observations.[27]

[21] *Al-Khawaja and Tahery v The United Kingdom* App nos 26766/05 and 22228/06, [2009] 49 EHRR 1 (ECtHR, 20 Jan 2009). The judgment in *Al-Khawaja* (2009) was in turn based upon the earlier jurisprudence of the ECtHR, including *Lucà v Italy* App no 33354/96, ECHR 2001-II (ECtHR, 27 Feb 2001) [40] (Art 6 is infringed upon 'where a conviction is based solely or to a decisive degree on depositions that have been made by a person whom the accused has had no opportunity to examine or to have examined').

[22] See also (n 76) below and corresponding text.

[23] *Mexico v Metalclad Corporation* (2001) 2001 BCSC 664 (The Supreme Court of British Columbia, 2 May 2001). For a detailed analysis, see ch 4 (Hamamoto) of this volume.

[24] Human Rights Committee (HRC), Committee on Economic, Social and Cultural Rights (CESCR), Committee on the Elimination of Racial Discrimination (CERD), Committee on the Elimination of Discrimination against Women (CEDAW), Committee against Torture (CAT), Subcommittee on Prevention of Torture (SPT), Committee on the Rights of the Child (CRC), Committee on Migrant Workers (CMW), Committee on the Rights of Persons with Disabilities (CRPD), and Committee on Enforced Disappearances (CED). On UN human rights treaty-monitoring bodies, see, eg, Philip Alston and James Crawford (eds), *The Future of UN Human Rights Treaty Monitoring* (Cambridge, Cambridge University Press, 2000).

[25] On the analysis of binding character (under international and national law) of the instruments adopted by UN human rights treaty-monitoring bodies, see Rosanne van Alebeek and André Nollkaemper, 'The Legal Status of Decisions by Human Rights Treaty Bodies in National Law' in H Keller and G Ulfstein (eds), *UN Human Rights Treaty Bodies: Law and Legitimacy* (Cambridge, Cambridge University Press, 2012) 356.

[26] See further ILA, Committee on International Human Rights Law and Practice, 'Final Report on the Impact of Findings of the United Nations Human Rights Treaty Bodies' (2004). See also Machiko Kanetake and André Nollkaemper, 'The Application of Informal International Instruments Before Domestic Courts' (2014) 46 *The George Washington International Law Review* 765.

[27] *Jones v Saudi Arabia* [2006] UKHL 26; (2007) 1 AC 270 (UK House of Lords, 14 June 2006); UN Committee Against Torture, 'Conclusions and Recommendations: Canada' CAT/C/CR/34/CAN (7 July 2005) paras 4(g), 5(f). In *Jones v Saudi Arabia*, having noted the Committee's critical remark regarding Canada's state report, Lord Bingham dismissed the relevance of the Committee's observation, noting that '[w]hatever its value in influencing the trend of international thinking, the legal authority of the Committee's recommendation is slight' (*Jones v Saudi Arabia*, ibid [23]). Lord Hoffmann found 'no value' in the Committee's position (ibid [57]). The Committee's interpretation was further disagreed with by the ECtHR

Finally, treaty provisions and customary international law themselves are also subject to national contestations. As analysed in this volume by Mateja Steinbrück Platiše, the jurisdictional immunity of international organisations, which international law protects under the broad notion of functional necessity,[28] has met the jurisprudence of national courts that attempt to restrict it.[29] The German Constitutional Court in *Solange I*[30] and *Solange II*[31] famously conditioned the human rights review of the acts of the European Community (EC) on the availability of comparable protection at the European level. The *Solange* reasoning has been applied to the acts of the EC/EU and other international organisations by several domestic courts in Switzerland, Italy, the US, Argentina, and Columbia.[32] As illustrated by these examples, the subject matter overlap has created the opportunities for both the harmonisation of national regulation according to international law, and the occasions in which national organs encounter difficulties in absorbing it into the domestic legal systems.

B. Domestic Actors Engaging in Contestations

In expressing certain dissatisfaction about international law, various state organs do not speak with one voice. Executive, legislative, and judicial bodies have varied interests using and challenging international law and decisions of international organisations and courts.[33] Rene Urueña in this volume suggested that international legal scholars tend to overlook the variance at the domestic level.[34]

National courts, although there is nothing novel for them to encounter a conflict between domestic law and the rules of international law,[35] may be becoming less hesitant in placing stronger trust in their own domestic

in *Jones v UK*: see UN Committee Against Torture, 'Concluding Observations of the Committee against Torture: Canada' CAT/C/CAN/CO/6 (25 June 2012) paras 14–15; Committee Against Torture, 'General Comment No 3 (2012): Implementation of Article 14 by States Parties' CAT/C/GC/3 (13 Dec 2012) paras 22, 42; *Jones and Others v The United Kingdom* App nos 34356/06 and 40528/06 (ECtHR, 14 Jan 2014) [208].

28 See ch 3 (Platiše) s II.

29 See ibid s III.

30 *Internationale Handelsgesellschaft v Einfuhr- und Vorratstelle für Getreide und Futtermittel* [1974] CMLR 540 (Germany, Federal Constitutional Court, 29 May 1974).

31 *In reapplication of Wünsche Handelsgesellschaft, Federal Constitutional Court,* [1987] 3 CMLR 225 (Germany, Federal Constitutional Court).

32 For details, see ch 3 (Platiše) s III(C).

33 In relation to the national implementation of the IACtHR, Huneeus observes that the implementation involves 'disparate state actors whose interests, ideologies, and institutional settings differ': Huneeus, 'Courts Resisting Courts' (n 18) 495.

34 Ch 6 (Urueña) of this volume.

35 See Jonkheer HF van Panhuys, 'Relations and Interactions Between International and National Scenes of Law' (1964) 112 *Recueil des Cours* 1, 34–48.

constitutional law and avoiding and rejecting internationally binding rules and decisions.[36] Domestic courts contest directly or indirectly such rules and decisions even against the willingness of political organs to give domestic effect to them. The contrast of *Medellin*[37] before the US Supreme Court and the Italian Constitutional Court's decision no 238/2014[38] illustrates this point. While both the US Supreme Court and the Italian Constitutional Court declined to give effect to the ICJ's judgments in *Avena*[39] and *Germany v Italy*[40] respectively, the US court in *Medellin* left it to the Congress to decide whether a non-self-executing treaty—in this case, the ICJ's decision in *Avena*—could be enforceable at the domestic level.[41] By contrast, the Italian Court declined to defer to the decisions of the Italian Parliament which had obliged judges to give effect to the ICJ's judgment.[42]

Political resistance against international law can stem from legislative and executive organs as well as from the wider public. As pointed out in the chapter by Rene Urueña, while lawyers tend to focus on the role of national *courts*, non-judicial national organs obviously play a crucial role in accepting or rejecting international law at the domestic level.[43] For instance, there have been longstanding political oppositions against the ECtHR and its particular decisions. The UK initiated the public debate on the possible withdrawal from the ECHR in 1956,[44] and the opposition persisted in the 1990s especially after the ECtHR's decision in *McCann v UK*.[45] In response to in *Hirst v UK (No 2)*[46] over the prisoners' voting entitlement, in which the ECtHR concluded that the general restriction on the rights

[36] Waters observes that judicial dialogues—both vertically between national and international courts and horizontally among national courts—may have incrementally altered the identity of national courts not only as domestic legal agents but also as contributing to international legal norms: see Melissa A Waters, 'The Future of Transnational Judicial Dialogue' (2010) 104 *Proceedings of the Annual Meeting (American Society of International Law)* 465, 465–66.

[37] *Medellín v Texas* (2008) 128 S.Ct. 1346 (US Supreme Court, Judgment of 25 March 2008).

[38] Sentenza no 238, Anno 2014 (Italy, Constitutional Court, 22 Oct 2014), English translation is available at: www.cortecostituzionale.it/documenti/download/doc/recent_judgments/S238_2013_en.pdf.

[39] *Avena and Other Mexican Nationals (Mexico v United States of America)* [2004] ICJ Reports 12 (31 March 2004).

[40] *Jurisdictional Immunities of the State (Germany v Italy: Greece intervening)* [2012] ICJ Reports 99 (3 Feb 2012). In this case, the ICJ found Italy's internationally wrongful acts in disregarding the international customary law to grant Germany immunity from civil suit.

[41] *Medellín v Texas* (n 37) 1368.

[42] Legge 17 agosto 1957, no 848 [Law no 848 of 17 Aug 1957], Gazzetta ufficiale (GU), no 238 (25 September 1957) art 1; Legge 14 gennaio 2013, no 5 [Law no 5 of 14 Jan 2013], in GU, no 24 (29 Jan 2013) art 3 ('Esecuzione delle sentenze della Corte internazionale di giustizia').

[43] Ch 6 (Urueña) of this volume, s III.

[44] The debate was in relation to the case brought by Greece against the UK: *Greece v The United Kingdom* App no 176/56, Decision of the Commission on the Admissibility of the Application (2 June 1956).

[45] *McCann and Others v The United Kingdom* App no 18984/91, Ser A no 324 (ECtHR, Grand Chamber, 27 Sept 1995).

[46] *Hirst v United Kingdom (No 2)* App no 74025/01, ECHR 2005-IX (ECtHR, Grand Chamber, 6 Oct 2005).

to vote exceeded any acceptable margin of appreciation,[47] the UK Parliament expressed its resistance to the ECtHR by stating that the decisions on the prisoners' right to vote 'should be a matter for democratically-elected lawmakers'.[48]

Political resistance also continues to surface with regard to the particular decisions of international investment tribunals, dispute settlement mechanisms under investment treaties, and even such treaty mechanisms themselves. As exposed by Prabhash Ranjan's chapter, Ecuador denounced several bilateral investment treaties (BITs), South Africa terminated several BITs, Bolivia and Ecuador withdrew from the ICSID, Australia decided not to have an investor-state dispute resolution mechanism, and India reviewed the existing BITs in order to better secure the host state's regulatory power.[49]

As Ji Li argued in this volume, these contestations from judicial and non-judicial fora cannot be separated from wider social norms that underline such contestations against international law and institutions.[50] Governmental officials decide whether and how they use international law and the decisions of international institutions at the domestic level, and such officials' attitude towards international law is constructed by their social and cultural backgrounds.[51] Domestic legal, political, and cultural factors alter the level of compliance by states with the judgments of international courts.[52]

C. Standards of Review

The contributions to this volume further suggested that relevant actors can contest international law on the basis of national and/or international law which, in substance, can overlap one another.

i. National Law

The reliance on national law indicates that domestic constitutional law and other national legal principles and rules *themselves* allow space for contestations. In the Italian Constitutional Court's aforementioned decision no 238/2014,[53] for instance, judges conducted review on the basis of

[47] ibid [82].
[48] House of Commons Votes and Proceedings, Sessions 2010-11, No 115, 10 Feb 2011, available at: www.publications.parliament.uk/pa/cm201011/cmvote/110210v01.htm (234 in favour, 22 against).
[49] See ch 5 (Ranjan) of this volume, s III(B).
[50] Ch 7 (Li) of this volume.
[51] See, in the context of trade dispute resolution, ch 7 (Li) of this volume.
[52] Huneeus, 'Compliance with Judgments and Decisions' (n 8) 453–57.
[53] Sentenza no 238 (n 38).

the fundamental principles of the domestic legal order, including the principles of protection of fundamental human rights,[54] in light of which the relevant laws were found disproportionately restricting the 'fundamental principles of the constitutional order',[55] including the constitutional right of access to justice.[56] Likewise, albeit in the context of EU law, the Court of Justice in *Kadi I* upheld the autonomy of the EU legal order based upon the 'rule of law', which allowed the Court of Justice to conduct the 'full review' of the contested EU (then EC) regulation.[57]

At the same time, the review of the national implementation of international law, formally based upon the national standards of review, can also provide feedback to the international legal order. First, as indicated by Veronika Fikfak in this volume, in the course of ultimately reviewing the relevant implementing legislation, judges may critically analyse the original decisions of international courts and international organisations.[58] For instance, the Court of Justice in *Kadi II*, having intensified the level of full review, scrutinised the UN's listing process in detail,[59] although the Court of Justice's review was ultimately for EU regulation on the basis of the fundamental rights in the EU legal order. Also, as demonstrated by Mateja Steinbrück Platiše in this volume, national judges examine the purpose

[54] See ibid [3.1].

[55] ibid [3.2] ('i principi fondamentali dell'ordinamento costituzionale').

[56] See ibid [3.4], [4]–[5]. The Italian Constitutional Court found the general provision of the domestic law that obliged the national judges to comply with the ICJ judgments were contrary to the judicial protection which is guaranteed by Art 24 of the Italian Constitution. According to the Italian Constitutional Court, the fact that the Court is not in a position to examine the ICJ's qualified interpretation of customary international law does not mean that the Italian Court does not decide upon the conflict between international norms and constitutional norms and principles: see Sentenza n 238 (n 38) [3.1], [3.3].

[57] Cases C-402/05 P and C-415/05 P *Kadi and Al Barakaat International Foundation v Council of the European Union and Commission of the European Communities* [2008] ECR I–06351 (ECJ, Judgment of 3 Sept 2008). On the 2008 judgment, see, eg, Deirdre Curtin and Christina Eckes, 'The Kadi Case: Mapping the Boundaries between the Executive and the Judiciary in Europe' (2008) 5 *International Organizations Law Review* 365; Christina Eckes, *EU Counter-Terrorist Policies and Fundamental Rights* (Oxford, Oxford University Press, 2009) ch 5; Paul James Cardwell, Duncan French and Nigel White, 'European Court of Justice, *Yassin Abdullah Kadi and Al Barakaat International Foundation v Council and Commission* (Joined Cases C-402/05 P and C-415/05 P) Judgment of 3 September 2008' (2009) 58 *International & Comparative Law Quarterly* 229; Gráinne de Búrca, 'The European Court of Justice and the International Legal Order after Kadi' (2010) 51 *Harvard International Law Journal* 1.

[58] See ch 2 (Fikfak) of this volume, about the different modalities of judicial review.

[59] The Court of Justice assessed (1) whether one of the reasons (for listing) stated in the summary provided by the UN's Sanctions Committee was sufficiently detailed and specific and (2) whether it was substantiated: see Joined cases C-584/10 P, C-593/10 P and C-595/10 P, *Kadi v European Commission* [2013] ECR (ECJ, Judgment of 18 July 2013) [114]–[16], [118]–[19], [125]–[28], [130]. (1) With regard to the former, the Court of Justice acknowledged that some of the reasons stated in the Sanctions Committee's summary were sufficiently detailed and specific: *Kadi* (ECJ, 2013), ibid [140]–[50]. (2) Nevertheless, for the latter, the Court of Justice found that information or evidence which might have substantiated the reason for listing was absent, and thereby annulled the contested EU regulation that implemented the decisions of the UN Sanctions Committee's decisions: *Kadi* (ECJ, 2013), ibid [151]–[64].

and scope of the immunities traditionally granted to international organisations under international law; by so doing, domestic courts highlight the shortcomings—in the eyes of national courts—of international law concerning the immunities of international organisations.[60]

Second, the national standards of review can be enriched by international treaties, especially international human rights treaties. Although the Italian Constitutional Court in its decision no 238/2014[61] employed the constitutional right of access to justice as a basis for declining to give effect to the ICJ judgment, the decision, through the substantive connection between the constitutional right in question and the right to access to justice under international law, effectively provides critical feedback to international law on state immunity as interpreted by the ICJ.[62]

ii. International Law

International law itself has been a facilitator of national contestations. As examined by Mateja Steinbrück Platiše's chapter, the fact that the ECtHR in *Waite and Kennedy* has effectively adopted the *Solange* reasoning at the international level further empowered domestic courts to condition the grant of international organisations' immunity on the availability of alternative remedies; for instance, the Belgian Court of Appeals in *Siegler v Western European Union* resorted to the *Waite and Kennedy* test[63] and found the organisation's jurisdictional immunity incompatible with Article 6(1) (the right to a fair trial) of the ECHR.[64] While relying on the ECtHR's jurisprudence, the Belgium Court conducted a more detailed assessment of the internal procedure of the international organisations against the essential conditions of the right to a fair trial.[65]

As reminded by Veronika Fikfak in this volume, national and EU courts also directly reviewed the decisions of the UN Security Council on the basis of *jus cogens* norms.[66] In the September 2005 judgment in *Kadi I*, the General Court (then the Court of First Instance) engaged in *jus cogens* review while recognising the UN Charter's primacy which structurally

[60] See ch 3 (Platiše) of this volume.

[61] Sentenza no 238 (n 38).

[62] See Pasquale De Sena, 'The Judgment of the Italian Constitutional Court on State Immunity in Cases of Serious Violations of Human Rights or Humanitarian Law: A Tentative Analysis Under International Law' (2014) *Questions of International Law, Zoom Out II* 17.

[63] *Siegler v Western European Union*, Journal des Tribunaux (JT) 2004, 617, ILDC 53 (BE 2003) (Brussels Labour Court of Appeal, 17 Sept 2003) [50]–[51].

[64] ibid [63].

[65] ibid [59]–[62]. See Maarten Vidal, 'Analysis: *Siedler v. Western European Union*' ILDC 53 (BE 2003) paras A3–A5.

[66] Ch 2 (Fikfak) of this volume.

limited the Court's judicial review.[67] This is the case in which the EU Court employed, as a standard of review, the international rule of law standards regulating authority exercised by the UN Security Council. The use of *jus cogens* also illustrates the formalistic and thin character of the international rule of law regulating the UN, as contrasted with more substantive and thicker rule of law standards applicable to national organs.[68]

II. INTERNATIONAL DEFERENCE

As noted at the beginning of this chapter, national contestations may appear to be a threat to the international rule of law if the latter is understood as requiring full compliance. However, as demonstrated by this volume, domestic contestations incrementally invited procedural or substantive changes on the part of international institutions. As suggested by the chapters of Jennifer Easterday and Stephan Schill, national and international law are dependent on each other in order to achieve certain purposes; this inter-dependency renders both national authorities and international institutions receptive to each other's demands. On this basis, we argue that this cycle of national contestations and international responses is an essential feature of the international rule of law.

A. International Procedural Reforms

Such a cycle can be seen first with regard to the practice of the political organs of international organisations. National contestations against the decisions of such organs can encourage the organs' reforms to improve the transparency and accountability of international decision-making procedures by taking into account the national rule of law standards. As a good illustration, *Kadi* and other judicial contestations facilitated

[67] See Case T-315/01 *Yassin Abdullah Kadi v Council of the European Union and Commission of the European Communities* [2005] ECR II–03649 (CFI, Judgment of 21 Sept 2005) [226]. The CFI's *jus cogens* review was, however, based upon the extremely brief assessment of the concept and scope of *jus cogens* norms and proceeded with its own notion of *jus cogens*: see Joris Larik, 'Two Ships in the Night or in the Same Boat Together? Why the European Court of Justice Made the Right Choice in the Kadi Case' (2009) *College of Europe EU Diplomacy Paper No 3/2009* 6–10. *cf* Andrew Hudson, 'Not a Great Asset: The UN Security Council's Counter-Terrorism Regime: Violating Human Rights' (2007) 25 *Berkeley Journal of International Law* 203, 216–222 (observing that the right to a fair hearing is part of *jus cogens*, and that the 1267 sanctions regime breaches the core procedural guarantees protected by the right to a fair hearing).

[68] See Machiko Kanetake, 'The Interfaces between the National and International Rule of Law: The Case of UN Targeted Sanctions' (2012) 9 *International Organizations Law Review* 267, 286–87.

political momentum at the UN for procedural reforms,[69] leading to the incremental procedural improvements at the UN Security Council's sanctions committees.[70] Domestic contestations with regard to the scope of immunities in part encouraged international organisations to revise the scope of immunities. Such a trend can also be seen in the jurisprudence of international courts on the immunities of international organisations.[71] This is accompanied by the provision of internal procedures through which affected private parties can bring their claims to international organisations.[72]

B. Adjusting the National Margin

International courts and treaty-monitoring bodies showed deference to national legal practices by adjusting the margin accorded to them. The deference to democratic legitimacy is one way to alleviate the democratic deficit in the operation of international judicial bodies themselves. As suggested by Andrew Legg in this volume, the margin of appreciation is in fact an integral part of the international rule of law.[73] Birgit Peters pointed out that the principle of subsidiarity, the margin of appreciation, and the European consensus provide the frameworks through which the ECtHR engages in and respond to national courts' decisions.[74] The UK Supreme Court in *Horncastle* also characterised its own contestations as a gateway to a 'valuable dialogue'[75] between the UK judiciary and the Strasbourg Court, which indeed invited adjustment by the ECtHR's Grand Chamber in *al-Khawaja*.[76] As Shai Dothan argued in this volume, the ECtHR derives its own normative legitimacy by deferring to democratically accountable

[69] Among various political initiatives, noteworthy is the UN High-Level Panel's call in 2004; the Panel noted that '[t]he way entities or individuals are added to the terrorist list maintained by the Council and the absence of review or appeal for those listed raise serious accountability issues and possibly violate fundamental human rights norms and conventions': Report of the High-Level Panel on Threats, Challenges and Change, *A More Secure World: Our Shared Responsibility*, A/59/565 (2 Dec 2004) para 152. For various political initiatives to call for procedural reforms, see further Machiko Kanetake, 'Enhancing Community Accountability of the Security Council through Pluralistic Structure: The Case of the 1267 Committee' (2008) 12 *Max Planck Yearbook of United Nations Law* 113.

[70] For procedural reforms, see Kanetake, 'The Interfaces between the National and International Rule of Law' (n 68) Annex II (The Procedural Development of the Al Qaida Sanctions Committee).

[71] Ch 3 (Platiše) of this volume.

[72] ibid s IV(B).

[73] See ch 10 (Legg) of this volume.

[74] Ch 8 (Peters) of this volume.

[75] *Horncastle* (n 20) [11] (Lord Phillips, in a judgment agreed upon by all judges).

[76] *Al-Khawaja and Tahery v The United Kingdom* App nos 26766/05 and 22228/06, ECHR 2011 (ECtHR, Grand Chamber, 15 Dec 2011). The Grand Chamber, having analysed relevant English criminal law provisions and jurisprudence (ibid [40]–[62]) and the practices of other common law jurisdictions (ibid [63]–[87]), presented the jurisprudence relevant to Art 6

institutions, which also conditions the ECtHR's deference on democratic decision-making at the national level.[77] The cycle of contestations and deference can be seen in the context of international investment law. As analysed by Prabhash Ranjan, national contestations have facilitated both national and international debate as to how the balances can be better struck between investment protection and the host state's right to regulate in the public interest.[78] Of course, the degree of deference significantly varies depending on international courts and case-specific circumstances. Owing to its extensive remedial orders and the continuous monitoring of compliance, the IACtHR is known for being less deferential to the region's national legal practices which, when presented before the Court, often involve large-scale state-sponsored crimes.[79]

International treaty-monitoring bodies also show deference to state-specific circumstances, by engaging in a form of *dialogue* between the Committee on the Elimination of Discrimination against Women and states parties. As argued by Yvonne Donders and Vincent Vleugel in this volume, the dialogue enables states to challenge the way in which universal human rights are understood by treaty-monitoring bodies, which in part induced the changes on the part of treaty-monitoring bodies.[80]

One particular aspect of international human rights law which is negotiated in this way is reservations to human rights treaties. Ekaterina Yahyaoui Krivenko's chapter suggested that the practices of negotiation and their outcomes constitute one of the essential elements of the international rule of law.[81] As argued in her chapter, the 'reservations dialogue' allows for a constructive negotiation of diverse national legal orders into international human rights law.[82]

III. PROBLEMS OF UNCERTAINTY AND PARTICULARITY

As illustrated by this volume, national contestations and international deference are part of the process for developing international law. At the

(fair trial) of the ECHR in a more flexible way than did the *al-Khawaja* decision in 2009. Considering the 'overall fairness of the proceedings' (ibid [144], [146]), the Grand Chamber considered that a hearsay statement as the sole or decisive evidence does not 'automatically' lead to a violation of Art 6(1) (ibid [145], [147]). On this basis, the safeguards in the English law were found to be in principle strong safeguards designed to ensure fairness (ibid [151]). The Grand Chamber also noted that it is not the task of the ECtHR to make abstract or general assessment on the common law rule against hearsay (ibid [126]).

[77] See ch 9 (Dothan).

[78] Ch 5 (Ranjan) of this volume.

[79] See Huneeus, 'Courts Resisting Courts' (n 18) 496, 500–02.

[80] Ch 13 (Donders and Vleugel) of this volume

[81] See ch 12 (Yahyaoui Krivenko) of this volume.

[82] ibid.

same time, such a nuanced process involving a dialogue has several shortcomings. In particular, it appears to compromise the certainty of law (A) and to allow a particular version of the rule of law to contribute to the formulation of international legal practices (B).

A. Uncertainty

One of the consequences of balancing competing demands for international law is to undermine certainty and foreseeability; for instance, the meaning of legal rules may be unclear when international human rights law tries to balance the demand for universality and diversity.[83]

One of the common criticisms for leaving greater space for cultural diversity at the national and sub-national levels is that this undermines sufficient clarity and predictability in international human rights norms, as pointed out by Yvonne Donders and Vincent Vleugel in this volume.[84] Legal certainty as part of the rule of law requires treaties and treaty provisions to be sufficiently clear and precise to be predictable and foreseeable.[85] The terms of human rights treaties leave the space for flexibility and diversity at the level of national implementation. Human rights treaty-monitoring bodies, such as the Human Rights Committee (for the ICCPR), provides a vital role in balancing, on the one hand, the flexibility and diversity in international human rights law, and, on the other hand, the certainty and foreseeability in the substance of human rights law.[86] More specifically, the dialogue created between human rights treaty-monitoring bodies and national officials has the role of formulating international human rights norms in a way which is still acceptable for states parties.

B. Particularity

There is also another question whether the cycle of domestic contestations and international deference would increase the disparities among states in terms of their contribution to the development of international law.

The thickness of the rule of law at the domestic level is by no means uniform among states and regions. For instance, the rule of law in one country does not weight the protection of human rights in the same manner as another country does in its domestic legal order. The crux is that

[83] See ibid, introduction.
[84] Ch 13 (Donders and Vleugel) of this volume.
[85] ibid s II(B).
[86] ibid.

the different approaches to the rule of law at home may affect the ability of states and regions to review and criticise the decisions of international organisations and international courts at the domestic level, including before domestic courts. The adoption of the relatively thin rule of law at the domestic level might, albeit still a hypothesis, reduce the opportunities for domestic organs to directly or indirectly review and criticise the decisions of international organisations and international courts on the basis of the states' national rule of law standards.

Certain rule of law standards can be proactively pursued at the international level by the governments of some politically influential countries and regions, and the international political impact of national judicial decisions greatly varies depending upon the countries. Large disparities in political influence become problematic if certain standards of review employed by one state or one region can be presented as universally applicable and agreeable without the involvement of wider states. In this sense, judicial contestations at the domestic level, whose legal effect of the decisions is formally confined in respective legal orders, should be understood as part of political influence and initiatives vis-à-vis international organisations, international courts, and international treaties.

IV. THE INTERNATIONAL RULE OF LAW BEYOND COMPLIANCE

The picture that emerges from the combination of parts I and II of this book thus allows us to revise a compliance-based understanding about international law's approaches to national law and the national rule of law. International law, and international institutions that interpret and apply it, do not always command blind national obedience to international law. Instead, they incorporate a process of adjustment and deference to national law and the rule of law embedded therein. International law and institutions (eg, international human rights treaty-monitoring bodies and human rights courts) respond to *national contestations* (as discussed in part I of this volume) and show *deference* to the national rule of law (as analysed in part II).

This process of adjustment and deference across the legal orders is arguably part of the rule of law integrated in the international legal order itself. In other words, the 'international' rule of law, as evidenced by and supported by the practices discussed in this volume, is not merely about ensuring national compliance with international law; instead, the international rule of law appears to accommodate the cycle of national contestations and international responses to them. While this flexibility might come at the expense of the certainty of international law, the practice suggests that the international rule of law in relation to the national legal order seems to allow flexibility, national diversity, and pluralism.

The notion of the international rule of law presented by this volume finds further support in the statement of South Africa in 2009 during the debate on the rule of law at the UN. The South African delegation pointed out that the concept of the rule of law does not simply refer to compliance with international obligations.[87] The South African delegation suggested that the concept also implies the fair and inclusive law-making process, using the non-inclusive Security Council as a point of critique.[88]

Ultimately, behind national contestations and international deference, there lies a much wider problem of legitimacy and accountability deficit on the part of international law and international institutions. Study of the feedback of national legal practices on the international rule of law highlights how international law and institutions pay deference to, and rely upon, political legitimacy attached to the national rule of law.

[87] UN GA Sixth Committee, Summary Record of the 8th Meeting on 14 Oct 2009, UN Doc A/C.6/64/SR.8 (11 Nov 2009) paras 73–74 (Mr Tladi of South Africa) (at the debate on 'the rule of law at the national and international levels').

[88] UN GA Sixth Committee, on 14 Oct 2009 (n 87) para 75; *United Nations Juridical Yearbook 2009* at 219 (the summary of the debate) ('It was pointed out that, in addition to ensuring compliance with international obligations, the concept of the rule of law implied a law-creating process that would involve all States, thereby strengthening the fairness and legitimacy of international law').

Index

References such as '178–9' indicate (not necessarily continuous) discussion of a topic across a range of pages. Wherever possible in the case of topics with many references, these have either been divided into sub-topics or only the most significant discussions of the topic are listed. Because the entire work is about the 'rule of law' the use of this term (and certain others which occur constantly throughout the book) as an entry point has been minimized. Information will be found under the corresponding detailed topics.

www.ingramcontent.com/pod-product-compliance
Lightning Source LLC
LaVergne TN
LVHW052215200926
848481LV00001B/115
* 9 7 8 1 5 0 9 9 2 4 5 8 5 *